SERGEI M. EISENSTEIN

By the same author
PAUL ROBESON
PANDITJI. A PORTRAIT OF JAWAHARLAL NEHRU
PORTRAIT OF A DIRECTOR. SATYAJIT RAY

Sergei Mikhailovich Eisenstein

SERGEI M.
EISENSTEIN

a biography by
MARIE SETON

Revised edition

London
DENNIS DOBSON

First published in Great Britain in 1952 by The Bodley Head
Revised edition first published in Great Britain in 1978
by Dobson Books Ltd, 80 Kensington Church Street, London W8
Printed in Great Britain by Whitstable Litho Ltd, Whitstable, Kent
ISBN 0 234 77440 1

To
my former husband, Donald Hesson,
without whose understanding help
this book could never have been written.

Acknowledgements

I wish to express my thanks to the following individuals and institutions for the great help they have given me in the preparation of this book:

Ernest Lindgren and Norah Traylen of the British Film Institute; Roger Manvell and the members of the Publishing Committee of the British Film Academy; Judith Todd and Mrs. Fox of the Society for Cultural Relations Between the U.S.S.R. and England (S.C.R.); Lotte Eisner (Lotte Escoffier), Librarian, and Henri Longlois of the Institut du Cinema, Paris; Mrs. Elizabeth Barrett of the Theatre and Film Collection of the New York Public Library; Alfred H. Barr Jr. and the staff of the Museum of Modern Art Film Library, New York; Miss Vernoy and members of the staff of Harper Library and the Archives Department of the University of Chicago.

Albert Einstein, Lion Feuchtwanger, Fritz Lang, Hans Richter, Hans Feld; Leon Moussinac, Georges Sadoul, Jean Georges Auriol; Jean Mitry, Armand Panigel, Nino Frank, Eugene Jolas, Robert Aron, Roland Tual, Jean Lods; Paul Rotha, Thorold Dickinson, Jack Isaacs, Roger Burford, Oswald Blakeston, Kenneth MacPherson, H. P. J. Marshall, Freda Brilliant, the Hon. Ivor Montagu; J. Alvarez del Vayo; Jean Charlot, Agustin Aragon Leiva, Mr. and Mrs. Brooks Atkinson, Mr. and Mrs. Conrad Seiler, Joseph Freeman, William Gropper, Margaret Bourke-White, Joseph Wood Krutch, Sara Mildred Strauss, Herman G. Weinberg, Christel Gang, Lincoln Kirstein, Witter Bynner, Agnes Jacques, Dr. Lawrence Jacques, N. Napoli, George Kraska and Zina Voynow. Also to Gabriel Fernandez Ledesma and the editors, Vinicius de Moraes and Alex Viany, of *Filme*, Brazil.

For translation: Alexander and Rita Spaulding, Grigori B. Lotsman, Mrs. von Meck; Joseph M. Pyle, Fernando Penesola; James Hodgson, Maria Kende and Marvin Peisner.

Messrs. Faber and Faber, London and Messrs. Harcourt, Brace, New York for permission to include extracts from *The Film Sense* by Jay Leyda.

I wish to extend my special thanks to Seymour Stern for the invaluable source material and illustrations which he loaned to me; for his permission to publish letters written to him by Sergei M. Eisenstein, Agustin Aragon Leiva and others, and for his checking of details in chapters viii, ix and x. To Dr. Charles Kligerman, formerly of the University of Chicago, for checking the manuscript from a psychological point of view. To Jay Leyda for the invaluable material and illustrations which he made available and for his checking of all details in the manuscript. I am indebted to the late H. W. L. Dana who made available important source material shortly before his death.

Finally, I am deeply indebted to Grigori Alexandrov for his confirmation of many vital dates and facts, and to Richard Ainley and Marvin Peisner who gave hours of their time to criticizing the manuscript and, lastly, to Basil Wright for his expert advice.

Contents

List of Illustrations

Frontispiece

Sergei Mikhailovich Eisenstein

Between pages 54 and 55

List of Line Blocks in Text

Foreword to the Revised Edition

BETWEEN the death of Sergei Eisenstein in February 1948 and
the first publication of this book in September 1952, it seemed to
me presumptuous to claim that Eisenstein's films and theoretical
writings were bound to exert an influence. Only time would prove his
creative value and the force of his theories and research. If he were but
a flash in the pan of cinematic experiment, his films and his thoughts
would soon become dated.

Even now, thirty years after his death, it is still too early to set him
in a final perspective because all of his writings, fragments of projects
and drawings have not yet been made available for study in the Soviet
Union, or internationally. However, it is now evident that Eisenstein's
influence is expanding and it is not confined to film makers. As to
what contemporary film makers can draw from him, especially in
regard to audio-visual combinations, an extensive study is required to
examine these traces. Eisenstein was far ahead of his time. In consequence, it is interesting to find that almost everywhere members of
young audiences, those born since his death and not professionally
concerned with the techniques of cinema, frequently comment that
Eisenstein's films appear singularly contemporary and undated.

Sergei Mikhailovich's phenomenal range of interests and research,
together with his 'feel' for cultures other than his own, were stressed
in this book as dominant facets of his complex personality. But now
readers can grasp this range and 'feel' from his own vivid, flowing, and
associative-thought autobiography. As autobiography it is unique and
dynamically conveys how Eisenstein thought and, indeed, talked
when he was in the mood freely to express himself. The emotional
Eisenstein, seldom glimpsed by those who met or knew him, emerges
poignantly, because, as his PS., PPS., reveal, he wrote his 'memoirs'
realizing he was threatened by death. Until the publication of this
volatile, gay, sometimes pathetic testament, there existed absolutely
no confirmation of what I had written about Eisenstein's parentage,
childhood and youth. I had only Eisenstein's word for it. When a man
is only alive by a 'miracle', as was the case when he wrote his autobiography, he is unlikely to lie about himself, even if he jests about
his sufferings.

The most enthralling and exciting aspect of Eisenstein's expanding influence today (and it would thrill him in his pursuit of being useful to unborn generations for a couple of hundred years), is his capacity to inspire creative artists in fields other than cinema.

It is detailed in this book how the 1926 release of *Potemkin* in Berlin was immediately reflected in the structure of Lion Feuchtwanger's novel *Success*, with a screening of the film included. But it is mainly since Eisenstein's death that his synthesis of the arts as applicable to film has sent out a powerful ripple to capture other artists' imagination. In my chapter, 'The Eternal Circle', it is mentioned how Eisenstein was inspired to use the composition of David Alfaro Siqueiros' mutilated mural, *Burial of a Worker*, for shots of a burial in *Que Viva Mexico!* Subsequently, as Bernard S. Myers relates in *Mexican Painting in Our Times*, Siqueiros acquired from Eisenstein not only an interest in film which 'he felt could increase space elements, especially volumes in space', complex movements and further the idea of mobility, but in the inter-relation of psychology, chemistry and biology and their relation to the plastic arts. Siqueiros fused these elements in his later murals executed in Mexico, Chile and Cuba. Hardly a single Siqueiros painting after his meetings with Eisenstein is lacking in cinematic elements.

On the evidence available, it must be said that Eisenstein has markedly inspired those within the Spanish-Mexican orbit. It is significant that the magnificently diverse and contrasting Mexican Exhibition seen in Paris, Stockholm and London in 1953 was arranged by Fernando Gamboa, who had sat in his youth at Eisenstein's feet. For the understanding of the background context of the Exhibition, Gamboa requested special screenings of *Thunder Over Mexico* and *Time in the Sun* my own skeleton editing of the mutilated *Que Viva Mexico!* Gamboa claimed that Eisenstein had brought an awakened perception of Mexico to receptive Mexicans, headed, of course, by Siqueiros. In turn, Eisenstein claims in his autobiography that he was not only in love with Mexico, but that it was there that his own drawings flowered and flowed as never before.

Eisenstein's influence penetrated into Spain with equal power though he was never within the borders of Spain.

When this book was first published in 1952 there existed in Valencia a group of young students filled with questioning. The group had existed for some time and one of the original members, Juan Genoves, had left for Madrid where he became a painter. At the age of eight, during the Spanish Civil War, the little Juan had seen *Potemkin* and other Eisenstein films projected in a hall. For ever they left their mark upon his visual concepts of Man in the throes of terrible action and movement. The very texture of his evolving canvases, black and white, give the effect of film being projected on a screen. Other pictures are tonally in sepia, as if he were using sepia stock. It would be hard to find compositions which are so acutely reminiscent of Eisenstein's use of masses moving along architectural forms as Genoves' *Laberinto*, nor the lasting impact of Eisenstein's images in relation to the film strip like composition of terrified people running to escape the symbol of brutal authority in action with truncheons. Here is political art transmuted into the most compelling painting. He has transferred to canvas scenes scarred on his mind in a similar manner to Eisenstein's recreation in *October* of the 1917 Revolution he witnessed in St Petersburg at the time; only the Age of the H-Bomb and Space has entered Genoves' pictures. One understands his comment that Eisenstein's films 'represent a real part of our lives'.

Sometime after Genoves' departure to Madrid, the centre of the small questioning group was taken by the girl art student Angeles Ballaster. She and her group read of *Eisenstein, a Biography*, in an Argentine newspaper. They had never seen an Eisenstein film. They wrote a collective letter to me in search of obtaining the book and a copy was sent. They sent me a set of drawings by the Mexican painter Tamayo. The folder was wrapped up in a tatty sheet of paper on which there were the tracings of a powerful drawing by Angeles. She married one of her fellow students in the group—Rafael Bosch—and they, to find more liberty, went to Venezuela to become active in a film society. Angeles' talent constantly expanded. She and her husband found their way to the United States and back to Spain and back again. I was curious whether Angeles was a 'disciple' of Eisenstein. Her reply:

'Just like Eisenstein, I have tried to contrast in my work the peaceful happiness that man tries to achieve in this world and the violent horrors to which he is condemned by the very structure of an unjust society—as well as the necessary fight that man has to engage in to free himself from the sombre powers above which try to destroy him . . . For instance, "Menaced Lives" . . . you will recognize here the memory of the mother falling down the Odessa stairs . . . By the same token, some of my Maternities, Children Lovers, are themes influenced by the scenes of the Mexican film. But it is not only the subjects that matter . . . As Eisenstein put the accent on montage, I put it on composition . . . What Eisenstein especially taught me is that composition must be based on contrast, in order to achieve a more powerful image and impression . . . I always read his theories on the principle and types of rhythm and I try to learn from them. Also, his lessons on the relationship of Oriental painting and writing, on the one hand, and, on the other, montage have affected me deeply. The "shot" quality he discovered in the partial perspectives of a Japanese painting I tried to carry out in the elements of structure in my painting.' [Plate 18].

Born into so utterly a different culture pattern as Spanish, Mexican and Russian, one English painter, who is extremely reflective of this tortuous period, admits to the impact of individual Eisenstein 'shots', particularly those of *Potemkin*. This is Francis Bacon, beset with the drive to implant with paint the instant image—the twisting mouth, writhing body, the twitching of animal muscles and the distorting expressions transforming the human face. Bacon says that he could find little to help him in the painting of the past, or even of the present. Instead, he found a more dynamic expression of this time in photography and film. These images spurred him on. At some point he saw *Potemkin*. The woman in the pince-nez whose eye streams blood transfixed his imagination. He was so haunted by this image that it inspired a picture. In his opinion, this attempted approximation of intensity failed dismally. But he began to feel that even if one painting failed he would not discard the vital inspiration derived from Eisenstein. He began to transmute the influence along a line more individual to himself. The three heads now reproduced were selected by Francis Bacon as representative of the more lasting impact of Eisenstein's images upon his painting. [Plate 10].

But the most unexpected influence of Eisenstein's ideas of editing, arrangement of images and even scenario structure, is that cast upon the British composer Alexander Goehr, who, failing in traditional composition, turned towards Schönberg. It was the failed student's manner of looking at material in musical terms which set him on course to become receptive to the work and ideas of Eisenstein. He came to think of sound related to sound like the relation of image to image in Eisenstein's films. He was seeking to isolate tones, instruments and the use of the voice, isolate yet combine. As a musician he was attracted to the audio-visual aspects of the Eisenstein-Prokofiev experiments no less than to Eisenstein's silent films. Goehr stumbled upon this biography. Reading of Eisenstein and his ideas gave rise to the most unexpected concrete response in Goehr. First he decided upon a composition for voices based upon the second half of the fourth reel of Eisenstein's scenario of *Sutter's Gold*, the film that Paramount failed to make. The singers sing Eisenstein's words of the terrifying discovery of gold in California in 1848. Thus, a fragment of unrealized film took on another life in another medium and was heard at the Leeds Festival in 1960.

Goehr then made a second attempt under the inspiration of Eisenstein's ideas—a fourteen-minute Cantata utilizing Leonardo da Vinci's description for his unrealized fresco 'The Deluge' for the sung words. Eisenstein had broken this description down into a shooting script. This, together with some of Eisenstein's montage ideas, touched a chord in Goehr to be reflected in his instrumentation. Throughout the Cantata there is the shadow of Eisenstein and da Vinci transferred to another medium.

These daring attempts give an amazing perspective to the creative process in terms of time and receptivity: da Vinci sets down his images for his unrealized fresco; Eisenstein siezes upon the *Notes* as a forerunner of a cinematic concept; he attempts to utilize Leonardo's vision to depict flooding in the film *Ferghana Canal*, which again is never made. Goehr, aiming to find new musical methods, manages to achieve two compositions under the stimulus of Eisenstein and da Vinci in another era and another country. Here is an exciting immortality of thought and image.

In 1934, Eisenstein insisted to me that everything had been created already, but there were always new ways of recreating in a new form what had gone before. If he were alive today Eisenstein would be overjoyed and making delicious jokes about his usefulness to others. It was this very hope that kept him going through every trial and tribulation. He was far-sighted in his sensitive toughness and not deluded by the hardship of his own life. He had faith in the future of his efforts and, as his *Autobiography* reveals, his sense of humour and passion for knowledge enabled him to transcend 'the slings and arrows of outrageous fortune'.

M.S.

London, 1977

Introduction

SERGEI M. EISENSTEIN, whose art sprang from the vortex of the Russian Revolution, is already assured a place among the few great pioneers of cinematography. He was one of the adventurers striving to mould a mechanical means of entertainment—the moving picture—into a dynamic form expressive of a new society in our era of unprecedented scientific investigation and social conflict.

In Eisenstein, the genius of an artist and the fervour of an inspired scholar were united; and his six completed films, though they represent but a fraction of his creative activity, reveal him as one of the most important artists of the 20th century.

As a film director, Eisenstein's contribution to the development of cinema is as distinctive as that of such directors as David Wark Griffith, Charles Chaplin, Robert Flaherty or René Clair. But Eisenstein was not only a film director. He was a scientist searching for the roots of artistic expression. This led him to the development of a body of theory relating to the creative process and film aesthetics.

However, since a great part of his research and theoretical work is still unpublished, it is difficult to set Sergei Eisenstein accurately in the perspective of the short history of his chosen medium. When all his unpublished work is assembled it is possible that posterity will rank Eisenstein the scientist and philosopher as high as or even higher than Eisenstein the film director. Indeed, he may be generally recognized as a universal genius.

Eisenstein the man was no less remarkable than his work. He appeared to some as a cynical egotist bending everything and everyone to his own will; others declared with equal conviction that he was the victim of insincere and merciless men. To some people he appeared as the embodiment of the scientific materialist of a communist society; while others saw him as the embodiment of the individualist whose way of thinking was saturated with mysticism and symbolism. He impressed many people who knew him as the most intelligent man they ever encountered.

This biography is a personal portrait of Eisenstein. It relates the man to his work and attempts to answer the many questions asked about him. The basic material used in this book was given me by Eisenstein himself between 1932 and 1935. He dictated some of the material to me, particularly that relating to America and Mexico. Other material

13

concerning his ideas and his life I noted down at his request, and a great residue remained imprinted on my memory.

When I began to write this biography, a few people said that the greatest service I could render to the art of film, and to Eisenstein, would be to record his work as an artist and theoretician. These people feared that the stature of Eisenstein and the film medium would be lessened if the more difficult and complex aspects of his life were included. They thought that many details of his life should not be fully revealed at this time.

However, I felt that such an approach would do Eisenstein an injustice for it would serve to perpetuate the legend of a confusing personality whose life has been surrounded by exaggerated stories and innuendo. Because I had a deep respect for Eisenstein as a person, I decided that I would not evade the more difficult and complex aspects of his character.

I have, therefore, attempted to explain his personal conflicts as he explained them to me. If at times the personal aspects are detailed to a point where some might call it indiscretion, my answer is that the understanding of a great artist as a human being is more important than the creation of a formal record of his achievement. It is for this reason that I have omitted only those things which might injure people who are still living, or those things of such an entirely personal exchange of thought and feeling that they would have no meaning except to those people intimately involved.

Other biographers may interpret Eisenstein differently from myself. They may have access to some material which is not yet available and they may stress other aspects of his life and work. But, if Eisenstein and his work are to be fully understood, it would seem that a personal portrait, such as I have presented, has its place.

The psychoanalyst, Eduard Hitschman, recently said 'To understand [character] by tracing it back to inborn instincts and their transformation by the ego, and the influence of parents and early events in life, is legitimate and scientific characterology which is the most important part of biography.'

It is my hope that in the future there will be other studies of Eisenstein so that ultimately a just estimate can be reached of one of the most brilliant and profoundly interesting figures of the first half of our century—a man spanning two social and political systems; an artist rushing forward to the future; a genius whose aim was to make himself a worthy member of a new society and serve generations of artists as yet unborn.

Seeing that I cannot choose any subject of great utility or pleasure because my predecessors have already taken as their own all useful and necessary themes, I will do like one who, because of his poverty, is the last to arrive at the fair, and not being able otherwise to provide himself, chooses all the things as being of little value. With these despised and rejected wares—the leavings of many buyers—I will load my modest pack, and therewith take my course, distributing, not amid the great cities, but among the mean hamlets, and taking with such reward as befits the things I offer.

Many will believe that they can with reason censure me, alleging that my proofs are contrary to the authority of certain men who are held in great reverence by their inexperienced judgements, not taking into account that my conclusions were arrived at as a result of simple and plain experience, which is the true mistress.

The natural desire of a good man is knowledge.

LEONARDO DA VINCI, C.A. 199 v.a.

12 14 '44

CHAPTER ONE

The Clown . . . and Leonardo

Pre-imagining is the imaginings of things which are to be.
LEONARDO DA VINCI, Fogli B. 2 v.

SERGEI MIKHAILOVICH EISENSTEIN was born on the 23rd of January 1898 in Riga, Latvia, where for centuries opposing streams of culture had clashed and finally fused into a precarious unity. The Letts and Jews strained restlessly under the repressive laws of Imperial Russia and the oppression of the German Balt Junkers, who were permitted to retain their privileged position. From time to time the Lettish peasants made futile attempts at revolt and the workers, ever growing in numbers, existed in the hope that some day they could drive out their masters. As the attempt at Russification intensified towards the end of the nineteenth century, the less militant middle class sought spiritual refuge in the tradition introduced by the Swedes and Germans before Latvia became a fragment of the Russian Empire.

The tolerance shown to the Jews during the reign of Tsar Alexander II was swept away in 1885 by repressive laws which prohibited Jews from living in Riga unless they held a university or technical college degree. Marriage was in the hands of the Church and it prohibited marriage between Christians and Jews unless the Jewish partner first obtained a certificate of baptism and agreed that the children would be given a Christian education. For christianized Jews there were no legal restrictions on government employment, and once a family had been christianized a Semitic family name ceased to be much of an official handicap.

In such a setting it was rather unusual for a Jew to marry a Russian lady of independent means. But, according to Sergei Eisenstein, such was the case of his father and mother. Whether it was his father, Mikhail, who had renounced Judaism, or his paternal grandparents, is not clear. So far as is known, the family did not suffer any direct handicap because of their Jewish ancestry. His father, Mikhail, whose family came from Germany, was a successful engineer employed by the city of Riga. Although many christianized Jews retained their Jewish faith in secret, Judaism exerted no hold upon Mikhail Eisenstein and his son grew up without allegiance to the traditions of his father's people or the

Jewish creed. Judaism lay outside the pattern of the Eisenstein family, which was prosperous and cosmopolitan.[1]

Mikhail Eisenstein was a robust man with a Kaiser Wilhelm moustache spread over a broad face which topped a stocky body—the physical structure he handed on to his son. He was possessed of a sense of humour. It was the kind of humour which delighted in puns, pranks and flamboyant nonsense. Each time *Die Fledermaus* played in Riga, Mikhail Eisenstein would take his friends to the theatre, occupy the front-row seats and yell with the chorus while it sang, 'Eisenstein has gone to quod, gone to quod, gone to quod!'

Julia Eisenstein must have winced at her husband's exuberance. She was entirely too refined to be anything but shocked at broad humour; in fact, any act which did not fit into her pattern of a charming, orderly middle-class life greatly disturbed her. A small, pretty woman who retained her charm into late middle age, she was concerned with the elegant and less exhausting things in life—pretty clothes, flowers, and gossip. In her youth she yearned for the niceties of life as a protection against the dark barbarities of peasant life in Latvia. Perhaps she sought to ward off the slightest thought of the scourge which now and then struck indiscriminately at her husband's people—the pogrom. She cultivated every refinement and her home was run as a cultured Russian home embellished with an awareness of things German, French and English. As early as Sergei could remember he had a nurse to look after him, a Russian nurse, who later became his housekeeper.

She brought a warm, earthy atmosphere into the house and when she arrived she took almost total charge of the beautiful little boy whose forehead was unusually large and whose blue eyes often gazed into the far distance. In place of learning or refinement, she brought the child an intimate feeling for the Russian speech of the moujik and knowledge of something deeper, more persistent than the educated wit of his engineer father and the pretty femininity of his mother. From his nurse, Seryozhenka learned to feel at home with simple people, those who could neither read nor write. [Plate 1]

But with this gift, which served him later as an artist, his nurse brought him a sense of the mysterious, the superstitious. She instilled into his childish consciousness the idea of a great power residing in icons, amulets and little holy figures, and she said no one must ever part with his good-luck tokens: he must carry them with him wherever he went. In trouble, a good-luck charm could save a man—his love, his reputation, even his life.

Very early she taught Sergei to pray before the icon with its ever-

[1] Sergei Eisenstein told me that he knew nothing about his paternal ancestry beyond these meagre facts.

burning candle. She told him the stories of the saints and their wonder-ful visions and the miracles they performed. These people with powers which reached beyond the visible world were different from other people; their souls were especially precious to God and the Saviour. From his nurse little Sergei also learned to love the Virgin and the Child Jesus.

A hypersensitive child, brimming over with lovingness and a desire for love, he possessed a vivid imagination. In his mind the delicate figure of his own Mamochka often appeared intertwined with the image of the Virgin. Since she flitted constantly through the childhood scene, but never stayed near Sergei long enough for him to know her in the deep and affectionate way he knew his nurse, she appeared elusive. She and the Virgin were beings inhabiting a world beyond the boy's power to grasp. Only the nurse stood firm, planted in the real world.

Beneath the veneer of family decorum, the relations between Julia and Mikhail Eisenstein were strained. Mikhail took no action to improve or alter the situation and it was Julia who made the first step. In 1905 she moved to the imperial capital, St. Petersburg, and took the seven-year-old Sergei with her. Events gave her action the coloration of reason, for during the 1905 Revolution, which sprang up in the wake of Russia's defeat by Japan, the provincial town of Riga was shaken to its foundations. In the vain hope of gaining independence, Latvia revolted and the Revolution was put down with appalling bloodshed. Safe in St. Petersburg, Julia Eisenstein took a flat and bought fine furni-ture with her own money.

For a little while Seryozhenka was alone with the Mamochka he adored. He cherished her every kiss and the touch of her hand was reassuring; it gave him the most pleasurable sensation in the world. But one day his idol turned inexplicably cruel. She sent him to his father in Riga and ordered that he be locked up alone in a railway com-partment. He never forgot that journey, the meaning of which he could not understand. At the other end his nurse met him, and when it was time for him to return to St. Petersburg, his father kindly sent the nurse with him. That he remembered as a happy journey. But the nurse returned to Riga and the next time Sergei went to see his father, again his mother sent him alone.[1] Once more he was locked up in a com-partment by himself and tasted a recurrence of fear and despair.

Thus, he began to feel loneliness and lack of love. Already he was proud and shy, so he tried to bury his tender and passionate feelings. When he came into the company of people he pretended to be aloof

---

[1] Eisenstein gave an account of these journeys to Grigori Alexandrov, who later said it was all Eisenstein ever told him about his early childhood.

and sometimes he gave the impression of being a sulky boy who did not wish to have anything to do with anyone. Though dressed in costly clothing, he often had the expression of a perplexed, rather hostile waif.

[Plate 2]

During one of his visits to Riga, Sergei Eisenstein first met his lifelong friend Maxim Shtraukh, the actor, with whom he later worked and shared a flat. Without etching in the background of the Eisenstein family Shtraukh wrote: 'I was seven or eight. . . . I remember the sand dunes and pine woods along the Riga seashore, the seashore highway lined with resort cottages where people rented rooms for the summer. In the garden of such a cottage one could often see a boy of about ten, his large head with close cropped hair, bent over a thick sketch book. His hand, sure and quick, produced fantastic drawings. The boy was Seroyzha Eisenstein. Drawing was his favourite pass-time and his sketch books were filled with his drawings. . . . We saw each other for several years and gradually became friends.'[1]

Some time before 1910, Mikhail Eisenstein moved to St. Petersburg, where he continued his career as a city engineer. With the family pattern re-established, Sergei's nurse, who had come from Riga, once more became his protector, comforter and chief companion.

Perhaps it was her wide-eyed wonder at the city's grandeur which first led Sergei to see St. Petersburg with a sense of wonderment. His excitement at its architectural magnificence was never blunted; the clarity of his impressions carried over into adult life to serve as the basis of some of his most intricate imagery in the film *October*. The character of Russian Baroque with its ornate decoration, which was rooted deep in his childhood, became a passion with him. He was never to outgrow the first charm of the voluptuous neo-classical figures on the roof of the Winter Palace. All his life the sweep of massive façades, spiralling curlicues and floral scrolls retained an irresistible fascination, even though their social significance later filled him with a loathing which drove him along the road of the iconoclast.

As he was sensitive to the characteristics of Baroque, so he was always intensely aware of the artificial, rococo appearance of Petrograd's gentry. Among them the figure of his nurse stood out humble and human. Like the architecture, the upper classes in St. Petersburg emulated foreign fashions and lived in a world decorated by the *beaux mots* delivered in French. They appeared as foreign to the Russian people as the outward face of Petrograd was foreign to the visitors from other Russian cities. This 'foreignness' of St. Petersburg pleased the Eisensteins, who spoke French and German as easily as they spoke Russian.

Since they were not of that turn of mind which led to any profound

[1] *Encounters* by Maxim Shtraukh, Iskusstvo Kino, Nos. 1–2 (Moscow, 1940).

questioning of the autocratic *status quo*, they were not touched by any awareness that beneath the seemingly impregnable magnificence of the imperial city there lurked the termites of constant follies in the Government accompanied by unrestrained cruelty towards all who dared to organize opposition. When the Eisensteins heard the whispered tales of the flogging of political prisoners exiled to the far north and Siberia, they accepted it as the regrettable but natural punishment meted out to dangerous agitators.

In order that their son should grow up to be a man of cosmopolitan culture, the Eisensteins followed the fashionable procedure of many well-off Russian families. They engaged one of the English governesses who had come to St. Petersburg. Seryozhenka learned English quickly and became familiar with the literature read by English children. From his governess he received his elementary education at which, in later years, he sneered because he disliked to admit he was the child of privileged parents. The governess had also stood in the way of his doing things he enjoyed. He expressed his childhood 'fate' in a poem written in English in his composition book:

WINTER (Big Poem!)

The snow is falling,
I hear my sport friends calling,
With them to skate,
But I can't skate so very late,
Because I have to wright [*sic*] a composition.
That is my poor position,
And it has to be done
Or else I won't have so great fun.
And so I have to wright [*sic*]
Or else my miss will fight.

Already Sergei Mikhailovich showed an ability to express himself in a foreign language. And while skating, he enjoyed a feeling of mastery; the blades of his skates added to his height, a fact which pleased him. On holidays he played 'cops and robbers'. His 'followers' were usually younger boys smaller in stature than himself. In the role of leader he assumed the expression of a mature, brooding man and it is possible that he imagined himself as the hero of *Prince Serebryani*, a story about Ivan the Terrible and his Lifeguards, the Oprichniki, which towards the end of his life he said had made a great impression upon him in childhood. [Plate 59]

Sergei had grown a little taller each year. But he felt that his forehead was too large and his body too small. His ears with their pricked tips looked to him like those of a hobgoblin, or some other creature from a world where mortals could not go. Though he frequently felt out of place, nothing momentous happened after his father came from Riga until 1910.

One day, which had begun like every other day, Sergei came home from the school he was now attending. He found a sudden and terrible change had taken place in his home since morning. His mother had left, but for what reason he did not know. She had stripped the flat. Nothing remained but his bed, his father's bed and the nurse's bed. In the empty drawing-room stood his father's piano and piano stool. For weeks the flat remained bare for at that time Mikhail Eisenstein had insufficient money to refurnish the home. In the eerie emptiness, his father nightly pounded on the piano, giving vent to his grief and resentment at his wife's departure. She had gone away to France to lead her own life.

Sergei was stunned. His love for his mother had long been betrayed by a frivolous neglect. That he had borne hoping that some day he could draw nearer to her. But her deliberate withdrawal from his life brought him an intense sense of rejection, a feeling that she had never loved him. During the long nights he prayed to the Virgin, holding the Child in her tender embrace. She was the mother of Heaven and she would send his mother home to him. But nothing happened. His mother failed to return. The world became a cold, harsh place for him and his faith in human loyalty withered and almost died.

Perhaps his mother was not wholly to blame; there may have been things she suffered which her son could not comprehend. Maybe her only sin was the possession of a small, silly mind. She was never able to understand how her act warped the personality of her son, who stood in need of assurance and affection if he were not to suffer all the days of his life.

Gradually, Sergei felt his love for his mother turning into hate. It made him feel guilty. It was very wicked to hate one's mother. 'Honour thy Father and thy Mother.' . . . His hatred began to turn upon himself; he tried to find excuses for the mother who had deserted him. Already over-sensitive and on the verge of adolescence, Sergei grew to feel that his mother had gone away because she could not bear the sight of him any longer. He saw himself as a creature so unworthy of tenderness and love that even his own mother was compelled to reject him. He shrank before this humiliating image created by his overwrought imagination. Like an outcast he would stretch his imagination towards the warmth flowing from the love and affection other boys received. Yet he dared not attempt to participate lest he be rejected.

He believed that only his nurse could accept him, and during the unhappy days of his youth she kept a small flame of warmth burning within'him. She was a good soul, simple and kindly, and he felt at home with her as with no one else. He found beauty in a good heart and homely peasant ways. All his life he was to find a place with humble and simple people upon whom he would shower the kindness and affection he feared to show to others. If it had not been for his nurse, Sergei might have become what many people thought him—a man without a heart.

One day she took him to the circus in St. Petersburg. Most boys enjoyed the circus and she thought he ought to have a little pleasure. This simple soul could not have known that her kind act would bring a great influence into Sergei's life. She could not divine, and never did accept the fact, that her Seryozhenka was different from most boys; that in him lay the most wonderful and tragic of seeds—that of genius.

From the first moment he watched with avid attention—the acrobats with their beautiful, perfectly co-ordinated bodies swinging lithely upon the trapeze; the tightrope walker balancing upon the wire with death waiting below. The spectacle carried Sergei into a new world, one which seemed to lie beyond all logic. He was aware of the intensity of his own excitement and that of the people around him. He dreaded lest the tightrope walker fall to his death, yet he could not turn his fascinated gaze away. His emotions intensified until it seemed that he was himself involved in these extraordinary feats of balance washed by the glaring floodlights. The acts ended.

Into the ring tumbled a host of clowns, creatures Sergei had never seen before. They folded up and rolled about like apes; threw out their arms in grotesque gestures which set the crowd roaring with laughter. Beating each other over the head, every clown was every other clown's butt for mirth. Sergei wondered if these curious creatures had human faces under their fantastic masks of grease-paint. What kind of eyes, noses and mouths? He tried to detect the outlines, but all he could see were the great stylized grins which hid their own faces. No one could know what went on in the heart of a clown. Their bodies were scarcely human in the swathes of their chequered, baggy costume; very fat, very thin, no one could see the real body of a clown.

'There was one clown I could not forget,' Sergei Mikhailovich told me years later.

The image of this clown, small of stature with a large head and a wig of upstarting hair, had remained in Eisenstein's memory for more than twenty years.

As he had watched the antics of this queer little figure who could not be separated from his fanciful costume, Sergei had felt himself to be of the same substance as this clown. If he could change places with this clown, he imagined he would be freed from his shyness and escape his loneliness. Disguised as this clown he would make the crowd laugh at his own wit and the wonderful and fantastic scenes of comedy he often felt swell up within him. At home the fantasy conjured up by the clown did not fade; instead the feeling of identification grew.

'He was no bigger than I was and his head was like mine.'

Never melodramatic when he spoke of the things closest to him, there was the sadness of childhood in Eisenstein's face; in his voice a tone which asked for understanding.

'Can you not understand how it came about? I wanted to escape from my body, hide it. . . .'

Each time the circus came to Petrograd, Sergei Mikhailovich went to it over and over again. Though he was fascinated by the acrobats, he really returned in order to watch the antics of the clowns, especially those of the clown whom he had made the *alter ego* of his physical self. Yet it never entered his head at the time that he might translate his subjective feelings into the overt act of a circus performer. His feelings were more complex. He felt himself to be like his special clown, not as a performer, but as a person. He must act out the part of clown in life, so he began to construct a character to clothe his physical features.

As the years passed he built a role with words, gestures and on occasions a costume all carefully contrived to give the impression of an aggressive person to whom all things were a matter for mirth. Soon he became dependent on this role, for through it he could establish a seemingly easy contact with people. In time it was to impress many people as being the real Eisenstein.

The irony of this identification was that any disproportion in Eisenstein's physical structure was not as evident to others as to himself. True, he had short legs and arms, small hands and feet and a large head and torso, but expressiveness and vitality gave him harmony. Far from looking ridiculous as he thought—and sometimes sought to appear—when he was at ease, Eisenstein radiated such richness of spirit that it lent him an aura of beauty.

He found relief from unhappiness and his sense of inferiority in books and becoming a bitterly acute observer. He continued to draw and began to express himself in dramatic terms. It was at this time that his mother made an attempt to re-establish contact with him by sending him first a present and then three roubles and a photograph which she thought was of his father. Sergei's response to her was ambivalent. He drew a biting caricature of a rich man sparkling with diamonds in the act of receiving homage from an old Jew. Between the proud rich man and the bowing Jew stands a 'little nigger boy' holding a placard with the word 'Merci!!' This he intended to send to his mother. It conveyed the vague

Drawing by Eisenstein on postcard, about 1912

suspicions and hostilities he could not put into words. On the back, he
wrote a note couched in quite a different tenor:

MY DEAR MOTHER!

Thank you very very much for the parcel for which I waited so
impatiently. Also thanks for the 3 roubles and forgive me for not
thanking you before.

I was so eager to get the parcel, that I forgot about the money.
Furthermore I am now very busy with the production of two acts
from Hebbel's tragedy of 'Die Nibelungen' which will be presented
after Lent. I am invited to two parties during Lent, one at Depreo and
the other at Taylava. The music of the navy band is wonderful and I
must learn to play the balalaika.

Father and I examined carefully the photograph of the German
embassy and the person in front of it is not father.

The clipping may be of some use to Vova. I kiss your hand.

X 1000
KOT (TOM CAT.)

But he could not bring himself to send it to the mother he both
loved and hated. Instead he kept it with a few photographs and
'mementoes' of his youth. As for the heroic saga of the *Nibelungen*, it
remained dormant for some twenty-eight years, until he produced *The
Valkyrie* at the Bolshoi Theatre in Moscow. The attraction of mythology and its symbolism already had a hold on him.

Sergei was unable to find security with his father, who expected him
to follow in his footsteps. Mikhail Eisenstein enjoyed life and had many
acquaintances, but Sergei made no close friends and felt ill at ease in the
body Nature had given him. Perhaps he envied his father's ability to
rid himself of grief and anger through the simple act of pounding on the
piano. Mikhail, who was able to adjust himself to living without his
wife, may have grown tired of his son's moods and unwillingness to
confide in him. Unable to comprehend suffering which burst out in
sarcasm instead of tears, he felt his son was an ungrateful boy who
showed too little appreciation for his own efforts to refurnish and keep
a home for him. Finally, he sent Sergei back to Riga for a time where
he lived at No. 6 Nikolajevskaya Street. Here he most probably stayed
with his mother's sisters; he told me twenty years later that he disliked
them and hoped 'they would die in Siberia'.[1]

In Riga, Sergei had the companionship of Maxim Shtraukh who
says that they 'became infatuated with the circus. We gave full performances in the garden and the two of us played all the parts,
including the animals. . . . In 1914 we were separated by war and lost
sight of one another for about six years.'

[1] Eisenstein's parents were divorced in 1909.

Dominating influence

During this time in Riga, Sergei attended the Lycée, but his studies were directed by no overriding passion. He read avidly, with a love for knowledge but little inclination to win scholastic honours. The only marked talent that he showed in his early teens was that of drawing and for a time he attended the School of Fine Arts. But very soon the suffocating atmosphere of academic training, shrouded as it was in superficiality and romanticism, stifled his sensitive and perceiving spirit. Revolted, he turned away to what he thought was a nobler and more intelligent conception—that of literature—and algebra. At the outbreak of the First World War in 1914, Sergei Mikhailovich returned to St. Petersburg to live with his father.

He was sixteen and his father had no patience with his inclination towards art. He expected his son to study engineering and become an engineer like himself. Too timid to argue about the plans drawn up for him by his father, Sergei was enrolled in the University's Institute of Civil Engineering. But, as he later wrote, a 'subconscious and unformulated inclination to work in the field of art induced me to pick a course within engineering that led, not to mechanical, technical fields but to one closely allied to art—to architecture'. (App. One.)

Once he began his studies, he found the scientific approach increasingly fascinating, yet his yearning for art and an interest in philosophy developed hand in hand with his passion for the circus, which never waned. He also discovered the popular variety theatres with the particular humour characteristic of vaudeville comedians and eccentric turns. In every thing he saw, Sergei was extremely conscious of the setting—the circus ring, the stage properties used in the variety shows, the period background of paintings. 'Old things' enchanted his imagination.

In 1916, Sergei Mikhailovich found a focal point in a serious study of the Italian Renaissance. It was not only the liberation of painting which impressed him with the kaleidoscopic character of a culture in its flowering, but also the free dramatic expression which developed simultaneously. Thus, Eisenstein became aware of the Italian Commedia dell'Arte and thought he detected techniques descended from it in the style of comedians in the vaudeville theatres he visited.

While Sergei Mikhailovich was studying at the University, war raged on the Russian Front. Bad as the conditions became for the Russian Army, and grave as the errors committed by the Government, daily life in Petrograd retained a semblance of order until the beginning of 1917, when the Tsarist autocracy began to crack. The voice of protest and revolt crying for a hundred years had not been heeded, nor the undercurrent of prophecy in Russian literature understood. Even at this eleventh hour many people turned deaf ears, thinking that the crumbling regime would check the tide of rebellion before it engulfed them.

In this first period of revolution, the sporadic rumblings roused little response in Sergei Eisenstein. Nineteen years old, he was without political allegiances. This was unusual, because Russian university students had been for decades the most sensitive barometers of political opinion. So preoccupied was he that on the first day 'of the February Revolution, Eisenstein walked through the fighting in the city to attend a performance of Lermontov's *Masquerade*, produced by Vsevolod Meyerhold at the Imperial Alexandrinsky Theatre. The première was postponed and he found the theatre closed. It was closed for ever as an Imperial theatre, when it reopened it was as a State theatre.'[1] While the Empire crumbled around him and innumerable 'splinter' groups rose up offering different panaceas, Eisenstein remained immersed in studies. He continued to live within the routine framework of his life. Nightly he went home to his father's flat.

Since no intimacy had grown up between Sergei and his father, neither discussed any serious matters with the other. Life went on as though the future were assured and it did not strike Sergei Mikhailovich that he, and everyone he knew, including his relatives, were being inexorably engulfed in the volcanic eruption of the Russian people. He had no foresight that in a few months his life would be torn asunder. It did not enter his head that his father would choose one political side and he would be hurtled on to the opposite side of an ideological barricade.

Nor did Sergei feel a sense of his own destiny. He went about his own business without any premonition that out of the chaos he would rise meteor-like to reveal a unique talent. He knew only one thing, that no matter how successful he might be as an engineer, the expression of his innermost self in terms of personal relations would be a difficult, tenuous matter. At nineteen he still had no close friends, no sweetheart; he had never kissed a girl.

Sergei Mikhailovich's emotions were blunted to the impact of external events; he was no longer aware of his loneliness, because he had been struck by the second and greatest influence in his life.

As he had seized upon the small clown as the image of his physical self when he was twelve, so now at nineteen Sergei found his intellectual and spiritual image reflected in Leonardo da Vinci. It was not only Leonardo the painter, whose early 'Benois Madonna' hung in St. Petersburg's Hermitage Museum, that Sergei felt to be his *alter ego*, but Leonardo, the engineer and architect, anatomist and physicist; the man

[1] An article on Sergei M. Eisenstein by Maxim Shtraukh; manuscript in the possession of Jay Leyda.

of many parts, of whom the most exaggerated stories were told by his contemporaries, and who is yet the most mystifying, aloof and impersonal figure in the history of art.

'I was pierced to the depths of my being when I read Leonardo's words about his earliest childhood memory,' Eisenstein told me. He remembered these words: 'It seemed to me, while I lay in the cradle, as though a kite had come down to me, opened my mouth with his tail, and struck me several times between my lips.' He did not understand why then.

He became obsessed with a need to know everything about da Vinci, the man whom he was never to discard as the affinity of his intellectual self. The more he read, the more surely he felt there was some inner connection between da Vinci and himself; that he was to be Leonardo's heir in the twentieth century. An even more compelling connection seemed to him to be established when, at last, he came upon the psychoanalytical study of da Vinci by Freud. In certain features this analysis of Leonardo seemed to apply to himself.

In an interview twelve years later in Paris, Eisenstein told a journalist how: 'He thumbed through it casually [Freud's study of Leonardo da Vinci] and viewed it at first without great conviction and then suddenly "the memory of childhood" exploded like a bomb in the middle of his consciousness. He was staggered. A new sun was on the horizon. All swollen with love; it was a revelation. He threw himself headlong into the "Libido" which carried him into the most sombre regions, into the most distant territories of the human soul. He would go to Vienna in order to follow the courses of this most learned professor, but October 1917 was not far off.'[1]

Sergei Mikhailovich was never conscious of the audacity—the possible effect—of this identification. He accepted it as natural that he, who had accomplished nothing at nineteen, and had no immediate prospects or plans for creative or scientific work, should see his own spirit, almost his very being, in the figure of one of the most encyclopaedic minds that history has recorded; the man whose visions were doomed to remain unrealized because of their magnitude.

Like Leonardo, who, as a young man, had walked through the streets of Florence on Sunday, April the 16th, 1478, and watched the people rioting after the murder of Guiliano de' Medici and later went to the gallows and made a careful sketch of the assassin, Bandino Baroncelli, as he hung by the neck, so Sergei Mikhailovich, caught by the spirit of scientific inquiry, watched and stored up impressions as to how the Tsarist Empire collapsed. He observed with the coolest precision how

[1] Report by 'A.M.' of an interview with Eisenstein, *Cinemonde* (Paris, No. 59, December 1929).

antagonistic classes of people behaved during the days, weeks and months of the political and social earthquake shaking the world.

On Friday, March the 9th 1917, crowds of workers gathering, dispersing, hovering, waiting—like migratory birds expectant of their long-delayed flight into a new climate—thronged the streets. In the shifting crowd, Sergei Mikhailovich observed faces which symbolized to him the nature of the crowd. On other streets he watched the faces, gestures and emotions of the Petrograd gentry confronted by the fear-inspiring spectacle of thousands of people who yet showed no signs of doing violence. The strangely passive behaviour of the people was more terrifying than overt violence. What storm would come when the unnatural calm broke? The bridges of Petrograd were suddenly raised.[1] As if the collapse of feudal Russia could be prevented by the medieval method of raising the drawbridge of a castle!

Each day a new blow was dealt to the old order. The Tsarist regime was growing feebler. Officers no longer knew how to control their men. Soldiers, ordered out to disperse mobs, broke rank, surged forward and, handing over their rifles to anyone who wanted them, kissed their striking comrades from the factories. 'For the people or against the people' was becoming a salutation. On March the 15th, 1917, Tsar Nicholas abdicated. The power of autocracy was shattered.[2]

The Provisional Government took office with Kerensky as Minister of Justice. Soviets of Workers' and Soldiers' Deputies, patterned after those of the 1905 Revolution, were formed throughout the city, each entitled to send one representative to the Taurida Palace, where the new Government was installed with responsibility towards the Soviets. With the autocracy abolished and a democratic system in potential formation, the people's thoughts turned to the question of peace. The imperialist-minded bourgeoisie wanted Constantinople as the price of peace, the masses simply wanted a just peace without annexation. Peace, land, bread was what the people wanted.

During the spring, summer and early autumn of 1917, this question was debated while the Provisional Government vacillated. Leadership of the people hung in the balance. Over this restless period when mobs wandered from one political speaker to the next, Sergei Mikhailovich continued to attend the University. Professors stood up and went through the motions of education like clockwork. Outside the academic halls, the Government fumbled and withheld peace from the milling crowds. Sergei watched these movements of the crowd. There was

[1] When Eisenstein came to interpret this incident in the film *October*, only one bridge was raised.

[2] In the film *October*, Eisenstein symbolized the Tsar's abdication by the pulling apart of a statue of the Tsar.

nothing in his heart or mind against the Revolution as it ebbed and flowed. He merely found no focal point to engage him in politics. He knew nothing of the theories of Karl Marx, and the name of Lenin was not yet known to most of the people in the streets; he was no more politically informed as to the future than the people, even the most illiterate. All he felt was the pulse of Revolution—shift, pause, movement to and fro. His impressions were vivid, though he could not understand exactly what was happening. The rhythm of this early period seeped into the pores of his skin so that ten years later he was able to recreate it out of his consciousness with a force and sense of reality such as never had been seen on the screen.

The hated war on the Western Front continued. The victories of Brzezany in the first week of July and that of Zborow in the third week brought demonstrations from the well-dressed and the well-to-do, who had inherited power through the Provisional Government and dreamed that it was now theirs to keep. But the people clamoured for peace, peace, peace as food grew scarcer and scarcer. Opinions shifted from day to day. Workers would not work; they were searching for democracy, for socialism among the conflicting voices. The voice of a small man with a russet-tinted beard and a high-domed head spoke over and over again to the ever-shifting tides of human beings broken loose from bondage. Lenin promised the Russian people, and the proletariat and peasants of the world, a new society in which the oppressed should inherit the earth and all should have land and bread and freedom from oppression.

To the people who had not yet found a leader, he said quietly, decisively: 'The workers' revolution, a workers' government, means work, that all shall work. When you are ready to go back yourselves to work and you want a government that will go to work and not only think socialism and talk socialism and mean socialism—when you want a government which will do socialism—then come to the Bolsheviki.'[1]

In time they came in ever greater numbers to these Bolsheviks who worked tirelessly within the precincts of the Smolny Institute, which had once housed a school for noble girls. By October 1917, the Bolsheviks (meaning the larger part), under the leadership of the returned exile Lenin, had gained a majority in the Petrograd and Moscow Soviets. The conflict between the Soviets and the Government under Kerensky grew sharper. A trial of strength was coming.

As the Government drifted further out of touch with the popular will of the people, the people's committees coalesced around the Military Revolutionary Committee set up by the Petrograd Soviet and the

[1] *Autobiography of Lincoln Steffens* (New York, Harcourt, Brace and Co., 1931), p. 761.

Central Committee of the Communist Party. Everyone was looking forward with hope—or dread—to November the 8th when the second All-Russia Congress of the Soviets was to meet. Kerensky, as head of the Directorate into which the Provisional Government had evolved,[1] demanded extraordinary powers for the purpose of suppressing the Congress, together with two Bolshevik newspapers. In reply the Military Revolutionary Committee ordered the troops to protect the newspapers *Pravda* and *Izvestia*. On the 7th November, detachments of workmen and soldiers occupied Government buildings, while the Congress of Soviets declared the Government of Kerensky overthrown. The Council of People's Commissars took the place of the former Government. The Second All-Russia Congress of the Soviets accepted the new government headed by Lenin. The first steps taken by the Congress were decrees to end the war with Germany and to distribute the land among the peasants. Thus opened a new chapter in the history of Russia and the World.

Kerensky was able to escape and joined the 1,500 Cossacks under General Krasnov, whom he had ordered to suppress all revolt. Most of his ministers were left behind in the besieged Winter Palace, where the last bulwark against the overthrow of the bourgeois-liberal regime was a regiment of amazonian women. The first phase of the proletarian revolution ended when the sailors of the *Aurora* from the naval fortress of Kronstadt entered St. Petersburg and helped defeat Krasnov's Cossacks. The General was taken prisoner, but released in a burst of enthusiastic generosity and relief that the proletarian revolution had ended with so little bloodshed.

Not even the victory of the Bolsheviks closed the University. Following the few hectic days after the People's Commissars took power, Sergei Mikhailovich returned to his classroom along with his fellow students. Everyone now felt certain that peace would soon be signed with the Germans and the promised dream—peace, land, bread—fulfilled. The people were joyous, but every day the propertied classes became more fearful. Eisenstein, who was neither 'of the people' nor with the Bolsheviks, but yet disinterested in the bourgeoisie, came into no conflict with the new regime. He continued in his role of spectator and student. He was still engrossed with his 'table books', those books he had chosen as his guide. Varied as they were—the works of Freud, Oscar Wilde, Aubrey Beardsley, Maurice Maeterlinck, *Memoirs of Saint Simon*, Ibsen, Weininger, *The Tales of Hoffman* and Schopenhauer—they probed men's souls rather than the nature of society.

Had no civil war developed and no war of intervention, Eisenstein

[1] In the film *October*, Eisenstein interpreted this change as a return to the past. With trick shots, he reassembled the shattered fragments of the Tsar's figure.

might have concluded his studies in engineering and architecture peacefully and followed in his father's footsteps under the new regime. During the winter of 1917–18, he had every reason to feel that the Revolution had been accomplished with remarkably little disruption to his life as a student. But after the peace treaty was signed with the Germans at Brest-Litovsk on the 3rd of March 1918, and the Government moved to Moscow, the old governing classes began to consolidate their forces with the intention of recapturing power. In this late rally they sought the aid of Russia's former allies, France and England. Fighting broke out first in one district, then another.

The first act of intervention came when the Czech prisoners of war in Russia put themselves under French commanders and were supposed to proceed to Vladivostok and, hence, to France. Instead, they broke from the trans-Siberian train and began to fight for the White Russian forces concentrated in western Siberia. Pushing westward, the Czechs captured the Volga city of Samara on the 8th of June 1918. Five weeks later, General Krasnov, whom the Bolsheviks had released, commenced to fight the 'Reds' in the Don region. The Germans, with whom the Bolsheviks signed a peace treaty, had already moved eastward through the Ukraine. The area held by the Soviets began to shrink. Civil war and intervention broke out in Archangel; the Japanese sent warships to Vladivostok. American troops joined the Japanese at Vladivostok and the British at Archangel.

Soon civil war tore homes, country and the relatively peaceful Revolution to pieces. Each day, every week and the succeeding months brought terror, battles, victories, defeats, atrocities to both the 'Reds' and the 'Whites'. The feeble Army of Workers and Peasants, ragged, untrained, fought like tigers. Partisan groups formed in the woods, stalked the old regime across the endless steppes. The ranks of the Red Army swelled, the revolutionary army retreated, attacked, held the advantage, advanced, only to be thrust back again. . . .

Arriving one morning for his class at the University, Sergei Eisenstein found its hallowed precincts in an uproar. Every student seemed to be in the corridors, milling about, bent on his own business. Pushing his way through the crowds, Sergei Mikhailovich went in search of his class. When he found his fellow students, they had just voted to enter the Red Army for the defence of Petrograd. For all his confusion it never entered his head to dissociate himself from his comrades. He could not set himself against the Revolution. Even though he had no clear political opinions, he knew that he was on the side of the people.

Almost the same day his father came to an independent decision. Mikhail Eisenstein decided to support the counter-revolution. Thus, Sergei and his father parted; the one fighting to preserve and further the Revolution, the other in a vain effort to destroy it. With the defeat of the 'White' Russian forces, Mikhail Eisenstein fled to Germany.

As Sergei Mikhailovich and his University comrades moved up in the rear of the ragged bands of workers and peasants to face the re-assembled officers of the Tsarist regime equipped and aided by Russia's former allies and enemies, a profound emotion swept even the most irresponsible of the recruits. The hopeful emotions of the first months following the October Revolution now stiffened the resolve of millions of young people. They were willing to die to save Russia from a return of the old regime and the grip of the Interventionists. Death rather than the defeat of the people's will as in 1905.

From this spirit, intensified by each defeat and increased by the smallest victory, miracles sprang. Not the least miracle was how such an ill-armed, ill-trained, nondescript band as the Army of Workers and Peasants managed to hold together in the face of privation and the gradual breakdown of communications. The only explanation for the final triumph of the people's army is that its supporters were filled with such passionate conviction that there was nothing too hard or too terrible for them to endure. These people—millions of whom had shown no great qualities before—felt themselves as a unit. They were part of a new fraternity cemented by a new faith. In this moment of history numberless people found a love greater than any personal love. They loved the Revolution, this striving, sprawling, spawning new idea which was in mortal danger of being strangled. Such sentiments reached white heat at the front and in the immediate rear of battle.

In this atmosphere it is easy to understand how all that was humanistic and philosophically far-sighted in Sergei Eisenstein responded to the struggle in which he now found himself a small unnoticed cog. From the Petrograd front he moved with his detachment eastward to the Vologda front and from there to Dvinsk. Even in the filth and stench of troop trains and overcrowded barracks he experienced an elation, if not a happiness, he had never known before. Comradeship became his for the first time in his life, and he shared with his comrades a sense of destiny. Somehow everyone knew he could withstand the concentrated attack of the foreign capitalists and the consolidated remnants of the old regime. They were conscious of being a liberated people who were going to defeat autocracy, national or international.

Caught up in the tide of revolution, he could only suffer a profound sense of shock at the world which had fashioned him when most of its members sided against the Russian people. It seemed all the more terrible when most reasonable people the world over had long agreed that a revolution in Russia was necessary and inevitable. To Sergei the shock was very close. By siding with the 'White' Russians, his father had become 'an enemy of the people'. This was the most heinous crime a man could commit—one which can be understood only in times of revolution and war. It appeared like the murder of the long-cherished hopes of an oppressed people who at last had gained their freedom.

Sergei Eisenstein, as part of the intelligentsia, wished to be one of the new men worthy to build the rich and free world lying beyond the anguish of civil war. A new-found brotherhood between the literate and the illiterate—between the intelligentsia and the humblest worker and peasant was being cremented. But in actuality this newly discovered brotherhood—being rough, harsh, coarse—was often difficult for him to master. He witnessed his comrades doing things which lacerated his soul; he saw people with good hearts do terrible things to people who had done evil. Peasant girls skinned alive a village priest who had raped them. To escape, to save the chastity of his spirit, Sergei Mikhailovich often shrank into himself, yearning for the gentle and beautiful things in the world going down to destruction.

He hated his shrinking feelings, despised his sensibility. There must be something soft and decadent in him to make him seek dreams of beauty and desire tender and reverent sentiments. Disgusted by what he thought was his weakness of character, he longed to rip from his nature the moral precepts and refinements instilled into him by his traitorous father and the mother who had rejected him; he wanted them to be consumed by the fire of his growing hatred for all manifestations of the bourgeois world. He wanted to be freed from his innate physical modesty, his reticence, his secret feeling that he could only give up his virginity as an act of sacred love and not as an act of bravado to be flung in the face of bourgeois conventions.

Unable to endure the good-natured, uninhibited jeers of his robust comrades, Sergei Mikhailovich took refuge in his role of clown to conceal his mortifying sensitivity and romanticism. He clowned with the humour of Rabelais; his wit was barbed with such pornographic imagery that it caused the more natural and simple Russians to blush. Since it was God, the Virgin and the Child who constrained him from action and set in his soul a sense of sin, he lashed them with blasphemy.

As revolution and service to the growing Red Army released a flood of contradictory emotions in Sergei Mikhailovich, the great events of the moment also released his natural talents. To be of service to the Revolution—to the people—replaced the age-old admonition 'Honour thy Father and thy Mother'. At this precarious moment there were many degrees of service. Those performed by Sergei Mikhailovich and his comrades were often very humble ones; the only thing which made them memorable was the passion with which they were performed.

At first Sergei Eisenstein's knowledge of engineering was utilized in building defences, but later he was engaged in decorating troop trains and freight cars moving up to the front. He made banners, painted slogans and executed drawings explaining or glorifying the Revolution. Not infrequently he castigated the old regime with a flourish of uproariously funny satire, made all the sharper because of his intimacy with it and his subjective feelings that the bourgeois world had made a weakling of him.

These were crude ways of trying to give substance to the idea of a new society, but they were an effective means of cutting the ground from under the feet of the counter-revolution. Thus, from the very beginning of the Revolution, pictorial and dramatic propaganda was exceedingly important. In this work, so humble, elementary in terms of 'art', Sergei Mikhailovich found a niche and developed his great latent talent for design. With bold, flowing, economical lines he could reduce an idea to a witty, wicked, powerful image. In 1920 his talent for agitational propaganda was recognized and Eisenstein was transferred to the political command and sent as a poster artist to the front at Minsk.

Even at this time Eisenstein's ability to give his ideas visual form was balanced by intense analytical activity. In the most violent period of civil war, Sergei Mikhailovich would withdraw into himself and concentrate upon some abstract idea or interest. In this way his intellectual curiosity led him to the most unexpected of subjects. At the Minsk front, he lived in a freight car with other members of the political command. Among them was a former instructor in Japanese.

Many a Russian student might at that time have shown a passing interest in Japan. At least a part of the intense international-mindedness in Russia was due to the belief that the workers of the world would rise up in revolt and thus bring the intervention to an end. Yet not one student in a thousand would have set himself, as Eisenstein did, to understand the nature of the Japanese language and to learn three hundred characters. He became intoxicated with the hieroglyphics, and traced them back to their Chinese origin. There was the one of 'ma', retaining in a formal design a depictive image of its meaning—a horse. Still more fascinating was a second category of hieroglyphics, the 'huee-i', which Sergei called 'copulative'. These united two depictables—for example, 'to weep', the stylized picture of water and an eye; 'to listen', an ear near a drawing of a door; 'to sorrow', a knife and a heart. From the building up of Japanese hieroglyphics, Eisenstein discovered the essential character of the Japanese Kabuki Theatre and its corresponding technique of building up effects. In a few years this was to serve him as one of the cornerstones for his own theatrical and film technique of 'montage'.

Sergei Mikhailovich concluded that Japanese was one of the most interesting languages on earth. It followed he must devote his life to its study. Immediately he decided to abandon his career of architecture and engineering and become a professor of Japanese. This would take him to Japan, where he could study Kakubi Theatre. In the throes of revolution and civil war this never struck him as a curious choice of a profession; nor did anyone else consider it the least odd. Such a sudden switch in interest conflicted with no plan. Sergei Mikhailovich, like every young man who had once had plans, was now free to remake his life if he so desired. Nor was Eisenstein's choice of Japanese in conflict with the larger plan of the Revolution; indeed, its study was in the spirit of the Revolution.

By the middle of 1920, it was clear that the tide of battle was turning in favour of the Red Army. The pressure of intervention slackened and the 'White' armies were in retreat all over the country. The Bolshevik Government was now firmly established, and attention had to be directed to the urgent problem of what to do with millions of uprooted people and the problem of reconstruction.

As part of the move towards the reconstruction of the shattered country, it was decreed that those university students who had supported the Red Army be demobilized. As a reward for their services they could return to their studies at the Government's expense. They could study whatever they pleased at the university of their choice. This decree enabled Sergei Eisenstein to apply to study Japanese at the University of Moscow, the only place in Russia where Japanese was taught. After some waiting, Sergei Mikhailovich received his discharge papers and a pass to Moscow.

As he later wrote:

> The revolutionary tempest . . . freed me from the inertia of the course I had marked out, and let me develop inclinations which by themselves did not have the strength to free themselves. . . .
>
> It took the shattering of the foundations of the country . . . to make the timid student break the chains of the career marked out for him by solicitous parents from early youth, abandon an almost completed education and assured future, and plunge into the unknown future of an artistic career.
>
> From the front I returned not to Petrograd to complete studies begun but to Moscow to start something entirely new. (App. One.)

Note 1977. See Eisenstein's *Autobiography* (London, Dennis Dobson, 1978) for confirmation of parents' conflict and Eisenstein's relations with each of them. [See also pp. 126, 318–21.]

CHAPTER TWO

From Hieroglyphs to Acrobatics

The muscles which move the lips of the mouth are more numerous
in man than in other animals; and this order is a necessity . . . in
whistling, laughing, weeping and other actions like these. Also in
the strange contortions used by clowns when they imitate faces.
LEONARDO DA VINCI, Fogli B. 29 r.

ARRIVING in Moscow in the autumn of 1920, Sergei
Mikhailovich found that life in the mother city of Russia had
reached its lowest ebb. The almost complete destruction of the trans-
port system had left the people with nothing to eat except the crumbs
left over from the soldiers' miserably small food supplies. The only
shops which remained open were the State bookshops and the few
half-empty co-operative stores. To keep from freezing to death people
were burning their furniture and demolishing the wooden houses; lack
of electricity had brought most tramcars to a standstill. People died in
great numbers from typhus.

Every stranger arriving in Moscow was regarded with fear and suspicion. They might be spies or saboteurs. The battlefield was in the
minds of people rather than in the exchange of shots. There were many
cases like that of Sergei Eisenstein where father and son stood and
battled on opposite sides; brother fought against brother and wives
became the enemies of their husbands. The atmosphere of terrible
hardship was shot through with suspicion, caution, hostility.

Sergei Mikhailovich found his way to an address given him by a
comrade. He asked if he could have a room; without explanation the
door was closed in his face. He went to several other houses, but no one
would give him a room. Bewildered, he did not know where to go
next. He knew no one in the whole city. Soon he discovered he could
not even eat. Food was rationed and he had no ration book. The University had not opened. Applying for a ration book he was informed
that ration books were given only to people who had a job. Helplessly
he walked the unfamiliar streets. Other men went to a soldier's committee and demanded aid. But Eisenstein was so filled with loneliness
that he felt stripped of all identity. Suddenly he realized all his ties with
the past were broken. Nothing held him to the future except the
thought that he knew some Japanese and that the University must open

soon. He wondered why he had not changed his name like many of his comrades who realized they belonged to no one and so took new names with which to begin a new life.

He forgot how long he wandered in the starving city wondering where he could find a place to sleep for the night, a crust of bread and some practical advice. Then chance flung him in the way of a young man who took him home to share his room. That night not only were his immediate problems solved, but his life turned into yet another channel.

In relating his experiences to me, Eisenstein did not mention the name of the young man; but from an account given by Maxim Shtraukh of his chance reunion with Sergei Mikhailovich, Shtraukh may well have been the person. 'Our next meeting', after Riga, says Shtraukh, 'happened under rather unusual circumstances. One evening I wanted to attend a performance at the Kamerny Theatre and was to buy a ticket from a "scalper". In those days these speculators were subject to prosecution and were usually arrested while in the act of illegal sale of tickets in front of the theatre just before the performances. I almost made a deal with one of them when I suddenly felt the intense stare of a man in military uniform upon me. I assumed that he was a member of the militia whose duty it was to arrest not only the ticket seller, but also the people who bought the tickets from him. I became very uncomfortable and quickly entered the theatre. I was quite surprised when the stranger appeared nearby again. He stared at me from under a frowning brow, and was obviously observing me. I moved away again. This was repeated several times until the persistent stranger approached me and asked uncertainly—"Aren't you Shtraukh?"

'The stranger turned out to be not a militia man at all, but Eisenstein. It is not surprising that we didn't recognize each other. We had not seen each other for several years. We had known one another as boys, but were now young men. In addition Eisenstein was wearing a military overcoat and cap. He had just come to Moscow from the Western front.

'Our meeting was a happy one and we walked the streets of Moscow all night. We shared our past experiences and our dreams about the future. We were still interested in the theatre and decided to work together. However, we wanted to create and serve an art that was an expression of the fighting mood of the times and which would be a weapon of the revolution. It was this that led us to the Proletkult."[1]

Before the night was over a plan had been worked out. Eisenstein should paint the scenery for the Proletkult Theatre until the University of Moscow opened; this work would entitle him to a ration book, and a

[1] *Encounters* by Maxim Shtraukh, Iskusstvo Kino, Nos. 1-2, (Moscow, 1940).

room. Money as a means of exchange having ceased to function, food and a room was all a man needed. The next morning Eisenstein went to see Valeri Pletnyov, the Chairman of the Proletkult Theatre, who immediately gave him a job.

As the name implies, Proletkult was dedicated 'to promote culture among the workers, and to encourage gifted young men and women from the common people, largely factory workers, to express themselves freely in art, drama, poetry and literature'.[1] Proletkult was striving to create a new culture to take the place of the withering bourgeois culture, which, according to Proletkult theorists, no longer had a place since the class under which it had grown, and which it represented, was now replaced in power by the proletariat.

Shortly before Sergei Mikhailovich joined the Proletkult, the theatre had evolved from its first crude stage of so-called agit-prop productions when its 'workers during acute moments of the Civil War were in the position of danger at the fronts . . . even stepping straight from the theatre to the trenches'. Now it was equipped with a building in Moscow—the Central Arena of the Proletkult—where agit-prop performances were gradually evolving so that they required more elaborate staging. Eisenstein's experience in decorating troop trains for the Red Army had allowed him to develop a technique suited to the Proletkult Theatre. Though he was a former bourgeois, there was no feeling that his ideas clashed with those of the Proletkult people.

Pletnyov was a proletarian writer with considerable experience in organizing. As they talked of the purposes of the new theatre in the Soviet Union, and particularly the Proletkult, Sergei Mikhailovich became more and more intrigued with the possibilities of his new-found work. He was extremely sympathetic to the idea of propagandizing the ideas of the Revolution in terms of drama. He thought it necessary for such a theatre to struggle against the ideas and techniques of the old, supposedly dying theatre, where personal problems dominated and carried the audience away from the present into the past, or into preoccupation with 'romance'. A new theatre expressive of the classless society must be created.

Sergei Eisenstein then went to work, or perhaps it would be more accurate to say that he was swallowed up in a vortex of activity among eager people intoxicated with the ideas of the Revolution and of experimenting with ways of presenting those ideas. All of them were always half-starved, yet they made merciless mirth of food and plenty. In a half-hysterical state of creative excitement, they forgot their hunger and the terrible cold that racked their bodies in the winter of 1920-1.

[1] *New Spirit of the Soviet Theatre* by Huntley Carter (London, Chapman and Dodd Ltd., 1924), p. 81.

Sergei too was hungry, but he forgot this gnawing hunger along with his plans to become a professor of the Japanese language. However, his interest in, and study of, Japanese theatre and art continued.

The passionate desire of the Proletkult people to create a new art reflective of their revolutionary ideology was not, at this time, much above politically conscious vaudeville, with the accent on the satirical and the eccentric. Their agit-prop sketches were performed by factory workers after a day's work; other workers would come and sing, dance or play instruments. There was much fun-making and comic horse-play. The best of the agit-prop skits were a kind of 'living newspaper' enlivened by a great vitality and unpolished originality. However crude the Proletkult performances might be by any professional standard, they revealed that the people had taken hold of the idea that art belonged to them and that everyone who wanted to participate in creating 'theatre' had the undisputed right to do so.

With Eisenstein's arrival at the Proletkult his star had risen. Before this moment he had lacked direction. Hovering between engineering, architecture and languages, his genius had found no focal point. But setting foot in the 'theatre', even his first work emerged as a distinct creative act. He served no period of apprenticeship but was immediately appointed a designer. He also became co-director, or co-regisseur in Russian terminology.

B. Arbatov had made what they called an 'agit-poster' from Jack London's story *The Mexican*, the direction of which was in the hands of Valeri Smishlayev, a theorist of the Proletkult. Eisenstein was appointed to design the scenery and costumes for this production, the story of which indicates the extreme simplicity of the group's aims—indeed the crudity of what they regarded as revolutionary subject-matter: A group of Mexican revolutionaries require money to carry on their activities. A young Mexican offers to get the money through manipulating a boxing match. He trains for the fight and conspires with the champion to let himself be beaten for a small part of the prize. But when he gets into the ring, he beats the champion and thus wins the entire prize.

It is interesting that Eisenstein, generally considered the most objective of directors, began his creative career by clothing this simplest of 'agit-posters' with the trappings of his subjective passion—the circus. Both scenery and costumes for *The Mexican* were derived from the circus, the clearest derivative being in the style of the costumes—baggy and heavily padded—so that many of the characters appeared in the guise of clowns. Likewise, some of the movements of the actors reflected what Sergei Mikhailovich had seen in the circus ring when he was twelve years old.

Not content with clothing *The Mexican* with circus costuming and injecting certain formal movements, Sergei Mikhailovich added elements of his own embryonic genius—the spirit of reality which was to develop into the powerful imagery of his films. The climax of the Jack London 'agit-poster' was the fight. This, Smishlayev, the regisseur, intended to produce in the conventional manner—an impression conveyed to the spectator through the reactions of the characters observing the supposed fight going on off-stage. Eisenstein, present in his capacity of designer, could not refrain from making a far more dynamic suggestion of his own. He proposed to stage a real fight in sight of the audience. His idea struck everyone as highly original. Encouraged by the acceptance of his first directorial attempt, he thought it would be appropriate to stage the fight on a dais in the middle of the auditorium, in order to create the illusion that the fight was a real one in a boxing ring. But this suggestion was summarily crushed by the theatre's fireman. Writing of the fight many years later, Eisenstein remembered this scene as employing 'realistic, even textual means—real fighting, bodies crashing to the ring floor, panting, the shine of sweat on the torso, and finally, the unforgettable smacking of gloves against taut skin and strained muscles'. Analysing the course of development which led him towards the cinema, Eisenstein said that the roots could be detected in the production of *The Mexican*. 'Here, my participation brought into the theatre "events" themselves—a purely cinematographic element, as distinguished from 'reactions to events'—which is a purely theatrical element.'[1]

Yet other elements of Eisenstein's talent found tentative expression in *The Mexican*. The groupings of actors—unmistakably of his design—already suggest his superb sense of composition. It is as though he saw movement broken down into 'shots' and edited. Compared with other Proletkult productions of this period, *The Mexican* stood out for its sharpness and style—as if marked by the hand of a great artist. With this production, Sergei Mikhailovich not only commenced his career, but with it there began his consuming interest in Mexico, the subject which was to culminate in the most tragic and devastating experience of his life. Thus, in this very first work, Eisenstein at twenty-two years of age created a working sketch of his creative life.

It is difficult to say whether the Proletkult Theatre had of its own volition reached the point in its development where it must go forward to more ambitious productions, or if the sudden crystallizing of Eisenstein's ideas pushed the theatre into a technical advance. In later years he claimed it was due to him. At any rate, from the moment of his association with the group, the productions began to develop style,

[1] *Film Form* by S. M. Eisenstein (New York, Harcourt Brace and Co., 1949 and London, Dennis Dobson, 1950), p. 6.

rhythm and a certain startling eccentricity. After *The Mexican*, 'agit-prop' and 'agit-poster' productions gave way to adaptation of both traditional and new plays.

Pletnyov had written a play called *Precipice* concerning an inventor caught in the web of a big city still in the grip of capitalism. The play was given to Smishlayev to produce with Eisenstein designated as co-regisseur as well as designer. Sergei Mikhailovich, who had not experienced the reality of Western urbanism, nor the heart of capitalism —the American city—had some very strange and startling ideas about how to convey theatrically the helplessness of the individual in the 'big city'. Some very wild notions came pouring into his head. He wanted to have moving scenery, 'running scenery', parts of which were to be attached to the actors who should wear roller skates! His designs, which were subsequently lost, resulted from a study of the current cubistic paintings of Picasso, which integrated man and his physical sur-roundings into a unified composition. Some of the details long sur-vived in Eisenstein's mind after his disagreement with Smishlayev and the abandonment of their joint production.

The legs of two bankers were to support a stock exchange with two top hats atop the roof. The policeman was to wear a costume decorated with streets, automobiles, trucks and tramcars; while the costumes of other characters were to blaze with lights—street lamps and electric signs shown in perspective. In effect these unrealized ideas for scenery and costumes hinted the components of film montage before its 'inven-tion'. Finally, the production was shelved for more than a year before being assigned to another director. Eisenstein, who was never to allow the breakdown of a working collaboration to fill him with personal bitterness, was assigned to V. Tikhonovich as designer for the produc-tion of the play *King Hunger* by Leonid Andreyev. [Plate 7]

The production of this play at the Proletkult Theatre was in accord with the Marxist and Leninist concept that art to be real must reflect the actuality of life. It was an integration of dramatic subject with the events of life. At the moment of its production in 1921, drought had brought 25,000,000 people in the Volga region to the verge of starva-tion. The people crowded to the river's bank to die. To postpone the death of their children, women fought for scraps of horse dung which they cooked in the contaminated water of the Volga. Yet the artists of the Moscow Proletkult went on working feverishly. It was as though the steel-tipped words of Vladimir Mayakovsky, poet of the Revolu-tion, gave them courage:

> Who can match the glow of our golds?
> Will the waspy bullets bite?
> We strike back with songs for weapons.
> Massive god—our thundering voices.

The third production designed by Eisenstein was *Macbeth*, a production of V. Tikhonovich, produced at the Polenov Theatre in Moscow. In his designs for *Macbeth*, Eisenstein revealed the versatility of his style as a stage designer. Nothing could be more naturalistic than the Victorian setting, nor subtly suggestive than the figure of Lady Macbeth with the cat whom she resembles. Indeed, this could be the work of a designer for Stanislavsky's Moscow Art Theatre. In striking opposition is the costume design for Duncan, which is a foreshadowing of the symbolic use of costumes which Eisenstein developed during the final decade of his life. [Plate 4]

The longer he watched his friend Maxim Straukh and a girl named Judith Glizer, the more he was impressed with their talent. They could adapt every style of make-up as though it were a mask, yet wear it as if it were their own face. Judith Glizer revealed a strong sense of eccentric acting blended with a rich observation of life. The longer Sergei Mikhailovich watched this expressive pair, the more it seemed to him they echoed the spirit of the Commedia dell' Arte. Soon they married and for many years Eisenstein lived in the next room to theirs at Chysti Prudi 23.[1]

Following *Macbeth*, Sergei Mikhailovich went to work for a short time at a small studio theatre—Mastfor, or Free Studio of Forreger, which was entirely devoted to satire.[2] Forreger's first success, with Eisenstein as designer, was a programme of three *Vaudevilles*—*A Good Relation with Horses* by V. Mass; *Thieving Children* by Dennery; and *The Phenomenal Tragedy of Phetra*. Each parodied a current production in one of the old, or 'art', theatres of Moscow.

The most famous production burlesqued in *Vaudevilles* was that of Racine's *Phèdre*, which had recently been produced by Alexander Tairov at the Kamerny Theatre with his wife, Alice Koonen, as the classical heroine. Illustrative of Tairov's theories of the 'aesthetic' theatre (he himself called it the 'synthetic' theatre) where the actors were trained to perform classic tragedy, musical comedies and modern European and American plays with equal ease and skill, the movements, gesture and speech were synthesized with the synthetic (or aesthetic) *décor* and musical accompaniment. The highly styled gesturing of *Phèdre*—like a ballet performed to words—lent itself to hilariously eccentric burlesque in *The Phenomenal Tragedy of Phetra*, a stab at the theories of Tairov.

To critics who reverenced the art theatres and their respective

---

[1] Maxim Straukh and Judith Glizer later became the leading actors of the Theatre of Revolution and of the Moscow Dramatic Theatre. Straukh acted as an assistant on Eisenstein's films *Strike*, *Potemkin*, *October* and *General Line*.

[2] Which became the Theatre of Satire and lasted until the mid-1930's.

traditions, Forreger's studio 'was degraded to a series of acrobatic tricks and variety turns.' Forreger's view, which was shared by Eisenstein at this period, 'was that the old world could best be destroyed by making it ridiculous, so he tried to pour scorn on the theatre by parodying it.' In his productions, of which '*Vaudevilles* was an early example,' the orchestra was replaced by the 'noise band', and the ballet by 'machine dancing' and for a long time these two new art-forms were accounted the highest achievements of the Revolutionary Theatre.[1]

But Eisenstein's contact with the art theatre, albeit via burlesque, engendered in him the ambition to create his own special kind of theatre. He ceased to think in terms of 'voluntary' or 'amateur' theatre and was seized with the desire to excel any professional director in Russia. In order to accomplish his ambition, he realized he must learn theatre craft. Since he had found his place in the so-called Left theatre ideologically dedicated to the Revolution, he joined the recognized leader of the Left, Vsevolod Meyerhold, the most brilliant, volatile and revolutionary figure in the Russian theatre since 1900, around whom constellations circled including poets, painters and dramatists.

Meyerhold was pleased to accept Eisenstein as designer for his production of G. B. Shaw's *Heartbreak House*. Thus, Sergei Mikhailovich found himself surrounded by the sophisticated *avant-guard*, all of whom believed they had now inherited the earth and it was their special function to develop entirely new art forms which would sweep out the old styles from Russia and the world. Their criticism was levelled particularly at the nineteenth century and the pre-Revolutionary years of their own era. [Plate 7]

Meyerhold and Eisenstein had much in common—their wit and volatility, their intense interest in experiment and a mutual understanding of satire. In Eisenstein, Meyerhold saw a young disciple and poured out his knowledge of the theatre to him.

Most important to Sergei Mikhailovich, who had carried his bent for science into the theatre, was Meyerhold's concept of drama. Years before the Revolution he had discarded the idea of theatre as a place of initiation where the actualities of life were reshaped to appear 'natural', where the audience was in the position of peeping through a keyhole to watch the subtle emotions of individuals weaving their way through episodes of 'life'. To Meyerhold the theatre was not a static form dedicated solely to the drama of individuals; it was an expression of an evolutionary process, hence the theatre must constantly discard old forms to attain the essential form suited to a given period. He also sought to break down the gap between the stage and the auditorium

[1] *The Russian Theatre* by Rene Fülop-Miller and Joseph Gregor (Philadelphia, Lippincott and Co., 1930 and London, George Harrap & Co. Ltd., 1930), p. 70.

which had developed with the traditional proscenium arch. By drawing the spectator into closer contact with the action on the stage, Meyerhold believed that the actor and spectator would become united in such a way that for the period of the performance the spectator would identify himself with the action on the stage. This was a concept Eisenstein at once began to apply in his own theatre work and later in the making of films. It was the problem he attempted to solve throughout his career and discussed twenty-six years later in his theoretical writing concerning stereoscopic cinema, which he thought would '"cover" the breach . . . separating the spectator and actor'.[1]

By the time Eisenstein joined the Meyerhold Theatre early in 1922, Meyerhold was working in terms of his latest and final theory of the theatre. This he called 'bio-mechanics', which 'established a principle of analysis by which each movement of the body can be differentiated and made fully expressive'. He considered it to be the projection into the theatre of the scientific spirit motivating the life of Russia at that period when the Machine had become the symbol of the new world. Applied to acting, mechanical theory and the biological experiments of Pavlov, bio-mechanics was in direct opposition to the emotional and psychological approach of Stanislavsky's Moscow Art Theatre where internal, contemplative study of a role produced in the actor the natural externalized expression of emotion in his gestures, facial expression and voice inflexion. According to Meyerhold, the same emotions could be stimulated in the actor and conveyed to the spectator by an external method—bio-mechanics which considered the actor as a complex machine composed of many interlocking parts. The problem of mastering bio-mechanics was how to obtain maximum performance of each part—for example, the muscles and tendons which equalled flexible piston rods and cylinders.

Replacing the emotional theory of acting, bio-mechanics was intended as a scientific education for the actor, training his intellect and developing his body control through sport. As a theory it had its social basis (a fact exceedingly important in post-Revolutionary Russia) in the physical organization of the workers. It also incorporated into the modern theatre some features developed by the Italian comedians of the Commedia del'Arte and the techniques of the circus performer, 'where precision, dexterity, steel nerves, courage, daring, judgement and an engineering exactitude' were essentials.[2] The many facets of bio-mechanics were profoundly fascinating to Eisenstein. He 'sought

---

[1] S. M. Eisenstein 'Stereoscopic Films' (*Penguin Film Review*, No. 8, Penguin Books London, 1949).

[2] *The New Spirit of the Soviet Theatre* by Huntley Carter (London, Chapman and Dodd Ltd., 1924), p. 52 *et seq.*

the same sphere of exact knowledge that had succeeded in captivating [him] during [his] short experience in engineering'. (App. One).

In 1922, Meyerhold's theory resulted in productions which exactly reflected the tempo and spirit of the time. It suited the presentation of expressionistic plays where characters symbolized ideas. As a method it was highly effective when used in satirical interpretations of the Russian classics.[1] The exaggerated movements, reflective of mechanical motion, the rhythmical, stylized speech of the actors created a harmonious dissonance when set against the stark futurist, constructivist and functionalist *décor* characteristic of the Meyerhold theatre. All 'naturalism' was bourgeois and Meyerhold eliminated it entirely from his stage, except as a symbol. Thus, there would appear on a stage lighted by unconcealed spotlights and equipped with some gaunt wooden abstractions symbolizing bridge, path, forest or machine such an object as a perfect mid-nineteenth-century footstool or an exquisite antique chair.

For some nine months Meyerhold rehearsed *Heartbreak House*. As designer, Eisenstein was constantly present at conferences and rehearsals. He worked hard, determined to learn as quickly as possible because he was already developing ideas for a theatre of his own. With no intentions of being an imitator of Meyerhold, he began to extend the theories of Meyerhold in his own mind. The theory which gradually evolved was that of the Acrobatic Theatre. This was an extension of his first production, *The Mexican*, and the further evolution of some aspects of Meyerhold's bio-mechanics.

Soon Sergei Mikhailovich became aware that though Meyerhold was a very great director possessed of vast originality, he was a dictator in his theatre. It was Meyerhold and not his actors who created each character complete to the last gesture and tone of voice. He would rush on to the stage from his seat in the auditorium and act out every character in each scene; hence what his actors produced was a mere copy of Meyerhold's own interpretation. Eisenstein quickly noted Meyerhold's Achilles' heel. As a pupil he learned that when he became a director he must avoid dictation and draw out from student or actor what is in him. He also noticed, and turned to his own use, the fact that the actors in Meyerhold's theatre with the greatest amount of individuality were not happy; they wanted scope to develop their own ideas.

While at Meyerhold's theatre, Sergei Mikhailovich met a young actor who was soon to play an important role in his life. This was Grigori Alexandrov, who was identified with Eisenstein as his collaborator until 1932. According to Sergei Mikhailovich, it was a moment

[1] Meyerhold's most noted productions were of Ostrovsky's *The Forest* and Gogol's *Ravizor* (*Inspector General*).

of unbearable hunger which drove Alexandrov, generally known as Grisha, into his orbit.

The actors brought what food they could scrape together to the theatre and hid it. One day Eisenstein brought a chunk of bread but forgot to conceal it. The stark days of famine affected Alexandrov more intensely than Sergei Mikhailovich, whose physical hunger was allayed by his burning passion for creative work. Alexandrov could not forget the void in his stomach and when he saw Eisenstein's bread lying by the theatre switchboard he was unable to resist his ravenous hunger. Grisha had almost finished the sour black mass when Sergei Mikhailovich appeared. They fought like beasts over the remaining fragment. But suddenly Alexandrov went limp and explained how he had not eaten for two days. Eisenstein, who had eaten the day before, gave the remains of the gnawed bread to Grisha.

After that Eisenstein, who had merely greeted Alexandrov in the morning and said farewell when rehearsals broke up, became aware of Grisha's social and physical charm. He was nineteen and his body was beautifully co-ordinated, his features strong and regular, and he had handsome golden hair. Clever and gay, he glowed with magnetic animal energy and love of life. He was the social success of the Meyerhold Theatre and whenever he played the piano he attracted a crowd.

He was resourceful, and even the most obtuse subject appeared simple when Alexandrov explained it. A few years later, he married the beautiful Anna Sten, the young Soviet actress who was brought to Hollywood in 1932.

Alexandrov may have felt the superiority of Eisenstein—the curious, cold justice he had displayed over the bread. They began to exchange ideas and, contrary to Eisenstein's expectation, Alexandrov showed an extraordinarily quick grasp of what Sergei Mikhailovich was talking about. It seemed he could reduce the complexity of Eisenstein's concepts to a simple statement. Their discussions were joined by Sergei Mikhailovich's Proletkult friends, Shtraukh and Glizer. Amid the play of these personalities, Eisenstein confided his plans for an Acrobatic Theatre, while Meyerhold continued to rehearse *Heartbreak House*.

Alexandrov was fascinated by the possibilities of applying and extending the technique he had learned from Meyerhold in a freer environment. If Eisenstein could put through his plan, he was entirely willing to act on a tightrope or the trapeze. Carried forward on a wave of enthusiasm, they all saw this new advance as yet a further step towards destroying the hated naturalism of the old theatre.

In this period of intensive experiment no theory, however wild, was buried without heated argument. The Acrobatic Theatre did not arise in a vacuum. A great storm of discussion had arisen about the future character of the circus. The central question was how to bring the circus into line with current life. The circus must become socially conscious, for if it remained outside the influence of contemporary life, then it would divert people from the urgent problem of building socialism. In short, a non-Marxist circus constituted a place of escapism. Yet even the most socially conscious workers flocked to it to watch elephants, acrobats and clowns performing according to the old traditions of their calling. The appeal of the circus was seemingly irresistible. As if intoxicated, the eyes of even the most revolutionary spectator were riveted upon the tight-rope walker and the trapeze artist.

Sergei Mikhailovich and his friends often went to the circus in search of those elements they could incorporate into the embryonic Acrobatic Theatre. For Sergei Mikhailovich, the circus was a link with his boyhood, a thread leading him back to the clown with the big head. A sense of identification with the clowns remained. But the years had changed his feelings about the acrobats. Now he watched them with a scientific eye. Their physical control no longer appeared mysterious, miraculous. He was intent on understanding the reactions of the audience to their feats of balance. It seemed that each and every person in the audience identified themselves with the performers. Clearly, the fascination of the circus had much to teach the theatre man seeking to captivate his audience.

As Sergei Mikhailovich listened to the arguments about the circus in a socially conscious, classless society where everyone would ultimately find satisfaction in his life and work and, in consequence, not require the stimulus of vicarious excitement in watching feats of balance, he came upon a problem which to him Marxism could not explain. It seemed to Eisenstein ridiculous that man's reaction to feats of balance would ever wither and die. The fascination was not grounded in man's ideology, it was independent of economic and political laws; its roots lay in the biological make-up of man. Many years later, towards the end of his life, Eisenstein wrote: 'The perfection of skill, strength, self-control, will-power and daring which gives brilliance to the circus will always be an expression of the natural urge for the fullest development of the qualities which are of the essence of our physical nature.'[1]

The attraction of acrobats could be utilized, Sergei Mikhailovich thought, to stress the play of emotions between characters in the theatre. Working from this idea, Eisenstein was, in less than a year, to create the most remarkable of all his stage productions.

His idea was that he would return to the Proletkult Theatre and bring that theatre up to a professional level. He was so certain of his

[1] S. M. Eisenstein, 'Stereoscopic Films' (*Penguin Film Review*, No. 8, Penguin Books, London, 1949).

direction and the future of his theatre that his new collaborators, Alexandrov and Shtraukh, who were to be identified with him in his greatest work, never doubted his ability to carry out his plans for a theatre 'collective'. Eisenstein—whose only experience was in terms of the creative 'collective'—was eager to give his colleagues a share in the creative process.

Although he was only twenty-four, Eisenstein spoke and laid down his plans as if he were already an artist of recognized stature. He experienced none of the doubts and hesitation of young artists and few of the frustrations, and this confidence he communicated to others. The creative process enlarged his consciousness to a state approaching ecstasy; often it seemed to him that he possessed powers beyond sensory perception. The breadth of his vision, seeking always a balance between erudition and originality, held people spellbound. A formidable figure for all his youth, many people assumed he was older than he was.

When Sergei Mikhailovich appeared at a gathering, his gestures—a wide sweep of the arms counterpointing a faint, hardly perceptible flick of his delicate, sensitive fingers—focused all eyes upon him. His small agile body—almost as expressive as that of Chaplin—sprang into motion with his words. It was as if a marvellously contrived dynamo drove streams of golden, laughing energy through his veins. His eyes laughed and probed in turn. His head with its fluffy hair not yet receding from the luminous expanse of forehead, was set on his still thin shoulders as though it were the head of a god. It would not have sounded foolish had he murmured, as he often did later in jest, 'I would I were Zeus to give birth to demi-gods out of the top of my leonine head'.

Yet Eisenstein had confidence in himself only as an artist. As a man he was uncertain, too conscious that within him ran a stream swarming with childish fears, the nightmare images of adolescence; and against this poisoned stream a more healthy current flowed—an abiding desire for the spiritual enrichment of his nature. Strange, contradictory, he yearned for the mystic's sense of grace to expand his consciousness into an equilibrium of wholeness. If excessive pressures had not squeezed Sergei Mikhailovich into further conflict, he might have reached a just esteem of himself and thereby shed the lingering sense that he was Nature's Clown.

But a state of almost intolerable conflict arose between Sergei and his mother when she came back into his life. Following the Revolution, Julia Eisenstein had returned to Leningrad in search of her son. Unable to find him, and with her source of income swept away, she had been forced to work. But when she finally found Sergei in Moscow she immediately turned to him expecting him to share his life with her.

As if risen from the grave of childhood memories, Julia Eisenstein's presence brought a flood of contradictory emotions to Sergei Mikhailovich. Try as she did to convince him of her affection, he could not believe her. What seemed pretence of solicitous affection filled him with loathing. It was evil for a man to hate his mother; but even Sergei's hatred could not obliterate the taste of tender love his mother had inspired in childhood. Fearful that somehow she would break down his resolution to keep her at arm's length, he reacted to her pleas to live with him as though he were still an enraged and hysterical child. Such exhibitions of weakness caused him anguish.

Although he kept a room for her in Leningrad, nothing could uproot the thought that his mother wanted to exploit him. He deeply resented her complaint that she could not be expected to work; he refused to understand her constant grumbling and abuse of the new regime. Most of all, he writhed against her ceaseless efforts to dominate him with the rod of her helpless femininity.

The position of Madame Eisenstein was the more pathetic because she could not grasp the dreadful results of her conduct. She was appalled by her son. She thought at first he must have abandoned himself to what she considered the licence of the New Morality. When she could find no such evidence, she accused him of being unnatural because he had not married as befitted an honourable professional man.

Year in and year out Sergei Mikhailovich resisted his mother's plea to come and live in the same flat with him. The eternal argument was that she could look after his needs better than his old nurse, Totya Pasha, who came to act as his housekeeper. Often he drove his mother out of the house by shocking her sensibilities. Seeking allies, he would beg them to keep his mother away from him.

In this endless battle of wills, Eisenstein always won. On innumerable occasions he drove his mother back to Leningrad in floods of tears. Returning to the flat Sergei kept for her in Leningrad—one which she said she hated more than any place on earth—she would write beseeching or upbraiding letters. Sergei was a cruel, unnatural and wicked son; he would suffer damnation for his outrageous conduct. She had borne a monster—but still she loved him.

Preserving the appearance of gentility, she was driven in later years to pursue the coarsest, most insensitive means of humiliating her son. With a dreadful tenacity she clung to her maternal rights. If she heard anything which she thought called for her presence, she would suddenly appear in Moscow. With effrontery clothed in motherly sweetness she would demand answers to the most personal questions. She would open his letters in an effort to pry into his life. Finding nothing, she set in motion a system of spying on him through people in Moscow. Thus she kept vigilant track of her son, even though he forced her to live in Leningrad.

Despite the conflict with his mother, Eisenstein's neurotic fears were potentially balanced by an entirely normal desire for affection. She did not succeed in causing him to hate women, only to fear them. Deprived of trust in his mother, he felt a need to be cherished by a mother who would be kind to him, as his nurse-housekeeper was kind, but with whom he could share his problems and his work. He dreamed too of some day finding a wife who would release the concealed reservoir of tenderness which kept gathering within him. His loneliness of spirit heightened and strained his normal desire to share himself with a wife and muffled desire to make alliance with any available woman. The slightest emotional attraction towards a woman called forth a hyper-sensitivity to the woman's smallest reaction. Imagining himself unlovable, he knew no way to reveal himself except by small protective acts so fleeting and out of character with his general brilliance that they startled rather than reassured.

Such complexity of emotions interwoven in an idealistic nature would not have been unique nor abnormal in a sensitive man, except in the historical moment when they were manifested in Sergei Mikhailovich. His complex nature was hopelessly at variance with the free and easy Russian morals of the early 1920's. The paramount human relationship was a frank comradeship in the building of socialism. Romantic and ideal love between a man and a woman had given way to simplified relations. Two people met; if they were attracted to each other they made love without many subtle preliminaries. No one thought the worse of them for that. Often they set up house together without pretence of being bound together by eternal love or conventions. Thereupon they were automatically regarded as man and wife. Sometimes they registered their union at Z.A.G.S., the marriage and divorce office; more often they saw no need for registration. If and when they did not get along together, or when their desire to sleep together abated, or they found they were sexually incompatible, they parted without recriminations. Changing partners was common. Not infrequently it was done without changing rooms. The housing shortage flung people into extraordinary tangles which they solved by the yardstick of common sense rather than sentiment. This period was reflected in Kateyev's comedy of manners. *The Squaring of the Circle*, and the film *Bed and Sofa*. Since the Revolution had made women the equal of men (and in Russia women had always been surrounded by less mystery than elsewhere), it was common for virginity in either a man or a girl to be regarded as the badge of the bourgeois. Virginity was a constant joke, and among Eisenstein's generation it was very nearly a social disgrace to be thought a virgin.

This popular interpretation of revolutionary morals was extreme; Lenin deplored the licence to which it first led. But it was a natural phase, only slightly more extreme than the post-war loosening of conventional moral standards in the West. In time, exaggerated sexual freedom was to pass; yet while it lasted it heightened and bruised the sensitivity of Sergei Eisenstein. In such an atmosphere, he became acutely aware of his inner conflicts and the conflict between his reactions and the accepted new morality. Had he not aggressively identified himself as a man with the new world, he might have reconciled his inner conflicts more easily. Hating the old world and all traces of bourgeois morality with a deep sincerity, he knew his inner conflicts were yet its stepchildren. As one of the positive builders of the new society, he was plagued by the sense of inner division and unfitness. The only person who seemed to shed light on his predicament was Freud. Still the limitation of Freud's work was its confinement within the conditioning of foreign capitalist society, and the more Sergei Mikhailovich discovered about himself through Freud, the further he seemed to recede from the norm of a healthy man in a Soviet society.

His comrades were singularly frank and uncomplicated. Having dedicated themselves to honest striving in the building of a new society and to the development of a new type of man, they expected an equal frankness and honesty from Eisenstein and everyone else. No one except a man out of step with the times invested personal and sexual relations with metaphysical implications. With sex entirely free and a matter of personal responsibility, suggestiveness was as taboo as too great preoccupation with the mystery of sex and the connection with sin with which the bourgeois world and Puritanism had endowed it. St. Paul's declaration, 'I would that all men were even as I myself'—a celibate, met with fierce contempt and derogatory mirth.

Surrounded by the new society to which he could not adjust his inner needs, his chastity of spirit grew into a scourge. Sergei Mikhailovich was revolted and wounded by the promiscuity around him. Agreeing with Leonardo that uncontrolled lust put 'man on a level with the beasts', Eisenstein took refuge in driving his intellectual passions to a point where sexual energy was sublimated. In time continence was to become a fetish for him; if he renounced its discipline he would lose his genius. Yet he had to make an intellectual compromise with the morality of the time. He had to defend himself against jeers and the accusation of being a bourgeois moralist; thus, he was led to

Maternal Grandmother

Maternal Grandfather

Seryozhenka with his parents,
Mikhail and Julia Eisenstein,
about 1900

Modern Art, New York

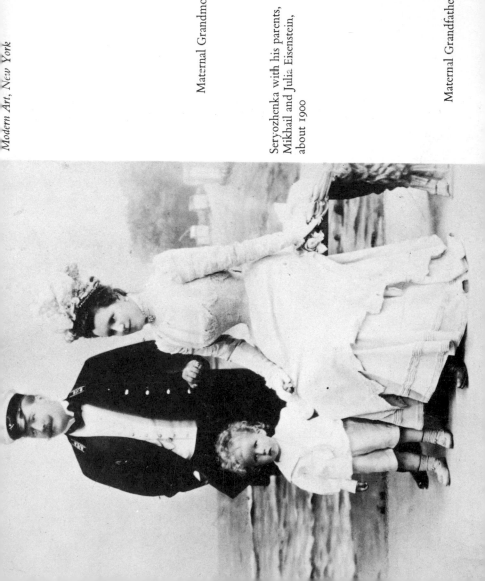

Eisenstein (*centre right*) about 19

Skating, about 1911

With Maxim Strauk

By courtesy of Kenneth MacPherson

Eisenstein at the age of 27,
following the completion of
Potemkin

Pera Attasheva, about 1932

By courtesy of Zina Voynow

Eisenstein Collection, Museum of Modern Art, New York

1921. Stage design, probably for the production by V. Tikhonovitch at the Polenov Theatre, Moscow

Eisenstein made designs for *Macbeth* throughout his life though he never produced it. (Originals in the Moscow Theatre Museum)

1921. Costume design, King Duncan   1931. Mexico. 'Macbeth motifs'

Eisenstein Collection, Museum of Modern Art, New York

By courtesy of the Society for Cultural Relations with the USSR, London

Eisenstein (*third from right*) with a group of the Proletkult Workshop, autumn, 1922

5

The Wise Man, The Acrobat Theatre, Proletkult Theatre, Moscow, March 1923

Grigori Alexandrov (on tight rope) in Eisenstein's adaptation of Ostrovsky's *Much Simplicity in Every Wise Man*

By courtesy of the Society for Cultural Relations with the USSR, London

Eisenstein in front of a poster for this production which he designed and directed

Theatre designs,
1921–22

Costume design for
the ex-lawyer in *King
Hunger* by Leonid
Andreyev

senstein Collection, Museum of Modern
, New York

signs for a projected production of Shaw's
artbreak House, Meyerhold Workshop,
2

Boss Mangan

'The cart fell to pieces and the driver dropped into the cinema'—Eisenstein

Gas Masks by Sergei Tretiakov, directed and designed by Eisenstein and staged at the Moscow Gas Factory, 1924

Eisenstein's first film, *Strike*, 1924. The child motif seen here is carried through to the end of his life

The Priest in *Potemkin*

Eisenstein's humour—a wink as the Priest feigns death

Eisenstein being made up for the part of the Priest

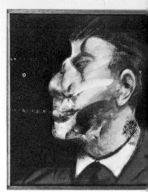

Marlborough Fine Art, Ltd

Pictures selected by Francis Bacon as a later example of Eisenstein's influence upon him

'Study for the Nurse in the film *Battleship Potemkin*'

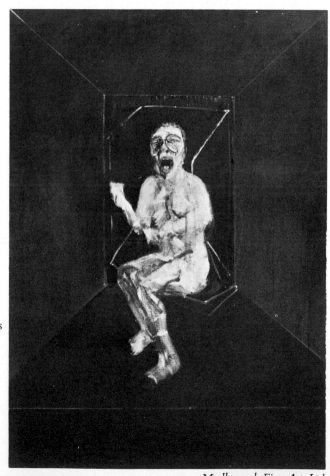

Bacon was intensely struck by the shot where the Cossack hits the woman in black with glasses on the Odessa Stairs

Marlborough Fine Art, Ltd

y courtesy of Paul Rotha

he Odessa Stairs in *Potemkin*,
25

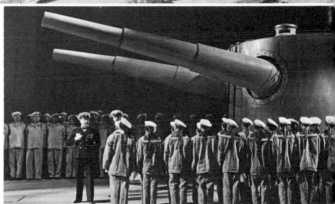

e opera, *The Armoured
uiser Potemkin*, produced at
e Bolshoi Theatre, Moscow,
ecember, 1937

e direct influence of *Potemkin*
evident in the stage setting
d make-up of the actors
aying characters which
peared in the film

By courtesy of H. W. L. Dana

The New York Theatre Guild
production of *Roar China* by
Sergei Tretiakov, 1930

When Eisenstein saw this
production he said the stage
setting was an adaptation of h
own composition in *Potemkin*.
Lee Simonson, the designer,
admitted the influence of the
film

By courtesy of H. W. L. Dana

October (Ten Days that Shook the World), 1927

Eisenstein lolling in the Tsar's throne in the Winter Palace

Eisenstein Collection, Museum of Modern Art, New York

A small boy welcomes the Revolution in the closing scenes

By courtesy of the British Film Institute

12

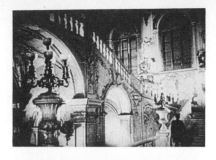

October, 1927—The Intellectual Cinema

Kerensky entering the Winter Palace. 'A comic effect was gained by subtitles indicating ascending ranks . . . and the "hero" trotting up the same unchanging flight of stairs'—Eisenstein

Minister of War and
Marine --

Prime Minister --

By courtesy of the British Film Institute

Old and New (*General Line*), 1929
The Religious Procession—Fourth Dimension
'A multiple series of lines, each maintaining an independent compositional course
and each contributing to the total compositional course of the sequence . . .' Eisenstein

*Old and New
(General Line),*
1929

Marfa Lapkina

Peasant types

The old woman

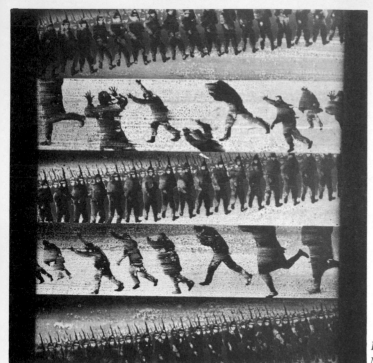

Juan Genoves

Here is the direct influence of the movement of the masses from the Odessa Stairs
sequence upon the Spanish painter. He saw *Potemkin* at the age of 8 during the
Civil War

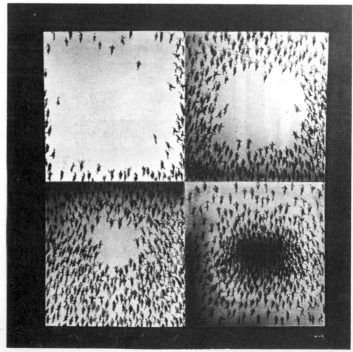

pay extravagant lip-service to eroticism. The painfully anamolous
character of his behaviour did no great damage to his life until he
fell in love.

After he joined Meyerhold's Theatre, Sergei Mikhailovich met his
young daughter who was training as an actress. She must have
possessed some unique quality since for many years she remained as an
image of perfect beauty in his memory. It seemed to him that she was
surrounded with an aura of purity and belonged in the ideal world of
his imagination, a world of gentle, subtle sentiment. With this girl he
could share love as the most unique and special experience, the sacred
expression of his personality and hers. Sergei was enchanted by her.
Perhaps he never saw this girl as a woman, only as a symbol which
called forth a shining, romantic reaction. She was the girl he wanted to
marry.

Month in and month out he hovered around her, waiting for the
right moment to make each faint advance. He must have lost a thousand moments. A hundred expressions of his love failed to strike with
certainty, so exceedingly subtle were they—a slight inflexion, a fleeting
glance, words threaded on a string of double-talk. A whole pattern of
action and reaction had to be established like the pillars of a bridge to
span the abyss of his shyness and loneliness.

At the end of some nine months, the young actress had gained sufficient admiration for Sergei Eisenstein to leave Meyerhold's Theatre
when Meyerhold abandoned *Heartbreak House*. She joined Sergei
Mikhailovich's 'collective' which included Grigori Alexandrov, Judith
Glizer and Maxim Shtraukh. Now the Acrobatic Theatre was to be
catapulted into existence and Eisenstein was on the road which was to
lead him through theatre to cinema.

CHAPTER THREE

Through Theatre to Cinema

For having given a beginning, what follows from it must necessarily be a natural development of such a beginning, unless it has been subject to a contrary influence.

LEONARDO DA VINCI, C.A. 154 r. b.

SERGEI MIKHAILOVICH returned to the Proletkult Theatre as a director in the autumn of 1922. His plans for the Acrobatic Theatre were as many-headed as a Hydra. Meanwhile, one of the Proletkult's directors, M. Altman, had produced Pletnyov's play, *Precipice*. Though Eisenstein received credit as designer, the original designs he had drawn up while working with Valeri Smishlayev more than a year before were much modified.

In returning, Eisenstein made no attempt to take over the Proletkult Theatre. It remained a 'collective' in which many of its former personnel continued to work, although he now became the centre of the theatre's development. The over-all scheme he brought back with him from the Meyerhold Theatre was so complete that it constituted the outline for his life's work. He considered that it was necessary to institute a training programme for the worker actors as preparation for the plays to be presented. Revolutionary as the training programme was, the concept was a turn in the direction of tradition rather than a breaking away. Every major Russian theatre had developed as a result of such a concept.

Beginning with the classic and histrionic Maly Theatre, whose style dominated the Russian theatre until 1896 (and has persisted as one of many styles down to to-day), each successive style emerged as a result of individual genius. In 1922, though in formal revolt, Eisenstein's embryonic Acrobatic Theatre was basically in the tradition of the great theatre men, all of whom had instituted schools for the training of actors in accord with their distinctive theories. Each moulded dramatists and classic plays into vehicles expressive of his theories of dramatic presentation. The more positive the theory, even the more extreme— the greater the likelihood of its taking root. The average English or American company of actors, having no cohesive theory, could not have survived in the climate of the Russian theatre.

Theatre in Russia was never a profession, but the passionate pursuit of a vocation—the engagement of the whole personality in a highly evolved creative process. The reverence of actors for their craft was so well recognized that the theatre had long been like a temple where actresses were as dedicated vestal virgins and actors fervent acolytes. Hence, the Russian audience regarded the theatre as a noble institution and they entered its portals in as serious a spirit as a student entering the Bodleian Library. Discussion of styles, hair-splitting criticisms of details and a grave appraisal of theatre audiences kept the theatre in a constant state of creative excitement, including the revolutionary Proletkult.

Eisenstein was, therefore, not an isolated phenomenon. His ideas, which would have struck the theatre managers of England and America as outside practical consideration, met with no such attitude in Russia. New ideas in art had always been listened to with attention. Eisenstein had no difficulty in promoting his ideas at the Proletkult. It would have been hard to disagree with his reasoning that the Proletkult workers had reached a point where they must conscientiously discover and learn to project the actor in themselves. Maximum effectiveness could be achieved only through the study and mastery of fully comprehended principles of acting. The idea of a deeper participation in a consistent and evolving creative process, reflective of the new proletarian culture, called forth a tremendous response from the Proletkult workers.

'In our first theatrical undertaking in the Proletkult, we gave ourselves completely to the study of the methods employed by the people's circus and acrobats,' wrote Maxim Shtraukh. 'The actors, fascinated with the circus technique, developed a great love and passion to produce the greatest precision in their work; it taught them to hate carelessness in art.'[1] Because the Proletkult people considered themselves workers, at this time and for many years, Sergei Mikhailovich designated himself as 'Worker' Eisenstein because, as he said, if he were a shoemaker he would go about his work in the same manner. [Plate 5]

Probably the first account of Eisenstein to reach beyond the Soviet Union (where he worked in virtual anonymity during the early years of his career) was a passing mention by Huntley Carter in his book *The Theatre and Cinema of Soviet Russia*, which appeared in London in 1924. It is a reflection of the working attitude in the Soviet Union in the early 'twenties that though Eisenstein was recognized by everyone connected with the Proletkult Theatre as the most brilliant mind in the organization, he was not presented to Carter as the creative leader, although the work for which he was the spokesman was discussed in great detail. Carter heard of Eisenstein only as one of many Proletkult workers. The chairman, Valeri Pletnyov, explained how the actors were developing

[1] *Encounters* by Maxim Shtraukh, Iskusstvo Kino, Nos. 1-2 (Moscow, 1940).

their own original theories and instruction in acting technique. Through their elected representative, Eisenstein, they had also 'invented' a new type of stage.

This stage, which now made the Proletkult Theatre the outstanding *avant-garde* theatre of the world, was an arena platform derived from the circus. This was Eisenstein's method of breaking away from the limitations of the formal proscenium arch and giving the maximum fluidity to his ideas. This step was far beyond Meyerhold; not until the early 'thirties did that great innovator propose to build a theatre with mobile stages and no proscenium arch.[1]

Thus, within a very short time, Eisenstein's plans had led to the development of a school for actors and an entirely revolutionary stage, which brought the audience into a new spatial relationship with the actor. While still at Meyerhold's Theatre, he had adapted the classic comedy of Ostrovsky, *Enough Simplicity in Every Wise Man*, to conform with his Acrobatic Theatre. Directed and designed by himself, this play, under the title *The Wise Man* (or *The Sage*), was first presented at the Proletkult Arena in March of 1923. [Plate 6]

Taking his cue from Meyerhold, whose disregard for the sacredness of classic plays was notorious, Sergei Mikhailovich's Ostrovsky was even harder to recognize than Meyerhold's classical productions. He turned the play inside out, stripped it down to skin and bones, injected the lifeblood of the ancient and topical Commedia dell'Arte, added a sauce of his own incomparable social satire and sense of fun and nonsense. Then he served the whole up as a circus performance, with most of the characters appearing as clowns, the rest as acrobats. Since 1923 was a year of increasing anti-religious sentiment, Eisenstein added a slashing commentary on religion. With the rapier of his wit and reason, he hoped to accomplish a double mission—enlightening his audience by ridiculing religion and killing the irrational yearnings for God within himself.

On entering the 'theatre', the spectator found himself in what was once a large, elaborately decorated ballroom. At one end there was a gallery, from which the ramped seats descended towards the stage occupying one-third of the room. This stage took the form of a small circus arena edged with a red barrier. The audience surrounded three-fourths of the arena, on which stood a small raised platform, several steps high. The remaining fourth, behind the arena, was hung with a striped curtain—echoing a circus tent—and serving to blot from the spectators' eyes the disconcerting frieze of neo-classical figures pushing

---

[1] Eisenstein's acrobatic stage was experimented with in a variety of forms at the Realistic (Krasni-Presni) Theatre under the direction of Okhlopkov in the 1930's and by E. F. Burian in Prague.

their heads against the ceiling. (These were objects of much mirth during rehearsals and certainly most curious ornamentation for the proletarian theatre.) On either side of the platform were two curved approaches—symbolic segments of a circus ring. Such was the structural setting for the production of *The Wise Man*.

The stage properties were unique. The floor of the arena was covered with a soft carpet, as necessary physical protection for the actors. Attached to the ceiling was the high trapeze. Scattered about for easy use were rings, horizontal poles, vaulting horses, slack wire and other instruments used as the contiguous extension of a stage gesture. Thus, the actors, commencing a line of dialogue with relative dramatic formality, ended with a gymnastic twist. In place of the dramatically formalized expression of rage as hitherto employed in the theatre (even in the Meyerhold Theatre), the climax of rage became the lightning flash of a somersault; while exaltation found expression in a *salto-mortale*, and lyricism in a delicate pirouette along a tight-rope. With the exception of a few characters, all the actors, as mentioned above, were attired in costumes derived from those of the circus clown. In their style of acting, however, acrobatics was combined with a whole galaxy of other traditions drawn from beyond the circus—echoes of Italian Commedia dell'Arte, French comedians of the music-hall and the pantomime style of Charlie Chaplin.

In this multi-brewed form, the Ostrovsky comedy of family intrigue was parodied in a pattern of utmost complexity. The audience could enjoy and appreciate the parody on the Russian comedy of manners, which transformed a comedy of money-making into an absurd children's game carried on between uncles and nephews, aunts and their gallants. Such was the surface veneer of *The Wise Man*.

But Sergei Eisenstein was incapable of taking any work at its face value. It was the essence of his method to seek to relate each fragment of creative work to other expressive manifestations. Having done so, he must relate the interconnected fragments with the processes observable in the real world. Hence, the character of Glumov appeared to him as one face on a coin—the mask of comedy. The other side of the Glumov coin was represented for Eisenstein by Balzac's character Rastignac, who, on a serious, even tragic plane, echoed the situations, passions and financial intrigue inherent in the Ostrovsky character. In establishing this connection, Sergei Mikhailovich dipped into the ocean of philosophic speculation which was to link his myriad theories into a whole philosophy of art.

The plot of *The Wise Man* offered a delightful fluidity for Eisenstein's pursuit of the experimental. For example, Mamayev giving his nephew instructions, and the nephew's interpretation, made it possible for the characters to skip about and play upon various sections of the 'stage' or manœuvre on the circus apparatus. The dialogue, retaining some of Ostrovsky's lines and including many quips from Sergei Eisenstein, was carried from one acting area to another; in fact, from scene to scene, without the conventional pause or 'curtain' to mark, as it were, 'another part of the forest'. This technique approached the time-space fluidity of the film medium. Actually, Eisenstein was practising an elementary 'montage' throughout the production of *The Wise Man*, though no thought of the cinema was in his mind.

A direct use of the cinema medium was, however, introduced by the inclusion of a short film. This was a pictorial interpretation of Glumov's diary, an important dramatic element in the original play. The inserted 'film-diary' whirled off into a volatile parody of the currently developing Soviet newsreel.[1]

An account preserving the reaction of both a trained critic and an untrained audience to this *pot au fer à la Eisenstein*, is given in Huntley Carter's book. It is inaccurate in one detail, in that Carter assumed the production to be a work of collective creativity rather than what it was —collective creativity under the direction of Sergei Eisenstein.

Assuming the parody of Ostrovsky's play to be the work of the actors themselves, Carter writes how 'they'—he does not mention Eisenstein —'had left only sufficient of the writer to allow anyone who knew his work to recognize him'. The audience—mostly workers—were not concerned as to whose play they were witnessing; it mattered not at all that it had once been a revered classic. The spectators 'could feed on the eccentric and exciting circus acrobatics. It was a parody on number two ["White"] Russia and the émigrés [like Eisenstein's own father and in the spirit of his mother], who believed they represented the real Russia. The mime also made sharp attacks on well-known foreign politicians and militarists, Mussolini, Joffre, etc.' This, of course, carried into the theatre, and transferred to motion, the types of pictorial propaganda Sergei Mikhailovich had executed while he was in the Red Army.

As to the anti-religious moments, Carter goes on to say 'there was a procession of caricatures carrying candles, chanting church service and bearing boards with the inscription "Religion is the opium of the people"'. The character of the whole production was full of wit and gaiety and it 'went at a great speed, almost too quick for some spectators. It took many shapes and colours like a kaleidoscope'. The vitality of the players astounded Carter, particularly as some of them were workers who had worked all day in factory and workshop. His conclusion, after seeing Eisenstein's first independent production, was that

[1] At this time Eisenstein's future cameraman, Eduard Tisse, was making just such newsreels as Eisenstein was parodying.

'various forms of representation were passing from the circus to the conventional stage'.

There were things which Carter seemingly missed in the performance, particularly that which was uppermost in Eisenstein's mind— the connection between the circus apparatus and the emotional content of the scenes in which they were most daringly employed. For Eisenstein the most important scene in his *Wise Man* occurred when he had Grigori Alexandrov (who had accommodated him by mastering the tightrope) play the scene in which Glumov makes love to his uncle's wife, Mamayeva, balanced on the tightrope. Glumov had, among other improprieties, stolen Mamayeva's purse and to avoid her finding out, or about his designs on her niece, he made love to her. Glumov's precarious position on the tightrope was symbolical of the emotional situation. Delicately trying to balance and keep her attraction to save himself from detection, the balancing on the tightrope was an external objectivization of the inner content. Eisenstein was to attempt to solve just such problems in art for the rest of his life.

More orthodox critics observed that 'senseless as this method seems at first glance, we cannot ignore it as sheer insanity. . . . An interesting theory lies at the root of this resort to circus tricks and clowning, though the forms which this theory has assumed in practice are often absurd and futile. The manager of the Proletkult (Eisenstein) started from the fact that in Russia the circus was older and nearer to the people than the theatre which had been imported much later from the West. Revolutionary art, therefore, aiming at something new clung to the tradition of ancient popular buffoonery.'[1]

Beneath all the gaiety, froth and audacious nonsense of *The Wise Man*, Sergei Mikhailovich's intentions were serious. In connection with the Ostrovsky production, he was invited to explain his theories in the magazine *Lef*,[2] among whose editors were Mayakovsky and Sergei Tretiakov, whom he had met at the Meyerhold Theatre. This was his first statement of theory.

'The basic materials of the theatre arise from the spectator himself', wrote Sergei Mikhailovich, 'and from our guiding of the spectator into a desired direction (or desired mood).' After listing a variety of elements likely to hold the spectator's attention, he comes to the core of his theory, that of attraction. 'Attraction (in our diagnosis of the theatre) is every aggressive moment in it, i.e. every element of it that brings to light in the spectator those senses or that psychology that influences his experience—every element that can be verified and mathe-

[1] *The Russian Theatre* by Rene Fülop-Miller and Joseph Gregor (Philadelphia, Lippincott and Co., 1930), p. 70.
[2] S. M. Eisenstein, 'Montage of Attractions' (*Lef*, No. 3, Moscow, 1923).

matically calculated to produce certain emotional shocks in a proper order within the totality—the only means by which it is possible to make the final ideological conclusion perceptible.'

'I establish attraction as normally being an independent and primary element in the construction of a theatrical production', he wrote. Defining this attraction as a molecular or compound unity of the efficiency of a specific theatre in relation to the theatre in general, he gave as analogy the 'pictorial storehouse' employed by the German artist, George Grosz, and of the current photo-montage. 'As difficult as "compound" may be to limit, it certainly ends with that fascinating noble hero (the psychological moment) and begins with the concentrated moment of his personal charm (i.e., his erotic activity), for the lyric effect of certain Chaplin scenes does not in the least affect the attraction communicated by the specific mechanics of his movement; it is just as difficult to fix the boundary line where religious pathos moves into sadist satisfaction during the torture scenes of the miracle plays.'[1]

'Approached genuinely, this [attraction] basically determines the possible principles of construction as an "action construction" (of the whole production). Instead of static "reflection" of an event with all possibilities for activity within the limits of the event's logical action, we advance to a new plane—*free montage of arbitrarily selected, independent* (within the given composition and the subject links that hold the influencing actions together) *attractions*—all from the stand of establishing certain final thematic effects—this is montage of attractions.' Going into further details of how the director gathers together his pieces of attraction, Eisenstein stated that the job of the Proletkult Theatre 'was to establish this way as a production method'.

'Schooling for the montageur'—as Eisenstein now termed himself— 'can be found in the cinema [a medium which he had not yet explored] and chiefly in the music-hall and circus, which invariably [substantially speaking, Sergei Mikhailovich added] puts on a good show—from the spectator's point of view.' These theories underlying *The Wise Man* had been put into practice at the Proletkult Workshop, the school which had been founded in the autumn of 1922.

While Eisenstein was writing in this probing and by no means simple language for the readers of *Lef*, a worker journalist writing in the *Rabochaya Gazeta* described how 'a big training of proletarian actors is taking place' at the Proletkult Workshop. 'In the first place, it is a physical training, embracing sport, boxing, light athletics, collective games, fencing and bio-mechanics. Next it includes special voice training, and beyond this there is education in the history of the

[1] S. M. Eisenstein, 'Montage of Attractions' (*Lef*, No. 3, Moscow, 1923).

class struggle. Training is carried on from ten in the morning till nine at night. The head of the training workshop is Eisenstein.'[1]

These expositions, which appeared almost simultaneously, reveal an enormous discrepancy between the level of Sergei Eisenstein's theories and the bald account of his workshop by a journalist writing for the average Russian worker. Proletkult was the centre for the development of a new proletarian art and culture; yet to understand Eisenstein an extensive education in the arts was necessary. With such an educational gap between Eisenstein and his audience, how was he going to fare? How was he to make himself understood? Even Huntley Carter was conscious that the production of *The Wise Man* 'went at a great speed, *almost too quick for some spectators'*. If this was the impression left by Eisenstein's first independent work, what would be the general reaction to his work as it became more complex?

Had it not been for the experimental character of the time, Government support would not have been lavished almost indiscriminately upon any Workers group who wanted to develop some theory. Artists, and people who wished to become artists, were enjoying a hey-day, because a man of considerable personal culture— Lunacharsky, the dramatist—was Commissar of Education, and in that position could allocate funds. Though Lunacharsky—himself a supporter of middle-of-the-road styles—probably recognized that the tornado of experiment would have to wear itself out before the new culture and art would assume any steady or permanent form, he thought it necessary, and desirable, for every new idea to gain a hearing. Without Lunacharsky, the artists might have suffered great frustration.

With large-scale private property swept away and private investment ended, there was only one fountain-head for funds—the State. True, the temporary retreat from socialism instituted in 1921 when N.E.P., the New Economic Policy, was put into effect revived and prolonged the existence of many bourgeois economic trends, but it did not herald in a softening of revolt against the old regime; it merely made physical existence a little less stark in a period of transition from Military Communism to the period of Socialist Construction.

During the early 1920's, Marxism exerted a tremendous influence in every branch of art, particularly where the young held sway. Art in their hands was moulded to reflect the class struggle; the masses were regarded as a collective hero. Yet any man's interpretation was almost as good as the next. The creative workers like Eisenstein seized on Marx, read a few statements and rushed to interpret this, that or the next thing in the light of a single sentence. Few people had read Marxian theory, and still fewer had stopped to analyse what it meant. Mighty battles

[1] *Rabochaya Gazeta* (Moscow, 22 April 1923).

were fought over interpretation; criticism and discussion were furious
and the interpretations of Marxism were as varied and lively as the
experiments being carried on in the arts.

In this atmosphere, Sergei Mikhailovich eagerly pursued the
theory of the 'Montage of attraction' still further. He turned at once
to a modern play specially written to meet the requirements of
what he termed 'agit-Guignole'. This was his adaptation of the currently popular French Grande Guignole, a style of short play confined
to a theme of exaggerated horror. Fascinated by the likely emotional
response of an audience to the spectacle of 'where an eye is gouged out,
an arm or leg amputated before the very eyes of the audience; or a telephone communication is incorporated into the action to describe a
horrible event taking place ten miles away; or a situation in which a
drunkard, sensing his approaching end, seeks relief in madness', Sergei
Mikhailovich found a willing dramatist in Sergei Tretiakov, an editor
of *Lef*.[1]

Tretiakov's specially written 'agit-Guignol', *Listen Moscow*, was produced at the Proletkult a few months after *The Wise Man*. In formal
design it had much in common with the Ostrovsky extravaganza; but
Eisenstein soon became conscious of something disquieting about his
new production. As he sat and watched the play, it appeared he was
carrying the intersecting movement of actors to a point where the
ultimate limit of his new theatrical form was approached.

Since Eisenstein created from deep springs of spontaneous inspiration rather than by holding to a line of didactic theory, he turned to
study the intricate patterns he had woven in *Listen Moscow*. It seemed
the eyes of the spectators became glued to a group of characters, thus
dissociating them from the general stream of stage movement. A hand
holding a letter blotted out everything but itself. The play of an actor's
eyebrows, or a glance, appeared magnified into an enormous close-up.
Eisenstein felt that 'the technique of genuine mise-en-scène composition was being mastered—and approaching its limits. It was already
threatened with becoming the knight's move in chess, the shift of
purely plastic contours in the already non-theatrical outlines of detailed
drawings'.[2]

Eisenstein's situation was paradoxical. There was nothing he feared
to create; he would destroy and rebuild classic works to suit his purposes,
while criticism of him as an artist held no terrors; yet he had not dared
to tell the young actress from the Meyerhold Theatre that he was madly

[1] Sergei Tretiakov, best known for his play *Roar China* and the biography
Chinese Testament.

[1] *Film Form* by S. M. Eisenstein (New York, Harcourt Brace and Co., 1949
and London, Dennis Dobson, 1950), p. 15.

in love with her. He longed to ask her to marry him, but whenever she came near him he dreaded that she would laugh at him as a lover and wasted the opportunity by parading in the armour of his intellectual brilliance. Thus, it was only too easy for the girl to believe what many people said: that Eisenstein was so coolly, cruelly scientific that the emotion of love could only be a disease for him to diagnose and then forget. Others hinted he must be more satyr than man, interested only in orgies of strange practices.

Had she sensed Sergei Mikhailovich's fear of rejection she might have cured his inordinate shyness with a positive show of affection, for within him lay an exceptional capacity for the marriage relationship he wished to establish. But she did not fathom him, though she may well have been in love with him. Eisenstein did not know.

About this time Sergei Mikhailovich fell prey to a subjective turmoil over his reactions to art, all art. Iconoclast from the inception of his creative life, he again found himself enthralled, by those works of art which were to him the most beautiful and spiritual. Each seemed to fasten upon him and lead him to dreams. It was as if a hundred smiles of Mona Lisa promised him the unfolding of mysteries—of the human heart, the human spirit and the nature of Godhead. Such Art was evil, because under its spell Eisenstein felt himself growing deaf to the voice of the Revolution.

He was not the only man to suffer pangs of nostalgia at the ineffable, magical impact of the old world's art. Art of the past made the contemporary world look harsh and horrible to many people who had intellectually dedicated themselves to the building of a new society. In private, sometimes in public, the poet Mayakovsky denounced the insidious influence of art. Likewise Sergei Tretiakov, who was now in close contact with Eisenstein. The people around the magazine *Lef* talked much about what seemed the sickness of their emotional responses. As they talked they began to find themselves pushed to wage a new crusade. From the first they had been crusaders against the forms and subject-matter of bourgeois art. Now they saw Art itself as the reflection of a profound sickness of the spirit.

The men of the new world must be set free from Art's sickly thraldom. If they were not liberated, Art would lead them away from reality and cause them to wallow in the ideal world of art. Art must be destroyed, then men could grow in healthy realism. But how was Art, the immemorial accompaniment of man's journey up the spiral of evolution, to be stamped out? A stark and devastating creative landscape opened out before them.... They must destroy Art by the weapon of Art itself. They must create works so violent, so permeated with reality, that the spectator, seeing their works, would tire of Art and prefer the drama of reality itself. Thus, Eisenstein and Tretiakov, the dramatist, planned the play *Gas Masks* as a death-blow to the last remnants of theatrical tradition.

During rehearsals it seemed that this play transferred *real* workers of a *real* gas factory to the stage; that here was the unvarnished 'life' and labour of the masses. Had *Gas Masks* been acted in the Proletkult Arena, Sergei Mikhailovich might have continued to believe he had reached rock-bottom realism in the theatre; that his production would indeed aid in the destruction of Art. But instead he brought his career in the theatre to an end by staging it in the Moscow Gas Factory. In doing this he imagined he was carrying the theatre into the real world and anchoring Tretiakov's play to reality. [Plate 8]

What happened? Actuality knocked the dramatic fiction of *Gas Masks* on the head. The conflict between the 'play', which was supposedly 'life' rather than 'art', and the factory setting, which was part of actual life, appeared so sharp that in Eisenstein's own words, 'the cart fell to pieces and the driver dropped into the cinema'.[1] As he watched the play being performed in the gas factory, Sergei Mikhailovich realized that the interiors of the factory, the smells and the workers had nothing to do with the fictional representation he had mistaken for a slice of 'life'. The real factory, and the audience of real workers, made *Gas Masks* look patently artificial. 'The turbines, the factory background, negated the last remnants of make-up and theatrical costumes, and all elements appeared as independently fused. Theatre accessories in the midst of the real factory plastics appeared ridiculous. The element of "play" was incompatible with the acrid smell of gas. The pitiful platform kept getting lost among the real platforms of labour activity. In short, the production was a failure.' Sergei Mikhailovich turned his eyes upon the structural features of the gas factory, wondering how he could find his way out of his artistic dilemma.

All around in the factory he saw the spirit of the times manifested. Here was the way the triumphant people worked in a factory which now belonged to them. As he searched the faces of the workers, each of whom he thought of as subscribing to the revolutionary ideal, 'All for one, one for all', he saw how the mass was composed of distinctive types of people in whose faces and bodies the story of life was dramatically told. This was reality. He must capture its spirit and form so that the world could see and understand the nature of revolution. A true depiction of reality would destroy 'art' with its own strength.

An explosion occurred within Eisenstein. The first intense elation seethed through him. It was the same excitement that he had experienced

[1] S. M. Eisenstein, *Film Form.*

when he suggested to Smishlayev that a real boxing match should be staged before the very eyes of the spectators in the production of *The Mexican*. Ideas garnered over the years, experiments already made rushed into his conscious mind and fused with his new impressions of the factory and the workers. Plunging out of the Moscow Gas Factory, Sergei Mikhailovich sought refuge in his small square room, next to that of Shtraukh and Glizer at Chysti Prudi 23. He knew in what direction he must now go.

He thought of the newsreels he had parodied in *The Wise Man*, of the film *Intolerance* by the American, D. W. Griffith. He too must master and mould the undeveloped film medium. The film was the means whereby he could pursue reality and create an 'art' to destroy Art, adapt his pursuit of composition—the *mise en scene* (now to be transferred to the *mise en cadre*) and develop the 'montage' he had already applied in the theatre. He remembered how shortly after the production of *The Wise Man* he had assisted Esther Schub in re-editing Fritz Lang's film *Dr. Mabuse* for Russia.

Out of his head between sleeping and waking—this border area of consciousness being Eisenstein's period of greatest creative activity— came the primary ideas for his first film, *Strike*. This was to be unlike any film the Russians (or anyone in the world) had seen before. It was to cut across the two developing lines of the Soviet cinema—the newsreels, exemplified by Dziga Vertov's Kino Pravda, and the story film of which Lev Kuleshov was the theorist and Vsevolod Ilarionovich Pudovkin the most talented pupil. Eisenstein considered both tendencies crude, primitive and beneath contempt. But in Kino Pravda there were certain elements of camerawork. There was a wonderful human eye behind the camera-eye.

They were the eyes of Eduard Tisse, who had been working in the cinema since 1914. He was of Swedish origin and had studied painting in his youth. In 1914 he was making films in Sweden; with the outbreak of the First World War he was designated as an official war photographer. In May 1918 he joined the Soviet Central Cinema Committee and subsequently worked in Dziga Vertov's unit, Kino Pravda. Eisenstein, who had met Tisse during the production of *The Wise Man*, sought him out and listened carefully to what he had to say about his camera, and Tisse in turn listened to Eisenstein with an inner excitement which did not show very much on his quiet, thin, old-maidish-looking face. They agreed that photographic reproductions could be combined in various ways. 'Both as reflections and in the manner of their combination, they permit any degree of distortion— either technically unavoidable or deliberately calculated. The results fluctuate from exact naturalistic combinations of visuals, interrelated experiences to complete alterations, arrangements unforeseen by nature, and even to abstract formalism, with remnants of reality'.[1] Then they consulted with Pletnyov and the Proletkult collective. All agreed that they should collaborate in the making of a film which should bring 'collective and mass action on to the screen, in contrast to individualism and the "triangle" drama of the bourgeois cinema'.

Under the guidance of Sergei Mikhailovich, Valeri Pletnyov prepared a scenario which eliminated a very vital element of both theatre and ordinary story films—the subject-story. The place of subject-story was taken by images of collective action to picture the concept of 'collectivity' and allow the camera the greatest virtuosity. There were some 'characters': 'The Organizer' (acted by A. Antonov), 'The Worker' (Mikhail Gomarov), 'The Spy' (Maxim Shtraukh), 'The Foreman' (Grigori Alexandrov) and members of the Lumpenproletariat (Judith Glizer, Boris Yurtsev and other Proletkult actors). These stock 'characters', who constituted the origin of 'typage' developed by Eisenstein in later films, had their genesis in his idea of the Italian Commedia dell'Arte, where the seven stock characters had been immediately recognized by the audience as soon as they appeared on the stage. In the same way as to-day a music-hall or film comedian is known as soon as he puts his head around the proscenium arch or into the film frame. None of the seven stock characters were individualistic, but composite portraits of 'types' of people who had been synthesized into one image by and for generations of faithful playgoers. They were, Eisenstein thought, a projection of the audience's own consciousness and an expressive manifestation of the people themselves.

Set up as signposts of conflicting social forces, the characters—'types' —stood out sharply in a series of episodes during a strike resulting from the suicide of a worker accused of stealing tools. The episodes selected depicted the most typical methods used by the revolutionary underground movement among the workers, and the equally typical methods of provocation and brutality employed by the Tsarist police to break the spirit of the strikers. In contrast to these scenes of political action of two groups in the throes of class struggle, Sergei Mikhailovich introduced lyrical imagery, a small child polishing a samovar and her father's large boot and a rook sitting on the factory chimney. The restlessness of an average factory worker, who does not know what to do with himself while on strike, is contrasted with pigs, hens and a kitten basking in the sun. The episodes—like many camera lenses recording the happenings of life from different angles—culminated in the final sequence, where the slaughter of a bull was intercut as symbolic commentary on

[1] *Film Form* by S. M. Eisenstein (New York, Harcourt Brace and Co., 1949 and London, Dennis Dobson, 1950), p. 15.

the slaughter of the striking workers. [Plate 8] The last twenty shots of *Strike* brought to the screen Eisenstein 'montage' in its first violent form.

The butcher moves past the camera (panning) swinging his bloody rope.

A crowd runs to a fence, breaks through it, and hides behind it (in two or three shots).

Arms fall into the frame (film-frame).

The head of the bull is severed from the trunk.

A volley (of bullets).

Soldiers' feet walk away from the camera.

Blood floats on the water, *discolouring it*.[1]

(Close-up) Blood gushes from the slit throat of the bull.

Blood is pouring from a basin (held by hands) into a pail.

Dissolve from a truck loaded with pails of blood to a passing truck loaded with scrap-iron.

The bull's tongue is pulled through the slit throat (to prevent the convulsions from damaging the tongue).

The soldiers' feet walk away from the camera (seen at a further distance than previously).

The bull's skin is stripped off.

1,500 bodies (lie) at the foot of the cliff.

Two skinned bulls' heads.

A hand lying in a pool of blood.

(Close-up) Filling the entire screen: the eye of a dead bull.

(Title) THE END.[2]

In this, and other sequences, the 'theme' was carried in images calculated to produce a chain of 'shocks' in the spectator. For some time, Eisenstein had been interested in the application of Pavlov's theory of the conditioned reflex as a means of engaging and directing the emotions of the spectator. He knew that a class of people whose attitudes had been conditioned by the social and economic pattern of their class are shocked by images which violate those attitudes.

Sergei Mikhailovich had used the 'shock' technique in his agit-Guignol production, *Listen Moscow*; but the film medium, being more fluid, gave him an opportunity to create a chain of 'shocks' integrated in a pattern of contrasts through montage. As Eisenstein wrote at the time: 'Maximum intensification of aggressive reflexes of social protest

[1] Already Eisenstein thought in terms of colour films, though not until the end of his life did he evolve a complete colour theory, which he used for two reels in *Ivan the Terrible*, Part II.

[2] Published by Alexander Belenson in *Cinema To-day* (Moscow, 1925), p. 59.

is seen in *Strike*, in mounting reflexes without opportunity for release or satisfaction, or, in other words, concentration of reflexes of struggle, and heightening of the potential expression of class feeling'. But when *Strike* was shown to various audiences, it became clear to Sergei Mikhailovich that 'a given shock can produce a certain reaction or effect only in an audience with a specific class identification . . . for instance, metal workers and textile workers react entirely differently and at different points to the same presentation'.

Reactions to the 'shock' of seeing the slaughter of the bull juxtaposed with the shooting of the striking workers varied. 'An American who saw *Strike* regarded such violent effects as unacceptable and pointed out that these scenes would have to be deleted for foreign audiences'. But the same scene 'did not have the effect of blood or violence on worker audiences, for the simple reason that for a worker, cattle blood is generally associated with the production of by-products in slaughter-houses. To a farmer, who is accustomed to killing cattle, the effect is zero'.

From these observations, Eisenstein reached the conclusion that 'the choice of shock is its class probability. A negative example is the assortment of sexual attractions which constitute the basic theme of the majority of bourgeois films, and which merely serve to divert attention from concrete reality. This can be demonstrated by the expressionism of *Dr. Caligari*, the sweet poison of middle-class psychology in the Mary Pickford films, all of them exploiting and intensifying by systematic shocks'. Therefore, 'the science of shocks and their "montage" in relation to these concepts should suggest the form. Content, as I see it, is a series of connecting shocks arranged in a certain sequence and directed at the audience. . . . All this material must be arranged and organized in relation to principles which would lead to the desired effect. Form is the realization of these elements in terms of specific material, by means of certain shocks and their arrangement in such a way that they can produce the desired reaction in correct proportion. This is the concrete and realistic aspect of composition.'[1]

Upon the completion of *Strike*, which was intended as the first of a series of films on the history of the working-class struggle towards revolution in Russia, Sergei Mikhailovich was disgusted by his 'failure'. He thought the camera tricks employed were painfully reminiscent of his crude designs for the play *Precipice* and that the whole film 'floundered about in a flotsam of rank theatricality'. Ten years later, he labelled *Strike* as an example of 'the infantile malady of leftism'.

'Failure' following 'failure'. It seemed to Sergei Mikhailovich he

[1] S. M. Eisenstein, *Method of Production of Proletarian Films* (*Kino*, No. 21, Moscow, 1925).

had failed twice—with the play *Gas Masks* and now with the film *Strike*. Perhaps his sense of defeat was not so much a result of what he saw in his work, but the sense of defeat that came into his own life.

According to Sergei Mikhailovich, it was some time during the making of *Strike* that Grisha Alexandrov detected that he was romantically in love with the young actress from the Meyerhold Theatre. To Grisha it was a great joke that the scientific Eisenstein should make a ridiculously elaborate comedy of manners, a great chivalric romance out of life's most simple biological urge. All this talk about idyllic love was nothing more than the natural need to copulate. There was nothing esoteric about sex attraction. In Grisha's opinion there was no girl who couldn't be induced to make love with almost any man—not even this virginal young woman. . . . Virgins weren't sacred, only ignorant.

Eisenstein was incapable of adopting Grisha's simple view, while Grisha, imbued with the ideas of the time, had no sympathy with Sergei's concept of love. Though Sergei Mikhailovich told him he wanted to marry this girl, Alexandrov came in time to Eisenstein and assured him with a good-natured gesture that Sergei too could conquer the young actress with ease. Just as Eisenstein never knew whether the girl loved him, so he never knew why she went to Alexandrov.

Sergei Mikhailovich concealed his humiliation very well and only a few people ever knew about it; but emotionally it irretrievably crippled him. Soon he felt he had been betrayed by no one but himself. All his short life he had been an exile from the happiness enjoyed by other men. A wandering spectator of life gifted with creative and intellectual powers, he could not bring himself into normal relations with people in the world as it was. He felt he must renounce the attempt to live like an ordinary man and thereby escape the bondage of the world around him.

Envy grew within him until with all his being he envied Grisha Alexandrov's physical attraction. Not only had it won him the young actress, but every day it brought him social success which Grisha accepted as his natural right. As in his boyhood, Sergei Mikhailovich's imagination stretched towards the warmth of the enjoyable, sensual world in which Alexandrov moved with complete naturalness. He imagined with all the power of his vivid imagination the joy he would experience if he could be transformed into Grisha, receiving the smiles, the embraces.

Suddenly he was incapable of fighting with Alexandrov as he had fought with him in Meyerhold's Theatre over a crust of sour black bread; instead, Eisenstein felt the greatest need to keep Alexandrov close to him. Grisha's physical beauty meant nothing to him of itself; he denied that any homosexual attraction existed. Still, Grisha Alexandrov appeared as a facet of himself—only clothed in physical beauty. He wanted to live as Grisha lived; but he knew he could never bring himself to do so, therefore all he could hope for was to live on the periphery of life through Alexandrov.

Thus, the most disastrous psychic twist was given to the ancient tragicomedy of Pierrot, the eternal clown, Harlequin, the mercurial lover, and sweet Columbine, who could not distinguish between true love and counterfeit.

But as it was always to be in the life of Eisenstein, sorrow, fear or failure could not quench his spirit; he had to create in one field or another and go on striving up to the moment of his death. Soon he was at work again, while *Strike*, his 'failure', was ranked a great success in Paris. Startling, extraordinary, it won a prize at the Exposition des Arts Decoratifs in 1925. Germany showed it publicly and people in Europe began to wait for the next film of Sergei Eisenstein, the revolutionary voice of Soviet Russia.

Note 1977. Eisenstein, who later dubbed *Strike* as 'infantile leftism', did his utmost to prevent the preserved copy of the film being shown to anyone. After his death copies were made and circulated, the first, I think, being made available to the British Film Institute.

CHAPTER FOUR

Film Language—*Potemkin*

Intellectual passion drives out sensuality.
LEONARDO DA VINCI, C.A. 358 v.a.

THE small clown first. Then Leonardo da Vinci, Sigmund Freud, Karl Marx. Each occupied the attention of Eisenstein, revealed to him facets of himself and of society. From childhood he had felt the weaknesses permeating his strength—the timidity he covered with a show of bravado; the mystic's reverence, which he had tried to submerge with laughter and scientific research. Despite his confusion, Sergei Mikhailovich was bound—like Leonardo—to a star. Through inner conflict and the misunderstanding of others, he found whole areas of himself imprisoned in a chest filled with treasures likely to buy him further pain in life, but honour in posterity.

He had surrendered himself to living one level of his existence vicariously, with Grigori Alexandrov as his window. Sergei Mikhailovich regarded this as the road to perversion. He realized the abnormal deviations of personality to which he could be led by his inability to achieve emotional maturity in relation to women. His position was not unique. Such men often became part of the community who called themselves the 'third sex', and it included many great talents. This world had its intellectual attraction, because of those who had been its illustrious citizens. According to Freud's analysis, Leonardo da Vinci was disposed to be one of its members. da Vinci had been brought to trial for his alleged association with a young man and, though acquitted, he was psychologically crippled.

The problem for Sergei Mikhailovich was how to hold the perversions he thought had developed in him at a minimum. Severe concepts of 'good' and 'evil' were rooted in his consciousness. It was his weakness, and he knew it, that he had no power at this time to make any further frontal attack to solve his personal life. All that he knew of Leonardo at this moment helped him, though the momentary blessing was in time to become but another curse. From his study of Freud, he knew that man could transform sexual energy into intellectual curiosity and creative activity. He recognized that to a certain extent he had always been sublimating his physical passions into the passion of his intellect. Now it was essential for his survival to make the fluctuating sublimation a permanent state of consciousness. By an effort of will Eisenstein dedicated himself anew to creative work. One step up or one step down?

The next creative step was the film *Potemkin*, the work by which Sergei Eisenstein ascended to the pinnacle of world acclaim.

As originally planned, the film *Potemkin* was one of eight episodes in a panoramic picture entitled *1905*. It was authorized by the Central Committee of the Communist Party on the 19th of March 1925, as one of a series of films commemorating the 1905 Revolution. Another film of the series was *Mother*, based on the novel by Maxim Gorky, and directed by Vsevolod Pudovkin.

The scenario for the film *1905* was written by Nina Agadzhanova-Shutko. It portrayed events newly disinterred from the Tsarist archives. They were the warp and woof of the history of a new class—the working class which had risen to power in 1917. As Eisenstein later said: 'We tried to take the historical events just as they were and not to interfere in any shape, manner or form, with the process as it was actually taking place.'[1]

On the 31st of March, Eisenstein, Tisse and some members of the Proletcult—Maxim Shtraukh, Grigori Alexandrov, A. Antonov, Mikhail Gomarov and others—began shooting the episode of the 1905 General Strike in Leningrad under the auspices of the First Studio of Goskino. They worked there until August when the weather turned bad. Everyone felt dissatisfied. As Maxim Shtraukh later said: 'The danger was not the unfavourable weather, but the wide scope of the material in the scenario. Everyone was aware of it but no one had the guts to say "Dear comrades out of the eight parts of the scenario we must take only one and from it create the entire film." '[2] Nature, however, imposed this dictum. The approaching autumn in the north drove the unit southward to the sun along the Black Sea.

On arriving in Odessa, Eisenstein saw for the first time the steps leading from the promenade to the beach where the populace had been massacred in 1905. It so fired his imagination that he promptly discarded the work already done and concentrated on one episode—the mutiny of the sailors of the Armoured Cruiser *Potemkin*. He wrote a new scenario expanding this episode and continued direction on the second version—*Potemkin*—with Grigori Alexandrov as assistant director.

Sergei Mikhailovich threw himself into the development of the details of this episode, and the events of the year 1905 became synonymous

[1] S. M. Eisenstein, speech delivered at the All-Union Creative Conference of Workers in Soviet Cinematography, Moscow, 8-13 January 1935.

[2] *Encounters*, by Maxim Shtraukh, Iskusstvo Kino, Nos. 1-2 (Moscow, 1940).

with the Cruiser *Potemkin*. During the first few days, he delved into the history of the mutiny of the sailors.

Of the original ship Eisenstein says, in an unfinished manuscript written in 1945, 'The *Potemkin* herself had been knocked apart many years before', and that he therefore used *The Twelve Apostles*, a ship of the same class which, in 1925, was tied up in Sevastopol habour and used for storing mines.[1] The mutiny was staged on this ship though other scenes were shot on the Cruiser *Komintern*. Maxim Straukh's belief that Eisenstein found *Potemkin* still in service as a training ship and so used the original ship seems to have been mistaken.[2]

In his researches Eisenstein found a series of sketches by a French artist who had witnessed the massacre on the Odessa stairway. He talked to survivors whose accounts gave him the 'feel' of what had happened twenty years before. 'The only thing I need is contact with the people,' he said later. 'How many times have I gone out with a preconceived plan of execution, all thought out, with sketches and drawings, and then, on finding myself among the masses, on feeling their nearness, I have changed the idea completely. It is they, in their spontaneity, who actually imprint on the film the great tone of reality.'[3]

Eisenstein wanted the film to portray the history of the 1905 Revolution in terms of the masses. He wished to show the nature and meaning of the Revolution made by the masses; his Hero was the Mass itself in the throes of action. No episode of history was simpler, and in his film Eisenstein presented the events of revolutionary struggle according to the laws of tragic composition in the most canon form—a five-act tragedy.

Among the hundreds and thousands of words describing *Potemkin*, the most compelling description was written by Lion Feuchtwanger as a chapter in his novel *Success*.[4]

'The crew's sleeping quarters. Hammocks slung close together. A petty officer nosing about among the restlessly tossing sailors.' A young sailor turns away, his shoulders heaving from a bullying remark. Faces of men. And here one—Vakulinchuk—the voice of protest.

'Sailors gathering round a bit of meat hanging on a hook. They examine it with disgust. More and more come to look at it. . . . A close-up of the meat: it is crawling with maggots. . . . The ship's doctor is brought along, a somewhat perky gentleman. He puts on his pince-nez, does his duty, inspects the meat, and announces it is not unfit for con-

---

[1] Published posthumously in *Iskusstvo Kino*, No. 4 (Moscow, 1950).

[2] 'Encounters', by Maxim Straukh, *Iskusstvo Kino*, Nos. 1–2 (Moscow, 1940).

[3] *Rusia Alos Doce Anos*, by J. Alvarez del Vayo (2nd Ed., Madrid, 1929).

[4] *Success*, by Lion Feuchtwanger, translated from the German by Willa and Edwin Muir (London, Martin Secker, 1930, and New York, Viking Press, 1930).

sumption. The meat is cooked. The crew refuse to eat it and grumble again. Trivial occurrences, simply portrayed, with emphasis. A bit of stinking meat, sailors, officers. . . .

'The resentment on board swells; one cannot rightly tell how. But there is no doubt that an outburst is bound to come: everybody in the audience feels it. . . .

'The threatening, insistent music continues,[1] the tension increases. The captain parades the crew on deck and asks: who has any complaints to make about the rations? A few men step forward. Suddenly . . . these malcontents, the best of the crew and the leading spirits on board, are isolated; a broad and dangerous space yawns between them and the others. . . . The main body of the crew stands in a frightened mass. The little group of leaders is roped off, penned up in a corner. . . . A piece of sail-cloth is spread over them: one or two pathetic grotesque movements are visible through the canvas. Rifles are trained upon them. Commands ring out, cold and precise. One of the men in the main body of the crew opens his mouth and screams in horror.' A priest appears. He holds high his crucifix. 'The order to fire is given. But no shot follows it. The rifles do not go off.

'A frenzy seizes the people, both those on the screen and those in front of it. . . . And the people in front of the screen cheer and applaud those on the screen. They overwhelm the relentless, triumphant, insistent, horrible music with their clapping hands while on the screen a wild orgy begins as the sailors hunt the officers out of their ridiculous hiding-holes and pitch them overboard into the merrily plashing waves, one after another, the perky ship's doctor among them and his pince-nez after him.' The pince-nez swing from the rigging to and fro, to and fro.

'The flags are pulled down. A new flag flutters up the mast, amid tremendous enthusiasm, a red flag. Sailors take over the officers' duties: the machinery doesn't function any the worse for that. Flying the red flag shyly, the ship sails into Odessa harbour.' Ahead goes a small tender with the body of the sailors' leader, Vakulinchuk.

An appeal from the Dead: Mist over the harbour. Fishing smacks heave as if suppressing a sigh. The slow flight of alighting gulls creates the impression of their mournful cry. The breeze stirs, flaps the tent where Vakulinchuk's body lies with hands clasped. A card tells the legend of his death—for a spoonful of soup. His mother weeps. With the dawn, the trickle of people moving towards the beach becomes a

[1] For the German presentation of *Potemkin*, a special musical score was composed by Edmund Meisel after consultation with Eisenstein. It was played by a large orchestra, but the score was not put into general circulation with the film. For presentation in other countries, including America, a list of musical items was suggested by the distributor.

stream. The stream becomes a torrent. The dead sailor becomes the focal point for the people of Odessa.

From mourning to protest. A daughter of history's most oppressed people speaks for the dead Russian. The Odessans listen. Workers, petty business men, women and children. One listening man with teeth like a ferret raises the cry: 'Down with the Jews!' Workers, whose seaman comrade died for a spoonful of soup, silence the man who lives by finding scapegoats. The scene shifts from the beach to the promenade. Now the people look towards the Cruiser Potemkin'.

'Odessa regards the red flag shyly at first, and the people open their mouths and cheer. They breathe more freely, they break out in rejoicing, they cheer loudly and clearly. At first one by one, then in crowds, the whole city comes in pilgrimage to the ship with the red flag, . . . they swarm in rowboats round the ship with the red flag, and bring some of their own meagre provisions to give to the sailors. . . .

'A flight of steps is shown. An enormous broad flight of steps which goes on for ever. The populace in an endless train are (moving down them) to bring their sympathy to the mutineers. But not for long; for the others are on the steps. A line of Cossacks advance down the steps slowly, menacingly, invincibly, their rifles under their arms, barring the whole breadth of the stair. The people waver. The wavering movement quickens, they hasten, they run, they take to their heels, they fly. A few have not noticed anything or do not understand. . . . The soldiers' boots are shown descending the stairs slowly, step by step; the boots are gigantic, and a little smoke issues from the barrels of the rifles. But now the crowd . . . flings itself down (the steps) as fast as its wind and its legs will permit. But a few are rolling down, and it is no longer their will that propels them, or their limbs or lungs, but simply the law of gravity: for they are dead. And the boots of the Cossacks go tramping on with the same regularity and more and more people roll down the steps. A woman who had been pushing a perambulator is no longer doing so: . . . but the perambulator goes on alone of its own impetus, down one step, and then another, and a sixth and a tenth, until finally it comes to a stop. And behind it, slow and enormous, the boots of the Cossacks.

'On the sea, too, they haven't been idle meanwhile. Other ships have been summoned, gigantic, powerful ships. They surround the . . . (Potemkin). On the ship with the red flag everything is cleared for action. Her huge smooth glittering guns are being trained, and rise up and down like threatening fabulous monsters; the needles on the dials fly backwards and forwards wildly. All around they come on, the great steel vessels of destruction, powerful and perfect to the last detail. The . . . (Potemkin) advances towards them. The ships which are surrounding her, hunting her down, are of the same class as herself, six, eight, ten of them. There is no chance for the . . . (*Potemkin*) to get through, for her guns carry no farther than theirs. She cannot win, she can only in dying drag the others to the same destruction. On the screen and in front of it reigns a wild, agonized suspense as slowly the gigantic ships close in a circle around the . . . (*Potemkin*).

'Then the condemned ship begins to send out signals. Tiny coloured flags rise and fall. The . . . (*Potemkin*) signals: 'Don't fire, brothers.' She steams slowly towards her enemies, signalling: "Don't fire, brothers." One can hear the laboured breathing of the audience; the suspense is almost unendurable. . . .

'A boundless joy fills everybody's heart when the circle of enemy ships lets the . . . (*Potemkin*) pass. . . .'

When he made *Potemkin* in 1925, Sergei Eisenstein was not only a man with his total personality dedicated to creative work—albeit a creative work aimed at destroying all orthodox concepts of 'art'—but he was also a revolutionary fighter, a propagandist for the Russian Revolution. Thus, his work had a utilitarian purpose as well as an artistic one. He was educator and artist. At its most obvious level, *Potemkin* was regarded as propaganda for the Revolution; at a deeper level it was a highly complex work of art which Eisenstein thought would affect every man who beheld it, from the humblest to the most learned.

To Sergei Mikhailovich the most important thing was to affect the spectator. By its portrayal of revolutionary heroism, *Potemkin* must electrify the masses, inspire them in their effort to build a new society. His attitude was that of a scientist. As he later explained: 'The cinema can make a far bigger contribution and a far stronger impression by projecting matter and bodies rather than feelings. We photograph an echo and the rat-tat-tat of a machine gun. The impression is physiological. Our psychological approach is on the one hand that of the great Russian scholar, Pavlov, with his principles of reflexology, and on the other, that of the Austrian Freud—the principle of psychoanalysis.

'Take the scene in *Potemkin* where the Cossacks slowly, deliberately, walk down the Odessa steps firing into the masses. By consciously combining the element of legs, steps, blood, people, we produce an impression. Of what kind? The spectator does not imagine himself at the Odessa wharf in 1905. But as the soldiers' boots press forward he physically recoils. He tries to get out of the range of the bullets. As the baby carriage goes over the side of the mole he holds on to his cinema chair. He does not want to fall into the water.'[1]

[1] S. M. Eisenstein, *Mass Movies*, an interview written by Louis Fischer, *The Nation*, New York, 9 November 1927.

A vivid description of Eisenstein's handling of the great mass of people who participated in the massacre on the Odessa stairs was recorded by Maxim Shtraukh: 'In the period of one week people in panic pushing and trampling each other ran down and rolled down the stairway in order on the signal of the director—'stop!'—to stop and again go up and begin the panic, the pushing, the trampling, the running down and the rolling down of the bodies. Above, they were squeezed by the measured steps of the soldiers' boots and below by mounted Cossacks cutting into the people. This canvas of fabulous slaughter by the will of the director again brought to light the reality of the past as in a nightmare.'[1] [Plate 16]

Eisenstein and Tisse worked with magnificent energy and inspiration. They infected everyone and everything with their own feelings. 'They went tirelessly up and down this stairway of 120 steps all the time finding new and different possibilities of expression.' By the standards of Hollywood of 1925, their technical equipment was exceedingly primitive. But they overcame these limitations by original experiments. They used mirror reflectors for the first time in the Soviet Union, and Tisse devised out-of-focus photography. For the mass scenes he employed a change in lenses in place of a change in camera set-ups. This prevented camera self-consciousness in inexperienced people. In order to shoot the downward movement on the steps, invention was resorted to. A movable wagonette, large enough to hold the cameras, Tisse, Eisenstein and his assistants, was constructed. It was shuttled up and down alongside the stairs on specially built wooden rails. By this means the camera could follow the downward motion of the soldiers and the crowd on the steps.

From the film *Potemkin* there arose a school of revolutionary cinematography in the Soviet Union as distinctive as any school of painting. Also arising from it came the major lines of Eisenstein's art and his theories of film constituents which, in their impact on world cinematography, produced an artistic revolution. The one line was 'typage', the other 'montage'.

Eisenstein's first primitive ideas of 'typage', as mentioned earlier, were derived from the traditions of the Italian Commedia del'Arte. He had attempted to realize the idea with actors in *Strike*. But now in applying his theory of 'typage' to the film *Potemkin* and his later work, Eisenstein discarded the professional actor, and replaced him by people from the streets, fields or workshops who manifested the physio-psychological characteristics of the personages, or crowds, necessary to interpret the action. By employing 'types', Sergei Mikhailovich sought to bring to his art the greatest possible measure of reality based upon

[1] *Encounters*, by Maxim Shtraukh, Iskusstvo Kino, Nos. 1-2 (Moscow, 1940).

his ceaseless research into human behaviour, both in the physiological and psychological spheres.

The first step in the discovery of a 'type' lay in Eisenstein's mind. He conceived the role to be played with all its physio-psychological characteristics, the creation of his image being composed from the united force of imagination and observation. As he once explained to me: when he wanted to create a character, a street cleaner, for example, he went out into the streets and there observed the characteristics of people who were engaged in cleaning the streets. From the general characteristics he observed, he formed a composite image of a typical street cleaner. Then he searched for the individual who possessed the greatest number of traits observed in the many street cleaners, though he might in fact not be a street cleaner. When he found that person, he considered him as the best and truest image of the 'type'.

In practice, 'typage' required the attribute of great patience. It was a time-consuming method of work. In order to find one of his most important characters for *Potemkin*—the small part of the ship's surgeon— he searched endlessly in Odessa but could find no one who exactly fitted his concept. When the unit moved on to Sevastopol to shoot the scenes on board the *Potemkin*, again he searched in vain and was forced to conclude he would have to use the best of the people he had already seen. But none of them was the 'type', only an approximation. Almost at the end of his search, he saw a man shovelling coal in the Sevastopol hotel where he was staying, and in this man Sergei Mikhailovich found each and all of the characteristics of his 'type'. The man who had been shovelling coal became the surgeon in *Potemkin*—an image few people who have seen the film forget. In the same way he discovered the 'type' of the priest in the physiognomy of a gardener who had never acted in his life. But when Eisenstein came to shoot the scene where the priest raises his crucifix in an attempt to quell the mutiny and is then knocked down the stairs by a sailor, the shooting was temporarily halted. According to Jay Leyda, Eisenstein later told him that the gardener was frightened of acting the fall down the stairs, so Sergei Mikhailovich was made up as the priest to enact the scene. While the gardener watched, Eisenstein enacted the scene which Tisse shot. According to Leyda, the gardener, encouraged by Eisenstein's demonstrations, then enacted the fall and went on with his part. [Plate 9]

The publication of the photograph of Eisenstein being made up as the priest, and of reports referring to him as the 'actor-director' of *Potemkin*, led to the story that he acted the role of the priest. It is possible that the footage of Sergei Mikhailovich falling down the stairs shot by Tisse was used when the film was edited. A still from the scene of the priest lying at the foot of the stairs reveals a wink that is characteristic of

Eisenstein, and there is also a faint suggestion of the mole which Eisenstein had above his left eyebrow. Despite the story Eisenstein related to Leyda, it is very possible that he intended to play the priest in this short scene which held an ironic, religious meaning for him. If he did not intend to play it, it is very strange that a suitable wig and beard should have been available since the gardener was selected as a 'type' and wore no make-up.[1] [Plate 9]

Behind the theory of 'typage' was philosophical reasoning. As Sergei Eisenstein later expressed it: 'A thirty-year-old actor may be called upon to play an old man of sixty. He may have a few days' or a few hours' rehearsal. But an old man of sixty will have had sixty years' rehearsal.'

'I do not pick my actors from the profession. . . . They do not act roles. They simply are their natural selves. I get them to repeat before the camera just what they have done in reality. They are hardly conscious of any artificiality, of any make-believe. . . . And in the mass action of my films, different as the individual persons are from each other, they are significant not as separate human organisms, but as parts working together in a social organism, like the separate cells working together in the human body.'[2]

The second, and perhaps more important, theory realized by Sergei Mikhailovich through the film *Potemkin* was his subsequently ever-expanding concept of 'montage'.

In film language, 'montage' means the uniting of shots of seemingly dissociated objects in such a way that they take on a new qualitative relationship to each other in the mind of the spectator. A simple example of montage lying outside the film medium which influenced Eistenstein may be found in the hieroglyphs of the Chinese language. The idea 'to weep' is depicted by an eye and water. Taken separately, these images bear no necessary relationship to the idea 'to weep', but when united a new quality emerges—a new idea is evoked in the mind of the beholder. It should also be borne in mind that on occasion Eisenstein's method of montage included the editing of very closely asso-

---

[1] In an unfinished manuscript by Eisenstein written in 1945 and published posthumously in *Iskusstvo Kino*, No. 4, Moscow 1950, Eisenstein recounts the 'legend' that he played the role of the Priest in *Potemkin*, which arose from the photograph of his being 'made up as the Priest. He says: 'I was being made up to double for him [the Priest]: the respectable old man was supposed to fall down a companion-ladder. The camera was to be behind him during the fall. And I could not refuse myself the satisfaction of "personally" performing this *cascade* !'

[2] *Revolution in the World of Make-Believe*, by H. W. L. Dana, Boston Evening Transcript, 1 March 1930.

ciated images, for example, the film pieces used in the 'fog over the harbour' sequence in *Potemkin*.

The term 'montage' was brought into wide use in European languages by Soviet films; first by *Potemkin* and later by such films as *Mother* and *The End of St. Petersburg* by Vsevolod Pudovkin; *Earth* by Alexander Dovzhenko, and others. Before this time, montage was associated with the principle of building and construction in the field of engineering and of photography in the word 'photo-montage'.

Although it was Eisenstein who developed the theory of montage based on aesthetic principles, the roots of the idea lay in an attempt to overcome a practical problem facing the early Soviet film industry. From the outset Soviet film makers had been faced with a shortage of raw film stock. Thus, they were compelled to look for ingenious ways of using the short ends of negative and positive that were lying about studios and laboratories. During the early experiments of Kuleshov and Vertov, mentioned in the previous chapter, it had been shown that a definite principle of editing could be established by the utilization of short ends.[1] For example, Vertov discovered as early as 1920 that a shot of even two or three frames was visible to the human eye.[2] It was against this background of technical experiment that Eisenstein began the development of his subtle theory of montage.

In *Potemkin*, montage of film pieces, or of 'shots', served as the basic constituent of the work—the very method from which the finished film emerged. Montage plus captions superseded in importance formal composition, 'acting', even 'story' in any orthodox sense. There was in fact no motion picture until Eisenstein himself united one piece of film with another. Montage existed in his head. It was not an element of film construction which could be outlined and expressed on paper, for it came into actual existence only in the moment of editing. Thus, if all the pieces of film 'shot' for *Potemkin* had been hung up around the work room of another director for him to edit, they would have made little or no sense to him in terms of a potential motion picture. Only a part of the pieces of film had recognizable continuity in the manner of the accepted story film; that is, where the scene recorded dovetails into the next in a simple and obviously coherent series of shots.

Since montage depended upon individual creative vision, no separate film editor had a place in Sergei Eisenstein's scheme of film making. Through montage the hitherto mechanical character of film production with its separation into different technical jobs was largely transformed

[1] 'The Film in U.S.S.R.—1937' (Report of A.C.T. Delegation to the U.S.S.R., headed by Thorold Dickinson, May 1937, in the *Cine-Technician*, August–September 1937).

[2] According to Dziga Vertov in an interview with the author in 1934.

into an almost wholly individual creative act. Eisenstein wrote his own scenarios with Alexandrov as his collaborator, designed and directed the scenes and, finally, by his various methods of montage, edited the film. Eduard Tisse, as cameraman, acted in the capacity of a third eye, achieving the ideas conceived by Sergei Mikhailovich during the pre-montage stage—the stage of direction. Sometimes it was Tisse who realized the full possibilities of a fleeting idea. Since in the early films Eisenstein often digressed from the scenario, much shooting was extempore.

Such an instance occurred while Eisenstein and Tisse were in the Crimea shooting the scenes on the Cruiser *Potemkin*. One day they went south from Sevastopol along the coast and came to Alupka, once a palace of the Tsars of Russia. Walking around the formal garden, they saw the marble lions decorating the flight of steps leading from the palace to the lower garden. The first lion lay asleep. The second lion had awakened. The third was rising. Montage!

Three pieces of film recording three of the lions could be edited to cause a stone lion to move! Tisse became excited. A sense of anticipation ticked feverishly inside him. But Sergei Mikhailovich was enjoying the sun and the resplendent semi-tropical flowers. Momentarily he was bored with the many ideas that coursed through his mind. He felt lazy; he didn't want to be bothered with work.

'We have too many ideas. We can throw some away. There will always be more.'

But after they returned to Sevastopol, Tisse kept urging Sergei Mikhailovich to go back to Alupka so they might shoot the three lions. To humour Tisse, they returned and Tisse shot his lions. In time, Sergei Mikhailovich took the three pieces of film in his hands, studied them, and three inanimate lions became one stone lion which sprang up.

He achieved this effect by a correct calculation of the length of the second shot. The waking lion was juxtaposed with the sleeping lion. This established the first action on the beholder's eye. Juxtaposed with the waking lion was the rising lion, which produced the second action. Thus, the lion seemed to rise in a single swift motion.[1] Transforming the static into the dynamic was simple. What was infinitely more interesting to Eisenstein were the thoughts and feelings engendered in him by the rising lion—the symbolic significance of marble become dynamic. Even stone cries out in protest? . . . The final and complex montage of the rising lion in *Potemkin* was as follows:

Cut into the thunder of *Potemkin's* guns, a marble lion leaps up in protest against the bloodshed on the Odessa steps. Such combinations,

[1] *Film Form* by S. M. Eisenstein (New York, Harcourt Brace and Co., 1949 and London, Dennis Dobson, 1950), p. 56.

such philosophical and emotional interpenetration of 'things' with other 'things' stamped the individuality of the twenty-seven-year-old Eisenstein upon his work.

When at last they had finished shooting *Potemkin*, they returned to Moscow and then the work of editing commenced. Patterned with different montage methods, two of the five distinctive methods later developed by Eisenstein were used in *Potemkin*. In an essay written four years later in London, he explained what he meant by montage and how he had employed different methods in *Potemkin*—in particular those which he designated as 'rhythmic montage' and 'tonal montage'.

In rhythmic montage 'formal tension by acceleration is obtained here by shortening the pieces [of film] not only in accordance with the fundamental plan, but also violating the plan. This most effective violation is by the introduction of material more intense in an easily distinguished tempo.' In the Odessa steps sequence—approximating act four in classic tragedy—'the rhythmic drum of the soldiers' feet as they descend the steps violates all *metrical* demands. Unsynchronized with the beat of the cutting, this drumming comes in *off-beat* each time, and the shot itself is entirely different in its solution with each of these appearances. The final pull of tension is supplied by the transfer from the rhythm of the descending feet to another rhythm—a new kind of downward movement—the next intensity level of the same activity— the baby-carriage rolling down the steps. The carriage functions as a directly progressing accelerator of the advancing feet. The stepping descent passes into the rolling descent.'[1]

All who have seen *Potemkin* remember the mounting tempo of this sequence with its fearful introductory shot—the legless man hopping out on his hands from behind the lace skirt of a lady with mincing shoes —to the equally shocking closing shot of the woman whose eye suddenly streams blood. Between these two shots of horror— an application of Grand Guignole—nameless people are senselessly slaughtered and their slaughter driven into the spectators' minds most fiercely by the figure of the crazed woman carrying her dead child *up the steps towards the soldiers* to meet certain death. This figure is the focal human principle pushing, as it were, against the force of blind destruction; while the baby-carriage seems animated with desire to escape destruction—to flee ever faster and faster. [Plates 10, 11]

In Eisenstein's rhythmic montage 'movement within the frame impels the montage movement from frame to frame. Such movements within the frame may be objects in motion, or of the spectator's eye directed along the line of some immobile object.'[2] But in his tonal

---

[1] *Film Form* by S. M. Eisenstein (New York, Harcourt Brace and Co., 1949 and London, Dennis Dobson, 1950), p. 74. [2] *Ibid.*, p. 75.

montage, Eisenstein sought to penetrate deeper into the inner nature of his images and reveal 'the characteristic *emotional sound*'. For example, the fog sequence preceding the mourning for the dead leader of the mutiny.

'Here', Eisenstein said, 'the montage was based exclusively on the emotional "sound" of the pieces—on rhythmic vibrations that do not affect spatial alterations. In this example, alongside the basic tonal dominant, a secondary, accessory *rhythmic* dominant is also operating. This links the tonal construction of the scene with the tradition of rhythmic montage, the furthest development of which is tonal montage. . . . This secondary dominant is expressed in barely perceptible changing movements; the agitation of the water; the slight rocking of the anchored vessels and buoys; the slowly ascending vapour; the seagulls settling gently on to the water.'[1]

The montage was completed in two months and on the 1st of January 1926, *Potemkin* was premièred in Moscow's gilded Bolshoi Theatre—symbol of Tsarist magnificence. *Potemkin* marked an advance in film development comparable to that made in painting when Giotto's frescoes first appeared. Like Giotto, Eisenstein ushered in a new period of expressive realism in art.

In this one work the 'creative ecstasy'[2] of Sergei Eisenstein and the creative impulse of the society to which he belonged merged in an harmonious unity. He identified himself with the revolutionary struggle of his country to an intense personal degree; in a manner akin to the religious devotee who believes he has come into contact with a higher reality and tries, thereafter, to create a symbolic testimony of his experience. The sailors on the *Potemkin* became through their mutiny, and with the aid of Eisenstein's art, the symbolic image of the total revolutionary struggle.

Sergei Mikhailovich, who had written a little less than three years before of attracting and engaging the emotions of the spectator, now found he had created a work which accomplished his desire. In a few months *Potemkin* was released in Berlin where it ran for a year at the Kamera Theatre alone. 'It caused a tempest that equalled, in the literary world, that unleashed by Goethe's *Götz von Berlichen* one hundred and fifty years before.'[3]

The impact of *Potemkin* went deep into the consciousness of many German artists. As the novelist Lion Feuchtwanger later wrote: '*Potem-*

---

[1] *Ibid.*, p. 76.

[2] Eisenstein used this term in his writing and in speech to convey the nature of his inspiration, particularly as a description of a heightened state of consciousness.

[3] *Gestalter der Filmkunst*, by Ludwig Gesck (Amandus, 1948).

kin had an enormous influence especially on the German literary youth, and the result was that one did not only see events of revolutionary character as Eisenstein had shown them in *Potemkin*, but the film technique of rapid sequence of pictures, the simultaneousness of different situations was also tried in literature.'[1]

Max Reinhardt, the theatre director, said that 'after viewing *Potemkin*, I am willing to admit that the stage will have to give way to the cinema.' Germany's leading newspaper, the *Berliner Tageblatt*, wrote: 'For the first time there has appeared a film that is felt to be not of merely transitory but of permanent value. This is not a picture—it is a reality. Eisenstein has created the most powerful and artistic film in the whole world.'

Eisenstein later wrote that the '"crushing" effect' which *Potemkin* had in Germany was intensified by the musical score composed by Edmund Meisel. Sergei Mikhailovich went to Berlin for a few days before the release of *Potemkin* in Germany to work with Meisel who 'agreed at once to forgo the purely illustrative function common to musical accompaniments at that time . . . and stress certain "effects", particularly in the "music of the machines" in the last reel', where the *Potemkin* prepares for battle. Thus, the music 'stylistically broke away from the limits of the "silent film with musical illustrations" into a new sphere—into *sound-film*'.[2] From his collaboration with Meisel came Sergei Mikhailovich's central ideas for the sound-film 'where true models of this art-form live in a unity of fused musical and visual images'. Eisenstein was one of the very first film directors to see the creative possibilities of sound but, ironically, he was not to complete a sound-film until 1938.

Beyond the borders of the Soviet Union people who had seldom entered a cinema went to see this reputedly remarkable film, this work of Soviet art which had burst unexpectedly on an astonished world. Some reactions to it were violent. Fearful and frightened film censors cringed before the power of *Potemkin*, imagining it as the match to set ablaze a world revolution. Intellectuals and artists saw in it a whole new philosophy of art. For some it was the commencement of a new political philosophy. But Eisenstein could not remain content to express himself through the medium of film alone. He was to become engaged upon a larger mission—creating a theory for the unification of the principles of science and art in an age when men were being forced into a new relationship with their environment and many branches of knowledge were unfolding.

[1] Lion Feuchtwanger in a letter to the author, dated 30 May, 1950.

[1] *Film Form* by S. M. Eisenstein (New York, Harcourt Brace and Co., 1949 and London, Dennis Dobson, 1950), p. 177.

The Viennese psychoanalyst, Dr. Hanns Sachs, recognized the importance of Eisenstein the psychologist. It greatly interested him when a friend, after seeing *Potemkin* three or four times, explained that at one point in the film 'he had been very strongly moved without being able to discover what it was that moved him. On each occasion this experience came when, at the captain's command, the sailcloth is being carried on board. In the midst of this operation the head of the fugleman of the guard, called up for the shooting [of the mutinying sailors], emerged clearly for a moment and turned to watch. This watching head seems to have no particular expression, and any expression it might bear would, owing to the fractional time during which it appears in the picture, be lost on the spectator. . . . By looking round at the sailcloth as it is being carried past, [the fugleman] betrays, however slightly, his character of a human being involved in the proceedings. . . . We know that even the guard, in its totality of unfeeling machine, is made up of men capable of sympathy, and we begin to hope.'[1]

Douglas Fairbanks and Mary Pickford, who saw *Potemkin* in Moscow during their visit in July, 1926, declared upon their return to America that Eisenstein had mastered the 'science of motion'. Fairbanks' opinion hastened the release of the film in New York, where it was presented at a spectacular première on Sunday, the 5th of December, 1926, at the Biltmore Theatre, with seats at the fabulous price of 5.00 dollars each.

American critics and literary figures seemed to vie with each other in proclaiming *Potemkin*. Fannie Hurst delineated it as 'magnificent. Lean, high-strung, this strange story pinions the interest and grips the emotion.' The discerning critic, Richard Watts, Jr. said that '*Potemkin* simply compels the attention of anyone whose interest in modern artistic expression is even casual. It is a film blazing with vitality and dynamic power. It is one of the notable achievements of modern art. The National Board of Review selected it as the finest film of the year, and commented that it was 'the perfect cinematic re-creation of an event'. The *Christian Science Monitor* predicted 'There is no doubt but that *Potemkin* is going down in screen history as one of the way-making films. Mr. Eisenstein has established a new technique for making motion pictures.'

In December, 1926, the Cine-Clubs of France began to show *Potemkin*. It made such a profound impression that it soon led the critic Leon Moussinac to write the first serious book on Soviet films. In analysing the work of Eisenstein, Moussinac saw 'self-discipline, passion for truth which leads at times to a certain brutal realism and to a cruelty in which one easily recalls some memories of Dostoievski, breadth of a

[1] Dr. Hanns Sachs, 'Film Psychology' (*Close-up*, November 1928).

rare amplitude, poetry of the collective élan, emotion springing directly from the mind and heart of men, eternal rhythms of the great media of expression which every age creates in its image and on the scale of its design. Griffith has given the diverse sides of tragedy but only from the psychological and individual aspect, Eisenstein by the same artistic process evisages the collective and social aspects'.[1]

Although *Potemkin* was not shown in England until the autumn of 1929, much was written about it by English critics. In appraising Eisenstein's use of imagery, Robert Herring said: 'He gives us the material *as it is*, not as it seems, or might seem to individuals. As it is, so that we can't mistake it. He intensifies it. He heightens the drama. . . . In fact, Eisenstein makes our consciousness fully aware, brings it fully into play, by playing on it until the subconscious is awakened; dragged up to reinforce the conscious'.[2]

Meanwhile, in Moscow, Sergei Mikhailovich, long immersed in his creative dreams, was faced with the reality of his own achievement. With no preparation for world fame, he found himself alone and very much disturbed by the notoriety heaped upon him. Painfully shy, he did not know how to behave with moderation. At first he behaved like a boor. Not infrequently he appeared to others in the guise of a gargantuan caricature of vanity and egotism—an exaggeratedly aggressive personality.

Inside he was trembling with anxiety, yet he was consumed with an insatiable desire to know how the world appraised *Potemkin*. To obtain copies of the foreign Press he would haunt the office of V.O.K.S., the cultural and scientific exchange organization set up as a clearing house for foreign information. He felt uncomfortable, fearful of exposing his uncertainty.

Recently he had learned to what lengths people would go in an effort to discover the nature of his psychological quirks. He shrank from the memory of the frontal attack which had been made upon his private life. This incident lay upon him like a cold hand, and was to do so for many years.

Not long before *Potemkin's* triumph, practical joking had been turned upon him. Two of his comrades devised a scheme to unmask Eisenstein. Was he a virgin? Would he submit to a woman's advances? His comrades, mystified by Sergei Mikhailovich's resolute continence, arranged with a prostitute to go to his room on the Chysti Prudi and wait for him while they lurked in another room. Their practical joke had inconclusive results. All they ever knew was that Sergei Mikhailo-

---

[1] *Le Cinéma Soviétique*, by Leon Moussinac (Gallimard, Paris, 1928), p. 150 and *seq.*

[2] 'Imagery-Eisenstein,' by Robert Herring, *Close-Up*, December 1928.

vich flew into a rage of extraordinary disgust marked by all the symptoms of hysteria.

If his friends would do such a thing to him, what were strangers thinking? His sensitivity grew ever sharper and he ever more wary. He felt his silent interrogators towering over him waiting to expose all his weaknesses. In a gesture of defiance, he combed up his mane of hair until it bristled like a halo of electric force. His high, bulging forehead glowered at the world as if to keep it at bay. His naturally expressive and beautifully chiselled features assumed an alternating expression of mocking mirth or a remote scowl. He would stride through life as an Olympian clown whose wicked humour would demolish all things foolish and small and sacred to the petty-minded. [Pl. 18, p. 96].

One day Sergei Mikhailovich strode into V.O.K.S. flaunting his most Olympian manner. He wanted the German reviews of *Potemkin*. To his chagrin, the precious reviews had just been given to a young film worker—Pera Fogelman—who used the professional name of Attasheva. In egocentric, overbearing tones, Sergei Eisenstein demanded that Pera Attasheva let him have the papers first. [Pl. 19, p. 96].

It seemed to Pera that Eisenstein was the most arrogant man she had ever met. It would do him good to wait. He might have made *Potemkin* and that admittedly was a great film, but he lived in a society where people were supposed to act in a comradely manner towards each other.

'But I need them,' he said.

'I have work to do with them and it can't wait,' she answered.

She was small, with rich dark hair and dancing black eyes. But Eisenstein was impervious to her charm. He demanded she telephone him the moment she had finished with the papers. Taking his telephone number, Pera Attasheva departed. She did not hurry with her translations. Eisenstein must learn he was not a god—or a temperamental bourgeois artist—in anyone's eyes except his own.

In the meantime, Sergei Mikhailovich contracted influenza. His resistance was low, because for more than eight years he had never really had enough to eat. Added to lack of food, he suffered from nervous tension and the exhausting excitement caused by the prospect of his future in a state which would now reward him with limitless opportunities to express his ideas. Plans swarmed in his great skull. But he could not fight off the 'flu and was forced to crawl into bed in his bleak room as miserable as a sick child. There was nothing to console him but the sight of books, books and more books, and two concentric circles, one red and the other blue, which he had painted on the ceiling above his bed.

After several days of feeling miserably sick, the telephone rang. Pera

Attasheva had finished with the foreign papers; he could come and get them any time he liked. She lived at Naschokinsky Pereoulok 14. He told her he was ill. Being ill, his aggressive mannerism had withered. He was too miserable to preserve pretence, so Pera offered to bring the papers to him.

Arriving that evening in the cold, carpetless room, Pera was sorry for the fallen and humbled god she found. Cold, hungry and with a fever, he was as pitiful as a lost waif. No one would leave a person unaided in such a state—not even a person one disliked.

Briskly Pera set about putting Sergei Mikhailovich and his room in order. She obtained food, cooked and fed him, then did a little elementary nursing. None of this was an effort for her. It was part of the pattern of her home life, where her mother was often ill and she had to look after her younger sister. Pera was inclined to laugh at trouble, and her laughter was so gay and infectious that it was a key to renewed hope. That she was taking a man, and an almost total stranger, under her wing did not trouble her. She knew that a man with 'flu was only a child in need of comfort. Sergei Mikhailovich was frankly and utterly grateful and did what he was told without argument.

His gratitude went deeper than his 'flu. It sprang up like a young tree from a long-sleeping seed, for until the bustling entrance of Pera, no one but his nurse had ever been truly and humanly kind to him. Indeed, he had made it difficult for people to feel he needed kindness. Many thought he would bite them like a vicious dog if they offered him such a poor and mortal thing. Overwhelmed by the sudden warmth of Pera's kindness and laughing bossiness, he was filled with a sense of security. He relaxed. It was comforting to be taken hold of by competent hands and made to understand that men usually did not die of 'flu. Though she was only twenty-five and laughed a great deal, Pera was like a mother.

Within the space of a few hours, a singular relationship, changeless and irrevocable, was established between Sergei Eisenstein, possessed by Promethean dreams, and Pera Attasheva, possessed to the full with love of life and an immeasurable capacity for devotion. She came next day and the next to carry on the job of pulling Sergei Mikhailovich through his illness. She was in and out until he was again on his feet. Now he raged at the time he had lost and the work which had piled up for him to do. What he needed was someone to help him keep things in order.

Eisenstein asked Pera to become his secretary. He thought that with the success of *Potemkin* he would now be able to earn enough money to pay her. She knew German, French and English, and could do research for him. Pera accepted on the condition that she have time to work for herself as well. She liked to write and translate; she had ambitions too and was not by nature a secretary. The arrangement was agreeable to Sergei Mikhailovich.

So Pera took over the affairs of the Old Man, as she called him 'because he knew so much', and she managed them with the same competence as she had nursed him. At first it was a job done for some-one she had come to admire; soon it became part of her whole being —for with familiarity the Old Man became ever more fascinating; the more known, the more possible—indeed inevitable—was it to fall in love with him.

It was not long before storms broke all around her. Boris Barnet, who was in love with her, implored her to forget this crazy passion which must end unhappily, since Eisenstein had always been mystifying and unpredictable. Would she not forget and come back? She shook her head. Her mother wept, warning her she was throwing her life away on an extraordinary man who behaved most oddly and was un-necessarily rude. Pera held her peace and closed her lips. She was tactful with Sergei Mikhailovich's own mother, who attempted to gain her confidence so she might win back the affection of her son. In spite of these warnings, she could not believe the Old Man would be so good to her, so comradely towards her or so trusting, if he did not love her. There was a lot of time. . . .

But for Eisenstein the days were too short. *Potemkin* drove him to new plans; it also brought him into subtle though violent competition. Shortly after the triumph of *Potemkin*, the first film of Vsevolod I. Pudovkin, the pupil of Lev Kuleshov who had been experimenting for five years with story films, burst on Moscow as a second bombshell. This was the beautiful and humane film *Mother*, also a story of the 1905 Revolution. Pudovkin, whose work was poetic and humanistic, was compared with Eisenstein, the brilliant intellect and technical virtuoso. There were some people who favoured Pudovkin's personal portraiture as a means of portraying revolution over Eisenstein's relentless vision of historical mass movement. An emotional man who doubted the intel-lectual approach and trusted to the heart, Pudovkin collided with the scientific approach of Eisenstein; while Eisenstein retreated sarcastically from Pudovkin's uninhibited emotionalism. A secret contest arose, each seeking to prove the superiority of his artistic theories over the other.

Although the contention between Eisenstein and Pudovkin resulted in part from a conflict of personalities, they genuinely differed in their theoretical approach. In an article written in 1929, Sergei Mikhailovich analysed his theoretical differences with Pudovkin in the following words:

In front of me lies a crumpled yellowed sheet of paper. On it a mysterious note:

'Linkage — P' and 'Collision — E.'

This is a substantial trace of a heated bout on the subject of montage between P (Pudovkin) and E (myself).

This has become a habit. At regular intervals he visits me late at night and behind closed doors we wrangle over matters of principle. A graduate of the Kuleshov school, he loudly defends an understanding of montage as a *linkage* of pieces. Into a chain. Again, 'bricks'. Bricks arranged in a series to *expound* an idea.

I confronted him with my view point on montage as a *collision*. A view that from the collision of two given factors *arises* a concept.

From my point of view, linkage is merely a possible *special* case.

Recall what an infinite number of combinations is known in physics to be capable of arising from the impact (collision) of spheres. Depending on whether the spheres be resilient, non-resilient, or mingled. Amongst all these combinations there is one in which the impact is so weak that the collision is degraded to an even movement of both in the same direction.

This is the one combination which would correspond with Pudovkin's view.[1]

The film *Potemkin*, with its concept of the Mass as Hero, and *Mother*, with its highly personalized interpretation of the Mass through the unforgettable characters of Mother and Son, proved the declaration of Lenin that 'the cinema is the most important of all the arts', because of its power to reach great masses of people. Thus, Eisenstein and his rival, Pudovkin, stood shoulder to shoulder in the public eye and were pointed to as examples of Soviet artists whose work revealed to the highest degree the social reality of their time. Each had created a work of art peculiarly unique and expressive of the new social base from which the future culture and art of the Soviet Union must spring.

They might be brothers in revolutionary art in public, but high aims could not overcome their natural animosity and rivalry. When together in public or private, each showed-off in an attempt to get the better of the other—Eisenstein extolling the virtue of the scientific and intellectual approach, Pudovkin the emotional and humane. Eisenstein claimed privately that Pudovkin had imitated certain of his methods of montage; Pudovkin claimed, also privately, that Eisenstein was an untrustworthy man who 'stole' other people's ideas and failed to give them credit. Eisenstein hinted that Pudovkin was a fool; Pudovkin that

[1] *Film Form* by S. M. Eisenstein (New York, Harcourt Brace and Co., 1949 and London, Dennis Dobson, 1950), p. 38.

Eisenstein was an over-intellectual man whom he pitied because he was incapable of human feelings. As the feud grew beneath the surface of solidarity, these two remarkable artists became as spiteful towards each other as little boys engaged in a senseless battle for supremacy of the school 'gang'. Finally, each bought a dog and gave the poor beast the name of his rival. Pudovkin taught his dog, Eisenstein, to beg for titbits, while Eisenstein shouted at his dog, Pudovkin, to make it obey him.

Potemkin having been released before *Mother*, Eisenstein went to work on his next film ahead of Pudovkin—a fact which was to be most unfortunate for him. He was working in a society where art was bound by political philosophy to be responsive to social aims and demands; where, at a given moment, all social thought and effort was directed through the Press, literature and the fine arts towards goals which did not remain static. Following the completion and release of *Potemkin*, the two problems uppermost in the minds of Soviet planners were the future of China and the future of Soviet agriculture. These problems were a source of inspiration to Sergei Mikhailovich. His thoughts soared. China! What could be a more wonderful subject.

Sergei Mikhailovich planned a mighty film of China in three parts. The strange, exotic, the unknown, the ancient and the new revolutionary stirrings in China made an irresistible appeal to his imagination, as a few years later the same elements in Mexico were to take almost demoniac possession of him. But this, his first unrealized dream, was suddenly terminated. For technical reasons the film was too great a project to be undertaken by the still undeveloped Soviet film industry. In this decision, foreshadowing other such decisions in Eisenstein's career, political consideration may also have played a part. The close association between the Russians and the Chinese was breaking down. Chiang-Kai-Shek's putsch turned the country from the road of revolution to that of reaction; thus the future of China became a highly speculative and precarious matter.

However, Eisenstein's study of Chinese culture continued throughout his life, and his interest in the country from the point of view of a film revived for a short time early in 1935 when he considered the possibilities of making a picture based on the novel *La Condition Humaine* by André Malraux.

Sergei Mikhailovich was too responsive to social demands to make an issue of the matter. He spent no time in complaining, but plunged with equal passion into the alternative subject—Soviet agriculture.

Though a city-bred man, he was bound to the peasant consciousness through his nurse. To Eisenstein the earth was a source of great and mysterious strength. He loved the earth with a mystical passion which was more primordial than poetic. Nature was cruel as well as beautiful. Her children, the peasants, were animals gradually evolving towards the status of humanity; they were like himself, filled with elemental feelings. He loved these people as his brothers.

Yet he was also a scientist and at this time extremely proud and boastful of his scientific methods. He recognized that Soviet society must mould the earthy peasant into a new rational and constructive human force—else the Revolution would end in failure. This enormous task—to revolutionize the thinking of one of the most backward peasantries in the world—could only be accomplished through the mechanization of the land and through the growth of agricultural co-operatives. 'It is', he wrote, while at work on this task of picturing the agricultural revolution, 'imperative to raise the village from the slough of ancient custom and bring it into line with the Soviet system as a whole.'

Together with Tisse and Grisha Alexandrov, Sergei Mikhailovich set about mastering his new subject. They rushed into the country and took up residence in a village for a month—a gloriously happy month for Eisenstein, who could speak to the peasant in his own colourful, if crude, language. In his first creative contact with the village, Sergei Mikhailovich was pulled between his instinctive response to the symbols of folk culture and his intellectual conviction that science would, and must, create a new world for the peasants. He led his assistants to model farms, where he became entranced with modern experimental methods. With the meticulous care of a reporter on hard facts, he interviewed the editors of peasant newspapers and invaded the Commissariat of Agriculture, where he studied masses of complaints and agricultural reports coming in from the countryside.

The scientific fever possessed him. He had to know everything, and everything he discovered must go into his film document of Soviet agriculture. He visited peasants of the agricultural trade union and attended their meetings. He went to schools, biological laboratories and the growing co-operatives. From his preliminary research, two symbols emerged of the peasants' future—the Cream Separator and the power of the Tractor. The machine was the means of breaking through into a new era. To crown his efforts, Eisenstein went to the 14th Congress of the Communist Party and saw that his film must enable 'the official terminology of theses, resolutions and decisions [to] come to life on the screen in herds of fat cattle, in the movement of harvesters and tractors, in warm stalls, in the opening earth under the spring snow'.[1] His film was to be *The General Line* of collectivization, as it affected the life of the peasant and the village. To remind himself of his main thesis, Sergei Mikhailovich obtained an American placard advertising a new

[1] *Voices of October*, by Joseph Freeman (New York, Vanguard, 1930).

cream separator and pinned it on the wall above the table in his room on the Chysti Prudi. The placard would watch over his work—like an icon.

Eisenstein, Tisse and Alexandrov went to work in a great flurry to pour into one film all the details of the changing agricultural scene. The clear, concise line of *Potemkin* was discarded in favour of a freer form, an almost entirely documentary concept.

Meanwhile, Pudovkin's success with *Mother* had resulted in his being assigned the direction of a most important film to commemorate the tenth anniversary of the October Revolution. He was busy working on this film—*The End of St. Petersburg*—which told the story of the last days of the Russian Empire. It was being produced under the auspices of the film trust Mezhrapom; while Eisenstein was working under the auspices of Sovkino, who had drawn up no plans for an anniversary film. Sovkino hastened to remedy their oversight. Eisenstein was their luminary. They asked him to halt work on *General Line* and rush through an anniversary film, which was to cost 500,000 roubles, an astronomical sum for the early years of the Soviet film industry. So Eisenstein switched from the revolution taking place in the village to reconstruct the 1917 Revolution as it took place in the imperial city of Petrograd where, ten years before, he had been a student in the University. The result was the titanic film *October*, or, as it was known abroad, *Ten Days that Shook the World*. This title and some of the details were taken from the book of the same name by the American journalist John Reed, who had died in the throes of the Russian Revolution.

CHAPTER FIVE

Fourth Dimension—*October* and *General Line*

You who speculate on the nature of things, I praise you not for knowing the processes which Nature ordinarily effects of herself, but rejoice if so be that you know the issue of such things as your mind conceives.

LEONARDO DA VINCI, G. 47 r.

WHEN Eisenstein arrived in Leningrad to direct *October*, the city was put at his disposal. He strode through the streets and took possession of its palaces like the Tsar whose catastrophic collapse he had witnessed. With the impishness of an incorrigible child, Sergei Mikhailovich lolled in his workman's clothes on the late Emperor's throne in the Winter Palace. With a mock gesture of His Majesty waving his hand, he ordered photographs to be taken of himself in his role of iconoclastic emperor of a new art form. But as he sat on the throne, his short legs did not touch the floor. Defiantly he flung his legs over the arm of the throne and was photographed again. [Plates 12, 50]

Still, the Winter Palace filled him with glee and he collapsed into paroxysms of childlike laughter such as had seldom shaken him in childhood. He revelled in his freedom to thumb his nose at marble goddesses (who at other times ravished him with a sensual delight in their baroque imaginativeness), and his power to turn the imperial bed into his director's seat. The jester side of his nature ran riot. His greatest find, one which threw him into a stream of ribaldry, was the late Tsar Nicholas's crested chamber-pot. Master of fun-making at one moment, Eisenstein was master of the populace the next. Three thousand inhabitants of Leningrad nightly gave their services in the re-creation of revolution. Old revolutionaries once more stormed the Winter Palace at his bidding, and in the process more windows were broken than during the actual ten days that shook the world. The battleship *Aurora* steamed up the Neva River from Kronstadt and once more bombarded the Winter Palace.

History—the days of history through which Sergei Mikhailovich had lived ten years before served as the outline of his scenario. He had but to gather up the threads of what had happened in 1917 between March and November and reawaken the vivid impressions he had stored away. And this he did. Between somersaults of mirth, the vision of Revolution returned to Eisenstein. Once more he experienced the sensations of

96

an Empire tottering and falling in ruin. But now he saw the events through the telephoto lens of ten years during which he had changed from a young student who dreamed of becoming the da Vinci of the twentieth century, to a man who in actuality had manifested the power of genius. In the film *October* a multitude of impressions and ideas peculiar to Eisenstein were grafted on to the tree of history. He built up each image of the Revolution according to the laws of his own nature and moulded them in accordance with his own will.

The film *Potemkin* had embraced one episode in the history of the 1905 Revolution. But its successor, *October*, encompassed events covering eight months when the course of modern history took a turn the end of which we have even now not seen. In its own medium—film— *October* had no parallel, though it may have been foreshadowed in literature by Tolstoy's *War and Peace*, and in a less passionate tone by Thomas Hardy's *The Dynasts* where, likewise, the tapestry of history served as the woof and warp of art.

Political action rather than personal passions was the source of Eisenstein's inspiration; yet he pursued the line of political action according to his inner vision, one curiously responsive to philosophic stimulation. He was also driven on by the tail wind of his experimental passion to carry the exploration of his chosen medium to its furthest horizon. From these two driving forces, *October* was born—a work as difficult to understand without explanatory notes as *Potemkin* was simple.

History marched across the screen as never before. But historical action suddenly became suspended while Eisenstein wove a visual commentary, the nature of which was nearer to Socratic discourse on the nature of things than to Art, as it was later to be interpreted in the light of Marxism, Leninism and Stalinism. *October* was an esoteric work of art permeated with symbols of ambiguous meaning to the majority— a work on several levels all developing simultaneously. Being diffuse as well as monumental, *October* had the power to tire all but the most inquiring mind. No human character served as a focal point and no single emotion ran as a thread through the whole. An encyclopaedia of images, the imagery rose to a crescendo that could too easily leave many spectators exhausted by the mental gymnastics required to follow the discursive line.

As in *Potemkin*, montage was the method used to construct his vision of the ten days that shook the world; but the montage became more complex and the imagery far more subjective. He could not append an explanatory commentary to his visual commentaries, and only a small fraction of the people who later saw *October* read his analysis of his own work.

October would have fared better had Sergei Mikhailovich been in the position of a man like James Joyce, whose literary experiments were explained while he worked on and published fragments of *Finnegans Wake*. But Eisenstein was a film director standing at the beginning of a new art form with his audience unprepared for experiments in 'cine-dialectics'. He was trying to convey what was in his mind through images at a time when education in such imagery was almost non-existent. There was, as he might have remarked with a wry smile, little cinema culture. Even now, more than four decades after the creation of *October*, when Sergei Mikhailovich is but a handful of ashes sealed in an urn, his words, painfully penned in an effort to explain his aims, remain in advance of the general concept of film.

In *Potemkin*, Sergei Mikhailovich developed what he termed rhythmic montage and tonal montage, methods exemplified in the editing of such sequences as the massacre on the Odessa stairs and the prelude to the mass mourning for the dead leader of the mutiny. He also introduced symbolic imagery, the stone lion rising in protest against the massacre. The first two methods of montage—rhythmic and tonal—continued to develop logically in *October*, while methods stemming from the stone lion symbolism evolved further and in great profusion. This increasing complexity appeared perfectly natural to Sergei Eisenstein. No less a thinker than Goethe had observed that 'in nature we never see anything isolated, but everything in connection with something else which is before it, beside it, under it, and over it'. Sergei Mikhailovich was consciously striving to bring *October* closer to life than *Potemkin*, which he termed a poster.

Thus, he sought to heighten historical actuality by relating it in '*emotional* combinations, not only with visible elements of shots, but chiefly with chains of psychological associations'. In this way his montage became 'association montage'. The purpose was to point up a situation emotionally. As an example: 'The sugary chants of compromise by the Mensheviks at the Second Congress of the Soviets—during the storming of the Winter Palace—are intercut with hands playing harps.'[1] At one level he united images to produce a psychological reaction and create an emotional effect; at another he pushed technically ahead of his time—in a silent film he created a montage of audio-visual effects.

October was spangled with such effects. Another example was 'the dramatic movement of the union of the Motor-cycle Battalion with the Congress of Soviets [dynamized] by shots of abstractly spinning bicycle wheels, in association with the entrance of the new delegates. In this

---

[1] *Film Form* by S. M. Eisenstein (New York, Harcourt Brace and Co., 1949 and London, Dennis Dobson, 1950), p. 58.

way the large-scale emotional content of the event was transferred into actual [visual] dynamics.'[1]

From these comparatively simple picturizations of mental associations, Eisenstein moved to more complex processes of thought. 'A trench crowded with soldiers appears to be crushed by an enormous gun-base that comes down inexorably. As an anti-militarist symbol seen from the viewpoint of subject alone, the effect is achieved by an apparent bringing together of an independently existing trench and an overwhelming military product.'[2]

With the emergence of each new idea and its realization in a sequence of images, Eisenstein's desire to make manifest the abstract became ever more imperative. He thought that his audience would follow him up to the apex of his intent—where the film became expressive of purely intellectual discourse: an arena for debate regarding intellectual concepts. At this moment it might be said that Sergei Mikhailovich shared with Robert Browning an heroic philosophic courage—that 'a man's reach should exceed his grasp, or what's a heaven for'. He actually thought that the following examples of his intellectual deduction would be followed by the average man.

In tracing Kerensky's rise to power and the establishment of the so-called dictatorship after July of 1917, Eisenstein sought to explode the whole of Kerensky's personality and political significance on the intellectual level. As Kerensky rose in power 'a comic effect was gained by sub-titles indicating regular ascending ranks ("Dictator"—"Generalissimo"—"Minister of Navy—and of Army"—etc.) climbing higher and higher; [and these sub-titles were] cut into five or six shots of Kerensky, climbing the stairs of the Winter Palace, all with exactly the same pace. Here a conflict between the flummery of the ascending ranks and the "hero's" trotting up the same unchanging flight of stairs yields an intellectual result: Kerensky's essential nonentity is shown satirically. We have the counterpoint of a literally expressed conventional idea with the *pictured* action of a particular person who is unequal to his swiftly increasing duties.'[3] By this visual presentation and appraisal of Kerensky, Eisenstein hoped that his audience would arrive at a purely rational, intellectual understanding of the historical role of Kerensky between March and November 1917. [Plate 13]

He went even further in seeking to make his audience *think*.

In depicting the historic event of the White Russian General Kornilov's march on Petrograd, made under the banner of 'In the Name of God and Country', Sergei Mikhailovich 'attempted to reveal the religious significance of this episode in a rationalistic way. A number of

---

[1] *Ibid.*, p. 58.   [2] *Ibid.*, p. 58.   [3] *Ibid.*, p. 61.

religious images, from a magnificent Baroque Christ to an Eskimo idol, were cut together. The conflict in this case was between the concept and the symbolization of God. While idea and image appear to accord completely in the first statue shown (that of the highly evolved Christ figure), the two elements move further from each other with each successive image. Maintaining the denotation of "God", the image increasingly disagrees with our concept of "God", inevitably leading to individual conclusions about the true nature of all deities.'[1]

In these two sequences in *October*, Sergei Mikhailovich felt convinced that he had taken the first embryonic steps towards a totally new form of film expression. He thought he was approaching 'a purely intellectual film, freed from traditional limitations, achieving direct forms for ideas, systems, and concepts, without any need for transitions and paraphrases'.[2] Here was the beginning of the synthesis of art and science at which he aimed. He expected that on the 7th of November 1927, his tenth anniversary film in honour of the Russian Revolution would be recognized as heralding in a new epoch in the history of art. Working like a fiend, he completed *October* in time.

When he talked to Alvarez del Vayo, the Spanish writer whom he had met during the production of *Strike*, Eisenstein said: '*Potemkin* has something of the Greek temple, *October* is a little Baroque. There are parts of *October* which are purely experimental. Methods of intellectual film making that I think will develop. For me, from the experimental point of view, *October* is more interesting'.[3]

But on the day *October* was scheduled to be released all over the Soviet Union in commemoration of its closing scenes—the storming of the Winter Palace and the fall of the Kerensky Government—its public release was held up by events which strained the inner structure of the Soviet State almost to breaking point.

While Sergei Mikhailovich was immersed in his work, events of which, unfortunately, he had not taken adequate notice were working inexorably beyond the immediate confines of the film industry; in fact, in the highest circles of the Soviet system, in the Central Committee of the Communist Party.

The struggle between Leon Trotsky, the hitherto acknowledged military hero of the October Revolution, and Stalin, Lenin's successor as secretary of the Communist Party, had broken out in open hostility during October 1926. Trotsky had been read out of the Politburo and sent south as a disciplinary action. In July 1927, while Eisenstein was

[1] S. M. Eisenstein, *Film Form* (New York, Harcourt Brace and Co., 1949 and London, Dennis Dobson, 1950), p. 62 and, for subjective source, *Autobiography* (London, Dennis Dobson, 1978).   [2] *Ibid.*, p. 63.

[3] *Rusia Alos Doce Anos*, by J. Alvarez del Vayo (Madrid, 2nd ed., 1929).

working on *October*, Trotsky returned and attacked Stalin in violent invectives which he followed up by setting in motion underground groups dedicated to the overthrow of Stalin—groups similar in composition to those which Trotsky had once used in an attempt to overthrow the Tsar. To crown this struggle, just when *October* was about to appear, Trotsky organized street demonstrations against the Communist Party, which had emerged as leader of the Revolution. Trotsky was expelled from the Communist Party and sent into exile.

Sergei Mikhailovich, occupied with matters of montage, had failed to follow this struggle, or foresee the extent of the schism growing daily wider in Marxist interpretation. Suddenly, instead of his work being acclaimed, it was held up. It was pointed out to him that *October* could not possibly be released as scheduled because it showed Trotsky as a hero of the October Revolution when now Trotsky was regarded as a betrayer of the Revolution.

The delegates to the Tenth Anniversary celebrations who had expected to see *October* as part of the ceremonies did not see it. Pudovkin instead of Eisenstein received acclaim for his film *The End of St. Petersburg*, while Sergei Mikhailovich was left with the ordeal of deleting Trotsky from his epic of revolution. It took him five months to re-edit *October* so that it was not pro-Trotsky history, pro-Trotsky propaganda in its historical interpretation. In his diary, Alfred H. Barr, Jr., now director of New York's Museum of Modern Art, who was in Moscow at the time, records his meetings with Eisenstein:

December 28, 1927 (visit to the house of the writer Tretiakov)
    Among the company on our arrival were Eisenstein and two Georgian Kino men. The former was just on the point of leaving, but M. arranged with him so that we hope to see parts of his new films in a fortnight, *October* and *Generalya Linya*. Both were intended for the October celebration but were delayed.

January 14, 1928
    . . . to the Russkino to see Eisenstein. He was extremely affable—humorous in talk, almost a clown in appearance. . . . We saw four reels of *October*, his revolutionary film which was supposed to be finished three months ago—and may be ready by February. His mastery of cutting and camera placement was clearly shown, especially in the July riot scenes. We didn't see the storming of the Winter Palace which is the high point of the film. Certain faults appeared—he seemed to yield to the temptation of the fine shot— viz., the drawbridge scene, the strangling [of the horse as the bridge opens]. At times the tempo was too fast. The film seemed however a magnificent accomplishment.

February 2, 1928

To Eisenstein's to see about stills for articles on *October* and the *General Line*. Found him very weary. 'Will you go on a vacation after *October* is finished?' 'No. I'll probably die.'

Later Barr wrote: 'I think the clown simile which several people seem to have used in connection with Eisenstein is based on his general physiognomy, the tipped-up nose, the baldish head, the wide mouth, the expressive face . . . the continuous sense that he was playing a rather self-mocking role. His phrase, "No, I'll probably die", I assumed at the time was simply exaggerated humour mingled with a certain self-mockery.'[1] Not until March of 1928 did *October* appear.

As the people watched its extraordinary imagery unfold, they grew more and more baffled. Critics stirred uneasily; they had no idea what to say about it. This was the Revolution as they knew it. All the salient elements were present—except Trotsky. Trotsky's deletion was not the problem they had to pass on, but the extraordinary visual commentary was their artistic affair. Was Kerensky merely a human image of a peacock as Eisenstein inferred in a series of scenes? What was this business of Kerensky walking up and up the same stairs in a repetitive movement? What was intended by the gods and Kornilov? What was the meaning of that sequence with all the statues? Had Kerensky examined every piece of statuary in the Winter Palace as he ascended the stairs to take office as head of the Provisional Government? What had happened to the director of *Potemkin*? They all knew something had happened, but what exactly it was they did not know. The reception was uncertain. This was the Revolution of 1917 according to Sergei Mikhailovich Eisenstein. In 1931, however, the first chipping away at Eisenstein's edifice began in the Soviet Union. (App. Four.) Later a Soviet critic did not hesitate to say that Eisenstein failed 'because for an objective picture of the historic events of the Great October Revolution he substituted his own individual, subjective reaction. [*October*] strikingly demonstrated the utter incorrectness of Eisenstein's creative method, the falsity of the theory he then held.'[2]

With the passage of time and the stabilizing of revolutionary ardour, *October* may indeed have come to appear as mythology; yet no man had worked with a deeper passion for truth than Sergei Mikhailovich —truth as he saw and felt it.

The perceptible change in Eisenstein's art was not accidental. He had simply fallen in love with his art, the art he had once designed to destroy all art. He had become captive of his own thought processes

[1] Alfred H. Barr, Jr., in a letter to the author, dated 19 April 1950.

[2] 'A Failure and its Reasons', by Timofei Rokotov, *International Literature*, No. 8 (Moscow, 1937).

and his extraordinary vision of what the art of film could become. He was sliding away from the practical reality of Soviet life even though he loved the Revolution with a great love. His loyalty was above question. He was, as the novelist Theodore Dreiser wrote in his book on the Soviet Union, 'a more communistically convinced person' than any other Soviet artist Dreiser met. Because Eisenstein had great faith in the Revolution and his revolutionary art, he possessed the courage of his convictions.

When the film was released abroad under the title of *Ten Days that Shook the World*, reactions were mixed. In Germany, it was selected as the best film of 1928; but in America, Alexander Bakshy writing in *The Nation*, remarked that 'with the magnificent material in his hands —material pictorially and dramatically as striking as that in his *Potemkin* . . . [Eisenstein] could have easily achieved success if he had only chosen to repeat himself, or to follow the more conventional methods. Deliberately he steered his course to a different goal . . . [to] a recital of events with the recitalist's personal "angle" conspicuously in evidence. . . .

'The problem which engaged his special attention was that of the cinematic equivalent of metaphors and other figures of speech and qualifying clauses which in the verbal language serve to express the speaker's personal attitude to the subject of his narration. In the present case Eisenstein confined his personal reaction to satirical comment on the enemies of the revolution: he points a mocking finger at self-opinionated Kerensky by introducing the statue of a woman holding a wreath as if about to crown the hero, . . . he stresses the moral of a telephone conversation between Kerensky and a Cossack stableman by showing the buttocks of munching horses as a sign of the latter's "neutrality" [Plate 13]

'It is impossible to deny considerable interest to Eisenstein's experiment. It is suggestive. It may add to the resources of the cinema. It may bring about a new, essentially descriptive genre of the screen art. But it is fundamentally anti-dynamic and anti-dramatic, and as such lies off the main road of artistic progress in this medium. Far more important than these exercises in linguistic ideography are some of Eisenstein's startling visual effects produced by purely dynamic means. Such is the effect of machine-gun fire with its rapid staccato beat which is conveyed almost with the reality of sound. . . . It remains to be added that in spite of its rococo discursiveness and its lack of organized dramatic development, *Ten Days that Shook the World* is replete with magnificent scenes of mass movement.'[1]

[1] 'The Language of Images', by Alexander Bakshy (New York, *The Nation*, 26 December, 1928).

If Sergei Mikhailovich was disturbed by his *October* troubles, he did not show his perturbation. Not a word of public complaint passed his lips. Yet the mixed reception given *October* was as a lash upon his sensitive spirit, because, as he was later to realize in a period of deepest anguish, he had no life save in terms of what he could create. His reaction to the *October* difficulties was that which he was to adopt again and again: he turned his attention to a new field of activity in which he felt certain he would succeed. He returned to the matter of completing the film *General Line*, which was renamed *Old and New*.

But even here the events of life encroached upon him. During the time he had been working on *October*, collectivization of the farms had moved forward and most of the footage he had directed earlier was already out of date. So he set to work all over again. This time he was to complete his film of the changing village, the changing peasant psychology in the film *Old and New*.

The American placard advertising the cream separator still hung on the wall of Eisenstein's room. Tractors and cream separators were still the means of transforming the countryside. These machines would bring plenty where before only poverty had existed.

He wrote a new scenario on which, as in the case of *October*, Grigori Alexandrov was a collaborator. By this time Eisenstein had become dependent upon Alexandrov in the preparation of his scenarios.

'As my ideas became more complex, I had to have someone to explain them in simple words. Grisha could make my plans sound simple,' said Sergei Mikhailovich years later. By then Alexandrov had gone his own way and Eisenstein was alone. He did not know how to explain his aims to the heads of the film industry who had to approve his work.

As the new scenario began to take shape, deep new springs of creative insight began to well up in Sergei Mikhailovich. He was groping towards the creation of fuller characters instead of the scientific construction of 'types'. Pity, compassion: a sense of beauty began to break through and find expression in a humanism which was barely permitted to draw a breath in *Potemkin* or *October*. Thus, early in the scenario of *Old and New*—in the old village, in the rotting houses, 'on the stove, on the floor, on chests, bags, wall-benches, sleep human beings, sheep and children. Chickens hatching their eggs, chicks fluffing their feathers in their baskets.' Then, as if ashamed to express such tenderness which the peasants called up, Sergei Mikhailovich, the harsh realist and boastful scientist, noted how 'the breath steams heavily out of the mouths. The lungs inhale heavily the humid air.' [Plate 15]

In shooting this sequence, Sergei Mikhailovich inserted into the scene of human beings living like beasts a comment upon his own thoughts.

Intercut with the image of the torpid peasant woman inhaling heavily in her sleep is a shot of da Vinci's 'Mona Lisa'. This shot remains on the screen long enough to shock the spectator into thought as to the range of human development—from the animal-like peasant woman to the enigmatic 'Mona Lisa'.[1] Later in the film Eisenstein reversed the comparison by cutting the repulsively obese wife of the kulak with the china figure of a sow standing on its hindlegs dressed as a woman.

Yet to-day thousand-year-old customs prevail.

If brother parts from brother, then they divide the estate, tear it apart in two, destroy the power which could create wealth.

They break the wagon between the wheels, they tear the colt away from its mother, the plough rusts with no horse to draw it, the rooster crows for the hen.

It must be half, half remains.

The brothers saw their house through the middle. Each must yield up half.

It must be half. Everything must be reduced to half.

The marker is drawn through the fields, breaks up the ground in little pieces.

Here a fence springs up, then a second, a third, a net of poles cuts up the land.

In the second episode, Eisenstein sets down words which, though they had no poetic intention, still echo the pages of Walt Whitman's *Leaves of Grass*, a work beloved and cherished by Sergei Mikhailovich:

Dreary dampness eats about—wraps heaven in wet diapers.

A woman among many; Marfa Lapkina.

She has a plough, but no horse.

She has a cow, but no stable.

She has not much which is necessary to plough the ground and reap the bread.

Time passes.

The dandelion is blowing.

Those who are employers, the owners, have sown their seed.

But there's no seed for the peasants.

Time speeds onward. Marfa Lapkina wishes to try her luck at the rich farm owner.

She comes at noon, the labourers are sleeping on straw under the barn, the strong horses of the owner lie in the cool shade, the rich farmer himself is enjoying leisure.

[1] To the author's knowledge, the only copy of *Old and New* outside the Soviet Union which contains this shot is the one in the Institute of Cinematographic Archives in Prague, Czechoslovakia.

On what thick pilings rests the barn! How the roof of white tin
shines! What rich carvings ornament the walls!
The owner did not lend her a horse. Marfa must return home back
to her rusty plough. . . .

This Marfa Lapkina—the first film heroine of the new Soviet society
—was discovered by Sergei Mikhailovich. She was twenty-eight years
old and had worked on a farm since she was nine. Fearing he might
destroy the simple life of this woman by diverting her from her place in
the real world, Eisenstein insisted that at the end of the film she go
back to the farm, or not act in the film at all. It was as if he knew there
were pitfalls, dangers and griefs attached to becoming an artist and he
wanted to save this young peasant woman, the look of whose expressive back had caused him to notice her. Farm life, as he told her, was
emerging from the slough of the past when

> Marfa hitched her emaciated cow by the collar to the plough and
> drove her over the field, while the perforated heads of the dande-
> lions sadly stretched their necks to heaven.
> Both woman and cow were devoid of every bit of strength. The
> plough tore only shallow grooves. The crows scarcely picked up
> a worm. . . .
> Bending over the handle, pushing the plough ahead, spending in-
> human effort in the hellish, heavy work of the earth.
> The poor cow while stepping plucked a few of last year's blades of
> grass. Marfa poured a bucket of water over the cow's head and
> the cow made a last attempt to draw.
> The last strength of peasant and cow was spent.
> The sun shone, the fields spread out unconquerable.
> The cow could not withstand the labour, and fell down.
> They had to unhitch her to prevent her from dying.
> Marfa tore at the handle with both hands, causing the plough to
> upset and screamed,
> No!
> No!
> This can't continue!
> This
> can't
> continue. . . .

Marfa's words were integrated as captions into the expressive movement and became images of sound as they filled the screen. In this and
other sequences, an element in Eisenstein's nature doomed never to be
revealed in his art as he wished to reveal it was shown in all its great
creative potentialities—his ability to feel and respond with the whole

of his being to simple, naked human emotions. But his task was not to create a film about the anguish of Marfa Lapkina in the old days, but to show Marfa emerging into a new world. [Plate 15]

So Sergei Eisenstein sends Marfa to an agriculturists' meeting, such as he himself had attended during his research period, and Marfa joins the embryonic co-operative. Then follows perhaps the most remarkable symphonic passage in all of Eisenstein's completed work—the Religious Procession. In this sequence, where he said he felt a relationship between his use of imagery and the music of Debussy and Scriabin, Sergei Mikhailovich reached the apex of his original style—that of montage.

Sun, sun again and again, sun enough to famish.
The country dries up.
Harvesting is dead.
The chickens gape with open bills. The flanks of the sheep fly in and out like bellows. The huge bell resounds, the small bells ring like mad.
Flags wave under the cloudless, dust-saturated sky.
Perspiring, vicious, the prayer-procession drags itself over the fields. The church candles soften and bend over. Women cry, enough to burst their throats. The children drag the small holy pictures with difficulty, the grown-ups under the larger ones.
Vagabonds, the village feeble-minded, old women, follow the priest in ceremonial clothes. The bells ring madly, human voices sing in a sing-song fashion.
Covered with brocade, glittering with silver, the priest raises his hand to heaven, the multitude does likewise.
As if out of their senses, the people throw themselves in the dust and load their backs with holy pictures.
A cloud forms into a ball. The priest falls into ecstasy.
The people are lying prone on the ground digging their faces in the dirt, the ringing becomes mad. The cloud increases, raindrops fall, the wind blows, a whirl of dust envelops everything. The people turn their faces to the light, open their thirsty mouths to catch the spare drops. However, the cloud separates, the barometer rises. Disappointed, the people get up out of the dust. Sun again and again—enough to famish.
Deception?
Suspiciously the farmers look at the priest. Trust has disappeared from their faces. The women too look distrustfully. . . .

The torrent of images with which Eisenstein clothed this sequence was saturated with fearful reality, and edited with such extraordinary imagination that many who have seen *Old and New* have carried the memory of the sequence as an experience they have been unable to forget. Religious hysteria was revealed in all its fascinating orgiastic reality. [Plate 14]

Writing many years after the creation of *Old and New*, Sergei Mikhailovich attempted a logical analysis of the component lines he had used to create the Religious Procession. At a distance it seemed to him that he had woven 'a multiple series of lines, each maintaining an independent compositional course and each contributing to the total compositional course of the sequence'.

'Thus:

(1) The line of heat increasing from shot to shot.

(2) The line of changing close-ups, mounting in plastic intensity.

(3) The line of mounting ecstasy, shown through the dramatic content of the close-ups.

(4) The line of women's "voices" (faces of singers).

(5) The line of men's "voices" (faces of the singers).

(6) The line of those who kneel under the passing icons (increasing in tempo). This counter-current gave movement to a larger counter-stream which was threaded through the primary theme—of the bearers of icons, crosses and banners.

(7) The line of grovelling, uniting both streams in the general movement of the sequence, "from heaven to the dust". From the radiant pinnacles of the crosses and the banners against the sky to the prostrate figures beating their heads in the dust. This theme was announced at the opening with a "key" shot: a swift camera pan downwards from the belfry cross glittering in the sky down to the church base from where the procession is moving.

'The general course of the montage was an uninterrupted interweaving of these diverse themes into one unified movement'[1] which swept the audience into the centre of a vortex of religious emotion.

In planning this sequence, Eisenstein deliberately sought to expose the exploitation of superstition and religious fanaticism in Russian life. He was acutely aware of the influence of religion, for had not ceremonies and the use of images played upon his own susceptible imagination as a child? Was he not still prone to religious feelings in unguarded moments? He wanted to dispel this influence from Russian life as he was constantly trying to banish its lurking influence within himself. This desire to aid in clearing religious and mystical practices out of the way so that a healthy rationalism could grow was strictly in accord

---

[1] S. M. Eisenstein, *The Film Sense* (London, Faber and Faber, 1945), p. 65.

with the revolutionary principles of the time. He was, in fact, acting like a good Bolshevik who preferred scientific truth to vague 'other-worldliness'. But Sergei Eisenstein was not the man to handle religion versus rationalism. Religion was like a marshland in which he could too easily make a false step because he could not retain his scientific objectivity when he approached the matter.

Though Sergei Mikhailovich wished with all his reason to escape the clutches of religion, there were elements in every phase of religion which lured him. Filled with hatred towards what he felt to be the false practices of the Church, he was yet irresistibly fascinated by the inner philosophic aspects of religion and the primary figures and symbols which man worshipped. At bottom his attitude echoed that of his Leonardo, who argued scientifically against the existence of ghosts and deplored the salvation of souls through the sale of candles, yet felt that the Creator had indeed taken a hand in the formation of man's muscular system.

Phases of religion had appeared in three of Eisenstein's earlier works: in his Proletkult production of *The Wise Man*, where 'there was a procession of caricatures carrying candles, chanting church service and bearing boards with the inscription "Religion is the opium of the people"'; in *Potemkin*, where the priest uses his crucifix in an attempt to stop the mutiny and is knocked down by a sailor; and again, in *October*, where he attempted to create intellectual concepts to rationalize 'God' out of existence.

In *Old and New*, manifestations of religion began to occupy a more prominent place. Religion, or formal composition hinting religious feeling, began to assume a distinctive character in Eisenstein's work which was in time to bring him into head-on conflict with authority. In his role of aggressive rationalist, Sergei Mikhailovich was afraid to expose the paradox into which his mind and emotions were leading him when he came to religious subject-matter. Instead of admitting an interest in religious manifestations, he clothed his oblique references to it in a most curious mixture of tongues—the language of science, dialectical materialism, mystic phrases, even film terminology—which rendered him almost incomprehensible to anyone not possessing the key to what was in his mind.

At the time of editing *Old and New* early in 1929, the Religious Procession called up in him a quite extraordinary state of mind. As he handled the many film pieces he had directed, their combination with each other set up a fever of 'creative ecstasy' within him; each piece appeared to be animated by special 'psycho-physiological' vibrations of its own. As he proceeded with the editing, his state of mind grew more and more receptive to the content of his images, until his conscious mind seemed to be overwhelmed by deeper layers of his consciousness. In this state he seemed to 'hear' and 'feel' the emotional quality of each piece with great intensity so that in effect he edited them in what seemingly amounted to a sensual trance akin to the religious ecstasy portrayed in the sequence.

Later, when he first came to look at his editing in a calm and objective state of mind, Sergei Mikhailovich said: 'I could not fit the combination of its pieces into any one of the orthodox categories within which one can apply one's pure experience . . . the reasons for their choice seem completely incomprehensible. The criteria for their assembly appear to be outside formal, normal cinematographic criteria.'

According to his practice, he returned again and again to an analysis of his work. Gradually he saw in the Religious Procession and the methods of his montage 'visual overtones' which conveyed to him an element of a fourth dimension.[1] Fascinated by the possibilities of the film as a means of perceiving the invisible fourth dimension, Eisenstein asked the question: was he not penetrating through film into the province of Einstein?—Or was it mysticism? Or a joke?[2]

Eisenstein began to probe into the intense and varied states of consciousness he experienced under creative stimulus, as if within himself he would find the secrets of all ecstatic states and supernatural powers. In 1932 Eisenstein admitted this preoccupation in an article. 'For some time,' he wrote, 'for years, I worried about those certain supernatural powers, transcending common sense and human reason, that seemed indispensable for the comprehension of the "mysteries" of creative film direction.'[3]

During the direction and editing of Old and New, further aspects of Sergei Mikhailovich's personality commenced to find expression in his work through symbols.

Following the Religious Procession, and indeed juxtaposed with it, is the sequence of the cream separator, Eisenstein's original symbol for the transformation of the Russian peasants' poverty into socialist wealth. The separator has been acquired by the new co-operative of which Marfa is the most devoted member. This separator plays an impressive role on several levels of interpretation. In its socio-economic role, the separator makes the processing of butter possible; butter will not turn sour; it can be taken far away and sold in the city. But in this sequence Sergei Mikhailovich created most amazing visual impressions to convey this simple economic-political idea.

[1] *Film Form* by S. M. Eisenstein (New York, Harcourt Brace and Co., 1949 and London, Dennis Dobson, 1950), p. 69.
[2] *Ibid.*, p. 69.   [3] *Ibid.*, p. 86.

In the middle of the room, a thing was wrapped in coarse linen. Four members of the co-operative proudly sat around the thing.

The agriculturist came into the room. The whole village pressed themselves upon the steps of the entrance.

The agriculturist pointed to the thing.

The first acquisition of the new co-operative on credit.

A cream-separator!

The farmers gape. The linen (cover) dropped off. A gleaming fire-work shot up into the air. The cylinder of the separator glitters white, sparkles! Everything around sank into darkness. The machine gleamed, her light became as a symbol. Its glittering took away the breath of the peasants. . . .

The agriculturist turned the handle. The cylinder purred, faster, and faster. Marfa poured a can of milk into the machine, thin, transparent fatless milk—the milk of poor people's cows.

The poor people stared eagerly. Would it produce a wonder? . . .

The wheel turns, the machine gleams, the multitude whispers. . . .

The farmers wait. . . . They wait for the drop of cream, eyes, noses, mouths and hands, all wait for the wonder. Convinced the agriculturist turns faster. How the membership of the milk co-operative wavers.

Just now it consisted of six, now only one remains, the first member, Marfa Lapkina.

The drops increase. Joy spreads over their faces . . . now the stream comes faster, thicker—and drips heavily down on the tin (bucket).

A storm of rejoicing bursts from the multitude. The membership increased to fifty people immediately.

Four at the beginning—now fifty. . . .

Because of the symbolic intensity and the sensations it called up in the sensitive spectator, the separator sequence provoked much speculation as to its meaning. To at least one critic it appeared as a phallic symbol—an abstract presentation of an orgasm.[1] True, it could have symbolized the physical orgasm, but for Sergei Mikhailovich it was eroticism transmuted on to another level—as he transformed his own eroticism and made it serve as energy for his intellectual striving.

Actually, the cream separator had become associated in Sergei Mikhailovich's mind with a curious symbol—the Holy Grail. This symbol in its very earliest form—its purest folk form—had been connected with the concept of a magical food-providing, self-acting talisman, the

[1] Oswald Blakeston's review of William Hunter's 'Scrutiny of Cinema' in *Close-up* (December 1932).

exact nature of which was not specified. But it was probably known to Eisenstein at that time only in its later christianized form as the dish or chalice of the Last Supper miraculously given to Joseph of Arimathea by Jesus Christ. Its quest was to the good Christian Knights of the Round Table, the greatest means of salvation. For a man seeking to be a rationalist the association of a machine with the Holy Grail was certainly a paradox, particularly when earlier Sergei Mikhailovich had contemptuously dismissed the Grail as 'just a bit of Spanish pottery!'[1]

Writing after the completion of *Old and New*, Eisenstein proceeded to turn the Grail symbol upside down. 'It is not the Holy Grail that inspires both doubt and ecstasy—but a cream separator.'[2] Nothing explains this curious reference to the Grail, except a consciousness that what he had actually created on the screen was a visual impression which might well have conveyed the strangeness and intensity of emotion experienced by people witnessing a miracle.

He *must* push the thought of the Holy Grail away, and in 1929 Sergei Mikhailovich pushed hard. This, however, was not the end of the Grail in his mind. Six years later it re-emerged in his thoughts and he talked to me with awe and reverence of this symbol, which had become for him that of humanity's ceaseless quest to come into the presence of God.

To return to *Old and New*. Following the cream separator sequence, Marfa and the co-operative plan to buy a bull. But the men want to drink up the money and Marfa has to fight them in an effort to preserve the co-operative. With the money for the bull at last in her hands she falls asleep and dreams of the young bull, Fomka, which she will purchase from the experimental farm. In the dream

an immense powerful bull begins to grow in such a manner that he conceals the entire heaven, a milk-white rain streams from heaven, gushing milky waterfalls. The houses rival each other to appear snow-white, and out of the earth grow cow stables, pigsties, chicken coops. . . .

This sequence in which Freudian symbols and Marxian theses flow together emerges into real village life with preparations for a wedding. Excitement mounts as garlanded girls wait for the bride, who at last steps through the door.

Flowers adorn her head, the ends flutter in the soft wind.

[1] *The Russian Theatre*, by Rene Fülop Miller and Joseph Gregor (Philadelphia, Lippincott and Co., 1930), p. 112.
[2] *Film Form* by S. M. Eisenstein (New York, Harcourt Brace and Co., 1949 and London, Dennis Dobson, 1950), p. 77.

She waits until the outburst of unrestrained merriment of the laugh-
ing girls subside.
Now her voice resounds.
'Moo!'
It is a cow. . . .

A twist. The presentation of the unexpected. In this way Sergei
Mikhailovich entertained, shocked and gave vent to his special brand
of humour. Humour and eroticism were linked together in his make-
up; they see-sawed in his consciousness, the impulse towards one often
ending in an upsurge expressive of the other. Thus, the comedy of the
bride changed its character from shot to shot:

The bridegroom!
Was he not, a little while ago, a chubby milk calf? Look then, look
how he grows, how powerfully he roars, how his muscles swell,
how the blood runs together under his eyes.
How he resembles more and more the heavenly animal which Marfa
had dreamed about.
The bride notices her bridegroom. Does he not resemble her adorned
with ribbons? Don't large white flowers grow beneath his feet?
The bride trembles—the bridegroom rushes in a swift gallop towards
her.
A powerful jump joins him with her.
Thereupon the earth wants to tremble. Fiery flames shoot out from
her ruts in all colours. It bursts as an earthquake.
Out of the dark cloud which slowly dissolves march countless rows
of young cattle. . . .[1]

Sergei Mikhailovich had rigidly controlled his passions through
sublimation but his inhibitions could not always hold eroticism in a
strait-jacket, hence this scene which had social sanction in that it produced the beneficial and necessary results—a herd of cattle for the good
of socialist agriculture. Until he went to Mexico a few years later, the
intensity of his personal inhibitions prevented him from expressing
eroticism between human beings in his art.
From the sequence of the bull *Old and New* proceeded in a relatively
simple line showing the struggle between the old forces and ways and
the new ways and machines in Russian village life. Only once did
Sergei Mikhailovich digress into another sharp, personal commentary,

[1] *Old and New*, scenario by S. M. Eisenstein and Grigori Alexandrov, was
published in Germany by Schmidt, Berlin, 1929; in French in *Revue du Cinema*
(Paris, No. 15, September 1930), and in English from the German in *Film
Writing Forms* by Lewis Jacobs (New York, Gotham Book Mart, 1934)—the
translation used here.

this time in terms of satire. He had satirized the kulaks earlier; now he turned a visual venom upon the bureaucrats of the tractor factory, where the peasants go to insist on the fulfilment of their order for their tractor. Here 'the pillar of industry' is a typewriter around which the secretaries hover preening themselves!

But while following to the end a fairly simple 'plot' ending in the triumphant procession of tractors drawing wagons across the land, Sergei Eisenstein revealed many subsidiary facets of his artistic vision. In the harvesting sequence—one of the most beautiful ever recorded on film—he directed effects as if he were the twentieth-century Cézanne; and in one scene, Sergei Mikhailovich summed up the total processes of nature: a pregnant peasant woman stands between two winter-stripped boughs, her eyes upon a single leaf heralding spring.

Sergei Mikhailovich may have been moved to shoot this scene by the fact that during the production of *Old and New*, Marfa Lapkina became pregnant and towards the end of the shooting only close-ups and scenes of her back were photographed. Almost on the last day of the shooting schedule, Marfa gave birth to her baby. Sergei Mikhailovich, who had a most singular feeling for children and never made a film without introducing at least one child, held the baby as if he were the young, inexperienced, peasant father.

At the completion of *Old and New*, Sergei Eisenstein looked at his film and prized it above his other work. It was, he thought, his real beginning—his mastery of the intellectual film. He saw in it the line he wished to develop. He said to Alvarez del Vayo, 'I will not hide from you that I have put some hopes into this film. You will see what diversity there is in the midst of its simplicity. I have tried to show the transformation in our villages, the revolution has changed its soul and physiognomy.'[1] But he did not see that such a tapestry of images as he had woven would prove too rich for the many; that because of its very many-sidedness, it could only strike the head and heart of the few who in some measure were reflections of himself.

While he was editing *Old and New*, Sergei Mikhailovich received a visit from several Americans. Among them was H. W. L. Dana, with whom Eisenstein was to be in periodic contact until his death.

In writing of Eisenstein's method of work and thoughts at this period —1929—Dana recorded two features of Sergei Mikhailovich's attitude towards his work which constantly evolved from the beginning to the end of his career. The first was his approach to what is called realism, the second was his attitude to each of his works when completed.

When one of the Americans with Dana asked Eisenstein if he took

---

[1] *Rusia Alos Doce Anos*, by J. Alvarez del Vayo (Madrid, 2nd ed., 1929).

his actors from the Moscow Art Theatre, Sergei Mikhailovich answered ' The Moscow Art Theatre is my deadly enemy. It is the exact anti-thesis of all I am trying to do. They string their emotions together to give a continuous illusion of realism. I take photographs of reality and then cut them up so as to produce emotions.

'I am not a realist,' continued Eisenstein. 'I am a materialist. I believe that material things, that matter gives us the basis of all our sensations. I get away from realism by going to reality.'[1]

However far Eisenstein moved away in later years both in subject and form from the accepted definition of 'realism', he never abandoned the pursuit of those elements which would call up real emotions in the spectator. Nor did Sergei Mikhailovich's attitude towards each new creative venture greatly change from that reported by Dana.

' By the time *Strike* had won a prize in Paris I had already outgrown that kind of film and had started a new technique in *The Armoured Cruiser Potemkin*. By the time you in America were admiring *Potemkin* I had got sick of it and had gone on to something entirely different in *October* and now *October* already seems out of date and I have developed a new method in *General Line*.'

'We got', said Dana, 'such a sense of his rapid progress in scrapping each bridge as soon as he had crossed it that we got the feeling that if we should go back a little later . . . he would have gone on again to something new.'[2]

Once more he waited hopefully, expecting his work to move the masses, as *October* had failed to move them. *Old and New* was released in September, 1929. It was reported that at a private showing of the film at a Red Army Club 'the judgement of the soldiers, themselves Russian peasants, was rather cold. They said the film could not be understood by peasants and that is why the film had not fulfilled Eisenstein's aim.'[3] When *Old and New* was released in New York on the 2nd of May 1930 (a few days before Eisenstein arrived in America), the *New York Times* critic wrote:

'Although this picture possesses in most of its scenes a fund of interest, there are times when Mr. Eisenstein dilates too long on some of his sequences, and consequently they become a trifle tedious. . . . In quite a number of instances he delights in extravagances, either in por-traying the abject poverty of the people or in depicting the greed and laziness of the more fortunate farmer. One is impelled to think . . . that

[1] 'Revolution in the World of Make-believe', by W. H. L. Dana (U.S.A., *Boston Evening Transcript*, 1 March 1930).
[2] *Ibid.*
[3] Moscow Correspondent, *Film Kurier* (Berlin, 5 October 1929).

Mr. Eistenstein has selected isolated cases to make his film impressive. (See App. Four.)

'His ability to show the expanse of country on a relatively small screen is marvellous, and so is his work in close-ups. As in *Potemkin*, which is infinitely more dramatic, the director in this current work is usually careful in the choosing of his types. There are never two persons alike among those who appear in the film. The woman, Martha . . . turns out to be a kind of Joan of Arc of the soil. . . . She encourages the acceptance of new inventions, the first of which is a separator. There are some remarkable views portraying the hopeful persons and the doubtful ones watching the working of this machine. It is during a stretch in which the priests and peasants are praying for rain that Mr. Eisenstein makes a target of the Church.'[1]

In contrast, the French film critic, Cecile Pierrot, in *Revue du Cinema*, said, 'In the group, each individual retains his importance. Each individual, even each animal, each object. That man passes, we will not see him again. He has but figured accidentally; his every day life continues, the film ends. Now come others and others, who, for an instant, express everything that a face contains, moulded by its daily life, with which we are not familiar. . . . The film is built with the elements which exist outside of the scene designer.'

But Eisenstein had already gone abroad as the honoured representative of Soviet art when *Old and New* was released in Moscow. In the three and a half years since *Potemkin* was released, the greatness of Eisenstein's art had brought honour, interest and new friends to the Soviet Union. To the world, Eisenstein and likewise his rival Pudovkin stood as symbols of the creative genius of the new Soviet society.

He had gone away with a seemingly endless vista of creative possibilities and opportunities before his eyes. Unfortunately those eyes of his were too unworldly, too far-sighted to see the pitfalls just beyond his sensitive feet in the canvas shoes which allowed him to walk with a strangely elemental gait not at all in keeping with his reputation as a man of great intellect, a representative of Soviet art.

Note 1977. See Eisenstein's *Autobiography* for the subjective origin of the dismembering of the figure of Tsar Alexander III, the women's use of parasols to stab the worker and religious impressions translated into objective cinematic interpretation in *October*.

[1] Review, *New York Times*, 3 May, 1930.

CHAPTER SIX

Outside the Frame

Fame should be represented in the shape of a bird, with the whole figure covered with tongues instead of feathers.
LEONARDO DA VINCI, B. 3 v.

LIKE H. G. Wells's 'hero,' Mr. West, foreigners began to venture into the Land of the Bolsheviks to see the new society rising on the ruins of the old. During the first few years after the Revolution, only the most enterprising came; but in 1926 more and more people flocked to Moscow. With the triumph of *Potemkin*, foreigners interested in the arts began to seek out Sergei Eisenstein.

Sergei Mikhailovich revelled in the surprise he usually afforded his visitors when he addressed them in their own language—English, French or German. It interested him to note how they gazed around his room, astonished at its modesty. It was in an old flat and the odds and ends of furniture looked like salvage from a great wreck. But Eisenstein was proud of it—a small room allotted to a working man. He wanted the foreigners to appreciate and comprehend the great efforts and new ideals of his country which, fortunately, he could explain more easily than many since he had no need to use an interpreter. Eagerly he would explain Soviet art. Through making them understand its character, he hoped to influence their opinion of socialism. A few of his visitors noticed the rare seventeenth-century books and the collected lithographs of Daumier stacked on the unpainted shelves.

On the other hand, Eisenstein was eager to learn about the outside world. He read everything that was available to him about the arts and sciences in Berlin, Paris, London and New York. He was especially interested in Hollywood. It was the world centre of the film industry with superior technical resources. Hollywood was the place where D. W. Griffith had commenced to mould the film medium into a powerful mode of expression, and Sergei Mikhailovich had learned much from Griffith, particularly from *Intolerance*, which he had seen more times than any other film. In Hollywood there was Charlie Chaplin; Hollywood produced spectacles by the mile and heroes flew on magic carpets. It would be interesting to go to Hollywood. He could learn a great deal there in the way of technique. Russia was rich in ideas, but exceedingly poor in technical equipment; Hollywood rich in technique if somewhat short on ideas.

No one in Moscow was more excited in July of 1926 than Sergei Mikhailovich when Mary Pickford and Douglas Fairbanks arrived. He waited for them with great expectation, longing to meet and talk with them and learn from them. Whatever he had managed to achieve in *Potemkin* was in spite of great technical handicaps, whereas the achievements of Mary Pickford and Douglas Fairbanks had all the technical aid so far developed.

When at last Eisenstein met them, in a way the tables were turned. It was they who were anxious to talk to him, question him and load him with praise for *Potemkin*. They had never seen any film remotely resembling it; they said it was the greatest film ever made. They must introduce it to America. Sergei Mikhailovich was thrilled, and also not a little amused at Fairbanks' astonishment when they first met.

'I pictured you as being old, very serious and wearing eye-glasses and a beard,' said Fairbanks.

To the Hollywood visitors this young Russian seemed charming and almost one of themselves; besides, he knew a great deal about their films and the pictures being produced in Hollywood. They liked his eager appreciation of America's technical skill and immediately invited him to come to Hollywood. But he had no money to go to Hollywood. He had nothing but his modest salary. So Fairbanks promised to arrange for him to make a film for United Artists, the company in which he and Mary Pickford held the controlling financial interest, together with Charlie Chaplin. When they left Moscow, they took with them a print of *Potemkin*.

Thus *Potemkin* was introduced to America by Douglas Fairbanks in the autumn of 1926 after a then unknown young Scotsman, John Grierson, had been engaged in New York to edit it for the American market. Meanwhile, Fairbanks wrote to encourage Eisenstein. In a few months he must come to America; Fairbanks was working on arrangements for him to come to United Artists. With each letter Sergei Mikhailovich's anticipation soared. But the United Artists' contract never materialized, though at last an invitation did arrive—from the Film Arts Guild of New York. By the time it came, Eisenstein was already at work again.

Yet he held fast to the thought that he must, and would, get to America, if not by the end of 1926, then in 1927. His hopes were again raised towards the end of 1928 when Joseph Schenk of M-G-M. communicated with him about coming to Hollywood the following year. As the prospect of his going abroad increased, Sergei Mikhailovich became more and more interested in the foreigners visiting Moscow. He talked at length with the French film critic, Leon Moussinac, who was writing a book about the Soviet cinema. When the Mexican painter, Diego Rivera, came to Moscow, his accounts of his country impressed the receptive Eisenstein so much that he began the study which led him four years later to make *Que Viva Mexico!*

Anxious to spread knowledge of the Soviet film abroad, Eisenstein collaborated with Louis Fischer, then the Moscow correspondent of America's leading liberal weekly, *The Nation*, on the first comprehensive article explaining his current attitude towards cinematography.[1] He became friendly with Fischer and his Russian wife, Marcoosha, and often went to parties at their home. But on occasions his conduct was somewhat disconcerting to Marcoosha Fischer: instead of entertaining her guests with his wit, Sergei Mikhailovich retired to the kitchen to talk to the Fischers' peasant houseworker about her village.

Eisenstein met other Americans. There was William Gropper, the young artist and cartoonist, and Joseph Freeman, who had come to Moscow to prepare a book called *Voices of October*, in which the Russians should speak about their new society for themselves. But with Joe Freeman something more than a casual acquaintance was established. An understanding sprang up the first day Freeman arrived at Chysti Prudi 23.

Sergei Mikhailovich was talking on the telephone to his old friend, Sergei Tretiakov, who was writing a biographical article on Eisenstein. Walking into the small, cluttered room, Freeman saw him standing by the phone, etched sharply by the light from the uncurtained window, 'his pale face intent, ascetic and ironical, his curly hair standing high like a shako. He was saying the most curious things in a tone of a man declaiming from the rostrum.

'"Had it not been for Leonardo, Marx, Lenin, Freud and the movies, I would in all probability have been another Oscar Wilde."'

Eisenstein hung up and greeting Freeman with a whimsical smile explained what he had said to Tretiakov with a frankness that life would soon almost completely extinguish in him.

'I urged Tretiakov to include a chapter on Freud, whose influence on me has been enormous,' he said; then as if sensing Freeman was not a man to misunderstand him, he continued, 'Without Freud, no sublimation; without sublimation, a mere aesthete like Oscar Wilde. Freud discovered the laws of individual conduct as Marx discovered the laws of social development. I have consciously used my knowledge

---

[1] 'Mass Movies', written by Louis Fischer on the basis of conversations with Eisenstein (*The Nation*, 9 November 1927).

of Marx and Freud in the plays and movies I have directed in the past years.'[1]

They talked long of Soviet films and out of the talk emerged the plan for Eisenstein to write a section for Freeman's book, *Voices of October*.[2] Three years later, when the book was published in America and Eisenstein was in Hollywood, it helped to arouse the howl against the 'Red Dog' Eisenstein who, it was claimed, had come to the United States to undermine free enterprise with his Bolshevik movies. But in 1927 Sergei Eisenstein was extraordinarily innocent as to the ways of the world. At that time he could not have envisaged the complexity of his life, as it was to develop, once he made the attempt to live in two worlds and retain his own integrity. Already he was curiously immune to all but his own standard of conduct. He had selected his own path and he walked along it even if it estranged him from his fellow Russian film workers. In little things as well as big he deviated far from the normal pattern. He neither drank nor smoked and, as Joseph Freeman observed, he was like Hamlet—'man delighted him not nor woman neither', though 'he took an almost sensual delight in logic and humour'.

During their long talks in the room overlooking the Chysti Prudi, Sergei Mikhailovich and Freeman discussed what the Russian Revolution meant to each of them, and what were the truly important events in their lives. Sergei Mikhailovich explained to Freeman how he felt intellectually and spiritually akin to da Vinci and his ideas concerning the film on which he was then working—*General Line*. Already the image of the cream separator and the Holy Grail were connected in his mind.

Generally when visitors came, Eisenstein went to considerable pains to be genial, witty and brilliant. Never missing an opportunity to stress his scientific approach, he would talk about going to find and study his 'stars' in biological laboratories. Hollywood would hardly make a 'star' of a grasshopper or a fly; but he could—to illustrate the genetic theory. Yet the very next instant—just as if the whole world were his natural domain—he would talk enthusiastically of America, its great resources and his forthcoming visit there.

One of his visitors—Alfred Richman—asked him if he intended to emigrate. Emigrate? Until that moment Sergei Mikhailovich had not imagined that his desire to go and work in Hollywood could be interpreted in any other way than as he thought of it—as a natural phase of his experience.

[1] *An American Testament*, by Joseph Freeman (New York, Farrar and Rinehart, 1936 and Victor Gollancz, Ltd, 1938).
[2] *Ibid.*

Yet it was an obvious question for Richman to ask. Coming from America and seeing Eisenstein's room, he could not imagine a man of such great ambitions being content with hardship and poverty. When Sergei Mikhailovich answered, it was in words no one could have foretold.

'I should not want to leave the soil that has given me strength and substance,' Eisenstein said. 'I believe that if I remind you of the story of Antaeus, the Greek hero who lost his strength as soon as his feet left his mother, the Earth, you will understand better than if I discussed the relations between artistic creation and the socio-economic theories of Karl Marx and Lenin.'[1]

Sergei Mikhailovich liked to draw on myths and classic heroes to explain his feelings. In ancient man there was harmony between man and Nature; his arts and games were united in a religious and social organism full of meaning. Now once more in Soviet society, Sergei Mikhailovich saw a unity of man enfolded by society and fashioned by new forces, with art serving the welfare of mankind.

Already Eisenstein's reading was prodigious. Everything he read, he passed through the fine sieve of analysis in search of those elements which could be used to enrich his special field. He was particularly interested in the techniques used in novel writing, especially those developed by novelists seeking to convey social reality through the medium of words. Almost, if not at the very apex of the pile of contemporary realistic novelists, Eisenstein set Theodore Dreiser, who portrayed the American scene in terms Sergei Mikhailovich could understand. Dreiser's characters were the result of their environment; social and economic forces pressed them and deformed them. Hence, Sergei Mikhailovich was excited by Dreiser's visit to Moscow, and by his subsequent visit to Chysti Prudi 23.

Meeting face to face, Dreiser and Eisenstein, whom fate was to draw together in Hollywood in connection with the filming of Dreiser's *An American Tragedy*, did not immediately understand each other. Dreiser was not the dynamic man Sergei Mikhailovich had expected; his ponderous manner of speaking appeared slow and provincial for so great a literary figure. Patiently Dreiser tried to comprehend Eisenstein's new work; its imagery moved him to wonder, but it seemed most strange.

Generally it was Sergei Eisenstein's brilliance and wit which impressed people; but not Dreiser. What Dreiser remembered about Eisenstein was his communicativeness and his communist convictions, which were stronger in him than any other Russian artist Dreiser met. 'He was', as Dreiser wrote, 'Bolshevik, young, barely twenty-nine,

[1] 'Sergei M. Eisenstein', by Alfred Richman (U.S.A., *The Dial*, April 1929).

and handsome.' Then with his sense of fidelity, he added, 'a little short and stout, but with a fair boyish face and blue eyes, and a mass of thick curly hair'.[1]

Sitting on Eisenstein's one chair, while his host sat on a backless stool, Dreiser compared the room to the luxurious dwellings of Hollywood directors. The room was very small. 'To make it more habitable and presentable, Eisenstein had decorated the walls with a series of fantastic bull's-eye convolutions in colour.' With some surprise, Dreiser noticed the American placard of a cream separator above the table; he supposed it was for purposes of ornamentation. The thing which really impressed him, however, were not the priceless books which already lined the bookshelves, but the bed. He envied that, because it was the largest and most comfortable-looking bed he had seen in Moscow.

When Dreiser left and walked down the dimly lit passage to the front door, Sergei Eisenstein did not dream that it was this man's greatest novel which would lead him into a maze of disastrous events, the effects of which he would never entirely escape. Perhaps if he had asked Dreiser if it was wise for him to go to America, Dreiser might have warned him of the nature of American commercialism in practice, of the narrow vision of art he would encounter and the provincial political bigotry which could be hurled at him. But Dreiser left and Sergei Mikhailovich continued to dream of going to Hollywood.

On each of his periodic visits to Moscow, Alvarez del Vayo came to Chysti Prudi to see Sergei Mikhailovich. During the production of *Old and New*, Eisenstein told him of his interest in the intellectual film. 'It must be absolute as to material, authentic in presentation and emotional and pathetic in form. I am going to incorporate all this in a film I propose on Karl Marx, designed to show the dialetic method of the intelligentsia.' But Einsenstein said he would not begin this project 'within two years'. Before he made such a film, he wished to go to America to orientate himself.[2]

As he waited, Eisenstein was too deeply involved in work to appraise calmly the step he planned to take. He did not objectively analyse his position in relation to his own country, whose development could not stand still while he was gone; nor how his identity with the Soviet system would affect his relations to another social system. Capitalism in its highest stage of development was a theoretical matter for him. He did not understand its nature as a practical system of society which afforded the setting for the individual's work. It never crossed his mind that the statements he so freely made to foreigners, and which they reported abroad because of his growing fame, made him appear to

[1] *Dreiser Looks at Russia* (New York, Liveright, 1928).
[2] *Rusia Alos Doce Anos*, by J. Alvarez del Vayo (2nd ed., Madrid, 1929).

many as the agent of world revolution. Neither did he stop to consider too carefully that whatever he did, or failed to do, as an individual could have repercussions far beyond himself. Greatness endowed him with a rare kind of innocence. He could not calculate the impression he made upon others and the possible results of his uniqueness.

By 1928, at the age of thirty, Sergei Mikhailovich had developed into a very remarkable man, one who stamped his image on the memory. As Joseph Wood Krutch put it to me twenty years later, he 'was a man who, if met by accident in a doorway while sheltering from the rain, would give the impression of greatness—a man perhaps like Goethe— one who could not help but make a contribution to any work in which he engaged'. Seemingly bold and determined, he gave the impression of being proud, possibly even brutal in his strength. He seemed to know his powers, yet he was devoid of the vulgarity of ordinary vanity. There was no narrow fanaticism in his make-up, and with the years he had apparently grown beyond the confines of race or nationality. His reservoir of culture made it appear that the world was his domain. Young, he yet seemed to hold any great intimacy at bay; his imper- sonal manner caused him to appear as one standing above and beyond his fellows. Other Russian artists were cautious in expressing what they thought of Eisenstein, or of his opinions as they thrashed out with the crack of a whip. Even in Moscow where unusual theories were every- day conversation, the ideas of Sergei Eisenstein were startling.

The contrast between Eisenstein's revolutionary views on art and those of Lunacharsky, the Commissar of Education, with all art projects in the Soviet Union under his control, reveals how far Sergei Mikhailovich stood from the more moderate official view. Lunacharsky believed that Soviet art had to build upon the best of the old art. To him the life of the factory worker was narrow, even under the best circumstances, and art must counteract this narrowness. Eisenstein, on the other hand, declared that 'in the perfect state there will be no art'. To him all bourgeois art was a vicarious fulfilment of unsatisfied desires, while communist art was purely practical. No such thing as a 'perma- nent aesthetic value' existed and every work had to be judged accord- ing to its usefulness at a given time and a given place. As the perfect state emerged there would be no unsatisfied desires and the ordinary processes of life would be all-sufficient in themselves. Art, therefore, would disap- pear.[1] Even though Lunacharsky appeared to Eisenstein as a half- assimilated bourgeois, and Eisenstein appeared to Lunacharsky in the role of a new barbarian, no open conflict existed.

'In the perfect state there will be no art!'

[1] 'The Season in Moscow (III): Eisenstein and Lunacharsky', by Joseph Wood Krutch (*The Nation*, 27 June 1928).

Yet even while Sergei Mikhailovich thundered that art would disappear, he knew perfectly well that he had fallen in love with his art designed to destroy art. Little by little he tried to rationalize his position: if Art and Science could be united, then man's response to art would not be vicarious. The rooted conviction in his mind was that he could, and would, unite them. Aggressive in both the theory and practice of his art, Sergei Mikhailovich still remained uncertain in matters outside his work.

As the months stretched into years, he had grown ever more dependent on the only close human relationship he had established. In every crisis, minor or major, he turned for advice and comfort to Pera Attasheva. Since no other woman had gained any foothold in his life, most people surmised that Pera was Sergei Mikhailovich's wife, though her public relationship was that of secretary. There was sly discussion and much speculation about them. Eisenstein did not explain the place of Pera in his life; Pera did not discuss the bond which held her to Sergei Mikhailovich.

With time and much testing, their relationship assumed a complex pattern. Pera's love was of the simplest: Eisenstein was the only man with whom she wanted to live and whose children she wished to bear. It tormented her that the Old Man could not bring himself to love her in the way she loved him. Though he deprived her of her greatest desire, he yet loved her with an indestructible devotion. So deeply did he value Pera that there was to come a moment in his life when she assumed an even greater importance than his work.

Eisenstein did not wish to hurt Pera, yet it was impossible for him to avoid doing so. It was beyond his power to rid himself of the rooted fantasy that Pera was the embodiment of his mother image; at other times a sister. The thought of making love to her filled him with dread. Sometimes it was the feeling that a sexual act with Pera would be incestuous; at other times the equally poignant horror that he would be impotent.[1] He begged her to understand and accept the affection he was able to give her.

And Pera tried to understand. She strove to find contentment in the Old Man's companionship, compensation in his trust and pleasure in making his life less stark; even in cooking him the most delicious meals

---

[1] 'Psychiatric Aspects of Impotence', by E. B. Strauss, *British Medical Journal*, 25 March 1950: 'Experience has proved to my satisfaction that many men may find themselves impotent because they have unconsciously identified their sexual partner with their mother or sister; and the incest taboo has asserted itself. A mother fixation and a sister fixation are very real concepts, and not merely Freudian whimsies. These men are struck impotent in the same way as Peeping Tom in the Coventry legend was struck blind.'

she could devise. But there were sides of Eisenstein which Pera could not understand, or accept. It was her sense of humour and the affection she called forth in many people which saved her from despair. She lived in hope that some day the Old Man's feelings towards her would change. When at last in the summer of 1929, it was decided that Eisenstein should go to Berlin for the German première of *Old and New*, and that he and Tisse and Alexandrov could spend a year abroad investigating the new developments of the sound film, Pera was almost glad to see him leave. She thought a separation might alter their relationship.

The decision that Eisenstein should go abroad was influenced by the fact that sound films had not as yet been produced in the Soviet Union, although they were already superseding the silent picture in America and were being produced in considerable numbers in both Germany and France. In August 1928, one month before the first tests of the Russian-developed sound system of Shorin, Eisenstein, Pudovkin and Alexandrov had issued a collective 'manifesto' on the future of the sound film.[1] The statement, being both prophetic and far ahead of anything previously written on the subject of sound, was immediately published abroad.[2] It set forth artistic principles for the use of sound in cinematography and made the important distinction between 'the saleable merchandise, *talking films* . . . in which sound recording will proceed on a naturalistic level', and provide 'a certain "illusion" of talking people, of audible objects etc.', and sound '*directed along the line of its distinct non-synchronization with the visual images*', leading 'to the creation of an *orchestral counterpoint* of visual and aural images. . . . Sound, treated as a new montage element.' Clearly Eisenstein, who had proposed the statement, was the man to investigate the development of sound systems abroad.

Before leaving for Germany, Sergei Mikhailovich put some of the theories advanced in the sound 'manifesto' into a plan for the synchronization of *Old and New*, which he expected to record in Berlin with Edmund Meisel once again as his musical collaborator. As he worked out his ideas for the montage of sound, he could never have imagined that a whole decade would elapse before he would complete another film and finally realize the concept of 'orchestral counterpoint of visual and aural images'. His future, as he prepared to leave, looked

[1] 'The Sound Film', a joint statement by Eisenstein, Pudovkin and Alexandrov published in *Zhizn Iskusstva* (Leningrad, 5 August 1928).

[2] 'The Sound Film', translated from the Berlin *Vossische Zeitung*, appeared in the *New York Herald Tribune*, 2 September 1928; *New York Times*, 7 October 1928; *Close-up*, October 1928. A French translation appeared in *Cinéa-Ciné* (Paris, 1 February 1930).

entirely different. He thought he might go from Germany to America to direct a picture for Joseph Schenk, who had been negotiating with him to come to Hollywood. He had also received an invitation from the French *Revue du Cinema*, which was organizing a congress of independent film producers to be held at the Swiss château of La Sarraz from the 2nd to the 7th of September. He knew he had a great reputation in Germany, and from what his friend Leon Moussinac had told him, he was regarded by thousands of Frenchmen as the standard-bearer of a new approach towards art. Though Eisenstein had been widely acclaimed as a great film director, perhaps even the greatest, he later told Ivor Montagu that when he left Moscow for Berlin he had only $25 in foreign currency in his pocket. Tisse, the self-appointed 'father' of the trio, and Alexandrov also had $25 each. Seventy-five dollars and no practical experience of the entirely different world to which their train was carrying them. . . .

Eisenstein, however, was not a total stranger in Berlin. He had spent a few days there in 1926 working on a musical score for *Potemkin* with Edmund Meisel. At that time he had visited the Neubabelsberg film studio of Ufa, where Fritz Lang was directing scenes for the film *Metropolis*.

Eisenstein was interested in the methods Lang was using 'to free the camera from static angles.' Lang had prepared a shot in which the camera—focused on two actors—was mounted on a kind of children's swing to be pushed forward in the direction of the two actors during an explosion and then would automatically swing backward to its original position. In this way Lang was trying 'to give the audience the impression of what the two actors would feel under an impact of a pressure wave.' The conversation regarding the pros and cons of static or moving cameras, was cut short by the shooting schedule. He planned to meet Eisenstein again, but never did as Sergei Mikhailovich left Berlin in a few days.[1]

In 1926, Mikhail Eisenstein was still living in Berlin, and his son's name had been mentioned in the German press in connection with the film *Strike*. It is probable that Sergei Mikhailovich saw his father. He told me that his father was working as an engineer in Berlin and that he died there later in 1926 or early 1927. This conversation took place in 1934, but even then Eisenstein could not talk about his father except in halting phrases.

On arriving in Berlin, Eisenstein immediately contacted Hans Feld, the editor of *Film Kurier*, whom he had met on his visit to Germany in 1926; he also cabled to Joseph Schenk saying he was on leave from the Soviet Union and was now able to come to America. Schenk is alleged

[1] Fritz Lang in a letter to the author, dated 4 July 1950.

to have replied that his offer made more than six months before was off and that he could do nothing for Eisenstein. So Sergei Mikhailovich received his first rebuff in the city where his fame made Schenk's indifference look ridiculous.

To thousands of German artists and intellectuals struggling feverishly to survive and create in the mesh of the post-war German debacle, Eisenstein's films symbolized the triumph of their own revolutionary dreams, which had failed to come to fruition. Since Eisenstein portrayed the revolutionary struggle more clearly and forcefully than perhaps any other living artist, he stood in the minds of many Germans as the artistic leader of the new revolutionary age. He was a prophet whose visions would be re-enacted in Germany and around the world. That Eisenstein used a new form—the film—with such mastery in itself attracted attention and added to his stature, which in Germany was far beyond life-size. To a section of Germany he was scarcely a man—rather a demi-god whose figure symbolized the total force of the Soviet Union.

That Sergei Eisenstein should come to Berlin for the first presentation of his new film *Old and New*, or *General Line* as it was alternatively called abroad, had great political significance. It seemed to testify to every German communist and socialist sympathizer that the Soviet Union stood shoulder to shoulder with the German people in their increasing struggle against German capitalism and reaction. Thus, Sergei Mikhailovich was received in Berlin with a show of honour such as had never been accorded to him in Moscow.

On the 23rd of August, Eisenstein wrote to Kenneth MacPherson, the editor of *Close-up*, where the Sound Manifesto and his article 'The New Language of Cinematography' had already appeared:

> I am arrived to Berlin with the first copy of *The General Line* and am passing to Switzerland to the Independent Film at La Sarraz (the 3rd of September). Meanwhile I will be at Berlin, cutting the German version of the picture. I should be very glad to know in which way we could see each other—
> . . . I beg your pardon for my bad english and wait for your answer.
> My heartiest regards and greetings to Mrs. Bryher
> > Sincerely yours for ever
> > > S. M. Eisenstein.
> PS.—I have a manuscript of a book written by me about film theory. We could discuss about it also. . . .

The meeting with MacPherson took place after Sergei Mikhailovich returned to Germany from Switzerland. Their 'long chats in Berlin cafés where Eisenstein drank chocolate with a lot of cream and delighted in eclairs' led to the publication, over the years, of his basic theories in English, first in *Close-up* and later in *Life and Letters To-day*. Within a few days of his arrival, Sergei Mikhailovich received an offer from Wechler of the Praesans Company of Zürich to direct a film in Switzerland. It was to be a semi-scientific picture aimed at the legalization of abortion. Wechler suggested that Eisenstein, Tisse and Alexandrov come to Zürich after attending the congress of independent producers at La Sarraz. So they set off for Switzerland in the company of Hans Richter, the *avant-garde* director, whose experimental films Eisenstein found most interesting. Like Eisenstein, Richter, Walter Ruttman, the director of the symphony of a city—*Berlin*, and several other independent German directors had been invited to the congress at the château of La Sarraz, which belonged to the aristocratic and influential Madame Helène de Mandrot. But when the train arrived at the Swiss border, Eisenstein was confronted by his first political difficulties.

The Swiss authorities considered Sergei Eisenstein and his two comrades as political undesirables. His film *October* had been regarded as so politically incendiary that it had been released in Switzerland eight months before only after 25 per cent of the total footage had been cut. They were held at the border for twenty-four hours before Madame de Mandrot was able to persuade the Swiss authorities to allow Eisenstein to enter the canton of Vaux. Meanwhile, the gathering of intellectual *avant-gardists* from France, England, Germany, Switzerland, Holland and Spain, who regarded film as an art and a social force, waited for Sergei Eisenstein to make his first appearance at an international gathering in the West.

Only Hans Richter and Leon Moussinac knew Eisenstein, but everyone present accepted him as one of the greatest figures the cinema had so far produced. When at last he arrived, Sergei Mikhailovich made the most diverse impression even upon the people who later became his friends. Jack Isaacs, then a lecturer in English literature at London University, was struck by his quiet manner and reserve. To Isaacs, he never appeared to relax into the British idea of 'matiness'. When everyone else was having a good time, Eisenstein remained slightly impervious and obtuse. In contrast, Ivor Montagu, who later worked with Eisenstein in Hollywood, recalls how 'three strange figures arrived dressed from head to foot in blue zipper boiler suits',[1] and in the twinkling of an eye the gathering found themselves drawn into a hilarious display

[1] *Eisenstein*, a memorial pamphlet published by the Society for Cultural Relations with the U.S.S.R., in conjunction with the British Film Institute and British Film Academy (London, 1948), p. 7.

of intellectual slapstick presented in the guise of practical film production.

Eisenstein and Richter did in fact take over the conference and make a film ostensibly for the purpose of showing the delegates Eisenstein's method of directing crowd scenes. With a flourish, Sergei Mikhailovich cast the *avant-gardists* in their roles. The Commercial Cinema 'type' was Jack Isaacs, who was directed to stand guard at the foot of the castle turret where the elegant Janine Bouissounouse acted imprisoned Film Art in the composite guise of Rule Britannia and La Belle France, with breastplates made of film spools. The rest of the company, decked out in the castle's armour and thrusting lances wildly about, stormed the citadel to release Film Art. Unfortunately, the volatile Richter consigned this joyous film charade to the care of the still more irresponsible Eisenstein who, somewhere between La Sarraz, Zürich, Berlin, Paris and London, lost the historic document of nonsense. It survives only as a legend of Sergei Mikhailovich's exuberant sense of fun in the middle of a conference called to discuss the Art of Cinema, its Social and Aesthetic Purposes. [Plate 17]

But during his stay at La Sarraz, Eisenstein interested not only the *avant-gardists* but the police, who haunted the village 'because of the Russians', and the Protestant Church, whose lights went out of order. For some reason no one could repair the church lights, so the pastor sent to La Sarraz thinking that 'film people' must know something of the mysteries of electricity. Eisenstein and Alexandrov went to the church and, while the pastor and others looked on, repaired the lights. On another day, he amused the congress by requesting two Japanese film distributors to devise the staging of a Japanese Nō play with him, about which he clearly knew much more than they did. The scope of his interests and knowledge surprised the gathering, but his candour on the one hand and mystifying reticence on the other left some people a little confused.

Jean-Georges Auriol remembered an incident which he thought somewhat strange. One day he and a few men, including Eisenstein, went for a walk. Finding a stream in an isolated spot, they decided to take a swim. They stripped and plunged into the water. When Eisenstein did not join them, Auriol asked, 'Why don't you join us?'

'I'm not belonging to myself,' Eisenstein said. 'I'm too old.'

'So you think you are wiser than we are!' someone remarked.

Still Sergei Mikhailovich remained standing on the bank.

'You must see me as an older man,' he said. 'I have done so many things I think it is too late for me to go by an alternative way. You can't live two lives at the same time. I feel old because it is too late.'

Auriol could not understand what Eisenstein meant by these

seemingly enigmatic remarks called forth by a few men taking a swim in which Eisenstein, as a man of thirty-one, would not take part. Some months later in Paris when Irving Shapiro, the independent American film distributor, was visiting Eisenstein in his hotel room, he was surprised when Eisenstein asked him to turn his back while he changed his clothes.

While at La Sarraz, Sergei Mikhailovich arranged with Ivor Montagu and Jack Isaacs to go to London with Hans Richter in December and lecture under the auspices of the London Film Society. Then he left for Zürich with Tisse and Alexandrov to discuss the film on abortion. But after arriving in Zürich, the prospect of making the Wechler film appeared less and less interesting. Finally, Sergei Mikhailovich dismissed it with one of his quips.

He said: 'Look, let me abort all Zürich, then I'm interested; but abortion for only one woman, definitely no!'

But Tisse demurred. Having appointed himself the 'fatherly' protector of Eisenstein and Alexandrov, he accepted the job of cameraman for the sake of earning some money. Sergei Mikhailovich then returned to Berlin where he found a pension near the Wittenplatz where he lived for several weeks.

Once more his thoughts turned to his plan to synchronize *Old and New*. Edmund Meisel, who had been in London when he first arrived in Germany, had returned, and with Hans Feld and his wife, Eisenstein went to see Meisel. They spent an evening playing Spanish music, which interested Sergei Mikhailovich because of its rhythm and the special 'sound effects' counterpointed in the musical pattern. But no collaboration with Meisel arose from this meeting and Eisenstein, who had spoken to Feld about his sound montage for *Old and New*, was suddenly silent about synchronizing the film.[1] For weeks no one heard anything definite about Eisenstein's plans for future work, though a rumour circulated in Berlin that he was involved in the direction of a film called *Poison Gas*. In October, Sergei Mikhailovich asked Feld to publish a letter in *Film Kurier* concerning these rumours, in which he said:

> I thought I was morally obligated to give some advice as to types and trick camerawork for the nearly finished film of a young, hopeful director whose work had pleased me. I would never endeavour to interfere more profoundly in the creative work of another. I hope that I will have more opportunity through these lines to interest

[1] It is probable that after the cool reception of *Old and New* in the Soviet Union in September 1929, the Soviet film industry dropped the plan for the synchronization of the film.

myself in the work of young directors without people giving too much attention to it.[1]

Later it was said that Eisenstein was asked to do advisory jobs by people who realized he was, in fact, having financial difficulties. It was a curious situation since Eisenstein's fame was at its height. But he did not use his position to win the interest of the financial investors behind the film industry. When he was interviewed on the Berlin radio by Felix Mendelssohn,[2] Sergei Mikhailovich talked about the scientific base of the Soviet film and how 'his actors are the masses and his script writers and critics are also the people'. He explained how the scenarios of Alexandrov and himself were 'read in the factories and commissariats'. Just at this time when he wanted to experiment with sound, and talking pictures were the new vogue, Eisenstein 'categorically declared "I am against the talking film, which I see as a transitory form and a false form". On the other hand, sound is for him only a sort of element of editing which makes a harmonious composition with the image possible.'[3]

These views, so diametrically opposed to the film industries of Europe, who thought in terms of making money, made Sergei Mikhailovich a hero to *avant-gardists* and politically conscious groups struggling against the dictates of commercialism. Instead of cultivating the influential heads of the U.F.A. film company, or even the successful German film directors, he spent his time with the *avant-gardists* who were full of creative ideas but short of money with which to realize them. Day in, day out, Sergei Eisenstein was surrounded by painters, writers, dramatists, theatre directors, film directors, actors, dancers and a host of people, many of whom were communists and many more forced into a temporary revolutionary mood by the painful economic and political realities of German life. Much talk, many theories and a heated, delirious atmosphere attended these meetings. To Sergei Mikhailovich, sitting enthroned as the centre of attraction at the Romaniches Café, or some other haunt of Berlin's impoverished Bohemians, it appeared that German capitalism was descending into chaos and power must ultimately pass into the hands of the German people, whose artistic representatives were Eisenstein's new acquaintances and eager admirers.

If possible, they found him even more dynamic than his films. He seemed a tower of strength—cool, objective, with a poise that may

[1] Letter from Sergei M. Eisenstein appearing in *Film Kurier* (Berlin, 17 October 1929).
[2] Reported in *Film Kurier* (Berlin, 27 September 1929).
[3] *Ibid.*

have seared them with a dreadful awareness that Germany was on her knees and did not know how to rise again. That he spoke German flawlessly gave them the illusion that Eisenstein was one of them. One young writer transformed Sergei Mikhailovich's initials into the highest honour—*Seine Majestät*. Thus, for a time, Eisenstein became 'His Majesty' to the German intellectuals.

But Hans Feld, whom Eisenstein saw on his first day in Berlin, came to feel that despite his show of brilliance and levity, Sergei Mikhailovich was a shy, unhappy man. He was struck by his friendly and unassuming manner when he was alone with Feld and his wife, though the moment other people were present Eisenstein became egocentric and scurrilous in his speech.

The first time Eisenstein came to his home, Feld discovered that they shared a common passion for the tales of E. A. T. Hoffman, particularly the story *Princess Brambilla*, illustrated with the etchings of the 16th-century artist Jacques Callot. As they discussed Hoffmann, whose stories had been one of Sergei Mikhailovich's 'table books', Feld realized that Eisenstein's intellect and emotions were on tenterhooks. Suddenly he had the impression that Sergei Mikhailovich had never known what it was to be happy; that in his nature ran an undercurrent of conflict and sadness which he strove to conceal with irony and sarcasm.

In the feverish city, intellectuals introduced Sergei Mikhailovich to the strange and fascinating by-ways of Berlin life. Just to sit among them and listen to them was an excursion into the vagaries of the human mind. These people were personalities using modes of creative expression quite new in the experience of Eisenstein. Most of them were arrant individualists idolatrously worshipping the ideal of socialism. Dreaming of revolution in the midst of a society on the verge of disintegration, they revealed infinite contradictions within themselves and their art.

Ernst Toller, the poet and expressionistic playwright, who later committed suicide by hanging himself in New York, was a melodramatic, burning, tortured figure. Having been in gaol as a leader of the disastrous Bavarian Revolution following World War I, Toller now lived with elegant mistresses while yet preaching an idealistic revolutionary solution for distraught Germany. To Eisenstein, Toller appeared strange and undisciplined. Equally curious, even a little repellent, was the dry, bloodless energy he felt in Berthold Brecht, whose sharp verses and satirical plays coolly, exactly bored into the bowels of social hypocrisy. Brecht, Sergei Mikhailovich thought, was a persistent professor wielding a political pneumatic drill against the stone wall of conscience, which he could not fire with passion. There was Erwin Piscator,

didactically, blindly modelling his revolutionary theatre on that of
Meyerhold, whose roots were buried in Russian, not German soil.
Such film directors as G. W. Pabst and Fritz Lang displayed a certain
science in their pursuit of the strange. Sergei Mikhailovich felt
drawn to their work, much of which was shot through with exploration into the abnormal twists of personality.

The general phantasmagoric tendency in German art was fascinating.
Eisenstein wavered between condemnation of the decadent, unscientific
outcroppings of Freudianism turned pornographic and sentimental,
and curiosity about the neurotic artistic expression of feverish Berlin.
Several years later, Eisenstein wrote that the German cinema was
saturated with 'mysticism, decadence, and dismal fantasy . . . showing
. . . a future as unrelieved night crowded with sinister shadows and
crimes'. It reflected 'the confusion and chaos of post-war Germany.
All these tendencies of mood and method had been foreshadowed in
one of the earliest and most famous of these films, The Cabinet of Dr.
Caligari (1920), this barbaric carnival . . . of silent hysteria . . . unnatural broken gestures and actions of monstrous chimaeras.'[1]

As he well understood, this art grew out of the state of German
society which was sick.[2] Eisenstein was shocked by Berlin life. For all
the licence of the Russian Revolution, it was not sophisticated
viciousness let loose, and perversity had long been driven from the
public view. People in Russia might still be promiscuous, but sex
was not openly for sale. Brothels and pornography were outlawed, the
former by legislation, the latter because it offended the average Russian.
But in Berlin vice and perverse practices were exotic, highly advertised
delights, each specimen with its own price. The exaggeration of
eroticism was comic. At the same time it allured with its strangeness.

Some of the people Sergei Mikhailovich mixed with in Berlin were
extraordinarily exotic in their behaviour. Vice and perversions
afforded them no profit, only escape from the haunting insecurity they
felt as defeated people. Numbers of intellectuals and artists behaved
like the frenzied figures depicted in German films and plays. There was
an astounding lack of reticence. It was seemingly quite socially
acceptable to display bi-sexual passions. Women made love to women
in the presence of their husbands or lovers. He went to the Eldorado
the most fabulous café in Berlin.

For the first time in his life, Sergei Mikhailovich witnessed the
extreme end of the road for homosexual men and women. It was

[1] Film Form by S. M. Eisenstein (New York, Harcourt Brace and Co., 1949
and London, Dennis Dobson, 1950), pp. 202–203.
[2] From Caligari to Hitler, by Siegfried Kracauer (Princeton University Press,
1947).

fascinating yet revolting: men and boys made beautiful with women's make-up, wearing exquisite evening gowns and rubber breasts which, with a coy look, they would slip out and deposit on the table beside their drink. His preoccupation with the causes and extent of his own fears and rejection of normal sexual behaviour crystallized.

In Moscow, even if he could, Eisenstein would not have searched out the perverse in an effort to discover what lay within himself. Reticence would have forbidden it. But in Berlin, where perversity was entirely open to inspection, he attempted to find an answer to his own problem —if there was one. Why could he not love a woman? Why did he dread the sex act? Why was he gripped by the fear that intercourse with a woman would rob him of his creative ability? What made him dread impotence? Freud had given him some speculative answers and led him to sublimation, which now itself might be his secret vice.

Sergei Mikhailovich clothed his search to understand himself in the most impersonally conducted scientific investigation. He went to the Magnus Hirschfeld Institut für Geschlechts Wissenschaft, where every phase of sexual abnormality was being analysed. There he spent much time studying the phenomena of homosexuality, his reason being the thought that if he had command of knowledge he would detect the signs within himself and control them. In spite of all the great artists who had come into the circle of homosexuality, he felt its practice could lead only to creative death.

Once when discussing this research with me, and his reasons for undertaking it, Sergei Mikhailovich said: 'My observations led me to the conclusion that homosexuality is in all ways a retrogression—a going back to the state where procreation came with the dividing of the cells. It's a dead-end. A lot of people say I'm a homosexual. I never have been, and I'd tell you if it were true. I've never felt any such desire, not even towards Grisha, though I think I must in some way have a bi-sexual tendency—like Zola and Balzac—in an intellectual way.'

While in Berlin, Eisenstein met Dr. Hanns Sachs, the representative of Sigmund Freud. This was the same Dr. Sachs who had written about the psychological aspects of *Potemkin*, particularly the impression created by the fugleman. Sachs was thus the closest personal link that Sergei Mikhailovich ever established with Freud, 'the learned professor', with whom he had desired to study on the eve of the October Revolution. It is unfortunate that no record remains of what took place at the meeting between Eisenstein and Hanns Sachs.

But still research did not release Sergei Mikhailovich from his conflicts, though for a time he grew less rigid in his attempts to sublimate. A limited freedom came to him in the midst of licence. He may have been deliberately seeking to find some way to make love to a woman. But by his very nature the choice was limited. His behaviour towards women was so correct and formal that it chilled interest in him as a man. He had no idea how to start a flirtation or pay compliments. When in an intellectual mood, his impersonalness was so complete that only a woman intrinsically interested in his ideas could enjoy his company for any length of time. Art, mutual interest, some penetrating, instant communications with another alone could stir him out of his shell. In Valeska Gert, Berlin dancer, he discovered a kaleidoscope of sensuality, humour and pathos.

As artists, Sergei Eisenstein and Valeska Gert had an affinity. For both the panorama of the world was a fusion of the comic and the tragic; they found inspiration in the real world; both possessed symbolic minds and could not be anything but revolutionary in what they created. Yet their methods of creation were exactly opposite. Sergei Mikhailovich consciously transformed the sensual into intellectual energy; Valeska Gert instinctively used sensuality for direct creation to a degree Sergei Mikhailovich never saw in any other artist. So self-intoxicated was Valeska Gert in her dancing that in rehearsal, if she were stopped, she could only continue by starting at the beginning again. In every dance she portrayed some facet, be it comic or tragic, of the erotic side of woman. Often it was the prostitute and the gallery of figures she created formed a frieze of passion expressive of the over-wrought imagination of the Berlin intellectuals.

Like Sergei Eisenstein, Valeska Gert went her own way filled with pureness and innocence of heart. Had Valeska been corrupted by a self-conscious sophistication, her every gesture and the slightest movement of her stocky body would have screeched an unbearable lewdness; instead she engendered an elemental beauty composed of passion, comic or moving in its expressive depths. Her dancing captivated Sergei Mikhailovich. When he met this woman, who appeared to alternate with each mood between ugliness and beauty, she was for him the symbol of primal physical attraction heightened to an almost paralysing intensity. Devoid of affectation, or any attempt at glamour, Valeska Gert charmed Sergei Mikhailovich with her sturdy goodness as well as her passion. He liked her very much as a human being and consequently forgot temporarily to be afraid of her.

She had such a genuine liking for men that it never seemed to her necessary to create a subterfuge. She knew herself and could detect immediately any man who was interested in her. She detected Eisenstein's interest at once. He appealed to her on every level: the physical, the artistic and the intellectual. But the thing she did not detect was his shyness and his genuine lack of sophistication. She blundered. She made him feel her interest in him was only for a new experience and not for the affection he wanted to share with her. Though he turned to other matters, Valeska Gert remained in his mind, for the passion she had aroused in him brought him a little closer to life.

His thoughts turned to creative work. He was, as he once remarked, a working Bolshevik, not a capitalist bum. Two ideas occupied him: a film to explain Marx's *Das Kapital*, which he had mentioned to Alvarez del Vayo, and the book by Albert Londres, *The Road to Buenos Aires*. In the hope of finding financial backing for the Londres film, Sergei Mikhailovich decided to go to Paris by way of Zürich. There was also the matter of the lectures in London which Ivor Montagu was arranging.

Before leaving Berlin, Eisenstein met two people who for different reasons left a lasting impression on him. One was the Italian playwright Pirandello, whose plays interested Eisenstein because he had brought the role of Narrator back into European drama, a device which Sergei Mikhailovich saw as having great possibilities for the development of sound films. The other was Albert Einstein, whose theory of relativity he had studied while directing *Old and New*. He was flattered when Einstein gave him a signed photograph, one which he kept through his subsequent wanderings and, finally, hung in his flat near Moscow, where he worked and died. But twenty years later, Einstein wrote: 'My acquaintance with the great film director Sergey Eisenstein was very short. I am unable to recollect anything of our conversation.'[1]

Eisenstein's departure for Zürich and Paris was delayed for a few days. He contracted food poisoning. According to Hans Richter he did not respond to treatment as rapidly as was usual in such a case. He worried the doctor and the doctor worried him. At that time Sergei Eisenstein told Hans Richter it was dangerous for any great strain to be put upon his heart. For a long time he had suffered from a heart weakness, a fact which he hated to admit since it rendered him more than normally vulnerable to mortality, while his mind seemed tuned to endless life. Perhaps life churned in him so intensely because the shadow of an early death lay in the centre of his physical organism. Of death, Eisenstein never spoke—except in connection with *Que Viva Mexico!* where death was conceived as Nature's dual process with birth.

[1] Albert Einstein in a letter to the author, dated 18 October 1949.

CHAPTER SEVEN

The Contradictions of Being

You do ill if you praise but worse if you censure what you do not rightly understand.

LEONARDO DA VINCI, C.A. 76 v.a.

EARLY in November, Sergei Mikhailovich arrived in Paris with Tisse and Alexandrov. The money Tisse had earned on the abortion film in Switzerland solved their financial problem for the moment. They went to stay at the Hotel Astorg, where Eisenstein met Leon Moussinac, and some of the people who had been at La Sarraz—Auriol, Jean Mitry and Alberto Cavalcanti. But Eisenstein did not mention *The Road to Buenos Aires* to anyone except Auriol. He told Auriol he was going to present the idea to the Société Générale du Film, the company which had produced the remarkable picture directed by Carl Dreyer, *The Passion of Jeanne d'Arc*.

Presumably Sergei Mikhailovich thought it would be easy to find a sponsor for the film. *Potemkin* had been a sensational success in France in 1926, and Soviet films attracted as many as three thousand people each time they were shown in Paris by the Friends of Spartacus. If he had heard that M. Eduard Herriot had received requests to prohibit the activities of the Friends of Spartacus, Eisenstein did not take it as a warning that there were people in high places who would use their influence to convince the French film industry that it would be unwise to employ the creator of *Potemkin* to direct a film. Moreover, Sergei Mikhailovich was not sufficiently familiar with the cinema in France to realize that French art films were singularly 'non-political', while the major films were produced for such ulterior motives as making money or advancing the reputations of the *chères amies* of bankers and other gentlemen who had no love for socially-conscious art.

In a very short time Eisenstein began to learn in practice the sharp difference between directing films in the Soviet Union and trying to arrange the production of a picture in France. The criterion for a film in Russia was the importance of its theme at a given time and the manner in which it portrayed social and political reality. Its commercial value was of minor consideration; if it made money for the film trust which produced it, so much the better. The impact of the West, great as it already was on Sergei Mikhailovich, in no way altered his conviction that as an artist he was first and foremost responsible to society. He was shocked to find that though his reputation in France rested upon the power of his art and his realistic portrayal of social and political reality, no one in Paris was willing to invest a single franc in a film commensurate with the concepts which he held.

He was told that since his revolutionary films appealed only to the French intellectuals and Leftists, and not to the masses, he would have to make more 'popular' pictures. If he would make a 'popular' film, it might be possible to find money provided it had an attractive role for some young actress.

'But', protested Sergei Mikhailovich, 'I don't use actors. I use people. Actors are too artificial.' He did not know what else to say, since his whole concept of film production excluded the theatrical.

His prospective backers melted away and the sharp tongue of Eisenstein rasped like a razor. Was he to become an artistic pimp? The trade Press of the French film industry was silent about his presence in Paris.

At this moment Grigori Alexandrov asserted himself. He thought that Eisenstein was so intractable in his views on art that Tisse and he would gain little experience from their period of leave from the Soviet Union unless he sought ways and means apart from Eisenstein. So Alexandrov began to circulate on his own in Paris while Sergei Mikhailovich plunged into a discovery of the city to which all the world flocked for recognition of its talent—the city that had at first denied Balzac, Zola, de Maupassant, Proust, Picasso. . . .

As he looked about, interest triumphed over disappointment. Paris was a new world where at each corner his thirst for discovery was titillated by things he had heard of but never seen. He was as a child let loose in a playground where every path led to a different garden of enchantment. The *quais* along the Seine, an integral part of Parisian consciousness, acted as strong drink upon him. Each book-box had its mysteries which he must uncover—an unknown commentary of Balzac here, a Daumier print hidden there. In these boxes the obscure literature and art of France lay waiting to be seized upon by his hungry curiosity. This mind open to all impressions—alien, dangerous—yet certain of its own persistent direction. As he knew, Paris was the world's metropolis, the modern Damascus, where the things of East and West changed hands.

He dived into cellars in the Rue Bonaparte in search of paintings, into antique shops for prints. He wanted a print of Hokusai, the Japanese master. But when he found a print, he was too poor to buy it. Though his way of living was modest, he could not scrape together more than 10,000 francs. With 10,000 francs he bought two or three prints from the school of Hokusai. Meanwhile, in the heart of Paris, he talked to his companion, Jean Mitry, of the Kabuki and Nō theatre. From Japan he had taken his original ideas of the montage of attraction, to which he had added the reflex theories of the biologist Pavlov. He talked with a fervour mounting to exaltation.

But soon came the nights when Eisenstein sat in the Café Dome with his compatriot, Ilya Ehrenburg, and scarcely said a word. At least one of Ehrenburg's friends, Nino Frank, had the impression that Eisenstein did not speak a word of any language except Russian, His grimness as he sat deep in his chair seemed impenetrable while the people around him talked alternatively in Russian and French.

Sergei Mikhailovich was pierced by an anguish he had not known before. The beauty and gaiety of Paris changed to a *danse macabre* before his soured gaze. Never since he was a small boy and his mother had left him to come to this city had he felt so graceless; not since the day when Grisha conquered the girl Sergei Mikhailovich wished to marry had he felt so much like a clown who could not find the right quip to save his face. For the second time the social charm of Alexandrov had succeeded where his own sincerity had failed. Grisha had found a way to make a film in Paris.

Alexandrov's peregrinations had led him into an acquaintanceship with Mira Giry, a Russian who dreamed of becoming a singer. Under romantic circumstances Mira Giry had met and married the Paris jeweller known as the King of the Pearl. He was willing to finance the production of a short sound film in which his wife could sing. Tisse argued that at least it would pay their expenses and allow them to experiment with sound.

Unwillingly, Sergei Mikhailovich joined his comrades and the gay people who proposed to produce the film *Romance Sentimentale*. He watched Grisha dancing and drinking, and felt like a mound of awkwardness among these people whose gaiety was not his, whose feelings were wholly dominated by their senses. In turn, they saw him as a short, fat little man who behaved as if he were already middle-aged.

Ten years of creative work had overlaid the feelings of his youth. But now, with no outlet for his creative impulse, the conflicts of his youth rose to the surface. He felt a need to belong to someone, so to make-believe that he did, he told Jean Mitry that he was married. To others he talked about the sights he had seen in brothels. He sounded to sophisticated Frenchmen as if he were a boy of sixteen. They speculated about him and concluded that he lived 'like a priest'. He grew lonelier than in all his adult life. In search of escape he turned to the age when the dreams of men soared heavenward as their hands laid stone upon stone.

Long he recalled the sensation of mystery which passed into his body as he found his way into the cathedral of Notre Dame. The great doorway, the dim vault and in the distance, the altar set in the stone body like the secret organs of woman. It was like being absorbed back into the womb that gave him birth. The edifice dedicated to God seemed to Sergei Mikhailovich like a woman waiting for man.

Sergei Mikhailovich was profoundly moved, yet a little shocked by the blasphemy of his feelings. It seemed that everything he felt was strange, incommunicable in the ordinary course of life; the very intensity of his feelings sealed him within himself. If there were just one person in the world with whom he could share his inner self, life would be quite different for him. Pulling himself from the trance which seemed to possess him, he sought to reorientate his mind to the reality of Notre Dame. This was but one of many Gothic churches; the first which he had actually seen. He observed the details. Every stone, each nobly rising column was beautiful and all the lines flowed into one another harmoniously. Every rib of stone united with another rib as it sprang upwards, bending at last in the vaulted roof. As one who understood the structural nature of the building, its details became the richer for Eisenstein as they united with each other and with the primary form. It seemed that here in stone was manifested the nature of life itself, where all things were somehow related to one another. He had felt this unity of scattered pieces of knowledge for a long time; now he was certain of its truth and it was like a revelation. The guiding principle of his life must be to learn the pattern and try to put the pieces of the puzzle together so that his art, the poor impoverished, uncultured film, could some day rise to the expressive heights of Gothic architecture.

This thought revitalized Sergei Mikhailovich. It brought him a sense of perspective. No longer did it matter so much that he could not find financial backing for *The Road to Buenos Aires*, or all that was opened to him was to work on a little film while his dreams remained unrealized.

When Sergei Mikhailovich recounted this experience to me, he spoke as if he had gone alone to Notre Dame. But, as I later learned, he had asked Jean Mitry to go with him. Mitry did not know what feelings had passed through the man at his side, but he remembered the scene as they left the cathedral.

A little old woman had come up to Sergei Mikhailovich with pictures and trinkets in her hand. She pressed him to buy a picture of Our Lady.

'No, little old one,' said Eisenstein. 'It is all fetishism!' And he laughed sarcastically until the small, motherly woman retreated from him. When his laughter died away, he said to Mitry, 'I am interested in the why of the sacrament. I must know why the ancient meaning has gone and all that remains is the totem.'

For several days he spent much time with Mitry. He seemed to be in a constant state of exaltation. His jovial, almost childlike delight in small things contrasted strangely with his serious, even pessimistic conversations about the paroxysms of emotion that stabbed through the course of life. He spoke much about the art of Rembrandt, Goya, Daumier and the ecstasy of suffering in El Greco which appealed to him. He talked often of the mathematics at the base of his own art in *Potemkin* and when they went to the Louvre he said his composition in *Old and New* had been influenced by 'Mona Lisa' and the 'Madonna of the Rocks'.

After he had looked at da Vinci's pictures for a long time, Eisenstein spoke of the obsessional aspects of the works—the inescapable smile haunting Leonardo. It was not 'Mona Lisa' which held him enthralled, but the 'Madonna of the Rocks', which seemed to Eisenstein the most complete, the most symbolic of da Vinci's paintings. The mathematical substructure and the geometric proportions created for Eisenstein an overwhelming mystical impression.

It must have been terrible for Sergei Mikhailovich to experience the full reality of Leonardo's painting which had influenced him while he worked on *Old and New* and to go from that to work on the little film *Romance Sentimentale*, built around a little song. Yet there was nothing else for him to do, because Tisse and Alexandrov and he had long been a unit and they had to have money to live.

So Eisenstein worked on the tawdry script of a woman singing a nostalgic Russian song while a storm raged to symbolize the great upheaval that had cast her adrift. He spent some ten days at the Tobis Klangfilm Studio at Epinay devising ways of using sound. He composed some shots, beautiful in themselves, like the echoes of Japanese painting. But one day he walked out, leaving Tisse and Alexandrov to do what they could with the film. 'It was like being on the moon!' he told Mitry.

At the end of November 1929 Eisenstein left Paris with Hans Richter for England, where he was to lecture for the London Film Society. At last he had come to the land which had seeped into his childish consciousness through the pages of Dickens and the 'miss' who had been his governess.

With the Englishman's sense of propriety, a member of the Communist Party had booked rooms at an expensive West End hotel for Hans Richter and Eisenstein, even though neither of them had an extra penny with which to bless themselves or tip the braided porters. Sergei Mikhailovich rebelled at the luxury of his surroundings and summarily persuaded Richter to move with him to the Lincoln Hall Hotel in Bloomsbury, just off Russell Square. There, in the atmosphere of patterned lace curtains, aspidistras and antimacassars, Eisenstein was quite content. He came and went without ruffling the reserved quiet and to some people he appeared as a courteous and benevolent professor.

This side of his personality may have emerged because the British were not brittle, clever people given to hyperbole. He soon noticed that few Britishers idolized him as most Germans had, nor did they find him as formidable or mystifying as the French. Being circumspect, the British measured him, not allowing themselves to be overawed; a kind of orderly, respectful attention was paid him in this country of paradox.

On arrival, Ivor Montagu told Eisenstein that the intensive efforts to persuade the British Board of Film Censors to pass *Potemkin* for public exhibition in the Central London area had failed. The story circulated that as a last resort Mr. Stanley Baldwin, the oak-hearted Prime Minister, had been requested to view *Potemkin*. It was said that he had thought the film most interesting, but persisted in regarding it as too politically inflammatory for the masses to see; though, of course, it could be shown privately by the Film Society.[1] However, the Central London prohibition on *Potemkin* was circumvented by the enterprising Mr. Wurzle, who induced the Labour Borough Council of Walthamstow to allow *Potemkin*, and other Soviet films, to be shown publicly in their local borough. Even the reporters of the popular Press treated Sergei Eisenstein with courtesy. They might not agree with his politics, in that they would beg to differ; but in the country where Karl Marx had died an exile and Lenin had been granted temporary asylum, Mr. Eisenstein, Soviet Russia's great film director, was an honoured guest whose film had raised the medium of cinematography to a new level.

It was a new experience for Sergei Mikhailovich not to meet with extreme reactions. Time would prove his experience in England to be unique in his life. The sense of security which he felt may have led him to create a fiction about himself. He left Jack Isaacs with the impression that his parents, though not Orthodox Jews, were still not Christians; that they were a happily married couple and that his mother had always surrounded him with kindness and affection. On one occasion when he was in a London pub with an over-enthusiastic admirer, who started questioning him about his theories of montage, Eisenstein cynically waved aside the theories he had created with the assertion that he and his Russian colleagues had merely invented montage to cover up the fact that half the time they didn't know what they were doing when they were obliged to work with short ends of film.

But when Eisenstein gave his lectures to the Film Society, he spoke

[1] As late as 1974 a copy of *Potemkin* was confiscated in Brazil.

of cinematography as if it were not only an art which had reached as high a level of development as the older arts, but as a science grounded on philosophic and higher mathematical knowledge. As Basil Wright recalled: 'There we were, with notebooks and pencils, thinking passionately about Film, Film the great new art-form. . . . There was he, with blackboard and chalk, about to expound the inner, the Eleusinian mysteries of Film Art.

'He talked about the Japanese Kabuki plays, about William James, Darwin, Toulouse-Lautrec, Daumier; about Kenyon's proposition that two opposite reactions can be provoked by the same stimulus; about Duchelle's studies of the muscular movements, and his conclusion that 'L'action musculaire *isole* n'existe pas dans l'expression humaine'; about de Terrail's *Rocambole*, le Blanc's *Arsène Lupin*, about Stefan Zweig, Zola and James Joyce.

'It was at first a little disappointing, a little shocking. I remember spending a few minutes alone with him, carrying some tins of film from Manetta Street to Wardour Street. He asked me, as an aspirant to film-making, "Have you read Ben Jonson?" "Only *Volpone*," I confessed. He told me to read it again, and to read the other plays. It was hardly what I expected. But I did.

'And as the lectures progressed one began to understand and appreciate all those surprising references. Eisenstein never forgot that the film is a synthetic art. He made it clear that for him the approach to film theory, and in particular to montage, was not something in a vacuum. He claimed, in fact, that film montage was the *cinematic* aspect of a particular form of expression used by artists in other media— particularly poetry, painting, drama and the novel. He said: "Only recently have we begun to feel the real type of filmic film which is to come. So far films moving in this direction have been purely experimental. . . . But now the historical moment has come at which we are to find *the synthesis of art and science in an entirely new form of picturization:* The new form is not symbolic, but vital and picturesque. The method of expression is purely dynamic, like music, but not so impressionistic as music. In the new film sound will play a very big role: but the big development will *not* come from the sound tecnhique. Sound will in fact come in as one of the elements of the new montage system. . . . The different elements of art are not opposites; the essential thing is to find out the law belonging to *all* forms of impression and expression. . . . Montage in all its aspects, and they are many, is derived from one single principle."[1] [App. Two.]

It suddenly became impossible for anyone present to continue to

[1] 'Eisenstein's Lectures in London'; a reconstruction by Basil Wright and Jack Isaacs, B.B.C., Third Programme, 17 December 1949.

think of the lecturer as simply the creator of the revolutionary films *Potemkin*, *October* and *Old and New*. Eisenstein was more than an artist inspired by the Russian Revolution; he was pre-eminently a philosopher and scientist experimenting with a new medium of expression. As Eisenstein spoke—and even his mastery of English was remarkable —he ploughed deep into the receptive minds of those present. The seeds he sowed took root in the thoughts of those who heard him. Perhaps the adaptation of his ideas was possible because none of his British listeners considered for an instant that they could, or should, directly imitate Eisenstein's films.

Amongst those attending his lectures were Anthony Asquith, Basil Wright, Arthur Elton, Ivor Montagu, Thorold Dickinson, H. P. J. Marshall, Jack Isaacs, Robert Herring, the film critic and—darting in and out—John Grierson. After re-editing *Potemkin* in New York, that stormy petrel had returned to his native Scotland and with the knowledge gained from *Potemkin*, he had produced the picture of Scottish fishermen, *Drifters*. This pioneer British documentary had been shown by the Film Society on November the 10th together with *Potemkin*.

The impact of Eisenstein's lectures following upon the first showing of his film *Potemkin*, and Grierson's *Drifters*, produced what Sergei Mikhailovich would have termed a creative explosion in the minds of quite a number of the Film Society Study Group. They were given a stimulus towards the making of films based on real life—the realities of British life which had not found expression in the trite story films and ponderous historical pictures made by British studios. The honourable work of the men and women who kept the wheels of industrial Britain turning was important and dramatic. The men who dug the coal in the pits of Wales and Lancashire were never heroes in their own person. Only now were the weatherbeaten men of Scotland, sailing out into the North Sea in trawlers, whole images on the screen. Eisenstein's attentive listeners, some of them socialist-minded and some of them not, were as conscious of the strength and ceaseless contribution of the British masses as Sergei Mikhailovich was conscious of the Russian masses.

Instead of writing long books on film aesthetics, or making experimental films of dubious value (as some of Eisenstein's followers did on the Continent), when Sergei Mikhailovich departed from England, some of his listeners came together to discuss the practical possibilities of utilizing some of his ideas. A few of them went to work with Grierson and thus helped to create the British Documentary Film movement. Eisenstein did not overshadow them; they seldom, if ever, tried to copy his vivid technique. They honoured him the more by not attempting to become the slaves of his style.

During the period of Eisenstein's lectures, and as the second course of the Film Society Study Group, Hans Richter had been conducting the production of an *avant-garde* film in a tiny studio above Foyle's bookshop in Manette Street. This film, which was never completed, because Richter carried it away with him and left it in a Swiss laboratory, was one day interrupted by Eisenstein, who injected his own interlude. Dressing himself up in the uniform of a British policeman, he performed a ballet of the bobby on point duty directing traffic. From the isolated frames which Eisenstein clipped out of the film and later gave me, he appears to have caught the spirit of British bobbies: their dull, paternal benevolence touched sometimes with a Cockney whimsicality; their little gesture of hitching up their belts, the reproachful eye gazing down upon the small offender from the eminence of six feet. In the comic mask which Sergei Mikhailovich designed for his ballet, he captured a fragment of British character, sharp as a Dickens cameo. [Plate 17]

That he should catch the gestures and expressions of a classic British 'type' was natural considering how Eisenstein became a sponge absorbing the atmosphere of any culture to which he was exposed. He had formed the habit of finding 'guides', whom it seems that he himself guided, perhaps for the purpose of observing their reactions. Early in his London visit, he invited Oswald Blakeston, a frequent contributor to *Close-up*, to show him London. But when Mr. Blakeston arrived for the appointment, Sergei Mikhailovich had made his own plan. They boarded a tram on the Embankment and in proper British silence rode to the end of the line and back again. Blakeston was perplexed by Eisenstein's satisfaction with what appeared to him as a pointless and dull ride which had led them nowhere. Then they visited Whitechapel and went on a 'pub crawl', during which Eisenstein consumed several glasses of beer and absorbed the characteristic conversations going on around him.

In the company of Jack Isaacs, with whom he spent much of his time, Sergei Mikhailovich sensed the pulse of London: its beat in the open markets and the streets; the tones of the auctioneer's voice at Hodgson Auction Room. There they bought a parcel of prints for £5 and divided the contents between them. Among the prints were French portrait engravings and, to Eisenstein's joy, some prints by Jacques Callot. Again he searched for Japanese prints. He wanted to find a print of an actor by Sharaku, so Isaacs took him to a Japanese art dealer on New Oxford Street. But they searched in vain. Often they spent hours browsing in the bookshops along Charing Cross Road, discussing art and English literature. The only area of literature that seemed closed to Sergei Mikhailovich was lyric poetry. He wanted to sense and understand this mode of expression which at this time appeared to elude him.

Some years later, Eisenstein wrote to Isaacs for an account of 'the origin, progress, and function of the dumb show in Elizabethan drama'. 'My answer', said Isaacs, 'was the inevitable one to most problems of serious research: "I wish we knew." It was only the answers which didn't exist that he wanted from the experts—everything else he could work out for himself.'[1]

At one point Tisse and Alexandrov came to London for a few days. Then they went about 'as a team', and during this time Isaacs noticed the affection and respect which Tisse had for Eisenstein. When his comrades returned to Paris, Isaacs continued to show Sergei Mikhailovich the England that too frequently remains an enigma to those not born to its tradition. Their circuit widened. They went to Hampton Court. On another day they journeyed to Windsor to see the castle and Eton.

'Now I know why there will never be a revolution in England,' said Eisenstein.

It seemed that only when he had absorbed the feel of England did his thoughts turn to his own medium of expression. While walking in the streets, he one day observed that in the life of London lay the material for a documentary film which could convey the essence of this complex civilization, which he admitted held great appeal for him. But he made no effort to interest anyone in producing such a picture. When Sidney Bernstein, the cinema proprietor and member of the Film Society council, gave a party for him, he merely stood in silence until, wearied by the atmosphere of the smart, sophisticated crowd, he made a few tersely blasphemous remarks, which left some of the people who had come to meet him with a slightly uncomfortable feeling. Yet when alone with someone he became expansive.

One day he sat for many hours in the small, unpretentious Lyons' teashop next to the Holborn Underground with Paul Rotha. He drank several cups of coffee and 'smoked like hell'. Normally he never smoked. But he had been with Rotha to the museum of the Royal College of Surgeons. He talked about the Russian Revolution and drew incessantly upon the marble table-top to illustrate the camouflage ideas used by the Red Army during the Civil War. From the museum of the Royal College of Surgeons to the Russian Civil War. . . . There was a psychological thread linking the sights he had seen at the front and the sights in the museum. As he had once tried to conceal his innocence from his Red Army comrades by Rabelaisian talk, so now Sergei Mikhailovich camouflaged his frustrations by speaking of psychoanalysis and smoking endless cigarettes. But his ideas spread out in an

[1] 'Eisenstein's Lectures in London'; a reconstruction by Basil Wright and Jack Isaacs, B.B.C., Third Programme, 17 December 1949.

ever-widening circle until they reached to the *Mysteries of Paris* by Eugene Sue and Zola's novel *Germinal*, which he told Rotha he would like to make into a film. Time seemed to have no meaning for him; only the pursuit of knowledge. It was his only outlet for the mounting tensions within him: his only defence against the disappointment that gnawed at him.

Before he left England, Eisenstein received an invitation to address the students of Cambridge University on Russian films. There he stayed with the economist, Maurice Dobb, who showed him around the hallowed precincts where generations of England's youth had studied. A thinking man, be he Bolshevik or otherwise, was acceptable at Cambridge. It is said that Eisenstein made such an impression on the members of the faculty whom he met that one of them jokingly remarked it was a pity such a man as he was not a Cambridge don. On returning to London, Sergei Mikhailovich told Richter that someone had suggested he should become a professor at Cambridge. He was not joking, for Cambridge had stirred in him a desire to abandon his career in the cinema.

The colleges and halls, the libraries and the chapels, stimulated the urge rising inexorably within him—to devote himself to research, philosophic speculation and pure learning. As he walked the Cambridge streets and sat in the rooms of dons, he thought of the end of life. How pleasant it would be to retire from the world and in obscurity study the things which interested him. It would be good to die peacefully in a passionless, cloistered court of Cambridge. To dream his dreams undisturbed. . . . But he was only a film director with a year's leave from his country, where everyone was engaged to the uttermost in building a new society.

It came to Eisenstein in Cambridge that he had won fame in a field where he could at best only fulfil a part of himself—the artist part. He felt constrained by limitations he had not foreseen when he left the Soviet Union; his reputation as a film director caused him a deep sense of dissatisfaction. For all the richness of his creative imagination, he realized it was now only a facet of his larger purpose. Like da Vinci, who had outgrown the desire to paint and sculpt, Sergei Mikhailovich was beset by a thousand ideas which pulled him this way and that: he wished to delve deeper into psychology, become a philosopher, pursue research in anthropology. Thirty-two years old, Eisenstein was already burdened with a brain nagging to break the bonds of human capacity.

'I'm outgrowing films,' he said to Hans Richter. 'The medium is too primitive for me.'

Shortly before the New Year, he returned to Paris. His lectures in London had stimulated further theoretical work. He revised and added a new section to a long article—'The Fourth Dimension in the Kino'.[1] On the 2nd of January 1930, he wrote to Kenneth Macpherson from Paris:

'Tis only today that I have received the copies of my article. . . . I'm afraid that it will be very difficult to translate the articles because they are very complicated being of big theoretical importance.

Let Herring help in explaining the english translation—because he has heard the whole thing in my lectures. . . .

It would be fine if it could be done before the 13th, when I am leaving Paris for about 10 days, coming back again after that time. . . .

It is a great pity—Switzerland does not give me a visa, and I shall not pass my holidays there. . . .

Then he went with Alexandrov to Holland to lecture for Film Liga, whose representatives had been at La Sarraz. Eisenstein was met at the Rotterdam airport by a large group of reporters and Press photographers who had confused his name and were expecting to interview Albert Einstein. Questioned about his plans, he said he expected to go to America in March or April with Tisse and Alexandrov. He knew that Douglas Fairbanks was coming to Europe and he was still hoping that Fairbanks would make arrangements with him to work for United Artists. He added that later he would make a film of *Das Kapital*. A surprised journalist asked him what were his ideas for a film of Marx's *Capital*. 'That,' replied Eisenstein, 'is a factory secret!'[2] While in Holland he made some test shots 'for future films'. He also met a young Dutchman, Joris Ivens, the social documentary director, who was then experimenting with visual effects in his films *Rain* and *The Bridge*.

Leaving Holland, Eisenstein went to Germany for a few days to lecture at the University of Berlin. Then he returned to Paris; en route, in Brussels, he gave a lecture for the Cine Clubs.

Back in Paris again, Sergei Mikhailovich went to stay at the small Etats Unis Hotel on Boulevard Montparnasse, where Tisse and Alexandrov, who were still working on *Romance Sentimentale*, joined him. Though the film industry continued to ignore him, ever more people began to seek him out. He met Jean Cocteau and Ferdnand Leger, whose painting and personality made a strong impression upon him. Leger introduced him to the circle of La Reine de Montparnasse, the model Kiki, who surrounded herself at the Café Dome and La Coupole with a court of famous and near-famous men. She paid Eisen-

[1] S. M. Eisenstein, 'The Fourth Dimension in Kino, I and II' (*Close-Up*, March–April 1930).

[2] Report in *Film Kurier* (Berlin, 16 January 1930).

stein the compliment of drawing his portrait.[1] But of Kiki, who showed an interest in him, he never voiced an opinion. He was elusive. One day he was with one group, the next with another. Only a few people heard that he was interested in Blaise Cendrars' novel, *D'Or*, and that he discussed with the author this story of the American Gold Rush which later became the basis of his treatment of *Sutter's Gold*, a film Paramount refused to produce. Nor did many people know that Eisenstein and James Joyce discussed *Ulysses* as a possible film.

Eisenstein wanted to meet James Joyce, because in literature Joyce alone among living writers was breaking down the walls of literary tradition and creating new forms to express the inner processes of thought and emotion. The montage possibilities of the 'internal monologue' of Joyce's Leopold Bloom had long occupied the imagination of Eisenstein, for, as he later expressed it, he was fascinated by the process of listening 'to one's own train of thought, particularly in an excited state, in order to catch yourself looking at and listening to your mind. How you talk "to yourself", as distinct from "out of yourself". The syntax of inner speech as distinct from outer speech. The quivering inner words that correspond with the visual image. . . .'[2]

So in Paris Sergei Mikhailovich went to the home of James Joyce. Though he had already read and re-read *Ulysses*, and thought he had grasped its subtle nuances, he found he had only just begun to understand the book on an elementary level. Only when Joyce read passages to Sergei Mikhailovich (who never before had felt himself to be sitting at the feet of any living master) did its words and images take on their full significance. In Joyce, Eisenstein found a man to whom his aims and methods were intelligible. They talked of the future development of their mutual preoccupation—the 'internal monologue' how the processes of the mind could be made visible and comprehensible through the film medium. Despite his near-blindness, Joyce wanted to see those sections of *Potemkin* and *October* in which Sergei Mikhailovich had tried to reveal the inner core of man and, thus, convey reality to the spectator. Following these meetings, Joyce told his friend Jolas, the editor of *Transition*, that if *Ulysses* were ever made into a film, he thought that the only men who could direct it would be either Walter Ruttman the German, or Sergei Eisenstein the Russian.

But the time Sergei Mikhailovich spent in France was marked by the upsurge of one predominant passion. Often he had felt himself possessed of powers 'transcending common sense and human reason'. Now in

---

[1] Drawing of Sergei M. Eisenstein by Kiki reproduced in *Pour Vous* (Paris, 26 December 1930).

[2] *Film Form* by S. M. Eisenstein (New York, Harcourt Brace and Co., 1949 and London, Dennis Dobson, 1950), p. 105.

Paris these experiences became a focal point in his thinking. Away from the Soviet Union, where rationalism had controlled his thoughts to a considerable extent, Sergei Mikhailovich sought to wrench from life the secret of miracles and what lay at the root of estatic states of consciousness. Jean Mitry, who had gone with him to Notre Dame, had concluded that his desire 'to explain all manifestations of exaltation in life' must have sprung from the fact that he had transmuted a youthful mysticism and strong religious sentiment into a 'political mysticism'.

Shortly after arriving in France, Eisenstein heard that a 'miracle' had reputedly taken place in a village on the Normandy coast. He hurried to the village explaining he wanted to investigate the occurrence for a film on religion which he hoped some day to make. Later he said that the village was like a Russian village and what he had witnessed there was an extraordinary experience. He began to seek out psychologists and doctors with whom he discussed manifestations of ecstasy and French mysticism.

A little later he went with Roland Tual to Lisieux to see Anatole de Monzio, the former French Ambassador to Moscow, hoping that he would intercede with the French authorities who were threatening to expel Eisenstein as a political undesirable. Their visit to Lisieux coincided with a religious pilgrimage to the shrine of Teresa of the Little Flower. Sergei Mikhailovich, with the help of Alexandrov, spent much time taking photographs. Roland Tual noticed that despite Eisenstein's hunger for religious souvenirs—postcards and crucifixes—he seemed to go about the photographing of people in the grip of religious emotions in an objective manner, explaining that he was making this record for a comparative study of religious ecstasy. Though Sergei Mikhailovich appeared to be acting scientifically, the whole realm of experience lying within the compass of the mystics plagued him. He wondered if science could explain certain states of consciousness he had witnessed, or those he himself experienced.

While Tisse and Alexandrov worked on *Romance Sentimentale*, he went to Lourdes, hoping to understand the nature of its alleged miraculous cures. What had been the inner states of Bernadette, the girl whose visions had brought Lourdes into being? Was Lourdes nothing but the Church's exploitation of the credulous? There was that element; indeed it was very strong as he could well see. But what had happened *inside* Bernadette and the people whose ills were cured? Some, of course, were neurotics; but was it auto-suggestion in all cases? A self-induced illness resulting from abnormal tensions followed by a self-impelled cure? The unconscious mind could produce extraordinary things.

Eisenstein pursued his investigation. He studied the legend woven about the recent French visionary, Teresa of the Little Flower, hoping, as far as possible, to understand her state of mind. What was this state of consciousness which was the sign of alleged 'grace'? How did it correspond with his own curious states? In 'ecstasy' he sensed a dialectical movement of development as in the natural processes of transformation; in that *instant* when 'water becomes a new substance— steam, or ice-water—or pig-iron—steel'.[1] As the elements changed their quality under certain conditions, so man's inner self changed its quality through the experience of ecstasy. In some people the highest peak of ecstasy was reached in such a moving 'out of themselves' that they believed they had come into communion with the unknowable— God, Jesus Christ, the Virgin. Some even bore signs upon their flesh— the marks of Christ's crucifixion—the stigmata. They were wounded and they bled. Were the wounds self-induced, the visions but hallucinations?

Strive as he did, Sergei Eisenstein could not find entirely adequate scientific answers. His research drove him further into the no-man's-land of uncertainty where he stood alone with only the intensity of his inner experiences. Being a man given to logic, he might have considered himself mentally ill; but it is doubtful if such an idea ever struck him. He merely stood too often upon the brink of the unknown, convinced that some men were marked with a peculiar receptivity to supernormal experiences. He wanted a scientific basis, but he wanted still more to retain 'those certain supernatural powers, transcending common sense and human reason, that seemed indispensable for the comprehension of the "mysteries" of creative film direction'.[2]

But Eisenstein's need for creative expression, like his transcendent states of consciousness, worried him. Boycotted by the film industry, he scattered his energy in research which brought him into touch with members of the faculty of the Sorbonne. Finally, the Groupe d'Etudes Philosophiques et Scientifiques pour l'Examen des Tendances Nouvelles invited him to lecture on the Principles of the New Russian Cinema at the Sorbonne on the 17th of February 1930, and to show *Old and New*. Sergei Mikhailovich was pleased. But five hours before the lecture, Chiappe, the anti-Communist Prefect of the Paris Police, who had been making Eisenstein's stay in France difficult, notified the Sorbonne that the police must view *Old and New*. Leon Moussinac, who had custody of the film, took the print to the Prefecture and waited for the verdict.

At this time French newspapers were carrying stories about the

[1] *Film Form* by S. M. Eisenstein (New York, Harcourt Brace and Co., 1949 and London, Dennis Dobson, 1950), p. 173.
[2] *Ibid.*, p. 86.

alleged abduction by the Soviet Government of the White Russian General Koutiepov, and charges of espionage against the Soviet Ambassador in Paris. There was talk of breaking diplomatic relations with the Soviet Union. Interspersed with these stories were outbursts in the conservative French Press about Soviet persecution of religion in Russia. Cardinal Mercier had taken the opportunity to raise again the moral and political reasons for intervention during the Russian Civil War.[1] Despite this anti-Soviet atmosphere, several hundred people, including many professors and psychologists, crowded into a small hall of the Sorbonne to hear Eisenstein speak.

As he waited to step on to the platform, Sergei Mikhailovich knew that those who had preceded him as speakers back over the years were men of established learning, not film directors. Their subjects had not been the new language of cinematography but learned discussions on the nature of Intuition or the Transcendentalism of Kant. But he was a man from a new society, the representative of a system challenged by the whole world. Not a single degree followed his name; he had only his words and his beloved film to explain his own vision and the aims of his country.

Those who watched Sergei Eisenstein step on to the platform suddenly felt released from the severe demeanour of academic decorum. The man who stepped out warmed them with a friendly smile. They applauded him until he raised his expressive hands. The gesture seemed to say, 'You must hear me and see my work before you approve'. The charm radiated by Eisenstein was suddenly cut short. The embarrassed chairman raised his voice to say that the Parisian police had forbidden the showing of Old and New.

Sergei Mikhailovich remained quite still. So this was French democracy! This the city where once the spirit of the French Revolution had blazed. He heard faint murmurs coming from the chairman of the group devoted to examining the new tendencies in philosophy and science.

To the amazement of Eisenstein, the decorous people sitting in front of him were galvanized into a frenzy of protest. For a quarter of an hour they demonstrated against the repressive act of the French police.

Without notes, Sergei Mikhailovich began to speak. He could be himself, even though his flawless French, with its perfect accent, was slightly formal. Sometimes a word got lost in his memory, but he substituted it with a gesture comprehensible to all.

'I am sorry that you cannot see my film.' Restrained words to express the anger and disappointment which he felt. 'This makes my task much harder, as I will have to make up for what you cannot see

[1] Le Monde (Paris, 18 February 1930), Le Figaro (Paris, 18 February 1930).

with my limited French. When I am finished you may throw questions at me and I will try to answer as in a friendly ping-pong game. . . .'

Thus, Eisenstein introduced his discussion of the Soviet cinema and how it was designed to bring knowledge and a wider understanding of the social processes to the Russian people. 'We build our films in a scientific manner in order to make a specific impression on the spectators. Here we have developed a potent weapon for the propaganda of the ideas upon which our society rests.' He spoke eloquently of the achievements of his comrades, Pudovkin and Alexander Dovzhenko, Kuleshov, the pioneer, and Dziga Vertov. He explained his work, stressing what he meant by 'typage'. Lastly, he spoke about the project which had been straying in and out of his mind for several years, and of which he had written while in Berlin—the possibilities of making a film of Marx's *Capital*.

'The intellectual film is the only thing capable of overcoming the discord between the speech of logic and the speech of imagery,' explained Eisenstein. 'On the basis of the speech of kino dialectic, intellectual cinematography will not be the cinematography of episodes, not the cinematography of anecdotes. The intellectual kino will be the cinematography of concepts. It will be the direct expression of entire ideological systems and systems of concepts.'

'My new conception of the film', he continued, 'is based on the idea that the intellectual and emotional processes which so far have been conceived of as existing independently of each other—art versus science —and form an antithesis heretofore never united, can be brought together to form a synthesis on the basis of cinedialectic, a process that only the cinema can achieve. The scientific formula can be given the emotional quality of a poem. I will attempt to film *Capital* so that the humble worker or peasant can understand it in the dialectical manner.'[1]

Part of the audience was much impressed by what Eisenstein said, even though they may have felt uncertain as to the exact nature of the proposed film, *Capital*. Some knew that Eisenstein's views were given scientific validity by the observations of Claude Bernard, the French physiologist, whose own views on emotion and intellect echoed Eisenstein's. A smaller section had failed to hear his actual words. They were stridently hostile to him because he represented the Soviet Union and Bolshevism. They could not appraise him as an individual, only as a representative of a political and economic system which they abhorred. They flung bitter and malicious questions at him, seeking to entangle him in matters quite beyond the scope of his lecture.

To Sergei Mikhailovich these hostile barbs were a new experience.

[1] S. M. Eisenstein, 'Les Principes du Nouveau Cinéma Russe' (*Revue du Cinéma*, No. 9, Paris, April 1930).

He refused to retract his statements; he refused to be forced from his support of the Soviet Union. He stood by what he was: a Soviet artist and a disciplined Soviet citizen.

A man sprang up shouting: 'Will the speaker please tell me whether it is possible for an actor who is an individualist in his art and philosophy to exist in the Soviet Union?'

Eisenstein, the individualist, who was the voice of revolutionary art, replied with sarcastic wit: 'Stay here, young man, you will find French soil much more fertile than ours!'

There were other questions. One person asked if the reports were true that laughter had died in Moscow.

After a long laugh at this question, Sergei Mikhailovich answered: 'You should hear my Russian comrades laugh when I tell them about that question!'[1]

Such leading French newspapers as *Le Monde* and *Figaro* did not mention the banning of *Old and New*, or Eisenstein's speech at the Sorbonne. He wondered what acclaim would have been his had he joined the colony of White Russian *émigrés*. For some time rumours had been reaching him that the French film industry had ignored him for political rather than commercial reasons. When the Friends of the Soviet Union gave a dinner in his honour, not one of the two hundred people present was a representative of the French cinema industry. As Samuel Brody later observed, this exhibition illustrated rather well the remark of Leon Moussinac that 'jealousy and envy are one of the forms of the petty bourgeois mind. Cowardice is a form of decadence.'[2]

Shortly after the affair at the Sorbonne, Eisenstein was again confronted with the problem of having his permit to remain in France extended by the Prefecture of the Police. At first M. Chiappe refused to prolong his permit, and for some time Sergei Mikhailovich was faced with expulsion from the country.[3] But finally his permit was prolonged when the *Nouvelle Revue Française* protested and a letter signed by some sixty writers, painters, musicians and cinema artists was sent to the Ministry of the Interior.[4]

As spring approached, Eisenstein's future looked vague. Sometimes he did not have enough money to pay his hotel bill, but his friends always came to his aid. He was glad when Leon Moussinac and his wife suggested that he go with them on a motor-trip through France. In spite of his troubles, his curiosity and perception were not blunted. As they passed from one province to another going southward, Moussinac

[1] *Humanité* (Paris, 19 February 1930).
[2] 'Paris Hears Eisenstein', by Samuel Brody (*Close-up*, April 1930).
[3] *Cinemonde* (Paris, No. 75, 27 March 1930).
[4] *Revue du Cinema* (Paris, No. 10, 1 May 1930).

was moved to wonder by Eisenstein's sensitivity to the French spirit.
Many years later, Moussinac recalled how Sergei Mikhailovich knew
immediately when they reached a new region. 'He understood with
his very being the culture, history and art of each province and the
subtle differences between the people of one district and another.' By
now his French had grown fluent. He gave tit for tat whether to a man
of learning or a factory worker. He had assimilated the essence of France
and drawn close to the spirit of the French. During this trip, Moussinac came to feel that Eisenstein was 'a man of universal genius for
whom the costume of the time was too small'. It seemed he had
domination over all subjects, yet of the things that touched him the
most deeply, he spoke with irony.

Returning again to Paris with Moussinac and his wife, Sergei
Mikhailovich waited, still hoping that he would find a way of going
to Hollywood. He heard that Douglas Fairbanks was in London, but
there was no word from him. Then when it looked as if Eisenstein's
whole journey abroad was turning into an utter failure so far as
creative work was concerned, the executives of Paramount began to
talk about employing him to direct a film in Hollywood.

Note 1977. His *Autobiography* reveals that Eisenstein had visited and fallen under
the spell of Paris in his boyhood, a visit he never later mentioned to anyone, as
far as I know.

CHAPTER EIGHT

'An American Tragedy'

And often when I see one of these men take this work in hand I
wonder whether he will not put it to his nose like the ape, and ask
me whether it is something to eat.

LEONARDO DA VINCI, C.A. 119 v.a.

Savage is he who saves himself.

LEONARDO DA VINCI, Tr. 52 a.

THE dramatic power of *Potemkin*, especially the tempo and rhythm of the 'mob scenes', had quickened the pulse of America's producers of thrills and spectacles. Give Eisenstein the means and he would out-Mille de Mille. Fairbanks had praised Eisenstein and spoken of his enthusiasm for American technical skill and his eagerness to work in Hollywood.

Following the American première of *Potemkin* at the Biltmore Theatre in New York on the 5th of December 1926, and its sensational acclaim, the film was released in Hollywood. As *Potemkin* zinged through projectors in many Hollywood studios, superlatives were hurled about. Cutters thronged to study Eisenstein's montage, cameramen Tisse's angles. Soon Eisenstein's technical experiments were being imitated in American films. Thus, Eisenstein's name and major achievement had become known in the American film industry.

For some time, several studios had been considering the idea of bringing Eisenstein to Hollywood, among them M-G-M and United Artists. During the latter part of 1928 and early in 1929, talk about Eisenstein circulated inside Universal. Seymour Stern,[1] a production-assistant and special adviser to Carl Laemmle Sr., had been urging him to employ Eisenstein. At the same time, Paul Kohner, chief of Universal's European office in Berlin, was 'dickering' with Pudovkin.

Early in 1930, Ivor Montagu went to Hollywood, where he became a script writer for one of the studios. He talked about Eisenstein a great deal and spread the word that he was in Paris on leave from the Soviet Union. When the genial Mr. Jesse Lasky of Paramount arrived in France, he contacted Sergei Mikhailovich with the view to employing him to inject a dash of freshness and vigour into an American film. In the past European directors had brought originality and spice to certain

[1] Later the author of *The Griffith Index* and D. W. Griffith's authorised biographer.

types of Hollywood pictures,[1] while from long practice the importation of European stars—Vilma Banky, Pola Negri, Greta Garbo, Maurice Chevalier, Marlene Dietrich, etc.—had proved most profitable at the box-office. Paramount considered the services of Eisenstein desirable. So Mr. Lasky, a pioneer of American cinematography, offered Sergei Eisenstein, the pioneer of Russian art films, a contract for six months for which he would be paid $500 every seven days.

Sergei Mikhailovich knew almost everything there was to know about art, but almost nothing he should have known about business. Having lived the whole of his creative life in one small room in an old Moscow house with several other families, he had no solid knowledge on which to gauge what $500 could do for him, nor what he would be expected to do in return for such a salary. In a sense, he was acting out a real-life Hollywood romance—the poor boy who makes good. But he did not foresee that in his case he was to twist the romance of success inside out, because he was not the ordinary poor boy who makes good. It was not the money which excited him, but the realization of his long-held wish to work in Hollywood. He was pleased beyond measure, for this would mean as much to Tisse and Alexandrov as himself. He asked Lasky what about contracts for them.

Lasky was not interested in Tisse and Alexandrov, only in Eisenstein. He probably did not realize that the three had always considered themselves a unit, bound together by mutual effort so that where one went the others went as well. Paramount was unwilling to give them contracts. Sergei Mikhailovich argued and Lasky resisted. He continued to resist until Eisenstein announced that he would not go to America without Tisse, his cameraman, and Alexandrov, his assistant. Since Lasky wanted Eisenstein for Paramount, he offered him $900 a week, out of which Eisenstein could pay his assistants.

Nine hundred dollars a week! Sergei Mikhailovich was amazed. Unconsciously he had played the business man with astonishing results.[2] Eisenstein and Lasky shook hands on the 'deal', and it was reported in the French Press on May the 1st that Eisenstein had been engaged by Paramount.[3]

But Eisenstein could not leave immediately for America. In August 1929, the Soviet Government had given him a year's leave, and the

[1] Notably Erich von Stroheim and Ernst Lubitsch.

[2] The $900 a week was only a retainer while Eisenstein looked for a story and prepared a scenario. When the actual shooting on the film commenced, he would receive $3,000 a week. However, it was widely reported at the time that under his contract with Paramount, Eisenstein received $3,000 a week from the outset.

[3] *Pour Vous* (Paris, 1 May 1930).

contract Paramount had offered him would extend beyond this period. There was much correspondence before the film trust, Sovkino, finally gave Eisenstein, Tisse and Alexandrov permission to go to Hollywood. It was understood at the time that after working six months in Hollywood, Eisenstein would return to the Soviet Union, where he would work for the next six months, at the end of which time he would again return to Hollywood.[1]

As Sergei Eisenstein affixed his signature to the contract with Paramount, his imagination soared. He must investigate: Harlem and Negroes—gangsters and prisons—Chicago's slaughterhouses and steel mills. He would at last meet D. W. Griffith and Charlie Chaplin, and see Joe Freeman again. He would walk the earth Walt Whitman sang about . . . and study the society Theodore Dreiser portrayed in his novel *An American Tragedy*. The pinnacles of Manhattan rose up and up in the imagination of Sergei Mikhailovich—the tallest buildings in the world.

'Why don't they seem high?' The notion crawled lazily through his brain when he arrived and with wondering eyes surveyed the smooth surfaces of New York's skyscrapers. He had expected to be crushed into the pavement by their towering shadow and whizzed across the city in a high-powered automobile. The automobiles were high-powered, but they pulled him jerkily from block to block, like snails creeping, halting at every crossing for pedestrians and for the surging cross-traffic. Such congestion of machines and humanity he had never seen in all his life; nor had he ever experienced such a deafening roar, such a cacophony of shouting voices, purring traffic—and all of it suddenly driven into seeming silence by the wail of a fire-truck screeching warning of death.

Sergei Mikhailovich felt dazed. He wished that Alexandrov, who had remained in Paris to complete *Romance Sentimentale*, had come with them. Grisha could help ease the strain of the buzzing Press agents, movie journalists and people whose names and functions Eisenstein could not pin in his mind as they grabbed him, weaved about him, chattered, questioned, made irrelevant suggestions and loaded him with hospitality. The sea of lights at first seemed to drown out his sense of perspective so that he felt himself suspended in the air surrounded by a system of dazzling theatre wings through which the flood of headlights streamed down nameless streets.

Amidst the high-pitched impressions of strange things and unfamiliar people, the face of Joseph Freeman was a relief. With Joe, then the

[1] Leon Moussinac, with whom Eisenstein discussed this matter, later received a statement from Eisenstein while he was in Hollywood, explaining the arrangements he had made with the Soviet Government and Paramount.

editor of the *New Masses*, Sergei Mikhailovich could speak in his own idiom, hear words he could understand and be rid of the clackety-clack of movie jargon from the Paramount people. Freeman's America was altogether different. A rebellious world wounded and angry, conscious of the Depression that had brought bread lines, but failed to extinguish the lights of Broadway. Eisenstein had taught Freeman much about the Soviet Union; now it was Freeman's turn to teach Sergei Mikhailovich something about America.

Freeman's book, *Voices of October*, was at last in print. The publishers had held it up for two years because the book was considered too radical in 1928; with the Depression, it became acceptable. Sergei Mikhailovich was pleased that his statement, written for Freeman in Moscow, was included. Together with other statements he had made during the last four years to various Americans, Eisenstein's section made somewhat ominous reading to those who wanted to see in Sergei Mikhailovich's visit to America a danger to the capitalist system.

'Imagine a cinema which is not dominated by the dollar,' Sergei Eisenstein had written for Freeman's book. 'A cinema industry where one man's pocket is not filled at other people's expense; which is not for the pockets of two or three people but for the heads and hearts of one hundred and fifty million people. Every motion picture affects heads and hearts, but as a rule motion pictures are not produced especially for heads and hearts. Generally motion pictures are turned out for the benefit of two or three pockets; only incidentally do they affect the heads and hearts of millions.'[1]

In these words, Sergei Eisenstein had characterized the American film industry and contrasted it with the Soviet film industry from which 'the fat individual whales' had been driven out 'by a vast collective whale composed of little fishes' which the Revolution had released from oppression by 'a small body of masters'.[2]

Evidently the Press agents of Paramount had not read his words, or if they had, they had hastily forgotten them. Before Sergei Mikhailovich was allowed to draw many free breaths, the mechanism of building him into an impressive and respectable director began to operate. Dressed in an exceptionally elegant and correct suit, he was conducted to the photographers and posed against an elaborate, abstract panorama of lights and skyscrapers. Eisenstein must look the man he was: the modern genius in the modern world. The results of this art photography were striking. Sergei Mikhailovich's magnificent head and expressive face were wiped clean of all humour, intelligence and sensitivity. The retouch artist created a new man—dull as a model advertising expensive

[1] *Voices of October*, by Joseph Freeman (New York, Vanguard, 1930), p. 225.
[2] *Ibid.*

men's suiting; handsome enough to make the heart of American woman-hood beat just a little faster. He was turned into a fine hunk of noble-looking manhood.

The temperature of Sergei Mikhailovich's wit began to rise. It would take more than $900 every seven days to quench his humour and still his iconoclastic spirit. He had sworn to uphold the American Constitu-tion, including the Prohibition Amendment, but he had not sworn to shave himself every day, nor forsworn to wear his Russian workman's cap. So he omitted to shave. The second day he stroked his little stubble appreciatively and again omitted to shave; the third day he grinned with delight at his overgrown chin, stroked it tenderly and flipped on his Russian-made cloth cap. Arrayed in a baggy suit of tweeds, Sergei Mikhailovich sallied forth from his room in the Hotel Astor on Times Square to the luncheon at which Paramount was to introduce him to the New York Press.

As he rose to speak to the highly select gathering, he stroked his three days' stubble and smiled his most engaging, mocking smile; his eyes twinkled.

'I think,' said Sergei Mikhailovich, 'you picture all Russians with beards.' He slurred the word, whisking his small hands down his cheeks and chest in a lightning gesture. 'I did not wish to disappoint you, so I grew this beard of mine especially for you!'

The reaction of the gathering to this gibe has not been recorded. Eisenstein had flung his challenge to America. As quickly he turned off his wit and with perfect seriousness announced that he had come to America to make a real American film.

It was not long until all kinds of annoying things began to happen to Sergei Mikhailovich, and Paramount. Alexandrov sent word from Paris that his salary was being held up by the producers of *Romance Sentimentale*. The producers refused to pay him unless the film went forth to the world with Sergei Eisenstein's name attached.[1] With his indispensable comrade held in 'hock', Sergei Mikhailovich, without stopping to consider what *Romance Sentimentale* might do to his reputa-tion, cabled Alexandrov to put his name on and 'get the hell' to New York as fast as possible; he needed his company more than in all his life.

Old and New had opened in New York. It was premièred at the Cameo Theatre, a small cinema on Times Square where art films were shown. Since it was not another *Potemkin*, it made the people of Para-mount look at each other and wonder about their new director. *Old*

---

[1] The account of the circumstances under which Eisenstein's name came to appear as co-director of *Romance Sentimentale* was given to the author by Eisenstein. It is also confirmed by a letter written to Leon Moussinac by Eisen-stein while he was in Hollywood.

and New was a most embarrassing film. *Potemkin* could be labelled history, but here was Eisenstein extolling Soviet collectivization of agriculture when American journalists were writing reams about the horrors of this new Soviet plan.

Hurriedly Paramount began to consult with Eisenstein about a film. They proposed a story of the early Jesuit fathers, who converted the Indians of the South-west to Christianity. Sergei Mikhailovich was not interested. He suggested a film, based on Blaise Cendrar's novel *D'Or*, about John Sutter, the Swiss immigrant, upon whose Californian land gold was discovered in 1848. Paramount was not enthusiastic; but Sergei Mikhailovich continued to think about it. There was nothing for him to do but wait for Grisha to arrive from Paris. Then they would go immediately to the West Coast by way of Chicago.

With time on his hands, Sergei Mikhailovich began to sort out the many people he had met. As in Europe, he gravitated to those whom he liked rather than those who had power. He spent some time with D. W. Griffith, from whose work he had learned the elements of montage. He poked and pried about New York. Often he got lost. He was used to streets with names, not numbers. The avenues running north and south and the streets crossing east and west confused him with their sameness. Almost every street was a neutrality.

Eight years later, when Sergei Mikhailovich was immersed in speculation concerning man's response to words and the creation of images, he remembered how he taught himself to find his way around New York.

My memory assembled the theatres, stores and buildings characteristic of each of the streets I had to remember. This process went through definite stages. Two of these stages should be noted: in the first, at the verbal designation: 'Forty-second Street' my memory with great difficulty responded by enumerating the whole chain of characteristic elements, but I still obtained no true perception of the street because the various elements had not yet been consolidated into a single image. Only in the second stage did all the elements begin to fuse into a single, emerging image: at the mention of the street's 'number', there still arose this whole host of its separate elements, but now not as a chain, but as something single—as a whole characterization of the street, as its whole image.'[1]

The soaring skyscrapers appeared to Eisenstein 'to be built of a number of small-town buildings, piled on top of each other. One merely needs to go beyond the city-limits or, in a few cities, merely beyond the centre of the city, in order to see the same buildings, piled,

[1] S. M. Eisenstein, *The Film Sense* (London, Faber and Faber, 1948), p. 22.

not by the dozens, and fifties, and hundreds, on top of each other, but laid out in endless rows. . . . Where this provincial wave has swept in more than a cottage here or a church there (gnawing off a corner of that monumental Babylon, 'Radio City') . . . this good old provincialism has turned inward to apartments, nestling in clusters around fireplaces, furnished with soft grandfather-chairs and the lace doilies that shroud the wonders of modern technique: refrigerators, washing-machines and radios.'[1]

Before he left for Hollywood, arrangements were made by Monosson of Amkino, the Soviet film industry's agency in America, for Eisenstein to lecture at Columbia University and Harvard. On the 26th of May, Sergei Mikhailovich spoke at Columbia's McMillin Theatre with John Dewey, the philosopher, presiding. At Harvard he lectured under the auspices of the Department of Fine Arts.

During his visit to Boston, Sergei Mikhailovich stayed with his old friend, Professor H. W. L. Dana, at the house of Dana's grandfather, Henry Wadsworth Longfellow, on Brattle Street in Cambridge. It was here that George Washington had made his headquarters for part of the Revolutionary War, and where the literary circle around Longfellow had gathered. Every room contained intimate family trophies of American history and literature. Eisenstein would stand at the window of his room furnished in the elegant style of 18th and 19th century America and gaze at the wide lawn and the balustraded terrace below. Beyond were other houses which had not changed since colonial days. He thought of a film of American history woven around the house, every angle of which suggested a scheme of montage. George Kraska, then the manager of Boston's Fine Arts Theatre, took him to see more of colonial America—Lexington, Concord, and Bunker Hill. But, so far as Professor Dana knew, no word of such a film went down on paper.

To Dana, who had met Sergei Mikhailovich in the very different setting of his room in Moscow, it did not appear strange that he should be 'conventionally dressed in a dark blue business suit, soft collar, striped tie, with a corner of a handkerchief showing in the breast pocket of his coat'. Eisenstein seemed at home in the setting of Boston society who came to the Hotel Vendome to meet him at a luncheon. Among the guests were such notables as Mrs. Ralph Adams Cram and Mrs. Felix Frankfurter, the wife of Judge Felix Frankfurter. A slightly incongruous publicity stunt was introduced by the appearance of the canine movie star Rin-Tin-Tin with whom Sergei Mikhailovich was requested to share a loveseat while the press photographers clicked their

[1] *Film Form* by S. M. Eisenstein (New York, Harcourt Brace and Co., 1949 and London, Dennis Dobson, 1950), p. 197.

cameras. The dog's repertoire failed to impress Sergei Mikhailovich, who had made a study of Pavlov's reflex theory in relation to dogs. And he observed the reflexology of Bostonians during the space of an hour or so when he answered 'approximately 100 questions about Russia, Russian movies, the Russian soul and his own business. "You destroy illusions about Russia," one woman told him. "Illusions ought always to be destroyed," he said, "The truth is better."'[1]

At his lecture in the Baker Memorial Library of the Harvard Business School on the 26th of May, Eisenstein told his audience that the new type of films he planned to make as successors to *Old and New* (two reels of which were shown), 'will have the possibility of guiding not only the emotions of the audience but its process of thought'.

A number of Harvard psychologists listened attentively when Eisenstein remarked that 'the object of the new films is not to bring better sound effects to the audience, but to present abstract ideas. In this way the art of our time will have a new function and historical mission. The culture film, which makes people think, can bring a renaissance into the artistry of motion pictures. The new films provoke a new way of thinking in the audience and create new ideas.'[2]

Shortly after Eisenstein's visit to Boston, Alexandrov arrived from Paris and restored to each other's company the trio forgot their troubles. Before they set off for Hollywood they went to Abercrombie and Fitch and bought new camel-hair coats, several suits of good clothes, new luggage and the best cameras. As the train sped out of New York and across the continent, Sergei Mikhailovich saw the duality of America: 'the regiments of skyscrapers that moved deep into the countryside, with dense nets of railroads twisting around them; but at the same rate small-town agrarian America [appeared] to have overflowed into all but the very centres of the cities.'[3]

He was amazed by the unimagined 'abundance of small-town and patriarchal elements in American life and manners, morals and philosophy'.[4] The passengers on the streamlined train rushing through the night at a speed Sergei Mikhailovich had never experienced before were much more provincial than he had anticipated. He could not bring the women into focus; all individuality seemed to be lost beneath the paint and smart hair-styling. Yet he knew there were some who had personalities of their own. He had met one in New York, a dancer,

[1] 'Rin-Tin-Tin Does His Tricks for Noted Russian Movie Man', by Mason Ham (*Boston Herald*, 27 May 1930).

[2] 'Eisenstein Predicts New Type of Film' (*Globe*, Boston, May 27 1930).

[3] *Film Form* by S. M. Eisenstein (New York, Harcourt Brace and Co., 1949 and London, Dennis Dobson, 1950), p. 197.

[4] *Ibid.*, p. 198.

Sara Mildred Strauss, whose brother-in-law, Albert Rhys Williams, he had known in Russia. She was lively, warm and intelligent.

Arriving in Chicago on the 3rd of June, the Three Musketeers were met at the station by a young woman, Agnes Jacques, the executive secretary of the Society for Cultural Relations between the U.S.S.R. and America. No one was quite sure what to do with the distinguished guest, except that he had to be entertained in Chicago for several days.

Sergei Mikhailovich flummoxed Miss Jacques at the outset by ordering with a great gesture 'No museums!' and 'Take me to see Chicago'. So Agnes Jacques, her young doctor brother, Lawrence, and some of their friends bundled their disconcertingly exuberant guest into what they felt to be a too shabby car and took him to the ornate Palmer House Hotel. He barely sat down before he wanted to be off. For days they panted after him, each hour becoming more captivated by his energy and the charm of his childlike excitement, good nature and simple tastes.

First they took him to see Chicago's Gold Coast of North Michigan Avenue; but clasping his head he cried out: 'Take me away from these Babylonian things!' In an effort to show him the city, they took him to the top of the Chicago *Tribune* Tower. But he only stared uncomprehendingly at the sprawling industrial city.

'There's nothing to see!' exclaimed Sergei Mikhailovich.

His companions saw what he meant—an immense view of buildings, but no humanity, and he was seeking the details of American life.

They descended from the tower and took him to the small streets, the poor hideous streets—West Madison teeming with bums, Maxwell Street with its open markets, Halsted Street filled with Mexicans with striking faces, and the Black Ghetto, where the beauty and physical rhythm of the Negroes fascinated Sergei Mikhailovich. People enchanted him; forms intrigued his eye; a splash of light and shadow caused him to pause and speculate. He was thirsty for details, though he appeared to take little note of the social implications of what he saw, and he never talked politics.

Contrary to his former expectations, the steel mills of Gary bored him. He said to the Jacques that, since he was a Russian, everyone wanted to show him steel mills and factories. He preferred the municipal dance hall at Navy Pier, where he had a wonderful time dancing and stuffing himself with popcorn and cotton candy. He refused to be taken to fine places to eat and, in Chicago, he met for the first time the American institution—the cafeteria. The idea of waiting on himself pleased him enormously and, 'like a wedge', he headed into the Ontra Cafeteria on Wabash Avenue with his hosts following him.

Piling his tray high with food to satisfy what the others thought was a prodigious appetite, Sergei Mikhailovich draped a napkin over his arm and, hustling to a table with the best waiter's manner, unloaded his tray before an invisible patron with the expression and gestures of an attentive waiter. Tipping himself ten cents, he sat down to eat. His companions became almost hysterical with joy. What a man! They had never met anyone who gave them so much delightful fun, or one who was less demanding.

But Sergei Eisenstein did other things in Chicago than frisk and gambol like a child. Interested in the psychology and behaviour of criminals, he made contact with a University of Chicago criminologist, John Landesco, who took him to the lowest dives of the Al Capone gang in the Chicago suburb of Cicero. He also showed a very different side when he delivered a lecture at the University of Chicago in Mandel Hall on the 6th of June.

Nineteen years later, those who heard Eisenstein recalled with vivid clarity his extraordinary ability to explain his then almost unknown theories of montage, and his remarkable blending of humour and erudition. His vital personality and his crown of hair remained an unforgettable image in the minds of those who saw or met him. Even Eisenstein's gestures had remained as an after-image in the mind of Lawrence Jacques. An amazing man! In considered retrospect it suddenly struck Dr. Jacques that Sergei Eisenstein's legs and arms were possibly a little too short for his massive body. But what a magnificent head! [Plate 19]

More than a year later, when Eisenstein was in Mexico and in great trouble, he wrote to Agnes and Lawrence Jacques. But they did not answer. 'At the time we couldn't understand why a man as great as Eisenstein should remember us,' they said.

Leaving Chicago, Sergei Mikhailovich and his comrades travelled westward across Missouri and the prairie state of Kansas, flat as the far-horizoned land of the Ukraine. On the 13th of June 1930, the train stopped in New Mexico. Eisenstein bought a postcard of two Santo Domingo Indians and posted it to Leon Moussinac with the inscription 'The Family Moussinac!'

At last he arrived at the destination to which he had been bound since 1926; the place he later renamed 'Californica'. It was stranger by far than any movie: a fabulous world of Press agents, 'stars' and palm trees, where the only familiar thing was the tall, gangling figure of Ivor Montagu. Ivor Montagu and his wife became part of Eisenstein's retinue. They all lived in a hill-top house at 9481 Readcrest Drive in Coldwater Canyon, Beverly Hills, which Montagu had leased from Proctor ('Ted') Cook, the columnist. [Plate 34]

With $900 a week they could all live very comfortably together in the Spanish-style house with a swimming pool, employ the owner's cook, eat as much as they wanted and purchase a car. Rosie the cook was half Negro, quarter Irish, quarter Red Indian and wholly lovely; the car was an old secondhand De Sota, the most rattle-trap car in which a 'great' director ever rode about in the annals of Hollywood history.

Life was wonderful. Except when Sergei Mikhailovich was thrust into a role he did not know how to play, that of 'the man who has taken Europe by storm and whose pictures are to-day the subject of world discussion'. He played this role extremely badly; he 'fluffed' his lines; he danced where angels feared to tread. At a dinner given in his honour by a multi-millionaire, he is alleged to have invited the butler to exchange places with him, because, as he explained, it made him uncomfortable to be waited on. He committed heresies; he refused to drink, because he had sworn to uphold the 18th Amendment; he found Marlene Dietrich dull and Garbo a stupid woman, because she asked him who was this man called Lenin. He could not gauge what it was all about when Carl Laemmle asked him if Trotsky would write a scenario.[1] His refuge was Charlie Chaplin; but he could not understand how or why it was that Chaplin displayed all seriousness and had so little sense of fun. This disappointed him: he could not fathom it. Indeed, he really could not fathom anything of what went on around him except the fact that an enormous chasm divided the American film industry from the rest of American life. The very basis of film production in America was the exact opposite to what it was in his native land.

With optimism born of mixed idealism and a tragic ignorance, Eisenstein dreamed to fill this chasm by the creation of a real American film. So he commenced to run counter to nearly all the formulas of Hollywood and set himself in opposition to the accepted concepts of how to produce successful pictures. At the very outset he looked over the galaxy of stars presented to him for his choice with an eye chilled by utter indifference. Since he was basically opposed even to the use of professional actors on the screen, no star could rouse the least interest in him from an acting point of view. He was interested only in people and it was the people of America and California whom he immediately set out to study. He wanted to know the people and without any intention of personal affront Eisenstein cold-shouldered the stars. The only screen star, other than Chaplin, whose company he ever enjoyed was that of Colleen Moore, because she had a sense of humour and he thought she was so pleasantly natural. He had first seen her in Griffith's film *Intolerance*.

[1] S. M. Eisenstein, 'The Cinema in America' (*International Literature*, Moscow, No. 3, 1933).

This was, of course, not the behaviour Paramount had expected when they put Eisenstein under contract, nor when they set him up in a palatial office of two rooms, where he reminded an observant reporter who visited him a few days after his arrival, of 'nothing so much as a caged lion [who] was himself not yet conscious of captivity or restraint'. Never had Hollywood captured 'a robust genius' to 'whom this environment with its stark, unmitigated implications of commercialism seemed so great an impertinence as it [is] to this leonine Russian'.[1]

Paramount's campaign to 'sell' the name of Eisenstein to the American public was interrupted before Sergei Mikhailovich had been in Hollywood a week. On the 17th of June 1930, Jesse L. Lasky received the following telegram:[2]

If your Jewish clergy and scholars haven't enough courage to tell you and you yourself haven't enough brains to know better or enough loyalty toward this land, which has given you more than you ever had in history, to prevent your importing a cut-throat red dog like Eisenstein, then let me inform you that we are behind every effort to have him deported. We want no more red propaganda in this country. What are you trying to do, turn the American cinema into a communist cesspool? It won't take any Samson to pull down the bolshevik temple you are starting and at this rate it won't be long now Mene mene tekel upharsin. (signed) Major Frank Pease, president, Hollywood Technical Directors Institute.

This Major Pease, 'a professional American patriot', had looked up Eisenstein's origin and work and concluded he was a member of an alien and sinister political party. His next step was to circulate in California and throughout the United States a twenty-four-page document entitled 'Eisenstein, Hollywood's Messenger from Hell', in which Sergei Mikhailovich was presented as a dangerous alien, a Jew and one responsible for every alleged atrocity committed by the Bolsheviks since the October Revolution. Pease raised the cry: were Californians

---

[1] 'Eisenstein in Hollywood', by Clifford Howard (*Close-up*, August 1930).
[2] *Motion Picture Herald*, 28 June 1930. The article in which this telegram from Major Pease to Jesse L. Lasky was quoted reported that 'A group of men here [Hollywood] headed by Major Frank Pease, calling itself the Hollywood Technical Directors' Institute, is waging a vigorous campaign to stop national showing of *All Quiet on the Western Front*, and to railroad Dr. Sergei Eisenstein out of Hollywood. Their weapon is literature, correspondence and what little diplomatic contact they possess. . . . The argument set forth to combat the picture as well as the presence of Eisenstein in Hollywood is that both represent pacifist propaganda and that "there is no place in this country for such vicious propaganda or for representatives of it." '

going to sit idly by and let this 'Bolshevik murderer and robber' instil his insidious poison through American films?

In a Press release (typical of many put out by Pease), he said: 'We now learn of Lasky's importation from Moscow at a fabulous figure of "Eisenstein", to come here and make propaganda pictures for American boys and girls. It is this sadist and monster "Eisenstein", who has been glorifying in the red cinema the cutting of throats of Army and Navy officers. One is a trifle aghast that the rubber gates of Ellis Island were allowed to stretch wide enough to admit this vermin.' Major Pease went on to say that it was the holy mission of the Hollywood Directors' Institute to fight 'these Mesopotamian mongrels'.[1]

Pease was not speaking for himself alone; he was not merely an isolated 'crank' seeking publicity, although self-aggrandizement probably played a part in his activities. In linking 'Communists' with 'Jews', Pease reflected the anti-Semitism in California, and elsewhere in America, which increased as the Great Depression of the 'thirties deepened. He was the spokesman of many individuals and groups whose anti-Semitic attitudes had been expressed by innuendoes about the 'money changers' in the Temple and by advertisements in newspapers for the renting of flats and rooms—'Aryans preferred'—'For Gentiles Only'.

In characterizing Eisenstein as a 'Jewish Bolshevik' whom the successful Jews of Paramount had imported to make 'propaganda films', Pease created a focal point for the growing anti-Semitism. Eisenstein was the whipping boy for identifying 'Jews' with a 'menace' to 'the American way of life'. Major Pease, who was a product of the traditionally 'polite' New England variety of anti-Semitism, later vanished from the public scene, but his campaign brought the Fish Committee—the forerunner of the present House Committee on Un-American Activities—to Hollywood and helped to bring disaster to Eisenstein's efforts to make a film in America.

Hollywood began to shudder at the thought of being labelled unpatriotic for having brought Eisenstein to America. The publicity campaign to build him up as the world's most distinguished film director was now switched to a defence of him. The publicity writers riddled Pease's accusations with barbs of scorn. They argued that Paramount had brought Eisenstein to Hollywood for the sake of Art, and that Art was above political considerations. But in the executive offices of Paramount an uneasiness about Sergei Eisenstein began to grow. He was hastily photographed with Chaplin, Marlene Dietrich and Joseph von Sternberg. His friendship with Douglas Fairbanks was publicized, although at that moment Fairbanks, who was entertaining members of

[1] Rob Wanger's 'Script' (Hollywood, 28 June 1930).

the British Royal family at his estate, Pickfair, was attempting to avoid Eisenstein.

Mr. Krumgold of Paramount's publicity department arranged a banquet at the Ambassador Hotel in Los Angeles for Eisenstein and Alexandrov, to which the world Press was invited. In an atmosphere of cigar-smoke, Sergei Mikhailovich was presented by Paramount's B. P. Schulberg, but his speech was short. Some foreign reporters took offence at what they claimed were Eisenstein's derogatory remarks about European films. In a letter to Leon Moussinac,[1] Eisenstein claimed that in his report in *Cinemonde*,[2] Jacques Lory had entirely misinterpreted his statements.

The 'three Roossians', as Hollywood called Eisenstein, Tisse and Alexandrov, were objects of curiosity. The gossip columnists followed Sergei Mikhailovich's movements. One commented that he looked and thought like an Irishman. At a dinner given in his honour by Ernst Lubitsch, where the guests included Marlene Dietrich and Joseph von Sternberg, he was described as a man with 'a tremendous forehead that runs completely over and beyond the horizon; smiling blue eyes, a Harvey Thew nose, and a handsome mouth revealing teeth that could be tooth-pasted with profit by any advertiser'.[3] His witty quips were copy for bored journalists; his play on slang most entertaining: '"Boloney," mused Eisenstein, "I shall call my daughter boloney."'

Studios other than Paramount entertained him. He went to Walt Disney's studio where he met Mickey Mouse. In Boston, Eisenstein had said that the most interesting director in America was 'the man who directs the Mickey Mouse's films, animated cartoons with sound'.

Paul Kohner, then a leading producer at Universal, who had met Sergei Mikhailovich in Berlin, encouraged Carl Laemmle Sr., Universal's president, to arrange a luncheon for Eisenstein in the inner sanctum of the studio's commissary. Here 'Uncle Carl', who gave the impression of a baby octopus, suggested a 'big picture' to the slightly embarrassed Eisenstein who reminded Laemmle he *was* already under contract to Paramount. Not deterred, 'Uncle Carl' is reported to have waved this aside. With hands cupped as if full of gold, he wheedled 'just in case things don't work out with Paramount'. Sergei Mikhailovich glanced across the table at Seymour Stern, who had been hoping Eisenstein would come to work for Universal, and remarked

[1] 'Après le Banquet d'Hollywood', a letter by Eisenstein to Leon Moussinac, (*Cinemonde*, Paris, No. 103, 9 October 1930).
[2] Report of banquet in Eisenstein's honour in Hollywood by Jacques Lory (*Cinemonde*, Paris, No. 39, 31 July 1930).
[3] Rob Wanger's 'Script' (Hollywood, 9 August 1930).

irreverently something to the effect that 'the capitalists are beginning to cut each other's throats over me!'

The luncheon was followed by a grand tour of inspection of Universal's lot; introductions to innumerable people—Frederick Kohner, John Aurer, Werner Muller, Jack Ross and Werner Klinger, now a director in Eastern Germany—and the taking of photographs: 'Uncle Carl' and Eisenstein; Edward Cahn, the director, Seymour Stern, members of Universal's staff and Eisenstein, Tisse and Alexandrov. It was all a part of a day in Hollywood except for Eisenstein's meeting with Seymour Stern, who was fired with a passion for the possibilities of film as an art, and who later became one of the editors of 'Experimental Cinema', along with David Platt and Lewis Jacobs.

Because Sergei Mikhailovich found few people in the Mecca of cinematography who thought of the cinema as he did, he paid more attention to Stern than to the famous 'names' who formed the backbone of Hollywood. As time passed, he spent much time with Stern. They would meet and talk for hours concerning montage. Sometimes Stern brought along other people, other times Eisenstein and Stern would go down to the beach and discuss film art. Louis H. Sackin, an editor at Universal who later became president of the Film Editors' Union, forgets the exact details of some of these conversations, but recalls the impression Eisenstein made: a witty man of 'penetrating intelligence with some of the surface gaiety of a clown and also the underlying sadness. That high-domed, balding head, somehow accented the symbol of a clown.'

There is no record of what the seductive Marlene Dietrich, Greta Garbo, or any of their Hollywood sisters thought of Eisenstein. Set apart from these fabulous creatures, who failed to impress Sergei Mikhailovich, was a German girl, Christel Gang. She was a translator at Universal Pictures and also worked as secretary to Seymour Stern.

One day, Stern took her to the hill-top house in Coldwater Canyon because she had translated some of Eisenstein's essays, which had appeared in the German magazine *Querschnitt*, and also Pudovkin's book, *Film Technique*. To Christel Gang, Sergei Mikhailovich immediately seemed like an old friend. She found him warmly responsive, fascinating, attractive. Occasionally she went to the hill-top house and took notes for him and typed them up. She had a deep admiration for him and in time she felt a sincere affection for him.

They were interested in the same things and they talked much about art, cinema and photography. After some time, Christel Gang showed Sergei Mikhailovich a collection of abstract photographs by Edward Weston, whose work Eisenstein admired. She asked him to keep the one he liked best, and he chose an abstract nude of a woman's back. It turned out that the model had been Christel Gang. A play of sentiment began to grow. She became 'Gangster' to Sergei Mikhailovich and one day he presented her with 'a vibrant red heart with fancy sugar decoration all around it. It was a fat jolly-looking little thing and in a most suggestive spot he placed his bold signature.' She shared his delight in souvenirs and responded. But Eisenstein lived in a house surrounded with many people who made claims upon him, and Christel Gang was involved in her own work.

In the strange atmosphere of Hollywood, Sergei Mikhailovich set to work to find a story acceptable to Paramount. The first subject he attempted was an idea of his own which he called *Glass House*.[1]

Eisenstein was struck by the use of glass in modern building in Western Europe and America, especially where it was used for partitions to separate people in large offices. From this sprang the idea that the use of glass was symbolical of many people's attitude of mind in capitalist society. They appeared to be withdrawn and isolated from each other even when no glass partition physically separated them. Hence, the first dramatic climax in *Glass House* was to come when two characters became aware of their isolation and wished to break through the psychological 'wall of glass' surrounding them. At this point Sergei Mikhailovich found he could not develop his idea further.

Since neither Alexandrov, nor Ivor Montagu who had joined the unit, could devise a story to clothe this idea, Eisenstein sought the aid of Hollywood script writers. He selected those who had previously written detective and thriller films; but all their suggestions were too whimsical for a film which Eisenstein wanted to be a quite realistic story but with a philosophic undertone.

It is said that when he was unable to find a solution for *Glass House*, he consulted a psychologist to find out why he could not evolve a story around his idea. But getting nowhere, he abandoned both the idea and the psychologist. He returned to the idea of *Sutter's Gold*, although it had not appealed to Paramount. It was a wonderful theme: the very foundation of California's growth—the gold rush of 1849. He had found the main theme for his film in the French novel *D'Or*, by Blaise Cendrars, which he had brought with him from Paris.

According to his method, Eisenstein did no work on the script until he had read, marked and studied all the written matter which had any-thing to do with the theme. This took him three or four weeks, while his collaborators did nothing at all. Alexandrov went on a round of parties and, as in Paris, made friends. Tisse spent his time studying the

[1] The report of *Glass House* is based on an account of Ivor Montagu. Another account, given by Jay Leyda, is that *Glass House* was to have been based upon the novel *We* by Eugene Zamiatin.

technical development in camerawork. When Sergei Mikhailovich had finished his study, he sallied forth with his collaborators in holiday mood. They went to look over the scene in the country surrounding Sacramento and Sutter's Fort, where gold had first been discovered in February 1848. In the spirit of a biographer and antiquarian, Sergei Mikhailovich sought out everyone who knew anything about the gold-rush days. He collected stories and accounts of how people were said to have behaved; he talked with elderly ladies who, as children, had sat on Sutter's lap. Though he had never done this kind of research except in his own country, he knew what he wanted and how to get it. [Plate 19]

With these impressions fresh in his mind, he returned to Hollywood and wrote a draft treatment in three days, working almost without pause. Eisenstein dictated his ideas to Alexandrov, who wrote them in Russian, here and there simplifying the words. The script was immediately typed and translated. As the translations came through, Sergei Mikhailovich discussed it, and the script in general, with Montagu. Thus, Eisenstein would be dealing with a relatively complete first reel of the script while still preparing reel five or six with Alexandrov. As part of the draft treatment, he separately prepared his own director-designer's note-book, making basic sketches for settings with notes as to how many extras he needed for a particular sequence. He went so far as to decide essential properties, for example, 'frogs for frog races'. In fact, this man, who was interested in anything and everything, could be most exact and concise; though he lived in an untidy maze of books with ideas jotted on hundreds and thousands of scraps of paper, he could, when the time came, discipline himself to complete order.

When the draft treatment of *Sutter's Gold* was presented to Paramount, word got around Hollywood that it was a brilliant piece of work. But on the heels of the superlatives came the second and determining reaction: Paramount didn't like the moral imbedded in *Sutter's Gold*—that gold is the source of destruction to man and nature. Paramount could not accept a script which presented John Sutter, the first settler in Sacramento, a rich and prosperous farmer, reduced to the depths of ruin, ruin to his land and himself, when gold is discovered near his sawmill.

In recalling Paramount's rejection of his treatment, Eisenstein told a reporter later, 'I wanted to make *Sutter's Gold*. I had brought the book along. . . . They preached box-office to me. . . . Nice elderly ladies said Mrs. Sutter should be pictured as a nicer character than she really was. And the Daughters of Something or Another got interested and raised a row. And a Major Pease and his Blue Shirts said I was a "Red Dog" and shouldn't be allowed to stay in the country. And the producers

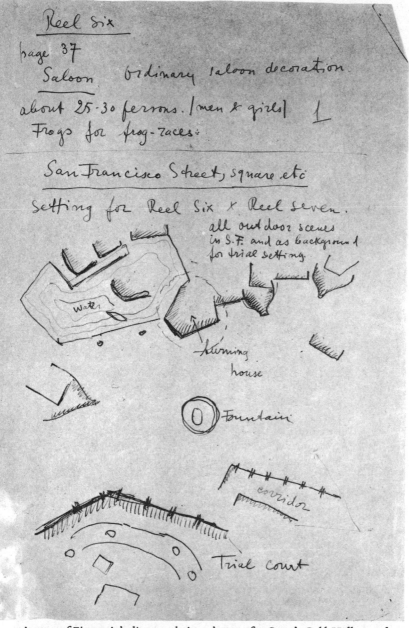

Reel Six

page 37
Saloon   Ordinary saloon decoration.

about 25-30 persons. [men & girls]   1
Frogs for frog-races:

San Francisco Street, square etc

Setting for Reel Six & Reel Seven.

all outdoor scenes
in S.F. and as background
for trial setting.

water

turning
house

Fountain

corridor

Trial court

A page of Eisenstein's director-designer's notes for *Sutter's Gold*, Hollywood, 1930. The most striking aspects of Eisenstein's scenario are, the spectacle element foreshadowing *Alexander Nevsky* and *Ivan the Terrible* and the vivid use of an imaginative range of sound including, in the earlier sequences, the refrain of a song which becomes the song of Sutter and of California. The whole concept, as well as the audio-visual style indicated in the script, suggests a film far ahead of its time; indeed a film full of experiment which might have been made in the 1970s.

complained that I didn't seem to get sex appeal into my films. And the race question entered into my difficulties, too, and I don't mean the Negro race.'[1]

Then Paramount handed Eisenstein a book they had kept on the shelf for a number of years. This was the monumental novel, *An American Tragedy*, by Theodore Dreiser, 'the old grey lion', who had visited Sergei Mikhailovich in his small room on the Chysti Prudi.

As he took the book, along with an unspoken ultimatum from the Paramount executives, Sergei Eisenstein knew it was 'a work that [had] every chance of being numbered among the classics of this period and place. That this material contained the collision of two irreconcilable viewpoints—the "front office"' and his own. Paramount wanted 'a simple, tight whodunit about murder' from Dreiser's novel 'as broad and shoreless as the Hudson . . . as immense as life itself'; yet Sergei Mikhailovich knew that 'this epic of cosmic veracity and objectivity had to be assembled in a tragedy—and this was unthinkable without a world attitude of direction and point'.

With $900 every seven days in his pocket, Sergei Eisenstein could oblige his employers with a film 'about the love of a boy and a girl'; or he could remember the philosophy of life in the land from which he had come where he had first read *An American Tragedy* and concluded that Clyde Griffiths, and the murder for which he went to the electric chair, resulted from 'the sum total of social relations, the influence of which he was subjected to at every stage of his unfolding biography and character'.[2]

While Eisenstein was deciding upon his course—his obligations to 'the old grey lion' and to himself—he made his usual tour of inspection. This included searching the filling stations and hotels of Los Angeles for a young man to play the part of Clyde Griffiths and a later visit to Sing-Sing prison where he saw the electric chair with 'the brightly polished spittoon' set for the convenience of men condemned to death.

The campaign instituted by Major Pease against Eisenstein had not abated. In recalling his experiences in America many years later, Eisenstein said: 'I had a certain foretaste of hostile people and their attitude

[1] It is thought by some well-informed people that an important contributory factor in Paramount's rejection of *Sutter's Gold* was the inter-office struggle between two factions, one headed by Eisenstein's sponsor, Jesse L. Lasky, the other by B. P. Schulberg, who opposed the projects in which Lasky had an interest. The Schulberg faction was in the ascendancy throughout the period of Eisenstein's contract with Paramount.

[2] *Film Form* by S. M. Eisenstein (New York, Harcourt Brace and Co., 1949 and London, Dennis Dobson, 1950), p. 96.

towards me and my country. . . . Besides that I had some disagreements and disagreeable attacks by forerunners of the Fascist Movement in the streets.'[1]

Eisenstein's reference to attacks 'in the streets' probably refers to a telephone call received by the Paramount office from a small town in the San Fernando Valley. The anonymous caller threatened Paramount that if they did not send the 'Moscow Jew, Eisenstein, back where he came from,' he would be kidnapped, if necessary from the streets of Los Angeles, and taken into the Mohave Desert and hanged on a Joshua tree.

The story was picked up by the movie trade journals and newspapers, but Sergei Mikhailovich merely joked about it to Seymour Stern and others. Yet he must have been shocked and filled with apprehension, even though it appears that nothing more than intimidation was intended. He was well aware of the 'iron hand' of the Better America Federation, which 'ruled' California, and of the activities of the Los Angeles 'Red Squad' under the leadership of Capt. William ('Red') Hynes. Eisenstein had every reason to suppose that if an attack were made upon him, the police might stand idly by because many were known to be anti-Semitic with a hatred for 'foreigners' and 'radicals'.[2]

Later, Sergei Mikhailovich concealed from me, and from others, that he had ever been made a personal target for anti-Semitism. He refused to let me read the pamphlet by Major Pease, which he kept. He said: 'It's not amusing; it's disgusting. The vilest things were said about me for political reasons.'

Major Pease, who had the support of many powerful people, sent telegrams demanding Eisenstein's deportation to Representative Hamilton Fish of New York and other congressmen and senators.[3]

[1] Report of an interview on 16 July 1946, between Eisenstein and Lee Bland for Columbia Broadcasting System, U.S.A.

[2] *Southern California Country*, by Carey McWilliams (New York, Duell, Sloan and Pearce, 1946), pp. 290-291.

[3] A copy of the following letter, part of a printed document put out by Major Frank Pease, National Commander, American Defenders, Marblehead, Mass., is in the file on Sergei M. Eisenstein in the Theatre and Film Department of the New York Public Library:

UNITED STATES SENATE

Committee on Mines and Mining

FROM U.S. SENATOR ODDIE   WASHINGTON, D.C.

My dear Major Pease:

This will acknowledge the receipt of your good letter of Dec. 3, making available information which will be of assistance in supporting the bill which I have introduced prohibiting Russian imports. . . .

But Sergei Eisenstein remained silent. What was there for him to say? He was a Russian; he did support the Soviet regime; his father was of Jewish descent; but he had not come to the United States to overthrow the system. To accuse him of such a thing was ridiculous.

So Sergei Mikhailovich went on with his work of preparing the first treatment of *An American Tragedy*. If he failed to write a script Paramount would accept, he would return to his native land as the distinguished son who produced not a single work as a result of a year's leave, which the Soviet Government had extended.

Strange as it may seem, Sergei Mikhailovich, the man of inner con-

---

I should like to learn if you have any objection to my using your letter on the floor of the Senate. . . .

I wish to thank you for sending me the Declaration of Principles of the AMERICAN DEFENDERS. . . .

All this work is very helpful in support of my bill to prohibit imports from Russia.

> Very sincerely yours
> (Signed) TASKER L. ODDIE (End)

The cuts in the above letter were made by Major Frank Pease.

The following letter is part of the document from the file mentioned before. It was addressed to Major Pease by the National Civic Federation of New York City:

Major Frank Pease,
   Marblehead, Mass.   Jan. 8, 1931.

Dear Major Pease:

Pardon me for not sooner returning the matter which you were good enough to let me have. 'Eisenstein, Hollywood's Messenger from Hell', is the most terrific piece of English I have ever read. In fact, you are the ne plus ultra, super-super slinger of invectives It is too bad you drove him out, because now you cannot issue such a letter. However, it ought to be published, anyhow, and with an introduction that would carry it over. . . . You talk about what the Government knows, but the Government did not know the things you thought it did, and it knows still less now—all of which I hope will be cleaned up by the legislation secured by the Fish Committee. It will not have much chance in this short session, because the Civil Liberties Union has already started its fight and can probably rally enough Red Senators to block it, although the Fish Committee may sweep it through.

> Sincerely yours,
> (Signed) R. M. EASLEY
> Ralph M. Easley
> Chairman Executive Council.

N.B. The above 'Eisenstein' matter is a document of 24 pages whose private circulation, both here and abroad, brought about this soviet propagandist's removal from our country. . . .F.P.

flict, never hesitated as to the character of his treatment of Dreiser's book. He had been born to a comfortable prosperity and he loved beautiful and expensive things; but he had lived a Spartan existence for thirteen years. Now he enjoyed luxury again and could eat all he wanted after years of bitter hunger which he never could forget. Still, it did not enter his extraordinary mind to deviate from his own vision.

'I could not compromise,' he said to me four years later. 'It was not virtue in me. I cannot destroy a work with compromise. I have to retain my integrity as an artist.'

Instead of extracting the murder story resulting from Clyde Griffiths' involvement with two girls—the factory worker, Roberta, and the rich girl, Sondra—Sergei Mikhailovich sought to retain Dreiser's total social setting, which implied that Clyde's personal tragedy was the symbolic tragedy of American society. Dreiser had shown Clyde pulled between love for the average girl and ambition to get on in the world through the rich girl who had fallen in love with him. It was the handling of the total socio-economic and political setting which had provoked such difficulties that Paramount had left the novel on the shelf for five years. It was approached—but no more than approached—by the patriarch of films David Wark Griffith, and by Lubitsch and many others. Now Eisenstein unhesitatingly reduced the very long novel to the dimensions of a film. Unlike many, if not most, film adaptations of long and important novels, Sergei Mikhailovich's treatment was not a rewrite of Dreiser's book. It was a remarkably faithful transcription of *An American Tragedy* from the novel form to the film form. Again Sergei Mikhailovich made director-designer notes, many of which were a break-down of shots with notations as to dialogue. (See page 178.)

With Dreiser's consent, Eisenstein made certain changes and clarifications. The major clarification was in relation to the actual circumstances of Roberta's death; how Clyde's intention to murder her was tangled by the *accidental* overturning of the boat. Dreiser presented 'the matter so impartially that the further development of events is left formally, not to the logical course of the story, but to the processes of law'. Thus it appeared to Sergei Mikhailovich imperative 'to sharpen the *actual* and *formal* innocence of Clyde within the very act of perpetrating the crime' in order to make 'precise the "monstrous challenge" of a society whose mechanism brings a rather characterless youth to such a predicament and then, invoking morality and justice, seats him in the electric chair'. To do this, Eisenstein chose the situation of Clyde wanting to kill Roberta but, like Hamlet, being unable to translate his wish into action, because, at the decisive moment, he falters through weakness of will.

However [wrote Eisenstein] before this inner 'defeat', he excites

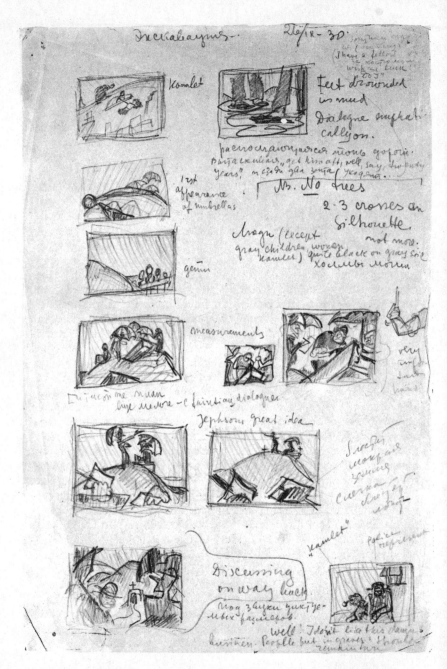

A break-down of shots for *An American Tragedy*, Hollywood, summer 1930

in the girl Roberta such a feeling of alarm that, when he leans towards her, already defeated inwardly and ready 'to take everything back', she recoils from him in horror. The boat, off balance, rocks. When, in trying to support her, he accidentally knocks his camera against her face, she finally loses her head and in her terror stumbles, falls and the boat overturns.

For greater emphasis we show her rising to the surface again. We even show Clyde trying to swim to her. But the machinery of crime has been set in motion and continues to its end, even against Clyde's will. Roberta cries out weakly, tries to retreat from him in her horror, and, not being able to swim, drowns.

Being a good swimmer, Clyde reaches the shore and, coming to his senses, continues to act in accordance with the fatal plan he had prepared for the crime—from which he had deviated only for a moment in the boat.[1]

This central episode of Eisenstein's first treatment of *An American Tragedy* afforded Sergei Mikhailovich an opportunity to experiment with the idea long in his mind—that of the 'internal monologue'. To him it was the means of revealing the internal processes of man's thoughts and emotions. Eisenstein had great knowledge of the inner nature of man and he wished to use his knowledge for the advancement of art. For years he had studied the development of 'streams of consciousness' in literature and the 'internal monologue', which had come to its fullest expression in Joyce's *Ulysses*.

Clyde Griffiths' inner struggle to murder or not to murder offered Sergei Mikhailovich the perfect psychological situation for portrayal of an 'internal monologue'. Thus, in Reel 10 of his treatment, Eisenstein was able to translate his long-held theory into specific form. Even on paper the first treatment pulsates with the inner life of Clyde.

(22) As the boat glides into the darkness of the lake, so Clyde glides into the darkness of his thoughts. Two voices struggle within him— one: 'Kill—kill!' the echo of his dark resolve, the frantic cry of all his hopes of Sondra and society; the other: 'Don't—don't kill!' the expression of his weakness and his fears, of his sadness for Roberta and his shame before her. In the scenes that follow, these voices ripple in the waves that lap from the oars against the boat; they whisper in the beating of his heart; they comment, underscoring, upon the memories and alarums that pass through his mind; each ever struggling with the other for mastery, first one dominating then weakening before the onset of its rival.

[1] *Film Form* by S. M. Eisenstein (New York, Harcourt Brace and Co., 1949 and London, Dennis Dobson, 1950), p. 99.

They continue to murmur as he pauses on his oars to ask:
'Did you speak to anyone in the hotel?'
'No. Why do you ask?'
'Nothing. I thought you might have met someone.'
(23) The voices shudder as Roberta smiles and shakes her head in answer, playfully letting her hand fall into the water.
'It isn't cold,' she says.
Clyde stops rowing and also feels the water, but his hand springs back as though it had received an electric shock.
(24) As he photographs her, the voices preoccupy him. While they picnic, or pick water-lilies, they possess him. As he jumps ashore a moment to put down his grip the voices rise and torment him.
(25) 'Kill—kill', and Roberta, happy, freshened by her faith in him, is radiant with joy of living. 'Don't kill—don't kill', and as the boat drifts almost soundlessly by the dark pines and Clyde's face is racked by the struggle within him, there rises the long-drawn-out booming cry of a waterbird.
(26) 'Kill—kill' triumphs, and there passes through his mind the memory of his mother. 'Baby—baby' comes the voice of his childhood, and as 'Don't kill—don't kill' rises he hears 'Baby boy—baby boy' in the so different voice of Sondra, and at the image of Sondra and the thought of all that surrounds her 'Kill—kill' grows harder and insistent, and with the thought of Roberta importunate it grows still harsher and shriller, and then the face of Roberta now aglow with faith in him and her great relief, and the sight of the hair he had so loved to caress, and 'Don't—don't kill' grows and tenderly supplants the other and now is calm and firm and final. Ending the conflict, Sondra is lost for ever. Never, never now will he have the courage to kill Roberta.[1]

In an analysis of his treatment of *An American Tragedy* Eisenstein wrote:

Only the sound-film is capable of reconstructing all phases and all specifics of the course of thought.
What wonderful sketches those montage lists were!
Like thought, they would sometimes proceed with visual images. With sound. Synchronized or non-synchronized. Then as sounds. Formless. Or with sound-images: with objectively representational sounds. . . .
Then suddenly, definite intellectually formulated words—as 'in-

[1] *An American Tragedy*, 'first treatment' by S. M. Eisenstein and Ivor Montagu, a copy of which is in the Eisenstein Collection, Museum of Modern Art, New York.

tellectual' and dispassionate as pronounced words. With a black screen, a rushing imageless visuality.

Then in passionate disconnected speech. Nothing but nouns. Or nothing but verbs. Then interjections. With zigzags of aimless shapes, whirling along with these in synchronization.

Then racing visual images over complete silence.

Then linked with polyphonic sounds. Then polyphonic images. Then both at once.

Then interpolated into the outer course of action, then interpolating elements of the outer action into the inner monologue.

As if presenting inside the characters the inner play, the conflict of doubts, the explosion of passions, the voice of reason, rapidly or in slow-motion, marking the differing rhythms of one and the other and, at the same time, contrasting with the almost complete absence of outer action: a feverish inner debate behind the stony mask of the face.[1]

From this point of the 'internal monologue', Eisenstein's first treatment pursued a psychological and tragic deepening until it mounted 'to an almost Grecian level of "blind Moira-fate"', that once conjured into existence will not relax its hold on the one who summoned it'.

In the novel, the hunting down of Clyde, his trial, conviction and death in the electric chair, take up almost the last half of the story. Eisenstein saw the endless game of advocacy in the court as based upon 'the sanctity of the *formal* principle in the codes of honour, morality, justice, and religion ... primary and fundamental in America.

'The defence lawyers have no essential doubt that a crime was committed. None the less, they invent a 'change of heart' experienced by Clyde under the influence of his love and pity for Roberta. ... But this is made far more evil when there *really* was such a change. When this change comes from quite different motives. When there really was no crime. When the lawyers are convinced that there was a crime. And with a downright lie, so near the truth and at the same time so far from it, they endeavour in this slanderous way to whitewash and save the accused.

'As part of the background of the trial it is indicated that the true aim of the trial and prosecution of Clyde, however, has no relation to him whatsoever. This aim is solely to create the necessary popularity among the farming population of the state (Roberta was a farmer's daughter) for the prosecuting District Attorney Mason, so that he may win the necessary support for his nomination as judge.

[1] *Film Form* by S. M. Eisenstein (New York, Harcourt Brace and Co., 1949 and London, Dennis Dobson, 1950), p. 105.

'The defence take on a case which they know to be hopeless ("at best ten years in the penitentiary") on the same plane of political struggle. . . . For one side, as for the other, Clyde is merely a means to an end. . . . Thus is tragically expanded and generalized the fortunes of the particular case of Clyde Griffiths into a genuinely "American tragedy in general."

'The whole tangle of design within the trial itself was almost entirely eliminated in the script's construction, and was replaced by the pre-election bidding, visible through the manipulated solemnity of the courtroom, being used as nothing more than a drill-ground for a political campaign.

'This fundamental treatment of the murder determines the tragic deepening and the strengthened ideological sharpness of yet another part of the film and another figure: the mother.

'Clyde's mother runs a mission. Her religion is a purblind fanaticism . . . her teachings and principles, her aim towards Heaven rather than training her son for work were the initial premises for the ensuing tragedy.

'In our treatment Clyde, in his death-cell, confesses to his mother (rather than to the Reverend McMillan, as in the novel) that, though he did not kill Roberta, he planned to do so.

'His mother, for whom the word is the deed, and the thought of sin equivalent to its execution, is stunned by his confession. . . . When she goes to the Governor with a petition for her son's life, she is startled by his direct question: "Do you yourself believe in your son's innocence?" At this moment that is to decide the fate of her son—she is silent.

'The petition is disregarded, and the dogma and dogmatism of its bearer are alike discredited. The mother's fatal moment of silence cannot even be washed away by her tears. . . . The more poignant these last scenes become in sadness, the more bitterly do they lash at the ideology that brought this sadness.

'Dreiser was the first to salute all that had been brought to his work'[1] by Eisenstein's treatment.

In the light of his subsequent life, it appears that with the completion of the Dreiser scenario with its motif of 'blind fate', Eisenstein's own life passed into a circuitous web of 'doom' which would not, it seemed, relax its hold on him for more than a few years at any one time. Over and over again he was to fail through a curious strengthening of the forces orientated, as they were, towards frustrating the fulfilment of his deepest desires in creative and academic work, and even in his personal life.

[1] *Film Form* by S. M. Eisenstein (New York, Harcourt Brace and Co., 1949 and London, Dennis Dobson, 1950), pp. 98, 100 *et seq.*

With Jean-Georges Auriol as 'machine-gunner'

Eisenstein 'directs' at the International Avant-Garde Congress at La Sarraz, Switzerland, September, 1929

As 'Don Quixote'

Eisenstein in an improvised *Ballet of the British Bobby*, London, 1929
Clips from negative given to the author by Eisenstein

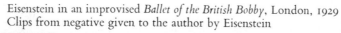

Angeles (See Foreword)

'Menaced Lives'

By courtesy of Mr & Mrs
    Sanford Shepard

She selects these paintings, alon
with many more to reveal
Eisenstein's influence upon her
work

'Death Falling from a Cloud'
(Atomic Death)

By courtesy of Mr & Mrs Nils Pal

Leaving Chicago for
Hollywood, June 10

On the way to Sacramento by steamer.
Inscribed on the back: 'I cannot escape the
religious'

Eisenstein in America, 1930

Meeting Upton Sinclair in
Hollywood

'The iron and fire of the Catholicism that Cortez brought' (Outline)

A symbolic ceremony—journey to Calvary—to be intercut in the 'Fiesta' story

'They pay with their lives' on the Day of Corpus Christi. A recurrent motif in the 'Maguey' story

The unfinished *Que Viva Mexico!* 1931-32

'The unity of death and life. The passing of one and the birth of the next one' (Outline)

By courtesy of Seymour Stern

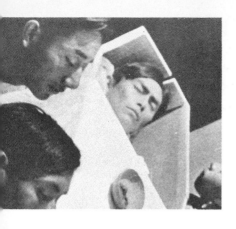
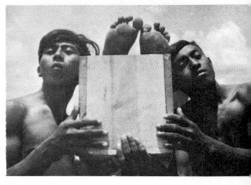

'In the realms of death, where the past still prevails over the present, there the starting point of our film is laid . . .' Prologue (Scenario, *Que Viva Mexico!*)

Siqueiros' 'Burial of a Worker' which inspired these shots

Sebastian and maguey

Conspirators

'Long before dawn . . .'

Sebastian awaits death

'The slow, sad tunes of a song'

Eisenstein's
sketch of peon

Maria finds Sebastian

Maguey plant

Peon drawing pulque

'Fiesta' story

'Sandunga' story

Women mourning
Christ 'bleeding like
the human sacrifices
that were made on
the top of pyramids',
(Outline)

Eisenstein's eternal
triangle

The unfinished *Que Viva Mexico!* 1931–32

'like serpents are the
waves of black and
heavy hair ...',
(Outline)

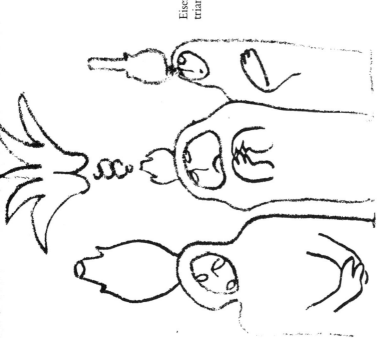

With Alexandrov directing the Prologue for *Que Viva Mexico!* at Chichen-Itza,
Yucatan, 1931

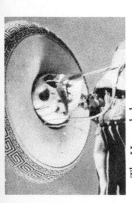

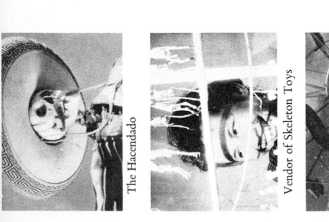

By courtesy of the British Film Institute
Dancers in death masks

The General removes his mask

The General

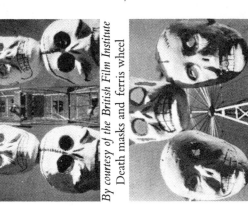

By courtesy of the British Film Institute
Skulls and merry-go-round

By courtesy of the British Film Institute
Death masks and ferris wheel

Triangle and circle

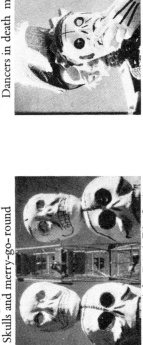

The Hacendado

Vendor of Skeleton Toys

Drummer in death mask

The unfinished *Que Viva Mexico!* 1931–32 Death Day and some of its motifs

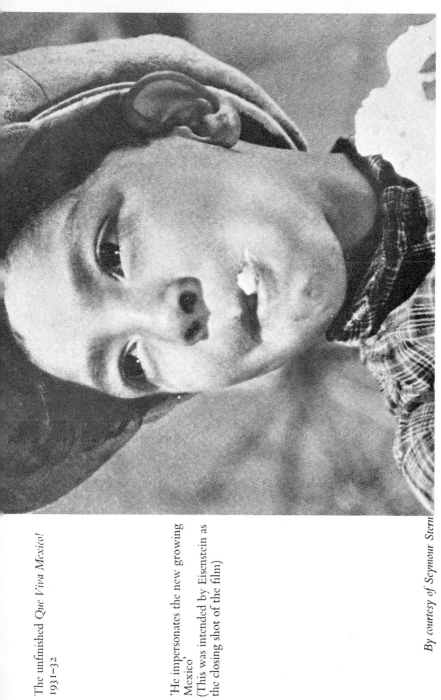

The unfinished *Que Viva Mexico!*
1931–32

'He impersonates the new growing Mexico',
(This was intended by Eisenstein as the closing shot of the film)

By courtesy of Seymour Stern

Calavera of the Zapatistas

One of the many works of Jose Guadelupe Posada inspiring Eisenstein's Death Day, the culmination of *Que Viva Mexico!*

The Hacienda of Tetlapayac, Mexico, 1931
Front row, left to right: Grigori Alexandrov (*second*), Don Julio Salivar (*third*), Eisenstein (*fourth*), Eduard Tisse (*fifth*). *Top of stairs:* Hunter Kimborough

gei and 'Doly', a skull made of sugar (Photograph by Jimenez)   *By courtesy of Seymour Stern*
gei and 'Sara' from the Mexico City Medical School   *By courtesy of Seymour Stern*

30

Eisenstein with Diego Rivera, Freda Rivera and a friend, probably Frances Flynn Paine

At the Palacio Nacional, Mexico City, 1931

By courtesy of Seymour Ste...

Sergei Eisenstein, a portrait by Jean Charlot, New York 1932

Travelling through the South on the way
from Laredo to New York, spring, 1932

Paul Robeson, Herbert Marshall and Sergei Eisenstein, Moscow, 1934

He was to remain mute until too late when he should have spoken clearly; he was to speak too fast and in the wrong tenor when he should have kept silent. But whatever his fate, and no matter how serious the work on which he was engaged, Sergei Mikhailovich's sense of humour was unquenchable. In the midst of completing the scenario his mind whirled off to a visual pun—'Roberta sitting on her trunk.'   [Plate 61]

On October the 5th, 1930, when *An American Tragedy* was completed and copies of the treatment were being mimeographed, Sergei Mikhailovich wrote the following letter on his personal grey-tinted stationery to Paramount to be enclosed with the script:

S. M. Eisenstein
An American Tragedy
First Treatment
GENTLEMEN:

So here we see the miracle accomplished—An American Tragedy presented in only 14 reels!

Still, we think the final treatment must not be over 12.

But we withdraw from the final 'shrinking', leaving it for the present 'in extenso', so as to have the possibility of making this unpleasant operation *after* receiving the benefit of notes and advice from:

1. The West Coast Magnates.
2. The East Coast Magnates.
3. Theodore Dreiser.
4. The Hays Organization.

Accordingly, gentlemen, we have the honour to submit to your 'discriminating kindness'

The Enclosed Manuscript
and . . . Honi soit qui mal y pense.

THE AUTHORS

Oct. 5th, 1930.[1]

Sergei Eisenstein was like a matador twirling his crimson cape before an already impatient bull. Why would a man act in this way when he knew, as Sergei Mikhailovich knew full well, that he had come to his last chance to make a film in Hollywood? Because he realized he could never fit into its commercial pattern? Perhaps. He knew he would not compromise; he would not produce a 'whodunit' film nor 'a boy meets girl' picture. So perhaps he was resigned. Yet not quite resigned;

[1] Carbon copy of this letter is included in the Eisenstein Collection, Museum of Modern Art Film Library, New York, with copy of first treatment of *An American Tragedy*.

he still betrayed a kind of faith that, maybe, his treatment would be acceptable.

On October the 13th, while en route to New York carrying the script with him for Paramount's 'East Coast Magnates' and Theodore Dreiser, Sergei Mikhailovich wrote a letter to his mother, one fated to be left unposted, as was, in his boyhood, his bitter drawing with its friendly note on the back:

The Chief
Santa Fe

13 X 1930
Arizona

En Route

DEAR LITTLE MOTHER!

... I am on my way to New York for the final decision regarding production of *An American Tragedy* and meeting with Dreiser and the executives of Paramount. If all goes well I will also go north of New York where the tragedy took place. You know, of course, that this is a true story and even the docks where the boats were hired exist.

The scenario came out very well 'excellent', which seems to be everyone's opinion. But there are many questions in connection with the 'propaganda' theme, particularly now when even my name, as always, is being knocked about by the committee of Fish (in investigation of Communist Activities).

Wish me well.

I kiss you affectionately
SON.[1]

The Fish Committee had convened in Los Angeles five days before— the 8th of October—to investigate 'communist activities' in California, and especially Eisenstein, 'the international Judas of the cinema', as Major Pease had characterized him. Among the people who testified was Lt.-Col. Leroy Smith, a representative of the Better America Federation, which had been waging a quieter and more subtle campaign against Sergei Mikhailovich. But the witness specifically questioned about Eisenstein was Fred W. Beetson, treasurer and secretary of the Motion Picture Producers' Association, and the West Coast representative of the Will Hays organization.

According to a report of Conrad Seiler, Mr. Beetson was asked if he knew 'that Eisenstein was going to make a picture in Hollywood. Yes, Mr. Beetson had heard something about it. What picture? He believed it was *The American Tragedy*. The American what? *The American Tragedy*, a novel. Chairman Fish declared he had never heard of the

---

[1] Letter in the Eisenstein Collection, Museum of Modern Art.

book and didn't know if it contained Communist propaganda or not. Did Mr. Beetson know if Eisenstein was making films of a propaganda nature? No, Mr. Beetson did not. "Do you think," asked Congressman Nelson, "that you'd recognize Communist propaganda if you saw it?" Mr. Beetson doubted if he could, but he assured the Committee that Eisenstein "will never be permitted to make a propaganda film in America. . . . We have all the machinery necessary to suppress Communistic propaganda in *The American Tragedy* . . ."[1]

Because of its treatment, the scenario did not please Paramount. Possibly no script Eisenstein could have written would have satisfied the Paramount executives, for they had grown sceptical of his ability to make a commercial film. He had stubbornly resisted doing what they wanted him to do, even turning down the studio's second suggestion, the film *Broken Lullaby*.[2] Moreover, Paramount was put out by his insistence that he would not use professional actors or stars.

'Stars are all right in their genre,' he argued. 'But I think the art of acting is a thing that ought to remain on the stage. The film has other fields.'

Meanwhile, the vilification campaign of Pease was having its effect. In New York there was a struggle inside Paramount. There were those who recognized the worth of Sergei Eisenstein's first treatment and those who, though they may have recognized it, were thoroughly intimidated by the campaign against Eisenstein. They wished to be rid of him, and his refusal to compromise over *An American Tragedy* opened the way.

On the evening of the 22nd of October, Sergei Mikhailovich met H. W. L. Dana. They went to the Theatre Guild's première of the play *Roar China* by Eisenstein's old friend Sergei Tretiakov. During the performance, Sergei Mikhailovich turned to Dana and pointed out that Lee Simonson's setting for the gunboat and the fleet of small junks was a stage adaptation of his own composition in *Potemkin* where the fleet of yawls swarm around the mutinying ship. [Plate 11]

Eisenstein seemed to be pleased with the compositional influence of *Potemkin* on Simonson's stage design. But he did not know how to tell Dana that all his efforts to make a film in Hollywood had ended in failure, although he knew that the executives of Paramount had prepared a public statement to be released the next morning. On the 23rd of October 1930, Paramount announced that 'the preliminary agree-

[1] 'The Red Mongers go West', by Conrad Seiler (*New Republic*, New York, 12 November 1930).

[2] The film directed by Ernst Lubitsch was made by Paramount in 1931; it was originally called *The Man I Killed*, but when released early in 1932, it was renamed *Broken Lullaby*.

ment between Paramount Public Corporation and Sergei M. Eisenstein has been terminated by mutual consent.'

In an article, Richard Watts Jr., the film critic, remarked sarcastically 'Perhaps he [Major Pease] persuaded Jesse L. Lasky and his colleague, Mr. Zukor, that Eisenstein was the threat to the popularity of Paramount and the Jew that his charmingly hysterical assaults suggested. Conceivably he provided the timorous Fish Committee investigating communist activities with proper proof that the presence of the Russian was overwhelming the bulwarks of our illustrious government.'[1]

Jesse L. Lasky's attitude towards the affair is recorded by the columnist Proctor ('Ted') Cook in a letter to Seymour Stern, dated the 14th February 1950. Cook tells of a cocktail party in New York where he 'spotted Jesse Lasky and I remember I made a point of asking him what had gone wrong with the Eisenstein assignment and I recall distinctly his reply in some detail. He said the studio was deluged with protests and they decided they could not go ahead successfully in face of all opposition.'

But it was not enough for Paramount to terminate the contract. The studio, with the curiously uncertain and envious streak of Hollywood movie concerns, was determined to get Eisenstein out of the country lest some rival company make a new contract with him and he was able to produce a successful film. Hence, Paramount arranged for Sergei Mikhailovich to return to the Soviet Union from the West Coast via Japan. They bought him his ticket and his departure was announced in the Press. The announcement was premature.

Freed from his contract, Sergei Eisenstein decided upon his own course. He made no temperamental scenes and refrained from making statements to the Press until more than eighteen months later. But he expressed his views on Hollywood by securing the Russian rights to George S. Kaufman's satiric comedy on the film industry, *Once in a Lifetime*. When leaving America for ever, Sergei Mikhailovich described this play as 'the most morbid thing I ever saw. Grim realism. When you know your Hollywood, it is a sort of *Mourning Becomes Electra*.'

With the great adventure seemingly ended, Eisenstein returned to Hollywood in the unpleasant role of the man who had failed. His reactions to this major disappointment in America were similar to his earlier reaction in the Soviet Union when he was unable to produce the great film on China—he turned his attention elsewhere. Back in Hollywood, Sergei Mikhailovich spoke with Charlie Chaplin and told him

[1] 'The Passing of Eisenstein', by Richard Watts, Jr. (*The Film Mercury*, 14 November 1930).

what he had in mind: that before he returned to the Soviet Union he wished to make an independent film laid in Mexico, the country which had profoundly interested him from the days of his first theatrical work —the Proletkult production of Jack London's story, *The Mexican*. But the question was to whom could he go for money? Chaplin suggested Upton Sinclair, the socialist.

Sergei Mikhailovich responded to this idea. As America's outstanding crusading novelist, Sinclair's works were extremely popular in the Soviet Union and this seemed to be a sufficient reason for Eisenstein to approach Sinclair. Full of hope, Sergei Mikhailovich went to see Upton Sinclair and his wife in their neat suburban house in nearby Pasadena. As he walked into the short imitation carriage drive with its un-Californian appearance, no shadow crossed Sergei Mikhailovich's mind as to the untoward results stemming from what seemed this most logical action. He wanted to make a film in Mexico and he could not do it by himself. Assuming that Upton Sinclair's social philosophy and desire for the creation of truthful art were the same as his own, Sergei Mikhailovich never considered going for aid to anyone but Upton Sinclair, not even to Dreiser, who had stood resolutely behind him in his uncompromising attitude towards Paramount, and subsequently sued the studio for distorting his novel in the film finally made by Joseph von Sternberg.

Thus, the sensitive and complex thirty-two-year-old Russian outlined his dream to the equally complex fifty-two-year-old American, Upton Sinclair, whose feeling for art was subordinated to his need to pamphleteer on political and social questions through the medium of novels. It was a most unfortunate incident in their respective lives, fated to embitter both of them as human beings, and enhance the reputation of neither.

Eisenstein was probably so immersed in his new Mexican dream that he was impervious to Sinclair's personality.

When Eisenstein first arrived in Hollywood, Upton Sinclair had paid him a call. 'He was,' Sinclair writes, 'polite but showed no special interest in me and did not ask to see me again.' (App. Six.) They had, however, met again casually. Sinclair and Eisenstein were both present at a dinner given in Hollywood for Rene Fülop-Miller, the theatre critic, who had written about Eisenstein's early work at the Proletkult Theatre.

Upton Sinclair came from a family who had once been estate owners and slave-holders in Virginia; but the ruin of the Civil War and alcohol had driven his father to vermin-infested slums, against which the young Sinclair turned rebel. While he came to espouse Socialism, he preserved a severe approach to matters of 'drink' and, as he wrote,

'I am glad that I did not waste my time and vision in sexual looseness'.[1] Sinclair was impervious to the culture of other nations. As he wrote of Italy: 'Places and events went by as if in a dream, and nothing had meaning unless it spoke of the pain and enslavement in America. . . . The grim castle of the Strozzi was an incarnation in stone of the Beef Trust or the Steel Trust.'[2] His second wife, Mary Craig Sinclair, was an aristocratic Southern belle, daughter of the Mississippian Judge Kimbrough. Of independent views as well as means, she participated in her husband's publishing ventures and bought and sold real estate in order 'to make money to pay debts'.[3]

Why Sinclair became involved with Eisenstein, a man whose attitude to art and culture must have made him feel uncomfortable, is hard to understand. They had nothing in common except one exceedingly slender bond: neither of them drank and they both thought drinking a disgusting habit. Yet Sinclair responded to Eisenstein's plea. He called upon his wife and some of his rich friends and persuaded them to become the financial backers of Sergei Eisenstein's proposed Mexican film.

In return for this 'comradely' assistance, Eisenstein said he personally wanted no salary; all he needed was a dollar a day to feed himself, Tisse and Alexandrov in Mexico. Mrs. Sinclair raised $25,000 and a contract was signed on November the 24th, 1930:[4]

This preliminary agreement between Sergei M. Eisenstein of Moscow, Russia, and Mary Craig Sinclair, of Pasadena, California, Witnesseth:

WHEREAS, Eisenstein wishes to go to Mexico and direct the making of a picture tentatively entitled Mexican picture; and whereas Mrs. Sinclair wishes to finance the production of and own said picture, THEREFORE, for the sum of ten dollars ($10.00) and other good and valuable consideration paid to Eisenstein by Mrs. Sinclair, Eisenstein agrees that he will proceed to Mexico City, with his assistant and his cameraman and equipment, and will devote himself, to the best of his ability for a period of from three to four months, to directing the making of the said Mexican picture; also that during the next eighteen months he will not make, or direct the making of, any Mexican picture for any other person.

Eisenstein furthermore agrees that all pictures made or directed by

[1] *American Outpost*, by Upton Sinclair (Girard, Kansas, Haldeman-Julius 1932; revised 1948), p. 1 and *seq.*
[2] *Ibid.*, p. 23.   [3] *Ibid.*, p. 106.
[4] A copy of this contract, together with the letter from Mrs. Sinclair to Eisenstein, was given to the author in 1939 by one of Eisenstein's Mexican advisers, Agustin Aragon-Leiva.

him in Mexico, all negative and positive prints, and all story and ideas embodied in said Mexican picture, will be the property of Mrs. Sinclair, and that she may market said material in any manner for any price she desires, and shall be the sole owner of all the world rights to said Mexican picture, and shall be free to take out copyright to the same in her name.

In consideration of the above agreement by Eisenstein, and in full faith that he will carry out his promise to direct the making of the best picture in Mexico of which he as an artist is capable, Mary Craig Sinclair agrees that she will put up the sum of not less than Twenty-five Thousand dollars ($25,000) and that after the original costs of said picture have been returned to her, she will pay to Eisenstein a sum equal to ten per cent (10%) of all sums which she may receive for the sale or lease of the picture; and that she will furnish to Eisenstein, or to his representative, a copy of all statements and accounts of payments made upon it.

This agreement is made upon the basis of Eisenstein's desire to be free to direct the making of a picture according to his own ideas of what a Mexican picture should be, and in full faith in Eisenstein's artistic integrity, and in consideration of his promise that the picture will be non-political, and worthy of his reputation and genius.

In WITNESS to the above the undersigned have hereunto set their hands.

So eager was Sergei Mikhailovich to make the Mexican film 'according to his own ideas' that he signed most of his rights away. He evidently failed to consider the legal implications of the contract and in particular showed no concern that he was to receive only ten per cent. of the profit or that the film was to be 'non-political.' Eisenstein clearly regarded the written document as a mere formality and, if he thought about the matter at all, was satisfied to depend on his notion of the spirit of the arrangement. But during the next few days, it struck Sergei Mikhailovich that he had failed to provide for free Soviet distribution of his film. He explained his oversight to Mrs. Sinclair and asked her to modify the agreement. In response to Eisenstein's plea, she wrote him the following letter:

Pasadena, California.
December 1, 1930.

DEAR COMRADE EISENSTEIN:

I am pleased to modify our contract of November 24th, 1930, in regard to the Mexican film, to provide that the Soviet Government may have the film free for showing in U.S.S.R.

MARY CRAIG SINCLAIR.

Still Sergei Mikhailovich failed to think of himself, or the very core of his artistic method. He did not realize that he had not reserved the right to edit his own film. He went on the assumption that the words 'directing the making of' a film meant that the film would be edited by him according to his theories of montage. He overlooked the words which were to 'doom' the work which contained his own essential vision and philosophy, the words 'that she [Mrs. Sinclair] may market the material in any manner . . . she desires, and shall be the sole owner of all the world rights'.

When all was settled and Eisenstein told Tisse and Alexandrov they could leave immediately for Mexico, Tisse was thrilled, but not Grisha. According to Eisenstein, Alexandrov had been offered a contract by one of the Hollywood studios and he wished to make a film before he left. Hollywood producers had found Grigori Alexandrov a person whom they thought capable of producing the kind of pictures they wanted.

Eisenstein flew into a rage. He castigated Grisha for thinking he could make a decent picture in Hollywood. His envy of Alexandrov's charm and social success may have flared into an uncontrollable jealousy of Grisha's opportunity to work in Hollywood where the door had been closed upon him. After some persuasion Alexandrov agreed to remain with the unit.

Ivor Montagu, who had worked with Eisenstein on *An American Tragedy*, disagreed with him over the Mexican project. He tried to convince Sergei Mikhailovich that the venture under the sponsorship of Upton Sinclair was likely to end in failure because the sponsorship was altogether too amateur. But Eisenstein, seized by the vision of a Mexican film, would not listen. Convinced that Sergei Mikhailovich was handling his affairs in a very foolish manner, Montagu left Eisenstein and returned to England.

On a quiet morning early in December 1930, Sergei Eisenstein left the Hollywood Hotel, where he had been staying. Salka Viertel, the scenarist, drove him and his comrades to the station. There, a small group including Upton Sinclair and his wife, Seymour Stern, Christel Gang and a few reporters gathered to see the departure of 'the man whose pictures had taken Europe by storm', but who was useless to the American motion picture industry. One of the reporters asked Eisenstein why he wanted to make a Mexican film.

'Mexico is primitive,' replied Eisenstein. 'It is close to the soil. In its missions alone there are many pictures. To make a good picture, one must have a positive approach. This is possible in a country like Mexico, where the struggle of progress is still very real. In the United States', continued Sergei Mikhailovich, 'there are motor-cars and miniature golf courses.'

He drew his eyebrows down and appeared to the reporter more than ever like an exaggerated drawing of the film star Victor Varconi. 'In my short visit I have witnessed the whole history of mankind,' he said. 'On the Tom Thumb golf courses there is symbolized the history of mankind. First the course was simple, lighted only for utility. Then they became more elaborate. Soon there was music. Backgrounds became magnificent, scenes were spread like panoramas instead of fences. Futurism crept in and flourished. Then came cold!' he declared. 'And with it devastation. Decadence and blight wrote a last chapter to history.'[1]

Eisenstein stood talking to the group until the last moment. 'The Chief Conductor twice called out "All aboard!" He was standing near our group, and at the second "All aboard!" he turned to Eisenstein and very courteously, and quietly, said: "We're pulling out now." Grisha and Tisse had already gotten on. Tisse excitedly ran to the vestibule of the car and called out to Sergei in Russian. Then Eisy got on. He walked through the car to his berth-window, near the centre of the car, and waved to as many of us as he could see. He looked somehow like a little boy. When I think of him, this is the 'image' that comes into my mind. It was my last impression of Eisenstein—and by far the most startling. For he seemed a very strange mixture then of many things: the smile was at once sad and sheepish—the peculiar shyness that various persons had often noted crept into it—yet at the same time he seemed excited and exuberant almost in an adolescent way, like a little boy taking his first big trip for a "good time". Eisenstein in that instant did not seem to belong to films, to the Soviet Union, or for that matter to the world: I can't easily describe what I mean, but I can only tell you that whenever I recall this scene, Eisenstein, the king and master of flaming images of turmoil and the world's war for freedom—seemed so completely, so pathetically and tragically, innocent. This was what stared from the Pullman window.'[2]

The train began to move. Sinclair and Stern trotted down the platform keeping pace with the slowly moving train. Sergei Mikhailovich kept waving from his window. He had no idea he would never see Christel Gang again, nor Upton Sinclair, nor Seymour Stern, who later said of him: 'He was the most intelligent human being I have ever met: he was intellectually free of illusion, politically free of dogma, and socially free of prejudice, and spiritually free of superstition. He was refreshingly clean of medievalism. He was an intellectual light, in a world and an age too often blinded by confusion, moral bigotry, political intolerance, religious tyranny and social authoritarianism. In Eisenstein I found a free mind.'

[1] Alice L. Tildesley in *Theatre Guild Magazine*, February 1931.
[2] Seymour Stern in a letter to the author, dated 20 July, 1950.

As the train turned and headed out to Alameda Street, popularly known as 'Death Avenue', Stern was hidden from view, and Sergei Mikhailovich's thoughts at once turned to his vision of a Mexican film. He did not foresee that Sinclair, his backer, and Stern, his friend, would soon become the spearheads in the bitterest struggle over a film in all the history of cinema.

TEXT

Adapted from Blaise Cendrars' novel " L'or " by S. M. Eisenstein

1. . . . the discovery of the gold on January 28th, 1848 : the decision of Sutter and the local inhabitants to keep the discovery secret : the prosperous landscape after rain . . .

CHORUS : Gold!

MALE VOICES : They say that the gold is the gift of the Devil.
(INDIANS) We have always known of it
And avoided it. Sutter, do not touch it!

BASS SOLO :
(SUTTER) Let us keep the discovery secret.

MALE VOICES : Pledge secrecy!

DOUBLE CHORUS : Gold!
Wealth and fertility of a prosperous landscape. The rains have ceased. Nature's garment is soft and sparkling. Myriads of raindrops glisten in the sunshine.

S & Co. 6362

Note 1977. The opening of Alexander Goehr's *Sutter's Gold*, A Cantata, 1961, based on Eisenstein's scenario.

CHAPTER NINE

The Eternal Circle

Supreme happiness will be the greatest cause of misery, and the perfection of wisdom the occasion of folly.

LEONARDO DA VINCI, C.A. 39 V.C.

EISENSTEIN, Tisse and Alexandrov had barely unpacked their bags at Mexico City's Hotel Imperial before the Mexican police came and led them off to gaol. A monsoon of rumours had arrived in Mexico with them: Eisenstein was sponsored by communists. . . . No, the Mexican Government had invited him to make a film. . . . Eisenstein was the most dangerous agent Moscow had ever sent on a mission. . . . On the contrary, he was on the point of becoming a Russian *émigré*. . . . Eisenstein was not a communist. . . . He was a German spy. Why Eisenstein and his comrades were arrested was never made quite clear, although it later appeared that the action resulted from telegrams sent by Major Frank Pease to the Mexican Government.

But the Mexican officials could not make up their minds what ought to be done with Eisenstein, and each of them sided a different way. In the meantime, Sergei Mikhailovich, in gaol for the first and only time in his life, pretended that his sole concern was the motion picture equipment they had brought with them. Yet beneath his seeming calm he was disturbed. No diplomatic relations existed between Mexico and the Soviet Union, and he and his comrades were without protection.

Alvarez del Vayo, then the Spanish Ambassador to Mexico, interceded and the next morning Eisenstein and his comrades were released from prison with muttered apologies that it had all been 'a mistake'. But no sooner had they returned to the Hotel Imperial than two police officers took up positions outside their rooms. For three days they were under police surveillance, by which time Eisenstein's plight was assuming the proportions of an international incident, and protesting cables arrived from Albert Einstein, G. B. Shaw and Charlie Chaplin. Again the Spanish Ambassador stepped in. He assured the Mexican Government that he knew Eisenstein and his work, and that he should be permitted to make a film in Mexico.

Finally, the Mexican Government announced that Sergei Eisenstein was an honoured guest to whom all assistance would be rendered in the making of a film. But the Government was not quite sure of his intentions, so they appointed several advisers, chief of whom was Adolfo Best-Maugard, whose job it was to see that nothing inimical to the Government got into the film. Agustin Aragon-Leiva, who was to become one of Sergei Mikhailovich's most loyal friends, was another adviser. He helped to introduce Eisenstein to Mexico's history, archæology, ethnology, music, customs and art. Leiva's love for his country was boundless. In him, the spirit of his ancestors had found a voice. He was proud of his forebears who were a mingling of Maya Indian, the astronomers and pyramid-builders, with a Spanish son of Levi, whose tradition was that of the keeper of sacred vessels and temple learning. His life was devoted to furthering art and science in Mexico.

In the course of his research, Eisenstein met Mexico's most celebrated painters: Diego Rivera, with whom he had talked in Moscow, Clemente Orozco and David Siqueiros [Plate 21], Jean Charlot [Plate 31] and Roberto Montenegro, who painted a portrait of Eisenstein in the role of a Spanish conquistador [Plate 62]. It was not long before every art-minded American in Mexico had come to discuss Mexico with Eisenstein and give him the benefit of their ideas. He was deluged with suggestions and loaded with information. But Sergei Mikhailovich knew what he was looking for. He had found his key idea in the book *Idols Behind Altars* by Anita Brenner. It was this book which had crystallized his dream of a Mexican film.

According to his contract with Mrs. Sinclair, Eisenstein was to devote himself for 'three or four' months to the making of a film. But at the end of three months he had not shot a single foot of film. He had merely travelled over much of Mexico and to distant Yucatan. He had discovered Tetlapayac, an old Spanish plantation, which was to become the centre of his work. In the three months his tentative idea had expanded into an all-embracing film based on Mexico's 'living history'. He envisioned it as four episodes or 'novels', as Sergei Mikhailovich called them, 'framed by prologue and epilogue, unified in conception and spirit'; each 'different in character, different in people, different in animals, trees and flowers. And still held together by the unity of the weave—a rhythmic and musical construction and an unrolling of the Mexican spirit and character.' He had in mind the literary form 'novella'.

Sergei Eisenstein, the creator of eccentric theatre, the revolutionary artist of *Strike, Potemkin, October* and *Old and New*, the social psychologist of the unproduced films *Sutter's Gold* and *An American Tragedy*, took 'a leap to a new quality'. Passing through an 'ecstasis', he emerged as a poet concerned with the Eternal—'the unity of death and life'. It is no exaggeration to say that he experienced such a profound revelation of his own being in Mexico that it seemed as if the 'soul' of a people had touched and become a part of his own soul. He found in Mexico in concrete form the place he felt to be his spiritual 'home'.

'The moment I saw Tetlapayac, I knew it was the place I had been looking for all my life,' Eisenstein told me.

I remember the tone of his voice. Singularly controlled and modulated even when speaking of his most painful experiences, Sergei Mikhailovich could not speak of Tetlapayac without his voice breaking into tones of excitement and pain though he had not seen the hacienda for years. He never spoke of any other place, experience or person in such tones. Like a man haunted by a lost love, he would carry in his pocket the letters he received telling him of what subsequently happened at Tetlapayac. He gave me one that I might comprehend this love and recognize Tetlapayac if I ever found my way to Mexico.

Tetlapayac was a lonely, beautiful and haunting building; changeless, yet changing with every movement of the sun. An old Spanish plantation belonging to Don Julio Saldivar, it lay some eighty-odd miles south-east of Mexico City in the State of Hidalgo. A fortress with coral pink walls—the shade of the Moscow Kremlin wall before it was whitewashed—and two high towers like sentinels rising above a sea of symmetrical, immobile grey-green cactus—the maguey—their spears as sharp as naked swords. In the distance the snowy head of Popocateptl, the volcanic pyramid.

Sergei Mikhailovich came along the barely distinguishable track through the maguey plantation at dusk. He saw the peons, the dark Indios—descendants of the Aztecs—who bore in their faces the memory of their ancestors as warriors. They were walking back to the hacienda for the night; ahead of them the little burros loaded with pulque barrels. Clip-clop, clip-clop into the first courtyard with the pulque-making sheds, the courtyard of the Indians. Beyond, through an arch, the smaller Spanish courtyard with its marble stairway leading to the long cloistered balcony, the many high-ceilinged, silent rooms, the chapel with the fiesta Santiago.

Every stone of Tetlapayac was sorrowful. Every shadow meaningful. Centuries of grief and generations of power and callous pleasure had moulded Tetlapayac and its people. Living within the tender-coloured walls—hundreds of Indians, many of mixed blood, a handful of pale-skinned, blue-eyed Spaniards. A deeply pagan note sounded in the morning prayer of the Indios to the sun god; in the chapel stood the incarnation of Christ's suffering carved by dark Indian hands.

The suffering child that Sergei Eisenstein had once been found solace in the golden sun of Tetlapayac. The thoughtful man gained peace in the smallest courtyard with its shaded garden hidden away beyond the chapel. The man who loved to play and make bawdy jokes discovered that the enduring Indians laughed more joyously than any other people he had ever known. The man who bitterly fought God's earthly representative—the Church—because he could not forget his love for Christ, communed with his innermost self in the dim chapel. Tetlapayac even held a deep social meaning for Sergei Mikhailovich.

From century to century, generations of Indios had passed silently across the courtyards to the maguey fields. There from sunrise to dusk they toil like sacrificial priests, attacking the thick protective leaves until they reach the centre of the plant. They cut out the heart leaving a round cavity where the heavy white sap collects drop by drop. They suck this into gourds, pour it into caskets which their patient burros carry back to the vats where it ferments into pulque. Pulque—'white like milk, a gift of the gods, according to legend and belief, this strongest intoxicator drowns sorrow, inflames passions'. But pulque will not drown all sorrows, all peons know that.

Like many other plantations in Mexico, Tetlapayac had originally been the estate of one of the early Spanish *conquistadores* led by Cortes. Its peons, whose ancestors had been enslaved by the Spaniards, had made vast fortunes from pulque for the landlords, the last of whom was Don Julio Saldivar's father. At the time of the Mexican Revolution the Saldivar family had retained the hacienda because they agreed to turn it into an agricultural co-operative. Gradually, after centuries of misery, the peons of Tetlapayac were slowly approaching what might some day become a better life.

Eisenstein found Tetlapayac strangely expressive of himself. So he settled into the hacienda. And something momentous happened. Something which never happened completely to Sergei Mikhailovich anywhere else. He was accepted as a human being. His contradictions worried no one, and he appeared neither forbidding nor out of place to the people of the hacienda. He was liked from the first day. As they grew to know him better, and to work with him, everyone came to love him as a dear brother. When at last he went away no one forgot him. They waited for him to return; but he was never able to come back except in dreams. This was a grief shared by all. Anyone who came to Tetlapayac afterwards with one word about Sergei Eisenstein was immediately included within the circle of affection he had established.

Tetlapayac: the whole land of Mexico—a love concentrated not upon an individual but upon a people—transformed Eisenstein's art. The scientist sank in him and the epic poet arose. The mode of expression merely hinted at here and there in *Old and New* blossomed into the most personal vision of his genius. Sergei Mikhailovich, who had been too inhibited to express a hint of love or passion on the screen, or give

expression to the gay, tender and truly reverent elements of his innermost nature, was now released into a passionate love of the beautiful, of
women, of the fulfilment of life itself; equally loving was he towards
the deepest religious feeling.

He prepared a brief outline of his film for Upton Sinclair. It overflowed with the spirit of poetry: life and death; the love of men and
women and worship of the gods. The dominant concepts: Death and
Love; the Body and the Spirit. Not all of Eisenstein's thoughts went
down on paper. The most sacred and daring he kept to himself.

Do you know what a 'sarape' is? A sarape is the striped blanket
that . . . every Mexican wears. So striped and violently contrasting
are the cultures in Mexico running next to each other and at the same
time being centuries away . . . we took the contrasting independent
adjacence of its violent colors as the motif for constructing our film:
6 episodes following each other. . . .

Death. Skulls of people. And skulls of stone. The horrible Aztec
gods and the terrifying Yucatan deities. . . . A world that was and is
no more. . . . Faces of stone. And faces of flesh. . . . The same man
who lived thousands of years ago. Unmovable. Unchanging. Eternal. And the great wisdom of Mexico about death. The unity of
death and life. The passing of one and the birth of the next one. The
eternal circle. And the still greater wisdom of Mexico: the *enjoying*
of this eternal circle. Death-Day in Mexico. Day of the greatest fun
and merriment. . . .

Eisenstein expanded this outline into a full length scenario.[1] He sent a
copy to Upton Sinclair and his wife who approved it.[2] They told
Eisenstein to commence work on the film, which he planned to edit
into ten reels. The Mexican Government also approved the scenario, but
some sequences were not mentioned. No cutting directions appear and
there are no indications of camera set-ups.

Later, Sergei Mikhailovich told me that had he edited the film, which
he entitled *Que Viva Mexico!*; he intended on the cutting-table to transfer the third episode, according to the scenario, into the place of the
first. But he would have transformed the third episode beyond recognition by montage: the story of the Matador was to be interlocked with

[1] S. M. Eisenstein and Grigori Alexandrov's 'Que Viva Mexico!' published
in *Experimental Cinema* (Hollywood, No. 5, 1934). In 1947, Eisenstein sent a
copy of this scenario, together with an introduction, to Armand Panigel, who
was preparing Eisenstein's selected works for publication in France.

[2] Grigori Alexandrov confirms Eisenstein's statement to the author that
Upton Sinclair approved both the synopsis and the expanded scenario in a
letter to Eisenstein.

the idea of Christianity. The scenario is poetry which only the creator, Sergei Eisenstein, could fully realize on the screen.

Prologue

Time in the prologue is eternity.

It might be to-day.

It might as well be twenty years ago.

It might be a thousand.

For the dwellers of Yucatan, land of ruins and huge pyramids, have still conserved, in feature and forms, the character of their ancestors, the great race of the ancient Mayas.

Stone—

Gods—

Men—

Act in the prologue.

In time remote. . . .

In the land of Yucatan, among heathen temples, holy cities and majestic pyramids. In the realms of death, where the past still prevails over the present, there the starting-point of our film is laid.

As symbols of recalling the past, as a farewell rite to the ancient Maya civilization, a weird funeral ceremony is held. . . . [Plate 21]

Sergei Mikhailovich's composition for the men carrying the coffin on their shoulders was a dynamic interpretation of David Siqueiros' unfinished and mutilated fresco, 'Burial of a Worker', commemorating the murder of the Governor of Yucatan, Felipe Carrillo Puerto. But life must follow death. In retrospect, Eisenstein said that he intended to conclude the Prologue with the promise of a new life. The dreamless sleep of death to the dreaming girl drifting along the river towards her mate. Together the man and the young woman go into the jungle and come to know each other in their innocent nakedness. [Plate 20]

In this sequence, Sergei Mikhailovich expressed the erotic side of his nature long sublimated in creative work which avoided all reference to physical passion. Here in the most simple and direct manner he created a symbolic, though realistic, scene in praise of the physical act of love. But death must follow life.

Suffering, repentance, bondage, and the contest of man against beast came to Mexico with Cortes and the Franciscan friars who, as Sergei Mikhailovich portrayed them, appeared like El Greco's paintings of St. Francis, with the ever-repeated motif of the skull. The theme of the Indians crushed by Spain was to be depicted through the montage of a multitude of seemingly dissociated shots and sequences, which Eisenstein did not define in the scenario. He deliberately concealed his true intentions for practical reasons: his Mexican advisers were watching to see that he violated no 'sacred taboos'. He also did not wish to express in writing the dual emotions which swept him. Mystical feelings rose within him; yet he was filled with passion against the evils of the Church which accepted the morality of the Cross and the Sword, and in that role aided in enslaving the Indian people. [Plate 20]

Thus, the words of Sergei Eisenstein in no way conveyed his passionate vision. The first novel, according to Eisenstein, but the third in the scenario, he ironically entitled:

Fiesta

Weirdness, Romance and Glamour constitute the make-up of the third [first] novel.

Like the Spanish colonial barroco—works the stone into fanciful lace-work on the wire-ribbon of columns and church-altars. Thus the complex designs, the elaborate composition of this episode. . . .

Spanish architecture, costumes, bull-fights, romance, love . . . manifest themselves in this story.

In the old pre-revolutionary Mexico the annual holiday in worship of the holy Virgin of Guadalupe is taking place. . . .

Dancers of ritual dances are getting their fantastic costumes and masks ready.

The bishops and archbishops are donning their gorgeous robes. . . .

And finally the heroes of this tale, the famous matadors, are putting on their gold and silk embroidered costumes . . . the carefree picador, the lazy Don Juan Baronito.

He is mindful of every detail, for an encounter more hazardous than the bull-fight awaits him.

He has a date with another man's wife! Having dressed, the matadors drive to the chapel of the Holy Virgin, the patron of their dangerous art.

Having knelt before her altar, whispered to her his prayer, and begged her benediction, the best of the great matadors drives over to the quiet home of his mother to bid her—

Good-bye!

Maybe for the last time.

In selecting the 'type' for the matador's mother, Sergei Mikhailovich either consciously or unconsciously chose a woman who bore a marked resemblance to his own mother. The character of Julia Eisenstein's face, the set of her head, the characteristic gestures of her hands, appear in the mother of the matador—a lady of Merida in Yucatan. The resemblance goes further, even to the gentility of her clothes and the style of dressing her hair.

During the parade the picador, Baronito, appears in full splendour, mounted on his white horse, and throws a stealthy glance in the direction where the queens [of the Bull Ring] are seated . . .

. . . The very famous David Liceaga displays all the beauty and elegance of the art of the matador.

Full of grace and valor he dances his 'dance' on the margin of death and triumph.

He does not stir from his place even when the bull's horns come within a hair's breadth of his body; he does not tremble, but smiles serene, and to top it all he pets the sharp horns of the animal and this provokes an endless savage outburst of delight from the crowd.

But the bull, enraged by the teasing of Liceaga, knocks down the horse of the infatuated Baronito. . . .

The ceremonial character of bull-fighting and the psychological reactions of the audience deeply stirred Sergei Mikhailovich. He shot thousands of feet of film in Merida recording the fine details of the ancient sport and the savage emotions of the spectators. But when he left the bull ring, it was the bull that remained in his mind and he made a series of drawings of bulls. Several times Sergei Mikhailovich drew a crucified bull. In other drawings the bull was grotesque, sometimes humorous and now and then the bulls were endowed with a pathetically human quality.

In the meantime, in the town square, fairs and market-places, a crowd of many thousands are contemplating the ritual ceremonial dances of Indians dressed up in gilded brocade, ostrich feathers and huge masks. . . .

There followed in the scenario an adulterous love affair between Baronito and a queen of the bull ring, but little of this material was actually shot. (App. Five.) Instead, Eisenstein concentrated upon the material he so lightly mentioned—'ritual ceremonial dances'. This included purely documentary material of strange and ancient ceremonial dances and enacted sequences where the composition was highly symbolic. The most remarkable sequence was one Sergei Mikhailovich never mentioned in the scenario, but of which he later spoke to me—the Penitente procession. This was a symbolic Journey to Calvary with Christ, the two thieves and the woman, Veronica, who according to legend, wiped the face of Christ on His way to Golgotha.

In this symbolic Crucifixion, Eisenstein took two ancient customs of Mexico and recreated them according to his own vision. In many areas of Mexico, the Crucifixion is re-enacted as a drama at Easter with three men interpreting the roles of Christ and the two thieves. At the sacred shrine of Amecamaca on Good Friday, so-called Penitentes do the

Stations of the Cross upon their knees to expiate their own sins, or the sins of another. Since these ceremonies are the most sacred in Mexico, Sergei Mikhailovich could not 'shoot' the actual ceremonies, nor re-construct them in the places where they were held sacred. He created his own 'dialectical' sequence based upon them, though transferred to a 'higher quality'. This he did in the town of Izamal in Yucatan, where the real ceremonies were unknown.

Eisenstein's setting for the Penitente procession embodied the concept of the pre-Christian idol behind the Christian altar. At the commence-ment of the procession, the Penitente mounted the ruined pyramid temple at Izamal, which Bishop Landa had razed to the ground, taking many of the stones with which to build his great monastery, which served as setting for the final shots of the procession. In directing this sequence, Sergei Mikhailovich gave expression to his deepest and most ecstatic feelings about the sacrificial nature of Christ's death. In the 'Fiesta' story the Crucifixion had a symbolic meaning. It was an 'overtone' which Eisenstein planned to reintroduce 'in reality' in the later Maguey episode, where, on the Day of Corpus Christi, three peons are buried up to their necks and their heads crushed by the hoofs of horses. [Plate 20]

Though the religious and symbolic was to play a very important role in *Que Viva Mexico!*—as indeed it does in Mexico—Eisenstein did not ignore everyday life. His theme: life must follow death. Thus, his second 'novel' (first in the scenario) was laid in the Isthmus of Tehuan-tepec, that area of Mexico where Spanish colonialism had made the least impact; so little, in fact, that the original matriarchal system of the Tehuana Indians remains to the present day. In this 'novel'—'Sandunga' —Eisenstein once more expressed the sensual and wholly human quali-tative thread he was to have established at the conclusion of the Pro-logue in the mating of man and woman:

Sandunga

The rising sun sends its irresistible call to life.

Its all-pervading rays penetrate into the darkness of the tropical forest. . . .

Indian maids are bathing in the river . . . and sing a song. [Plate 23]

Slow as an old-time waltz, sensual as a Danzon, and happy as their own dreams—an Oacaxa song—the Sandunga. . . .

Proud and majestic, like a fairy queen in her natural maiden beauty, is among them a girl by the name of Concepcion. . . .

A necklace of golden coins . . . is glimmering on her breast . . . this is the object of all her dreams. . . .

From tender childhood a girl begins to work, saving painstakingly every nickel, every penny, in order that at the age of sixteen or eighteen she may have the golden necklace. . . .

That is why the dreams of Concepcion are so passionate. . . .

Oh . . . we have let ourselves drift so deeply into dreams that we have not even noticed how the girls got to work when they went over to the market-place. . . .

As soon as a girl sells some trifle . . . she immediately begins to think of the necklace, begins to count the gold coins she still has to earn. . . .

The happy Concepcion tightly grips the long-wished-for coin in her hand. . . .

In the brilliance of her best dress . . . her beloved . . . Abundio proposes to her. And now:

The Bridegroom's mother is a practical woman!

She sends her women to the bride's house to take stock of the dowry and make sure that all is right. . . .

Experienced old women, nearly centenarians . . . they examine all her outfit, feel the velvet, smell the silk, count the gold coins. . . .

All is perfectly right! So traditional rites begin.

Concepcion's friends bring her presents. . . .

Entire Tehuantepec is stirred by the event. . . .

Under the sound of wedding bells the procession carrying palm branches goes to the house of the young couple.

And when left by themselves, Concepcion coyly allows her husband to take off her pride—the golden necklace. . . .

Time passes, new flowers bloom. Concepcion the woman is now a happy mother. . . .

With the peaceful lyric-song of dreaming beautiful girls ends the romance of tropical Tehuantepec.

In directing this 'novel', the ruthless artist of *Potemkin* and the intellectual experimenter of *October* and *Old and New* disappeared. There surged up the romantic young artist, whom Eisenstein had tried to kill during his years in the Red Army and later when his idyllic love drew forth jeers. This secreted personality flowered into a joyous and humane artist revelling in the unspoiled pleasure of primitive people. His delight in simple pleasures, the tender side of his humour, the reservoir of concealed lovingness which had survived in his nature found expression for the first and only time in his creative life. Traces of the gentle sentimentality that lay tightly controlled within him appeared. But most of all he revealed his love for simple human beings—old women like his nurse—and amidst so many beautiful girls and sweet-faced women, he found a woman who must have reminded him of Pera Attasheva.

Despite the joyousness and sensual delight of the Sandunga 'novel', and its praise of love and the goodness of life, Sergei Eisenstein found no personal experience of love in Mexico. He merely dreamed of man's profoundest need—a home. He could not fight to make his dreams come true; he was only rendered more receptive to emotional response. In later years the rhapsodic Sandunga episode of *Que Viva Mexico!* exerted the least hold upon his imagination. It may have grown dim, because an approach towards real happiness was more satisfying than the fulfilment of life in faraway Tehuantepec. Still later, he closed the door upon any memory of the story of Concepcion and Abundio and was concerned for the death sequences of *Que Viva Mexico!* rather than those of birth. (App. Five.)

Following his conception in *Que Viva Mexico!* that Death follows Life, the Tehuantepec episode gave way to 'a leap into opposition'. That is, it passed from joy to tragedy; the harmonious security of 'the female tribal system' being followed by the cruel conflict arising within 'the male tribe'. The third 'novel' (second in the scenario), entitled 'Maguey', revealed a dialectical evolutionary process. Set in the period of Porfiro Diaz's dictatorship of 1905–6, and the physical framework of the Hacienda of Tetlapayac, this is the story which, isolated from the total scheme of Eisenstein's film, later became known to the world as *Thunder Over Mexico*.

Maguey

Aggressiveness, virility, arrogance and austerity. . . .

Feudal estates, former monasteries of the Spanish conquerors, stand like unapproachable fortresses amidst the vast seas of cactus groves.

Long before dawn . . . over the high walls of the massive farm-house come the sad, slow tunes of a song.

'El Alabado' the peons call this song.

They sing it every morning before they go to work. . . .

In the maguey fields, where the peon Sebastian is working, a meeting takes place. Maria's parents bring their daughter to hand her over to her fiancée.

According to tradition, Sebastian will have to take his bride to the owner of the Hacienda as homage.

The 'charros' who are guarding the landlord's house won't let Sebastian in. . . .

On the terrace the landlord, in the company of a group of his nearest friends, is having drinks——

The 'hacendado' receives Maria; he is a good-natured old man; he fumbles in his vest pocket for a few pesos as a gift for the bride.

But at the moment an old-fashioned carriage drawn by six mules comes speeding along.

The old man's daughter, Sara, has arrived. . . .

Maria is forgotten.

Sebastian is restless while waiting in the front yard. . .

The forgotten, frightened, inexperienced Maria is awaiting her luck.

Bad luck appears in the shape of a coarse, drunken guest. . . .

He seizes Maria from behind a door and drags her into a remote room.

One of the servants, a close friend of Sebastian, witnesses this scene and runs with all his might to the yard with his startling news.

The Indian blood of Sebastian dictates his further course of action.

He rushes up the veranda knocking the guards off their feet, he breaks in like a storm among the merry guests. . . .

He demands Maria, his bride. . . .

Sebastian is sent rolling down the stairs for his insolence and effrontery. . . .

Vengeance germinates in his mind.

Vengeance begets conspiracy.

Three of his comrades pledge themselves to help him get revenge. . . .

Sebastian and his associates provide themselves with arms and cartridges out of the landlord's supplies and make an attempt to release Maria from confinement. . . .

The charros, however, on their finest horses, accompanied by the indomitable Sara and her cousin, make the pass (to which the peons have fled) and intercept the fugitives.

Cross-firing breaks out. . . .

Sara kills one of the peons and pays with her life for her daring. . . .

The fugitives are retreating into the maguey fields.

In the stronghold of a huge cactus, three of them seek refuge. . . .

The cartridges are exhausted.

The peons make an attempt to flee.

The agile charros fling their lassos around the fugitives and hold them captive.

Eye for an eye . . . they pay with their lives for their daring.

Among the maguey, where Sebastian had worked and loved, he finds his tragic end. . . .

Maria finds the remains of her beloved, of him who was to become her husband, who had raised his arm in her defence.

Eisenstein told me later that an important element in this 'novel' was not indicated in the scenario. This was a metaphysical and subjectively felt concurrent action which he planned to realize through montage. Probably it was the most complex concept he had up to that time wished to express. Since exact arrangement shot by shot existed only in his mind, it would be difficult, if not impossible, to lay out an authentic montage list on the basis of what he said.[1]

In the first episode—Fiesta—as mentioned earlier, Eisenstein had intended to show Christ crucified in the Penitentes' symbolic Journey to Calvary. In the 'Maguey' 'novel', the eternal Christ was to reappear in the symbolic festival of the Body of Christ—Corpus Christi. This festival was celebrated at Tetlapayac in 1931, and Eisenstein 'shot' it as it took place. He attached much significance to this festival—that of the Real Presence of Christ in the Sacrament; that is, when the bread and the wine are mystically transformed into the Body and Blood of Christ.

The festival at Tetlapayac, which, in 1931, culminated with one of the Indian peons of the hacienda 'going out of himself' into a state of penitential ecstasy, was to be intercut with the enacted death of the peon, Sebastian, and his two friends. Eisenstein's plan for the montage of simultaneous action was intended to reveal on the screen the concept that the symbolic ceremony was made manifest in the 'reality' of the hunting down and trampling to death of the peons. Their bodies and their blood were Christ's body and blood as symbolized in the Corpus Christi ceremony. Intersecting this mystical concept was irony: the formal, or Church side of the 'mystery', running parallel with the living mystery. [Plate 20]

Sergei Mikhailovich made sketches of key shots as ideas for montage came into his mind. (See page 206.)

The mysticism Eisenstein was seeking to express rendered him extremely sensitive to feelings of 'those certain supernatural powers, transcending common sense and human reason' which had haunted him from time to time. Hence, one of his moments of most intense awareness, indeed of a sense of 'revelation', occurred while he was directing the peons' death scene. The peons were to be buried up to their necks in the ground and their heads trampled by galloping horses. They dug their graves; they stepped in. . . . But Eisenstein was unconscious of having suggested any formal composition of the graves. When the peons were buried, he looked and then noticed they stood buried up to their necks in the form of a triangle—echoing the composition of Christ and the two thieves in the first story. [Plate 22]

In that moment Eisenstein said he felt the 'truth' lying at the base of composition. The 'coincidence' convinced him that primal form, particularly the pyramid, or triangle, symbolic of the relation between

[1] An approximation is to be found in the film *Time in the Sun*.

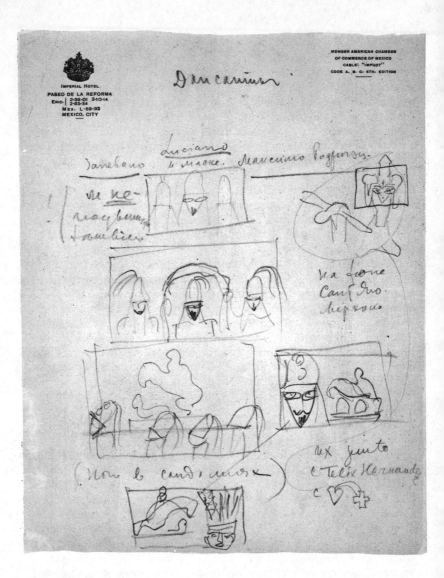

Montage sketches—Festival of Corpus Christi at the Hacienda of
Tetlapayac, 1931

God, Man and the Universe, was the sign of this higher truth. This form was the means of moving the emotions of men in such a manner that they felt the mysteries of an ordered universe even though they had no conscious intellectual grasp of the metaphysical concepts behind the form. Eisenstein no longer felt that his recurring use of the triangular compositional form was *his* work, his idea; instead he felt himself to be merely the instrumentality of a supernormal consciousness. So deeply did Sergei Mikhailovich feel this experience that subsequently the 'scientific' Eisenstein made no attempt to rationalize it. He accepted this seeming revelation as the discovery of profound truth and during 1933 and 1934 he constructed a theory of composition upon it. This theory existed in the form of extensive notes with many diagrams; but he hesitated to publish the theory and, so far, it has never appeared in print, although fragments from the theory have appeared in his writings.

Despite his increasing preoccupation with religion, Eisenstein was still extremely aware of and concerned with the social processes of revolution. Philosophical speculation and religious feeling had not submerged his wish for the creation of a new society. Hence the fourth 'novel'—'Soldadera'—was to portray new life in the midst of revolution and death. As in the 'novel' 'Sandunga', 'Soldadera' was realistic in conception and form. The period was 1910 when revolution broke out in Mexico:

Soldadera

Yells, shouts, general havoc seems to reign in the small Mexican village.

At first one gets bewildered, one cannot understand what is going on——

Women wrangling, fighting, shouting at each other. . . .

These are soldiers' wives, 'soldaderas', forerunners of the army, who have invaded the village. . . .

One of them is Pancha; a machine-gun ribbon hangs across her shoulder. . . .

The soldiers are breaking camp. . . .

A little girl is crying and to console her the mother, for lack of candy, gives her a cartridge. . . .

The weary army enters the village. . . .

Artillery soldiers release the donkeys and mules from the dust-covered machine-gun carriages. . . .

Pancha finds her soldier, Juan. . .

Supper over, Juan rests his head in Pancha's lap and hums the tune the guitars are playing.

'Adelita' is the name of the song and this song is the leitmotif of the 'Soldadera'.

When overcome by exhaustion he falls asleep. . . .

Pancha places five or six cartridges in Juan's gun and puts the gun by his side.

She packs her household belongings in her big sack.

Suddenly the loud voice of the author calls to Pancha:
Say, 'Soldadera'. . . .

'Where art thou going, woman?'

She turns pensively, smiles enigmatically, shrugs her shoulders. . . .
'Who knows?'

She is borne onwards by the strong current of women. . . .

Machine-guns are roaring.

Clatter of cavalry is heard.

A battle is raging.

Juan is fighting like the rest of the soldiers. . . .

Under the cars of a freight train the soldaderas are praying for their fighting men. . . .

The soldaderas go to the train, to the engine, and hence they look in the direction of the ending battle. . . .

Question. . . ! 'Have you seen mine?'

The excited Pancha is looking for Juan.

Here they bring him wounded.

Pancha runs up to him.

Uncovers his face. . . .

No, that is not he. . . .

Juan is safe and sound but worn out. . . .

Having seen him board the train Pancha gets on the engine platform.

The angry voice of the sentinel calls to her.

'What have you there under your shawl?'

And lifting her rebozo, Pancha answers quietly:

'Who knows, senor, it may be a girl or it may be a boy!' . . .

At daybreak, the soot-covered stoker leaps from car to car of the train in motion—jumps among the wandering women and children. . . .

Under the clothes hung out in the lanterns to dry, under soldiers' underwear waved by the wind, near the blazing bonfire, Pancha is sitting with her new-born baby. . . .

Another battle! . . .

Again the racket of machine-gun fire. . . .

Again the soldaderas are awaiting the returned wounded soldiers. . . .

This time Juan does not come back.

Pancha finds the body of her husband. . . .

She gathers a pile of rocks, makes him a primitive tombstone, weaves him a cross of reeds.

She takes his gun, his cartridge belt, his baby, and follows the slowly advancing, tired army. . . .

And then the same cross soldier walks up to her and takes the baby from her.

Pancha leans on the strong arm of her new husband in order not to fall and not to lag behind the army.

'Adelita' is the tune the tired bands are playing, falsely and out of rhythm.

The army has prepared for an attack, but the people from the city come up and explain.

The civil war is over.

Revolution has triumphed. . . .

The armies are fraternizing.

One might decipher on the banner—the last words of its device: Towards Revolution.

Towards a New Life. . . . (App. Five.)

'Soldadera' deeply moved Sergei Mikhailovich, for through this story he desired to convey the unity of human experience and the unity of death and life. As a young man, Eisenstein had moved from place to place with the ragged Soviet Army of Workers and Peasants; that the Mexicans had shared with him the experience of revolution was part of the great bond he felt with Mexico. In the figure of Pancha, Sergei Mikhailovich not only saw the flow of life but the evolutionary history of women. In Pancha there was the beginning of the independent woman sharing the common experiences of war and revolution with man. In restrospect, Eisenstein said that the birth of Pancha's baby would not have taken place as indicated in the scenario, but during the second battle, with the child's first cry coinciding with the death of Juan.

This story was the only one of the *Que Viva Mexico!* 'novels' which Eisenstein did not shoot. He planned to shoot 'Soldadera' last: before he was able to commence, Upton Sinclair ordered him to cease work on *Que Viva Mexico!* Fortunately, before the order came Sergei Mikhailovich directed and shot the culminating sequence—the Epilogue—in which, through montage, he planned to draw all the multi-threads of the 'novels' together and present his dialectically developed philosophy. This philosophic climax he had expressed in his very first outline: 'The great wisdom of Mexico about death. The unity of death and life. The passing of the one and the birth of the next one. The eternal circle. And the still greater wisdom of Mexico: the *enjoying* of this eternal circle. Death Day in Mexico.'

Eisenstein's scenario gives very little idea of the richness of his concept, or the character of the material which he finally shot. The idea of the Epilogue—Death Day on the 2nd of November—he had originally found in the book *Idols Behind Altars*. This section of the whole film was the one which he loved best and throughout his life it retained a tremendous hold over his imagination; so great that in the face of his own death he sought to emulate the Mexican spirit of *vacilada*, that curious blend of mocking denial, mocking belief that accepts anything as possible though admitting rationally that it is not; a heroic choice to attempt all and accept with grim humour the greatest tragedy.

Epilogue

Time and location—modern Mexico (1931–2).

Mexico of to-day on the ways to peace, prosperity and civilization.

Factories, railroads, harbours with enormous boats. . . .

The people of to-day.

Leaders of the country.

Generals.

Engineers.

Aviators.

Builders of new Mexico.

and

Children—the future people of future Mexico. . . .

New machinery.

New houses.

New people. . . .

And the Nation's leaders, the President, generals, secretaries of State Departments . . . you will behold in the land and in the cities the same faces—

Faces that bear close resemblance to those who held the funeral of antiquity in Yucatan, those who danced in Tehuantepec; those who sang the Alabada. . . .

The same faces—

but different people.

After the President's speeches and the generals' commands—

Death comes along dancing!

Not just one, but many deaths; many skulls, skeletons. . . .

What is that?

That is the carnival pageant.

The most original, traditional pageant, 'Calavera', death day.
This is the remarkable Mexican Day, when Mexicans recall the past and show their contempt of death.
The film began with the realm of death.
With victory of life over death, over the influences of the past, the film ends.
Life brims from under the cardboard skeletons, life gushes forth, and death retreats, fades away.
A little Indian carefully removes his death mask and smiles a contagious smile—he impersonates the new growing Mexico. [Plate 27].

Thus, Sergei Mikhailovich affirmed his belief in the great power of simple humanity to rise above the force of death and the oppression of the many by the few. But it had emerged as a cosmic process rather than a strictly political one. Now Eisenstein thought of life not in terms of single revolutionary movements or periods, but in great cycles of time, and for all the rest of his life he was to struggle to convey the magnitude of his vision of the life force defeating the forces of death and decay.

Sergei Mikhailovich had not the slightest intention of editing the Epilogue as it reads in the scenario. On the cutting table he had intended to turn the apparent glorification of 'modern' Mexico (material which some people later termed 'reactionary') inside out. The shots of 'Leaders of the Country, Generals, Engineers, Aviators, Officers, Technicians . . .' all of them composed with formality and a curious rigidity, were to be used, as it were, against themselves.

'Through montage,' Sergei Mikhailovich explained to me later with his most wicked smile, 'these shots were to appear satirical when intercut with the shots of Death Day figures. Death Day in Mexico has a unique character. In the past it had been the one day in the year when censorship was lifted and political satire permitted. Look at Posada's prints! Politicos were lambasted as skeletons and death's heads. And no one was sent to gaol!'

To carry out his ideas, however, Eisenstein shot material without telling the censors how he intended to use it. As his difficulties increased, Sergei Mikhailovich did not always take even Agustin Aragon Leiva into his confidence. At one point, Leiva was concerned by what he considered Eisenstein's seeming betrayal of the interests of the Mexican people. In a letter to Seymour Stern, dated the 7th of January 1932, Leiva says: 'Eisy [Eisenstein] has got in acquaintance with the racketeer in chief [General] Calles; he is in the film, altogether with the imbecile President [Obregon] we have. I see this as dangerous stuff for the stand-

ing of Eisy among the advanced people, as it is no more a secret that
Calles is the wealthiest Mexican, a fascist of the worst kind. . . . I cannot
imagine [him] in the film otherwise than in a sarcastic mood. We must
refrain of doing any comment until we'll see the film complete.'

But Sergei Mikhailovich later explained to Leiva why he was in
contact with these politicians, and that the material was intended to be
used satirically in the Epilogue. (See App. Five.) In an effort to aid
Eisenstein in his difficulties with Sinclair, who was complaining about
the cost, Alvarez del Vayo, the Spanish Ambassador, brought Eisenstein into contact with General Calles and President Obregon. To shoot
the 'Soldadera' episode, Eisenstein needed detachments of Mexican
soldiers and the use of railway equipment, etc., and it was through
Calles and Obregon that a detachment of the Army was put at his
disposal. However, Sinclair ordered Sergei Mikhailovich to stop work
on the film just when he was ready to shoot the 'Soldadera' story.

Even in retrospect, Sergei Mikhailovich chuckled over his plan for
evading the Mexican advisers, headed by Adolfo Best-Maugard, set
over him to see that he conveyed no unpleasant impressions of Mexican
politics. Yes, he understood very well the spirit of *vacilada*. [Plate
29]

In order to carry out his plans, Sergei Mikhailovich 'shot' many
'invented' death figures as well as the festival itself. He borrowed skeletons from the Medical School in Mexico City, took them to the roof
of the Hotel Imperial and dressed them up, some as the characters in
the Maguey story, others as a banker, a general, a hacendado and an
archbishop, each symbolic of the death of the past. [Plate 26] His
shots of the President, General Calles and the Archbishop of Mexico
were to be intercut with 'their' respective skeletons. This Posada-like
political satire embodying the underlying revolutionary tendency of
Mexico, was to be juxtaposed with the faces of laughing Mexican
workers and children who were the epitome of the future.[1] [Plate 28]

Throughout the Epilogue, the formal composition of the whole of
Que Viva Mexico! was reaffirmed in almost every shot; each motif
being dialectically introduced on a new level. The austere mourners
and ceremonial dishes on the coffin in the Prologue reappear in the

[1] The footage of the politicians, police, etc., later caused great dispute.
Eisenstein's supporters declared correctly that it was intended to be used
satirically, but Upton Sinclair maintained at one moment that there was nothing
in the picture that could be used against the Mexican Government and at
another hinted that some of Eisenstein's material was 'fascist in tone'. This dispute alienated some of Eisenstein's original supporters, who were later unwilling
to support the campaign against Sinclair to save *Que Viva Mexico!*

Epilogue as the gay, laughing lovers feasting by the grave and the little children playing with the sugar skulls. The skull motif of the first 'novel'—'Fiesta'—re-emerges in the bizarre Death Day toys, the dancing workers wearing death masks and the children playing with the symbols of death. Most interesting was the symbol of the ferris wheel, moving as a rhythmic focal point signifying the rotating of the 'eternal circle'. In the foreground of the ferris wheel—living figures, alternating with death masks arranged in the form of a triangle; the circle and the pyramid united; the eternal triangle and the eternal circle. [Plate 26]

The triangle dominated the compositional scheme of *Que Viva Mexico!* Its constant dialectical development was to carry forward the evolution of concepts beginning with the Prologue, passing into the first 'novel', taking 'a leap forward' in the third 'novel' and reaching a synthesis in the Epilogue. In the second 'novel' and the fourth (had it been shot), the pyramidal composition was not stressed, because in these two episodes Eisenstein's subject-matter was the real life of people rather than the depiction of concepts. The compositional character of *Que Viva Mexico!* was Eisenstein's distillation of the compositional essence of the country where the pyramidical form dominates: in the formation of the mountains, the pyramid temples built by the Toltecs, Mayas and Aztecs, the formal shape of the sombrero hat and the folds of the sarape hanging from the shoulders of the Indians. Sergei Mikhailovich also derived his use of three figures from the strikingly formalistic elements of Mexican daily life: three women customarily guarding the Cross at Easter and the common sight of three people sitting near a grave during festival days.

The significance Eisenstein attached to the compositional element in Mexico exerted a deep and lasting influence upon him. Under its impact he became convinced that for his future work composition within each 'frame' must be of equal importance with montage in forming the structural base of film dynamics. Montage remained as the method of giving rhythm and emphasis to an ever stronger compositional unity within the single 'frame'. Though the Eisenstein of *Que Viva Mexico!* was never to develop in accordance with his new concepts of film structure, yet without those concepts his later works—*Alexander Nevsky* and *Ivan the Terrible*—would probably not reveal the distinctive compositional character to be observed in them. [Plate 48]

Eisenstein's preoccupation with composition and mysticism was noticed by the painter Jean Charlot, who found the complexity of Sergei Mikhailovich's interests rather unexpected. According to Charlot, Eisenstein 'was studying mysticism and the works of Saint Theresa of Avila. The result was a series of drawings on the stigmata. . . . I was curious of this angle in his thoughts. I think he felt that he was missing something important, but could not fit it into an orthodox Marxist pattern.'[1]

Eisenstein tried to rationalize by comparing the desire to rest 'in the bosom of Abraham to the medical state in which adults, in their wish to return to the womb, adopt foetal positions. He made at least one symbolical drawing on those lines.'[2]

'Variation I—Werther's Death', Mexico 1931

---

[1] Jean Charlot in a letter to the author, dated March 1950.
[2] *Ibid.*, dated 1 April 1950.

There were many other drawings: the Bull series, mentioned earlier, which impressed the poet Witter Bynner as 'a remarkable perform- ance', and another on the Death of Duncan, which Eisenstein kept. Yet another series was on the theme of Salome and John the Baptist, a theme to which Sergei Mikhailovich returned some years later.

One of the series was entitled 'Ten Aspects of the Death of Werther'. Sergei Mikhailovich gave this set to Isabelita Villasenor—often known as Chabela—the young art student whom he selected to portray the role of 'Maria' in the Maguey 'novel', because she was 'like dark flames and so like the Virgin', and Gabriel Fernandez Ledesma, who later became her husband.

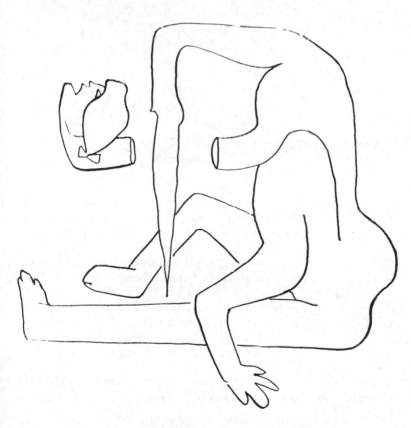

'Variation II—Werther's Death', Mexico 1931

Jean Charlot recalls watching Eisenstein draw 'very quickly so as not to disturb the subconscious elements. He planned to number the drawings in the order they were made and considered them as stills of a movie strip. Thus considered they are highly interesting documents to his mental workings'.[1] They impressed Charlot as being 'close to an automatic writing type of drawing', which Eisenstein said he would later analyse rationally in order to find out 'what had happened in this release of "stream of consciousness",' but Charlot did not know whether Sergei Mikhailovich did this or not. It did not appear to Charlot that there was a special mood in which Eisenstein turned to drawing, but as an 'intellectual search'.[2]

Some of the drawings which Eisenstein did in Mexico were later exhibited in New York at the John Becker Gallery.

[1] Jean Charlot in a letter to the author, dated March 1950.
[2] Ibid., dated 1 April 1950.

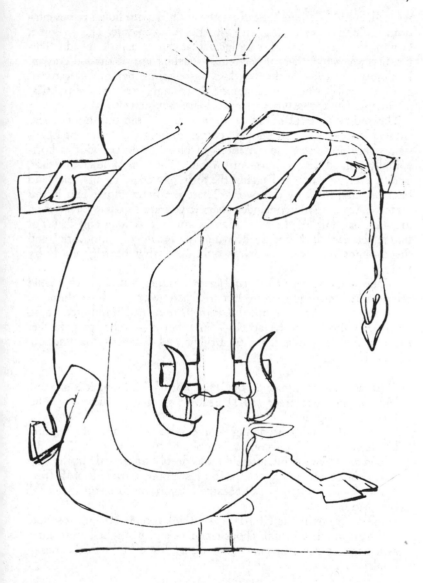

Alyce Wade, who saw this exhibition, described the drawings as 'a series of highly intriguing musings in red and black', which appeared 'like a devil-may-care launch into the æsthetically unexplored'. In the series 'labelled "Salome", he dispensed entirely with literal representation. St. John is seen toying with a disembodied Salome. The "Salome, Garcon de Café", has lines so lucid that one is a little awed.' This lucidity was achieved by Eisenstein's 'startling use of the red crayon. It is most noticeable in the drawings on religious themes, "Stigmata" and "Descent". These latter, amazingly enough, were free of political comment. The whole series are disturbingly sanguine.'

The most powerful of the series was that of the bull-fight where 'Matador and picador are doing yeoman duty in the service of Eisenstein's racy and eccentric variations in blood. The matador is horizontally pinned on the horns of the bull. Then, in another drawing, both are securely fastened against the form of a cross. Finally, man and beast are transfixed by the sword. There is a fierce movement in this theme.' Alyce Wade concluded that 'if you are looking for even an infinitesimal trace of the revolutionist, you'll look long and then not find it.' Instead, she found the drawings 'personal and iconoclastic', and she thought that some people would 'probably be frightened' by them.[1]

While working on *Que Viva Mexico!*, Sergei Mikhailovich would often retire 'into monastic seclusion . . . to work on his volume of esthetics'.[2] This book, entitled *Direction*, remained unfinished at his death. He also wrote an article—'Film Form'—embodying further theoretical ideas. In a letter to Bryher and Kenneth MacPherson, Eisenstein said:

At last I am sending you the 'Film Form'. . . . Hope it is not too. late for the September [1931] issue of your new 'heavy-weight' form of a magazine!

The style is also becoming of the sort: so in one of the three languages with which you are 'snobbing' the poor reader I am designed as '*Monsieur* Eisenstein'! I was deeply impressed! In the next days I hope to send you a pack of amusing pyramide-stuff from Yucatan—the oldest part of Mexico à condition that you won't call me 'Monsieur'! . . .

I hope you will like Film-Form—I think it one of the most serious and basic in what I think about cinema—and it might be presented as a page of my still (and I am afraid for ever!) 'forthcoming' book! . . .'

[1] Alyce Wade in a letter to Seymour Stern, dated 9 November 1932.
[2] 'Eisenstein's New Film', by Morris Helprin, *New York Times*, 29 November 1931.

But Eisenstein was seldom gay except when the eyes of strangers were upon him, or when he felt compelled to hide his feelings. His mode of life in Mexico made a deep impression on the man who worked with him and came to know him more intimately than perhaps any other. Agustin Aragon Leiva later wrote: 'In fourteen months of work, Eisenstein was known to live as a brother friar. Working and studying. He devoured books; he loves Science. He looks sixty years old and is only 34. His *raison d'etre* is to learn. He cares for nothing worldly. While we were all having the daily amusements of gay people, he remained in his cell, an actual cell, as we were in an old convent, reading Pavlov, [and] Eddington, Planck, Jeans, and other physicists'.[1]

In *Que Viva Mexico!* the inner dominants of Eisenstein emerged. He no longer feared the intensely emotional qualities of his creative nature; he no longer avoided the results of his highly original philosophic mind, which was attuned to the creation of works of art scaled to time-lessness rather than topicality. Though he remained a socially conscious artist, his revolutionary viewpoint was one that had become so highly individualized that it was no longer closely or clearly related to any existing group of artists. Sergei Eisenstein, the creator of the revolutionary film, now stood alone split off from Soviet cinematography and equally apart from American or European trends in cinematography. He was in actuality an artist isolated by the overwhelming force of his individuality and thus his position could only become extremely difficult. He stood outside the scope of cinematography under capitalism and it remained to be seen whether he would not also stand beyond the development of Soviet cinematography geared to the immediate problems of Soviet life.

From early on the production of *Que Viva Mexico!* encountered many difficulties. Since Sergei Eisenstein had no experience in making an independent film in the capitalist sense, independence went to his head. The result was that though he did not spend money in the lavish fashion of the Hollywood directors who later worked in Mexico, and even at Tetlapayac, Sergei Mikhailovich was not as economical as he might have been had he had previous experience. In all, he claimed that he spent $53,000,[2] or the equivalent cost of one sequence later 'shot' at Tetlapayac for the Hollywood production *Viva Villa*. Nevertheless, $53,000 was more than twice the amount originally discussed with Mrs. Upton Sinclair.

[1] Agustin Aragon Leiva in a letter to Seymour Stern, dated 22 June 1933.

[2] Eisenstein's statement to the author as to the amount he spent on *Que Viva Mexico!* was later confirmed by Grigori Alexandrov.

The basic costs were increased by lack of facilities in Mexico; Sergei Mikhailovich was obliged to send his rushes to Upton Sinclair in Hollywood for processing. He could not, therefore, look at his work and study it. To ensure that he would have a useable 'take' of every shot, Tisse photographed much duplicate footage and Sergei Mikhailovich directed many alternative 'takes'. This fact greatly disturbed Upton Sinclair when the film began to arrive in Hollywood. Just as Eisenstein was handicapped by lack of facilities in Mexico, so Sinclair was handicapped by his lack of knowledge about the technique of film production. Until he saw Eisenstein's rushes, Sinclair had never seen the rushes of a film like that proposed by Eisenstein. He did not understand why Eisenstein shot so much film, a great deal of which did not *look* in any way related. The distance between the two men, lack of facilities on the one hand and lack of technical knowledge on the other, prepared the ground for difficulties between Sergei Eisenstein, who was never very communicative during his creative work, and Upton Sinclair, whose attitude was predominantly that of a crusader rather than an artist.

At the end of eleven months, however, Upton Sinclair appeared to be enthusiastic about Eisenstein's work, at least to outsiders. Sinclair circulated a letter dated 26th October, 1931, a copy of which he sent to one of Sergei Mikhailovich's old friends :

Dear Mr. Dana:
    The Eisenstein expedition has been working in Mexico for eleven months; my wife and I undertook to raise the money; and my wife's brother, Hunter Kimbrough, is acting as our representative in the field. So far they have sent 110,000 feet of negative, which we have developed, stored, and insured in Hollywood laboratory. We have raised the necessary funds, and we did not intend to offer this picture until it was cut, and perhaps until it was synchronized. But developments appear to be forcing our hand. I will tell you briefly what these have been:
        1. The head of one of the big concerns in Hollywood heard of the picture and sent a representative to Mexico to see the work . . . and I have reason to think he is about to make an offer.
        2. There is in New York a lady who organized a Mexican Art Association, with the backing of the Rockefellers. . . . She took a batch of stills to New York, and recently being in Mexico again, she reported to my brother-in-law that she had shown them to the Rockefeller family who were delighted with them, and that old John D. had sat on the floor for an hour, looking at them and talking about

Mexico. A member of the Rockefeller Institute indicated his willingness to invest. . . .[1]

These steps were taken without my knowledge. But if a satis-
factory offer is made, I think the investors will want me to take it,
because we are none of us moving picture people, and went into the
undertaking as a matter of art, because we wanted to give a great
director an opportunity to make a picture according to his own
unhampered ideas.

. . . Every person who has seen the pictures has been delighted
beyond measure. Edmund Wilson, one of the directors of The New
Republic, said 'It makes one realize that there is something in art
after all'. . . . I will quote you a few passages from my brother-in-
law's recent letters: 'Eisenstein is trying to make a world sensational
picture'. 'The picture will be a great success. . . . The editor of
Ilustrado, the magazine which has been giving us publicity, saw the
picture a few nights ago, in company with the official from Gover-
nacion who is handling our business. Both were delighted. The
editor said he could not speak too highly of the picture; that it is a
masterpiece,—he is organizing a Mexican Picture Company, and
says he wants to use this picture as a model, a text-book for his
cameramen and directors to study before making any pictures in
Mexico' . . .

. . . When the best of it is selected and put together in the Eisenstein
fashion, the critics will go wild about it. . .

In the second half of this long letter, Upton Sinclair revealed that he
was informed as to Eisenstein's basic plan and approved his proposal to
make a full-length film composed of six interrelated episodes, instead
of a picture costing about $25,000 and one to be produced in three or
four months, as provided in the contract. These facts, Sinclair later
denied.

I will also quote a paragraph from one of Eisenstein's own letters,
as this explains his own attitude: '. . . the greatness of our gesture in
arranging the whole business was to try. . . . The absolute figure of
the footage has not obtained the footage of *October* (*Ten Days that
Shook the World*) (225,000 feet). The work with the natives takes

[1] The author has a letter written to her in which the statements referring to
the showing of stills to the Rockefeller family, their interest in the film and
willingness to invest money, and the reporting of this 'to my brother-in-law',
are characterized as being without any foundation in fact. For reasons wholly
beyond the control of the author, this letter cannot be published, nor the name
of the writer disclosed.

enormous quantities of it. . . . The episodes are planned to capture each a different part of an audience, and those who prefer lyric voluptuousness to tragedy may repose on the Tehuantepec scenes; lovers of girls might enjoy the Spanish episode with mantillas and adultery; real connoisseurs of plastic value the Yucatan scenes about which our Spanish Embassy audience was practically raving. I do not want to sing hymns to myself, but I know that a victory never will and never has been got on half ways. The actual shooting and arranging (what is much worse) takes all my forces and energies.'

I have a long and very detailed scenario of the story which was officially submitted by Eisenstein to the Mexican government and approved. . . .

Eisenstein has submitted to me a schedule of his future work from day to day, and he wants to shoot a total of 180,000 feet. This seems a great deal for one picture, but he is extremely fastidious, and we have felt justified in letting him have his way. I believe we are going to have one of the most marvelous pictures ever made, and one that will be a revelation of the possibilities of the art. The work is compared by Eisenstein to 'Decameron' by Boccaccio; or it may be compared to a musical suite: that is to say, it is a series of four episodes, with a prologue and an epilogue, all with a harmonious atmosphere and setting. Each episode is in a different place, and the total effect is a vision of Mexico through 5,000 years.

. . . . The first 75,000 feet of prints were sent back to Mexico and Eisenstein's assistant has made a rough selection of some of the best material and put it in consecutive form, about four reels. This was shown at the home of the Spanish Ambassador [Alvarez del Vayo], and the President of Mexico, the Minister of Foreign Affairs, and several other cabinet members were present. . . .

We have the last 35,000 feet of rushes in Hollywood, . . . you will have to bear in mind that Eisenstein has never seen these. He did not see the first 75,000 until five or six months after the shooting. . . .

Sincerely

(signed) UPTON

Attached to this letter was a report showing the status of the Eisenstein Picture as of the 2nd November, 1931:

The party has been in Mexico eleven months. They have sent back 100,000 feet of negative. . . . It has passed the censorship of the Mexican government and inspection by the United States Customs and is our sole property.

. . . The work has been delayed by wet weather, fevers and governmental red tape.

Eisenstein asks to be allowed to remain in Mexico another three or four months. He has submitted a complete detailed scenario of his picture, and a schedule of all scenes still to be shot, and of the costs to finish the work in Mexico. The total estimated cost of the picture is $90,000, and of this $10,000 has still to be raised.

The investment can no longer be considered speculative, as the developed film has been seen by many experts who have given it unqualified praise, and a picture can certainly be made out of it. The big distributors have all begun bidding for it. . . .

The enterprise had been organized under the laws of the State of California as the Mexican Picture Trust. According to Sinclair, the investors were to receive certificates of their interest, which were to be held in escrow until the film was marketed. The first sums received from the sale of the film were to be used to pay the investors in full. After that, the investors were to receive their pro rata share of fifty per cent of the profits, the other fifty per cent to go to the promoters and to Eisenstein and his party. The trustees were Mary Craig Sinclair and her younger brother, Hunter Kimbrough, who was business manager of the venture.

When the controversy over *Que Viva Mexico!* began a few months later, Sinclair changed his mind about Eisenstein and the film. In a letter to H. W. L. Dana, Sinclair said:

The talk about 'the great masterpiece' is all plain bunk. Eisenstein was making five pictures and he purposely kept them incomplete as a means of making it impossible for us to call him from Mexico. If this stuff were all to be shoveled into one picture it would make such a mess that no one would go to see it except out of curiosity. I look forward with great joy to the time when Eisenstein will at last be able to cut his own version of his 'great masterpiece' and we shall see what happens.

In the meantime, every month additional difficulties arose, many of them trivial and common to all film production. But the disastrous results of each were increased by the clash of personalities and interests involved in the making of the film. In effect, three groups crystallized, each with a different axe to grind. There was Eisenstein, whose sole consideration was the creation of a work of art, and his supporters, some of whom quite unrealistically thought that the Olympian Sergei Mikhailovich could do no wrong. Then there were the Mexican advisers, whose duty it was to serve their Government and lead Eisenstein, if they could, down a somewhat flowery path. Half of them were sensitive, touchy souls who required tactful handling. Lastly there was the storm centre—Mrs. Sinclair's brother, Hunter Kimbrough, who was acting as business manager of the project.

Mr. Kimbrough, though he held the purse strings and was supposed to look after the Sinclair interests, was inexperienced in film production. Still more unfortunate was the fact that he despised the Mexicans and had a natural suspicion of strangers and foreigners. To add to the initial difficulties, Kimbrough was not an artist, and Sergei Eisenstein, both as an individual and as an artist, was entirely incomprehensible to him. At best, the association was extremely embarrassing to Hunter Kimbrough, who strove with all his might to interpret Eisenstein's behaviour according to his own canons. He declared that Eisenstein was no communist and even implied that Eisenstein might not return to the Soviet Union. Altogether the situation was pregnant with trouble from the outset, so that in case of a serious rift a storm of charges and counter-charges was inevitable.

Admittedly it was easy to misunderstand Eisenstein, and unfortunately he often showed very little tact in handling people. His preoccupation with his work sometimes led him to ignore important people who came to see him, and his indifference as to what went on around him laid him open to exploitation. While in Mexico all sorts of irresponsible people attached themselves as a kind of fringe to Eisenstein. A fairly typical day at Tetlapayac during the direction of the Maguey story struck an uninitiated outsider as the escapade of a group of ill-assorted eccentrics.

Katherine Anne Porter recorded her impressions in a short story called *Hacienda*. Out of the mêlée the most rational person appeared to be Alexandrov. To Miss Porter, Eisenstein—Uspensky in the story—seemed an exaggerated figure who never said an intelligible word. He merely sat 'in his monkey-suit of striped overalls, his face like a superhumanly enlightened monkey's now well overgrown with a simian beard. He had', so Katherine Anne Porter thought, 'a monkey attitude towards life which amounted to a personal philosophy.'[1]

Gossip had it that Eisenstein visited the reputedly obscene theatres of Mexico City and complimented the Mexicans on the 'shows', and he amused members of the American bourgeoisie with sheaves of ribald drawings. He was alleged to have staged clownish performances of old Russian country comedies on the open roads, during which he would 'shout his lines broadly and be in his best humour, prodding the rear of a patient burro, accustomed to grief and indignity, with a phallus-shaped gourd'.[2] This kind of humour made no adverse impressions on

---

[1] *Flowering Judas and Other Stories*, by Katherine Anne Porter (London, Jonathan Cape Ltd., 1936 and New York, The Modern Library, 1940), p. 255.
[2] *Ibid.*, p. 253.

the Mexicans, but Sergei Mikhailovich was under the scrutiny of other people. Of Upton Sinclair it was often said: 'Scratch him and you find a Puritan.' Eisenstein possessed grandeur of personality but, lacking circumspection, he often did what he wanted without considering the consequences. His shyness sometimes led him into flights of exhibitionism.

Hunter Kimbrough was present during some of Eisenstein's escapades, but he was hardly the man to comprehend that men assume strange masks to hide their inner nature. The relationship between Eisenstein and Kimbrough degenerated as the months passed—three, six, nine, twelve. . . .[1]

Kimbrough was 'a young Southerner with very old-fashioned ideals of honour'. He disliked the smell of the highly-seasoned Mexican food, and lack of modern sanitation made him dread disease. Like most white men reared in the Southern States he felt superior to the dark complexioned Mexicans. He could not understand their tempo of life, and over the months the warm, mocking laughter of Mexico undermined the conviction that he was master of the situation.

The people of Tetlapayac still tell the story of a spectacular joke they played on Kimbrough one day when he was returning from Mexico City. A number of Mexicans, together with Eisenstein, Tisse and Alexandrov, dressed as 'bandits' and draped with cartridge belts and 'six shooters' [Plate 28], rode off to meet Hunter Kimbrough's train. They 'held it up' a short distance from the station and dragged Kimbrough off. Within a few seconds, Kimbrough realised he had been made the butt of a practical joke. Sometime later he told Upton Sinclair a tale which is most likely his version of this story—that he 'disarmed a Mexican who tried to kill him and took from the man Eisenstein's gun which Eisenstein had given him for that purpose'. (App. Six.)

One crisis followed another: at Tetlapayac, in Mexico City, in far-off Tehuantepec and in Yucatan. With each crisis a flood of stories circu-

---

[1] The first confirmation of the many rumours of serious trouble was a letter from Leiva to Stern, dated the 30th October, 1931, in which he said: Eisenstein 'is facing such troubles that he is in danger of producing an unfinished symphony. This is confidential to you only!' On the 14th of November 1931, Stern received a letter from Lalla Rookh Rogers, in which she said: 'I know the film of Eisenstein is going to be a knockout. I am sorry it is taking so long but those three men are working day and night and showing the strain somewhat, I think. And of course they have difficulties here in getting permission, etc., to film certain things that they want. It is not so much a matter of difficulties as a matter of time—it is always manana with the Mexicans—and "one moment, please," oftentimes means hours or days!'

lated. It was alleged that in Tehuantepec Eisenstein contracted to pay the people in the film, but when the business manager appeared he had no money with which to fulfil the obligation. Rumour had it that he had lost all the money in Mexico City. But the most serious 'incident' is said to have occurred in Yucatan towards the end of 1931. The story in Yucatan is that Kimbrough went to a jungle village near Chichen-Itza, where they were then shooting some scenes, and somehow or other became involved in a brawl with two Indians, whereupon the villagers intervened and the three men were locked up for the night.

By this time, stories concerning Eisenstein's difficulties in Mexico had spread abroad. In an effort to dispel any unfavourable comment, Sergei Mikhailovich wrote to Leon Moussinac as early as August 1931. He told Moussinac of the hostility he had encountered on arriving in Mexico and of the police surveillance to which he was subjected. In order to allay the rumour that he might not return to the Soviet Union, he stated that he had received permission from Moscow through Soyuzkino to remain abroad until January 1932. (His statement was confirmed by the Moscow correspondent of *Revue du Cinema*, 1 October 1931.) He went on in his letter to tell Moussinac of the style he was developing in *Que Viva Mexico!*, and of the book concerning film aesthetics on which he was working.

As the pressure upon Sergei Eisenstein intensified he went on joking and, in his own odd way, holding his peace. But inwardly his resistance was breaking down and he felt desperately alone.

At the beginning of December, he wrote to Seymour Stern:

<blockquote>
Mexican Picture Trust
S. M. Eisenstein
Collective Productions
                                    Please ask Stade if
                                    he has sent me Spinoza's
                                    'Ethics'
</blockquote>

MY DEAR SEYMOUR!

I was very happy to get your letter and *just now*. Some time later you will know why, when I'll let you peep in such profoundness of troubles I at the present moment have, and only a movie picture director can have!

I do not know what will be the future, but so far now I think it is the *most* serious (and I had many) situation I ever had. And I mean what I say. . . . Do not try to find out but wait when it will be over—I myself will let you know. And then you will believe in the reality of fairy-tales (not meaning pancies with that!)

I am terribly torn away from Europe: for instance I never knew that 'Perspectives' ('Intellectual Cinema') was printed in 'Querschnitt' and you will oblige me very much if you will ask Gangster [Christel Gang] (whom I sincerely thank for her front-view—as from another side I have her for long ago!) to make me a present of it (I mean 'Querschnitt')—it is a pure personal matter—when I was very young I was enormously impressed by 'Querschnitt' and having not had written one article at that time—it was my dream to see myself printed someday in the magazine of high-brow . . . bunk (this opinion belongs to to-day . . . but nevertheless I would be very pleased to have the number). . . .

It is a pitty [sic] that neither you nor I do not believe in god. . . . We might pray to him to get some little help in my situation. So far god seems the only one who could do something. . . . Sincerely

Eisenstein

(There are so few dreams made in the youth that become realized some day, even if somewhat too late—like the one with 'Q'!)

As the storm gathered his thoughts constantly turned towards Pera Attasheva; it seemed that she alone could help him. Finally Sergei Mikhailovich cabled for her to come to Mexico. But the Soviet authorities refused his request for Pera to join him. It was a terrible shock to Sergei Mikhailovich. No matter what the rumours circulating about him, he had never entertained the thought of deserting his country.

Thus, he was forced to face his increasing troubles alone. The storm was rising to its climax. Returning from Yucatan to Mexico City, Sergei Mikhailovich at last realized that he and his film were headed for a catastrophe. In a mood of despair he one day sat in a café and drew his commentary upon himself in a self-portrait—a crucified ape.

As the crisis grew over the film, some of Eisenstein's American admirers assured him of their support. It has been said that a few wanted to make affidavits stating what they witnessed in regard to the difficulties confronting Sergei Eisenstein at that stage. But he is said to have waved aside the offer on the grounds that he disliked 'pettiness', and to draw up affidavits for his own protection was 'petty'. Kimbrough left Mexico for Hollywood and Eisenstein returned to Tetlapayac.

Though he seemed incapable of protecting his own interests at crucial moments, Eisenstein showed a strident and blunt sincerity when anyone misrepresented him in terms of Soviet society. He would let anything pass that concerned only himself, but he would let nothing pass that cast a reflection upon the Soviet Union. In November 1931 he wrote the following letter to *The Nation* magazine:

SIR:

In your issue of November 4, you published an article entitled Eisenstein inHollywood', by Mr. Edmund Wilson, which described in friendly terms my tribulations, in the United States and Mexico. Unfortunately, the article fails to mention my two companions, Co-director Alexandrov and Cameraman Tisse, although they have collaborated with me for a period of ten years.

Mr. Wilson's article is on the whole very fine, but I regret to say that it contains a passage which misrepresents my whole attitude toward the work I have so far accomplished in the movies. In connection with the Mexican picture which we are now making, Mr. Wilson says: 'Eisenstein in Mexico, in the meantime *was having a free hand for the first time in his life.*' The italics are mine. . . .

Whatever the author may have had in mind, his words imply that the only way I could escape from artistic 'forced labor' in the Soviet Union was by a trip to Latin America with funds supplied by some 'radical millionaire' so that I could have a 'free hand' for the first time in my life.

I reject such a misconception. It profoundly dishonors those who give all their greatest efforts to the task of creating the Soviet cinema, and slanders the Soviet social system, the only system which could give free creativeness an opportunity to expand. . . . Even our most violent enemies cannot deny our creative growth.

We Soviet artists, compelled by nobody, make it our own duty and our greatest ambition to handle in the arts and to express in our pictures the problems, subjects and themes which are important and vital to the growth and development of our republic of workers and peasants. . . .

In fulfilling this task, it might indeed happen, as Mr. Wilson put it, that 'efficiency may rush and embarrass an artist . . . and a rigid political creed which is always demanding fables to point its morals may have its irksome side'. But this may only mean that we have not yet succeeded in completely mastering the wild horse of the cinema—the mad Pegasus—rushing so many a cinematographer outside of Russia to pure . . . hell! . . . And we are not ashamed to confess that it is only because of our own inability to master completely the art of cinema expression that the social problem or 'rigid creed' sometimes crushes the fragile beauty of cinema esthetics.

. . . Even a defeat on this path means immensely more to us than many a victory on the glorious path of the united box office. All the artistic achievements and progress of the Soviet film are due precisely to the fact that it has had to face and solve unprecedented problems for the first time.

Mr. Wilson also misunderstood my motives in going to Mexico.

'Eisenstein,' he said, 'entranced with the Mexican scenery, so different from the bleak Gulf of Finland or the flat expanses of the collective farms, became carried away with the ambition to make a perfect film. . . .'

It so happens that my complexion is the exact opposite of Don Quixote's, and this in itself would argue that in regard to my own work I would never use such quixotic fanfaronades as this. . . .

There is nothing especially Mexican in the desire to make a good picture. It is true, however, that in order to develop cinema methods and to approach new forms of cinema expression, an occasional experiment with quite new, unusual and even completely opposite material is not only permissible but of the greatest experimental value. Remember the Marxian theory of opposites!

We are extremely enthusiastic (to speak in Hollywood terms!) about things Mexican; but it seems to us rather presumptuous to suppose that our Mexican picture is an escape into the realm of 'complete liberty', exoticism and 'entrancing scenery' from the 'bleak Gulf of Finland' or the 'flat expanses of the collective farms' —which happen to be the scene of the greatest things being done in the world today.

Mr. Wilson displayed an exact knowledge of the footage we have shot and the footage we plan to shoot in our Mexican film. It would have been equally useful if he had applied his mathematical gifts to discovering our ages. We are no longer little boys who run away from home to see Indians stick feathers in their hair or cannibals pass rings through their noses.

SERGEI EISENSTEIN.

Guadaljara, Jalisco, Mexico.

When Sergei Mikhailovich wrote this letter there was, in fact, a growing breach between Alexandrov and himself. As the plan for *Que Viva Mexico!* took shape and the work proceeded, Grigori found he could no longer agree with Eisenstein's artistic ideas. He decided to break away from the unit as soon as the film was finished, and he had discussed the matter with Eisenstein. But Sergei Mikhailovich did not mention this disagreement to anyone; he hoped to win back Alexandrov's support.[1]

[1] Alexandrov's decision may have been influenced by the publication in the Soviet Union earlier in the year of a long and critical article on Eisenstein's

Kimbrough's return to Hollywood was followed by a period of silence. Alone at Christmas at the hacienda of Tetlapayac, Sergei Mikhailovich wrote to Seymour Stern:

25 XII 31

DEAR SEYMOUR!

Passing the Christmas holidays in the *best company I can imagine*—and that is completely *alone* on the hacienda Tetlapayac (having even nobody speecks english here—the owners being away, and Grisha and Tisse happening to be for these days in Mexico! [Mexico City.]

I, myself, am like the wandering Jew, or Dante, touring through hell—getting out of one trouble only to get in another—and usually worse one!—out of one mess in another. 'Mass movement'—the glorious title accompanying my career should be really written 'mess movement' and mean a continuous and uninterrupted movement through 'messes'! But I am really getting desperate of . . . not getting desperate and continuing to have the most stupid optimism in the world! So, I expect to be out of [this] one in the soonest time.

What do you think of reprinting Film Form in 'Ex. Ci'? [*Experimental Cinema*] . . . The article as such is so fundamental in itself, and, for my own writings, will remain probably for a long time as a basic thing for future references. I am adding a copy of it for you which happened to be in my papers. . . .'

In the middle of January 1932, just when Eisenstein was about to commence shooting the 'Soldadera' episode, the thing happened which he had feared. Upton Sinclair, who believed his brother-in-law's tales of Eisenstein's misconduct in Mexico, notified Sergei Mikhailovich to halt work on the film. All the rushes were in Sinclair's hands. Even though the last of the 'novels' had not been shot, Sinclair was 'through' with Eisenstein, who suddenly found himself without financial support in a country which had no diplomatic relations with the Soviet Union.

Later, when Upton Sinclair related his story of *Que Viva Mexico!* in his autobiography *American Outpost*,[1] he portrayed himself as infatuated with the film, but caught between two fires—his wife and

---

films made prior to his going abroad. Though this article by Ivan Anisimov was not considered as very important when it first appeared, and some people condemned Anisimov for publishing it when Eisenstein was abroad, and, therefore, unable to defend his theories, the reappraisal of his work was later to play a significant part in Eisenstein's career. (App. Four.)

[1] *American Outpost*, by Upton Sinclair (Girard, Kansas, Haldeman-Julius Publications, first published 1932, revised 1947), pp. 114 and *seq.*

Eisenstein. During the arrival of the film there came a moment when, according to Sinclair, his wife 'Craig began to cry out in protest, and to demand an end. Mexico is a land of difficulties and dangers and her younger brother was managing the expedition and her affections multiplied the troubles in her mind. "Bring them home!" became her cry'.

Concerning the final halting of the film, Sinclair writes: 'Again Craig clamoured, "Bring them home!" And again husband [referring to himself] and wife took up the issue, and this time the husband was seized by a deadly chill, and had to be taken to the hospital in an ambulance, and lay on his back for two weeks.'

At 'the beginning of the 15th month of this Sisyphean labour . . . Craig assembled the cohorts of her relatives and lawyers, and closed in for the final grapple with her infatuated spouse. "Bring them home!" she commanded, and for eight days and nights the debate continued. To avoid going to the hospital, the husband went to the beach for three days; then he came back, and there were more days and nights of conferences with the assembled cohorts.'

In closing, Sinclair says that his wife was with him 'in the dream of a picture—until she decided that Eisenstein meant to grind her husband up in a pulp machine, and spin him out in celluloid film. She thinks that 35 miles is enough for any picture. And now she stands and looks at her husband, and her hands tremble and her lips quiver; because she licked him in that last desperate duel, and she wonders if in his heart he can ever forgive her.'

Eighteen years later, however, Sinclair gave another version of the reasons for his decision: 'What first led us to distrust him [Eisenstein] was that when the money was spent he wrote us that we'd have to send more or we'd have no picture. . . . He kept that up, over and over, and we realized that he was simply staying in Mexico at our expense in order to avoid having to go back to Russia. All his associates were Trotskyites, and all homos. . . . Men of that sort stick together, and we were beseiged by them for several years. . . . I made a joke of our troubles in American Outpost [quoted above]. . . . We stopped the work because first my wife and then I had come to realize that Eisenstein was a man without faith or honor, or regard for any person but himself.' (App. Six.)

After halting work on the film, Upton Sinclair tried to silence Eisenstein's friends by threatening to expose Eisenstein's alleged misconduct in Mexico. When he heard of these threats, and the tales Sinclair was spreading about Eisenstein, Agustin Aragon Leiva said in a letter to Seymour Stern, dated the 15th November 1932: 'Concerning the perversions, I think that the charge is childish. Eisenstein is not a saint, yet he never drinks or smokes or goes to wild parties. He is suspected to be a homosexual, but you know that thousands of innocents live under that suspicion. He made here heaps of . . . drawings. But he never intended to publish them or to exhibit. They were just tests and if perverted had no influence upon his magnificent public work. I define behind all this (Sinclair's threats to expose Eisenstein) the hand of Sinclair's brother-in-law. . . . but here we have scores of witnesses about *his* . . . lack of good manners, of the most elementary decency and respect to the generous hospitality of the Mexicans. I believe that Sinclair must be questioned about his brother-in-law . . . '

Eisenstein was a man of great pride who had never sought to make things easier for himself. He had never begged. Yet he brought himself to implore Sinclair to let him come to Hollywood and explain what had happened. He assured Sinclair he could edit a film from the footage already shot, even without 'Soldadera'. But Upton Sinclair was obdurate. He would not see Eisenstein and he would listen to no explanations. He even refused to speak with people who approached him on Eisenstein's behalf.

At last Sergei Mikhailovich, Tisse and Alexandrov decided they must go back to the United States and talk to Sinclair. They left Tetlapayac, the 'home' where Sergei had temporarily found the echo of his dreams and the place he would never forget. He said farewell to the Indians, who would await his return year in and year out, and to his many friends in Mexico City to whom he had given a sense of inspiration they would long remember. The simple Indian people and the cultured and sophisticated Mexicans alike had received a gift from Sergei Eisenstein blended of many elements, the most powerful being his extraordinary awareness of their spirit and his sense of being one with them. And in exchange they had given him a memory which would never fade; for all his life the memory of Mexico would be like the sarape he carried away with him, a multi-coloured tapestry woven of crisscrossed threads. The dominant thread: the kindness they had shown him in accepting him as he was in all his complexity—his incomparable gaiety; his earthiness and his ecstatic aspirations. When he left Mexico City on the 11th of February for the long drive north to the Texas border, Sergei Eisenstein passed into a second stage in his life. He would never again have a sense of belonging anywhere with complete inner ease.[1]

They reached the frontier town of Laredo in the old car they had bought as part of their working equipment in Mexico. But the American immigration authorities would not let them cross, although,

[1] In 1977 the Ontario Arts Council backed the production of *Eisenstein's Mexico*, A Film Tribute, by Philip Hudsmith. Peter Kosovic interprets Eisenstein.

according to Grigori Alexandrov, when they left Mexico City they believed they would receive a visa at Laredo.[1] During the time they were held at the frontier, Eisenstein made a number of attempts to find a way to complete his film. A representative of the Mexican Government came to see him and it was proposed that the Mexicans purchase the footage from Upton Sinclair. According to Adolfo Best-Maugard and Grigori Alexandrov, Mr. Sinclair refused to sell the film. Eisenstein then appealed to the Academy of Motion Picture Arts and Sciences in Hollywood to intercede on his behalf with the American authorities. But, according to Donald Gledhill, then an officer of the Academy, no one was willing to vouch for Eisenstein.

Sergei Mikhailovich then turned for assistance to Amkino, the Soviet film agency in America. He asked them if they could make arrangements for him to edit *Que Viva Mexico!* in Moscow. He also communicated with Bogdanov of Amtorg, the Soviet purchasing commission. Upton Sinclair replied to this suggestion in the following telegram:

We applied to seven U.S. senators to assist us to obtain your entrance. We also asked Amtorg and others. . . . Trustees unwilling assume responsibility further delay. Trustees approve proposition you made Amkino to cut picture in Moscow. We have wired Bogdanov. We have wired Department of Labour cancelling our application for your entrance. Amkino can get immediately your transit visa for you to travel to Russia via New York. Please wire Bogdanov approving this proposition. Will ship film via Bogdanov also your trunk boxes. Your statements that picture incomplete are damaging. Insist you do not make such statements again. If New York papers question you hope you will be wise and explain it was your proposal to cut in Russia. Moscow will appreciate your anxiety to return. (Signed) Upton Sinclair.[2] [Plate 19]

But Amkino was not able to obtain a transit visa immediately. According to Grigori Alexandrov, Upton Sinclair failed to send money

[1] In 1934, Sergei Eisenstein told the author that he expected to receive a visa at Laredo. His statement was later confirmed by Grigori Alexandrov. It is also confirmed in a letter from Agustin Aragon Leiva to Seymour Stern, dated the 18th February 1932, in which Leiva says: 'At this moment Eisenstein must be arriving to Hollywood. He left Mexico [City] a week ago, by motor car. A painful and long trip. I didn't say them Good-Bye because I never believed they were really leaving. . . . You are certainly going to see them . . . I hope there is a little possibility that Eisenstein shall get back here to finish his film.'

[2] Eisenstein later framed this telegram and hung it on the wall of his room in Moscow, where the author saw it and, at his request, made a copy of it in 1934.

to cover their living expenses. Having spent the $3,000 they had taken with them to Mexico, Eisenstein and his comrades were obliged to borrow $200 from one friend and $300 from another.

The American immigration officials heaped indignities upon Eisenstein, but the constant interrogation and the charges and the counter charges flung at him and his work were nothing to his concern over *Que Viva Mexico!*, every foot of which was in Sinclair's hands. All that Eisenstein had left of *Que Viva Mexico!* were a few photographs of various scenes. The only promise of aid that came to him was from the editors of *Experimental Cinema*, headed by Seymour Stern, who promised to raise a public protest on Eisenstein's behalf if Upton Sinclair refused to permit him to edit the film. Stern sent telegrams to leading people in Hollywood asking them to sign a telegram to the Secretary of Labour requesting Eisenstein's admission to the United States. Among those to whom Stern appealed were Mary Pickford, Charlie Chaplin, Carl Laemmle, Samuel Goldwyn, Ernst Lubitsch, Joseph von Sternberg, Lewis Milestone, Cecil B. De Mille, Walter Wanger, Irving Thalberg, Norma Shearer, John Barrymore, Dudley Murphy, Frank Capra, Mervyn Le Roy, King Vidor and William K. Howard. But only one responded. Ironically enough, this was the man who had finally directed the film of *An American Tragedy* while Sergei Mikhailovich was in Mexico.

Joseph von Sternberg wired: 'Will be glad to sign collective telegram petitioning Secretary of Labour to readmit Eisenstein.'

Finally, through the aid of Amtorg, Sergei Eisenstein won a thirty-one-day fight for permission to re-enter the United States. Together with Tisse and Alexandrov he was permitted to cross the International Bridge on the 14th of March 1932, upon express condition that he engage in no remunerative work and that he proceed to New York. They went directly to the Hamilton Hotel in U.S. Laredo, where a reporter from the *New York Herald Tribune* interviewed Eisenstein. He merely said he expected to receive a telegram from Upton Sinclair when he reached San Antonio and upon that would depend his future plans. He made no comment about the charges that he had made a film saturated with 'communist propaganda', or the counter-charges that in supporting the present Mexican Government, or so it appeared from the unedited footage, that he had shot 'reactionary' material.

Having gained admittance to the United States, Sergei Mikhailovich might have been able to influence Upton Sinclair's actions but for a foolish prank he had played while waiting in Laredo.

According to what he later told me, Eisenstein had methodically packed up a trunk of unwanted things and sent them to Upton Sinclair. Since the trunk came from abroad, Upton Sinclair had to claim it from the Customs House. At the top, Sergei Mikhailovich had scattered sheaves of specially drawn sketches, each carefully designed to shock the customs officials and 'disgrace' Sinclair in the eyes of the Federal authorities. It is doubtful if Eisenstein ever learned of the tragic price he paid for this desperate outburst of satiric blasphemy. He could not have known when he told me; he chuckled and said 'Let Sinclair, the Puritan, explain that one!"

Sinclair never really forgave Eisenstein for this. Some unconscious feeling stood in the way of his ever understanding such a strange expression of despair and fury. Instead of drawing forth a sense of humour or compassion, it made Sinclair determined to circumvent every effort made to return *Que Viva Mexico!* to Eisenstein.

In August 1933, when the controversy over *Que Viva Mexico!* reached its height, Upton Sinclair said in a letter to H. W. L. Dana: 'Suppose also I should tell you that the great artist is a sexual pervert, and that he shipped into the United States an enormous mass of unthinkably filthy drawings and photographs, the former made on our time and the latter made with our money? He shipped this in the baggage belonging to us and including all the priceless stills of the expedition. The whole thing was seized by the United States Custom authorities, and we very nearly had all our property confiscated and a frightful scandal in the newspapers.' Eighteen years later, Sinclair had not forgotten the matter, although he gives quite a different version: 'Kimbrough had the job of getting Eisenstein's trunks out of Mexico to be shipped to Germany as per Eisenstein's request. The customs people opened the trunks and inspected the contents and said it was the vilest stuff they had ever seen—and they see a lot. Kimbrough persuaded them to let us have a few samples—for our own protection against the flood of lies these degenerates were pouring out against us.' (App. Six.)

From Laredo, Texas, Sergei Mikhailovich and his two comrades set off in their old car for New York. En route, Sergei Mikhailovich acted as he usually did when he met adversity—he turned his attention away from his immediate troubles and sought to find relief in other things. This time it was a study of the American comic strip. In every town on the southern route to Washington, D.C. and New York, he purchased newspapers in order to collect the comic sections. He assembled them by the hundreds and took them with him to Moscow together with an enormous number of comic magazines. American popular humour gripped him. It was his 'opium' at a moment when he was involved in the most tragic circumstances of his life. He also visited many Negro churches as part of his study of American Negro life. [Plate 32]

On arrival in New York, he went to stay at the Hermitage Hotel on Times Square. Now, Sergei Eisenstein was confronted with the most important decision of his creative and personal life. According to Upton Sinclair, he had 'made a precise deal with Amkino in N.Y. The stuff [film] was to be sealed and shipped to them and they were not to open it but ship it direct to Moscow where Eisenstein was to cut it and the government would then ship the negative back to us.' (App. Six.) At least a considerable amount of the positive print of *Que Viva Mexico!* reached New York soon after Sergei Mikhailovich arrived; but it is not clear whether any part of the negative was ever sent. In a letter written on the 2nd of April to Seymour Stern, who had asked Eisenstein to send him a certain still from the film, Eisenstein said: 'I am very sorry—but the photo you want can in no way be sent to you; I have but one uncut positive here (so far).'

When the film arrived in New York, Sergei Mikhailovich opened it because, without the 'novel' 'Soldadera', he had to reshape his plan for montage and he had not seen the greater part of his material, some of which he had shot a year before. He ran the film in a small projection theatre. He invited some people to come and see it, among them Lincoln Kirstein, the editor of *Hound and Horn*, who after seeing 30,000 feet, wrote: ' These "rush" shots were shown in the sequence in which they happened to be filmed. . . . Sometimes the scene appeared four or five times in succession, each time altered and improved as the direction demanded. . . . I am sure that anyone would agree with me in thinking I had seen perhaps the richest material from a human and artistic point of view, that ever was the potential substance of a film.'

Then, as if sensing the tragic fate of *Que Viva Mexico!*, Kirstein concluded: 'Eisenstein is that, in our time so much sought after and denied being—a genius. . . . If anything should happen to *Que Viva Mexico!* between now and the time it is cut and shown, to rob it of Eisenstein's final fingering, it would be a loss of staggering dimensions. There are no catalogues of the Alexandrian Library which Caesar's fire ignited, and we have only the Rubens copy to show us what Leonardo's *Battle of the Anghiari* may have been. For us their loss would have been less crippling than this film of the heart of a consciousness, this testimony of extreme distinction.'[1]

Upton Sinclair was furious when he heard that Eisenstein was still in New York and had shown the film to some of his friends. He immediately had his lawyer, B. M. L. Ernst, recover the film and send it back to him. Later, Sinclair wrote: 'We never had any idea of shipping him [Eisenstein] a print or anything else after that. We'd as soon have

---

[1] 'Que Viva Méjico!' by Lincoln Kirstein (*Arts Weekly*, 30 April 1932).

shipped it to the devil. Any negotiations after that were for the purpose of trying to get back some of the money our friends had put in at our urging.' (App. Six.) Yet at the time, Upton Sinclair sent Eisenstein a telegram in which he said that if Eisenstein would return to Moscow, he would send the film *Que Viva Mexico!* 'on the next boat'.[1]

Meanwhile, a number of people, including Lincoln Kirstein who had followed the turbulent history of *Que Viva Mexico!*, realized that the chances of Sinclair sending the film to Moscow were growing remote. An influential New Yorker, who had watched Eisenstein at work in Mexico and held him in high esteem, rallied the support of interested people. They raised sufficient funds and offered to purchase the entire rights and footage of the film from Upton Sinclair. Eisenstein was assured that his visa could be extended so that he could edit the film in New York. A lawyer, Enos S. Booth of 74 Trinity Place, was employed to work out an agreement so that Eisenstein could take possession of the film and complete it without interference. Negotiations with Sinclair were begun.

But time was growing short and Upton Sinclair was silent as to his real intentions. In a telegram to Seymour Stern, dated the 28th of July 1932 (more than three months after Sergei Mikhailovich had left America), Lincoln Kirstein said: 'Will do anything humanly possible to save film intact. . . . Sinclair refused to answer Amkino or anyone else.'

The Soviet trade representatives in America (diplomatic relations had not yet been established) intimated to Eisenstein that it would be best if he returned to Moscow as already planned and leave the matter of *Que Viva Mexico!* to them. Still, Sergei Mikhailovich preserved an outward calm. He did not discuss the matter of returning to the Soviet Union with anyone. That was something he must decide for himself. His predicament was a most difficult one with *Que Viva Mexico!* entirely out of his control and he himself at the mercy of Upton Sinclair. He stood alone between his infuriated backer and the Soviet Government. He had borne such public humiliation and received so many shocks that he was strained beyond the point where he could analyse his position in relation to *Que Viva Mexico!* objectively.

He had assumed that among artists and intellectual people there was an area where individual morality and decency prevailed despite personal and political differences. The fact that Americans of international repute had extolled his work and a man like Douglas Fairbanks had introduced *Potemkin* to America, and Charlie Chaplin behaved in a

---

[1] Eisenstein kept this telegram and, during the years 1933 and 1934, he showed it to me several times. M.S.

friendly manner towards him, led him to suppose he had the support of many people on whom he could rely. Yet when the immigration authorities kept him at Laredo, the people who had honoured him were silent.

He realized that had he been a commercial minded man who was willing to make 'box-office' films, his money-making potential would have earned him respect and offset any charges made against him. This was a social law in America, but Sergei Eisenstein had somehow not foreseen that it would be applied to him. He had come to a new country full of curiosity and a naïve enthusiasm; but his experiences in America and Mexico left him with a feeling that no one in the world, save Pera, cared what happened to him. His individualism had led him to transgress the mores of capitalism and socialism alike. And his individualism led him in this moment of crisis to behave as though he was merely an interested foreigner on holiday in New York. He spent an afternoon with Seymour Stern's father, Harry A. Stern, talking about films and America. But his letter to Seymour Stern, dated the 2nd of April, reveals some of the tension he felt:

Hermitage Hotel
Times Square
42nd St. and Seventh Avenue
at Broadway
New York City

2 IV 1932

My Dear Seymour:

I am writing in a very great hurry—I have a lot (why do they not allow to say *two*, or even more—as in my case?) to do and hope to leave as soon as possible from here.

1. I think 'E.C.' [*Experimental Cinema*] in its actual shape is a brilliant achievement.

I hope that this statement from me is enough! I am sorry not to join the board of editors—but it could not be done in a magazine where such a lot of space is given to our activities! . . .

2. Very glad to hear that you seem to like the rushes. *Viva Mexico* in the theoretical research field is before everything a 'shot' (camera angle) picture: I think I have solved (anyhow for myself) the montage problem (as a system of expression). This picture has to analyse the same laws on their other degree—the 'shot'. It is a pretty hard problem—but a couple of emotional 'thru breaks' (like the ones you like) by their extravagance I suppose will help (and partly have allready helped) to solve the angle problem as well. I am allways very careful in 'my angles'—but in this picture *especially*—I am unrestful until I get into the nerve—basic nerve of a thing—and in this problem

there still are little odds and ends which escape and will not be clear to the moment of the release of the picture.

[He discussed at length a misuse of the idea of 'overtonal' montage, the vulgarization of the word and how his own use of the phrase 'film language' had later led to 'easy talking'—'the language of Trauberg is clearer than the film language of Ekk'.]

3. I am very sorry—but the photo you want can in no way be sent to you: a) because I have but one uncut positive here (so far) b) and that is unimportant I do not want this type of things to be shown *before* the picture comes out. There are some 'refrain' treatments through the whole picture made in the same manner and connected with the death theme going through it. I reserve the intersts of this for this theme. It is an 'overtonal' theme to the picture—besides the 'rough' social scheme of enslavement of the peons: the idea . . . well I'll tell you about that another time. c) I do not want *too* much talking about the picture *now*—there is too much trouble in finishing it and getting it in correct form. And that is why I would ask you to tell *nobody about all you know* about it. There are too many things involved d) Mrs. Sinclair's statements . . . well I never use *too* strong language (in letters) and as in this case it would be *exceedingly strong*— I withhold. Less understanding for film . . . I *never* met . . . Well that is personal. No word about that.

4. I object *in the most formal way* to publishing *one line of the script* a) in principle—that must *never* be done with an unfinished picture b) there are very important changes in the film (you know that part of the material has not been shot and the film has been reshaped in treatment)
c) Because of the 'style' of writing it and presenting the most decent things in the apple-saucyest way.

[He urged Stern to get the copy of the scenario which Paul Kohner had and post it immediately to him.]

I need to show the pictures on my trip through Europe . . . (I expect to leave the 16th of this month!)

5. Certainly you may publish the photo you have 'in stock'—sorry I can't send you more at the moment. And I suppose that if it should be proved that they were 'in work' before you get the telephone call even legally there can be no attack. (I do not know them to be even copyrighted so far.)

6. Well—and many thanks for the troubles you took about me— it is a good lesson! if not more

Thanks and regards to everybody—Chrystel more than anybody else—

Sincerely allways
yours
Eisenstein

Soon after writing to Stern, Sergei Mikhailovitch moved from the Hermitage Hotel to the Barbizon-Plaza. Here he spent some of his time in a rather curious way considering the circumstances. He sat for a portrait by Jean Charlot, whom he had met in Mexico. At the same time, David Burliuk also painted a portrait of him. Charlot says that Eisenstein 'gave me the impression that his government had scolded him for staying so long in the U.S.' and that this worried him.[1] [Plate 31]

Shortly before leaving New York, Eisenstein was riding on a Central Park West bus on his way downtown to meet Alexandrov and Tisse at Carnegie Hall. Sara Mildred Strauss, the dancer, who had met him two years before, saw him, but it was not until they got off the bus at Carnegie Hall and Sergei Mikhailovich met Grisha and Tisse that she recognized him. Delighted, she invited them up to her dance studio, and her casual act produced an immediate response in Eisenstein. He liked Sara Mildred Strauss. There was something very kind and comforting about her which drew him to remain within her shadow for eleven days.

Before Eisenstein had been in the studio very long, he asked Sara Mildred Strauss to take charge of him and show him New York. He listed the things he wanted to see before he left America: New York's hospitals, and, if there existed such a film, one tracing the development of the foetus in the womb. He wanted to visit the law courts, night clubs and the Negro district of Harlem. So Sara Mildred Strauss drew up an itinerary, made appointments and acted as Eisenstein's guide. Each morning she met him at her studio about eight-thirty. He was always ahead of time, sitting on the stairs outside the studio door having his breakfast—a bottle of milk. Because Eisenstein questioned and talked so much at each of his appointments, they were always dropping behind their schedule. It seemed he was determined to wring out every detail.

During this time, Tisse and Alexandrov sometimes came to Sara Mildred Strauss' studio to meet Eisenstein. On one occasion Sergei Mikhailovich turned choreographer and danced an impromptu ballet with Tisse and Sara Mildred which Grisha photographed. [Plate 33]

[1] Jean Charlot in a letter to the author, dated 23 April 1950.

Grigori Alexandrov, who was no longer a member of the unit, was not planning to leave America with Eisenstein and Tisse. His first wife, Anna Sten, who had made several films in Germany, including *The Brothers Karamazov*, following her success in the Soviet pictures *The Girl with the Hat Box* and Protazonov's *The White Eagle*, had attracted the attention of Samuel Goldwyn, who had contracted with her to come to America. She had arrived in New York early in April on her way to Hollywood.

Meanwhile, aware that criticism of his actions towards Eisenstein was increasing, Upton Sinclair drew up a remarkable four-page leaflet, which reads in part:

UPTON SINCLAIR
Station A
Pasadena, California

April 1932

DEAR FRIEND:

For many years my readers and translators in various foreign countries have been urging me to write an autobiography. This has always seemed to me an old man's job; but recently—after the completion of 'Boston'—I found myself feeling temporarily old, so I took up this easier work. . . . The title of the book is 'American Outpost', and it will be ready when you get this circular; price $2.50, cloth bound.

There is a new edition of 'The Wet Parade' now $2.00. The book has been doing very well, and had the usual mixture of praise and slams from the reviewers. . . . Judge Harry Neil, president of the Bible House, wrote me: 'I published and sold millions of Bibles. I would have done more good to humanity had I sold a million copies of 'The Wet Parade' . . .

'The Wet Parade' has been made into a talking picture by Metro-Goldwyn-Mayer. . . . Imagine me under the klieg lights! I am happy to be able to tell you that it turned out a very fine picture. It has been changed in a number of ways from the novel, but the spirit of my work has been kept. . . . Nobody is quite sure whether the picture is 'wet' or 'dry' . . .

The greater part of my time for the past year has been taken up with a project into which I got more or less by accident. When Sergei M. Eisenstein, the Russian film director, broke with his Hollywood bosses, he came to my wife and me for help. He had a project to go to Mexico and make an independent picture of native life, and we undertook to raise the money to make this possible. The project was supposed to take three or four months, and so far it has taken sixteen, and the end is not yet. As I write, Eisenstein is in New York, about to sail for Russia, where he will cut the picture. He takes with him some thirty-five miles of the most gorgeous film you ever laid eyes on. When it is assembled and released, it will make a revolution in the art. Incidentally, it should make a great deal of money; and as neither my wife nor I care to become promoters for profit, we have pledged ourselves to use this money for the purpose of putting sets of my books into public libraries all over the world. We have established The Sinclair Foundation for the purpose, and we are making over to it our interest in the picture. . . .

A group of academic persons, writers and scientists, have done me the honor to recommend my name to the Nobel Committee of the Swedish Academy, as candidate for the Nobel Prize for Literature this year. . . . Those who signed the original call on my behalf included Albert Einstein, Bertrand Russell, John Dewey. . . . There are 405 signers from the United States, 79 from Great Britain, several each from such countries as Austria, Brazil, Czechoslovakia, China, . . . and one each from such countries as Algiers . . . Gold Coast . . . and Tasmania. . . .

Sincerely,
Upton Sinclair.

Thus, Upton Sinclair began a publicity campaign in his own defence, while Sergei Mikhailovich made no statements and could do nothing but trust that Upton Sinclair would keep his promise and send the film to Moscow to be edited.

As time was running out, some people in New York sought to show Eisenstein honour and respect in an effort to wipe out the insults to which he had been subjected. Among his supporters was Mrs. Edith Isaacs, the founder and editor of *Theatre Arts Monthly*, who gave a party in Sergei Mikhailovich's honour. When Sara Mildred Strauss heard of this, she took charge of the guest of honour. Since Eisenstein's clothes now looked a little shabby, she hurriedly cleaned his suit and saw that it was pressed. She told him that Mrs. Isaacs' guests would be very cultured, rather conservative people—well-known patrons of the arts. Later she was sorry for what she had said. She had no idea that Sergei Eisenstein was such a sensitive man and that her warning would so disturb him that he shrank into his shell and barely said a word. The party to which the people had come to meet the legendary Eisenstein, famed for his wit and brilliance, was a deadly failure. The slightest hint that he did not know how to behave made Eisenstein so self-conscious that he appeared the dullest and heaviest of men with nothing the least entertaining or interesting to say.

According to Lincoln Kirstein, shortly before sailing from New York, Eisenstein made an appointment with him to go and 'see gangsters' in the speakeasies close to Brooklyn Bridge. Contrary to his habit, Eisenstein began to drink. He is said to have drunk enough to reduce any normal man to a coma; yet he remained seemingly sober.

On the day before Eisenstein sailed from New York, Sara Mildred Strauss says he dropped his cool, impersonal or humorous manner. For the first and only time he talked about himself. He told her that arrangements had been made for him to remain in America if he wished to stay, but he had decided to return to Moscow because of his mother. He also said he had a sister named Pera whom he dearly loved. Then Sergei Mikhailovich left Sara Mildred. He had chosen his course of action: *Que Viva Mexico!* must be risked; he must trust in the good faith of Upton Sinclair.

'In all the eleven days I saw Sergei', said Sara Mildred Strauss after Eisenstein had died, 'he never so much as touched my hand. He treated me with a deference I never met in any other man. Because of his behaviour, I couldn't understand the telegram he sent me from Russia. All it said was "Love Sergei". I never heard from him again.'

On leaving Sara Mildred Strauss, Eisenstein met Lincoln Kirstein and they spent the whole night in a speakeasy. Again Sergei Mikhailovich drank more than any man Kirstein had ever seen.

'He must have been blind drunk, yet he could walk and talk.'

On the 19th of April 1932, a farewell dinner was given for Eisenstein by the American-Russian Institute. There were the usual after-dinner speeches with Hendrik van Loon acting as toast-master. Theodore Dreiser, 'the old grey lion', was the main speaker. Two great men, each loyal to their integrity, and for their loyalty rejected and reviled by those who could not purchase their obedience.

Eisenstein went to the dinner with the New Yorker who was trying to reach an agreement with Upton Sinclair over *Que Viva Mexico!* Some of the people at the dinner were pained by Sergei Mikhailovich's ashen, stony face. Those who knew most about *Que Viva Mexico!* feared that Sinclair was avoiding a settlement. Others had heard rumours to the effect that Eisenstein's films had been severely criticized in Moscow.

A small group left the dinner with Sergei Mikhailovich. They went with him to the *Europa* on which he was to sail from Brooklyn at midnight. It was a beautiful spring evening; as they crossed Brooklyn Bridge, they paused so that Eisenstein could look at the New York skyline which two years before had astonished him. As the party reached the ship, the attempted gaiety cracked like glass dropped on concrete. Everyone was sober and sad as they waited to wave good-bye to Eisenstein, whom they would never see or hear from again.

He walked on to the *Europa* with Tisse and Alexandrov (though Grisha was not going to sail with them). On board, Eisenstein faced the inquisitive reporters with a mocking smile and treated them to his witticisms.

Calmly he announced that on return to Moscow he would whip *Que Viva Mexico!* into shape. Then he would make a film on some burning question: maybe *Mr. and Mrs. Smith in the Soviet Union*. He praised the co-operation he had received from Upton Sinclair (whose last telegram promising to send the film on the next ship was in his pocket), and the Mexican Government and Mexico's Archbishop. Using his iridescent humour as a triumphant shield, Sergei Mikhailovich spoke of his experiences in America. His last words tripped forth merrily.

'No,' he said, 'I didn't shoot one foot of film in Hollywood. My departure from Paramount after six months was amicable. When I went to take leave of B. P. Schulberg, the director of production, I said: "Well, now is the time to say something historic."

' "It was", Schulberg said, "a noble experiment!" '

As the *Europa* steamed out into the black void of a long night, the Sergei Eisenstein of legend began to die. He had come to America a young man full of enthusiasm with a sensual delight in laughter; but two years had added ten to his appearance. He appeared a middle-aged man, whose austere face might never be humanized by a smile which was not wry. He wrote in his *Autobiography*: '. . . During my encounter with Mexico, it seemed to me to be, in all the variety of its contradiction, a sort of outward projection of all those separate lines and features which, it seemed, in a tangle of complexes I had and have within me.'

Note 1977. In a letter to Eisenstein dated August 28, 1931, Sinclair wrote, 'The great advantage of this part of the material [*Thunder Over Mexico*] is that you have one consecutive story. You can make what the conventional screen world regards as a screen picture. . . . In this way you would get hold of the public, and you would also get hold of the money.' The next day he wrote to Kimbrough to put a definite limit upon the amount of film still to be shot if Eisenstein did not accept that suggestion. *Sergei Eisenstein and Upton Sinclair The Making and Unmaking of Que Viva Mexico!*, edited by Harry M. Geduld and Ronald Gottesman (Bloomington/London, Indiana University Press, 1970) pp. 122–23.

Professor Steven Hill, researching the Upton Sinclair Archive at Indiana University, wrote to me, August 13, 1977, that Sinclair, having read Eisenstein's *Bezhin Meadow mea culpa* [see pp. 372–77] in 1937, 'wrote an ironic article, apparently not published, pointing out the similarity between his own and the Soviet Government's inability to handle Eisenstein. This "unmanageability" provided the final confirmation of the Sinclairs' belief that Eisenstein should not and *could not* complete the Mexican film.'

CHAPTER TEN

Cinematography with Tears

*So in like manner you must grow in patience when you meet with
great wrongs, and they will then be powerless to vex your mind.*
LEONARDO DA VINCI, C.A. 117 v.b.

WHEN the *Europa* docked at Cherbourg on its voyage to Bremen,
Sergei Mikhailovich wrote to Leon Moussinac. He said he would
have liked to see Paris again, but it had not been possible. He told
Moussinac that he would edit *Que Viva Mexico!* in Moscow. As the
ship steamed through the English Channel, he recalled London and
Cambridge. He would have liked to return to England, but he had
made his choice. He was going home by way of Bremen, and Berlin,
where he had once been so loudly acclaimed.

On the surface, the German capital looked to him as it had in 1929.
But during the few days he stayed in Berlin, Sergei Mikhailovich
caught glimpses of the contending forces battling for control of Germany's fate. On arrival at the Golf Hotel on the Kurfüstendamm, he
was told that Adolf Hitler had a room two floors below him and that
Hitler's supporters had increased in number as the German crisis
deepened. But most people said that Hitler could never come to power.
To prove that the Left was a strong bulwark against Nazism, Eisenstein
was taken to see the old communist deputy, Clara Zetkin, open the new
session of the German Reichstag.

The people who saw Eisenstein on his journey home noticed a change
in his appearance and manner. His eyes seemed deeper set. The front of
his leonine quiff was receding, as if his thoughts were eating away at
the roots of his fluffy hair. To Hans Feld, who had last seen him in
January 1930, he looked more mature and his manner had grown
distant. He had ceased to clown. When amused, instead of his face
crinkling in a wide smile the corners of his mouth merely flickered upwards with a mocking or enigmatic expression. He dismissed Feld's
question about *Que Viva Mexico!* with the remark that there were
'heaps of it all over the place!' He did not mention Upton Sinclair, or
An American Tragedy, although Joseph von Sternberg's version of
Dreiser's book, produced while Eisenstein was in Mexico, was being
shown in Berlin at the time, where Sergei Mikailovich probably saw it.
But in an interview with Lotte Eisner,[1] Eisenstein talked at length

[1] *Film Kurier*, Berlin, 28 April 1932.

about his plan for editing *Que Viva Mexico!* He showed her some photographs and said he would synchronize the film in Moscow with records of Mexican folk music he had with him. Blended with the music would be sound effects which would accentuate the imagery. He said he hoped to have the film completed by the autumn, and that he had shot 213,000 feet of film.

Then he talked of a new film he planned to make in the Soviet Union which would 'show Russia with the same intensity as some good books'. He wanted to travel to 'all parts of Russia, especially the unknown parts', and make a picture explaining the Soviet Union to foreign audiences. As he spoke, Lotte Eisner had the impression that Eisenstein was tired and a little sad. She thought he was a man in his middle forties although, in fact, he was still only thirty-four years old.

One of his last statements before leaving Berlin and the capitalist world to which he was never to return, concerned a film satire he wanted to produce. This he called *The Twilight of the Gods*. In it the decline of capitalism was to be symbolized by the sensational disappearance of Ivar Kruger, the international 'match king', and Lowenstein, the financier, who threw himself out of an aeroplane. But this idea soon faded from his mind and he never mentioned it again until 1940 when he recalled it in connection with his production of Wagner's opera, *The Valkyrie*, at the Bolshoi Theatre in Moscow.

As the train carried Sergei Eisenstein towards the Soviet Union, he had no idea how greatly Soviet society had changed since he left in the late summer of 1929. Everything and everyone had become more stable. Through concentrated effort, the First Five Year Plan had almost reached its goals. New factories had been built, new houses, new schools, and people were very proud. Budding poets wrote lyrics to bathtubs for factory newspapers instead of praising the exploits of civil war heroes. Socialist Construction was the dominant theme in Soviet life; it served as the theme for plays, novels and films. The mass as Hero had given way to individual characters symbolic of the struggle to build industry even in the wilderness. The Russians had girded themselves to build up the country's strength, develop natural resources and lay the foundation for industrial self-sufficiency. Only in the Second Five Year Plan would light industry for consumers' goods be developed and the standard of living raised.

During Eisenstein's absence, Soviet cinematography had undergone a reconstruction. This meant 'not only a technical but also an ideological rearmament; not only the reorganization of the material basis of production but also a deep revolution in the social and economic relations. . . . From a half-artisan, technically backward organism [the] industry was called upon to become a powerful industrial factor of cultural revolution.'[1] The technical and ideological reorganization of the film industry brought to a close the first period of Soviet cinematography; the period in which Sergei Mikhailovich had created *Strike*, *Potemkin*, *October* and *Old and New*.

In 1932, the films of Eisenstein were characterized as representing only a stage in the evolution of the Soviet cinema. They were 'cinematographic poems . . . profoundly lyrical songs of artists enamoured with the heroics and the pathos of the proletariat's revolutionary fight. They sing not so much of life as of events. . . . They describe everything from the point of view of distant historical perspective. . . . They throw all the details aside and dwell upon the essential historical line. . . . They paint in large strokes and speak through generalizing figures.'[2] It was considered that the time had passed for such lyrical songs which dealt 'not with society and its division into classes but with enormous masses of people set in motion by the storm of revolution'. For the period of Socialist Construction, films were expected to embody 'a concrete revelation of present reality', and 'give the masses answers to the concrete questions which are agitating them'.[3]

Discussion concerning this change in emphasis had been initiated by the Revolutionary Cinematograph Workers, who had criticized 'sharply and severely all manifestations of formalism and simplification in the cinema'. Formalism was interpreted as 'returning from reality to formal research means', and simplification referred to 'the tendency to glide on the surface of events [and] represent reality in ready-made figures of bourgeois art by way of their . . . adaptation to Soviet thematics'.[4]

The immediate result of this new ideological interpretation was that scenarists and directors began to seek a new humanism in which personal character should find a greater expression. Events could no longer be portrayed through mass action but must be seen as the actions of typical individuals. It was now recognized that the building of a factory, the creation of a collective farm or the construction of the vast Dnieperstroi Dam involved people and their intimate emotions. Laughter and romance entered into the lives of people as well as struggle and heroic actions. The highly experimental period of the 'twenties was thus eliminated.

The year before, while Eisenstein was in Mexico, his films had been sharply criticized in an article by Ivan Anisimov. Anisimov contended that although Eisenstein was an artist in revolt against bourgeois art and

---

[1] 'Reconstruction of the Soviet Cinema', an article by K. Feldmann, sent by V.O.K.S., Moscow, in February 1932, to the late Huntley Carter. Original MSS. now in the possession of H. P. J. Marshall.
[2] *Ibid.*   [3] *Ibid.*   [4] *Ibid.*

was in sympathy with the working-class revolution, he did not as yet see life through the eyes of a proletarian artist. He did not succeed in showing that the collective was composed of individuals. The sailors in *Potemkin* were an undifferentiated mass lacking individual human characteristics. His films *Strike*, *October* and *Old and New* showed a tendency towards exaggeration: in *Old and New* the poor peasant's hut was too degraded to correspond to reality; likewise the rich peasant was too fat and rich to be typical. (App. Four.)

The *Soviet Encyclopædia* of 1932 stated that in '*October* (1927) and *The General Line* (*Old and New*) (1927-9) Eisenstein, despite his great ability, yet gave no deep analysis of the decisive stages of the Socialist Revolution and made a diversion to formal experiment'. He was classified as 'a representative of the ideology of the revolutionary section of the petty-bourgeois intelligentsia which is following in the path of the proletariat'.

The new trend of more personalized films and the injection of comedy was being encouraged by Boris Shumyatsky, the new head of the film industry, who visited Hollywood in the summer of '32. He thought that the Soviet cinema would exert a greater political and social influence upon the Russian people if more 'story-telling' were introduced. Inevitably this would lead to the development of films where the role of the professional actor would become more important. 'Typage' would decline and montage could no longer be the dominant method of film construction. Moreover, in 1931, the full-length sound films—Vertov's *Enthusiasm* and Ekk's *The Road to Life*—had been completed; and by the time Eisenstein returned to Moscow both Pudovkin and Dovzhenko were making their first talking pictures, *Deserter* and *Ivan*, respectively.

Under the very best circumstances, Sergei Eisenstein's absence from the Soviet Union during a period of such marked change and development of ideology would have posed a problem of readjustment. Had he experienced no difficulties in America or Mexico, he still would have found himself at least a step behind in understanding current trends.

Arriving in Moscow, Sergei Mikhailovich was confronted with a situation he had not foreseen. Upton Sinclair had sent a report to the Soviet Government complaining of his conduct in Mexico. With no Soviet representatives in Mexico to determine the facts and Upton Sinclair held in high esteem in the Soviet Union, Sergei Mikhailovich was privately told he had behaved in a way likely to bring censure upon his country. Since he had no way of clearing himself of Sinclair's accusations, he accepted the reprimand and tried to pretend that nothing had happened.

Boris Shumyatsky, who disliked Eisenstein, suggested to him the making of a musical comedy known as *Jolly Boys*. Sergei Mikhailovich refused, the subject being patently unsuited to his artistic aims. This first Soviet musical comedy, known abroad as *Jazz Comedy*, was immediately assigned to Grigori Alexandrov on his return to Moscow in June. By August he had his own production unit and was directing the picture at the studio of Potylika outside Moscow near the Lenin Hills. The style of this picture was an extension and adaptation of *Romance Sentimentale*, which, though his own work, bore Eisenstein's name, and had met with some unfavourable criticism. The leading role in *Jazz Comedy* was played by Lyubov Orlova, who became Alexandrov's second wife, and who was soon one of the most popular actresses of the Soviet screen.

So it came about that foreign visitors to Moscow in 1932, who, four or five years before, would have been invited to interview Eisenstein, were now invited to visit his former assistant on the Potylika set. Inquiries concerning Eisenstein drew forth vague remarks that he was not as yet working on a new film, while some of his fellow workers in the cinema intimated that he was 'finished' and no longer played a significant role in the Soviet cinema.

In the early months after Sergei Mikhailovich's return, people who sought him out could see him at his room overlooking the Chysti Prudi, or at the Institute of Cinematography, where he was now implementing his many theories in the training of directors. He had thrown himself heart and soul into this work because it took his thoughts off his many problems and served as an outlet for the research he loved. His manner towards his visitors was impervious, a little ironical; at times he strove to leave a debonair impression. Some of his old friends like Marcoosha Fischer were piqued when he appeared to avoid their invitations to gatherings. Only Pera Attasheva and Tisse knew what Sergei Mikhailovich was suffering.

For Pera, the Old Man's return was an experience of mixed joy and frustration. She was still in love with him, but though he had come back, their relationship was in no way altered. She had been slim and pretty when the Old Man left, but some condition not very clear to the doctors she consulted had caused her to grow heavy. Now she looked the plump, gay, comfortable mother from whom men sought comfort. This made her suffer more because now she felt herself to be the irrevocable mother-image to the Old Man. Sometimes she wished he could find someone else. She wanted to be free, but she did not know how to break the bond which held her to him.

From the moment he returned, Sergei Mikhailovich was tormented by the matter of *Que 'Viva Mexico!* The prints did not come 'on the next boat' as Upton Sinclair had promised in his telegram. Weeks passed and there was no word. In fact, Upton Sinclair never communicated again directly with Eisenstein.

From April to July 1932, Enos S. Booth, the lawyer employed by the group in New York who were interested in *Que Viva Mexico!*, together with Amkino, made repeated attempts to negotiate with Sinclair. But, as Lincoln Kirstein's telegram to Seymour Stern dated the 28th of July states, 'Sinclair refused to answer Amkino or anyone else'.

In July, Boris Shumyatsky visited Hollywood and went to see Mr. and Mrs. Sinclair at their Pasadena home. According to Sinclair, he and his wife told Shumyatsky their version of how Eisenstein had treated them. (See App. Six.) Presumably they told him the stories of Eisenstein's conduct in Mexico as they had heard them from Mrs. Sinclair's brother, Hunter Kimbrough.

Sinclair has not recorded in full what Boris Shumyatsky said to him. He had, however, found an ally. As subsequent events show, Shumyatsky disliked Eisenstein personally and was the leader of a clique who were determined to discredit Eisenstein's prestige in the Soviet Union. Later, Shumyatsky used the unfavourable tales told him by Upton Sinclair to justify his attacks on Eisenstein.

From the outset, Sinclair took the position that Eisenstein had broken his contract and, therefore, forfeited his rights in the film. However, Sinclair finally proposed that if the Soviet Government would make a guarantee involving more than $50,000, he would send the film to Moscow for Eisenstein to edit. Eisenstein and Alexandrov later told me that Sinclair made this proposition. That Sinclair did demand large sums of money is confirmed by a cablegram sent by Louis Fischer to Upton Sinclair in which Fischer mentions Sinclair's proposition 'involving many tens (of) thousands of dollars'. But Amkino and Enos S. Booth took the position that Eisenstein had not forfeited his rights in the film and that Sinclair's demand was unreasonable in view of the fact that Eisenstein said he had only spent $53,000 on the film.

Sinclair undoubtedly repeated his proposition of a guarantee to Shumyatsky. If he did, Shumyatsky too may have thought the amount unreasonable. In any event, Shumyatsky returned to Moscow without having made any arrangements with Upton Sinclair to send the film to Eisenstein.

Filled with fear that he would never complete the film, every shot of *Que Viva Mexico!* grew more vivid in Eisenstein's mind—and more beloved. He made no comment and his silence appeared extremely strange to people who felt there must be something to be said on Eisenstein's side. But he felt if he kept silent and did not antagonize Sinclair any further, Enos Booth, or someone else in America, might be able to make arrangements to send the film for him to edit. But early in August 1932 he received a clipping from Seymour Stern which announced in Hollywood jargon that Upton Sinclair had made arrangements with Sol Lesser to edit the film, which was now renamed *Thunder Over Mexico*.

For three weeks Eisenstein behaved like a man going out of his mind. Long periods of anguished silence behind his locked door gave way to storms of despair. It no longer mattered to him what anyone thought since no further harm could be done to him. Pera, who was at first the only person he would see, feared he could not stand the strain of his despair. Day after day he talked of killing himself and every night she dreaded to leave him alone lest his mind break. To shield himself, Sergei Mikhailovich asked Maxim Shtraukh and Judith Glizer in the room next to his, and whose telephone he shared through an extension, to tell all callers, except Tisse and Pera, that he was away. This service they faithfully performed, adding that they had no knowledge as to when he would return to Moscow. It was at this period that I first met Sergei Mikhailovich through Maurice Dobb, who had given me a letter and some magazines to take to him. Two telephone calls had elicited the story that Eisenstein was away. The third call brought him to the telephone.

To someone who knew nothing of the difficulties besetting Sergei Eisenstein, and had merely heard him described as 'a man all brains and no emotion', his manner on the telephone made a most unpleasant impression.

'I have exactly ten minutes to give you, so be here on time—three o'clock!'

His voice sounded not only exceedingly cold but also hostile. It appeared as though Maurice Dobb's thought of him was an interruption with which he would prefer not to bother.

It seemed that the coolness in Moscow about Eisenstein and the hints that he was 'finished' might be the result of an arrogant, intractable temperament which stood out in contrast to the warmth and friendliness of his fellow Russian artists. Pudovkin and Dovzhenko, who even though busier than Eisenstein, had time to be pleasant.

Chysti Prudi 23 was rather less accessible from the centre of Moscow than many of the houses in which Soviet artists lived. Most of them had their homes on or near Ulitza Gorky (the former fashionable Tverskaya), Tverskaya Boulevard, or off the Arbat. Many lived in new houses. Though Chysti Prudi 23 would stand a few more years, it had fallen into decay. The paint on the stairway was chipping off; the shallow stone stairs had many cracks and the bell for 'kvartira' No. 2 was broken. A note above the bell said to ring three times for S. M. Eisenstein; but three knocks had to be substituted. A number of people shared the flat.

A wizened peasant woman dressed in rusty black with a kerchief over her head opened the door. This was Totya Pasha, who had taught Eisenstein to love simple people and who now served him as a housekeeper. She peered out suspiciously from small, sharp eyes. Upon request for Tovarish Eisenstein, she grunted, moved back and pointed to a door down a narrow passage lighted by a dim and naked electric bulb. The dull neutral-coloured walls, like those in many old Moscow flats, needed a coat of paint as badly as the stairway. In comparison with the homes of many artists of less standing than Eisenstein, it was exceptionally down-at-heel.

There was no answer to my first knock on Eisenstein's door. A second knock brought a sharp 'Da!' Opening the door, I walked into a room which gave the impression of a medieval cell filled with a most incongruous assortment of objects.

The room was square. Two bare, uncurtained windows faced the street. The other three walls were lined with bookshelves reaching from floor to ceiling. The shelves were tightly packed and on the floor, filling all but the minimum of space for movement, were piles of magazines, newspapers and books. Jutting out into the middle of the room was another tall bookcase. Between it and the shelves against the inner wall was the large bed that Theodore Dreiser had envied five years before. Now it was covered with a multi-coloured Mexican blanket. Squeezed in beside the bed, to the left, was a rickety little table with a reading lamp.

In the half of the room towards the windows was a plain deal table smothered with papers, a kitchen chair and an unpainted stool. No drawers and no cupboard broke the panelling of books, though a small, nondescript curtain hung over a couple of shelves of the right-hand bookcase. Scattered about were a curious assortment of knick-knacks, like those cluttering obscure antique shops. There was a collection of beautiful miniature Japanese theatre masks, several gigantic, highly ornamented Mexican sombreros, some peasant pottery and an array of plaster figures of the Virgin and saints. Near the right window was a sculptor's pedestal supporting an unfinished head three times life-size. As Sergei Eisenstein rose from the table, this head, like an enormous close-up, dwarfed the short figure of the living man.

Kurt London's impressionistic description of 'the thick-set, choleric Eisenstein, with a face like a clever ape, behind which one feels the brain of an almost corporeal power',[1] caught the caricaturish side of Eisenstein's appearance. But it failed to hint at the complexity of his appearance as it gradually emerged.

[1] *Seven Soviet Arts*, by Kurt London (London, Faber and Faber, 1937), p.273.

His head and body appeared at odds with one another. The short, stocky torso was built to shrug, to wriggle, perch and tumble. There was no dignity. Nature had designed the apparatus for laughter and burlesque, and Eisenstein had exaggerated Nature, for he wore baggy trousers too large for him and a loudly checked shirt. There was something embarrassing about the outfit; but not as clothing for that body, not even as clothes themselves, only in relation to so monumental a head which could but mock the body to which it was attached.

A square, heavily moulded face with a skull which looked impervious to fire, worms or man's hard blows; yet the features were of a Gothic cast and clothed in alabaster fine skin. Deep-set blue eyes, the nose straight from the front view, slightly tilted in profile, a finely chiselled mouth, the corners quivering with expression, and large ears tapering to the faintly inhuman tips which artists bestow upon the Devil's ancestor—prophetic Pan—and the company of other reputedly disreputable satyrs.

The first impression was that the arrogant voice of the telephone did not belong to Eisenstein, whose words came with such a lack of affectation that they modified the formidability of his appearance. He spoke as though he had picked up an unfinished conversation. He was eager to talk and remember things he had seen. Out of the varied scenes of his consciousness, Cambridge emerged, though he made no mention of Dobb, whose letter he left unopened on the table.

'When I went to Cambridge I knew it was the place I wanted to die in.' Eisenstein's tone and the expression of his face showed a humorous seriousness, that double-edged quality which was most characteristic of him. 'Cambridge is a place where a man could study undisturbed. It would answer my every wish.'

The violent check shirt and the baggy trousers would have caused a raised eyebrow or two among the Cambridge dons, but even on a few minutes' acquaintance they could be accepted as but the costuming of a role. They were like Mr. Micawber's tall hat—a mark of distinction which would fit into the British tradition of eccentricity.

Sergei Mikhailovich continued to talk of Cambridge. The green sward of the Backs, the symmetry of King's Chapel rising majestically from the mown ramp of grass; the choir and the narrow streets through which a torrent of bicycles poured the black-gowned students at night. The bookshops were a paradise to him. From a Cambridge bookstore Eisenstein leapt in one word to London.

'I would drag Jack Isaacs to Charing Cross Road. To Zwemmers! What wonderful bookshops! A treasure trove of books!'

His apt use of English was delightful. He pulled the most expressive words out of his memory and would juggle with the language, rebuild it to suit his own imagination. Sometimes it was in the spirit of James Joyce, at other times he used twists like Lewis Carroll, whose works Eisenstein enormously enjoyed. But suddenly the vitality with which he had absorbed England was suspended.

'I was shocked when I came back. Everything is so ugly. The new architecture we are building is cheap and bad. There is no taste. If only they would think a little,' and he touched his great forehead.

No other Russian had made so cool and appraising a comment about the appearance of the new Moscow. Either they did not see the architectural errors as the penetrating eyes of Eisenstein saw them or they regarded the errors as an unimportant, transitory phase of the gigantic plan in which they were engaged.

'A great many things changed while I was abroad,' said Eisenstein. 'To-day youth is creating in engineering, in aviation instead of in the arts as it was in the 'twenties. If I were an engineer, I would be more of this time.'

There was no condemnation or complaint in his tone. He was merely stating facts; it was this clarity of Eisenstein's which imprinted some of his quite unimportant remarks in the memory of people who met him.

Laying down the chubby red and blue pencil he had been holding, he searched through a handful of letters, envelopes and scraps of paper. Then he handed me a small clipping from a Hollywood trade paper which informed the world that Sergei Eisenstein's film, *Que Viva Mexico!*, was to be edited in Hollywood and released under the title of *Thunder Over Mexico*. It was the one and only newspaper comment about himself that Eisenstein ever showed me.

'Please don't ask any questions,' he said. 'It is hopeless.'

He stood with the tips of his fingers resting on the table. The expression on his face was indescribably baffled and forlorn. But suddenly he broke the silence with a verbal pirouette of bitter, jesting humour. Picking up several of the little Mexican Virgins and saints, he scoffed at them. His satirical gibes appeared in keeping with what I believed for a considerable time to be his stringently atheistic spirit. Savagely anti-clerical, at that moment Eisenstein seemed savagely anti-religious as well.

The mood of bitter jest subsided. He put the figurines back on the shelf and returned to the table. An expression of resignation spread over his curious face, so strong and aggressive in its structure, but with features which expressed a painful sensitivity.

At that moment I felt a great sympathy for Sergei Eisenstein.

'I don't want to work any more,' he declared. 'I can't!'

His tone sounded as if he were speaking to himself. Then he turned away and, standing near the unfinished head of himself, looked out of the window.

'I'm thirty-five, but I feel an old man.'[1]

Indeed, Sergei Eisenstein looked a man in whom all youth had been crushed.

'I might as well die now,' he concluded.

Eisenstein turned and looked at me as though he were in great need of making himself understood.

'There is nothing for me to live for. The thing I loved and put everything I had into has been taken away. I haven't ever had any life except my work.'

He spoke with no emotional emphasis, but his feelings were so intense about *Que Viva Mexico!* that he could not bring himself to speak to me of it in detail again for two years.

Extraordinary as this conversation was between two strangers, it had a penetrating reality. Sergei Eisenstein could not be a man such as Maurice Dobb had described: 'all brains and no emotion'. Rather he was a complex and highly emotional man who, imprisoned in an insensitive-looking body, had assumed a mask which despair had shattered. He had to speak and it was perhaps easier to do so to a stranger he might never see again than attempt to speak of his despair to people he would have to face in the future.

In a moment he slipped on the mask by which the world recognized him. As he glanced up at the huge portrait head, he wore a very wise and witty smirk, like that of a classical jester poking fun at his royal master.

'A work of one of my students!' said Sergei Mikhailovich. 'Does it promise to be a good likeness of my leonine head?' The flippant tone and the quizzical expression were perfect artifice contrived to fit the baggy trousers and the noisy shirt.

There came a knock on the door and a young man from the Institute of Cinematography came in with a sheaf of papers.

A few days later I saw Eisenstein in a Moscow theatre. He was alone and arrayed in a hairy tan tweed suit, which howled with clownish exaggeration. He looked out of place among the dark-clad Russian people. He wanted to know if I would take a letter to Maurice Dobb when I left Moscow.

It was never clear if Eisenstein read Dobb's letter, or wrote to him. He had no answer ready when I went to see him before I left. On this second visit he was a different man. Not the king's jester, nor the man tormented, but the man he aimed to be—the artist-scientist—with

[1] Eisenstein meant that he was in his thirty-fifth year.

whom one could have a friendship of great value if one were interested in his encylopaedic world.

It is not easy to explain how friendship with Eisenstein grew when the pattern of his life had been the rejection of close contacts. I attribute the commencement of our friendship to factors which modified this life-long pattern. He was full of impressions of the foreign world and these he enjoyed talking about. He was oppressed with a sense of loneliness and he wanted companionship. All his life Sergei Mikhailovich had suffered from the respectful awe too many people had displayed towards him; often he mistook this for dislike and blamed himself for his hedgehog-like demeanour. More important, now he had nothing to hold to but his speculative thoughts and creative ideas in which there was little interest in Moscow. Eisenstein was grateful to find people who were interested in his theories, since it helped to defeat his sense of being unwanted as an artist and a person whom no one cared much about. Because our friendship was at first entirely impersonal, there was nothing to confuse or hinder its growth.

The disappointment over *Sutter's Gold* followed by *An American Tragedy*, and the even greater shock over *Que Viva Mexico!*, temporarily crippled Eisenstein's creative impulse. The only thing which kept him from complete disintegration was his tremendous intellectual curiosity and the passion for scholarship which now assumed control of his life.

But to feed this driving passion he needed books and more books. Many of those he wanted were not available in Russia, and for the rest of his life, Sergei Mikhailovich was beset with the problem of getting books from abroad. Remembering the treasure trove of books he had discovered along Charing Cross Road, he wrote a long letter to Kenneth MacPherson in England:

MY DEAR MCPHERSON! [*sic*]

. . . At the present time I am finishing the licking of my Mexican wounds—it looks as if the picture is lost for ever . . . my work is cut into . . . short subjects of travelogal type and is being sold by this way by my 'philantropists' who turned out to be more stupid, barbarous and idiotic than even the well-known Tykoons—only that about these we have no illusions!

Well that's *entre nous* and as soon as the thing is definite you will get an article about this 'che d'œuvre inconnu'—the film that nobody will see. It is worth while to describe it and its conception!

Besides that—(in the far future)—you will get very soon two long articles:

1 about the method of professional selection of young directors among those who apply to our Film University where I am now something that corresponds to your english [sic] deans on the Faculty of Directing. I am working very hard about the organization and reorganization of this Institution and am working on a Standard course of directing and creative methods in cinema. (This will probably give another article about the film method in creative work.)

2 about the 'American Tragedy' in connection with the planning of the work of the two last semestres of the University. . . the essential experimental part and value of the non-realized film . . . for these elements were *hidden* from the script!

Now I can publish them . . . for the comedy ['MMM'] on which I am working at present is the next theoreticall [sic] step after things which were worked out and discovered upon the American Tragedy.

Might be something about the comedy as well.

Well you see that you get a whole perspective of printed ideas from me in the very next future (50% of them are waiting only to be copied!¹

This gives me the right to ask you for a very big favour.

Between the work I am doing, I am rejoicing myself by some amusing little research work; and this is for the moment *D. H. Lawrence*.

This research work interests me enormously and will give a lot of interesting results.

But . . . I need some materials:

I need: by the author:

1. Psychoanalysis and the Unconscious   (1921)
2. Aaron's Rod   (1922)
3. Fantasia of the Unconscious   (1922)
4. Kangaroo   (1923)
5. The essays concerning animals
   (and poems about animals)

(*I have*: Apocalypse, Lady Chatterley's Lover, Women in love [sic], The Plumed Serpent, Mornings in Mexico, Obscenity and Pornography. If I omit something crucially important and representative about his works please add it as well).

Besides that I need the best things written *about* Lawrence: I have

¹ The articles proposed by Eisenstein subsequently appeared in *Close-up* under the titles 'Detective Work at Gik' (dated October 1932) in December 1932; 'Cinematography with Tears', in March 1933 and 'An American Tragedy' in June 1933. All three were translated into English by W. Ray.

only Stephen Potter's book. But the really most brilliant things said about him.

Psychoanalytik [*sic*] things as well, although in the case of Lawrence they must be very vulgar and flat and the case as such is much more profound and interesting.

Please do not miss to send Frederick Carters 'D. H. Lawrence and the Body mystical' [*sic*] which Close Up is advertising.

I am really ashamed and affraid [*sic*] to ruin the 'Pool' business, but:

1   I never cashed your second 5 pounds sent to Mexico (there was something wrong with the adress [*sic*], so I was not able to do it and you can get them reemboursed through the post)

2   You see that I have a whole list of materials for you!

You would oblige me very much with such a sort of compte courrant in books which I need much more than cash. And very urgently.

With sincerest regards to Bryher and yourself, I remain anxious to hear as quick as possible from you

Allways [sic] yours
Eisenstein

13 X 32

In any one meeting he would talk about such a variety of subjects and spin such fine webs of speculative thought that it was almost impossible to retain with any clarity more than a fraction of his conversation. Psychology was in the forefront of his thinking and he was elaborating upon the early theory of attraction he had developed at the Proletkult Theatre as early as 1923. One illustration which often recurred to him, and which he later incorporated into his lectures at the Institute of Cinematography, has always remained in my mind, because it seemed to throw light upon Sergei Mikhailovich's inability to make any statement in defence of himself regarding his Mexican film.

Attraction and repulsion, said Sergei Mikhailovich, pulled a man in opposite directions. A man is suddenly confronted by a rattlesnake ready to strike; simultaneously he is seized with the impulse *to run away from it* and also *to go towards it*. The contrary impulses force him to stand where he is regardless of the consequences. It seemed that such strongly opposing reactions bound a man at every crisis, even in relation to people when a powerful reaction was manifested: attraction and repulsion. On every occasion when he mentioned this theory, he would pace about his room, pause, then suddenly translate into gestures the contradictory desires of the man in his analogy.

Eisenstein talked with equally intense energy about the most obscure tribal customs which to him embodied the idea of the unity of form and content. These could aid him in his attempt to lay down a body of basic principle as to methods of realizing correct form and content in a given film. He always tried to find concrete ground from which to begin his independent thought. To prove man's response to correctness of form for the expression of content, Sergei Mikhailovich studied Frazer's *Golden Bough* in pursuit of early and primitive man's use of sympathetic magic. His discovery one day that at birth certain Pacific tribes opened the doors of their huts in order to aid the women in childbirth, was a cause for great excitement. How right it was! See, we must achieve that kind of unity in cinematography!

Soon it became clear that Sergei Mikhailovich did not talk solely for his own pleasure. He talked to me, and a year or so later to his American student, Jay Leyda, with creative purpose. It helped to clarify his ideas, prepare them for the moment when he would sit down to write an article, and, later on, one of the many books he planned. Lecturing too aided him to sort out his myriad theories. Since oral expression was natural to Eisenstein, questions and argument stimulated him to further development of his ideas.

Though Eisenstein wrote his scenarios with comparative ease, to set down his theoretical ideas, build a paragraph and complete a written exposition drove him almost mad. Like his *alter ego*, da Vinci, Eisenstein would start, discard and restart his writings many times. He would crumple up hundreds of sheets of paper in an effort to gain clarity and perfection; hundreds of others he would stow away. As a writer, he felt himself to be ungainly, like an elephant, and this maddened him when his aim was to write in a superbly translucent style. As he never showed me but the one small paragraph concerning *Que Viva Mexico!*, he likewise never showed me or referred to the many theoretical articles he had published. He was always thinking in terms of the future and what he could accomplish, not what he had finished.

Had it not been for Pera's encouragement and assistance, many of Sergei Mikhailovich's articles would have remained unfinished. She not only helped him find books and other research material he needed, but she also collected information concerning the production of films and the history of cinematography in general. She arranged for his manuscripts to be typed and discussed them with editors. Occasionally she succeeded in inducing Eisenstein to dictate his ideas which she wrote up in the form of brief articles. Often she corresponded with people abroad to obtain details about foreign films and make arrangements for the publication of Sergei Mikhailovich's articles. Frequently she had to badger the Old Man to get him to make corrections: a typical comment from a letter of Pera to me: 'I'll get a copy after 3-4 days, will correct it (1 day) and one day more I must have for S.M. to be persuaded to change the end of the article.'

It would have been a great deal easier for Sergei Mikhailovich to carry on his enormous theoretical schemes had he used a dictaphone, or been able to reduce his ideas to visual form. Whereas he would sit for hours over the wording of one sentence, in an hour he could produce a folio of drawings. Visual ideas tumbled out so fast and so complete that he drew the most complex caricatures, witty blasphemies or sketches for productions with the speed and economy of a lightning artist. His hand, which became clumsy when confronted with any mechanism, took on a certainty, swiftness and delicacy which was fascinating to watch. Of these drawings, only those which he considered slightly meritorious survived. He stuffed the wastepaper-basket with the lesser creations and liberally handed away masterpieces. These marvellous products of Sergei Mikhailovich's most intimate imagination were mostly drawn with pen or pencil with touches of red and blue crayon for emphasis. All but the production sketches were the expression of emotions he could not articulate in words: the pouring out of anger, comment on a secret joke, a bitter or pathetic thought, or a sudden autobiographical notation. They were not 'art' as Eisenstein conceived it. Many were his commentaries as a spectator of a very funny, very tragic world in which he did not know how to participate.

As intellectual spectator of the world, Eisenstein eagerly sought information of the arts and sciences in America, England, China, Japan, Germany, France. . . . The latest American comic strip took up a niche in his retentive memory beside his continued research into states of ecstasy. To understand Sergei Eisenstein one had to accept that triviality and greatness dwelt in his world. He read Henri Bergson or Freud one moment and the *New Yorker* and Ruthless Rhymes, the next. Sometimes there was no immediate connection in Sergei Mikhailovich's pursuit of knowledge. It might be months or even years before he analysed his many observations and exposed them to the X-ray of Marxist-Leninist theory which he began to study with deeper insight under the impact of capitalist America. Finally, each idea was set in or discarded, as one brick in the superstructure of knowledge—the idea of synthesis which had struck him with such force in Notre Dame in 1929.

Ever more possessed by the magnitude of his purpose, Sergei Mikhailovich found it hard to talk about his academic work to his fellow Russians, who, as he was well aware, were giving every ounce of their strength to aid Socialist Construction. His retreat into books and research widened the gulf between him and his fellow directors— Pudovkin, Dovzhenko, Kozintzev, Trauberg and others—who spent much of their free time in social activities beyond the scope of their creative work. These activities were aimed at furthering the development of socialist society and bringing culture to the masses. The art workers would go to factories and Houses of Culture to speak about the aims and methods of their particular art They would attend meetings of collective farmers and explain their work to them. In this way, the artists attempted to integrate their creative work into the scheme of current life. Since Eisenstein felt there was a lack of interest in his research, he avoided any social task outside his teaching at the Institute of Cinematography. He seldom went out except to teach, attend a theatre, film or concert. Inevitably many people in Russia concluded that since he had been abroad Eisenstein had no interest in anything but himself and his own ideas.

For all his lack of orthodox behaviour in terms of current Soviet society, Sergei Mikhailovich had profound loyalty to the idea of a new society. Unlike other Soviet artists who expressed their social convictions in enthusiastic acclaim of day-to-day achievement, Eisenstein's were expressed in philosophic terms. He had no illusions that existing Soviet society offered man the realization of his highest dreams; but even when he was most deeply hurt by the treatment he received from ardent Bolsheviks, he strove to understand. His colleagues showed little or no interest in the academic articles he wrote after returning from America and Sergei Mikhailovich made no further effort to explain what he was trying to achieve. He did not blame his fellow directors for being more concerned with immediate matters, but their lack of interest made him feel more than ever that he was a man standing between two worlds.

He would insist he could never be anything but half a new man, for he had grown up in the old world and was by upbringing the tag-end of a dead class. Yet he believed in the future of the new society. That it was hard upon him did not invalidate the socialism he dreamed would grow up to give man greater opportunity and he could bear to be grist for the mill when the society he foresaw was not confined to Socialist Construction of 1933, 1934 or even a decade later, but rather what would come to be in a hundred or two hundred years.

Had he spoken this way to his fellow artists, many of them would not only have considered him an arrant idealist chained to a Utopian dream, but an incurable individualist. The Russians recognized man as belonging to his own age. It was the artist's duty to express the spirit of his time, and because Eisenstein's academic work did not subscribe to this interpretation, there were many people who sincerely felt that he was betraying his great talents by laying such a heavy accent on research. Even such a fine artist as Alexander Dovzhenko came to feel this about Sergei Mikhailovich.

But by 1932 Eisenstein had become convinced that every creative work had its roots in the past. He devoted more and more time to an analysis of the older cultures—the Greek, the ancient Chinese and Japanese, the Italian Renaissance, Spain of El Greco, England of Shakespeare, France of Zola and Balzac, even the Pacific Islands of the mid-nineteenth century. He truly loved the creative work of others as much as his own. Above either he cherished the essence of the creative process. From this devotion Sergei Mikhailovich had come to think that no one was capable of creating any entirely original work, although he recognized that he had moulded a new medium of expression into an original form. Very often he would say: 'Everything important has been thought and done by someone before.'

This did not discourage him, for he considered he had a special function to perform. He expressed it in these words: 'All there remains for me to do is to analyse what has been done and from it create a synthesis of knowledge; an understanding of methods which can be applied to the art of cinematography.' This was Eisenstein's mission and he clung to it with relentless tenacity up to the moment of his death.

A mission of such magnitude made his readjustment to Soviet life more difficult than it might otherwise have been. It was not easy for the average official of the film industry, not even his fellow artists, to understand the importance Eisenstein attached to his theoretical work. The Soviet film, like Soviet literature and dramaturgy, had to keep abreast of the developing society. Pera understood the Old Man's difficulties. She tried to help him understand what had happened to their country during his absence. Had he been willing to follow her advice, Pera could have saved him many hard knocks because she responded to Soviet life with her whole being. It would have been good if the Old Man would do what other Soviet artists found extremely helpful: talk over their ideas with their fellow artists and, if necessary, discuss the problem freely with some member of the Central Committee of the Communist Party.

But for Eisenstein it was impossible to follow any such course. He would not know, as he explained, how to begin to express his ideas to an official, or to a political leader. In the past, Alexandrov had simplified his ideas and acted as an explanatory bulwark; that was why Grisha had been very important to the unit in the carrying out of their projects. He felt the loss of Alexandrov was a terrible blow to his future creative work. Though creative ideas circulated feverishly in his mind, he was not, as he lamented, 'Zeus to give birth to fully fledged children out of the top of the head'.

Early in 1933, however, it appeared as if Eisenstein's research and teaching at the Institute of Cinematography was going to be balanced by a resurgence of artistic work. A stranger meeting him at that time would have thought that his Mexican film was entirely forgotten in an upsurge of new creative activity.

Eisenstein the artist had a brilliant and imaginative sparkle as he talked and built up in words a work of art. His command of words was so remarkable, even in another language, that when he created *cinematic* and *theatrical* productions he had worked out in his head, but had only in note form on paper, the tempo of his speech and his instinctive selection of words were in themselves cinematic and at other times theatrical. One 'saw' in one's mind's eye the action he described in terms of film, or for presentation on the stage.

The first of these 'creations' to which I was treated in 1933 was the film *Moscow*, a picture which Sergei Mikhailovich then expected to produce as his first sound film.

'I'm starting to learn all over again. The past is finished,' he said. 'We're at the beginning of a new era in film development. In *Moscow* I shall endeavour to combine the methods of *Potemkin* and *October*.'

The proposed film was on a tremendous scale. As in *Que Viva Mexico!*, Eisenstein wanted to portray the 'living history' of Moscow: the city where the patterns of Asia had once met and mingled with the Slav-European patterns of the Middle Ages; the city where many vestiges of the past had been attacked and surrounded in less than a generation not only by modernity, but the visible signs of a new society. The very nature of Moscow's physical contrasts, yet spiritual continuity, appealed to Eisenstein.

The film was to commence with the emergence of Moscow, the tight-knit walled city of the days of Ivan the Terrible (this Ivan who was destined to be the subject of Eisenstein's last film). Moscow of Ivan's day was a labyrinth of dark, narrow streets where deeds of blood and tyranny were planned and executed by the powerful Boyars; and where the secret, silent horrors now and then burst forth into greater deeds of blood-letting.

The birth of Moscow as the Mother City of all the Russias was clearly developed in Sergei Mikhailovich's imagination. It was easy to picture his shot by shot embellishment of the period, for the architectural resources of Moscow were to be utilized by him in the same manner as he had used the buildings and furnishings of St. Petersburg in *October*.

Though Moscow spread out beyond the walled city during the centuries, it shrank in importance before the growth of the new city of St. Petersburg guarding with imperial dignity the bitter northern river, the Neva. The outer shell of European culture and technology was planted on the north-west gateway to Russia by Peter the Great, and now the Tsar came only to Mother Moscow to worship once a year in the gold-cupolaed churches closed within the Kremlin wall. Moscow seemed to sleep; yet it was a sleep troubled by bad dreams—dreams of frustration and revolt against the succession of Tsars whose autocracy in succeeding centuries rivalled that of Charlemagne and Louis XIV. Yet Moscow was the heart of Russia. Muscovites could rise up and fight when necessary. Thus, Sergei Mikhailovich would show the glory of Moscow's soul in the face of Napoleon's might. The people would set afire the body of their mother city and freeze the blood of Europe's conqueror until he retreated across the steppes. . . .

In all the generations that Moscow lived on dreaming her own dreams, only the families of the poor changed not at all. Frail huts had been their shelter in the days of Ivan the Terrible. The huts rotted and fell and were replaced by the same kind of huts, though there were more of them in each generation. At first the poor had served the individual princes; in time, the only change was that of master. The princes' power was slowly equalled by that of merchants; palaces and great houses shared the sweat of labourers with factories where the poor worked at machines.

In 1905, the workers, galvanized by the widespread upsurge of revolution, rebelled. The future was in their faces and the death knell of an Empire echoed in their marching feet. In 1917, the revolt of the Moscow workers, following that of the Petrograd workers, triumphed.

The continuity of theme for *Moscow* was to be a worker's family from generation to generation. Thus, Eisenstein planned to unite the fate of individuals with the dialectically spiralling currents of the historic scene, the social and political scene, with emphasis upon the role played by the working class in its struggle for liberation.

Boris Shumyatsky, as head of the film industry, rejected *Moscow*. He considered the film unsuitable for the new period of Socialist Construction, because Eisenstein had no personal hero in a time when the new humanism was in the ascendancy and there was an effort to portray the new socialist man, or history through the individuals who had contributed to the development of socialism. Sergei Mikhailovich accepted the decision without comment. He went on teaching, giving his students Shakespeare's *Julius Cæsar* for production exercises.

The students were required to prepare a stage presentation of Caesar's murder. His seventy-five-odd students, many of whom came from distant republics and could not speak Russian very fluently, had a hard time with Shakespeare and the professorial Eisenstein. He was often severe and unbending; sometimes he would snap at a student trying to explain his idea: 'Don't say "I think"! Until you *know*, I will not listen to you!' His face looked like granite.

Following the rejection of *Moscow*, the news reached Eisenstein that the mutilated version of *Que Viva Mexico!* called *Thunder Over Mexico*, had been previewed in Hollywood on the 10th of May 1933, at the Carthay Circle Theatre in Los Angeles. The conflict between Upton Sinclair and Eisenstein's supporters, which had been simmering for more than a year, now burst into the open in a sulphurous torrent of charges and counter charges. There followed the most bitter controversy over a film in cinema history. Committees were formed; open letters were circulated and for several months the protagonists flooded newspapers and magazines with protesting letters and explanations. But as from the outset, Sergei Mikhailovich remained silent, except for one brief public statement.

Edited according to established Hollywood methods, the Maguey story, originally intended by Eisenstein to occupy but *two* reels in the total film, was spun out to six reels—seven including the Prologue and Epilogue. The slow development of 'story', with, of course, no intercutting of the Corpus Christi festival as Eisenstein planned, was impressive only on account of the beauty of the individual shots. No one could have seriously believed that this was Eisenstein's film as he would have edited it.

Writing in the *Los Angeles Times*, Philip K. Scheuer commented: 'Of cinedynamics, if I may use the term, there is almost none. Rather is the effect that of series of exquisite still pictures, in reasonable (but conventional) dramatic sequence. It could hardly, without Eisenstein and his mathematics of montage, have been otherwise. As well score a Beethoven Symphony for a string quartet. As well explain relativity in terms of this column. . . .'[1]

William Troy in *The Nation* wrote 'The real seriousness of "cutting" the work of a director, whose whole technique and reputation rests on an elaborately worked-out theory of montage, can only be understood if one imagines a magazine editor who would dare to rearrange the episodes in a story or the images in a poem. By the wrong sort of cutting a novel by Proust or Mann could be made into something completely opposed to either author's intention. . . . The episodes or images, individually considered, would be the same, but the articulation of them into a deliberately conceived pattern would be destroyed. In an Eisenstein film, the montage supplies the syntax, the larger structural rhythm (as distinguished from the incidental rhythms of movement, which are, however, usually identified with it), and because this element is always the most intimately personal in any work of art, to interfere with it is to disturb what is the most inviolable property of any artist—his style. . . . In Eisenstein's case, it would be possible to go even

[1] Review of *Thunder Over Mexico* by Philip K. Scheuer, *Los Angeles Times*, May 14, 1933.

further and say that (montage) is the irreducible element of his style.'[1]

Sinclair vehemently defended his act in cutting *Thunder Over Mexico!* and resolutely maintained that 'the editing of the episode used has been done in accord with Eisenstein's ideas, and there is nothing in the picture that was not shot by Eisenstein.'[2] 'The material omitted . . . consists (of) everything a tourist wandering through Mexico might find picturesque and interesting.'[3]

In an effort to dispel criticism, Sinclair appeared on the screen in a foreword to the film. He was flippant and jocular about *Que Viva Mexico!* and the reasons why Eisenstein had not edited his own film. Among other things, he said that Eisenstein had landed 'a white elephant' in his backyard by shooting 35 miles of film, and that he had the right to release a section of this 'white elephant' in the form of *Thunder Over Mexico!*, which had been highly praised by Eisenstein's own friends Douglas Fairbanks and Charlie Chaplin. He ended by quoting from Rob Wagner's magazine *Script*: 'At last we are permitted to see the bastard child of the shot-gun marriage of Moscow and Hollywood and like so many illegitimate children it is more beautiful than either parent.'

Sinclair's attitude outraged those people who believed that the commercial Hollywood cutters had mutilated a great work of art. The editors of *Experimental Cinema*, headed by Seymour Stern in Hollywood, began a campaign of public protest. In June, 1933, Stern wrote and published a manifesto, which said in part:

There is now being released on the world market a movie called *Thunder Over Mexico*, which is what it is: a fragmentary and entirely conventional version of Eisenstein's original majestic conception. The story behind this commercialized version is without doubt the greatest tragedy in the history of film and one of the saddest in the history of art. . . .

We decry this illegitimate version of *Que Viva Mexico!* and denounce it for what it is—a mere vulgarization of Eisenstein's original conception put forth in his name in order to capitalize on his renown as a creative artist. We denounce the cutting of *Que Viva Mexico!* by professional Hollywood cutters as an unmitigated mockery of Eisenstein's intentions. . . .

Eisenstein's original scenario provided for *six* interrelated episodes. . . . What has happened to this material?

[1] 'The Eisenstein Muddle', by William Troy, *Nation* (U.S.A.), July 19, 1933.
[2] An open Letter: 'Thunder Over Mexico' by Upton Sinclair, dated July 5, 1933.
[3] Upton Sinclair in a letter to the *New York Sun*, September 22, 1933.

Eisenstein's original prologue . . . has been converted into a pseudo-travelogue.

Worse than this is the fate of Eisenstein's original epilogue. . . . Under the guidance of Eisenstein's backers, . . . the epilogue has now been converted into a cheerful ballyhoo about 'a new Mexico,' *with definite fascist implications*.

The remaining mass of material, consisting of more than 180,000 feet, is in danger of being sold piecemeal to commercial film concerns. . . .

For more than a year Eisenstein's friends and admirers in the United States have been appealing to his backers, represented by Upton Sinclair, to save the picture and to preserve it so that eventually Eisenstein might edit it. . . .

The purpose of this manifesto, therefore, is two-fold (1) to orient and forewarn public taste on the eve of the arrival of a much misrepresented product, *Thunder Over Mexico*; and (2) to incite public opinion to bring pressure to bear upon the backers in a last effort to save the complete negative, both cut and uncut, for Eisenstein. . . .[1]

A copy of the manifesto was sent to Sergei Mikhailovich, who had been waiting patiently for a year, hoping that a way would be found to save *Que Viva Mexico!* Although he had refrained from making any public statements about the Hollywood editing of *Thunder Over Mexico*, Eisenstein at last gave an interview to the Moscow *Daily News* in which he said: 'I deeply appreciate what *Experimental Cinema* has done. I feel that what is said in this manifesto is perfectly true and I am very glad that someone has said it.'[2]

But the protest of *Experimental Cinema* could not help Eisenstein legally, although the lawyer, Enos S. Booth, had already threatened to bring a suit against Upton Sinclair in an effort to save the film. Nor

---

[1] This manifesto was reprinted in *Experimental Cinema*, No. 5, 1934, together with the scenario of *Que Viva Mexico! Experimental Cinema* had been founded in 1930 by David Platt with financial assistance from Seymour Stern. No. 1 was published in Philadelphia in February 1930 with David Platt and Lewis Jacobs as editors. No. 2, also published in Philadelphia, appeared in June 1930, at the time of Eisenstein's arrival in Hollywood. By this time Seymour Stern had become the Hollywood Editor. No. 3, was published in New York in March 1931 with Seymour Stern as one of the three editors. No. 4, published in Hollywood, by Seymour Stern was largely devoted to *Que Viva Mexico!*, including many stills. David Platt objected to the character of this issue and resigned. No. 5 was published in New York in the summer of 1933 under the supervision of Lewis Jacobs.

[2] *Moscow Daily News*, June 20, 1933.

had the International Defence Committee for Eisenstein's Mexican Film, which had been set up in New York, more than a moral basis from which to act in circulating a second manifesto, written by Lincoln Kirstein and Seymour Stern.

The members of this Committee were the writer Waldo Frank; Lincoln Kirstein, who gave office space to the Committee and helped to finance the printing and circulation of the manifesto; J. M. Valdes-Rodriguez, who undertook to spread the manifesto through Cuba; and Eisenstein's loyal friend, Agustin Aragon Leiva, who aroused a great deal of protest in Mexico. The main organization of the campaign was undertaken by Seymour Stern in Hollywood, where he was assisted by a number of people,[1] chief among whom was a young Californian poetess, Maria Luisa Yerby. She edited the June manifesto, translated reports on *Que Viva Mexico!* from, and into, Spanish, and wrote about the film in the Mexican press under her nickname, 'Titi.'

Because of the Latin American setting of *Que Viva Mexico!*, the strongest protests came from the Spanish-speaking world. Brazil was informed of what had happened by Olympio Guilherme, the actor, film director, and critic, who broadcast the manifesto. Enrique Mobili and Jacobo Muchnick of the Cine Club de Buenos Aires also campaigned against *Thunder Over Mexico* in the Argentine, Uruguay, Chile and Brazil. In Peru, the Cine Club of Lima organized a protest. The Film Bureau Division—Hemerotica Municipal—of Madrid and Filmofono of the same city publicized the tragedy of *Que Viva Mexico!* in Spain.

Organizations and individuals in America, England, Italy, Ireland, Czechosolovakia, and Poland[2] supported the campaign against the mutilation of Eisenstein's work. In time, the Nobel Prize Committee in Stockholm received protests against Upton Sinclair's candidacy for the Nobel Prize. But perhaps the most interesting single group of people who expressed sympathy for Eisenstein were a group of political

---

[1] Other people who made efforts to aid Eisenstein in connection with *Que Viva Mexico!* were: A. C. Jensen, Charles Liversay, Jorge Juan Crespo and Thomas Moore. Two other people, Maria Luisa Yerby and Le Roy Robbins, spent much time and energy in assisting *Experimental Cinema* to make it known that Eisenstein had not edited *Thunder Over Mexico* and that it was, in fact, one 'novel' lifted out from the material with a Prologue and Epilogue in no way related to the original conception of Eisenstein's Prologue and Epilogue.

[2] Hallie Flanagan, Drama Dept., Vassar College, Professor William A. Orton, Smith College, Dr. Wallace A. Atwood, International Film Foundation, New York; Thomas Craven, author and art critic, Louis Adamic, Margaret Bourke-White, Robert Edmond Jones, Clarence W. Winchell and Edith Johnson, Hudson County Cine Club, Jersey City, N.J.

prisoners confined in the Penetenciarul Central in the town of Aiud, province of Transylvania in Roumania. Prisoner No. 391—by name M. Kriper—organized the protest.

Sinclair again made a vigorous, if challengeable reply. In a letter to Agustín Aragon Leiva, dated the 1st of June, 1933, he said.

UPTON SINCLAIR
Los Angeles West Branch
California

June 1, 1933

MR. A. A. LEIVA
5a Del Pino 215
Mexico City, Mexico.

DEAR SIR:

In the answer which I dictated yesterday to your letter, I forgot to answer one of your statements, to the effect that I am deliberately lying about Eisenstein when I say that he did not always cut his own pictures. My authority for this statement is, first the story which Eisenstein told to me and to other persons in Hollywood, whose affidavits I can obtain. This story is that when *Ten Days that Shook the World* was completed, the hero and central figure of it was Trotsky. The quarrel between Trotsky and Stalin broke out just as the picture was completed and the government cut out every foot of the picture in which Trotsky was shown. . . .

Second, my friend, Lucita Squier, wife of Albert Rhys Williams, spent many years in Russia and did a great deal of motion picture work, including the writing of two scenarios. She was employed by the concern which made *Potemkin* and she has told me a detailed story of how this picture was cut by various persons, and how at the end Eisenstein managed to obtain the public credit for the entire work. . . .

In his efforts to remain in Mexico City and avoid having to go back to Soviet Russia, which was Eisenstein's principal purpose in life for many months, he went to one of the members of the cabinet and stated that if he were not allowed to remain and complete the picture in his own way, the resultant product would be injurious to the Mexican government and people. That is the basis of many of the stories which have been circulated, and the cause of a great deal of trouble which we have had with the Mexican government and with patriotic Mexicans. Eisenstein prepared a scenario which was officially approved by the Mexican government, but he privately wrote to me (I have it in his own handwriting) that this scenario was only intended to get him by with the Mexican government. It so happens that I am not a person who breaks his word and the pledges which we made to the Mexican government have been kept. As a result of this some young hot-heads are accusing us of having made a fascist picture. They say that the scenes which Eisenstein made of modern Mexico were intended to be satirically treated and that it is for this reason that we are guilty of the crime of 'assassinating' the great work of the master. Well, you can have it either way you choose but you cannot have it both ways. We cannot at the same time be guilty of attacking Mexico and of refusing to let Eisenstein attack it. Yet strangely enough these two contradictory stories have been sent out from the same sources in Hollywood. One set of statements is made to Mexicans and the other set is made to communists. Please tell me which set has been made to you.

We are accused of having destroyed a great 'sociological' picture, a great propaganda picture, et cetera. I point out to you that Eisenstein's original purpose was to make a travelogue and he himself of his own initiative put into the contract the provision that the picture was to be non-political. He said that he knew a political picture could not be made in Mexico and could not be shown in the United States. Every dollar of the money that was raised for the picture was raised upon these guarantees, given in all cases in writing. It may be said that Eisenstein planned to break these pledges; but as I said before, I am not accustomed to breaking my pledges, and as my wife and I raised all the money among our relatives and friends and among strangers as well, we have seen to it that the pledges were kept.

While I am writing I may as well tell you a little about Eisenstein's purpose throughout the entire misadventure. He had contracts requiring him to return to Russia but he concealed these facts from me. His purpose was to make a picture in Mexico while negotiating contracts in Hollywood. He had agents trying to get him contracts with every big producing concern in Hollywood and in New York and the reason he kept dragging out the work in Mexico was purely and simply because he could not get a contract elsewhere. He tried to negotiate contracts in India, in Japan and he even had his passport visaed to Spain.[1] All this was for the purpose of not having to go back to Russia. I have in my possession a cablegram from Stalin telling me that everybody in Russia considered him a deserter and that they

[1] J. Alvarez del Vayo, who was Spanish Ambassador to Mexico during the entire period that Sergei Eisenstein was there, told the author that, to the best of his knowledge, the Spanish Embassy in Mexico did not issue a Spanish visa to Eisenstein. del Vayo also said that since no diplomatic relations existed between the U.S.S.R. and Mexico, he would have been consulted had Eisenstein applied for a Spanish visa while in Mexico.

had no further interest in him. I have cablegrams and letters from other high officials in Moscow making similar statements. Do you want to see all this material published in the capitalistic Press! (See App. Six.) If you are a Mexican, I tell you that I protected your country from a man who sought to traduce it. If you are a Communist, I tell you that at the direct request of Soviet officials in New York I brought it about that their great director had to return to his own country, thus saving Soviet Russia a scandal. And for a year now I have kept silent under a flood of abuse and misrepresentation. But I don't advise you or any of Eisenstein's friends to count upon my patience lasting for ever.

Very truly yours,

UPTON SINCLAIR.

On the same day, Sinclair wrote a letter to the *Modern Monthly*, which had published an attack on the Hollywood editing of *Thunder Over Mexico*. He said:

I should have thought that thirty years of service to the radical movement would have entitled me to have you display the decency to ask me whether there was any truth in the statements you proposed to publish. . . .

There has been a campaign of deliberate falsification carried on concerning the picture. . . . I have submitted to all these attacks for one reason and one only, because I do not wish to be put in a position of seeming to attack Soviet Russia in the capitalistic press. If I tell the truth about Eisenstein and those who supported him, my statements will be so interpreted by the capitalistic press. However, I have written to a few individuals privately setting forth a few of these facts. I enclose a copy of a letter I am writing today to a man who wrote me an abusive letter from Mexico City. . . . You may, if you wish, go and see Bogdanov of Amtorg and ask him whether he wants the facts which I have concerning Eisenstein and his backers made known to the capitalistic press. . . .[1]

This did not silence the criticism. Instead, Herman G. Weinberg wrote an answer on behalf of Eisenstein's supporters in which he said: 'Mr. Sinclair contends that there were certain personal elements involving S. M. Eisenstein, the Soviet Government, the Mexican Government, etc., which made it impossible for Eisenstein to remain here to cut his film. Mr. Sinclair further maintains that Eisenstein has never cut his own films. . . . This seems hard to believe on the mere face of it. . . . Virtually every film director of note has testified, over and

---

[1] 'Upton Sinclair and Eisenstein': letters, *Modern Monthly*, U.S.A., July 1933.

over again, to the revolutionary consequences of Eisenstein's montage technique on the modern cinema. . . .

'Mr. Sinclair contends that the campaign now being waged on Eisenstein's behalf is a campaign of deliberate falsification of the facts, and states that certain instigators of this campaign have seen "documentary evidence that the charges are false". I have not seen such evidence, nor has anyone else connected with the campaign—otherwise our allegations would have been tempered by these facts. It seems to me that if Mr. Sinclair has such irrefutable documentary evidence that it is highly important that he make it public at once so that he will not continue to be placed in an unfavourable light, nor continue to be the victim of any further misunderstandings, as is his present claim.'[1]

Sinclair did not respond and make public his charges against Eisenstein. Instead, he circulated a printed statement in which he said:

We have recently learned that 'the Master' was really making a cycle of five pictures, something like the 'Ring of the Nibelungs'. The total length of the Mexican work, with all repeats and waste matter eliminated, would have been thirty or thirty-five thousand feet, and would have taken six or seven hours to run. It may have been that Eisenstein expected to raise the money to build a Bayreuth temple of art in which such a work could have been shown, but our investors did not have this money, and we know of no such temple now existing.[2]

In July 1933, the pages of *The New Republic* and *The Nation* magazines became a forum for the protagonists. Sinclair's statement that Eisenstein shot footage for a film running six or seven hours was countered by Aragon Leiva, who wrote that 'It is absurd to believe what Sinclair says, that Eisenstein wanted to produce many films. It was a film divided into six sections. The film was calculated to last ninety minutes . . . he cannot make us believe that Eisenstein was an imbecile, or a newborn child.' In answer to Sinclair's charges of excessive costs, Leiva said, 'the film had a ridiculously small production cost. Why? Eisenstein got nearly everything free of charge. An immense lot of commodities, facilities and means were offered to him through wide spread publication in numerous magazines and newspapers that his film was to be *Que Viva Mexico!* and an epic of the evolution of this country through a period of five thousand years.'[3]

Adolfo Best-Maugard, the Mexican technical adviser, disclaimed all

---

[1] 'Upton Sinclair and Eisenstein': letters, *Modern Monthly*, U.S.A., July 1933.
[2] An open letter: *Thunder Over Mexico* by Upton Sinclair, dated 5 July 1933.
[3] Letter from Agustin Aragon Leiva, *New Republic*, 9 August 1933.

responsibility for *Thunder Over Mexico*. In England, Ivor Montagu came to Eisenstein's aid. Writing in the *New Clarion*, he said that Sinclair had impatiently ignored all offers to find a solution for *Que Viva Mexico!*, including an offer made by himself 'to help expedite matters.'[1]

In the meantime, leading newspapers and magazines in Mexico carried articles of protest against the mutilation of *Que Viva Mexico!* 'A WORK OF GENIUS BARBAROUSLY MUTILATED.' 'MANIFESTATION OF PROTEST AGAINST THE NOVELIST UPTON SINCLAIR.' 'MEXICO AND THE TRAGEDY OF EISENSTEIN.'

At a meeting of the Centro Nacional de Ingenieros in Mexico City, Augustin Aragon Leiva said: Eisenstein 'travelled and studied, like a new Humboldt, with discipline and good manners and once he had become acquainted with our country and its traditions he began creating his work. . . . Sinclair has made no revelation [of his charges against Eisenstein], nor can he make one because Eisenstein is an honest man whose only sin is that of being an artistic genius and a profound thinker.'[2]

Still, Upton Sinclair repeatedly defended his own action in releasing *Thunder Over Mexico*. In a letter to *The New Republic*, he said:[3]

Sir: For two years and a half my wife and I have been carrying the responsibility for the moving picture which Sergei Eisenstein made in Mexico. . . . It seems that the time has come for the facts to be made known and the misunderstanding cleared up. Here is the 'inside' story:

In October, 1930, Eisenstein came to us, stating that he had come to Hollywood intending to make a picture. . . . As a result of what Diego Rivera had told him concerning the marvelous screen material in Mexico, he desired to go there and make a travelogue, which he could do in three or four months. He wanted somebody to raise the money for this, and my wife and I, full of sympathy for a great Soviet director whom Hollywood had failed to appreciate, undertook this heavy responsibility, and the expedition set out for Mexico. . . .

Eisenstein had said that he wanted to 'lay his ear on the bosom of Mother Mexico and listen to her heartbeats and be guided by what

[1] 'Eisenstein and Upton Sinclair', by Ivor Montagu (*The New Clarion*, London, 29 July 1933).

[2] Front page report, *Excelsior* (Mexico City, 19 September 1933).

[3] 'Thunder Over Eisenstein', a letter from Upton Sinclair, *New Republic* (New York, 5 July 1933).

he heard'. It appeared that the heart of Mother Mexico is a largeone, and Eisenstein followed the sounds over an enormous territory. In truth he fell in love with the country and I think would have wished to stay there the balance of his days. . . . Suffice it to say that the three or four months extended to fourteen months, and the estimated amount of film, 75,000 feet, expanded to 232,000. [See Sinclair's letter and report to H. W. L. Dana, p. 222.] We begged and borrowed from all our friends; my wife mortgaged the home we live in. . . .

However, the time came when both money and health were completely exhausted. . . . Moreover, we learned that Eisenstein had contracts with his own government and had long overstayed his leave. . . . He and his expedition had to leave Mexico. He was hoping to come to Hollywood and cut the picture, but the United States government held him for five weeks at the border and effectually barred that chance. [See telegram from Sinclair to Eisenstein, p. 233.] He obtained a 'transit visa', enabling him to travel to Russia by way of New York, and we endeavoured to make arrangements whereby the picture would be sent to Russia for him to cut it there. . . . However, after eight months of futile negotiations we realized that the arrangement could not be made. [See App. Six.] . . . The present editing has been done in accord with Eisenstein's ideas, and there is nothing in the picture that was not shot by Eisenstein. . . . Its principal episode is a story of oppression of the peons in the time of Diaz, thirty years ago. . . . The epilogue gives glimpses of modern Mexico, with a special emphasis upon those elements of athletics, youth, machinery and labour which appeal to the Russians . . . [See App. Five.]

During the period of struggle over the fate of this picture, I was sick almost unto death over it; but now that I have seen the finished work, my attitude has changed. I believe that the picture speaks for itself, and I no longer have either regrets or apologies.

Los Angeles, California   Upton Sinclair

Copies of these charges and counter charges were sent to Eisenstein, but he continued to wait. He still hoped that the lawyer, Enos S. Booth, would work out a way for him to receive a print of the entire negative of Que Viva Mexico!

Sinclair had publicly stated that 'the total cost of a lavender print from which a duplicate [positive print] can be made, would be about $5,000'.[1] Lincoln Kirstein, and the group in New York, had raised

[1] Open letter: Thunder Over Mexico by Upton Sinclair, dated 5 July 1933.

funds and ever since April, 1932, they had been attempting to purchase the film for Eisenstein and send it to him via Amkino. But Sinclair had refused to negotiate with them, although Enos S. Booth had threatened to take legal action which Bogdanov, the head of the Soviet purchasing commission, Amtorg, had approved. Sinclair continued to demand a guarantee of payment from Amkino and everyone else who approached him on Eisenstein's behalf before he would relinquish his rights in the film and turn it over to Eisenstein.

In an effort to make some arrangement, Sergei Mikhailovich had talked to Louis Fischer, the Moscow correspondent of *The Nation* magazine, who was going to America, and asked him to speak to Sinclair. In April, 1933, Fischer had met Sinclair who said that he would not reopen negotiations unless the threatened lawsuit by Enos Booth was withdrawn. *Thunder Over Mexico* had not as yet been previewed. However, by the time Fischer returned to Moscow, the film had been seen and the protest against it had flared into the open.

The armour which Sergei Mikhailovich had so valiantly worn during the winter and spring of 1933, began to crack. He was once more as desperate as during the months of August and September, 1932.

On the 4th of July, 1933, Louis Fischer cabled from Moscow to Upton Sinclair:

. . . Eisenstein . . . prepared discontinue suit provided you forward Moscow copy complete footage of all material shot plus copy Lesser's version. Eisenstein promises edit material four months after receipt in consideration whereof Eisenstein urges discontinue commercial exhibition Lesser version. Eisenstein inquires whether he receive contracted percentage world distribution his version and Lesser version if shown. Cable Fischerlou Moscow confirming your oral offer to me and your reaction Eisenstein's proposals. Urge immediate reply and action so Eisenstein can keep free order commence editing immediately upon receipt material.

Four days later. Upton Sinclair answered:

. . . Trustees consider contract broken obligations cancelled welcome suit enabling establish artists' misconduct personally prefer avoid scandal will myself pay artists' percentage when earned [from distribution of *Thunder Over Mexico*] will furnish Soyuzkino complete print when Thunder established will pay percentage artists' version when earned suit will cancel these offers regards Sinclair.

On the 12th of July, Fischer sent another cable in which he said that Eisenstein would accept Sinclair's offer and instruct Enos S. Booth to discontinue the pending lawsuit 'provided copy all material sent immediately'. He added that if Sinclair would agree, 'Eisenstein will ask Amkino grant you credits for making prints', which Eisenstein would repay from his earnings from *Thunder Over Mexico*. To this cable Upton Sinclair made no reply. On the 18th, Fischer cabled him again requesting an answer. The following day, Sinclair replied: 'Trustees business arrangements make impossible consider Eisenstein proposition. Visiting New York hope arrange something with Bogdanov.'

Sergei Mikhailovich grew more and more bewildered by Sinclair's conduct. He read and reread Sinclair's telegram promising to send the film 'on the next boat' if he would return to the Soviet Union. It did not matter that he had laboured for endless months in Mexico without pay, while Sinclair planned to use the proceeds of *Que Viva Mexico!* to put copies of his books in all the public libraries of the world. He could not understand Sinclair. But now it did not seem to be a matter of money. Sergei Mikhailovich grew distraught.

On the 25th of July, Louis Fischer sent a fourth cable to Upton Sinclair:

> Since Eisenstein prepared arrange credit for making copy all material which credit repaid either by you or him from his percentage Thunder earnings and since you or trustees refuse I forced conclude you under all circumstances insist depriving great artist product his labor. Must warn you Eisenstein mentally extremely depressed may do something rash. . . . Cannot exaggerate earnestness situation please advise without delay.

Six days went by before Upton Sinclair replied. Then his answer was:

> Proposition for furnishing complete print Soyuzkino at Soyuzkino's expense for Eisenstein cutting has been before various Soviet officials more than year. This offer still stands. Print will be made available after Thunder release as promptly as distribution makes possible.

Once more, on the 4th of August, Fischer sent a cable in which he asked: 'Does your last telegram refer proposition involving many tens thousands of dollars. Eisenstein can only pay actual cost manufacturing copy.' Sinclair answered that he was sending a registered letter, but it appears that no such letter arrived. Shortly after this last cable, Sergei Mikhailovich broke down completely and was sent to a sanatorium in Kislovodsk in a state of nervous collapse.

On the 26th of July, Sinclair wrote to H. W. L. Dana, who had written to Sinclair in connection with Sinclair's letter in the *New Republic*. Dana said that it failed to answer the fundamental objections to the editing *Thunder Over Mexico*. 'It merely tries to shift the blame from those who have put up the money to the film director himself, and argues that a work of art is the property not of the artist but of the investors.' Dana also told Sinclair: 'Those of us who have recently been to see Sergei Eisenstein about this question in Moscow have found that with remarkable patience he has himself urged us to wait before denouncing you publicly and to give you every opportunity of your own accord to do the generous thing.'

In response to this letter, Sinclair said:

MY DEAR HARRY:

. . . . I am waiting for Eisenstein to do what you say he contemplates doing—that is to attack me publicly. When he does that my hands will be free and I will publish a book upon the subject. In the meantime his partisans have been lying vigorously and I am taking it all. . . .

As to the story of Eisenstein and our dealings with him, that cannot be even outlined short of an essay, and it will take a book to tell it. Suffice it to say that he exploited me shamefully, mainly for the purpose of keeping from having to go back to Soviet Russia. . . .

I had a long cablegram from Stalin, telling me that everybody in Soviet Russia considered Eisenstein a deserter and that no one had any further interest in him. [See App. Six.] But the Soviet officials in New York begged us to help get Eisenstein back into Russia, and we did so; then instead of displaying any gratitude, they turned around and tried to take the picture away from us, and ever since then we have felt that we are being besieged by bandits.

I must explain to you that I really have no control whatever over the matter. I am rather easy to blackmail because I do not care much about money and I would rather give up and dismiss the matter from my mind and write another book; but, unfortunately for Eisenstein, it was with my wife that he signed a contract, and my wife is a person who would die rather than submit to blackmail. At the demand of the investors, there was formed a body called the Mexican Picture Trust. My wife and her brother are the trustees. . . . They have decided what to do, and it is up to me to help them or quit. I have been helping them, simply because the actions of both Eisenstein and his supporters have been of such a criminal nature as to break down, time and again, all my efforts to work out a compromise. [See App. Six.] It looks as if they were going to force me to tell the whole painful story.

The talk about 'the great masterpiece' is all plain bunk. Eisenstein was making five separate pictures and he purposely kept them incomplete as a means of making it impossible for us to call him from

Mexico. If this stuff were all to be shovelled into one picture it would make such a mess that no one would go to see it except out of curiosity. I look forward with great joy to the time when Eisenstein will at last be able to cut his own version of his 'great masterpiece' and we shall then see what happens. It will be a good joke on Seymour Stern and the rest of the young fanatics! Eisenstein wrote Stern he was making 5 pictures.

Now to cover the business side: . . . most of the money belongs to friends and strangers. It was raised on the basis of Eisenstein's promise to complete the work in three or four months. [See Sinclair's letter and report to H. W. L. Dana, p. 220.] Among the agreements made to the investors was the pledge that the negative was to be kept in a vault in Hollywood as security for the investors' money, and that it would never be allowed to leave this vault until the picture was completed and marketed, and the money returned. . . . I have absolutely no power to send anything to Eisenstein and no money to pay for its manufacture.

The Russian Government got their great artist back and avoided having him turn into a White, as Rachmaninov and Chaliapin have done. They owe this solely to our efforts, and we thought they would be ready to do the fair thing about the picture. . . .

Altogether I delayed the Hollywood cutting for eight months, by pleading with the trustees and investors, sometimes with tears in my eyes. . . .

I might mention to you that at the very outset we freely promised the Russian rights to Russia. We also promised Eisenstein 10% of the profits of the picture. We did not have to do this at all. We have been generous idealists all the way through, and I will put it very mildly and say that our favours have not been reciprocated.

Louis Fischer was here two or three months ago and we told him the situation. I also personally told him what I have said to Bogdanov and to Seymour Stern, and to numerous other persons, that it is my intention to see that ultimately Soyuzkino gets a print of the entire film so that they can let Eisenstein cut his own version if they want to. I stated that I want to do this even if I have to pay the cost of the print myself. I intend to do it not so much to clear my good name, for I am not worrying about that—I believe the truth will prevail in the end. I intend to do it because my artistic conscience insists that the world should have a chance to see what Eisenstein meant to do.

Fischer is now in Moscow and I have had several cablegrams from him. He has repeated my statements to Eisenstein, and first came the usual imbecile demand that we should suppress *Thunder Over Mexico* and send a print to Eisenstein at once. . . . Nobody in Russia is going to have a sight of the film until *Thunder Over Mexico* has been released and established. . . .

You see I have written a long letter. I could tell the story to the capitalist press and prove every statement by documents and make quite a sensation, and also help to advertise *Thunder Over Mexico*. Only one thing holds me back, and that is my interest in Soviet Russia. I am sure that you will appreciate this.

Sincerely

Upton Sinclair

Dana sent a copy of this letter to Eisenstein, and again wrote to Upton Sinclair, who answered, on the 2nd of August:

MY DEAR HARRY:

You say that my letter made you sad—well, yours made me even sadder. . . .

And you go right on talking about 'my' preferring the rights of the investors over those of a great artist and 'my' refusing to send a print as 'suppressing evidence'. . . . Apparently it has not occurred to you that there are laws in this country which govern the rights of investors—even when these rights come into conflict with those of a 'great artist'.

Also I am wondering whether there are any crimes a great artist could commit which would deprive him of his rights, in your opinion. Suppose I were to tell you that at one time when the great artist was managing the enterprise himself, he was entrusted with some $6,000 by myself, acting in behalf of the trustees, and that he has accounted for less than half of this? Suppose I were to tell you that he, or one of his two intimates, stole 20,000 feet of raw film from us and sold it to a rival concern in Mexico City? Suppose I were to tell you that he shamelessly traduced the character of my brother-in-law, because the latter had committed one single offence, of obeying my orders and demanding that the great artist should conform to the schedule he had agreed to (and repeatedly broken)? Suppose I were to tell you that in his desperate efforts to be allowed to stay in Mexico and to avoid going back to his own country, he told a member of the Mexican Cabinet that the picture in its incompleted form would be injurious to Mexico? He knew this was false, because there was not a foot of the film injurious to Mexico; also he knew that we had at the time nearly 100,000 feet of the film in the hands of the Mexican government, and it was nearly lost to us, and it took us several months and cost us a good deal of money to get it out of Mexican hands—as a result of Eisenstein's treachery. Suppose also I should tell you that the great artist is a sexual pervert, and that he shipped into the United States an enormous mass of unthinkably filthy drawings and photographs, the former made on our time and the latter made with our money? He shipped this in the baggage belonging to us and including all the priceless stills of the expedition. The whole thing was seized by the United States Customs authorities, and we very nearly had all our property confiscated and a frightful scandal in the newspapers.

How many more things would I have to tell you about your 'great' artist before I made you begin to realize that I might have some difficulty in persuading the investors and their trustees and their lawyer to place their property again in his hands, or to rely upon any promises he made? You and your friends, whom you call friends, are doing your best to put me in a position where I have to tell all these stories in order to defend my own good name. . . .

Sincerely,
Upton Sinclair

On the 18th of August, 1933, Pera Attasheva answered H. W. L. Dana's letter to Eisenstein:

Your letter to Eisenstein of the 30th July received. As Eisenstein is now in a Kislovodsk Sanatorium in a serious nervous condition the last letter of Sinclair cannot be forwarded to him—it would only worsen his condition. So I take upon myself the responsibility of replying (being fully acquainted with the whole of his affairs and the Mexican tragedy, his assistant and close friend).

At the moment in the absence of Eisenstein I cannot go into the details of Sinclair's astounding letter, but just point out the simple and basic fact: that all Eisenstein wants is a complete copy of his material to cut. I enclose the correspondence of Louise Fisher [sic] to Sinclair and Dreiser attempting to arrive at some agreement whereby this material may be had. It is obvious from all this that Sinclair is avoiding letting Eisenstein have this material at least until 'Thunder' is sold and giving profit. But if only someone would make Sinclair realize that Eisenstein wants above all as an artist to finish his creation, and that he does not intend to break his contract by marketing such a copy outside the Soviet Union. So what then has Sinclair to fear if he lets Eisenstein have the material at once? According to contract he should have done this long ago, and it's a test of his sincerity now. . .

One point: please find out if you can whether quite definitely *all* the negative is complete and intact in Sinclair's Hollywood vaults, for we have news that the Spanish part was sold (directly or indirectly) to Metro-Goldwyn for 'atmosphere shots' . . .

With very best wishes,
Pearl (Pera) Attasheva

Meanwhile, the campaign against *Thunder Over Mexico* was reaching its climax. The public release of the film in September, 1933, was greeted by an Open Letter to Upton Sinclair. Lincoln Kirstein financed the printing of 10,000 copies which were circulated by the International Defence Committee for Eisenstein's Mexican Film. This Open Letter said in part:

> You have refused to come out in the open. You have refused to answer certain important questions. Instead, you have implied on various occasions that you and Mrs. Sinclair have 'personal' (sexual) charges to prefer against Eisenstein, which you say, will ruin his political position in the Soviet Union and which prevented him from cutting 'QUE VIVA MEXICO!'
>
> You also have made these statements: 'Eisenstein was disloyal to the Soviet Union.' 'Eisenstein has never cut any of his pictures.' 'Eisenstein was not serious about *Que Viva Mexico!*' 'He did not wish to edit his picture.'
>
> You know that each of these charges of yours is a preposterous lie. You know that you cannot prove a single word of these high-sounding and worthless charges, and yet, for over a year you and your wife have been trying to intimidate Eisenstein and his friends into silence by threatening to publish these charges in a book.

When the film was previewed at the New School of Social Research in New York, Lincoln Kirstein, who rose to protest, was forcibly ejected from the showing by Sol Lesser and a detective. Still, Sinclair refrained from taking up the challenge to expose Eisenstein. Instead, he continued to attack film critics whose reviews were unfavourable. In a letter published in the *New York Sun* on the 22nd of September, Sinclair attacked their critics, John S. Cohen, Jr., for commenting 'that there has been mutilation (in *Thunder Over Mexico*) is perfectly obvious', and that the Hollywood editors 'made it as safe as safe can be'. Sinclair said: 'I assume that you have no reason for wishing to give the public anyone's guesses when the facts are so easily available. The facts are as follows:' and he recapitulated much of what he had said before. He insisted that all the remaining material was 'everything that a tourist wandering through Mexico might find picturesque and interesting'. As to the epilogue, Sinclair said that the Hollywood editors followed the scenario 'using the least "Fascist" elements in that scenario'. From this remark it would appear that Sinclair was now seeking to alienate Eisenstein's supporters by implying that Eisenstein held Fascist sympathies.

Finally, in October, 1933, *Thunder Over Mexico* opened at the Rialto Theatre in New York. In a printed letter widely circulated by Sinclair before the opening, he said: 'After thirty-three months the chariot-wheels of Sergei Eisenstein have rolled on, and I have wiped the dust from my eyes. Before me lies the golden favour he tossed to America in passing. His Mexican picture is completed and is ready to be shown in New York.' Then he quoted Darryl Zanuck, Douglas Fairbanks, Charlie Chaplin and others who had praised the film. And once again he insisted that the film had been cut in accord with Eisenstein's scenario. 'We are coming to New York for the opening, and hope to see our friends there, after many years.'

Because of the controversy over the film, a number of policemen were sent to the theatre to stand by, while a handful of Eisenstein's loyal supporters handed out leaflets denouncing Sinclair and demanding that he make public his evidence in support of his charges against Eisenstein. Nothing happened. As the days passed, everyone who had hoped to save *Que Viva Mexico!* experienced a sense of defeat. But Upton Sinclair, having other interests now than Eisenstein's *Que Viva Mexico!* turned his attention to another field. He announced his intention to run for Governor of California in the 1934 election under the slogan *End Poverty in California*.

In time, Sergei Mikhailovich recovered and returned to Moscow. He realized at last that his silence had gained him nothing. He had obeyed Sinclair's telegram sent to him so long ago in Laredo, commanding him to silence: 'If New York papers question you hope you will be wise and explain it was your proposal to cut in Russia.' Since leaving New York, he had never communicated with anyone in America who had attacked Sinclair on his behalf—Seymour Stern, Lincoln Kirstein, or others. Only once—in April, 1933—did he write to Agustin Aragon Leiva.

Finally, Sergei Mikhailovich felt he must vindicate himself.

He turned for aid to Joseph Freeman, his old friend and editor of the *New Masses*. He sent Freeman a thirty-page letter asking that it be published as his official statement. At the same time he gave me a brief outline of *Que Viva Mexico!* and asked me to make a copy of Upton Sinclair's telegram to him. He also told me about his dealings with Sinclair and about the Sinclair Foundation. I was to release this information in England after the publication of Eisenstein's letter in America.

But Sergei Mikhailovich's letter reached the *New Masses* after Upton Sinclair had announced his intention to run for Governor of California in the 1934 elections. The *New Masses* was supporting Sinclair's candidacy and under the circumstances they could not put themselves in the anomalous position of serving as a mouthpiece for Eisenstein against Sinclair in the controversy over *Que Viva Mexico!* Joe Freeman laid Eisenstein's letter aside and it was never published.

In the meantime, Upton Sinclair had decided to edit another film from *Que Viva Mexico!* Sol Lesser produced a new two-reel picture called *Death Day*, composed of scenes shot on the Day of the Dead and intended by Eisenstein for the Epilogue. This film was used by Sinclair to raise money and promote interest in his campaign for Governor of California.

I PRODUCE · I DEFEND

END POVERTY IN CALIFORNIA
UPTON SINCLAIR FOR GOVERNOR

1245 SOUTH FLOWER STREET
LOS ANGELES, CALIF.
PRospect 5094

June 19, 1934

Dear Friend:

As you no doubt know, I have written a "one acter", kidding the depression. Three men, wrecked on a tropical island, fall to gambling and one of them wins the island, after which the other two, because they have caught too many fish and gathered too many coooanuts, find themselves invited to starve. In this play "Depression Island" you will recognize many amusing allusions to the difficulties of our current depression. It is being performed by a cast of profession actors.

At the same time, we are giving the world premiere of a new Eisenstein Mexican picture. You will recall the marvelous camera work of "Thunder Over Mexico." There is more of the same sort in "Death Day," a two reeler, just completed by Mr. Sol Lesser.

Wednesday, June 27 is the night, and the Shrine Auditorium is the place. The motion picture stars from Hollywood have been invited to attend and take a bow. The event is for the benefit of our "End Poverty in California" campaign, which is surely in need of funds to carry on. However, there will be no politics, just art, economics, and some fun. Lewis Browne will be master of ceremonies, and Sheridan Downey will greet you.

I cordially invite you to attend and bring your friends so that we may fill the house, and thereby be assured of state-wide radio facilities between now and the August primaries.

Seats are priced at 83¢, $1.10, and $1.65. Please write our headquarters, 1501 South Grand Avenue, Los Angeles, or telephone PRospect 8145. A prompt reply will oblige us and assure your being able to obtain seats.

Sincerely,

US/cm

Letter circulated by Upton Sinclair, June 1934

Sinclair might not have been so eager to use this film on his own behalf had he known that Sergei Eisenstein would someday write that 'in the Danse Macabre which I see, in my mind, whirling in front of my eyes, are intercut other faces. The faces of those who did not permit the complete realization of my film. Those do not drop their mask. I have no need of them. I know on which side they dance. And I know what is hidden under the cardboard mask which covers their superficial "radicalism".' (App. Five.) The chief among these Calaveras skeletons was without doubt Upton Sinclair, whose candidacy for Governor of California was bitterly attacked by those friends of Eisenstein who had attempted to save *Que Viva Mexico!*

Sergei Mikhailovich waited for his letter to be published in the *New Masses*, but it did not appear. Freeman did not answer and Eisenstein began to fear that Boris Shumyatsky had sealed off the channels through which he could explain his side of the controversy over *Que Viva Mexico!* He asked me not to publicize the things he had told me about Sinclair's conduct. He felt that any further attempt to refute the charges Sinclair made against him would be useless. He bore this turn of events with the same magnanimity as the other disappointments he had experienced. But he did not know how to explain to his friends in Mexico all that had happened. He felt he had betrayed them because they had put their faith in him and his work. Some of them had written to him and he had left their letters unanswered.[1]

The following letter from Agustin Aragon Lieva, written during the production of the picture *Viva Villa* at Tetlapayac, was almost more than he could endure. He carried it about with him, read it and re-read it.[2]

Mexico City, November 11, 1933

DEAR EISENSTEIN,

Dawn . . . the maguey fields are surprised by the revolutionary beams of sunrise . . . [how] beautiful the vulcano looks to day . . . he is like a dead sun . . . Tetlapayac . . . what [is] that activity in the front court? Cameras, photographers, reflectors, charros and peasants, indians and soldiers, Melesio, Martin . . . Augustin . . . Julio is mad dispatching every one of his servants to hell. . . . D. Nico is still asleep . . . so many horses . . . where would be the fight? . . . a balcony in the corner opens and Tetlapayac is expecting the sudden aparition of a fat, smiling muezzin who is going to fill the air with his lamentations. . . . Melessioooo . . . Melessioooo . . . but this man

[1] Nevertheless in 1977 Pedro Chascel, film director and critic, claims the presence of Eisenstein in Mexico has subsequently influenced the entire Latin-American cinema.

[2] Written in English, not his native Spanish, it is printed without correction.

of the sad-looking face never shows himself and instead of him a tall
son of Ireland whistles a police signal little syren. Are we in Tetlapayac or Tetlapayac is in Hollywood, rebuilt into every detail? . . .
the professional disciple of Max Factor comes out to paint any human
face at his hand . . . where is Eisenstein? . . . Tetlapayac is waiting
for him? . . . that corner's room is filled with his thoughts and his
tremendous devilish dreams . . . a strange light comes out from the
room through the curtained windows. The light of his mind . . . but
where is he? . . . Tetlapayac waits for him and when it is heard in the
tinacal the counting song of the peones it seems like an invocation . . .
Eisenstein, where are you? . . . are you dead . . . are you in oblivion
. . . don't you like any more the mexican tragedy? . . . did you flee
away from the smell of pulque and out of the mexican lices and
poverty? . . . the invocation is off . . . a terrible noice breaks the
sweetness of morning air . . . three cameramen are coming down
under the protective smile of Julio . . . where is Tissé? . . . and
Grisha? . . . I don't see Castro Padilla nor Fito Best (the saint he is).
Chabela, Gabriel are not here but I distinguis Judahs, that one that is
even unable to write the biography of his master, if he ever had any
excepting Calles, it is meant Adolphus, the licenciado, a true one, as
he sells himself to the ennemy.

An admiration shout cuts the air as Pancho Villa in person comes
out on the balcony to display his moustaches and his war indument
. . . has Eisenstein played one of his jokes and so disguised himself as
Pancho Villa. . . . The clarity of the rising sun allows to identify the
face of Pancho Villa as the unconfidble one of Richard, the Lion
Hearted, as that of the king of the heavies of Hollywood, the
astonishingly brutal face of Wallace Beery, first husband of Gloria
Swanson, brother of Noah.

The maguey leaves close their arms in despair . . . what a change
. . . is this Eisenstein in the role of a heavy. . . . No, Eisenstein is just
a memory of Tetlapayac . . . but when maguey weeps pulque runs
drop by drop into the heart of the plant—Melesio is too much a man
to have tears in his eyes . . . there is just one that is mourning in a
corner, behind an immense pulque barrell that he pretends to fill
with his water of the eyes and ship it to Russia . . . this is the poor
meuzzin that has no more that job . . . he cannot make tremble the
air with his imprecations nor shake any human will. . . . HE IS WITH
TEARS IN HIS EYES . . . BUT SUDDENLY HE GETS TRANQUILE . . . out of the
corner's room it is coming a subtle breeze . . . that formerly was a
light . . . and we are going away in that breath . . . Tetlapayac has
been profaned; Mexico is being linched by Hollywood cinematographers. . . . Aragon's prophecy in his Excremental Cinema article

is being accomplished. . . . They are following your footsteps . . . like babies . . . like poor destituted children of no-talent . . . oh . . . this time Julio is digging dollarrs . . . but he is sombre, he is lost . . . looking for a wit, for a devilish fancy, for a tremendous thought and he finds Wallace Beery with his worn out marine's jokes and the same jokes of a hundred million blonde people. . . . Julio is sad . . . I knoe it . . . what a difference in technique, what a difference in spirit . . . well . . . he feels himself dishonoured for Pancha Villa is being killed this time in conventions and Mexico betrayed.

Tetlapayac . . . Tetlapayac . . . Melessioooo . . . Martiiinn . . . Chabela . . . in the golden twilight a jobless muezzin makes the road back to Mexico City . . . the maguey fields open his arms to devour him with his welcoming attitude . . . write to Eisenstein . . . write all this . . . they seem to say . . . we need a restoration, we need a complete rehabilitation . . . with tears in his mouth the muezzin boards the train . . . Tetlapayac is black and dull . . . he has suffered a barbaric invasion . . . poor Julio that has opened himself the doors of his farm to the derelict of Hollywood. . . .

I hope you had not got tired with my fanciful story, that saddest one of Mexico. . . .

Despite Upton Sinclair's lengthy and repeated explanations for depriving Sergei Eisenstein of the right to edit *Que Viva Mexico!*, it is difficult to discern exactly what lay behind Sinclair's conduct. However, some light is shed upon his motives by a statement he made after Eisenstein's death: 'We never had any idea of shipping him a print or anything else. . . . We'd as soon have shipped it to the devil.' (App. Six.) Yet at the time, Sinclair insisted to H. W. L. Dana, and others, 'that it is my intention to see that ultimately Soyuzkino gets a print of the entire film. . . . I want to do this even if I have to pay the cost of the print myself. I intend to do it not so much to clear my good name for I am not worrying about that—I believe the truth will prevail in the end. I intend to do it because my artistic conscience insists that the world should have a chance to see what Eisenstein meant to do.' But in the fourteen years that followed before Eisenstein died, Upton Sinclair, the author of the book *Mammon Art*, never finally sent a print to Sergei Eisenstein.

Note 1977. Professor Hill wrote me, July 28, 1977, 'I'm coming more and more to the conclusion . . . it was really *she* [Mrs Craig Sinclair] who opposed Eisenstein, and who forced the decisions, and if I may say so she did a darned good job of it, if you consider a shy middle-aged woman going up against an international heavyweight like Eisenstein, and eventually whipping him good!'

CHAPTER ELEVEN

A Leap Into a New Quality

Every part is disposed to unite with the whole, that it may thereby escape from its own incompleteness.
LEONARDO DA VINCI, C.A. 59 r.b.

EARLY in 1934, Ivor Montagu gave me some shirts and ties to take to Sergei Mikhailovich. On receiving them, he went to his shelves covered by the nondescript curtain and carefully examined his 'wardrobe'. It had shrunk since his return from America and he was obliged to conclude that Ivor had done him a great service. The double-edged tone of his voice could not conceal the expression on his face.

'There aren't many things I have a craving for,' he said. 'Only ties. And bright-coloured pyjamas. My taste is for the vulgarist!'

He hung up his ties, and going to the table, stood with a half-hesitating, half-grave expression on his face. Then, as if it were difficult and dangerous to express what he wanted to say, he cautiously mixed statements with a question.

'I can't pretend to be a Valentino. But if I could get thinner, I'd look better, wouldn't I? I'm too funny-looking as I am.'

It was an unexpected remark, and it brought Eisenstein's painful sensitivity into sharp focus for the first time. Though he had always given the impression he would respond to the slightest expression of affection, or gesture of intimacy with freezing sarcasm, it seemed that only some positive act of friendship might ease the poignant concern which had disturbed his normally impersonal manner.

'There isn't anything very wrong with you as you are.' Contrary to expectation, Eisenstein neither recoiled nor made a satirical comment when I took his arm.

'You wouldn't say that to flatter me, would you?' His eyes gravely penetrated mine, requesting an exact account of what was being thought.

'No. You worry too much. Really you look quite presentable.'

The discussion ended and Sergei Mikhailovich slipped back into his usual manner, as if nothing had disrupted his normal poise.

Despite his uneasiness about his appearance, he was not in the least concerned as to the way he lived, though by American or Western European standards he lived at that time in drab discomfort, and by

Russian standards in a bleak and graceless manner. He felt no need for an impressive setting and had anyone suggested he should seek some privilege in housing, or attempt a show of elegance, his contempt would have known no bounds. Later, when he lived in luxury as compared to the average Russian, he went to great pains to conceal it from others.

He was not an exacting neighbour, and often Totya Pasha prepared his supper after the other people in the flat, who shared the kitchen in common, had eaten. Totya Pasha was a very skilled cook, but Eisenstein never had any more basic food than the average intellectual worker. Unlike most Russians, he seemed to possess no samovar for making tea, and, being averse to imposing on Totya Pasha or using the kitchen, he drank tea sparingly. He kept no wine. Even when sweets became available, Sergei Mikhailovich seldom had any, though if he were given a box he would eat them with delight. He never spoke of luxurious living and his only lapse at this time from the most Spartan taste was the pleasure he found a few months later in the Crimea, where there were many exotic flowers, and where he manifested a gargantuan love of fruit and highly spiced foods.

The many stories which circulated about Sergei Eisenstein made him appear an exaggerated or mystifying character. But as I came to know him, I realized that beneath his armour lay a reserve he had never allowed anyone to penetrate. He veiled even his friendly acts with an air of neutral detachment. Unable to express any real feeling with largesse, he revealed his sincere feelings in an unobtrusive thoughtfulness which, once detected, modified his formidable personality. He sought company—only by oblique means. He would say there was going to be an interesting session at the Institute of Cinematography, or mention some musical event. Only if I responded with interest would it then become a personal invitation to go with him. After a while, he wanted to share his only possession of value, the books to which he confessed his secret thoughts. But even this suggestion Sergei Mikhailovich made in such a way that it appeared casual and commonplace.

Often he would discuss a book with me, then say he didn't mind loaning his copy, as long as it wasn't taken out of his room. This was followed by his suggestion that I spend an afternoon browsing with it, or other books on his shelves. It was no inconvenience to him, for he had to go out and he would not return until six or seven in the evening. There would be enough food and there was no sense in his eating alone.

The first book Eisenstein 'loaned' to me was the anthropological studies of Malinowski. Bergson followed. Then Freud's study of Leonardo da Vinci, and his study of humour.

Since there was not the slightest order to Sergei Mikhailovich's library, and his untidiness as to papers and books knew no bounds, it took time to find one's way about the shelves. Technical treatises jostled the mysteries of Agatha Christie; philosophy was mixed up with *Ruthless Rhymes*; the Holy Bible and *Ulysses* made a pair. A vast number of books dealing with psychology, anthropology, physiology, the arts and studies of specific cultures were interspersed with treatises on languages and dictionaries of slang. Plato and Van Dine thrillers in company were no incongruity. Almost anything could be found with sufficient diligence. There were nearly as many books in German, French and English as there were in Russian.

It seemed impossible to find a book which Eisenstein had not read thoroughly. The margins were inscribed from cover to cover, very often in red pencil. Not infrequently the inscriptions jumped from English to German and French to Russian; sometimes all four languages appeared in the same book. The Greek and Roman classics, Dante, Cervantes, Strindberg, and Ibsen were in English translation. Many of the notations on the margins were cross references, but many more were the thoughts which the text called up in the mind of Eisenstein.

The comments brought some order to his seemingly chaotic assortment of cherished bric-à-brac. There was reason to the apparent irrelevance of what he had collected. For example, his enormous collection of comic postcards, though it caused him delight, was an important part of his study of the nature of humour. Again, his collection of miniature Japanese masks had a place in two of his studies dating back to his early twenties—the Japanese Kabuki Theatre and its methods of montage, and the stylistic representation of the human face.

But the most surprising revelation contained in Eisenstein's books was his preoccupation with religious matters and mystical experience. At first these comments appeared strangely at variance with the blasphemous jokes he made from time to time about his votive figurines, and the anti-religious sentiments expressed in his films. Clearly, he was enthralled with religious customs and the matter of 'faith'. In book after book (sometimes books which had nothing directly to do with the subject), he would throw a scientific searchlight upon some aspect of religion and the forms in which it appeared. Over and over again, he made references to the Holy Grail, the Grail which had so curiously appeared in his analysis of the Cream Separator sequence in *Old and New*. A reference to the Grail even appeared on the pages of some of his detective fiction, hinting some theory which only later was elucidated. Notes as to heightened states of consciousness and underlining of passages concerning ecstasy and the beatific vision were astonishingly numerous. One such passage was in *Idols Behind Altars*, by Anita Brenner:

> *Sobriety and discipline were practised* for power, for accuracy, for *ecstasy*, for self-control in the sense of being able to use the self to attain always a *greater skill at life*, and thus a greater delight.

Such books as Flaubert's *Madame Bovary*, the novels of Balzac and Zola were heavily pencilled with designs for both stage and film presentation. *Thérèse Raquin* was entirely conceived as action within an ever-tightening circle. In James Joyce's *Ulysses*, the 'internal mono-logue' of Bloom had been broken down into a rough shooting script.

In his writings and conversation, Eisenstein usually maintained an objective attitude, but the marginal notations in his books were often subjective. For this reason it was difficult to read his books without associating them with him. He had marked this passage from Havelock Ellis's essay on Eli Faure with three lines of approval:

> If we indeed believe in life, we need not fear to trample underfoot the ashes of those who struggled before us. 'My tenderness and my hate are merely the necessary elements of a religious enthusiasm for all that is life.' The most beautiful ideas are those which are not yet made. Only they who never hesitate to destroy are worthy to grasp the conqueror's laurels.

And beside the following sentence, again in *Idols Behind Altars*, Eisenstein had written the word '*Me!*':

> Here all styles are constantly repeated; there is primitive, renaissance, baroque, romanticism, impressionism, cubism, classicism, realism, conscious and unconscious, all simultaneously.

And later, marked with another 'Me', 'Laugh thereafter though they speak in much solemnity'.

Yet when he arrived home, his behaviour was so conspicuously impersonal one forgot that the Eisenstein who had come into the room was the same person as the Eisenstein of the marginal comments.

Quite frequently, Pera Attasheva also came for supper. But Tisse, the only other person in whom Eisenstein put his trust, never came and it seemed that Sergei Mikhailovich seldom saw Tisse except when they were working together. So far as it was possible to observe, Eisenstein's neighbours never came into his room, not even Maxim Shtraukh and Judith Glizer, who had lived in the next room since the Proletkult days, and tapped on the wall each time there was someone on the telephone for Sergei Mikhailovich. If he met someone in the passage other than Shtraukh and Glizer, he would greet them politely, but apparently he avoided any conversation with them.

Sometimes at supper Sergei Mikhailovich would cast aside his erudition and talk epigrammatically in the guise of a sophisticated Shavian character. At other times he would make a swift play on words. He was like a fencer seeking to trick his opponent into a false lunge and thus betray intellectual pretentions. But there were moments when his brilliant and bitter cleverness subsided into the echo of geniality. If Pera were present, these moments of well-being in Sergei Mikhailovich made her extremely happy. She would talk nineteen to the dozen and the Old Man would show his appreciation of her presence in an oblique way: he would induce her to cook, an art at which she was a consummate master.

Because of her goodness of heart, Pera was always involved in helping the many people who carried their troubles to her. Often she acted as an intermediary for people who wanted to see Eisenstein. Invariably she would bring him some work she had completed for him, or something she had found which would be useful to him. But her interests and talk were not confined to the Old Man's affairs. We would gossip and discuss our common interests and occasionally these were entirely feminine. Eisenstein would sit by with a quizzical expression. The atmosphere of triviality amused him and he would tease us about such nonsense, but not spitefully.

When we left, Pera would sigh. She was glad the Old Man seemed to have enjoyed himself for a few hours. Sergei Mikhailovich was an insoluble problem: a trouble to the heart as well as the head. Apart from his work, he piled every imaginable complication into her lap and expected her to put it in order. This was hard on Pera, for though she had boundless resourcefulness and energy, she also had to carry the responsibility of her mother and younger sister, Zina. As she had no telephone in her flat, and she refused to use her relationship with Eisenstein as a means of obtaining one, she had to run out to a public phone to reach Eisenstein or the other people who wanted to get in touch with her. Still Pera never lost her ability to smile.

Her only complaint was that she had too little time for her own work which gave her great satisfaction. In her own right, Pera Attasheva was a highly respected worker in the film industry and for all her femininity she had a penetrating mind and extensive knowledge of what went on in the world. Because she took pride in her independent work, she disliked to be constantly identified with Eisenstein and the Moscow gossip had led her to avoid going about with him very much in public.

Engaged in ceaseless research, Sergei Mikhailovich had an ever-increasing need for books, many of which could not be obtained in the Soviet Union. He became ever more anxious to write articles which could be published abroad, for these were his sole means of obtaining foreign money with which to pay for books. He would send his theoretical articles to Ivor Montagu or give them to me. One of the many articles had the whimsical title *The Difficult Bride*—the bride being the art of cinematography. When the articles were sold, the money was deposited at Zwemmer's bookshop on Charing Cross Road, from whom Eisenstein would order the books he wanted.

Sometimes a fraction of his *compte courant* was withheld for the purpose of his 'de-pimpization'—a term Eisenstein used to signify repayment of money spent to buy him odd items of clothing. Only once did he want some of his money spent for what he thought an inexcusably trivial item—handsome headed notepaper, such as he had used in America. His excuse was that if he had to write a business letter abroad, the recipient might think him careless or discourteous if he used any old paper; besides, the stranger would think that the Soviet Union lacked amenities.

Towards the middle of 1934, Sergei Mikhailovich became especially interested in Lewis Carroll. He was particularly intrigued by *Alice in Wonderland*. 'Alice', he wrote to me, 'puts you under a certain new job —and this is to find out if there exists any research work about her—I mean historical and *psychological*. If so will you please find the most striking of it.' As I was soon to learn, the fascination of Carroll's work was for more personal reasons than his wonderful anatomical chart of the absurd, which had such great appeal for Eisenstein. In Carroll's use of psycho-physiological symbols—Alice's shrinkage in size and Alice becoming awkwardly large—Sergei Mikhailovich found literary expression of the painfully acute psychic feelings which he experienced.

By August, when I went to Moscow again, several Carroll books went along with socks and a brilliant pair of red pyjamas and a vivid blue pair. But Eisenstein was away in the Caucasus. According to Pera, the Old Man had been sent to a rest home for several weeks; but the reason for this was not clear. It may have been because of a heart condition which a year later became more serious.

Shortly before the close of the Moscow Theatre Festival of 1934, Sergei Mikhailovich sent a telegram asking if I could meet him in the Crimea, where he was to act as scenario consultant to the Children's Studio at Yalta and the Ukrainian Studio in Odessa. Pera insisted that the conferences would be interesting and that the Old Man would enjoy himself more if he had company. He wouldn't ask for company unless he wanted it. My telegram of acceptance brought another wire fixing the date when Eisenstein would arrive by boat from the Caucasus and stating that a room would be reserved for me in the villa belonging to the Yalta studio.

At Sevastopol, where the Crimean railway line ended and bus connection for Yalta was established, I met Vsevolod Pudovkin, on holiday with his assistant. As a rule, he was generous with praise of his fellow artists, but at the mention of Eisenstein's name he raised his hands in horror and tried to convince me that Sergei Mikhailovich was nothing but a monster—an intellectual dynamo without a heart. Pudovkin cited many things Eisenstein was alleged to have done to his friends and to Alexandrov.

'You are bewitched by a man who is bad! Anyone who comes too close to Eisenstein always regrets it.'

'What makes you dislike him?' I asked.

'He makes me feel uncomfortable. There has always been something perverted, sick about him. He has an ill mind. I pity him that he has no feelings like other men.'

Two years before, Pudovkin had told me that Eisenstein was incapable of friendship and that he hated women.

When I arrived in Yalta, Eisenstein was not at the bus depot as arranged. It looked as if he had not come from the Caucasus, or had changed his mind. But at the Intourist Hotel, I was told that he had been looking for me and that he was waiting on the promenade near the sea. He had only arrived an hour or so before and a mistake in my telegram about the time of my arrival had confused him.

At a distance, Eisenstein was hardly recognizable. His hair was cut shorter than usual and instead of his slightly exaggerated clothes he wore the same unpretentious white shirt, linen trousers and canvas shoes as almost all the Russians strolling by the sea. With the hint of the grotesque sheered away, Sergei Mikhailovich's remarkable head ceased to look noticeably inappropriate upon his body. For the first time he appeared as one integrated person. The aloof, penetrating expression he had usually worn had melted into a look of kindness and gentleness.

In place of his previously rather halting greeting, he welcomed me with a sincerity I have never forgotten. After a friendship extending over two years, namelessness ended when he bestowed the Russian diminutive—Marushka—upon me. 'If ever you feel I'm Serozha to you—or Serozhenka—which means much more, I'd be glad. But I don't want to be given illusion of affection if it is not felt,' he said.[1]

---

[1] In speaking to, or about Eisenstein, practically everyone (except Pera and a few others, who called him the 'Old Man') used the formal version of his name —Eisenstein or Sergei Mikhailovich. The familiar form—Sergei—and the intimate and affectionate forms—Serozha and Serozhenka—were never used. This was unusual because artists like Vsevolod Pudovkin and Grigori Alexandrov were usually addressed by their friends, and even acquaintances, in the affectionate form—Ludya and Grisha, respectively. The familiar and intimate forms of a name are generally used unless a person appears to be cold, formal and unlikeable; or the person is held in such high esteem—for example Leo Tolstoy —that the use of the familiar or affectionate name would appear presumptuous.

As though it had always been his custom, Sergei Mikhailovich took my arm and we walked to the end of Yalta and climbed the steep road to the studio's villa perched high on a promontory overlooking the Black Sea.

Spontaneously he explained why he had asked me to meet him in Yalta: after weeks in the Caucasus he had grown extremely lonely. The thought of a holiday pleased him; it was his first in some seventeen years and he hoped he wouldn't prove too 'lousy' a companion. What people did with themselves on holiday when there was no work to be done, he didn't know, but time would prove.

Never before had he given the impression of having any warm or gentle qualities in his nature. In order to enjoy his company it had seemed necessary to accept him with detachment, because he might well become sadistic or entirely indifferent to affection at any time. Despite his intellectual appeal, he had not exerted the least attraction as a man. He had given the impression that any desire for personal attachment or passion had been sublimated in his work, or had died with his youth which had seemingly passed early. There had been an agelessness about him. Only now had he regained the quality of youth. But these new impressions were momentarily dispelled by the situation which we discovered at the villa.

Leading the way up to the second floor of the fantastic-looking structure built long ago by a China tea king millionaire, the old peasant caretaker, who had had no guests for months, ushered us into an enormous sun-parlour with two alcoves, one overlooking Yalta, the other the Black Sea. He explained how in honour of our visit he had fumigated the room. Positively there were no bugs! He hoped the furniture he had brought in would be comfortable—exotic and exceedingly vulgar Ming furniture—vases, a baronial couch, a refectory table, gilded candelabras and a gigantic tapestry-festooned bed. Bowing, he wished us a long and happy life; then he went away to bring the luggage.

Eisenstein moved from the doorway where he had stood in icy silence. He apologized for such a Russian comedy; he said he would go to the studio and explain they had made a mistake.

'Please don't feel I meant it to be this way. You know I'm no Don Juan. . . .'

The error, which was evidently due to his request for a room for me in the villa, was most embarrassing to Sergei Mikhailovich. The truth was that he had only once slept in the same room with a woman. It was years before when he had been directing in the Caucasus. Pera had come and there was nowhere for her to sleep except in the same room with him. Since he had never lived like other men, he had called forth derision from his comrades, who were natural people with few inhibitions. He recoiled from the unpleasant task of going to the studio to explain the mistake for fear he would be laughed at again.

'Would you be embarrassed if it appeared you were my wife?'

'No. But it would be a pity if our friendship were injured.'

'I wouldn't intrude on you. It would only be a game at real life—to avoid laughter.'

So, to avoid the gossip and derision to which Sergei Eisenstein had been subjected, we agreed to do nothing about the mistake. We would share a platonic life and try not to destroy our friendship which, being of gradual growth, had become valuable. But it was clear that in making such a face-saving gesture our friendship would either break up or become stronger. When the caretaker returned, we went with him through the villa in search of two single beds.

Sergei Mikhailovich's defensive attitude soon passed. When he did not know what to do, he asked. When he felt shy, he said so. He was effortlessly neat with his belongings and in his personal habits. Stripped of his defences, the real Eisenstein was very much at variance with the public figure he had created. There was nothing clownish about him, nor was he a man of dominating will. He was kind and sensitive in his spontaneous actions. When his gentle and affectionate acts did not meet rejection, he grew less fearful of being laughed at for his sensitivity. Only in public places did he sometimes retreat into self-consciousness and he was never able to bring himself to lie on the beach or swim if there were other people near. We searched for secluded spots along the beach, but if anyone came near, he would immediately put on his bath-robe and suggest we go home or find another place.

Each day had freshness. Everything Sergei did and devised was new and came forth untarnished. He had an extraordinary capacity for creating joy and happiness, and he was extremely easy to get along with because of his respect for the integrity of the other person.

Released from the captivity of a life strung upon a chain of pain and bitterness, he sometimes appeared transfigured. His inner nature seemed to be remoulding the character of his face, and speaking through his expressive hands. For all of his imagination and vitality, Sergei Mikhailovich had a stability which gave each day a comforting regularity. Once something pleased him, he liked to weave it into a secure pattern. Unlike many artists, he had a stringent sense of what was real between people and what was a game and this enabled him, at this time, to build a deep and stable human relationship.

After barely a day, Eisenstein instituted a game of hide-and-seek with the solicitous representative of the Children's Film Studio, who daily sought him out with offers of a car in which to go sightseeing, or invitations to dine with them at the studio. He felt no desire to see the sights of the Crimea; he didn't want to be an honoured guest—that could wait until his consultations commenced. He wanted to lie on the deserted beach below the villa and devise delightfully nonsensical games, eat grapes, poke and pry in the many odd souvenir shops of Yalta and occasionally 'steal' some of the semi-tropical flowers tumbling over the crumbling walls along the streets. He did not want to sit at the head of a large table and answer questions, or if no questions were asked, search among his thoughts for something to say. He felt that only his students at the Institute of Cinematography were concerned with his theoretical ideas.

'Half of them don't understand my psychology,' Sergei said regretfully, 'and I can't understand half of theirs. Yet it is only from them I can learn what I need to learn. In return for the materialism they give me, I must give them the best of my knowledge. They have none of my hate for the old; they are really not particularly interested.'

Every time he saw people in their late teens and early twenties, he wondered what they thought about and what they wished to make of their lives. But he showed near-contempt for people of his own generation, or older, who were of bourgeois origin. Like himself, they were the tag-end of a class and full of falseness. The young were the hope.

Eisenstein, who had disciplined himself from youth to two daily periods of creative thinking—the marginal region between sleeping and waking—continued his intellectual work with only one difference: he wished to share his thoughts and he found he could do so without difficulty. He awoke each morning self-collected, with his ideas and feelings ordered.

One morning he woke up and started chuckling. 'Are you awake?' he asked. 'I have a great joke to tell you.'

He came to my bed and lying down across the foot of it, said: 'Listen to what you are doing to me. For the last nights all my dreams have been in English. You see, you're ruining me. If you can change my dreams and make me dream in your language, I'll have to listen to you while I'm awake. You laugh at me because I like sleeping in a nightshirt and using pyjamas for daytime. You say nightshirts are old-fashioned, and you're ashamed of me for clinging to a nightshirt. I know it looks absurd, but I've always clung to my nightshirt—it comforted me. But I shall now give it up and sleep as well as walk in pyjamas!' Thereafter he bundled up his nightshirt and put it away.

But he could not relax into the lazy holiday mood he was enjoying until he had unleashed his creative thoughts. He talked of his speculative ideas over breakfast, which we took late in a circular glass restaurant perched out in the Black Sea from Yalta's promenade. Gastronomically, we developed a mutual passion for chiboreki, the highly spiced Crimean dish akin to ravioli, which, on Sergei's insistence, we doused with white vinegar. It was a peculiar choice for breakfast, but for Sergei Mikhailovich, who adored to create ritualistic ceremonies to 'immortalize' certain personal emotions and delights, chiboreki became a sacerdotal morning dish.

Only once, on the day when Vsevolod Pudovkin came through Yalta, did we eat chiboreki except for breakfast. Pudovkin found it a detestable dish and it set off such a murderous verbal fencing match between Eisenstein and Pudovkin that Vsevolod Ilarionovich missed his boat connection. Eisenstein won every verbal 'touch', demolishing each of Pudovkin's arguments. The final argument spiralled into the heights of theoretic fantasy: Pudovkin had read a fourteen-volume work written to prove that the Golden Age of Greece had never existed, that it was the creation of the pre-Renaissance Italians who wanted 'classical' support for their breakaway from the strict formulae of mediaeval thought and style. The argument this theory provoked was hilariously funny. It called forth all of Sergei's wit, erudition and logic, while Vsevolod Ilarionovich waxed romantic and insisted it was 'conservative' to reject any theory. At least, this one should be considered as a possibility. The discussion went on for hours until Eisenstein allowed Vsevolod Pudovkin the possible point that 'though the Greeks had a word for it, they never existed'! This remark was a play on words referring to the title of the comedy *The Greeks Had a Word For It*, which Eisenstein had seen abroad.

While they sparred, Yalta went to sleep, and Pudovkin said he would have to come and stay in the studio's villa for the night. So Eisenstein woke up the caretaker and explained that Tovarish Pudovkin had missed his boat and, being a most distinguished film director, he was entitled to have a bed even without a directive from the studio. After we left Pudovkin, Sergei discarded his urbanity. He was irritated, certain that Pudovkin had intentionally missed his boat for the purpose of prying into his life. Before he went to bed, he did a most curious thing, one which afterwards he repeated every night. He came into the alcove where I slept and, standing close to the bed, made the sign of benediction. It seemed a jest. But he silenced the beginning of my laughter.

'I'm not playing a game now. This is how I feel,' he said.

In the middle of the night pandemonium broke out. Pudovkin came banging on the door asking for lotion. The bed he had been given was infested with bugs. Eisenstein sounded icily polite as he offered Pudovkin his blanket, which had been fumigated; then he asked if I objected to Pudovkin sleeping on the baronial couch to escape the bugs. 'No, so long as you don't mind.' Still Eisenstein was confused. Each moment he looked older and more withdrawn. He could not stand this seemingly inquisitive intrusion; it was driving him back into his cold, impersonal shell.

It was essential for Pudovkin to leave; his presence had a visibly crippling effect upon Eisenstein. Before it was light, I woke Pudovkin up and asked him to go. But he said there would be no boat for hours. Finally, he consented to leave the villa if I would walk with him to the pier. On the way he begged me with what appeared the utmost sincerity to end my friendship with Sergei Eisenstein and go back to Moscow.

When I returned to the villa, Eisenstein was sitting at the desk in the alcove overlooking the town. He had been trying to continue with an article he had commenced the day before. Only a few words were on the page. His face, which had begun to lose its transparent whiteness, was ashen and he looked more mocking and bitter than he had ever appeared before. He made no comment. He merely took some sheets of paper and swiftly drew a series of very witty, erotic caricatures of Pudovkin, whom he designated Chop Suey. One showed Pudovkin trapped in a nightmare among the figures of the Parthenon frieze—the Elgin marbles—whose authenticity had been disputed at dinner the night before. Until his anger subsided he did not say a word.

'I only pretended to sleep,' he said. 'I expected you to leave. Pudovkin would have been pleased to conduct you out of my clutches. You might have had a more interesting and amusing time had you decided to go.'

I told Serozha I valued his friendship above that of anyone I knew. Without question he accepted this as the truth and said he had found happiness. Then he relaxed into joking about the 'Bed and Sofa'[1] comedy brought about by too many bed bugs.

The only perceptible change after this episode was that Eisenstein, who had formerly talked in an impersonal, scientific tone about his theoretical work, spoke more personally, sometimes with great passion. Often he would clasp my hand as he talked, as if he must physically transmit to me the great urgency he felt about his work.

He talked more and more of his plan to create a synthesis of knowledge for the development of film as an expressive medium. He hoped to realize this monumental task in a series of books, which he regarded as more important than any film he might make. Each was devoted to a different subject and its relation and application to the art of cinemato-

[1] An early Soviet comedy dealing with love and the housing shortage.

graphy. Already he had extensive notes for some ten volumes. The first volume, entitled *Direction*, he had commenced in Mexico, but though he had been working on it, this book remained unfinished at his death fourteen years later.

Another would be devoted to a study of psychology and film. In this book he intended to draw extensively upon Freud, although Eisenstein had come to the conclusion that Freud's system had certain inherent limitations, particularly in its application to an evolving socialist society. Freud's research, unfortunately, had covered only neurotic personalities in a decaying capitalist society; his system did not envisage a new dialectically developing society where in time neurosis might well become modified by more and more people enjoying a balanced life freed from many of the constraints of bourgeois society.

Another book was to be devoted to painting and what it could teach the cinematographer about the unity of form and content. The full realization of the importance of composition in the enrichment of the film medium had come to Sergei Mikhailovich in Mexico, where composition had become one of his primary concerns. It was then he told me of his conviction that primary form—the triangle and the circle—revealed to man the 'mystery' of higher truths in symbolic form—the triangle: God, Man, and the Universe, and the circle: immortality. He was also concerned with the emotional effect upon the spectator of the depiction of the human figure—full view or profile.

To Sergei Mikhailovich, the figure in profile conveyed spirituality. It was the formal means of portraying higher, more refined emotions, even the experience of ecstasy. The full view gave a more temporal, solid effect, it was for the portrayal of the earthy passions. Of artists seeking to convey ecstasy, El Greco was the most provocative to Eisenstein. For comparison, he constantly returned to Leonardo da Vinci, with his use of the interrelated triangle, for example, in the 'Last Supper': Leonardo, of all men, appeared closest in spirit to himself, so close that Sergei Mikhailovich felt that many experiences in his own life echoed those of Leonardo.

'The destruction of Leonardo's great horse and *Que Viva Mexico!*—they are the same thing. I am as doomed to disappointment as Leonardo. For me there will be no escape. I know I am doomed.'

Then Eisenstein told me he had received reports (which later proved to be untrue) that Upton Sinclair had sold sequences of *Que Viva Mexico!* to Hollywood studios for use as background material in their own films. Until now, Sergei Mikhailovich had resolutely clung to the hope that by some means he could get the film and edit it. Even incomplete, lacking one episode—Soldadera—he could edit it very nearly as he had originally intended.

'I loved Mexico. I was happy there. It was like a home. The people ... I was as one of them; of the same material.'

'But you can't be of the same material as a peon—a peasant,' I said.

A shocked expression came over his face. He looked at me as if I had insulted him.

'Knowing me, I shouldn't have to explain such a thing to you! You can't know the peasant or you would understand. I feel with the peasant. Any peasant understands me better than pretentious, half-educated intellectuals who are trying to impress!'

Because Eisenstein now thought he would never be able to realize his dream of *Que Viva Mexico!*, he wanted to create it as best he could in words. It might ease his terrible feeling of loss. As he began to reconstruct the film (some of which he had never seen), he seemed to be holding the rushes in his hands, editing them image by image. In speech he became pure artist, caught once more in the remembered emotion of 'the first moment of inspiration'. Filled with passion for what he had created under the spell of entirely new feelings, he was released into a rhythm lost to him for a long time. His dormant powers of creative expressiveness flamed and for some hours Sergei Eisenstein fulfilled himself in the creative ecstasy of his imagination. Having shared his vision, he was prepared to put *Que Viva Mexico!* away in his memory. Though he wrote of all his other films and discussed some of his unrealized works, he never wrote a word about his Mexican film until the year before he died. Too much of it was part of his most personal self.

In 1939 I tried to get the footage of *Que Viva Mexico!* into Sergei Mikhailovich's hands so that he might finally fulfil his creative vision of Mexico. Failing, I took the memory of what he had told me and attempted to reconstruct his dream in order that it might not be entirely lost. This became *Time in the Sun*.

Almost every day in Yalta brought another of Eisenstein's proposed books to light. In a fourth, he intended to examine the customs of people through the ages, analyse symbols and create a reservoir of research material for the film director. In connection with this book, he talked at length about the surviving customs of Greece and retraced the life of centuries to the age of myth, the age when it seemed to him there had existed a certain primal unity in all of man's activities. When I told Sergei Mikhailovich how I had watched the shepherds of Mount Parnassus come down at night to the village of Delphi and, scarcely half a mile from the ruined theatre and the place of the oracle, dance what appeared to be a derivative of a choric dance, he said: 'It echoes of Mexico.'

There was one book which he thought he would never write, though the notes for it existed on many pages of his books and on sheaves of paper. It was to cover the meaning of religious experience, of ecstasy and man's relation to his gods. In discussing this book, Eisenstein considered the possibility of uniting the dialectical approach with mystical experiences which seemingly lay beyond the scope of dialectics. He believed in dialectical materialism as a scientific instrument to aid in understanding the nature of the universe; but ever since 1918, when he entered the Red Army and had been inspired to become a new Soviet man free from the idealistic philosophy of the past, Sergei Mikhailovich had not been able to destroy his religious feeling. It was based upon his own perception in certain states of consciousness when he felt a higher reality.

One day a little later, after telling me that in all his life he had only put his trust in two people—Tisse and Pera—who he believed would remain loyal to him to the end of his life, he suddenly said: 'I want to tell you something I have never spoken about. I believe in Christ. I love Him as a Saviour whose Passion must be borne by those who believe in Him. I have tried to overcome this. Now I have given up.'

On other occasions he discussed his religious feelings. For him there was a 'mystery', and the 'mystery' was finding the meaning of God and Christ. The names evolved, the forms and symbols changed from place to place and epoch by epoch; but the 'mystery' remained. From this point the most extraordinary of any of Eisenstein's speculative theories had developed: to him the legend of the Holy Grail was a story of detection. To find the Grail and, thus, gain eternal life, was to solve the 'mystery'. Man was compelled by his inner nature to search for the clues which lead to 'God' and salvation. The men who found the way, notably the mystics, found it by 'intuition', not by reason alone. In certain states of consciousness approaching ecstasy, the jig-saw puzzle into which 'truth' had been broken came together and was at last seen as a whole. Such was the spiritual experience of Jacob Boehm and all the mystics of whatsoever race or creed who had left a record of their experiences.

Then the religious 'mystery' took an amazing turn in Eisenstein's mind. The mystery story of detection was as a 'tracing' of the higher form of mystical experience. All detective stories were constructed as a chain of scattered, seemingly unconnected clues which the major characters of detective fiction—from Sherlock Holmes down to more recent characters—fitted into place and, thus, solved the 'mystery' by intuition. They shared with the mystics a supernormal consciousness. Hence, Sergei Mikhailovich's insatiable passion for detective stories was not a response to their apparent plot, but a fascination with the processes they seemed to reveal to him.[1]

The relaxation of holiday-living caused Eisenstein to lose all sense of time. Every day the outside world receded a little further and disturbed him less. When at last he remembered he would soon have to begin his scenario consultations, he longed to play truant. It was not indifference to the work he had to do, nor an unwillingness to fulfil his obligations, only a yearning to remain free from the inner strain under which he lived. He feared the rhythm of a contented existence would be destroyed by intrusions and he suggested trying to postpone his consultations, at least for a few days.

Eisenstein had lived so much in his own thoughts that he had lost touch with the social *mores* of Soviet life. I felt obliged to tell him that he would be criticized—and with justification from the Soviet point of view—if he used a human relationship as an excuse to retire still further from the current stream of life. He gave up the idea of trying to postpone his consultations. All he asked was that he would not have to go anywhere alone.

It was clear that Eisenstein no longer knew how to handle his working relations with any confidence. Though he did not complain and understated everything that happened, he was haunted by the thought that he had no friends, except Tisse and Pera. Something was wrong, and not only in Sergei Mikhailovich's imagination. But still it was not evident on the surface of the Soviet film world how serious were Eisenstein's official difficulties. There was merely the same tepid atmosphere which had existed two years before and the continued implication that he had ceased to play a major role on account of his research work and teaching. He did not know what steps to take in order to catch up with the Soviet years that were lost to him.

His public behaviour, particularly since his return from abroad, had gained him a reputation for being an arrogant man, vain and cynical, with an overweening pride in intellectuality. A secretive man. Unsympathetic. It was quite frequently said that Eisenstein had been ruined by going abroad.

The new concept of the Soviet man, his virtues and character, which had begun to emerge while Eisenstein was abroad, included deeper features than the possession of revolutionary ardour. A representative Soviet man in the 1930's must seek to serve the welfare of the Soviet Union with all his strength and personality. He must understand the

---

[1] It is interesting to note that certain writers of detective fiction either always were, or later became preoccupied, with religious matters. These include Conan Doyle, Ronald Knox, G. K. Chesterton and Dorothy Sayers, and, more recently, Grahame Greene.

evolving society and its people with *love*. The Soviet artist must now create more than works reflective of a changed society; he must create images of the men and women developing new social concepts and personal lives. To do so, the artist had to draw closer to the average man who served as the backbone of Soviet society.

As leading representatives of the Soviet cinema, Pudovkin and Dovzhenko untiringly gave social service. Night after night they would visit factories and clubs to speak about the Soviet film. They did this work with a sincere belief and a very strong sense that they belonged to Soviet society. To them this was not so much an arduous task as a privilege bestowed upon them—a rich encounter with the real life of their country.

The Eisenstein who had attempted to bring art into the industrial scene of the factory by producing the play *Gas Masks* in the Moscow Gas Factory, had died. It would have been tortuously difficult for the Eisenstein of 1934 to go to a factory and deliver a talk. He would have lost himself after a few minutes in some obtuse subject and no one would have understood more than half of what he was trying to say. Yet this was the Eisenstein who must somehow try to evolve into a man capable of giving expression to the new upsurges of thought and feeling typical of the Soviet scene. The wound to his creative life which he had received in Hollywood and from Upton Sinclair was unhealed, and it could not heal because of the attitude of Shumyatsky, who had now caused him to shrink from the thought of returning to film production. But he could not explain any of these things to his colleagues.

Too many difficulties and disappointments had crushed whatever skill Sergei Eisenstein had had in public tact and common sense. He had grown wretchedly stupid about himself with his ever-increasing knowledge of things bigger than himself. He really didn't understand why the executives of the Children's Film Studio would want him to come and eat dinner, or use the studio car.

At last he saw the oddness of his conduct; he decided we ought to spend a day at the children's colony of Artek, where the studio was making a film. Young people from all over the Soviet Union were awarded holidays at Artek for outstanding achievements. There was also the Palace of Alupka and a vineyard which produced wonderful wine.

When the studio car came early on the last day of the holiday period, a man who was to act as guide brought a letter from Pera. After reading it, Sergei Mikhailovich put it in his pocket and tried to conceal his confusion. His face grew tense and he sat in the car taking no notice of what the guide was saying. At last he spoke in a deliberate tone. He looked as if he were combating a sense of shame, yet he must force himself to explain.

'My mother has come from Leningrad. She is staying at Chysti Prudi.'

Until that moment, Sergei Mikhailovich had never mentioned his mother to me. It had appeared she was dead, like his father, whom he mentioned curtly as having sided with the White Russians and having died as a refugee in Germany. The only relatives he had ever spoken about were maternal aunts who had been exiled to Siberia after the Revolution, and who could stay there so far as he was concerned.

'Pera says my mother insists upon living with me,' he said. 'But we can't live together. My mother and I hate each other. It is a horrible situation, for once I loved my mother very much.'

He said no more. But on arriving at Artek he made an effort to be natural and show an interest in what was going on. He behaved as though he had never felt awkward in his life and had had a constant companion not for ten days but for many years, and he enjoyed it when the camp officials presented us with flowers.

The atmosphere of youth and endeavour at Artek appealed to him, he threw himself into its midst with the same warmth and spontaneity he revealed when he was not in the public eye. The result was instantaneous. The directors dropped their slightly formal manner towards an honoured guest and were clearly very pleased that he had come, not because he was Sergei Eisenstein, but because he appeared to be a likeable man.

After walking around the main buildings of the camp filled with children of many complexions and cast of feature—Mongolian, Ukrainian, Georgian, Tartar, Byelo-Russian—Sergei Mikhailovich broke away from the directors and lost himself in a game with two small children—a boy and a girl—who roared with laughter at his funny gestures and the things he said. Suddenly they set upon him and pulled him down on to the soft, sandy ground, hugging and pummelling him as though he belonged to them. At last they got up. Dusting the sand out of their hair, Sergei Mikhailovich took the children by the hand and declared that since he had found them, they belonged to him. They went round with us, chattering and holding alternatively to his hand or tugging on his jacket until it was time for them to go and rest. Then he remarked that perhaps we ought to leave. But there were protests. A meal had been prepared. A film set was being built, and Eisenstein's opinion would be appreciated.

We strolled slowly through a wood towards the set. The other people drifted ahead and disappeared. Eisenstein was moved by the beauty of the trees, the play of light—and the stillness. But he could never speak of beauty; to do so appeared a sentimentality. (He always made jokes about the moon when it looked the most beautiful.)

Instead of words, he used his hands, running them over the branches, pointing out the rhythmic lines. He had studied the formation of trees and so he searched for primary form in their growth. He carefully removed the brambles from the unmarked path and noted the holes and boulders—harshness and dangers also had their place in the scheme of Nature. The thing which most enchanted him was an ancient fig tree loaded with swollen fruit. Life could be extremely good for a moment in a corner which people had refrained from touching too heavily.

But someone came from the beach, calling: 'Sergei Mikhailovich! Sergei Mikhailovich, where are you?' He looked at me regretfully. After inspecting the film set, he walked back with the group, which included some of the older boys who talked to him about various camp matters. A few of them joined the meal, which Eisenstein appeared to enjoy. But when we left the camp, Sergei retired to his own thoughts until we reached Alupka.

Even when we walked through the palace and around the gardens and stood looking at the stone lions, which served as one of his most famed examples of montage, he behaved as though he had never been to this place before. Only when the lions appeared familiar to me did he admit cynically that he remembered how Tisse had made him come back and 'shoot' them.

Suddenly he made a determined effort to appear gay. He ran up the steps and leapt on to the back of one of the lions and slid down the balustrade. But he could not pretend to be gay for long and immediately we left he withdrew into a shell of silence—something he never did while he was in the Crimea, except on this one day. At the vineyard, where the car stopped, he walked through the sheds without interest. When we returned to Yalta, he immediately wrote a letter to Pera asking her to tell his mother that she must go back to Leningrad. He would not return to Moscow while she was there and he would make no arrangements for her to live with him.

After he had posted the letter, and on and off over several days, Sergei Mikhailovich talked about his childhood: his mother's desertion of his father, and his despairing identification with the small clown. How he had found Leonardo da Vinci and his conflict between the sentiments of the old world and the new; how he had been laughed at for his bourgeois sensitivity when he fell in love with the young actress of the Meyerhold Theatre, and of Alexandrov's role in his life. He related the incident of the prostitute coming to his room at Chysti Prudi and how it had filled him with fear and revulsion at the sex act. He talked about his period of intellectual preoccupation with homosexuality and how he had solved his conflicts by sublimation.

But he did not dramatize his life; he treated his experiences as facts, the influence of which he had, unfortunately, been unable to overcome. Nor did he consider his life a secret never to be revealed. He put the most intimate details of his life into my hands and his motive, as he told me, was that he did not wish me to be hurt through lack of understanding him, nor that I, through lack of knowledge, should hurt him. The fact that I accepted his reactions without making him feel strange made it easier for him to express his intimate thoughts and feelings.

'All my life I've wanted to be accepted with affection, but I've felt compelled to withdraw and remain a spectator,' he said. And he explained why.

He felt beauty with the utmost intensity. Everything that was beautiful moved him and he lived much of his life with ecstatic poetic visions. But he had always pictured himself as he thought others saw him and the image paralysed his will to express his emotions overtly. Falling in love with Meyerhold's young daughter at his theatre had been only an agony. Fame had intensified his sense of being imprisoned. He felt increasingly that he was a man of great intellectual powers, and the longer he lived the stronger became his emotional response to beauty and passion. Yet all his æsthetic sense had compelled him to conceal his feelings because such power of thought and emotion as his belonged in a form which was beautiful and noble to look upon.

'When the people at Artek gave us flowers and looked admiringly at you, I knew what it was to have a life of my own instead of being a spectator. We began this as a game. But now I think I was compelled to such a game because I wanted to know what it would really feel like to live like other people.'

And during these days while Eisenstein was telling me about his thoughts and feelings, I saw him work in a concentrated way with young and aspiring artists at the beginning of their creative life.

Once begun, the scenario consultations which Sergei Mikhailovich had at first wished to postpone became a source of pleasure, for each was a creative act. After the first session, to which the young film workers came in a somewhat subdued and uncertain frame of mind, they were charmed and stimulated by Eisenstein.

The Yalta scenario conferences (and later the week of daily conferences in Odessa) were conducted informally. They took place in the garden of the studios, and at the villa. At the early conferences everyone connected with the film was present and it was understood that all had an equal right to participate in the discussion and criticism. The work was collective. Only in the later stages, when specific points in the scenario came up for discussion, was the group reduced to the core of the unit—director, scenarist and chief cameraman, who came to talk to Eisenstein privately.

Since the units were composed of people with little or no experience, they were not clear as to what exactly they wanted to portray in their films. Each unit had the outline of a story, but they had not approached it from a definite creative viewpoint. Moreover, the young workers wallowed in their own enthusiasm, but had no creative language for making their ideas articulate, or working them out creatively among themselves. They were frightened of *not* making a *good* film. Their difficulties sprang not only from lack of experience, but from what Eisenstein recognized as the major problem—the stumbling-block he was himself trying to remove through his directors' course at the Institute of Cinematography—a lack of knowledge of art and the creative process.

Here was the third generation of Soviet film artists. They were drawn largely from the families of workers and peasants and not from the intelligentsia as most of the first and second generation had been. They came to art, as Eisenstein said, 'without cultural biographies'. Because they knew almost nothing of painting, they lacked a general sense of composition. They knew a little more about the theatre, but Shakespeare was still something of a closed book to them; they were not aware of the mechanics of projecting action through individual characters, which had become the new orientation of the Soviet cinema. Their limited knowledge of literature left them weak in understanding how to portray the psychological development of characters, or how to use significant details to enrich both subject and form.

These problems, however, were the very ones which Sergei Eisenstein liked to handle. They gave him an opportunity to express himself in the area where he was the most articulate. First he turned psychologist.

Realizing the emotional tightness of the workers and their poverty in knowledge of expressive material, Eisenstein instantly discarded discussion of the scenario itself and tried to draw everyone into a general discussion. He wanted to draw out each personality and start a flow of discussion so that a spirit of participation would be created. He encouraged the members of the unit, sometimes dropping in jokes to create an easy atmosphere. Once he had created animation he began to challenge them; but in such a way as not to crush or alarm anyone. They needed to argue with him in order to uncover and strengthen their own ideas and feelings. Soon the members of the unit were as free in their treatment of Eisenstein as they were towards each other.

As the new generation, freed from many of the conflicts of Sergei Mikhailovich's generation, they accepted Eisenstein as a fellow worker, different from themselves only in the fact that he had greater knowledge. There was no indication that he was a 'great' man set apart. It was this which made him grateful for contact with the young generation of workers.

Having established a good working relationship and a creative atmosphere, Eisenstein would rise (he never sat in a conspicuous position), and in a casual manner would say that he had to leave. Everyone should get to work on the scenario and he would be back after a few hours, or next day. Only at an advanced stage did he deal with the specific construction of the script and discuss the episodes one by one in an attempt to strengthen the subject-matter and mould the form.

The moment he left the group his thoughts would turn to ways of extending the director's and scenarist's knowledge of creative processes. He wanted to catch their imagination and direct it along the path of studying creative works. He had brought only a handful of books with him to Yalta; one was a Russian translation of Balzac's *Comédie Humaine*, which the students at the Institute of Cinematography were studying. He gave this to the director and scenarist after talking to them at length about what they could learn from Balzac for their own films. At Odessa, where there were many obscure bookshops, Eisenstein bought several books for the Odessan unit. In this way, Eisenstein introduced new points of view, threw searchlights on the scenario from different angles and sought to educate the young workers.

In his role of teacher-consultant, Eisenstein revealed his greatness of character and achieved the pinnacle of practical usefulness. In laying the foundations for future works of art, he gained fulfilment. His step, which responded to his moods, grew buoyant and he looked extremely young. He was filled with confidence and hope.

Yet he avoided any intimate contact with the units. Though he had no objections to the film workers coming to the villa (or later, to the hotel in Odessa), and he appreciated the flowers and small gifts they brought, Eisenstein would excuse himself from going out with them, and he never asked them to come and join him as friends. Still, satisfaction affected his private world. His delightful sense of humour, almost buried except in a satiric form since his return from America, came to the surface easily in a more good-natured form of jokes and a play on words. There was less expression of rebellion. His humorous response to situations was expressed in an episode which might have left him hurt at an earlier period, because of its reference to himself and Mexico.

One evening near the end of our stay in Yalta, Sergei Mikhailovich thought it would be amusing to go to dinner at the hotel where the engineers and other important Soviet technicians stayed. For the first time in the Crimea he put on an ordinary suit, one he had bought in America. Suddenly a middle-aged couple hustled over from another table and greeted Eisenstein as a fellow American. They supposed him to be a tourist and to find someone from home was grand! Unasked, they sat down at our table, explaining that they had been in Soviet Asia and had not seen an American for two years. Eisenstein was the first!

Sergei, whose English at this time was almost flawless, launched into Americanese. He'd come to look over his parents' homeland and get the lowdown. So the engineer outlined the Soviet engineering plans and he wanted the news from home. Eisenstein supplied news of America most admirably. They asked him what was his home town? Brooklyn. His job? Sergei was rather vague, as if it were none too respectable. Then they turned their questions to me. Where did I come from? England. At which point Sergei explained that anything could happen to a man who bummed around; bumming broadened the mind.

The American agreed and told how he and his wife had learned to eat just about anything in Soviet Asia, and before that in Mexico. He recounted his experiences on various engineering projects and what it was like in Mexico. *Mañana* there; *sechas* here. On the whole, the Russians got the job done faster than the Mexicans, though some of them were crazy. What hadn't he heard about that Russian movie guy —Eisenstein—in Mexico! He must have been as crazy as hell, taking miles and miles of film until he got thrown out. Upton Sinclair had backed him. He didn't know what had happened to Eisenstein, but he'd been shipped back to Russia. Maybe he'd been liquidated.

'Sounds as if such a guy'd get in the dog-house any place,' remarked Sergei Mikhailovich with a shrug. 'I guess he was a no-good so-and-so!'

He was so convincing as an American tourist that the game could have gone on for ever. It was fascinating to watch until he began to play more boldly and then it became difficult not to laugh. There was nothing for me to do but kick the impostor and plead we must really go. Out of sight, Sergei was delighted with himself. He swore that it seemed the kindest thing to do. But the next day he was fearful as to what he had let himself in for from two lonely Americans, and he instituted a game of hide-and-seek to avoid meeting them again. But in trying to find him in the Intourist hotel, they stumbled upon his identity and a most apologetic note was sent up to the villa. Wouldn't he *please* come and have a cocktail? After some hesitation, Eisenstein agreed to go. Fortunately the Americans had a sense of humour and appreciated Eisenstein's game. As to the Mexican affair, he passed it off lightly with a discreet remark that it was unfortunate that Mr. Sinclair and he had been unable to agree.

But Sergei Mikhailovich resisted another encroachment. A group of foreigners arrived at the Intourist hotel, which was the gossip centre of Yalta. Among them was Ernst Toller, the poet and dramatist, whom

Eisenstein had met in Berlin. Now a refugee living in England, Toller sent a note asking to see Eisenstein. But Sergei Mikhailovich did not answer it, pleading there was only one more day in Yalta. Odessa would be different. We would have to live in an hotel and there would be many people.

On the last day we spent much time buying souvenirs—postcards and shells made into heart-shaped boxes, Cinderella shoes and quaint funnel-shaped containers for keeping hair combings—the sort of useless things which Sergei Mikhailovich found charmingly ridiculous and touching. He bought many of these mementoes of a world that only lingered in Russia in such far-off towns as Yalta. Some time he said I should take them to his friends in London and Paris. One of the shoes would delight Ferdnand Leger, the painter; another was for Jack Isaacs. They were the echo of the world in which he had been born; but the present was much happier than the memory of childhood.

As the ship sailed round the coast to Odessa, Sergei Mikhailovich developed a toothache. He hated pain and in the hope of escaping it he went to sleep. The day was gentle and the sun shone with the radiance of autumn. Sleep revealed Eisenstein as he seldom appeared to the world. He emerged as an image of contentment, his face was illuminated with a tranquil expression. He looked noble and filled with a life force powerful enough to destroy the forces of fear and despair which too often disturbed him in his waking hours. Such a man should live to a great age and realize his enormous dreams.

As he lay asleep, it seemed that unless some crisis again engulfed him, Eisenstein would not be driven back into his shell. The contradictions of genius were seemingly becoming reconciled; he had a great desire to live harmoniously and express in life the best and most constructive side of human evolution. But as he said one morning in Yalta, 'nothing evolves in a straight line. There is the upward thrust; the pause and a turn and another upward thrust forming a spiral. There is no certainty as to time. But, dialectically, the process must continue, for nothing remains static, everything is either dying or becoming.'

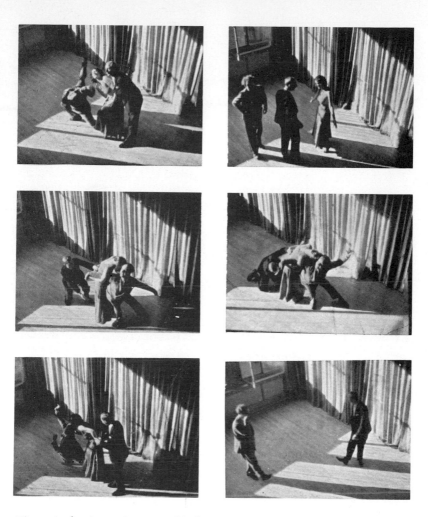

Eisenstein dancing an improvised ballet with Sara Mildred Strauss and Eduard Tisse, New York, 1932

Lecturing at the Institute of Cinematography, Moscow, autumn, 1934

With Mei-Lan-Fang, Moscow, 1935

Eisenstein Collection, Museum of Modern Art, New York

Ivor Montagu by Eisenstein, Moscow, 1936

34

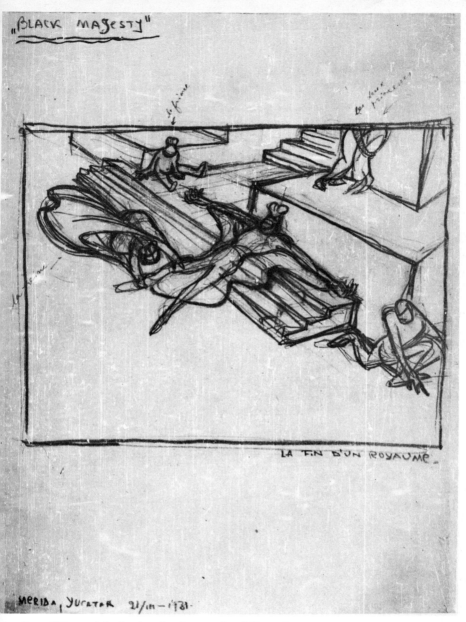

One of Eisenstein's sketches for the unrealized film, *Black Majesty*

With Dziga Vertov (*left*) and
Vsevelod I. Pudovkin at the
All-Union Creative Conference
of Workers in Soviet Cinematography, Moscow, January
8–13, 1935

With Pudovkin on
the *Ivan the Terrible*
set

Test shot of Judith Glizer for
Eisenstein's unrealized comedy
M.M.M.

36

Joseph
and
Photin's
Wife.

The Greeks had a word for it (p. 297)

Go ahead, old Greek! Whatever
you do' Chop Suey will say
we never existed!!

Eisenstein at the age of 37

Bezhin Meadow, 1935–37

'A new quality of film poetry'
—Eisenstein

(Photographs by Jay Leyda)

By courtesy of Jay Leyda

Bezhin Meadow,
1935–37

Vitya Kartashov as
Stepok and Boris
Zakhava, his father

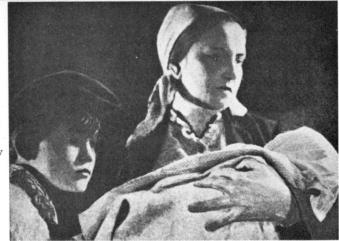

Elena Telesheva
and
Vitya Kartashov

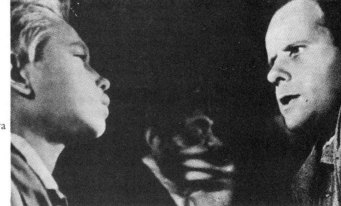

Directing Vitya
Kartashov

The Burning

The Hanging

Alexander Nevsky, 1938

The Teuton Knights in Pskov

By courtesy of Armand Panigel

Alexander Nevsky and *Henry V*

The Battle on the Ice

The Battle of Agincourt

Alexander Nevsky, 1938

Plan of the Battle on
the Ice

Nishi Novgorod

4

Parody on *Alexander Nevsky*
Left to right: Eduard Tisse, Eisenstein, Sergei Prokofiev

Eisenstein receives the Order of Lenin, February, 1939
Front row, left to right: Eisenstein (*second*), M. I. Kalinin, Chairman of the Presidium
of the Supreme Soviet of the USSR (*third*), Lyubov Orlova (*fifth*) and Grigori
Alexandrov (*sixth*)

44

By courtesy of the National Film Archive
A warrior

Eisenstein's sketches
for the Tamerlaine's
Tower sequence in the
unfinished film

Ferghana Canal, 1939

courtesy of the British Film Institute

From *The Deluge,* Alexander Goehr's Cantata after Leonardi da Vinci, derived from Eisenstein's shooting script.

By courtesy of Schott & Co. Ltd

The Valkyrie, 1940
Directed by Eisenstein and
produced at the Bolshoi Theatre,
Moscow, November 21, 1940

Directing Wotan (Innocent
Redikultzev) and Brunnhilde
(Marguerite Butenina)

Rehearsing Brunnhilde and
Fricka (Elena Slivinskaya)

The Valkyrie in performance

By courtesy of Jay Leyda

Characters from the miracle play, *The Cologne Cathedral Builder*, 1920
Note the connection in both style and attitude with *Nevsky* and *Ivan*

One of the sketches for Shakespeare's tragedy, *Richard III* made in 1944, during the
production of *Ivan the Terrible*

Studies in Composition

The peons in *Que Viva Mexico!* 1931–32

By courtesy of the British Film Institute

The Pskov Patriots in *Alexander Nevsky*, 1938

By courtesy of Artkino of New

The Three Kolichevs in *Ivan the Terrible*, Part II, 1941–45

By courtesy of the British Film Institute

CHAPTER TWELVE

Film Form—New Problems

Pray hold me not in scorn! I am not poor!
Poor rather is the man who desires many things.
Where shall I take my place? . . .
LEONARDO DA VINCI, C.A. 71 r.a.

IN the port city of Odessa, bustling with activity, time had meaning. The Intourist hotel thronged with Russians and foreign tourists. Some of the people at the hotel knew Eisenstein. The first person to find him was Maxim Shtraukh, who had been acting in one of the children's films in production at the Odessa film studio. But Shtraukh was not a possessive friend and he made no attempt to monopolize Sergei Mikhailovich's time. In any case, he was returning to Moscow the following day. Other people were more demanding, so life in Odessa had to be ordered, otherwise it would have run in a whirl of working and social demands.

Sergei Mikhailovich made an effort to avoid the restaurant of the hotel at crowded hours and he was unwilling to see anyone except at specified times. Though he was obliged to adjust to a more public life than in Yalta, his only conflict arose on two visits to the Odessa stairway, which he had not seen since directing *Potemkin*.

On the first visit he grew bitter and contemptuous because he could not recapture the feeling of inspiration which had once come to him at this spot. Nine years had numbed his recollection and all the words written about the massacre on the steps appeared as pretentious babbling which mocked him. He flung around incoherent remarks and fled away. But he could not resist returning the following morning. Then he stood at the head of the steps and punctuated the spitting of grape pips with obscene remarks. The painful reaction at last ended with Eisenstein trying to turn back to the present and deal with its problems.

Yet while we were in Odessa, Eisenstein was more concerned with his film and theatre projects than with his theoretical research. He talked about various projects at night while we walked near the harbour and along the pier, where he had found the imagery for *Potemkin*. But of *Potemkin* he spoke only now and then in halting sentences— typage, the Commedia dell' Arte, the classical form of the five-act

311

tragedy, and how his films of 'pathos' had grown out of his work at the Proletkult Theatre. Very often he grew hesitant in talking of his most daring innovations and of how they came about. His accounts were always couched in more modest terms than other people's stories of him and his work.

Stray memories of America came back to Sergei Mikhailovich. They were recalled by the presence of American business men drinking in the bar of the Intourist hotel. This place disgusted Eisenstein and he shunned it after one evening. He disliked the spectacle of Russian girls entertaining rich foreigners; to him it represented a kowtowing attitude on the part of Intourist in the handling of foreigners. His reaction to the Intourist organization, which had extended its activities while he was abroad, was reflected in a satirically philosophic comedy, M.M.M. He began to develop the plan for this film shortly after returning from America, but later, when he presented it, Shumyatsky rejected the project.

The barber shop, where Eisenstein had his hair cut so short that it was scarcely more remarkable than average wavy hair, set his recollection of M.M.M. in motion. The film was to commence with the sound of a razor scraping over a face, scrape, scrape, the sound growing in intensity until it blared and the first image appeared on the screen—the timid face of a little barber shaving an important official whom he was in great terror of cutting. He was so alarmed that the sound of his razor seemed to fill his whole head with its dangerous rasp.

Suddenly—through the patron he so greatly feared—the little barber was catapulted from his barbering into an important job—director of a foreign travel organization, about which he knew nothing. It was all very bewildering to the barber to find himself sitting in the director's chair at a big table surrounded by subordinates, all drinking one glass of tea after another and talking in a gibberish he could scarcely understand. They were outlining the 'plan' for tourists coming from abroad. The gibberish grew ever more mechanical in the mind of the man-at-the-head-of-the-plan-he-knew-nothing-about, until each mouth began to move mechanically and out of it came the monotonous sound of a stalled record repeating itself over and over again.

The little man was startled out of his wits. He began to see inside the men around the table and in the place where each should have had a heart there was a dollar sign. More bewildered than ever, the 'director' escaped into sleep, and dreamed a phantasmagoria in which the most extraordinary things happened to him and everything went topsy-turvy. He was asleep in a great bed canopied in silk and into his sleep came whispers: 'The Boyars are coming! The Boyars are coming!' The Boyars? But they had been driven out by the Revolution. There were no more Boyars. Sitting up, the little man rubbed his eyes again and again.

All around the walls he saw elongated painted figures of Boyars. 'The Boyars are coming!' The voice came from the walls and then a gigantic figure of a Boyar began to bend out from the walls. Gradually detaching himself, he stretched towards the bed. Then another and another worked his way loose, descended and stood—a living man—in the chamber. This made the little man indignant. THE BOYARS ARE DEAD. 'Oh, you think so!' said the Boyars scornfully. They enjoy their clever conspiracy very much and mock the little man, telling him how many Boyars who went away during the Revolution are now coming back—disguised as tourists. The little man is desperate in the face of this conspiracy. He *must*, and *will*, save the Revolution. He plunges into action. The returning Boyars must be prevented from crossing the border.

But who are the Boyars? How are they to be detected? In the midst of all his troubles, trying to detect a Boyar from a non-Boyar, something exceedingly unexpected happens: the Boyars who have managed to sneak in have taken a look at the new Russia. They rather like it. They don't want to overthrow the Revolution any more. No. For in their hearts, Boyars or no Boyars, they are still Russians. They would like to stay and help build the new society.

As Sergei Mikhailovich 'created' his film in delightful phrases and expressive gestures, the barber became a touching figure. He was comic, unheroic, yet couragously loyal. He had features of Eisenstein, who was afraid of being reprimanded because he gave to beggars and overpaid vendors who once had been 'Boyars'. He could not condemn these people as individuals, though he wanted to keep his kindly acts unseen. If observed, he flushed and said, 'It is weakness that I pity them'.

Eisenstein was not very clear as to what stage the script of this fantasy had reached before Shumyatsky rejected it as unsuitable. But he loved his idea and all the way through his verbal film 'creation' he chuckled, delighted with his own cleverness. His mischievous attitude and the way he played with it in the manner of a teasing boy never appeared when he talked of any of his other work.

That Eisenstein should have proposed this comedy to Shumyatsky showed how naïve he was in his estimate of an official policy towards the development of comedy. His reason for presenting such an idea was that laughter served as a healthy way of exposing stupid and vulgar things. In this point of view he was reviving the original philosophic base of the eccentric theatre which had flourished in the early 1920's as a means of making everything 'bourgeois' look ridiculous. Now he would like to employ a more sophisticated interpretation of 'eccentric comedy' against Soviet Philistines. To Eisenstein it was abominable for Soviet people to imitate the worst of bourgeois styles. He detested the 'compromise' of some of the Russian engineers' wives who dyed their hair, painted their finger nails and showed themselves off in clothes designed to look 'foreign'. To Sergei Mikhailovich they suggested the prostitute, and the sale of love, like the sale of talent, was a target for his lashing sarcasm. To him the imitation of bourgeois attitudes was a degradation of the men and women of a new society in which the exploitative character of the bourgeois world must be overcome.

Moscow the Second, another project of which Eisenstein talked, was a play by Nathan Zharki. In an article he had sent me earlier in the year, he explained how 'we are facing the important and fascinating problem of grasping new themes and discovering new ways of carrying them out'. The play was 'built around a person in whose honour a statue is erected for his outstanding work. This fact initiates in him a whole gamut of contradictory feelings and actions, which reflect the conflict between old and new emotional concepts. Thus the theme of the play becomes the struggle for the new man, the new personality and new attitude towards labour and fame.' There were only six characters, five people and one monument. In the process of work, the relationship between the central character and the statue was changed. In the first draft of the play, the statue was to represent an individual Hero of Labour. In the second draft the statue was to represent an ideal Hero of Labour with the central character acting merely as the physical model for the figure.

The play was to open with the setting up of the monument in Pushkin Square. The model for this figure was a factory worker, who looked like the noble image in the sculptor's mind. Overnight this unknown worker became famous as an image, though there was nothing remarkable about his character. It had never mattered before that he was not a hero; he had worked averagely well, got along averagely well with his wife, drunk a little but not too much. But with the unveiling of the statue, everyone expected him to set an example and this was very difficult for him. There was his physical form set up on a pedestal, while he, standing down on the ground and looking up at it, did not feel its equal. Hence he began to look very poor in his own eyes and everything soon went wrong for him. His wife complained when he behaved just as he always had; his comrades thought he slacked at work when really he worked just as hard as he had before. When he wanted to take a drink as he always had, he wondered if he should. It was not long before his average virtues seemed to turn into very serious faults. Thus, he fell into disgrace with everybody, and his wife, seeking a hero, deserted him. Finally, life became such a tangle that he ran 'mad', cursing the day he was chosen as the model for the ideal Hero of Labour. Wishing he could die, he escaped into vodka.

Alone, miserable, cursing and roaring drunk, he comes to Pushkin Square to have it out with that damned image of himself. He weeps: how hard it is to live up to himself. He yells rebellion against himself until a comrade finds him and seeks to resolve his problems by explaining that he was merely the physical model for the statue. He *looked* right. That was his contribution to the figure. But the figure itself symbolized the efforts of many men no better, no worse than himself; the statue was a composite image to which he had contributed the typical physical features of the current Soviet man.[1]

This philosophic comedy reflected the effort of Russians to discipline themselves as representatives of a society developing new standards of personal and social conduct. Humorously treated and subtly wise, *Moscow the Second* sprang in part from Eisenstein's own experience. Though he did not wield the individual power he might have in another country, he had, nevertheless, been pointed out as a famous figure since his middle twenties, when to be stared at made him self-conscious of his shortcomings. But his situation had to a certain extent been inverted in *Moscow the Second*. There the hero's character and intelligence fell short of the perfection of his physical form, while in his own case Eisenstein felt that his inadequate height dragged his inner being down and, therefore, he could not appear the man he really was.

In the idea for both *M.M.M.* and *Moscow the Second*, Eisenstein moved

[1] In a lecture on 25 October 1934, at the Institute of Cinematography in Moscow, Eisenstein mentioned *Moscow the Second* to his students: 'The moment Zharki told me his play was about a statue of a living man, I knew it was the subject for me. Think of the problem of a statue of a man still alive. When a man becomes famous we have the bourgeois problem of fame. The comparison between the real Udarnik (Hero of Labour) and the ideal Udarnik, hence the relations between the man and the monument. If the real man has a moustache there is disillusion. The play concerned the Udarnik's mistakes because of the monument. People considered him as the abstract idea of an Udarnik.

'The composition of the monument is repeated through the whole play. After three days the skeleton of the play was ready. We took literary traditions. I recalled after years Don Juan meeting his own funeral, so the monument [in the scene where the worker is drunk] appears to be removed in a coffin. This reflects the internal relations of the man at the time.

'I was infatuated with the subject because it embraced so many of the problems in which I am interested—mainly the man and his image. Such infatuation forms a basis for future work; it is the powder for an explosion. But you must not simply let your feelings explode, you must direct them in a definite direction. . . .'

(From notes taken by the author at the lecture.)

into a more personal vein than in his previous work. Realizing that the time had passed for films of the Mass, his characters contained a new dimension. He had great hopes for *Moscow the Second*, for not only did he have a desire to find new images expressive of Soviet society, but also the idea of working again in the theatre fascinated him. Even though very little of the dialogue was written, Sergei Mikhailovich had worked out an almost complete plan of the *mise en scène*. The *décor* too was integrating itself into the total production scheme. For example, in the last act laid in Pushkin Square, the scenery must have motion and change with the changing state of intoxication.

In planning to use scenery in motion to reflect a changing psychological state, Eisenstein was extending a theory of *décor* which he had originally devised for the Proletkult production of the play *Precipice*, over which he and Valeri Smishlayev had disagreed. In *Precipice* 'the task was to solve the dynamics of city streets—the intersection of man and milieu'; in *Moscow the Second* this 'intersection' was the state of man's mind in relation to the world around him. Unfortunately, Zharki was to die before the play was completed, so that Sergei Mikhailovich's ideas for scenery in motion were not to be realized until 1940, when he produced Wagner's opera *The Valkyrie* and finally utilized his theory to reflect the mental states of Hunding and Siegmund.

A third project stirred quite different passions in him. Ever since 1931 Sergei Mikhailovich had been hoping to make a film on Toussaint L'Ouverture, the liberator of Haiti, entitled *Black Majesty*. The original idea for this film was derived from the book by Vinogradov, *The Black Consul*,[1] in which Eisenstein had discovered the remarkable character Touissaint, who appeared to him not only as one of the most dramatic and noble of historical figures, but also a man in whom a stage in cultural evolution was reflected. To Sergei Mikhailovich, a slave—one generation from Africa—who was capable of organizing an army and defeating the troops of Napoleon was more than a unique individual; he must reflect the developing genius of the Negro people.

'If a race is biologically and psychologically inferior in its roots such a man could not appear in its midst,' Eisenstein said.

Toussaint L'Ouverture held great appeal, because Sergei Mikhailovich desired to express his admiration of the Negro people, whom he had studied while he was in America. In connection with this proposed film, Eisenstein hoped that he could somehow make arrangements to work with an American actor he had never seen, but of whom he had heard a great deal—Paul Robeson. From what he had been told, it

---

[1] Other books which Eisenstein was using as background for his projected film were *Black Majesty* by John Vandercook and *The Black Napoleon* by Percy Waxman; also Otten's play *Der Schwarz Napoleon*.

seemed to him that Robeson was an artist whose qualities would respond to his own creative methods.

'Then you should write to Robeson,' I said. 'He's in London, and being interested in languages, he's learned some Russian.'

Sergei Mikhailovich looked surprised, then pleased; but finally doubtful.

'He doesn't know me,' he said. 'He wouldn't be willing to come all the way here to talk to a man he doesn't know. I'd be embarrassed to ask him.'

So the matter was dropped for some weeks. Meanwhile, the scenario conferences ended. The autumn term at the Institute in Moscow loomed up and Eisenstein knew he must return to his cell-like room.

He explained his responsibility—to his mother and Pera and Totya Pasha. He was able to manage, though sometimes he was fearful lest he might not be able to make enough money to buy the only things essential to his life—books. Without books he did not know how he would live. Yet he did not complain, although it would have given him great pleasure had he been free to go back to Yalta. It was delightful to live in a house alone, to take as long a time as he desired over shaving, or to sit half the night among the pine trees in the garden. Had it been possible he would have liked to go on living for a long time as we had in Yalta.

If he had been a successful film director living in another country, he could have ordered his life in any manner he saw fit. But in the Soviet Union, Eisenstein was a worker with duties to perform. Though he was a great artist, and recognized as such throughout the world, he could not go out and buy or rent a larger place in which to live. He was conditioned to accept the fact that he could not do the things which men of his standing in a capitalist society took for granted. His relationship with any foreigner could only continue on Russian soil or through letters.

Sergei Mikhailovich was in an unfortunate position. After a life of extreme loneliness, he now had my deep affection. But only by a ruthless turning aside from his integrity could he continue to enjoy the pleasant life which had taken shape in Yalta and Odessa. He would have to abandon the standard of conduct he had imposed upon himself: that of a man who did not seek privileges. He only had the assurance that if he were ever able in the future to suggest a way of continuing this life, his suggestion would not be rejected. When he had something hard and difficult to do, Eisenstein behaved with iron-bound restraint. As at other times in his life, he tried to occupy his mind with impersonal matters. When the studio in Odessa paid him, we spent most of the last day poking about the secondhand bookshops. The books he retrieved from under the counters and from among stacks of discarded volumes filled two large crates, which members of the film unit brought to the station and put on the train. Two other young workers ran down the platform waving a cooked goose as the train started to move. They flung it in and Sergei caught it.

On the surface no one would have supposed Sergei Mikhailovich to be a competent traveller, but he was extremely efficient. He thoroughly enjoyed travelling. On a long journey he seemed possessed of the steady, untroubled nervous system of a peasant, the stamina of a man who tilled the soil. His stamina should have been broken down, for he lived day after day, month in month out consuming books, a life which should have blunted his acute sight and weakened him. He had no desire to be pampered, and his own considerateness did not include fussing around. One thing was absolute: equality in all things except in a matter requiring a man's strength. Though he never expressed it in words, he behaved as though there were no difference in human worth between a man and a woman; the one was not entitled to more than the other.

At a point between Odessa and Moscow, Sergei Mikhailovich found the last apple in a station restaurant. He brought it back and handed it to me. Without thinking, I ate more than three-quarters of it.

'I wouldn't forget you!' He took the apple from me as if I were a selfish child, swung up to the upper berth, and retired to the furthest corner. Perching in the shadow he assumed the contemplative expression of a monkey who found humanity a poor parody of itself. Having finished the remnant, he returned to his human identity.

'People don't forget if they want to share!' He made it clear he could not tolerate a person who became insensitive to the demands of a personal relationship.

'It's your turn to go and find an apple for me,' he said when the train stopped again. 'You let me go alone to hunt your apple, while you sat here expecting me to wait on you! It isn't easy to be conscious of another person at all times,' he continued, 'but if there's indifference there isn't anything.'

On arriving in Moscow we were met at the station by some of Eisenstein's students. One of them told Sergei Mikhailovich that his mother was still at Chysti Prudi.

The years of conflict with his mother rushed to the surface and he said he could not face her alone. He turned spiteful and truculent towards her, for he knew exactly what was going to happen.

Though it was only seven o'clock, Madame Eisenstein was waiting. She was dressed in a style resembling past elegance. Her dress was a gentle purple with old lace arranged fluffily at the neck. Her fair hair, not yet entirely grey, was attractively arranged. Like a gentle mother she received me with utmost graciousness, yet without any preliminary word to her son, Madame Eisenstein demanded in French an explanation for what she termed Sergei Mikhailovich's outrageous conduct. If what she had heard about us from Maxim Shtraukh was what it appeared—an example of the disreputable New Morality—what was Sergei going to do about it? He could not transgress decency with someone younger than himself who was obviously not an immoral woman. Or were we married?

With restraint, Eisenstein told his mother that our conduct was our own affair and she could make no demands or try to force answers or commitments from him. Her reaction was unexpected. She dropped her attack instantly and went out of the room to see if Totya Pasha was preparing breakfast.

The moment she was gone, Sergei Mikhailovich dropped his restraint. He begged me not to leave him alone with his mother even for a few minutes. He wanted her to believe he was married so she would be induced to return to Leningrad. He was also upset because Pera had left no note. He must see Pera immediately after breakfast.

When Julia Eisenstein returned from the kitchen, her attack upon Sergei Mikhailovich took another turn. Ignoring his presence at the table, she complained of the awful conditions in Russia under which she had to live.

'The Bolsheviks destroyed all the feelings my son ever had,' she said. 'Now he refuses to understand how I suffer! He makes me live alone in Petrograd in a horrible room without any comforts.'

She recalled with elaborate detail her former life in Riga, Petrograd and France before the Revolution. As she talked, the mannerisms of a cosmopolitan society woman appeared. When she had finished she glanced at Sergei Mikhailovich, who had listened in silence.

'My mother would sell her soul for a roll of lavatory paper!' he commented in English.

Though she did not understand English, Julia Eisenstein's manner changed.

'If only I could leave Russia like you!' she exclaimed. 'It is foolish of you to stay here. Go back to your home! My son is like all Bolsheviks —without feelings!'

Leaving Chysti Prudi immediately after breakfast, we walked to Pera's home. Sergei Mikhailovich was relieved when Pera told him she had not left a note because she was angry with his mother for refusing to return to Leningrad. His face became radiant with such devotion that it was evident he found in Pera the security which his mother had never given him.

After a while the Old Man went to the Institute of Cinematography. When he was gone, Pera talked more freely about him than ever before. She said she wanted him to be happy and if he could complete his life with another woman she would be content. She asked me if Sergei Mikhailovich and I were lovers, and when I told her we were not, she shook her head.

'I wish I did not love him,' she said.

Pera then told me how she was worried about the growing criticism of Eisenstein. Since returning from America he had evaded discussion of his work with the heads of the film industry. When asked to explain why he was devoting almost the whole of his time to theoretical research work, he failed to give any explanation. He ignored the criticism of his theories of the 'intellectual film' and the suggestion that he produce a new picture. By his conduct, Eisenstein was putting himself in an inexplicable position. The fact that Boris Shumyatsky disliked Eisenstein personally and (as subsequent events show) was attempting to destroy Eisenstein's reputation, made the situation even worse.

If Eisenstein were accused of irresponsible conduct, and the charges were proven, he might be sent out of Moscow. I knew that if this ever happened the only person who would be entitled to accompany Sergei Mikhailovich would be a wife with whom he had registered at Z.A.G.S., and who was a Soviet citizen. I asked Pera never to leave Eisenstein to face any such a problem alone. She said that if it ever appeared necessary she would try to persuade him to register with her at Z.A.G.S. But she knew that such a registration would not change their relationship.

Later the Z.A.G.S. registration did take place. Although Pera told me, it was not made public and she withheld the fact even from her mother and sister. But in the autumn of 1934 it was difficult to estimate how serious were the criticisms of which Pera spoke, and Sergei Mikhailovich insisted that she was exaggerating.

The night after our return from Odessa, Julia Eisenstein decided to return to Leningrad. The scene Sergei Mikhailovich dreaded was averted. His mother had supper with Maxim Shtraukh and Judith Glizer, and she came into his room once to ask if there was anything he wanted. He behaved quietly and made arrangements for her to be taken to the station. Only now and then when he caught the sound of voices in the next room did he flare up and say his mother would set everyone in the flat to spy on us. But when she came to say good-bye, it was polite—with half a room between them.

After she left, the taciturn and unsentimental Totya Pasha came in to see Sergei Mikhailovich. She discarded the frigid manner she had adopted while his mother was in the flat. Her bright little eyes twinkled.

Short of speech, she treated Eisenstein as if he were her nephew, whom she consented to feed. On this evening she brought two glasses of tea; it was the first time she had done this so late at night and it was her way of expressing her pleasure at being again in charge of his comfort. He made a joke and she chuckled with the same kind of pleasure as he expressed in his own chuckles. As she went away she smiled and it was the same sly, cryptic smile that sometimes flitted over Eisenstein's face. Clearly, he had learned his own peculiar sagacity and honesty with himself from Totya Pasha. She made it difficult for him to become a spoiled, petulant man. Adroitly she eased Sergei Mikhailovich back into the pattern of life in his small, bleak room. Even when he came to the flat of the dramatist Alexander Afinogenov and his wife, where I went to stay, Sergei Mikhailovich made no reference about how comfortably they lived in comparison to himself. He became very welcome there, because the Afinogenovs now found him a much more likeable man than he had formerly appeared.

With the opening of the autumn term, I spent much time with Sergei Mikhailovich and went to the Institute each day he lectured. At last a heavy fall of snow came and that afternoon I went to Chysti Prudi in borrowed snowboots. I struggled to undo the clasps as I had done at Chysti Prudi many times during the previous winter. Suddenly Sergei Mikhailovich knelt down, unfastened my boots and drew them off.

Never again was I allowed to take off my own boots; it made no difference whether we were alone at Chysti Prudi, in a crowded theatre, or in the house of Maxim Litvinov.

A few days later he said he had been assigned a flat in a new building which was to be built near the Potylika film studio some miles outside of Moscow. The house would be ready in six or nine months.

'It will have four rooms!' he said. 'But I can't live in four rooms alone. One room is for you, if you'll make it your home. You will always come back to Moscow, won't you?'

'Yes, always,' I answered.

We did not discuss this matter any further. It was a quiet arrangement for the future which involved no declaration on either side. But the future appeared as certain as day following night, and in time we told Pera of this plan and Alexander Afinogenov and his wife, Jeanya, also knew of it.

The moment Eisenstein's classes commenced at the Institute, he felt he was fulfilling himself. Every day that he taught was a pleasure, for he regarded his students as the hope of the future. One of them was the young American Jay Leyda, who later translated and edited Eisenstein's two theoretical books, *The Film Sense* and *Film Form*. Another of his students was the Englishman H. P. J. Marshall, who completed the full course of study at the Institute of Cinematography.

Day after day, Sergei Mikhailovich poured his genius into his Directors' Course. His total plan for the four years of training included every aspect of film production and gave the student a complete theoretical and practical training in the creative processes of art as a basis for the production of films.

This broad pedagogic plan had evolved over twelve years. Its roots were grounded in the training programme Eisenstein had instituted for the workers of the Proletkult Theatre in the autumn of 1922. It had grown from the lectures he had given at the Institute of Cinematography before he went abroad in 1929. By the beginning of 1934, Eisenstein had attempted to relate his knowledge of the arts and sciences, as well as his practical creative work, to his ever-increasing study of Marxist dialectics. Thus, he presented his entire course as illustrative of, and in line with, the thesis of Lenin: '. . . From co-existence to causality and from one form of connection and interdependence to another more profound, more general. . . .'

'This', Eisenstein wrote, 'is the only path which will enable us to embrace all the varied and at first sight independent themes and divisions which enter into the composition of the discipline of film direction. As the basis for the method of passing through all the stages of directoral knowledge we undeviatingly observe the thesis that we have "a repetition of each higher stage of certain features, qualities, etc. of the lower state" (*Lenin Selections*, Vol. IX, p. 258, Russian edition).'

Division I of the course began with what Eisenstein called 'Work on Oneself'. This meant a training period in which the student developed knowledge of his own mind and body. Such primary study was broken down into four subdivisions. First: Physical control and training of the organ most important for the visual artist—the eye. Second: 'The Development of the Necessary Gifts for Directed Perception', which was a highly complex series of exercises designed to train the mind to the discovery and organization of material. It commenced with the reporting of eye-witness accounts and culminated in a study of how such artists as da Vinci, Emil Zola and Gogol handled the reconstruction of events and phenomena. Third: A study of the Creative Process, beginning with an examination of the features and qualities of the creative personality, and ending with the student arranging for himself an 'accumulation of creative material' such as extensive notes and an illustrated collection of world art. Fourth: 'Work in the Group and on Production', where the students studied how the artist functioned and realized his work in different societies—the bourgeois world and a socialist world.

In Division II discussion of cinematography commenced with a study of the director's role in the production of a film. The study included world cinematography as well as Soviet cinematography. Two terms were devoted to Surveys. The third term opened with a study of 'Expressive Manifestations'—the 'Practice of Expressive Portrayal' and the 'History of the Development of Expressive Manifestations'. These two subdivisions carried the student through the history of art with an historical background, as well as a study of evolution within nature itself, culminating in the appearance of man upon the earth and his subsequent psychological and social development.

In Division III, the 'Theory of Expressive Manifestations' was studied from the philosophic point of view, commencing with the system of Plato and tracing the development of philosophic thought up to the reflex theories of the biologist Pavlov. Division IV was devoted to the 'Process of Expressive Manifestations', which was, in effect, a combined study in sociology and psychology.

The fourth term began with 'Teaching Concerning the Image,' in which Eisenstein trained his students in mastering theatre technique, absorbing a detailed knowledge of theatrical development and the sociological and philosophic interpretations of the meaning of imagery. At the end of this term the student, after presenting a practical report, qualified as Assistant Director on the Artistic Side.

The fifth term to the final term—the eighth—were devoted to training in all branches of cinematography. The close of the eighth term brought the student to the point where he was required to present a number of fully worked out plans for production and, when his plans had been passed, he had to work on a professional production either as an 'assistant practicioner' or as co-director. After making a report upon his production practice, the student received a diploma and the title Qualified Director.[1]

Throughout the training, Eisenstein laid special emphasis on visualization in all phases of the student's work. In the very first division they were required to do free sketching for the purpose of developing 'visual judgement', and had to draw and sketch from memory in order to stimulate their powers of visual conception. In the divisions devoted to 'expressive manifestations', and those concerned with the study of theatre technique, many drawn plans were required. For example, on one occasion when Eisenstein had his students present dramatic sketches based on a single simple idea, two students working together appeared with 139 drawings for the *mise en scène*. When the students, divided into groups, executed one scene from *Julius Cæsar*, each group had to pre-

[1] Eisenstein's detailed plan for his Director's Course was published in *Life and Letters To-day*, Nos. 6 and 7, 1936.

pare a complete series of drawings recording the *mise en scène* as it was to appear on the stage. This was in preparation for the still more extensive drawing of the *mise en cadre* necessary in their later study and practice in film production.

H. P. J. Marshall, who participated in this particular exercise in practical work, explains how the students' conception of the social and creative process was gradually expanded and deepened under Eisenstein's guidance. They proceeded to the organization of the sequence in space and time: the composition of the dynamic environment, i.e., light, skies, sound, things, people. The composition of the movement of the individual characters and the masses: the *mise-en-scène*. The formless movement of the masses in conflict with the purposeful movement of the conspirators.

'Finally the artistic image of the whole production: the image as the unity of form and content. The development from the seed of the theme to its final external expression.

'We saw the compositional relationship between the *encircling* of Cæsar and the semi-circle of the Senate, the conspirators completing the rest of the circle. The disappearance of Cæsar half-way through the play, the semi-circle uncompleted, and the appearance of Cæsar's spirit towards the end, the completing of the circle. Personal assassination cannot kill a social force, Cæsar is dead, Cæsarism lives!'

And, as a 'close-up' of Eisenstein's mode of analysis, Marshall remembered his question: 'Why did Shakespeare suddenly go into Latin? 'Et tu, Brute!' Another example, Eisenstein said, of the law relating to the changing of quantity into quality. At the highest tension-point of the sequence (he was always very particular about the tension-points, 'That's your closest-up point') there is a leap into another dimension. How to express in words the anguish and tragedy of a man receiving his death-blow from his greatest friend? Ordinary language no longer suffices, the leap into the next dimension could be silence or music—or (brilliant stroke of Shakespeare's genius) *another tongue!* Cæsar's mother tongue!'[1]

The development of the students' individual work was also preserved in large scrapbooks. For example, a student 'had stated that he wished to do an episode of the French Revolution. The subject was duly approved of and he began his work. First, he had to ... familiarize himself with every phase of French history during the Revolutionary period—and not only history: but customs, architecture, costumes, furniture, kitchen utensils, etc. Having already chosen his episode with an eye to cinema treatment, he wrote a brief synopsis, then a detailed scenario which he proceeded to illustrate with small pen and ink drawings about three inches square. He pasted these in his scrapbook, one beneath another, down the centre of the page, so that as your eye travelled down the page, you saw the salient points of a moving picture. When the book was completed, the student was permitted to go out and actually shoot a few scenes. These were then shown to Eisenstein who passed judgement on them. If the verdict was favourable, the student got a diploma and a job in some film studio.'[1]

In her diary, Gwen Seiler, whom Sergei Mikhailovich had met in Hollywood, goes on to record the scene of one of these 'judgements'. 'At the back of the projection room was a sort of pulpit where Eisenstein stood and watched the film work of the students. The author and director of the little film we were about to see was as nervous as a cat. And well he might be, for Eisenstein does not choose his words; if the film is bad the student will be told so in no uncertain terms.

'The lights went out and the film began. . . . The student had striven so hard for effects that he had defeated his own purpose. When the lights went on again, there was a long, tense moment of absolute silence. Although the room was full of students, no one made a sound. At last Eisenstein spoke. He asked the young man, quite kindly, what he had tried to convey. The answer was given very hesitatingly; the student attempted to defend his brain child. After he had finished, there was a veritable storm of discussion among the other students. . . . They were certainly blunt and to the point. Then Eisenstein asked us all to go into one of the big class rooms; he wanted to speak in detail about the film we had just seen. As we passed into the other room, I asked him if he was going to annihilate the poor young man.

'Yes, it is necessary,' he replied.

'. . . I could tell by the quiet way in which he questioned the student that he was trying to get at what was in the boy's mind when he made the picture. The young director got up and defended his film in a long and impassioned speech, to which Eisenstein retorted:

'Please do not defend your work merely because you are the author of it. You must have a better reason than that.'[2]

Eisenstein regarded his programme of training as a laboratory and, as he once said, his students were like guinea pigs to prove or disprove his theories as to the synthesis of art and science. In order that nothing should be lost, two stenographers took down all that he and the students said. The report was then transcribed. One copy was kept in the library for reference, another was given to Eisenstein so that he could utilize

[1] From the diary of Gwen Seiler kept during her visit to the U.S.S.R. in 1936.
[2] *Ibid.*

it in the future for writing the series of books which he planned. In December of 1934, one stack of these reports alone stood three feet high.

To watch Sergei Mikhailovich working with his students upon various sections of his tremendous training programme was to witness the breadth and majesty of his genius. It was more impressive because he thought of his students first and not of his self-aggrandizement. He seldom invited people to come and see what he 'was doing. [Plate 34]

It seemed that since Eisenstein had been assigned a new flat the criticisms of the film industry could not be very serious. Though his real desire was to work on the numerous books he planned and to teach at the Institute, his thoughts turned again to *Black Majesty*. He re-read his books on Toussaint L'Ouverture. But this film could not be produced without Paul Robeson, who was completing a film in London and would soon be free. I suggested going to London to establish a contact between Sergei Mikhailovich and Robeson. This idea pleased Eisenstein.

There was another matter which he wanted arranged. This was the publication of an 'Open Letter to Joseph Goebbels'. Seldom expressing violent emotions, Sergei Mikhailovich burned with indignation because Germany's Propaganda Minister had dared to hold him up as an example of a truthful artist to the Nazi film industry, declaring that *Potemkin* was a film for Hitler's German directors to use as a model for their own films.

In this letter, published in *Film Art*, the *Pariser Tageblatt* and in Moscow, Eisenstein, who had never written on anything but art and cinematography, declared:

What a work of art a truthful film of the Germany of to-day could be! But truth and National Socialism cannot be reconciled. He who is for truth cannot line up with National Socialism. He who is for truth is against you!

How do you dare, anyway, to talk about life any place? You, who are bringing death and banishment to everything living and everything good in your country with the executioner's axe and the machine gun! You, who are executing the best sons of the German proletariat and are scattering to the four corners of the earth all those constituting the pride of real German science and of the cultured people of the whole world!

How do you dare to ask your film artists to give truthful pictures of life without enjoining them, first of all, to trumpet forth to the world the torments of the thousands who are being tortured to death in the catacombs of your prisons and in the basements of your jails?

Where do you find brazenness enough to talk about the truth at all after you have erected such a Babylonian tower of infamies and lies in Leipzig?

And Sergei Mikhailovich was to write further and more passionate denunciations of National Socialism in 1938, following the completion of his film *Alexander Nevsky.*

Apart from his concern over the rise of Nazism in Germany, Eisenstein was happy and optimistic in November of 1934. He had ceased to speak of his sense of 'doom'. The thought of a flat of his own and the belief that his loneliness had ended filled him with a sense of security such as he had never known before. He was overjoyed when Paul Robeson decided to come to Moscow in the middle of December in order to discuss the film *Black Majesty.* From the moment he met Paul Robeson, Eisenstein found one more person with whom he felt at ease.

On the first evening when Robeson and his wife, Eslanda, came to supper at Chysti Prudi, Sergei Mikhailovich went to endless trouble to make his room homely. He transformed the room by lighting it with candles in antique holders and borrowing comfortable chairs and a white linen tablecloth. At last a long-secreted elegance of taste emerged in the setting he created for the good food and wine. He, too, was transformed. He wore a plain, dark suit which he had just bought. And after dinner when we went to Meyerhold's theatre to see Gogol's *Government Inspector,* Sergei Mikhailovich forgot to assume the harsh mannerisms he had usually adopted in public.

That evening he sat up half the night with Robeson discussing the evolution of languages. Then they turned to music as the expression of comparative cultural development and played the African and Chinese records which Paul Robeson had brought as a present for Eisenstein.

The first evening set the tenor for the next fourteen days of Robeson's visit to Moscow, when Sergei Mikhailovich became more sociable than at almost any period of his life. A round of parties began on Christmas Eve when Ivy Litvinov, who taught Basic English to Eisenstein's students, asked him to bring the Robesons and Albert Coates, the British conductor, to a family dinner at the Litvinovs' country house. Not until we arrived was it clear that the Commissar of Foreign Affairs regarded Eisenstein as an intimate friend.

From then on Sergei Mikhailovich went gaily to parties and receptions; he instigated special film showings and began to issue invitations to his old friends. Many evenings began with supper at Chysti Prudi. Eduard Tisse, whom I had never met, was included in the intimate circle. He also asked his friend, Professor Luriya, of the Medico-Biological Institute, to come and meet the Robesons. It was on this evening that Eisenstein first heard of the man with the phenomenal visual memory, of whom he later wrote in his analysis of colour and meaning.[1] Being in an expansive mood, Sergei Mikhailovich began to tell Jay Leyda, who was also present, about the inner significance of some of the compositions he had created for *Que Viva Mexico!*

Though Sergei Mikhailovich never discussed Paul Robeson as a Negro, he knew what it meant to any man's inner feelings to be a Negro in America. He admired Robeson as a member of the Negro race, but he appreciated him most because he instantly discovered that he was like himself a raceless and classless member of that section of humanity who looked forward to a society based on equal opportunity for all. Eisenstein, who accepted in the simplest way that he himself possessed genius, dearly loved the unique quality of Paul Robeson (and, later, Mei Lan Fang, the Chinese actor). To see honour done to his peers was a joy to him; for he was free from the taint of envy, save in the longing he had once felt to be possessed of Grigori Alexandrov's physical attraction. When a man he admired was honoured, Eisenstein stood by with an expression closely akin to that of love on his face.

[Plate 34]

On the 26th of December, Totya Pasha cooked a turkey to celebrate Christmas and the Robesons' visit. Tisse came, but Pera said she must stay with her mother and sister. Late in the evening, Eisenstein took us to Dom Kino—the House of the Cinema Workers—where he had arranged a party with all the accoutrements of a banquet in honour of the Robesons. He wanted his fellow workers to meet them.

The cinema workers took Paul Robeson to their heart when he sang—unaccompanied—two songs from Mussorgsky's *Boris Godunov*. When he finished the people rose and, surging around him, grasped his hands and kissed him. Through all this tumult, Sergei Mikhailovich sat perfectly still, smiling. Tisse told me he had never seen Eisenstein so happy.

On New Year's Eve, there was another party at the Dom Kino. Again Eisenstein appeared as the evening's host and for a moment it seemed as if he were once more the most important figure in the Soviet film industry. The atmosphere of friendship and affection had transformed him into a delightful man whose grace lent him a kind of freshness and a subtle dignity. He was sufficiently attentive to everybody for them to feel they had been paid a compliment by the host.

During the evening, a small incident occurred which revealed the human perception with which Sergei Mikhailovich was endowed.

Sitting at the end of the main table was a young American violinist, Helen Airoff, whom Eisenstein had met at lunch with Albert Coates.

[1] S. M. Eisenstein, *The Film Sense* (London, Faber and Faber, 1948), p. 118.

Sergei Mikhailovich watched her with the particular expression which came over his face whenever he wanted to know something deep and personal about anyone—a looking through the flesh and into the mind. Turning to me, he said: 'Don't you see something very unpleasant has happened to her? She's trying to hide it, but New Year's Eve makes it harder.'

He got up and going to the end of the table he asked her to dance—a thing he had been too self-conscious to do after his return from America until a few days before. He returned; then we went to dance and Eisenstein explained how Albert Coates, who had brought Helen Airoff to Moscow as his violinist, had gone to London leaving her to travel alone to Soviet Asia to give some concerts. She was distressed and wanted to leave. We sat down and presently Eisenstein drifted off and made arrangements with someone to take Helen Airoff to the Metropole Hotel.

When the Robesons left Moscow early in January 1935, Paul told Sergei Mikhailovich he would let him know as soon as possible when he would be free to return to Moscow and make the film *Black Majesty*. The matter appeared certain except for the date.

In January 1935, the Soviet film industry celebrated the fifteenth anniversary of its founding in 1920. In connection with the celebration a five-day conference was called to discuss the creative and political problems of the Soviet cinema.

The simmering criticism of Sergei Eisenstein was coming to a head. He was appointed chairman of the conference and was told he must explain his future plans. Shortly before the conference he had written an article for *Izvestia*. In this article commemorating the Fifteenth Anniversary, Sergei Mikhailovich divided the history of the Soviet cinema into three periods and analysed the characteristics of each period and its contribution to the development of cinematography. The article called forth fresh criticism on the grounds that Eisenstein's division was too schematic and that he had over-estimated the contributions of the period 1924-9 when *Potemkin, October* and *Old and New* were made.

For the few days before the conference, Sergei Mikhailovich was contented and undisturbed. He was, perhaps, too hopeful and happy to be deeply concerned about the mounting criticism for not having produced a film since returning from Mexico. There was now *Black Majesty*. But even so, he admitted that his heart was dedicated to his larger purpose of synthesis. The production of any film, no matter how creatively exciting for the moment, would impede the more important task he must perform in order to fulfil his greatest service to the future. The compelling need to teach and write his ideas ate away inside him. The longest life would not complete his work.

As Eisenstein called the conference to order on the 8th of January 1935, he looked as if no power on earth could disturb him, or deflect him a fraction from his own purpose. The legendary Eisenstein of the wild shock of hair, who had once ordered his photograph to be taken as he lolled on the throne of defunct Tsarism, had become at thirty-seven a man of ageless dignity whose magnificent head no longer appeared in the least out of keeping on his body, short as it was. Of late he had kept his hair cut to a reasonable length and had abandoned his exaggerated clothes so that he looked more of a scientist than an artist. [Pl. 52, p. 327.]

The conference opened with a four-hour speech by Dinamov, the representative of the Central Committee of the Communist Party. He spoke of the creative problems of the Soviet cinema; his two main theses were: first, that the time had come for Soviet artists to give new consideration to the matter of beauty in art; second, that the time had come for the development of characters rich in emotions, whose feelings and actions would reflect human behaviour in a changing epoch. With a marked degree of artistic appreciation, Dinamov analysed a number of recent films and the styles developed by Soviet directors since the organization of the Soviet film industry in 1920.

Dinamov made many references to Eisenstein's work. His chief criticism was directed at Eisenstein's theory of the intellectual film. 'The incorrectness of Eisenstein's theory consists in the fact that he separates thought from feeling. Such people do not exist. People who only think remind me of creatures with an exaggerated colossal head, but without arms, legs or a heart.' The current Soviet cinema must be the cinema of actors and not of 'typage', which had come in as a method as a result of Eisenstein's films. 'In *October*,' said Dinamov, 'there was only a crowd.' The film without characters was only an experiment. 'Characters disappeared in the cinema because the directors did not know the people and they thought the film must be based upon the Mass.' Finally, Dinamov characterized Sergei Eisenstein 'as an intellectual artist who mainly takes ideas' which could stop the world. But the Soviet cinema of 1935 required rich emotions and the beauty of real life.[1]

Boris Shumyatsky, head of the film industry, did not speak. The second speaker was Eisenstein, who had sat at the chairman's desk throughout Dinamov's speech with an expression of impersonal interest on his face. Some two hundred of his fellow workers were facing

[1] The account given here of the All-Union Creative Conference of Workers in Soviet Cinematography, Moscow, 8–13 January, is based upon notes taken by the author and the report of speeches and general discussion published under the title: 'Za Bolshoye Kinoiskusstvo' (Moscow, 1935).

him. There was a nerve that occasionally throbbed in his cheek when he was moved or excited. It did not throb.

As Sergei Mikhailovich rose, he knew why he was the second speaker and what was expected of him. Though he controlled any outward sign of confusion, nervousness or doggedness, he was the prey of all these feelings. But he had the ability to relax his hands and shoulders, even under the greatest strain, so that he looked comfortable soon after he began to speak. He had trained himself to speak in a controlled and modulated voice, even when he was filled with the deepest emotion. Now faced by his fellow workers and aware of what the Soviet authorities thought of him, Eisenstein did not honestly know what to say about his work. He could not say that Boris Shumyatsky had discarded his suggestions and that each rejection had made it more difficult for him to understand what kind of creative work was expected of him. It was beyond his power to stand up before a number of people and explain that for six years every creative idea he had developed had been shattered and all he now wanted was to be left alone to work on his synthesis of the arts.

He was in a position to announce that Paul Robeson had promised to let him know when he would be able to come to Moscow and make the film *Black Majesty*. Such a statement would probably have ended the criticism of Eisenstein for his lack of creative plans. But of this he could not bring himself to speak. He had announced too many pictures which he had been unable to make. If Paul Robeson failed him . . . He was unnerved, not just for a few moments or on the surface, but deep down inside himself. He felt he had only one thing to hold to: the great body of knowledge he had accumulated.

Eisenstein began:

It is very risky to receive applause at the beginning of one's speech as one never knows what will happen at the end of it. My intention was to take up with you rather briefly a few important matters. But the preliminary conference and the speech of Sergei Sergeyevich [Dinamov] has made it imperative for me to discuss with you a great number of problems, some of which I thought had passed into eternity long ago. . . . I hope that as a result of this it will be possible to put an end to some of these problems; on the other hand, it is quite possible that they will still persist. (Interrupter: 'I insist that it is recorded in the report that Eisenstein has a smile on his face.') No such remarks, please, it is simply dishonest. A whole lot of questions have been raised here about my attitude towards our cinematographic heritage. . . .

. . . It seems to me that in my last article in *Izvestia* I stated quite definitely my position on cinematography as a whole. There was no intention to minimize or to underestimate any of the periods. . . . It also should be noted that *Izvestia* cut a great deal of my article due to the shortage of space, and it seems to me if they had not done this, my ideas would have been much more fully developed and there would be less possibility of any misconstruction of my divisions. My point of view expressed there is that the change in the style and the general structure which our cinematography has followed in the process of its development, was specifically complex and reflected that revolutionary development which characterized the development of history itself.

Our cinematography begins with the protagonist represented by the movement of the hero-mass. Then at the conclusion of this fifteen-year period this style of a hero-mass gives way to the types of individual figures. A whole series of Bolshevik personalities and characters make their appearance . . . in the business of building socialism. . . .

. . . I blue-printed a three-cornered scheme which I must say has provoked a great deal of challenge, gossip, hurt, irritation, etc. I do not claim that my scheme is exhaustive; like all plans it is relative and schematic. . . .

You know that in a relative way I divide our cinematography into three separate stages of development. The third or fourth stage is that synthetic stage which began recently and which has already shown definite achievements in the films *Chapayev* [directed by S. and G. Vasiliev] and *Counterplan* [directed by Frederick Ermler].

Then Eisenstein discussed at great length the period 1924 to 1929—the period of his own films *Strike, Potemkin, October* and *Old and New*; Pudovkin's *Mother, The End of St Petersburg* and *Storm Over Asia*; and Dovzhenko's *Arsenal* and *Earth*. This period was characterized by attempts at typage and montage. Throughout these years artists sought 'to take the facts and the people and show them as they really and actually were with the minimum of reorganization and adaptation'. He analysed the theories evolved by the documentary group, 'Kino-Eye', Lev Kuleshov, Pudovkin and his own methods of applying 'typage'. He discussed the various styles of montage, including his own. As the individual tendencies developed, he had arrived at the theory of the much-disputed 'intellectual film'.

What was this intellectual film about which I am forced to speak here because it is spoken of as a sort of norm which contains within itself a certain actuality and seduces a great number of men to apply it? In the first place it is imperative that we cleanse this notion from

the inside out. The nub of the matter is that under the vulgar definition of an intellectual film there was an attempt to bring any kind of
film which was suffering from complete absence of emotionalism.
When some kind of fantastic film was presented it was called an intellectual film. . . .

When we spoke about an intellectual film, we thought primarily
of the kind of a structure which would direct the thinking of the
spectator and would lead to emotional understanding. If you remember my article 'Perspectives' then you can see that this emotionaliza-
tion of thought was becoming one of the fundamental problems. To
accuse me of tearing the emotional from the intellectual is without
any foundation! Quite the contrary! I wrote: 'Dualism in the sphere
of "feelings" and "rationale" must be completely overcome by this
new form of art. It is necessary to give back to the intellectual process its fire and passion, to dunk the abstract thinking process into
the boiling material of reality.'

Then Sergei Mikhailovich explained how in a period of revolution
artists engaged in all kinds of experiments with form in order to portray the life around them.

Let us say there are opinions such as Anisimov's [App. Four] in
which he explains the tendencies of my work as a result of my
belonging to the technical intelligentsia. But I do not think that these
explanations are very weighty and convincing. When I tried to
understand what we really saw and imagined in the world around us,
it remained for me to examine honestly the feelings within myself
which dictated the form through which I attempted to express the
content of the times. . . . The majority of the people (I speak auto-
biographically but yet widen the question beyond my personal biography) came to cinematography after having served in the Civil
War in a technical, not a leading capacity. We were like 'fellow
travellers' in literature. With the end of the Civil War we saw for
the first time the great sweep of history in which we had participated, but we were not conscious of the fact that our experience had
left a certain stamp upon our attitude to the material of reality. This
is the socio-psychological explanation as to why we 'typaged', . . .
and accepted the events and people of our revolutionary reality
without wishing to reconstruct them. . . .

He asked his fellow workers to remember how they had felt. Some
of them had been in the same position as himself. But, as the country
developed politically, their 'sideline' approach had been broken up.
More politically conscious people had entered the film industry and

then there grew up a more critical appraisal of all work. This brought about 'an entirely new sense and a new thirst to dig into the reality' of life. Now the epic form of film began to give way to the dramatic form. It was at the very beginning of this change that Eisenstein had gone abroad in the summer of 1929. 'Here my position becomes rather difficult.'

I have done not a little serious creative work, creative work which to my regret no one has ever seen and for which you will have to accept my word.

When I began to think after *General Line* [*Old and New*] about further lines for my future productions, I took a stand on the matter of characters. I had introduced into *General Line* Marfa Lapkina who was in embryo a 'hero' for my future work. This coincided with my going abroad. . . .

In a few words he mentioned *Sutter's Gold* and *Black Majesty*—which 'developed in a rather Shakespearean and tragic' manner. He did not say, however, that now he hoped to make this film. All he said was that a 'part was intended for a remarkable Negro artist, Paul Robeson, whom we greeted as our guest recently'. He passed immediately to the third important scenario 'which was almost completed and ready for execution—Dreiser's *American Tragedy* in which the whole problem converged so as to represent a very complex growth of human character'. Of *Que Viva Mexico!* Sergei Mikhailovich said not one word. He talked instead about how he had introduced Yutkevich's film—*Golden Mountains*—to New York just before his return to the Soviet Union.

He groped his way on and on through the maze of his own and other people's theories. It was painfully evident that only a small proportion of his fellow artists were following his thoughts. He compared *Mother* to Ermler's new film *Counterplan*: 'We know the service of *Counterplan* is great—that it shows the new type of man we wanted to underscore. But we also know that formalistically it leaves a great deal to be desired.' He went back almost begging his listeners to remember how passionately they had made films in the first 'typage-montage' period. The '100 per cent' aim had been reached again in *Chapayev*. He thought this film commenced the new Synthetic Period,

which absorbs within itself all the culture and results of the creative work accomplished in the periods preceding it. . . .

I think that a great many of the elements which characterized the first period (1924–9) will enter into the new quality at which we are aiming.

In this connection I wish to point out certain problems which face me in relation to the materials on which I am now working. However, I want it understood that the material which I'm now going to speak about should not be discussed at this time. Let us get together on that point first: it is only going to be some of the ideas about which I'm thinking at present—ideas which are not yet fully formed and which are as yet quite disputable, but which still represent material for my study and work. On this particular matter, I do not intend to accept your attack until this material is supported by full documentation. Until that time I will tell you about my thoughts as if 'on credit'.

It is interesting to look into what can be done further with the considerations which were expressed in our discussion of the intellectual cinema. Should they be thrown out completely or have they certain possibilities of developing into a new quality and, thus, begin to play a further positive role.

To start with I would like to say the following: it is very interesting that certain theories and points of view which in a given historical epoch represent the expression of scientific and theoretical learning, in a later epoch decline as science, but continue to exist as a possible means not along lines of science but along lines of art and imagery. . . .

Then Eisenstein plunged into the subjects with which he was really concerned—anthropology, the origin of language, the 'internal monologue', etc. In a study of these subjects the artist could find the 'laws governing the construction of the form and composition of art-works'. He declared that the cinema worker could make use of mythological figures in order to understand the phenomena of imagery. He passed to an analysis of the forerunners of the detective novel and the influence of James Fenimore Cooper on such writers as Balzac, Zola and Eugène Sue, who transplanted the metaphor of 'the dark forest' and 'the pathfinder' to stories of intrigue and detection laid in Paris. This led him to the evolution of the 'internal monologue'. 'We know that at the basis of creation of form lie sensual and imagist thought processes.'

He went on to explain how years ago, when a man was given the tooth of a bear, he thought he had possession of the bear's strength. And, in his opinion, this early mode of thought had passed into creative work. He himself had symbolized the whole personality of the surgeon in *Potemkin* in the swinging to and fro of his glasses. Then there was the Polynesian custom of throwing open the windows and doors to aid the birth of a child: 'everything must be opened, untied, to give maximum ease to the appearance in the world of the new child'. He spoke on and on, explaining how the film worker could find sources of creative knowledge in research materials and an accumulation of general knowledge. At last he turned back to the Anniversary and said: 'I consider that we are now on the threshold of the most remarkable period of classicism in our cinematography.'

Sergei Mikhailovich could not help himself. He had chosen his course even though it was the most impractical one he could have selected. He had the courage to stand by his ideas. Like a wise fool, he concluded with the perfectly true, but for the occasion utterly inconclusive, statement: 'My art is dedicated to no particular tendency but to the analysis of certain phenomena and ways of thinking.'[1]

Soon it was clear to Eisenstein that he had given those who honestly disagreed with him, as well as those who disliked him, an opportunity to humble him.

At every conference on the arts in the Soviet Union, the styles of individuals were appraised in terms of current trends and all problems discussed. Thus, each aspect of Dinamov's speech was analysed by the speakers, and the films of Pudovkin, Dovzhenko, Frederick Ermler, Lev Kuleshov, Grigori Alexandrov, and other directors, were criticized almost as severely as those of Eisenstein. But Eisenstein drew forth personal criticism because many of his fellow workers suspected him of setting his interests apart from the general line of Soviet cinema.

The first person to speak after Eisenstein was Leonid Trauberg. Interspersed in his analysis of the current creative problems, were comments on Eisenstein: 'If we take *Potemkin* out of its period and analyse it from the point of view of to-day, then undoubtedly a great number of critics could be found who will mercilessly criticize the film. But if we leave it within the limits of that period then we must say that for that period it was great and brilliant. . . . However, to-day it is necessary to destroy some of the legends which were created around the period which has passed.'

Alexander Dovzhenko spoke on the second day of the conference and brought the whole question of Eisenstein into focus. 'Now about Eisenstein: All who speak about him usually begin with trepidation and excitement. . . . We all know the role of Eisenstein in cinematography. . . . However, I was rather disturbed by his report yesterday: On the one hand, Eisenstein revealed himself as a deeply principled master and thinker . . . on the other hand, Eisenstein has failed to tell us what he intends to do. He no longer occupies the position in cinematography which he could. Standing here by his side, loving him with loyalty, I

---

[1] The second part of Eisenstein's speech, with introductory paragraphs, was published as 'Film Form, 1935—New Problems' (*Life and Letters To-day*, September–December, 1935); and in *Film Form* (New York, Harcourt, Brace and London, Dennis Dobson, 1950) pp. 122 *et seq.*

will tell you and him my view of his work. I do not want Eisenstein to tell tales about Polynesian females. All this is too far away from us. . . .

'I think that for Eisenstein it would be better to look into the living females surrounding us. They are closer to us and they are much more important. They are giving birth too and in a sort of modern way. I hope you will understand the metaphor as intended.

'When I heard the report of Eisenstein I was afraid that he knows so much, and his head is so "clear" that it looks as if he'll never make another film. If I knew as much as he does I would literally die. [Laughter and applause.] I'm sorry you're laughing. I'm afraid and I hope that Eisenstein will not chew up his own tail. I'm also afraid that his laboratory may explode from an overwhelming confusion of complicated, mysterious, and enigmatic material.

'I'm convinced that in more ways than one his erudition is killing him, no! excuse me, I did not mean that word; I wanted to say is disorganizing him. . . .

'Sergei Mikhailovich [turns to him]: If you do not produce a film at least within a year, then please do not produce one at all. It won't be needed by us and it won't be needed by you. . . . With your films you must unravel the disputed knots around your person. You must unravel the entire Freudian complex. It is necessary to put an end to it all. . . .

'I have done everything possible to soft-pedal what I wanted to say so that Sergei Mikhailovich would not feel too badly. But it is imperative for him to feel that there is a tremendous job ahead for him. [Turns to Eisenstein]: For me your production, Sergei Mikhailovich, is a thousand times dearer than all your theories. All this talk about the Polynesian females, all your unfinished scenarios I will gladly exchange for one of your films.'

Sergei Mikhailovich listened quietly. Dovzhenko might have been speaking about someone else. He knew that Dovzhenko had been criticized for the remote quality of his own film *Ivan*, which had been considered as an unsatisfactory portrayal of the building of the Dnieperstroi Dam.

The young director Yutkevich said: 'In conclusion—about Eisenstein. . . . Eisenstein is a genius and a master, but quite frequently he is a mistaken theoretician. . . . Without judging the interesting matters about which Sergei Mikhailovich spoke, I will direct my remarks to a certain circumstance. Eisenstein spoke with unusual pathos but he disturbed me because the thinking of this remarkable artist is going on only in regards to the inner processes of art and he is not coming out of the limits determined by the frame. . . .

'If George Sand had known Eisenstein she would have addressed to him, and not to Flaubert, the lines noted in January 1876: "One must not despise any of the powers of the human brain directed towards a search for truth." I speak because [turns to Eisenstein] you have many decisions to make but you talk only in extreme language. In reality you read and study, you labour more than I and more than most of us. You have received a better education than I will ever have; you are a hundred times richer than any of us; you are a millionaire and you are complaining like a pauper. Please help the poor one with alms! Your mattress is stuffed with gold and yet you want to live off nothing but beautiful phrases and deftly chosen words. But you, fool, why don't you dig into your mattress and eat your gold. Feed on ideas and feelings found in your head and in your heart; words and phrases, form with which you pride yourself so much will disappear as a result of your digestion. Investigation is your aim, but it should be only a by-product. A happy sincerity develops only out of emotions and emotions develop only out of convictions. Unless you feel a thing very passionately you cannot be aroused by it.'

Still Eisenstein appeared as enigmatic as a sphinx; his eyes almost invisible beneath the massive ridge of his brow. Only the flush under his eyes betrayed the intensity of his anger and nervousness.

After a long speech concerning his own place in the Soviet cinema, and the new problems confronting it, Vsevolod Pudovkin raised the question of Eisenstein's speech. 'It was complex, like a galaxy I would say. Galaxy—it is the system which is star-like, fascinating, greater than our solar system (Laughter). His report is rather foggy, unclear. . . . The gist of his communication was something like this: the road of our perception of the world through the arts like all manifestations of reality—is dual. On the one hand, there is this complex imagery in his thinking, on the other, a determination which is intellectual, analysing, atomizing. These are the two things, only the unity of these two can give fullness to perception. This type of thinking, this complex imagery, is found in a particularly intense form only among people who are still at the dawn of culture. Keep in mind his Polynesians. Eisenstein finds within himself the sharpness of intellectual attainment, and says that if he unites the sharp edge of his intellect in the order of polarity with the total imagery created by mankind, he can construct scenes of tremendous tension in his art.

'Comrades, as you know, in the tremendous works of art created by Goethe, scientific thought was united with myth and fable. Eisenstein approximates Goethe in a somewhat foggy form. . . .'

Pudovkin's speech came in a torrent of words punctuated with many gestures. At one point, Eisenstein caught my eye and from his expres-

sion I wondered if he too was thinking about the argument in Yalta—
'that the Greeks had never existed'.

The main speeches ended with that of Sergei Vasiliev, one of the
directors of *Chapayev*, who said to Eisenstein: 'You have always been
our teacher, Sergei Mikhailovich, and I speak as your pupil. I want you
to understand that the theoretical and scientific matters in which you
are immersed in your study where you sit wrapped in your remarkable
robe covered with Chinese hieroglyphics, and surrounded by a great
many books, wonderful statuettes and many other beautiful things, is
not everything, because it keeps you from participating. Until you
make up your mind to enter into the thick of our reality and to feel
that which is being felt by the entire Soviet people you won't be able
to create anything truly significant. You have created *Potemkin*. You
possess an unusual revolutionary passion and a burning feeling, but
something has happened to you. I do not care to enter into the causes,
but I do want you to discard your Chinese robe and participate in our
Soviet reality of to-day.'

When the conference was thrown open for general discussion on the
third day, Lev Kuleshov, the veteran of Soviet cinema, whose recent
work had met with serious criticism, made only one remark concerning Eisenstein: 'And about Sergei Mikhailovich—you have talked
about him here with very warm, touching, tearful smiles as if he were
a corpse which you are burying ahead of time. I must say to him, to
one who is very much alive, and to one whom I love and greatly value:
My dear and beloved Sergei Mikhailovich! Yutkevich said that one
can burst from too much knowledge, and he was afraid that would
happen to you.[1] Dear Sergei Mikhailovich no one ever bursts from too
much knowledge but from too much envy. That is all I have to say.'

The discussion continued. Yukov said: 'Undoubtedly Eisenstein has
helped us, and himself, to examine his own mistaken notions, but in
his self-criticism Sergei Mikhailovich did not go far enough to enable
him to formulate a positive platform on the basis of his own self-
criticism. . . .

'How can we understand this position of Comrade Eisenstein unless
it is an attempt to justify the whole set of theoretical principles in our
cinematography over which there have been disputes. . . . Such posing
of the question proves that everything in life is repeated outside of the
class struggle and outside of the dialectic view of scientific thesis. . . .

'His inability to take account of the fundamental tendency [of
socialist realism] leads Sergei Mikhailovich to the last incorrect conviction—that we are entering into a period of so-called classicism. I'm
not going to discuss this notion of classicism. . . . I consider his in-

[1] This remark was made by Dovzhenko not Yutkevich.

sistence upon such a view as quite dangerous and incorrect, because he undermines our conception and understanding of socialist realism.'

Then Lebedev, the head of the Institute of Scientific Cinematographic Research, who had had the opportunity to watch Eisenstein at work as a teacher and in the theoretical field, said: 'Eisenstein is a typical scholar, a great theoretician, a chemist—even an alchemist. . . . In his attempt to create the logarithmic tables of art there is something akin to alchemy. . . . Eisenstein has absorbed the theories of Freud, Marinetti [the Futurist], Pavlov, the physiologist, Bogdanov of the Proletcult and many bourgeois psychologists and philologists. Only in the past few years after his return from abroad did he begin to study Marxism. So it is only now that we can speak of him as a theoretician who has mastered the methods of Marxism.

'Eisenstein frequently compares his work to the work of Marr. Just as Marr seeks the roots of the development of the spoken language, Eisenstein seeks the roots and forms of the development of a cinematographic language. . . . If you examine his entire creative activity, you will be surprised to see that, with the exception of *Potemkin* which stands by itself, each and every one of his works is only an experiment serving as a foundation for one or another of his theories. . . .

'[But] his material is taken from the Revolution. He is always defending revolutionary ideas and his films always remain within the framework of a Soviet theme. No one can accuse him of resorting to classicism, or pure literature or the problems of the West. His themes served only as the material for the investigation of a scholar to whom the basic end was a search for a common denominator in the language of film form. Well, is it not a respectable problem to be preoccupied with film language and to experiment in this field in order to create a new theory and to test it in his own film production? . . . Just because Marr is a great academician and a master of language it does not necessarily mean that he can write poetry. It would be better for us to be patient and wait until Sergei Mikhailovich finds the kind of subject which will completely absorb him.

'I feel that it would be well to furnish Eisenstein with an empty studio and let him experiment to control his theories.' And, warned Lebedev, 'you can't force him to make a picture. Eisenstein's work in any case is not a trifle; from an historical point of view it is very important for the students of cinematography.'

Sergei Mikhailovich maintained an external calm throughout the three days of speeches and discussion. To his colleagues he presented the façade of an unfeeling man motivated by a monstrous stubbornness. But the strain he felt showed in his voice, which lost its lilt, and in his eyes, which seemed to fade from a clear blue to a stormy grey.

Before each session, and during recesses, Eisenstein would come to me and say that he was all right; and he asked me repeatedly not to interpret what was being said about him in terms of a personal attack. He knew that most of his fellow workers had little or no sympathy for him personally, but he could not understand why they did not realize the importance of his study. He felt that he had presented his case very badly and this bewildered him even more.

But he did not seek comfort, not even reassurance; instead it was he who reassured me. He was much concerned about my feelings and his personal conduct towards me was never at any time more considerate. I do not think he realized the full seriousness of what was happening, nor did I. Each of us tried to minimize it. We tried to push the implications of the conference away.

On the second and third day, Eisenstein asked me to sit where we could see each other without moving. Only once did he confess he must get away before further demands were made upon him. It was at the close of the open discussion on the third day. He asked me to go with him to look at something which would help him.

Some months before, Sergei Mikhailovich had discovered a monograph of da Vinci's studies of human proportion in the foreign currency store, Torgsin, in the National Hotel. He had made many visits to the shop and pored over it. But he could not buy it because he had no foreign money or gold objects to trade for it. Now we went to see his treasure. He stood looking at it for a long time before he picked it up and handled it with love, pointing out to me the fine lines of each drawing. In one, Leonardo had compared the child in the womb with the hazel nut imbedded in its sheath.

'I know that some day I will come to look at it and it will be gone,' he said.

Eisenstein had never borrowed foreign money, yet now he felt so great a need to possess this work that he asked me to lend him enough foreign currency to buy it on the condition that he would later pay back the debt from the proceeds of an article.

As we carried away the monograph with the figure of the perfectly proportioned man upon the cover, Sergei Mikhailovich said that at last he could look at it all he wanted and learn from it how Leonardo carried on his ceaseless work in the face of great obstacles. To possess anything from the hand and mind of da Vinci set Eisenstein an example of how a man could remain steadfast to his ultimate purpose.

Arriving at Chysti Prudi, Sergei Mikhailovich explained how he had discovered the earliest recorded memory of Leonardo visually concealed within the picture of St. Anne and the Virgin. 'It seemed to me, while I lay in the cradle, as though a kite had come down to me, opened my mouth with his tail, and struck me several times between my lips.' He took his copy of Freud's study of da Vinci and, opening the book at the reproduction of this picture, traced with a pencil the outline of what appeared to be the form of a bird whose tail touched the lips of the child Jesus.[1]

In the evening Totya Pasha brought us supper and we talked for a long time without, however, mentioning the conference. On Eisenstein's suggestion I had made arrangements to leave Moscow the following evening—the 11th of January. He had said earlier that everything interesting would be over by the 11th and for this reason I had not had my visa, which would expire on the 12th, renewed. He did not want me to return to Moscow until the flat at Potylika was completed and we could resume the life we had lived in the Crimea.

This arrangement had taken on a significance it had not had when we first discussed the idea of my having a room in the Potylika flat. While I was in London at the end of November and early in December 1935, our tranquil friendship had changed to an emotional attachment of a much greater intensity. Yet even now we were not lovers. But we hoped that in the atmosphere of new surroundings, the curiously effortless attachment which had grown up between us would develop into a complete relationship. Realizing that it would be a misfortune if Sergei Mikhailovich again suffered frustration because of the memories associated with his life at Chysti Prudi 23, I too thought it would be easier for us if I returned to London until his new flat was ready.

Early the next morning, Sergei Mikhailovich came to the National Hotel where I was staying. We took my luggage to Chysti Prudi so that I could leave directly from there for the station in the evening. No sound came from the boulevard where the deep snow dimmed all noise of traffic; the flat was perfectly silent since the neighbours were away at work.

The impression of our being completely alone was so startling that I suddenly saw what the preceding days had done to Sergei Mikhailovich. He looked so exhausted that his natural sturdiness seemed to have been used up. He appeared fragile, hurt. The realization that I was going to leave him was unbearable.

'I don't want to leave to-night,' I said.

'It won't be for long. This will all be over when you return,' he answered. 'I can bear it. Please don't insist on staying.'

---

[1] In trying to re-establish the concealed bird-form as Eisenstein traced it out in da Vinci's 'St. Anne and the Virgin', I have not been able to find a complete form, only the suggestion of a tail formed by the draperies covering the Virgin's left arm.

'But what are you going to do?' I asked. 'You must try to explain your position so that people understand it better. . . .'

'Marushka! I've never been anything but happy with you. Let us be happy for to-day. Don't force me to talk about the conference! I can't explain it, but when we're together I feel what I was always trying to do in art—to unite content and form. I don't know if I ever succeeded but when we are here—with no sound coming from outside—I feel everything is as it should be. Please forget that you're going to leave to-night and that some people regard my work as something only to be condemned. Let us believe there is no limit to the time we have.'

I could not resist. So we talked, we laughed and soon our mutual delight in being together caused everything else to sink into insignificance.

Suddenly the telephone rang in the next room and it continued ringing until Eisenstein answered it. When he hung up he said he had to go out immediately, but hoped he would not be gone too long. He picked up a manuscript from his cluttered table.

'I have to make a speech at the Bolshoi Theatre to-night when awards are made to our workers,' he said. 'I worked on my statement all night—in case I was required to speak.' He hurried out.

Eisenstein must have known for some time about the Bolshoi Theatre ceremony, but he had kept silent, though with me he had ceased to conceal things which affected him. Such a silence appeared strange when he now admitted he had sat up half the night preparing a statement. Later secretiveness was one of the many faults of which he was to be accused.

When he returned he was in a state of terrible nervousness. All that was clear from his incoherent sentences was that his prepared speech was not acceptable. He must rewrite it, but he felt sure that nothing he said would sound right. He dreaded the necessity of standing up to speak from the stage of the Bolshoi Theatre, where *Potemkin* had first been shown. Only ten years had passed. But now he had only a tenuous grasp of what was expected from him in this new period when Socialist Realism was the dominant idea in art. Everything that seemed real to him appeared as mere formal experiment to others, while what appeared to others as realism seemed to him as static and unnatural work of superficial and ignorant men.

Eisenstein had been in despair on the first day we met; but then he had known the cause of his despair. Now his despair was one of bewilderment. That the work he wanted to do—and was doing with all his heart—was regarded as of no importance, was incomprehensible to him. For some time it seemed he would be unable to force himself to go to the theatre in the evening.

'There's nothing for me to say, other than what I've said before,' he insisted. 'I feel like a dead idol.'

If he failed to appear, his position would become still worse. There were several hours for him to reword his statement. So Sergei Mikhailovich sat down and rephrased his speech. He knew that his way of explaining himself was weak, he did not know how to use facile, politic phrases. Though he did not express it in words, because to do so would have seemed to him disloyal, Sergei Mikhailovich was in terrible conflict. He could not resort to playing the role of an opportunist spinning out phrases which might have been acceptable, but which he himself knew were half-truths of little social or artistic consequence. Having rewritten his statement, he felt much better.

In this most serious moment he tried to still his anxiety by pushing away the impending ceremony. He sought to give the few hours left to us the same quality, only more poignant and personal, than the quality of the days we had spent in Odessa and Yalta. He did not wish me to change my plans and stay: it was not necessary. He wanted to share his ideas, the flat at Potylika, which would be ready when I came again to Moscow; but he must face the crisis concerning his work in his own way.

But after supper, when there was almost no time remaining, panic seized him. For the first time since we met he resorted to the hope that supernatural aid would come to him. He felt it was irrational; he was ashamed that pressure drove him to grasp the hand of what he intellectually condemned as superstition. He took his small Chinese Buddha from a shelf and put it in his pocket. It was his fetish. So long as he had it with him he would feel a power outside himself giving him strength.

'I've taken it with me in every difficulty. I can't go without it, not even if this act makes you think me ridiculous.'

To postpone the moment of leaving, Serozha asked which scarf he ought to wear. Should it be his 'baby' one, which Albert Coates had remarked was 'as long as his films', or his short blue one? Did he look suitably dressed?

At last we left knowing we would not meet again in the room at Chysti Prudi 23. The next time would be in the new flat at Potylika. As we drove to the Bolshoi Theatre, a sense of security held us encircled in contentment which seemed more real than any trouble.

'Wish me good luck,' he said, and he asked me to repeat the words after him.

For the first time he kissed me unreservedly. The ceremony at the Bolshoi Theatre, even our parting seemed unreal.

The car stopped near the theatre, Sergei hesitated. Then he got out and stood looking at me with a very strange expression—as if an aching pain were rising within him. He let go of my fingers slowly and turned away.

As he crossed the street towards the theatre holding his Buddha in his hand, I realized I had let him go in silence for I had no voice to tell him I had never taken his feelings for granted. But when he turned back and waved as though we would see each other in a few. hours, my sense of having omitted something important was submerged by certainty that he knew exactly how I felt. Then the car moved on to the station.

As Sergei Mikhailovich entered the theatre he may have known what was going to happen. In the glittering theatre he heard the decree of the Central Executive Committee of the U.S.S.R. commemorating the fifteenth anniversary of Soviet cinematography.

'For special services in the creation and development of Soviet cinematography', the Order of Lenin was bestowed upon Boris S. Shumyatsky, who headed the list of those receiving the highest order, Vsevolod I. Pudovkin, Alexander P. Dovzhenko, S. and G. Vassiliev, who had directed *Chapayev*, Eisenstein's former assistant, Ilya Trauberg, and others.

The Order of the Red Banner was awarded to fourteen people, including Grigori Alexandrov, Dziga Vertov, and V. F. Pletnyov, who had given Eisenstein his first job in the Proletkult Theatre.

Then came the awards of the third class, the title of People's Artist.

The fourth-class award, that of Honoured Art Worker, was given to sixteen people; among them were Eduard Tisse, Nathan Zharki, Lev Kuleshov, and Sergei M. Eisenstein.

Sergei Mikhailovich went home to Chysti Prudi. He knew that the next morning the Russian public and the world would know that he was considered to have neglected his duties. He had been shamed before all his fellow workers. He must make a film or . . .

Arriving in Leningrad in the morning I tried to telephone Sergei Mikhailovich. I was told he had gone out and it was not known when he would return. Then I saw the list of awards in the papers. I did not know what to do. My visa would expire at midnight and there was no way to get back to Moscow before it expired. It took several days to extend a visa and no one knew me in Leningrad. Again I telephoned to Chysti Prudi, but this time there was no reply. There was no way of reaching Pera. The hours dragged by. When at last there was an answer from Chysti Prudi, it was the same as in the morning.

I left on the night train and returned to England.

But Eisenstein did not deliver the speech he had prepared at the Bolshoi Theatre when honours were awarded. Instead, he delivered it as a part of his concluding speech when, as chairman, it was his duty to close the conference.

In his speech, Eisenstein revealed his character more completely to the world than at any other time. This was the real man, he was a challenge to the consciousness of both those who knew him for what he was, and also those who did not wish to see his true calibre. In this defeat he triumphed over his adversaries. He found the strength amidst his weakness to appraise himself and those who had done everything in their power to humble him.

It is frightening to take upon oneself the formulation of the concluding words for such a unique event as our conference about creative work. . . .

One of the most remarkable characteristics of our conference was that our discussion was held on a very high level and there was complete absence of what Lenin called 'pettiness'. . . . But I must take this opportunity to dispute Comrade Yukov's definition of classicism, the word I used to characterize the epoch in our cinema development beginning at this time. In his speech Comrade Yukov sounded quite 'petty' and it did not sound good when he permitted himself to interpret my definition of classicism as a substitution for the concept of socialist realism. On this score I am going to dispute his statement in full measure. As a matter of fact there was no such substitution. . . .

Then Eisenstein traced the origin of the word 'classicism' and showed its true meaning: that of perfection in the work of 'the first class'. He supported his definition by quoting from a Marxist paper dealing with the word as used by Gallia which had been delivered at the Institute of Philosophy.

Comrades, the highest and first class of to-day's society is the proletarian class. (Applause.) To the highest art of the highest class belongs the right to this term, the term of classical art.

Sergei Mikhailovich pointed out that Dinamov, who had not previously specialized in cinematography, had co-ordinated the problems of film development in his speech in a remarkable manner, but that too many of the professional cinematographers appeared to speak as if the highest achievements in cinema had already been accomplished. Eisenstein said this was a great mistake since the full development of the synthetic art of cinema was far from realized.

I want to speak sharply on this question because this, comrades, constitutes the danger and the error into which our theoretical thinking has already once fallen.

These feelings, seem to be concentrated in the last sentence of the speech of Comrade Yutkevich who quoted from the letter by George Sand as if it had been directed to me. You remember how he ended 'here is what George Sand writes . . . to Eisenstein'. There were these words: 'You're reading, studying, labouring, more than I and more than many others . . .'

and he repeated what Yutkevich had said to him.

Comrade Yutkevich has taken for his assistance George Sand. I began to search for some kind of a maiden to assist me (Laughter) but when I searched I found that what Yutkevich had found might also help me. I searched and searched and finally I found . . . the very phrase quoted by Yutkevich. The matter is that if he in his speech depended upon her then it looks like George Sand depended upon a great number of earlier thoughts which went something like this: As long as you are healthy everything else will be all right. And as also was said, search for the Kingdom of Heaven and everything else will work out right.

I have permitted myself such sharp formulations because in that phrase there sounded what Vladimir Ilych [Lenin] said in his time about the Proletcult line. I myself worked in the Proletcult of that period and at that time there was a point of view: Belong to the working class, be young, and . . . (from audience—'everything else will be all right!').

Eisenstein explained that in the beginning the directors of the Proletcult considered that the spontaneous expression of the young workers who came to them should not be interfered with. But after a while, it seemed to Eisenstein that much of this spontaneous expression was in imitation of the poorest examples of Russia's Tsarist's heritage. Finally he, and others, took a new tack on the basis of Lenin's criticism: that of inspiring the young workers who came to them to aim for 'the most perfect creativity and techniques'.

To escape the possibility of our making the same mistakes, I consider it my duty to remind you of this to-day. The self-same phrase of George Sand is directed against Comrade Yutkevich in yet a different way, and here I'm forced to operate not only with her letters but with the remarks which are found in the writings of her addressee—Flaubert. As a matter of fact, to Flaubert is attributed a remarkable additional comment, that imperfection of form is always an indication of indefiniteness in the grasp of an idea. However, I do not wish to use such polemics against Comrade Yutkevich. As I have said, and he agreed, and we all agreed, the film *Counterplan*

with all its remarkable ideational quality, is not the last word in perfection. Do you agree? (Voices from the audience—'Certainly. Certainly.')

I'm not going to draw from this any conclusions in reverse that if
it is not perfect in all its compositional qualities this stems from
the insincerity of the artist. This is impossible. I very much respect
the works of authors and in their interest I prefer not to quote George
Sand as a guiding principle but I will stand by what Lenin taught
about the Proletcult. This brings me to the question which had a
certain currency here, namely, that we greatly underestimate the
work and research in the technique of our particular art and the
solution to its many special problems.

No one here had to listen to so many compliments about high-
brow wisdom as I. Almost everyone spoke of it quite sweetly: 'Dear
Sergei Mikhailovich we hold you to be such a wise one, etc., etc.'
but when it came to concrete work by Sergei Mikhailovich there
was a kind of patting on the back, as if to say 'what you are doing
in the academy and in your study is nonsense. You've got to produce pictures. All your other work—all that is nothing.'

I feel that it is important to produce films, and I will produce films;
but I feel that the work of making films must go parallel with intensive theoretical work and research. (Voices: 'Correct. Correct' and
applause.) In this connection I want to say to Sergei Vasiliev: in your
speech you said 'I speak to you as a pupil to a teacher'. Permit me to
speak to you as a teacher to a pupil.

When you speak to me about my Chinese robe with its hieroglyphics in which I sit in my study you are making one grave error: it
does not have hieroglyphics. And when I am in my study I do not
look at my statuettes and contemplate abstractly. When I am in my
study I am working on problems which will help the growth of the
coming generation of cinematographers; and if I sit and work in
my study I do it so that you should not waste time in your study, but
continue to make such remarkable films as your *Chapayev*. (Applause.)

You're all familiar with the gossip about the ivory tower, and if
we are to speak about the ivory tower, then permit me to shelter
myself not in an ivory tower but in the thought that I live in one of
the fighting units from which I will break through to the themes in
our cinematography. And if in the past years I have worked on
theoretical and academic problems—over the problem of method,
theory and practice of bringing up young directors—from this time
on I include myself in the work of production and creation. (Continuous applause.)

Now in connection with this I would like to touch upon something which nobody speaks openly about and which disturbs you all. I want to place this question squarely. I want to speak about that point in the decision of the government which relates to the awarding of honours in connection with the 15th Anniversary of our cinema and which pertains to me. What are your feelings and what are my feelings about this decision?

Comrades, I consider this document which was given us by the government to be of the greatest import; and in that part which directly concerns me I think it is much wiser than in the other parts. I interpret it in this way: The nub is—and this you know—that I have not been engaged in productive or creative work for the past many years, and I consider the decision as a high-sign from the Party and the government that I must enter production.

I am a director and a pedagogue and it is possible that I would have acted similarly, not worrying that it might break someone's heart. Comrades, I am not broken-hearted. I am not broken-hearted because the heart which beats for the fulfilment of a Bolshevik aim cannot be broken. (Continuous and loud applause. Everyone stands up and continues to applaud.) Comrades, to-day you have given me much credit for my brains. I beg you from this day to give me credit for a heart. (Great applause.) Whether Comrade Yutkevich meant his remarks about me or not, such films as *Cruiser Potemkin* are produced with the heart's blood, and what I am saying to you now is aimed at putting an end to all the gossip and remarks about the one who was passed by and underestimated. These feelings should be torn from your heart by the roots with Bolshevik decisiveness. (Applause.) This interferes with our work. . . .

I want to say in conclusion that the great historical events in cinematography which have taken place in these days must mobilize us for the further study of all the colossal and difficult problems facing us. . . . This is the period of our greatest inner harmony. But this doesn't mean that we can sleep peacefully as if in Eden without vigilance and without struggle. Much has been done but much more lies ahead of us. . . .

Comrades, it is quite possible that we've mixed up the accents, maybe we have hurt certain directors because we did not speak enough about them. Maybe it is the directors, maybe actors, maybe cameramen. Comrades, this isn't so. Maybe we didn't speak of it in each session and in each of our speeches but we all feel and we all know that only a talentless collective can exist in the face of suppression of one creative individual by another (Applause), and comrades, you must not forget the colossal role our direct leadership plays in our work. You know that we have quarrelled and argued with Comrade Shumyatsky in our speeches and in the pages of the Press; but yesterday, at the meeting for those who were honoured by the government, we all embraced Comrade Shumyatsky, and Frederick Ermler said from this begins a new stage in all our work— the stage of direct co-operation and complete perception of the common undertaking of the creative workers (which at the time I had the honour to represent) in the direction which was decided upon by the Party and which leads our Bolshevik undertakings with all of us working together. (Applause.)

. . . No better concluding remarks, no better programme for the future can be applied to the medium of our work than that found in the socialist beauty with which Comrade Dinamov started his report.

I think, comrades, that with this we can conclude our conference. We firmly know what we will have to do in the future. (Tremendous applause.)

Note 1977. For the influence of Eisenstein and the Soviet Union on Robeson see *Paul Robeson* by Marie Seton (London, Dennis Dobson, 1958).

CHAPTER THIRTEEN

The Mistakes of Bezhin Meadow

Where there is most power of feeling, there of martyrs is the greatest martyr.

LEONARDO DA VINCI, Tr. 35 A.

'I KNOW of nothing more beautiful than the Appassionata,' Lenin once said. 'I could listen to it every day. Wonderful, immortal music. I always think, with perhaps a naïve, childish pride, how can man create such wonders?'

Lenin never pretended to be an artistic man; but he recognized, as did his Commissar of Education, Lunacharsky, that man did not live by bread alone. He realized, too, that the past had produced great works and fine institutions which must be preserved. It was this conviction which had led Lenin to save the Moscow Art Theatre of Stanislavsky from the young iconoclasts like Eisenstein, who would have decreed its dissolution in the early 1920's.

Though it was protected, the Moscow Art Theatre had declined in influence. Stanislavsky's leadership was overshadowed by Vsevelod Meyerhold, the leader of the revolutionary theatre, and for a moment by Eisenstein, who ripped apart the venerable Ostrovsky play, *Enough Simplicity in Every Wise Man*, and put its skeleton together again so that it might serve as the props for a circus parody upon itself.

By the protective foresight of Lenin, the belaboured Art Theatre survived, and by the late 'twenties it had taken on a new lease of life with the production of contemporary Soviet plays, into which its artists poured more human feeling than those who followed in the wake of Meyerhold. Thus, the Moscow Art Theatre began once more to touch the consciousness of young artists, and by January 1935 the adaptation of Stanislavsky's creative method had surplanted that of Meyerhold. Stanislavsky's followers were honoured, while Meyerhold was criticized as ruthlessly as Eisenstein for being a formalist. Unfortunately the Moscow Art Theatre, which Sergei Mikhailovich had always criticized, had now spilled its influence into the realm of cinematography and, therefore, was helping to create the limitations with which Eisenstein would now be compelled to contend. This was especially true when it came to the matter of acting. Fifteen years had brought great changes and ironic twists to creative lives in the Soviet Union.

The Lenin who had saved the Moscow Art Theatre from artistic vandals like Eisenstein and who was deeply stirred by the music of Beethoven continued: 'But I cannot listen to music too often. It affects my nerves and makes me want to say sweet nothings and stroke the heads of men who live in a dirty hell and can still create such beauty. But these days you can't go around stroking people's heads lest your hand be bitten. You have to smash them over the head—smash them without mercy—even though in theory we are against every form of oppression of mankind. . . . Ours is a hellish task.'

The followers of Lenin, growing impatient with Eisenstein, took Lenin's dictum and smashed him over the head, because, in their opinion, he had degenerated into a theorist who would not translate his theories into practice as a responsible Bolshevik should. Eisenstein was rendered the victim of a period which could not tolerate what appeared to be his recalcitrant bourgeois individualism. He had a duty to perform, even though to obey at first violated his every instinct.

But Sergei Mikhailovich was a sincere revolutionary, even though his understanding of Marxism was often not in accord with other Marxists. He realized he would have to make a film at once. He could not wait for Paul Robeson. To step back into the creative arena was difficult, because it meant he would have to abandon the teaching he so dearly loved, the research and writing to which he was dedicated. But Sergei Mikhailovich went to work.

During the remaining weeks of January 1935, and the first few weeks of February, he went through the preliminary steps for a film production. An idea was presented to him which became known as *Bezhin Meadow*. When he wrote to me on February the 5th, however, he was still thinking about his theoretical work:

> It's great to get all this Lewis Carroll stuff! And the finest thing in the whole is that his biography and character are just as they should be according to his work. Thanks immensely. If you should run across something else about him—especially in form of psychological research—send it as well.
>
> Now about G.I.K. . . . . I am probably entering production quite and very soon and that means that I shall work quite unsystematically in G.I.K.
>
> If there should develop something I'll let you know at once. . . .

Though Eisenstein was obliged to relinquish his regular classes, he had four students, including Jay Leyda, working with him on *Bezhin Meadow*. Their task was to express the scenario in a series of drawings which would clarify the concepts. In this way a great storehouse of drawings was prepared, the students' and Eisenstein's own. Pera Attasheva replaced Grigori Alexandrov as his assistant and Tisse, who had made one film with Dovzhenko, was once more cameraman-in-chief. As the production plan developed, Sergei Mikhailovich's creative artistry began to reawake and once more he began to reach out towards a new period of 'creative ecstasy'. There were great possibilities latent in *Bezhin Meadow*. It was not a conventional scenario and it could become the pivot for poetic film imagery.

A. Rzheshevsky, the scenarist, had been commissioned by the Young Communist League to write a story on the theme of the Young Pioneers and their contribution to Soviet collective farming. He recalled a story by Turgeniev called *Bezhin Meadow*, in which a group of horse-herders told Turgeniev their stories—tales revealing the psychology of the Russian child of 1850. Intrigued with the possibilities of contrast between the old and the new village, Rzheshevsky went to live in the village of Bezhin Meadow, which had now become a collective farm. There he composed his scenario, using Turgeniev's story to represent the past and the true-life incident of Pavlik Morozov, a Young Pioneer, to represent the children of the new age. Pavlik Morozov (Stepok in the film), the son of a kulak, organized his fellows to guard the collective farm harvest and by this act he incurred the fury of his father, who had planned an act of sabotage. The father killed his son and Pavlik became a hero throughout the Soviet Union.

For Sergei Mikhailovich the most important character of *Bezhin Meadow* was the boy Stepok, whose ideal image became vivid and fixed in his mind. Pera, and other assistants, picked out six hundred boys from more than two thousand; Sergei Mikhailovich summarily slashed the number down to two hundred, but even among these he did not find a single boy to whom he gave a screen test. So Pera went to Leningrad to see if she could find a Stepok there. She brought back a handsome boy whom the Old Man scornfully rejected as 'too pretty'. He was almost as desperate as he had been to find his ideal surgeon for *Potemkin*, because his first shooting expedition was due to start and Stepok appeared in the scenes scheduled to be shot. Only in the last viewing of children did Eisenstein find his ideal image in Vitya Kartashov, an eleven-year-old boy with a very odd face.

'He *is* Stepok!' Sergei Mikhailovich exclaimed.

No one could quite understand what Eisenstein saw in this boy who was quiet, had no particular interest in films, but had a pronounced liking for mathematics. But Eisenstein understood what was inside this boy who, according to Jay Leyda, had hair that grew in the wrong way and whose face and neck were blotched by lack of pigmentation in his skin. Freda Brilliant the sculptress, who used Vitya Kartashov for her figure of a Young Pioneer, however, says that she did not observe any pronounced skin defect in the boy, but when she examined her model figure upon completion, she found that Vitya's legs were out of proportion—they were too short for his torso.

At the screen test Sergei Mikhailovich heard Vitya's voice grow stiff and dull. Had he not known this feeling himself? Vitya should ask everybody riddles. And when he complied, his voice came out clear, fine, almost compelling. Vitya *became* Stepok in response to Eisenstein's direction: a real boy 'with intelligence, an expressive face and a great range of emotion'.

Eisenstein was now faced with the problem he had always avoided— the professional actor. His theory of 'typage' ran counter to Dinamov's opinion that 'without actors we can't do anything, for you can't base the cinema on "typage".' *Bezhin Meadow* was Sergei Mikhailovich's first sound film and he would be expected to use actors. So he compromised by engaging two: Boris Zakhava, the director of the Vakhantangov Theatre, and Elena Telesheva, an actress of the Moscow Art Theatre. [Plate 40]

Sergei Mikhailovich had met Elena Telesheva at the home of Grigori Alexandrov and his wife, Lyubov Orlova. According to Alexandrov, he avoided meeting Eisenstein after 1932, except in the course of work which occasionally brought them together at his home. Telesheva was a close friend of his wife and himself. She was a tall, masterful widow of about forty with one daughter. She was extremely active in the affairs of her theatre and had won a reputation as a teacher of acting. [Plate 40]

The first scenes for *Bezhin Meadow* were shot on the 5th of May 1935. The method of work was recorded by Jay Leyda in a Production Diary:

These first shots could not be taken before Turgeniev's place in and contribution to the history of literature and art had been thoroughly examined. Turgeniev bringing up the rear of romanticism, was attracted by the Paris Impressionists, who were in turn attracted by the Japanese print-makers; Turgeniev's introduction of impressionism into literature was the key the episode needed. As Turgeniev extracted the essence for literature out of the already (by the painters) extracted Japanese accent, on isolation, on the rounded perfection of an apparently chance selection, so out of Turgeniev's style and background was a cinema approach extracted. The problem for these first few compositions became the problem of showing the audience *how* Turgeniev saw the things around him. The resultant impression must not be that of turning over a collection of Japanese prints and Chinese water-colors, but of examining, lovingly, the corners and details of a landscape lit by the soft last light of romanticism and selected by an artist fascinated by the eye of the Orient.

Thus was logically brought into play all the culture of the world for every new problem. Thus the listening, waiting villagers assume the postures, even the sharp lighting of the listening, waiting disciples in the paintings of the late Spaniards. Thus the blanket arranged over the face of the dead mother reminds you of the death masks of Negro sculpture. A gorgeous embroidery brings along with it the composition of a Vermeer. Thus there are places in the film where an encyclopedic culture has been so integrally welded into cinematography that they remind you of nothing but Eisenstein. . . .[1]

This was the synthesis of the arts become dynamic through the film medium of which Eisenstein dreamed and talked. Here was what he had been striving to convey when he spoke at the January conference. Leyda's record reveals his approach and intent more exactly than Sergei Mikhailovich was ever able to state it except in intimate conversation.

He was pleased with these early compositions which set the mood for Turgeniev's Russia. He felt sure of himself and a few days after the shooting he made a public statement:

Many have reproached me for being an 'office scientist, for locking myself inside four walls'. This is incorrect. In studying, I have added valuable information to my present knowledge of cinema theory.

. . . Now I have received a really fine scenario. Like other fine scenarios, it is quite simple . . . 'Bezhin Lug' must serve as a means of mobilizing nation-wide Bolshevik vigilance, of mobilizing all our strength for the construction of socialism. . . .[2]

But soon *Bezhin Meadow* became a means of reaching back and trying to recapture some of the beauty which had stirred Eisenstein in Mexico and a pressing forward towards a 'revival "in a new quality" of film *poetry*'. As he worked, the sharpness of the criticism levelled at many of his original theories but four months before grew less important in his mind. Though he had not completed a film in more than five years and had suffered intense defeat and frustration, the original breadth of his genius and the freedom which had characterized his handling of large schemes in his youth, was not impaired. There was nothing he would hesitate to demand for the sake of his work. Once more he made demands on a scale unknown to his fellow directors. He knew what he wanted, as though he had never experienced a moment's hesitation in his life. Nothing but his vision would suffice.

[1] From the Production Diary of Jay Leyda, unpublished in 1951.
[2] *Moscow Daily News*, 14 May 1935.

Thus, when the real village of Bezhin Meadow proved unsatisfactory, Eisenstein made a map of an imagined village and sent forth his scouts to find the required elements. One location for the composite village was found 1,500 miles from Moscow on the Stalin State Farm in the Azov-Black Sea District. A second location was a road near Kharkov. Here the Kharkov Tractor Factory promised its co-operation for a month. On June the 15th the expedition set off by plane with four cameras which were in constant use during the shooting on the Stalin State Farm. Although sound equipment was not to be used until Eisenstein reached Kharkov, he considered the character of the sound for each day's work. Nightly he discussed his theories on sound with Jay Leyda and his assistants while they ate from large baskets of fruit:

'On the editing table this episode will be handled in the same way a composer works on a fugue in four voices. The material we're filming to-day is only one of the voices. Most of it will be used for rear projection and transparencies where the second voice will be created —figures and close-ups in the foreground. . . . The third and fourth voices (or themes or motives) are in sound—sound and speech.' Look at the riches that will be spread out on the table, the infinite number of combinations of these four voices. The episode must show the tempestuous, emotional, critical period of harvest preparation. . . . They will range from the simple forthright statements . . . to such combinations as the rear-projection image remaining constant while the quarrelling, singing, shouting figures in the foreground change repeatedly, and vice versa: the voices of the foreground figures drowned out by the clatter of the combines, and the images of the tractors accompanied by the voices of figures who do not appear. . . .[1]

Eisenstein had pledged himself to make a film aiding the construction of socialism. This was the first consideration in the production of *Bezhin Meadow* from the point of view of Boris Shumyatsky and the Soviet film industry. Unless he succeeded in conveying this point, the complex pattern of his film would only serve to arouse criticism. One critic at the January conference had said 'Eisenstein paid too much attention to things in *Potemkin*'. Another had asked, 'Why did he need to compare the tractor to many carts in *The General Line* [*Old and New*]?' Others had spoken of the generalizations of Eisenstein's art and remarked that 'instead of speaking of social realism [Eisenstein] talks of classicism which is still formalistic'. But these, and all the other statements which had been made to Sergei Mikhailovich, had faded before the onrush of creative excitement.

[1] From the Production Diary of Jay Leyda.

Instead of going out to talk to the collective farmers, he talked of the sounds forming like a symphony within his head. And the more he talked, the deeper he felt the upsurge of his own consciousness.

It was his tragedy that no one at this moment dared to tell Eisenstein he was losing sight of the objective purpose of *Bezhin Meadow*. No one present had a sufficiently strong will to protect him from his experimental urges. His ideas were so fascinating that they enthralled not only him but everyone else. So everyone listened to him and no one urged him to spend some days looking at the collective farmers, listening to them and understanding them in terms of daily life and work.

By the time the expedition reached Kharkov, Eisenstein's plans for sound had become ever more complex. For a sequence close to the end of the film (but which was shot almost at the beginning of the work), a procession of farmers recognizing the four saboteurs expressed their indignation 'by hooting, shouting and whistling. The sound indicated in the script becomes less and less realistic, until all sound is drowned out by the swelling whistling, which mounts to a volume where boat whistles and factory sirens take the place of human whistling. The sound track goes so far into imagery that the picture has to keep up with it—so now the new notation reads "the four under the wind", and then "the four under the hurricane".'[1]

Eisenstein had used sound metaphors in his silent films and some of these were the details for which he had been criticized—for example, the harps in *October*. Now engrossed in the problem of the 'orchestral counterpoint of visual and aural images' he evidently did not notice that his ideas were in the line of his theory of the intellectual cinema, the theory which Dinamov had advised him to discard.

As the work proceeded, Eisenstein's creative vision soared to extravagant heights. One day he suddenly saw that it was essential to refashion the road beyond Kharkov because its beauty had been defaced by telephone wires. With a flourish reminiscent of the day when he had taken possession of the Winter Palace and nightly had thousands of citizens of Leningrad at his disposal, Sergei Mikhailovich called for the telephone authorities, and down came two kilometres of telephone poles! The scenario was kept loose and elastic and 'more than one film day [would] pass without Eisenstein referring once to the script—so reliant is he upon the firm mental images he keeps with him'. He was employing a highly individual method in order to gain the effect of emotional spontaneity. Because *Bezhin Meadow* was a sound film, the actors and 'types' had to know their roles in advance, but still they were not informed as to what scene was to be shot until they arrived

[1] *Ibid.*

on the set. Thus, 'Eisenstein used their confusion for added emotion on the screen'.[1]

Of the children appearing in *Bezhin Meadow*, only Vitya Kartashov knew the complete story of the film. The others merely listened to Sergei Mikhailovich tell them the story of a particular scene which he then encouraged them to act out. In some of the scenes there were as many as forty children, half of them mere babies whom Eisenstein played with until they, too, responded to his games. There was 'no detail of the film from transplanting the wheat to placating the babies that Eisenstein does not supervise. Rehearsals for a single brief scene may last three hours, but the actual shooting is brief and there are few retakes.'[2] Before he had worked very long, Sergei Mikhailovich decided that when *Bezhin Meadow* was completed, he would make a second version on a simpler, less tragic and complex level specially designed for children.

During this first period from May to mid-September, Sergei Mikhailovich worked far ahead of schedule. He found time to write letters full of humour and nonsense about all kinds of small incidents which had caused us pleasure or laughter. He was in and out of Moscow, and between work he attended to the furnishing of his new flat at Potylika. This he never mentioned until it was completed. Having lived the whole of his adult life with nothing but a bed, a table, a chair and a backless stool, Sergei Mikhailovich decided to spend a large part of his salary on furniture for the flat.

By September he had almost completed the furnishing. His books were arranged in an orderly fashion in one room which he had set aside as a workroom; the rest of the flat was designed to be lived in as a home. Some people who saw the flat were surprised that Eisenstein who had lived in such a graceless clutter at Chysti Prudi should suddenly create a home.

But he never mentioned his efforts in his letters to me; not until the 7th of September did he write to say he had come into possession of the flat:

> Thank you for your sweet remembrance of Yalta-Odessa days past. I am working like hell—that's why I'm so poor a correspondent. . . . You are bombarding me with such a shower of gifts that I begin to become even more greedy than I ever have been. You know that I dispose at present of a 'quarteera' of four rooms and am building a little 'dacha' outside Moscow. This 'quarteera' lacks two things. . . .

---

[1] 'What I saw in the Film Studios' by Evelyn Gerstein, (*Moscow Daily News*, 10 October 1935.)

[2] *Ibid.*

These things are: 1 A small Victorian *globale* wall mirror—of the kind to reflect because of it curvedness (outside) the whole room it happens to hang in. [And he drew a picture of it.] There are lots of 'em to be seen in London homes. 2 A set of (also Victorian) wax-flowers: a sort of bouquet made out of artificial wax flowers. Do not grin. I want these things very much. . . .

There was no hurry; these things could be brought at leisure—perhaps by the November celebrations. 'Am building a little "dacha" outside Moscow' was understatement. When completed, the house was two stories with seven rooms. Thus, in all, Sergei Mikhailovich was to have eleven rooms when for all the years of his former creative life he had had but one.

By the time this letter reached me I had experienced some doubts about my own capacity to endure difficulties. My self-doubt was enhanced by my feeling that Sergei Mikhailovich deserved a love that would stand all tests. He must not be betrayed by an emotional attachment that would collapse under strain. It seemed to me I had no right to go to him unless I were able to bear all the problems of a new social system and his psychological difficulties with an enduring devotion.

While these doubts left me confused and unable to act with single-mindedness, events in the Soviet Union aroused Eisenstein's weakness —his compulsion to irony and understatement which ended in his retreating into silence for a time. Thus, I was left uncertain as to what was the best thing to do, even after I realized that my feelings for Sergei Mikhailovich were irrevocable.

Almost immediately after this letter the first of many misfortunes struck. It was announced in the Press that Eisenstein was ill, but no mention was made as to the seriousness of the illness. He had, in fact, contracted smallpox while searching for costumes. For Sergei Mikhailovich smallpox was extremely dangerous, because of his heart, the condition of which he had never mentioned.

In a moment of fear he told Maxim Shtraukh he felt he was extremely close to death. Yet it was impossible for Eisenstein to put such words on paper; instead, when he wrote to me after three weeks, he made the whole affair sound like a huge joke.

. . . I just escaped the Asylum (or do you call it otherwise) where I I have spent 3 weeks in bed with nothing beside them poxes to share the same blanket. Now I really do not know which kind of poxes they were. Small-pox, middle pox or something greater. According to my style it ought to be something of the third kind. My beauty is so far affected by the loss of my leonine hair which has been vandically cut. The surface of the front side of the upper part of my figure,

known as face, will probably have one or two unimportant spots to
remind me of this incident. I wonder if you will still like me, all-
though I never pretended much to be like Valentino (You know this
is one of the traits that makes a certain difference between Suey
[Vsevolod I. Pudovkin] and me. . . .)

Anyhow I am leaving for the Caucasus to regain some forces for
my heart (used to love and not small-pox!) is tired and needs some
rest. I will *not* return through Yalta; the gentle instrument (I mean
the heart) may crack in memento of the perfect harmony scattered
on the beach there in autumn 1934!

It was lovely to get your telegrams and the book about the sick
kittens. Also lovely that you realize my crazy wishes. I am eagerly
waiting for mirror and flowers. . . .

My film will not be too much afected by this sickness because we
were much ahead of our time shedule. Anyhow there will be pretty
hard work to be done from December on!

The great joke with my poxes was, that for about *7,000* people have
had to be—now I do not know the word—made immune by injec-
tions!! Imagine the publicity: all these imbeciles carrying the Sign of
Zorro, I mean S.M., on their arms! . . .

In October, he was sent to the spa town of Kislovodsk, where the
treatment was rigid and even the oldest Bolsheviks and toughest Red
Army generals were ordered around like little children by efficient
nurses determined to repair their hearts. It was a hive of medical clinics
with the palaces and villas of Tsarism turned into rest homes cradled in
the savage embrace of one of the most beautiful ranges of mountains in
the world. A place where the minds of most people became philosophic.

If their hearts permitted such a climb, people walked slowly to the
crest of one of the many ridges and gazed towards the highest peak of
the Caucasus—Elbruz. They would fall silent. Since all Russians love
their poets, Lermontov's name would be spoken, and, perhaps some
words quoted from 'The Dagger', his song of love forged in the wild
land of Georgian heroes with its last verse so harsh, so valiant and so
appropriate to be recalled by people who had survived a Revolution:

> You were to be my long companion.
> Give me your counsel to the end.
> I will be hard of soul and faithful
> Like you, my iron-hearted friend!

But for Sergei Mikhailovich, a closer brother was Aeschylus, whose
hero Prometheus had been held captive, chained to a mountain crag in
the Caucasus for daring to challenge the wisdom of Zeus. Prometheus,

the great rebel, who said: 'To speak is pain, but silence too is pain', and 'Neither in insolence nor yet in stubbornness have I kept silence. It is thought that eats my heart seeing myself thus outraged.' These thoughts of Aeschylus were not so pertinent for Eisenstein at the moment as they were to become. He could afford to look objectively upon the symbol of Prometheus, study him, turn him about for philosophic inspection, not for the purpose of self-example. The problem of the moment was not what an angry god might do to him, but how he could overcome the impediment of his weakened heart.

During this time, Pera Attasheva waited patiently for the Old Man to recover. Her fortitude was certainly equal to his and often she felt things more acutely because her spirit lived in the world and she could not escape to the peak of any ecstatic emotion. She had devoted ten years of her life to Eisenstein and now she knew that even the flat in Potylika was not to be her home.

When he returned to work in December of 1935, Sergei Mikhailo-vich worked feverishly. But after six weeks he contracted 'flu and was compelled to remain in bed for three weeks. His illness was serious and, according to later reports, he hovered between life and death for some time.[1] Yet in his letters he again made fun of his illness. Upon his recovery, Eisenstein returned to work on *Bezhin Meadow*, but soon his work was again interrupted.

Boris Shumyatsky, the head of the film industry, was dissatisfied with the results of Sergei Mikhailovich's first months of work. He directed him to re-write the scenario and re-shoot a large part of the film, because, as Shumyatsky later claimed, the socialist-realist por-trayal of the class struggle within the village during the period of col-lectivization of the farms had been submerged in *Bezhin Meadow* by a titanic struggle of good and evil portrayed through the conflict between an individual father and his son. In Shumyatsky's opinion, the father had assumed the unacceptable role of an Abraham sacrificing his son (the boy, Stepok).

However, no discussion of Eisenstein's protracted difficulties with the authorities over *Bezhin Meadow* took place for more than a year. He re-wrote parts of the scenario with the help of Babel, the writer. But he rejected other advice, even that of Alexander Dovzhenko, who later said he had asked Sergei Mikhailovich to show him the scenario because, being himself of peasant origin, he felt he could aid him.

In the second version of the film, the father and son motif was set as an episode within the larger framework of collectivization and the class struggle in the village. In an effort to achieve a greater degree of realism

[1] 'Films in Birth' by Leo Lania, *Die Neue Weltbune* (Prague, 4 June 1936); reprinted in translation, *Living Age* (Boston, November 1936).

in the second version, Elena Telesheva, who was playing a role in the film, and was a highly skilled exponent of the Stanislavsky school of acting, advised Eisenstein on the acting for the new scenes. Since the development of fully rounded characters, which had become the aim of Soviet cinematography, had not entered into Sergei Mikhailovich's original scheme of direction, modification of the style of acting was difficult. Moreover, he was still using mainly 'types' and he could not break away from his passionate interest in images, expressive faces or a gesture of significance.

Because Telesheva was skilled in the sphere where Eisenstein was most indifferent, he accepted her assistance with gratitude. Although she was a masterful woman who knew exactly what she wanted, it seemed that at this period he neither resented her nor stood in awe of her. It was noticed that he behaved towards her as any of her colleagues at the Moscow Art Theatre. It is probable that he liked her and appreciated her talents. But Pera, acting as the Old Man's assistant, deeply resented the role which Telesheva assumed. It is said that she saw in Elena Telesheva something she greatly disliked: the spirit of an opportunist which here and there survived in Soviet society. Soon an antagonism grew between Pera and Telesheva, whose career now became interwoven with Eisenstein's work.

Yet even in the second version of the film Eisenstein was unable to suppress his overriding interest in the conflict between Stepok and his malevolent father. It was impossible for him to sink his own feelings, nor could he control them even with the help of his Marxian studies.

The theme echoed his own life. In his childhood, Mikhail Eisenstein had played a negative, if not a positively destructive role; then when Sergei Mikhailovich was twenty, and fighting in the Red Army, his father sided against the Revolution. Moreover, *Bezhin Meadow* afforded him an opportunity to experiment with an idea with which he had long been preoccupied—the portrayal in art of ecstatic emotions of saints and sinners.

A break with the original concept of the scenario was made more difficult because Vitya Kartashov, Eisenstein's ideal Stepok, was in terms of daily contact a son as well as a sublimated image of his own boyhood. He lavished upon this child of a Red Army chauffeur the understanding denied to him by his own father. Unwittingly the quiet little boy, whose love of mathematics and riddles echoed the passions of Sergei Mikhailovich, had the power to inspire his creative genius and lead it into a more delicate and dangerous mystic path than it had ever trodden before, except in certain scenes directed for *Que Viva Mexico!* Thus one day Sergei Mikhailovich was moved in a moment of 'creative ecstasy' to place a source of light behind the head of Vitya in his role of Stepok, as if he were a consecrated child selected by God for the special task of protecting the collective farmers' harvest. And when he came to direct the death of Stepok, the body of the dead boy was carried as if he had met his death by crucifixion on the Cross. [Plate 40]

Gwen Seiler, who visited Eisenstein during the production of *Bezhin Meadow*, had the impression 'that Eisenstein was obsessed by the drama of the Christ story. There were Crucifixes and figurines of the Madonna' all over his flat at Potylika. In answer to the question as to 'why so many of these effigies, he told [her] he had brought them from Mexico. Then he described at length and with considerable enthusiasm some of the religious parades he had seen in Mexico.' 'The Christ story *plus* the religious ecstasy of the Mexicans caught his imagination. . . .'

'At dinner in his flat he started to tell the story of *Bezhin Meadow*. 'The ending stands out clear and sharp. I remember how he told of the death of the boy and that a dead tree with the sun setting behind it cast the shadow of the cross over his body. When he came to the death of the boy, he jumped up from the table and acted out the scene even to stretching out his arms to illustrate the shadow of the cross made by the trees.'[1]

According to what Grigori Alexandrov later told me, Eisenstein carried about a copy of the Bible while filming *Bezhin Meadow*. On one occasion when he invited a group of students, including H. P. J. Marshall, from the Institute of Cinematography, to watch him at work, he posed the character of Stepok's father on a small hillock against the background of a field. He kept the man in this static pose for more than three hours which, according to H. P. J. Marshall, gave the effect of a religious painting.

'Folk images equal human knowledge,' Eisenstein explained.

But some students commented about the slowness of Eisenstein's direction and the static composition. [Plate 39]

In July 1936, Jay Leyda left Eisenstein's unit and returned to America to accept the post of an assistant curator at the newly founded Museum of Modern Art Film Library in New York. At first Leyda hesitated, but Eisenstein encouraged him to accept this post, and before Leyda left Moscow, Eisenstein arranged for one of the rare, complete original prints of *Potemkin* to be sent to the Film Library.

He especially wanted the scenario of *An American Tragedy* to be available for study in America and he gave Leyda his personal copy which he had carried from Hollywood to New York. Stuck in among the pages of this manuscript was the letter he had written to his mother on the train and the drawing 'Roberta Sitting on her Trunk'. Together

[1] Letters from Gwen Seiler to the author, dated February and March 1950.

with the scenario Eisenstein also gave Leyda his copy of Dreiser's novel in which he had made his first notations which show the evolution of his ideas for a scenario. He added the scenarios of *Sutter's Gold* and *Que Viva Mexico!* with some of his director-designer's sketches. As a parting gift he gave Leyda some photographic 'mementos' of his childhood and youth as well as many photographs of his early theatrical work.

With this basic material Jay Leyda set up the Eisenstein Collection which is now a part of the Museum of Modern Art Film Library.

As the months passed, Sergei Mikhailovich avoided showing his work to his Russian colleagues. He felt that they disliked him and were, therefore, looking for errors in his work. Many were affronted by this action, more so since he showed sections of *Bezhin Meadow* to some visiting foreigners, who regarded it as a new step in cinematography.

Among the foreigners who saw *Bezhin Meadow* was Lion Feuchtwanger who was in Moscow in connection with the filming of his novel *The Oppenheim Family*. Sergei Mikhailovich found a sympathetic companion in Feuchtwanger, whose own writing had been influenced by *Potemkin*. In his novel *Success*, Feuchtwanger had used reactions to the film to reveal the clash of feelings in Berlin in 1926.

'He often talked to me about my novel *Power* (*Jew Suess*), and he also gave me the first Russian edition of my novel—which had been forbidden for a time.' 'I had the feeling that Eisenstein was rather frank and confiding in me.'

'He showed me *Bezhin Meadow* twice. The film was then completely uncut and took about five hours to run. He was afraid he would have to cut much from the scenes of the fire in which he was especially interested. He explained to me how happy he felt that he had succeeded in taking the scenes of the fire in *daylight*. He feared, however, that the film would not be understood. Obviously he foresaw many difficulties even then. He was also most depressed at that time because his close friend Babel [the poet who had helped Eisenstein to rewrite the scenario] was falling more and more deeply into disgrace.'

Despite his difficulties with Shumyatsky and 'the film bureaucracy', Sergei Mikhailovich thought, and Feuchtwanger hoped, that though 'it was not always easy for Eisenstein to get his plans approved', they might be able to make a film together because Feuchtwanger's work was popular in the Soviet Union at the time. Eisenstein wanted to film Feuchtwanger's historical novel *The Ugly Duchess*. 'I was under the impression that Eisenstein wanted to approach the problem of the ugly but gifted woman in his film from the pictorial angle.'

The Duchess was the grotesque looking Countess of Tyrol—Margaret Maultasch—whose sensitive and passionate nature became warped from lack of love and kindness. Imprisoned behind a gigantic forehead, ape-like face and a dwarfed body, she called forth only pity or mockery and was nicknamed 'Pocketmouth'. Centuries later her portrait inspired John Tenniel's illustrations for the comically awesome and intractible Duchess in Lewis Carroll's *Alice in Wonderland*. (This was the edition of *Alice* which I took to Sergei Mikhailovich, and which we read together in Yalta.)

Eisenstein did not tell Feuchtwanger about the anxiety his own appearance had caused him, but when I mentioned this to Feuchtwanger, he wrote, 'I am sure that your explanation is correct, and that Eisenstein identified the problem of the "Ugly Duchess" with that of his own'.[1]

Engrossed in his own creative world, Sergei Mikhailovich was hardly aware of the attitude of mind taking shape in the Soviet Union.

The aggression of Nazi Germany and Fascist Italy expressed in the Spanish Civil War, the collapse of the Popular Front in France and the subsequent failure of the democratic governments of France, England and the United States to aid Loyalist Spain, was daily turning the Russians more and more within themselves. They felt a passionate sympathy for the people of Spain, and Sergei Mikhailovich shared this feeling, but gradually it was being borne in upon the minds of the Russians that if they were attacked, no one would raise a finger to aid them. The Soviet leaders stiffened and the spirit of internationalism, which had characterized the Soviet Union since the days of the Revolution, hardened into disillusion. It was felt that the democratic and Left elements in other countries were too weak to create a bulwark against the menace of Hitler's Germany. With disillusion, a wave of suspicion arose. It was realized that Europe had become a honeycomb of Nazi intrigue in an effort to soften up the Continent for war, and that there were spies among the foreigners in Moscow. A general nervousness spread a cloud of anxiety over not only the Soviet Union, but the rest of Europe.

As *Bezhin Meadow* drew towards completion in January 1937, Sergei Mikhailovich again contracted 'grippe'. It gave him time to think and suddenly he felt compelled to reach out to those who believed in him and cared what happened to him. On the 1st of February 1937, he wrote a long letter to Jay Leyda in America:

MY DEAR JAY!

I was very, very happy to get news from you and all the lovely things you've sent me. It was a pleasure and a sorrow. For strange as it may

[1] Letters from Lion Feuchtwanger to the author, dated 30 May and 7 June 1950.

seem—I'm missing you here! You know I was never too sentimental—I'd say on the contrary—but you formed a certain link with
things I even have no opportunity to talk to anybody now! I mean
by that my theoretical ideas and the trend of thoughts surpassing the
purely professional side of producing! Most of the time with you I
was petty and disagreeable—but that was a sort of self protection
against . . . oneself: against things that drive me mad—things I cannot
put down in book form being chained to producing other things!
You were allways provoking and touching my most secret wounds
—*the* side of my work which is to my opinion the really most important of what I have to do—and which I am not doing. So that's why
our intercourse had a certain mixture of pain and pleasure . . . well
as any masochistic pastime! Now nobody and nothing is tickling me
in this way: and when I by accident jump out of production for an
hour or so, I feel like Peer Gynt in the scene where he watches the
rush of leaves on the earth which happen to be his ideas that never got
form. I hope that in three-four weeks I'll be through with the shooting. Quite a few people have seen the rushes and are very highly
impressed—all of them feel in it a return and revival 'v novom
kachestve' ['in a new quality'] of film *poetry* (that was the first
thing Feuchtwanger said when he saw them): As soon as I'm
through with the picture *I must* put myself at work on the book. But
there will start again a new tragedy: primo: there are plans for Spain.
Secundo: Paul Robeson who was with a concert tour here has just
put himself at my entire disposition for the time from July to October! Now both these things can fit marvellously together—taking
the race and national problems within the poem about revolutionary
Spain, but all that means . . . two more years of nothing doing about
the book!!! Well it is not quite sure about the next film—and if not
this film, then I hope to rob a couple of months out of my director's
biography and still accomplish what I ought to do.

Another feeling of sorrow overcame me in another direction:
Your letter made me feel out of touch with the outer world: I felt
myself in no connection with what is going along on the other side
of the ocean—what people think about, what they write about, what
is going along in the arts and sciences. Well I can imagine that not
much, if anything, is in progress there in the modern way. But discoveries, research etc must be going ahead. Couldn't you hold me a
little bit 'au courant' of what is happening in the fields I am interested
in. May be it wouldn't be too difficult to send me from time to time
even the 'Times' book review, so as to know what is published and
printed over there. Also some about what is going on in arts and art
sciences. You're in the center of all that there. Thanks for the books

you made notes of for me (the one promised to be sent never arrived).
And write me more often—not waiting for immediate answers. . . .

Only very great inward pressure, or the closest proximity and sense
of security, could so break down Sergei Mikhailovich's reserve. He had
liked Jay Leyda from the moment he became a student at the Institute of
Cinematography. He had felt his sensitivity and the sincerity of his
interest and had always been delighted whenever Leyda came to see him
at Chysti Prudi. Yet he had awed Jay Leyda, who had always been
careful, even a little fearful, lest he intrude on Eisenstein and strain his
patience. It was one of the ironies of Eisenstein's life that he called forth
the most sensitive response in the people for whom he cared, and who
cared for him, so that he created a bond which, though it could never
be broken, remained but half-realized because he never spoke clearly of
his affection until too late.

Three or four weeks and the immense strain of *Bezhin Meadow* would
be over, or so Sergei Mikhailovich hoped. Only the completion of
montage would remain. On March the 4th he wrote to me:

BELOVED!

I just got up from my bed where for three weeks enjoyed the company of the most fashionable disease of this season—the 'grippe'. I'm
probably growing quite old—jumping from sickness to illness and
back again. . . .

Why do you never write a word? You know my method: it is to
send *paperless* letters (in the style of wireless telegrams)—you must
have heaps (or heeps? or hipps?!) of them from me and the only
difficulty is that you cannot see, touch or read them—the next technical improvement is expected to make them readable—so believe
me (or not) that you dispose of lots sent from me.

Now you may suppose me to be crazy as result of the grippe:—
that is not true. I'm all right again and starting to shoot a new. . . .

I expect to hear from you very very soon and remain

Always
lovingly yours
SERGEI

Before he received an answer to this letter telling him I would come
to Moscow, the long-delayed collapse of all his plans came suddenly.
He had been unable to save himself, or to divert a single blow.

On March the 17th, 1937, the production of *Bezhin Meadow* was
halted by the Central Administration of the Cinema Industry. Two
million roubles had already been spent. The decision was followed by an
article in *Pravda* written by Boris Shumyatsky. It charged that Eisenstein, who had made a statement rejecting his former aesthetic prin-

ciples and who had expressed his intention to work along lines of social-realism, had misused his creative opportunities and the vast financial resources afforded him. Instead of learning from life, Eisenstein had placed too great a faith in his own 'scholastic profundities' and produced a film of 'harmful formalistic exercises'.

According to Shumyatsky, the theme of the Young Pioneer, Pavlik Morozov (Stepok in the film), had required intimate knowledge of the peasantry and a deep understanding of the class struggle in the village during collectivization. But Rzheshevsky's scenario had suffered such defects as poor construction, blurred characterization and ideological confusion. Eisenstein had been warned to improve the script and remove the defects from his picture; but, declared Shumyatsky, Eisenstein had always disdained criticism and, as a result, his whole conception of the social processes involved in collectivization was fallacious. 'The conception of the film is based not on manifestations of the class struggle, but on a clash of elemental forces of nature, on a struggle between "good" and "evil". The sharpness of the class struggle assumes in the film a Biblical character and features. The director shows here the senseless, brutal malevolence of some and the unctuous truthfulness of others.' [Plate 40]

Eisenstein's preoccupation with the elemental had led him to over-emphasise the destructive phases of collectivization and 'the motif of construction was revealed only as a means of showing the elemental character of the forces of revolution'. His presentation had failed to show people typical of the epoch or provide insight into the processes of social reconstruction; instead it depended upon 'a metaphor concerning the centrifugal character of unleashed elemental forces'. The head of the film industry singled out one episode, 'Smashing the Church', to illustrate what was wrong with the film as a whole.

This sequence which had been in Rzheshevsky's original scenario, showed a duly appointed committee of collective farmers dismantling a church. They entered in an orderly fashion and made an inventory of the contents. In shooting this episode, Eisenstein's own religious conflict rose to the surface. His hatred of the Church was counterpointed with ecstatic mysticism.

The farmers, swaying to the rhythm of a hymn which gradually changed to a broken revolutionary song, carried out the holy objects one by one until the church was bare. Then a 'Samson-like man' pulled down the reredos and pushed apart the pillars. The church collapsed. As it fell doves (which some people believed were symbolic of the Holy Ghost) fluttered from the cupola and soared heavenward.

According to Shumyatsky's article in *Pravda*, Eisenstein 'presents in this scene a veritable bacchanalia of destruction, and the collective farmers as vandals. Needless to say these scenes do not in any way reflect the real processes in the reconstruction of the life and social forms in the Soviet village in the years of collectivization. Depicting the Soviet village, Eisenstein never gave a thought to actuality. Among the personages of the film we find not images of collective farmers, but Biblical and mythological types. Eisenstein even hit upon the clever idea of portraying the chief of the political department as a man with an immobile face, enormous beard and the conduct of a Biblical saint.' The father, 'instead of being endowed with the features of the real enemy, appears like a mythological Pan from the paintings of the symbolist Vrubel' [Plate 40]

Shumyatsky then came to the matter of how Eisenstein had handled the central character of Stepok. He had presented the Young Pioneer 'in luminously pale tones, with the face of a consecrated holy child! To characterize this image, Eisenstein resorted to a trick intended to emphasize its quality of "other worldliness". For instance, in some of the shots, the source of light is placed behind Stepok so that this blond child in a white shirt seems to radiate a halo.'

Boris Shumyatsky, who in less than a year was removed from office and indicted for sabotaging the film industry, set himself as judge of Eisenstein. As a then trusted Bolshevik, he imposed his will on Sergei Mikhailovich and destroyed *Bezhin Meadow* as ruthlessly as Upton Sinclair had destroyed *Que Viva Mexico!* five years before.

The banning of *Bezhin Meadow* became a *cause célèbre*. The foreign Press reported the case in sensational terms. Rumour was piled on rumour. Since two of Eisenstein's early associates—Vsevolod Meyerhold and Sergei Tretiakov—had both been charged with political offences, and had subsequently disappeared from Soviet life in Moscow, the assumption was that Sergei Eisenstein was under political as well as artistic attack. Predictions as to Eisenstein's fate ranged from final disgrace as an artist, to exile and possible death. All accounts were garbled and added to by speculation as they were transmitted.

Later I was told that Sergei Mikhailovich's first reaction was to challenge the right of Shumyatsky to ban *Bezhin Meadow*. He is said to have insisted upon the verdict of a conclave of his fellow film workers. Whether at Eisenstein's request or not, a three-day conference was called on March the 19th.

During this conference not a single person came to the defence of Sergei Eisenstein, nor did anyone suggest that Shumyatsky's decisions be reconsidered. A great many people blamed themselves 'for kowtowing to big names and old reputations, for lack of candour and Bolshevik self-criticism'. But whereas the criticism of Eisenstein during the conference in January of 1935 had been confined to artistic matters, now his character came under attack. According to a report in the *Moscow Daily News*, 'Many accused Eisenstein of secretiveness, over-weening conceit, inability to co-operate with others, unwillingness to recognize the accomplishment of colleagues, and above all of aloofness from Soviet reality and the gigantic processes unfolding all about him'.

Since the age of twenty Sergei Mikhailovich had served the cause of revolution with complete sincerity. He had been vilified abroad as a 'Bolshevik'. Had he denied that he was he might have had a career in America with great material reward. He had refrained. Returning to the Soviet Union in May of 1932, he had encountered private criticism as to his conduct. Public criticism had come to him in 1935 and now it culminated in the banning of *Bezhin Meadow*. He was trained to accept criticism. At the three-day conference, Sergei Mikhailovich admitted many of the accusations made against him; but he did not repudiate his artistic theories.

According to the Moscow Press 'he admitted having been possessed of the intellectual's quixotic illusion that revolutionary work could be done individually, in segregation from the collective, in complete defiance of the general trend. "Fame came to me early," he said. "I thought that I could bear it gracefully, but it turned out that I couldn't. I over-estimated myself, and that was a major error. I never advanced beyond the stage of elemental revolutionism. I never achieved conscious Bolshevik revolutionism. Hence the many mistakes in my films."'

These were not words spoken to deflect official disapproval. Sergei Mikhailovich had known from the moment of his return to Moscow in 1932 that he no longer understood the trends of Soviet society and that he was profoundly out of touch with life, because he had never been able to resolve the conflict between the old and the new within himself. He was an individualist who wished to be part of a collective society, but did not know how to become a part of a collective. He believed in the future of Soviet society, yet he was pathetically afraid of close contact with individuals. He had never dared to come close to more than a handful of people since he was a child and he had suffered from a personality which made it difficult for people to understand him or to feel affection for him. He had lived tragically alone, though always longing to find himself accepted as an ordinary human being. Even at this late date he might have been saved from the anguish and trouble that was to follow him to the day of his death, if he had been able to translate into practice one remark made at the conference.

The director, D. Marian, said to him: 'Sergei Mikhailovich, in your statement you said that you were a Soviet man. No one doubts that. But one must understand simple things: only by starting from man, for man and in the name of man, is it possible to work in our art. Uproot the last vestiges of formalism from your consciousness, create a loved image of the Revolution, show the marvellous people of our epoch, learn to love them with a joyous love and then you will find yourself on a solid path, and then the banner of revolutionary art which you let slip from your hands will be yours once more.'

But where was he to begin? How was he to create a loved image of the Revolution when it had compelled him to hate what he had once loved? Sentiment had become as an anathema and he had lost the key whereby he could express human feelings and aspirations in terms which every man could easily understand.

With the conference ended, Sergei Mikhailovich knew he would never be trusted to work until he could convince the film industry he would not repeat the same mistakes. He returned to the flat he had put together in the hope of attaining happiness and he remained there alone for many weeks. No one was permitted to visit him except Pera Attasheva, who was registered as his wife at Z.A.G.S., and Eduard Tisse, who refused to work with anyone but Eisenstein.

During the summer of 1937, an opera, *The Armoured Cruiser Potemkin*, by the Ukrainian composer, Oles Chishko, was produced in Leningrad, and later at the Bolshoi Theatre in Moscow. Although the libretto followed the scenario of the film *Potemkin* very closely, and the same characters appeared with the actors made-up to resemble Sergei Mikhailovich's 'typage' characterizations, no mention was made of the film *Potemkin*, nor of the name of Sergei Eisenstein. [Plate 11]

Very occasionally he appeared at an official gathering. On one such occasion in May of 1937, Thorold Dickinson, who was in Moscow, attempted to speak to him, but Eisenstein appeared to be in 'an almost mindless state' and it was impossible to carry on a conversation with him. Frank Capra, who also met him at a public gathering about this time, had the impression that Eisenstein was entirely isolated from his colleagues.

Soon after Thorold Dickinson saw him, and when he had still made no official statement, he was sent to a rest home in southern Russia. While he was gone the attention of the whole country was concentrated upon the trials of the old Bolsheviks and generals accused of conspiracy. The trials submerged the case of Eisenstein. No further rumours circulated. He had not been charged with any political offence. He was merely rendered inactive. What his future would be no one could say.

In September 1937 I went to Moscow in the hope of seeing Sergei Mikhailovich. He was not at the station, and I was unable to reach him by telephone. A letter came from Pera in answer to my telegram. She said the Old Man was away, and she too was away for a few days, but he would soon return to Moscow.

Before his return, Marcoosha Fischer, the wife of Louis Fischer, who then appeared to speak with authority and as a pro-Soviet citizen, came and told me that Eisenstein was in very grave disgrace; that among other things he had been interrogated regarding his friendship with foreigners and about his relationship with me in particular. She said that if I made any attempt to see him, or if he attempted to see me, any chance of his being reinstated in the film industry would be destroyed, he might be exiled or even shot and if this happened I would be to blame. If I loved Eisenstein, I would prove it by leaving immediately and ending all further personal communication with him.

Against the background of events in the Soviet Union and the international situation, this sounded plausible, even if very hard to bear. I assumed that Marcoosha Fischer, who had never shown any ill will towards Eisenstein or myself in the past, was telling the truth and that Eisenstein knew about the situation and would understand. I left a note for him explaining that upon my return it had become clear that our plans had to be abandoned and that our personal relationship must end. I left Moscow the next day and held to this decision until a little more than a month before Sergei Mikhailovich's death, when I felt compelled to send a message to him through Jay Leyda.

Only after Eisenstein's death did I learn from his closest friend, Maxim Shtraukh, and others, that Marcoosha Fischer's statements to me had no foundation whatsoever in fact. What motivated her, however, is not clear. The truth is that at no time had Eisenstein's personal or private life come under official criticism and our continued relationship would not have injured him.

The matter of *Bezhin Meadow* ended when Sergei Eisenstein made the following official statement:

> How could it happen that ten years after the triumph of *The Cruiser Potemkin* I should meet with the failure of *Bezhin Lug*? What caused catastrophe to overtake the picture I had worked on for over two years? What was the mistaken viewpoint which, despite honesty of feelings and devotion to work, brought the production to a perversion of reality, making it politically unsubstantial and consequently inartistic?
>
> I have asked myself this question many times, and after repeated self-examination I begin to see it and to understand it.
>
> The mistake is rooted in one deep-seated intellectual and individualist illusion, an illusion which, beginning with small things, can subsequently lead to big mistakes and tragic outcomes. It is an illusion

which Lenin constantly decried, an illusion which Stalin tirelessly exposes—the illusion that one may accomplish truly revolutionary work 'on one's own', outside the fold of the collective, outside of a single iron unity with the collective.

This is the source of my mistake. And this is the first thing I must realize in my serious effort to explain the fundamental shortcomings of both my present and previous work.

This intellectual illusion was the main cause of mistakes and quixotic digressions from the right way of presenting questions and answering them. These individual digressions result in the political distortion of the events portrayed and a wrong political interpretation of the subject.

Unripened revolutionary feelings, which should have been replaced long ago by disciplined Bolshevik consciousness, is the source of errors that, subjectively mistaken, become objectively harmful, despite affirmative intentions and purposes.

This explains what happened to me in my understanding of realism.

By turn of mind I am much given to generalization. But is it that generalization which the Marxist doctrine of realism teaches us to understand? No. For in my work generalization destroys the individual. Instead of being derived through the concrete and the particular, generalization trails off into detached abstraction. This was not the case in *Potemkin*. Its power lay precisely in the fact that through this one episode I succeeded in giving a generalized presentation of the Revolution of 1905, of the 'dress rehearsal' for the October Socialist Revolution. This episode embodied all that was typical of that phase in the history of the revolutionary struggle. And the episode itself was typical in itself and its interpretation proved characteristic of the struggle as a whole. This was largely facilitated by the fact that *Potemkin* was originally conceived as an episode in a large epic of 1905 and subsequently became an independent picture which absorbed the entire complex of feelings and sounds that were intended for a panorama.

This did not happen with *Bezhin Lug*. The very episode which provides its basis—a dramatic episode—is in no way characteristic. A kulak father murders his son, a Pioneer; it is a possible episode, but not a typical one. It is on the contrary exceptional, unique and non-characteristic. However, when it is placed at the centre of the scenario it acquires an independent, self-sufficient generalized meaning. This anomaly distorts the actual portrayal of the civil war in the countryside, obscuring it with morbid pictures of a father 'executing' his son, which corresponds more to the subject of the 'sacrifice' of Isaac by Abraham than to the subjects which should interest our audience in connection with the last battles for the final consolidation of the victorious collective farm system. On this account the first version was utterly unsatisfactory since it treated this episode as basic and central.

In the second version of the scenario instead of making the drama between father and son a 'thing in itself', we tried to give it as one episode in the general course of the class struggle in the village. This was not done thoroughly and consistently. There was no complete break with the original concept of the scenario or with the director's interpretation.

The socially false emphasis in the situation inevitably led to a false psychological interpretation. The psychological problem of the father who kills his son became the centre of attention. And this generalized problem thrust into the background the main task—the portrayal of the struggle of the kulaks against the collective farms. The situation is solved in psychological abstraction, that bears no connection to a realistic investigation of actuality.

The first version deprives the father of all human elements; the father-beast is stilted and unconvincing. The second version goes to the other extreme: in depicting the 'human drama' of the son-killer it loses sight of the class hatred of the kulak, whose rabid fury in the struggle against Socialism does not stop at the murder of his own son.

This psychological conception, abstracted from reality, leads to political looseness; hatred for the enemy disappears, psychological nuances reduce the subject to that of a father's murder of his son 'in general'.

Mistakes of generalization divorced from the reality of the particular, occur just as glaringly in the methods of presenting the subject.

The first mistake is the detachment of the ideas from its concrete carrier, the character who embodies it in the film.

And this results in the underestimation of the human element and a negligent attitude towards the creator of the human image in the picture—the actor.

Hence the attention devoted to the people is not determined by the importance of their ideological role, but by the interest in them as personalities.

The beast image of the kulak thrusts itself into the foreground out of all proportion. The head of the political department is blurred, pale and rhetorical.

And at the same time the hero of the film—the village Pioneer—is developed out of all proportion to his real social importance. This results in the impression that the class war in the village is the work of the Pioneers alone, and in the picture, of one Pioneer single-handed (especially in the first version).

The same occurs in the artistic mounting of the film. Since attention is not fully centred on man, on his character, on his action, the role of accessory and auxiliary means becomes excessive. Hence the hypertrophy of the settings: the den instead of a hut, the distorted foreshortening in the camera shots and deformed lighting effects. Decorations, scenic effects, lighting—the setting instead of the actor. The same applies to the characters: the image displaces the actor. It is no longer a living face but a mask, the extremes of a generalized 'typification' divorced from the living face, a static image which resembles a frozen gesture.

These elements which were justly subjected to severe criticism, especially in the first version of the picture, are wholly the result of the postulates enumerated at the outset.

I write of all this in all sharpness, for during my two years of work, with the help of constant criticism on the part of the leadership of the cinematographic industry, I was moving in the direction of overcoming these elements. But I did not succeed in fully overcoming them. Those who saw all the fragments of the picture from the first scenes to the last, remarked that there was definite progress towards realism and the scenes 'at night' already testify to the fact that the author was abandoning the mistaken position with which he began work on the first version.

Exaggerated generalization, divorced from the particular and from reality, inevitably carried the whole system of images in the only possible direction—towards mythologically stylized figures and associations. The full-blooded, many-sidedness of the tragic clash was reduced to a duo-tone melodrama in 'black and white'. The reality of class conflict was transformed into a generalized cosmic struggle between 'good and evil'. It would be wrong to assume that the author consciously sought for a 'myth'. But we again see how failure to adhere consistently to the method of realist presentation and failure to master this method in practice becomes a matter beyond the bounds of aesthetics, and gives the composition a false political significance.

To whom, however, should the mistakes be attributed? And can it be said that political error is the result of a mistaken creative method? Of course not. The mistakes in the creative method nest in an error of a philosophic nature.

Philosophical errors lead to mistakes in method. Mistakes in method lead to objective political error and looseness.

This can be logically accounted for by every more or less intelligent artist in our country, including myself, but it required the harsh criticism to which the catastrophic *Bezhin Lug* was subjected in the Press and in meetings of the workers of the Soviet cinematograph industry, to make me not only understand it fully, but feel it.

A detailed scrutiny of all the consecutive scenes fully revealed to me the wrong approach to this subject. The criticism of my comrades helped me to see it.

What led to this? The failure to disclose the prime causes and the actual circumstances of the class struggle in the village. The situations in the picture did not follow from these causes and circumstances. On the contrary the situations in the picture were taken 'by themselves'. All this together could not produce the positive revolutionary effect which the author was striving for. On the contrary, mistakes of this sort are likely to produce the opposite effect objectively, and thereby to forfeit the sympathy of our spectators. Added to this the mistakes in method intensified these effects, and led to the unrealistic presentation of most of the material (with the partial exception of the last third of the new version which shows an improvement in method). Even without viewing the entire material, one may draw this conclusion from the scenario and the story in the separate shots.

Political carelessness was displayed by all who took part in directing the work. The work had to be discontinued. Additional shots and retakes could not save it. By now I clearly see the error, not only of various parts but of the conception as a whole. This wrong conception was contained in the scenario, but the director's interpretation did not revolt against it and continued to repeat the initial mistakes even in the second version.

The discussion of *Bezhin Lug* leads to the further clarification of the fundamental question: how could it happen that glaring incorrectness of concept should have developed in the production?

I shall explain this plainly and directly. I was somewhat withdrawn from life. In these years I worked intently with the youth, devoting all my energies to teaching at the Institute of Cinematography. But this work was confined to the school walls, without a broad, creative contact with the masses, with reality.

The fifteenth anniversary of Soviet cinematography gave me a sharp jolt. In 1935 I eagerly plunged into the work. But the tradition of introversion and isolation had already become rooted in me. I worked subjectively, within my own immediate group. I worked on a picture which was not one of flesh and blood with our Socialist reality, but was woven of abstract images of this reality. The results are obvious.

Now the development of severe criticism, truly Bolshevik

criticism, that is to say, criticism that is comradely and aimed at assisting and correcting and not at destroying, and the remarks of the workers of our collective at the Moscow film studio saved me from the worst—saved me from becoming embittered as a result of my mistakes with *Bezhin Lug*. The collective helped me first of all to see my mistakes, the mistakes of method, and the mistakes of my social and political conduct. All this overshadows even the natural sorrow over the failure of two years of work to which I had devoted so much strength, love and effort. Why am I firm and confident? I understand my mistakes, I understand the meaning of the criticism, self-criticism and self-check-up which proceed throughout the country in connection with the decisions of the plenum of the Central Committee of the C.P.S.U. in February 1937.

I keenly feel a profound need fully to correct the mistakes in my viewpoint, to root a new self in me, a need for the complete mastery of Bolshevism of which Comrade Stalin spoke in the above plenum.

And in this light I am confronted with the question: how can I accomplish all this most fully, profoundly and responsibly?

Detached from concrete practical tasks and perspectives this is impossible. What must I do?

I must seriously work on my own outlook, and seek a profound Marxist approach to new subjects. Specifically, I must study reality and the new man. I must guide myself by a carefully selected and solid scenario and subject.

The subject of my new work can only be of one type: heroic in spirit, militant in content and popular in its style. Regardless of whether it be material about 1917 or 1937, it will serve the victorious march of Socialism.

In preparing the creation of such a film I see the way whereby I shall rid myself of the last anarchistic traits of individualism in my outlook and creative method.

The Party, the leadership of the cinematographic industry and the collective of the cinematographic workers will help me to create new, lifelike and necessary pictures.[1]

When the world beyond the Soviet Union read this statement, many people thought that Eisenstein had written it to save himself from the fate of a 'heretic'. In contrast, the Soviet world read the document and most people felt that Eisenstein revealed himself to be a well-disciplined Bolshevik who could accept drastic criticism and come to an under-

[1] Sergei M. Eisenstein, 'The Mistakes of *Bezhin Lug*' (*International Literature*, No. 8, 1937). Originally published in the pamphlet *About the Film Bezhin Lug of Eisenstein* (Moscow, 1937).

standing of why he had failed to meet the requirements of socialist-realism. But in their interpretations both sides over-simplified Eisenstein's act.

Because of the tenor of his thoughts and feelings, the making of this statement was a complex process which involved Eisenstein's entire personality. It meant resolving the conflict between his sincerely felt duty as a Marxist artist who realized he was out of touch with the contemporary spirit in the Soviet Union and his profound need to express his subjectively felt ideas. The conflict had always existed, but had never previously been sharpened to the point of explosion.

His decision to repudiate his work was made in good faith. An intellectual grasp of Marxism and a stringently objective critical faculty led him to believe in the incorrectness of his work. But the danger to him in repudiating his own work was that it must shake the whole foundation of his adult life. Outside his work he had been unable to consolidate any real ties to life. All his forces had crystallized around his supreme devotion to his artistic vision and his theories of the creative process. Only his sense of dedication had given him an intellectual stability which had controlled his emotional immaturity.

In fulfilling his duty as a Soviet artist, he had to humble his vision of himself and his art. This rendered him more vulnerable to the influences of his childhood than ever before. Instead of building on the foundation he had attempted to lay down during his early creative work, Sergei Mikhailovich seems to have broken this chain of development and sought a difference course—one related to his earlier life. During the next nine years—1937 to 1946—he either consciously, or under unconscious compulsion, manifested in his mature life certain patterns which belonged to his childhood and adolescence.

Note 1977. After Eisenstein's death, and up to 1968, it was repeatedly stated that the negative and cutting copy of *Bezhin Meadow* was destroyed by water during the Second World War. It is still alleged that no other copy exists. In time, a series of frames kept by Eisenstein from the two versions were found. Introduced by a somewhat evasive and apologetic commentary, from these frames a brilliantly reconstructed film by Yutkevitch has been given to the world as a memorial to Eisenstein's film. Something of the original remains, echoing *General Line* and *Que Viva Mexico!* but still reaching forward towards the stylization of *Ivan the Terrible.* But, as in the case of *Time in the Sun,* the skeleton of *Que Viva Mexico!*, the exact meaning of Eisenstein's shot by shot correlation is only revealed in terms of approximation. As a postscript, the condemned symbolic fluttering of escaping doves at the collapse of the cupola not only appears in the reconstruction but may have inspired the flight of the single dove symbolic of Ophelia's death in Gregori Kozintsev's superb transcription of *Hamlet.*

CHAPTER FOURTEEN

"My Subject is Patriotism"

*One pushes down another: by these cubes (dice) are represented
the life and conditions of mankind.*

LEONARDO DA VINCI, G. 89 r.

IN a short biographical pamphlet on Eisenstein published in 1939
when he had again risen to the pinnacle of acclaim in the Soviet
Union, the author, Vsevolod Vishnevsky, says that following *Bezhin
Meadow* Eisenstein suggested two films, one on the Civil War in Spain,
the other about the creation of the Red Army in 1917. But 'his enemies
prevented the realization of either of these films'.[1] Then, according to
Vishnevsky, 'the Party and the Government, and Stalin in particular,
came to his aid'.

Eisenstein was permitted to resume work and in the autumn of 1937
he commenced the picture *Alexander Nevsky*; but under conditions
quite different from his previous films. He was surrounded by new collaborators whose task was to see to it that he did not lose his way again.
His use of non-professional 'types' ended and his work with a cast of
professional actors began. Nikolai Cherkasov, a member of the Supreme
Soviet of the U.S.S.R. from Leningrad, was selected to play the title
role of Prince Alexander Nevsky. He had previously made a great
success in several films—as Professor Polezhayev in *Baltic Deputy*,
Alexei, the tsarevich in *Peter I*, and Maxim Gorky in *Lenin in 1918*.

Piotr Pavlenko collaborated with Eisenstein on the scenario for
Alexander Nevsky and when completed it told a straightforward story
of the thirteenth-century rout of the marauding Teutonic knights by
the Russians led by Prince Alexander Nevsky. Except for the scenes
dealing with the role of the Church in the historic struggle, the scenario
had none of Sergei Mikhailovich's characteristic complexities nor intellectual twists.

Though *Alexander Nevsky* was an historical film, its Marxist approach
served a distinctly contemporary purpose. With the menace of Fascism
growing, the Soviet leaders thought it was necessary to arouse the Russian masses to a sense of their own historical development. *Nevsky* was
a patriotic epic designed to strike the heart of every Russian man,

[1] *Eisenstein*, a biographical pamphlet by Vsevolod Vishnevsky (Goskinozdat,
(Moscow, 1939), p. 20.

woman and child and prepare them to meet any war which came with a sense of optimism.

In preparing the scenario, Eisenstein and Pavlenko turned to popular epic. 'The spirit of the folk narrative was perceptible in the scenario. The figures of the Novgorod heroes, Vaska Buslai and Gavrilo Olexich, came from folk tales, as did their quick wits and the joyous and confident spirit with which they fought countless enemies. The biting comparison of the Germans to a fox caught in a crevass [was] also taken from folk tales.'[1] In the writing of the script and during direction, Sergei Mikhailovich gave the patriotic epic the distinctive form of a pageant-opera. In selecting this form, he appears to have picked up a thread from his adolescence when he was 'very busy with the production of two acts from Hebbel's tragedy of *Die Nibelungen*'.

Not even the presence of new collaborators who must restrain him from returning to the complexities of his past work could still Eisenstein's creative spirit.

When work on the shooting-script began, Eisenstein recalled Milton's *Paradise Lost*. Thus, Milton's imagery of the Battle in Heaven became the Battle on the Ice in *Alexander Nevsky*.[2] The line of Eisenstein's images almost exactly parallel Milton's imagery in the Approach of the 'Host of Satan' where:

> . . . at last
> Farr in th' Horizon to the North appeer'd [the Teutons]
> From skirt to skirt a fierie Region, stretcht
> In battailous aspect, and neerer view
> Bristl'd with upright beams innumerable
> Of rigid Spears, and Helmets throng'd, and Shields
> Various, with boastful Argument portraid,
> The banded Powers of Satan hasting on
> With furious expedition . . .[3]

and the Corresponding Movement of the 'Heavenly Hosts' where Nevsky, as leader of the Russians, mounts the rock with:

> . . . that proud honour claim'd
> Azazel as his right, a Cherube tall:
> Who forthwith from the glittering Staff unfurl'd
> Th' Imperial Ensign, which full high advanc't
> Shon like a Meteor streaming to the Wind,

[1] 'Alexander Nevsky, by Vsevolod Pudovkin (*International Literature*, No. 2, Moscow, 1939).

[2] Which in turn influenced Laurence Olivier in his production of the Battle of Agincourt in the film *Henry V*.

[3] S. M. Eisenstein, *The Film Sense* (London, Faber and Faber, 1946), p. 55.

With Gemms and Golden lustre rich imblaz'd,
Seraphic arms and Trophies: all the while
Sonorous mettal blowing Martial sounds:
At which the universal Host upsent
A shout that tore Hells Concave, and beyond
Frighted the Reign of Chaos and Old Night.
All in a moment through the gloom was seen
Ten thousand Banners rise into the Air
With Orient Colours waving: with them rose
A Forrest huge of Spears: and thronging Helms
Appear'd, and serried Shields in thick array
Of depth immeasurable: Anon they move
In perfect Phalanx to the Dorian mood
Of Flutes and soft Recorders; such as rais'd
To highth of noblest temper Hero's old
Arming to Battel, . . .[1]

The culmination of the Battle on the Ice in *Alexander Nevsky*, where
the Teuton knights are driven by the Russians across the ice which suddenly begins to crack, also seems to have been suggested to Eisenstein
by another passage in *Paradise Lost*. Without mentioning it in connection with *Nevsky*, Sergei Mikhailovich broke this passage down into
a shooting-script to illustrate how cinematic construction could be
found in poetry:

1. The overthrown he rais'd, and
2. as a Herd of Goats or timerous flock together throng'd
3. drove them before him Thunder-struck,
4. pursu'd with terrors and with furies to the bounds and Chrystall
   wall of Heav'n,
5. which opening wide, rowld inward,
6. and a spacious Gap disclos'd
7. into the wastful Deep;
8. the monstrous sight shoek them with horror backward,
9. but far worse urg'd them behind;
10. headlong themselves they threw down from the verge of
    Heav'n,
11. Eternal wrauth burnt after them to the bottomless pit.[2]

In working with Sergei Prokofiev on the musical score for *Alexander
Nevsky*, Eisenstein again seems to follow the sound and portrayal of
instruments suggested by Milton. Thus, there is echoed in the music and
imagery: 'Sonorous mettal blowing Martial sounds' and 'Of Flutes

[1] *Ibid.*   [2] *Ibid.*, p. 57.

and soft Recorders; such as rais'd to hight of noblest temper Hero's old . . .'

In an analysis of the relationship of the musical score to the images, Eisenstein later said: 'The audio-visual aspect of *Alexander Nevsky* achieves its most complete fusion in the sequence of the "Battle on the Ice"—particularly in the "attack of the knights" and the "punishment of the knights". This aspect becomes a decisive factor also, because of all the sequences of *Alexander Nevsky*, the attack seemed the most impressive and memorable to critics and spectators.'[1]

Prokofiev sought the objectivity of actual sounds . . . not the form of music, but its object. . . . At first, simple objects—'things' looked at from the viewpoints of their texture, material, materiality, structure . . . and, finally, they develop into images that embody pages of history, images of phenomena, of social systems—collective images of the people.

Thus the hoof-beats of the Teutonic knights in *Alexander Nevsky* do not merely 'hammer for the sake of hammering', but out of this 'hammer for hammer' and 'gallop for gallop' there is evolved a universal image, galloping across the thirteenth century to the twentieth—toward the unmasking of fascism.

In this inner relation of the spirit and nature of fascism, in this objectivization via fixed elements of tonal imagery, there is something akin to that period of modern painting when painters searched for the way to reveal the actuality of phenomena, through the physical composition of their materials—glass, wire, tin, or cardboard.[2]

To prevent Eisenstein from gradually transforming the script during production, Mosfilm, which had spent two million roubles on *Bezhin Meadow*, appointed D. I. Vasiliev to work with Eisenstein as his co-director. Vasiliev was to aid Eisenstein in keeping the film within the bounds of a clear political line and a story which everyone could follow, thus supplying the elements which the Soviet film industry felt had been lacking in Eisenstein's work since *Potemkin*.

Whether as the result of Vasiliev's presence or not, when completed *Alexander Nevsky* had an exceedingly close-knit and concise character, in spite of the fact that Sergei Mikhailovich injected echoes of his past qualitative style in the evolved pageant-opera form. The style is evident in the opening sequence where the land is strewn with skeletons symbolic of the battles fought with the Tartars.

[1] S. M. Eisenstein, *The Film Sense* (London, Faber and Faber, 1946), p. 136.
[2] S. M. Eisenstein, 'P-R-K-F-V'. Preface to *Sergei Prokofiev* by Israel Nestyev (New York, Alfred A. Knopf, 1946), pp. ix *et seq.*

Eisenstein's lifelong preoccupation with religion and the Church again burst out in his portrayal of the role of the Church in the Teutonic invasion. One sequence shows the part played by the Church during the sack of Pskov. Here the Black-robed Teuton Monk blesses two little Pskov children before they are thrown into the fire by a member of the Teutonic Order. This savage scene is followed by the hanging of a Pskov patriot. Surrounding the tower where the martyred man hangs above a carving of an angel is a forest of tall crucifixes held aloft by the white-robed monks accompanying the Teutonic knights [Plates 41, 48]

Eisenstein gave his further stamp to *Nevsky*, though again in a transmuted form, through his designs for the settings and costumes. The highly stylized costuming of the Teuton knights was the Eisenstein who had created such distinctive figures as the priests for *Que Viva Mexico!* and the symbolic characters in *Bezhin Meadow*.

Although the cast of actors included such artists as Nikolai Cherkasov, Nikolai Ohklopkov and Varvara Massalitinova, such talented artists could not arouse Eisenstein's interest in professional actors. Elena Telesheva, who had advised him on acting in *Bezhin Meadow*, was assigned to him as a 'consultant on work with actors'.

Pavlenko, Vasiliev and Telesheva had replaced Grigori Alexandrov, and Pera Attasheva who had stood by Eisenstein throughout his troubles over *Bezhin Meadow*. Only Eduard Tisse remained from the old days. Surrounded by new people, Sergei Mikhailovich was in a very different state of mind than he had been during the early months of directing *Bezhin Meadow*. Dreams of realizing a masterpiece and of perhaps leading a happier life were dimmed. Yet outwardly the situation was not markedly different from the *Bezhin Meadow* period.

Again enormous resources were put at Eisenstein's disposal. Working entirely with studio settings for the first time, he was denied nothing in the technical field. For the battle between the Russians and the Teutons on Lake Peipus, the Russian winter was reproduced on the studio lot near Moscow.

'My co-director, D. Vasilyev', Eisenstein wrote, 'proposed using a mixture of asphalt, water glass, white sand and chalk as a substitute for snow. Edouard Tisse, our chief cameraman, did a great deal to make it effective. . . . Water glass gave the complete illusion of a sparkling icy surface. Later on, such "ice" was used to cover an enormous field of 30,000 sq. m., where the battle scenes were shot.

'This experiment in shooting winter scenes in the summer proved successful. Of special interest are the episodes showing the knights sinking under the ice. These scenes were shot on a lake near Moscow. One part of the shore was covered with "snow", although a carpet of grass spread over the opposite bank. The shore was overlaid with sacking; "hoar-frost" on the trees was produced by covering the branches with white paint dotted with fluffs of cotton. The "ice", weighing 17.5 tons, was supported by pontoons filled with air and concealed under water. At a signal, the air was released from the pontoons and the "ice" submerged.'[1]

The 'Battle on the Ice' was shot during the torrid days of July 1938. As Tisse later explained, this created special problems. 'It must be remembered that in summer the atmospheric perspective is considerably greater and the flocks of clouds are less dense, all of which, when mixed with the sunshine, suggests warmth. In winter, on the contrary, the dome of the sky is nearer the earth and the clouds are thicker and darker.

'We created a "winter sky" by two devices: careful composition of the scene, and the use of the proper filters. As a general rule, we avoided filming soft clouds. A severe aspect of the sky was successfully transmitted to the screen with the aid of a filter combining orange and bluish light.

'Many people have asked why we chose not to use motor-cameras. Had we wished to use a motor-camera we could have filmed twenty-four and a half frames per second. But what we wanted was to accentuate and intensify the rhythm of the battle. It should be borne in mind that the weapons used—the swords, lances, axes, etc.—were mostly props, and if filmed at ordinary speed, would have given the impression of being exceedingly light. Consequently, we shot almost all the battle scenes at a speed of from eight to twelve frames per second, thereby achieving a highly dynamic quality in all the various episodes of the "Battle on the Ice".'[2]

Even though Sergei Mikhailovich was making a 'popular' film, he could not still the drive of his intellect and the seeking of his very being for 'creative ecstasy'. And once more he found it in the audio-visual effects created in collaboration with Sergei Prokofiev. As he revealed later in his writings, Eisenstein delved deeply into the matter of sound and imagery while making Nevsky, his first completed sound film. Through close collaboration with Prokofiiev, he was able to evolve new lines of theoretical thought which advanced his true interests. In this sphere, work on Alexander Nevsky was entirely satisfying; in fact, as creatively enriching to Sergei Mikhailovich as any of his earlier work.

Concerning their collaboration Eisenstein later wrote:

[1] S. M. Eisenstein, 'Director of Alexander Nevsky Describes How the Film Was Made' (Moscow News, 5 December 1938).

[2] 'How Winter Scenes Filmed' by Edward (Eduard) Tisse (Daily Worker, New York, 16 April 1939).

'You'll have the music by noon.'

We leave the small projection-room. Although it is now midnight, I feel quite calm. At exactly 11.55 a.m. a small, dark blue automobile will come through the gate of the film studio.

Sergei Prokofiev will emerge from the car.

In his hands will be the necessary piece of music.

At night we look at the new sequence of film.

By morning the new sequence of music will be ready for it.

This is what happened recently when we worked on *Alexander Nevsky*. . . .

Prokofiev is a man of the screen in that special sense which makes it possible for the screen to reveal not only the appearance and substance of objects, but also, and particularly, their peculiar inner structure. . . .

Among all the plastic arts the cinema alone, with no loss of expressive objectivity, and with complete ease resolves all [the] problems of painting, but at the same time the cinema is able to communicate much more. . . .

The camera-angle reveals the innermost being of nature. . . .

Montage structure unites the objective existence of the phenomenom with the artist's subjective relation to it. . . .

It is in this particular sense that Prokofiev's music is amazingly plastic. It is never content to remain an illustration, but everywhere, gleaming with triumphant imagery, it wonderfully reveals the inner movement of the phenomenon and its dynamic structure, in which is embodied the emotion and meaning of the event. . . .

Having grasped this structural secret of all phenomena, he clothes it in the tonal camera-angles of instrumentation, compelling it to gleam with shifts in timbre, and forces the whole inflexible structure to blossom into the emotional fullness of orchestration.

The moving graphic outlines of his musical images, which thus rise, are thrown by him on to our consciousness just as, through the blinding beam of the projector, moving images are flung on to the white plane of the screen.

This is not an engraved impression in paint of a phenomenon, but a light that pierces the phemonenon by means of tonal chiaroscuro.[1]

When *Alexander Nevsky* was finished, Eisenstein the creator of the intellectual film had evolved into the director of the spectacle film.

Completed in the record time of a little more than a year, *Alexander*

[1] S. M. Eisenstein, 'P-R-K-F-V', Preface to *Sergei Prokofiev* by Israel Nestyev (New York, Alfred A. Knopf, 1946), pp. ix *et seq*. In 1975 Kevin Brownlow and Andrew Mollo used Prokofiev's *Nevsky* 'Battle on Ice' music for their opening sequence of the Cromwellian battle in the historical film *Winstanley*.

Nevsky was released in Moscow on the 23rd of November 1938. It was a triumph exceeding even *Potemkin*, for it exactly suited the spirit of the time. Stalin is said to have slapped Eisenstein on the back and declared: 'Sergei Mikhailovich, you are a good Bolshevik after all!'

The triumph of *Alexander Nevsky* brought renewed honour and material rewards to Sergei Mikhailovich. Through this film he rose from the depths of public humiliation to an unchallenged position in the Soviet film industry. Many special honours and offices were bestowed upon him. He became a producer and the chief art director for Mosfilm. The degree of Doctor of Arts was conferred upon him by the Academy of Sciences of the U.S.S.R., Department of Cinematography. He was made a professor of cinema science, and in February 1939, he received the Order of Lenin, so long withheld from him.

For the official photograph of the awards to Soviet film workers, Eisenstein sat on the right hand of M. I. Kalinin, Chairman of the Presidium of the Supreme Soviet of the U.S.S.R. Sitting one away to the left of Kalinin were Grigori Alexandrov and his wife, Lyubov Orlova. Alexandrov smiled, delighted that he and his wife had been honoured. Everyone else looked pleased, except Sergei Mikhailovich, who sat beside the kindly Kalinin as though unconscious of his presence. Eisenstein, his sensitive mouth set into a hard, stubborn line, glowered straight into the camera as if he wished his hostile stare could break the lens to pieces. He felt that in reality he had not won the honour for himself, but had attained it under the guidance of Pavlenko, his co-scenarist, Vasiliev, his co-director, and 'Madame' Elena Telesheva. [Plate 44]

In 1940, Sergei Mikhailovich wrote an impressionistic description of the inner struggles he had faced after returning to the Soviet Union in May 1932. He set his experience as one scene in a panoramic survey of the Soviet cinema, which he depicted in terms of a ceaseless battle:

> Then would come a picture of the culminating, frightful battles, fights in the night, invisible, soundless. Not even illumined by the sudden searchlights of discussion and polemics.
>
> No more duels with an adversary, but a hand to hand duel with oneself. The most fierce of all duels, for it was fought for freeing oneself, to burn out of one's inmost self the last remnants of all that was not alive, of all that was alien, of all that draws one back and not forward, of all that leads to defeat and not victory. . . .
>
> And I would only try to forget all the clouds of suffocating gasses, with which the enemies, who managed to sneak into our cinematography, tried to slander the ideas of this or that seeker of ways, ideas of those, who, maybe, were making mistakes, but who remained

always honest and true, and who were stabbed in the back by cowardly hands.[1]

In an effort to explain Eisenstein's years of trouble to the Soviet people, VseQvolod Vishnevsky in his biographical pamphlet on Eisenstein tells how his enemies destroyed the 'important Soviet comedy *M.M.M.*', a film about Spain and the creation of the Red Army in 1917, and other projects. 'They [his enemies] suggested to Eisenstein ideas which were invalid, confused his goals, and offered useless material.'[2] Boris Shumyatsky, who had been removed from office in January 1938 and indicted, was not mentioned by name, but, according to Vishnevsky, the failure of *Bezhin Meadow* 'was due to a number of complicated factors in the process of the work itself, as well as continued efforts of enemies and saboteurs. . . . I am discussing this in detail', says Vishnevsky, 'so that the Soviet people will see concretely what great harm was caused by enemies and saboteurs in the area of the creative arts as in others. We can only imagine what Eisenstein and other great artists could have created if not hampered by these obstacles.'[3]

After its triumph in the Soviet Union, *Alexander Nevsky* was quickly released abroad. Unlike *Potemkin*, the film received a mixed reception, for it was not in the Eisenstein tradition. To many people it seemed that the Eisenstein of old was dead and in his place had risen a director with a magnificent flare for spectacle and patriotic pageantry. For some, the impression of change in Eisenstein's work may have been enhanced by the fact that the Pskov sequence, in which his savage realism and conflict with religion are evident, was partially cut in the prints shown publicly abroad.

Sergei Mikhailovich, who had said when he explained his 'mistakes' in *Bezhin Meadow* that 'the tradition of introversion and isolation had already become rooted in me', now tried to fulfil his social obligations in a way he had never done before. He learned all about the simple details attending the work of other directors, their relation with the public, and the letters they received from 'fans'. He wrote about these things in a straightforward and simple language.

In one article he said: 'I have been told that after the release of my film *Alexander Nevsky*, showing the struggle of the Russian people against the German invaders in the thirteenth century, notably the

[1] S. M. Eisenstein, *Twenty Years of Soviet Cinema* (Moscow, Goskinozdat, 1940).

[2] *Eisenstein*, a biographical pamphlet by Vsevolod Vishnevsky (Moscow, Goskinozdat, 1939), p. 20.

[3] *Ibid.*, p. 20.

famous battle of the Russian cohorts and German knights fought on the ice of Lake Peipus, there was a run on paper clips in the stationers' stores. Children have been buying boxes of paper clips by the dozen to make chain mail as worn by Alexander Nevsky. Every day, after school, young saviours of Russia armed with ply-wood shields and broom stick lances have been driving the Teuton invaders from their courtyards.'[1] While shooting *Alexander Nevsky*, Eisenstein himself could not resist the desire to don the chain mail and pose as the mighty Novgorod hero, Vasili Buslai. His utterly serious expression, like an 'overtone' to the joke, projects the image of his adolescent dreams [Plate 44]

In April 1939, Sergei Mikhailovich wrote to Jay Leyda after a silence of more than two years.

DEAR JAY!

It was a real pleasure to get your letter. I hope that from now on we will have a continuous and regular correspondence. The idea of your magazine is fine. I will let you know quite soon if I'll be able to contribute to it an article which I hope to finish soon—an article quite amusing in its ideas: 'El Greco y El Cinema'! Can you imagine a machine of some 26,000 words (!) solely occupied with the problem, how cinematic in all directions that old Spaniard behaves! C'est piquant! The thing will need quite a lot of Greco pictures and details as well as other illustrations. It is the result of a certain 'elephantiasis' undergone by one of the chapters of one of the books I'm constantly writing. I've started to work on 'Vol I' of *Rezhissera* but strange as it may seem, I'm still so tired after *Nevsky*—who was a hell of a job to be made on so short a schedule—that I cannot concentrate on the work, as concentrated I should be! Will see how everything will turn out. Also with the Greco article. Please write me *as much as you can* and *about everything of importance* and *interest* in *books*, in the *arts* and so on. . . .

What about the 'snobbishness' around Nevsky: I'd like to know as much as possible about everything—unfavorable even more than favorable (what is written in *Nation* and *New Republic*, what in magazines? What do people say about him?)

The next film will be not *so very* soon: it will probably take the whole of next summer. I'll try like hell to manage something with the book during the time the script and preparations are done. Awaiting news from you as soon as possible. . . .

---

[1] S. M. Eisenstein, 'The Soviet Screen' (Moscow, Foreign Languages Publishing House, 1939); reprinted in *Daily Worker* (New York, 25, 26, 27 September 1939).

Again Sergei Mikhailovich expressed what remained truly important to him—his theoretical work. Despite the pressure of work he had succeeded in writing a long article entitled 'Montage in 1938'. This incorporated vast research as well as originality of ideas and it had been published in January. Yet in his private life he had begun to play a new role. The honour *Alexander Nevsky* had brought him could not erase the years of defeat which had preceded it. He had furnished a home and built a dacha, but there was no one to share them. He was registered at Z.A.G.S. with Pera Attasheva, but an emotional gulf lay between them.

His contact with Elena Telesheva, which had begun during *Bezhin Meadow* and continued during *Alexander Nevsky*, now developed into a new relationship.[1] He began to appear as the 'husband' of the tall and masterful Telesheva on a round of parties and public gatherings. The assumption of this role set many people laughing and for years all manner of jokes circulated about it. It was laughingly said: 'He likes BIG women. Women six feet tall! Great grenadiers of women.'

Elena Telesheva continued to live in her own home with her daughter, while Sergei Mikhailovich lived by himself in his four-

[1] The first account I had of this relationship was given me by Marcoosha Fischer in New York. She gave me the impression that Eisenstein had married Elena Telesheva and that it was a normal, happy marriage.

But after Eisenstein's death many people, including Grigori Alexandrov, Maxim Shtraukh, and others, told me they had never understood this relationship and they gave various accounts which form the basis of what is related in the text.

In letters to me Jay Leyda says:

'I don't believe Eisenstein knew her [Telesheva] before he cast her in a role for *Bezhin Meadow*. But he must have found unusual sympathy between her (and the Art Theatre method of work with actors) and his aims, because she was soon his special assistant in the work with other actors. . . . Marriage after my departure. As you can see she is not mentioned in his letters to me.' 'Certainly it was a marriage with Telesheva—they knew each other well even when I was still there.'

In another letter to me, Margaret Bourke-White describes her impression of Eisenstein's relationship with Telesheva during the summer of 1941. 'I hardly knew Telesheva. I met her very briefly through Eisenstein. . . . I recall her as a large, unbeautiful and rather stout woman. But I recall that she had a very positive and likeable personality. You got the impression of an interesting person. . . . I remember meeting her backstage at some theatre and Eisenstein made a great point of stopping me as I rushed through, to introduce me to her. . . . Their manner towards each other was very informal and friendly, one of good companionship. As I recall it, his manner was, "Of course you must meet Telesheva", but I am afraid I paid so little attention that I hardly realized whether they were in love, living together as man and wife or what.'

roomed flat. Soon his flat at Potylika began to take on a slightly grotesque air, as if he had decided to parody the home of the woman whom he would not permit to live with him at Potylika, or in his dacha sheltered within a grove of pine trees some twenty-five miles from Moscow.

It seemed that Eisenstein's social whirl with his supposed wife was a mockery of the life he had once planned. All his tastes appeared to have become inverted. Happiest in pyjamas, or a shirt and linen trousers and canvas shoes, Sergei Mikhailovich now wore finely tailored clothes. His ties were formal rather than gay, but his hair shot up from his massive and balding skull like that of the classic clown. Apart from this strange array of hair, it was as though the elegantly dressed little boy of the Riga and St. Petersburg days had grown without a break into a man who had known nothing in life but comfort.

To Pera Attasheva this was a distortion of human relations and she could no longer bear to have anything further to do with Sergei Mikhailovich. It caused more pain because Pera had always said she was willing, even anxious, that he should find happiness and a normal life with anyone as long as the relationship was real. Perhaps Pera did Telesheva an injustice, but she felt that Telesheva was a hard, insensitive woman who had entered into this relationship because of the position Eisenstein now held in the Soviet film industry—there was honour and satisfaction in being known to the world as the wife of Eisenstein. To Pera, who had rejected all material advantages, Telesheva seemed to exploit Eisenstein and she thought Telesheva treated him as though he were an incompetent child. In spite of this, Pera accepted Telesheva gracefully.

The sharp-eyed Totya Pasha rebelled against this 'marriage'. Filled with anger, she would come to Pera's flat to ease her heart. She said that Sergei Mikhailovich, who had lived quietly, was now expected by Elena Telesheva to give fine parties equal to her own! The flat at Potylika—what it had become! She complained about Telesheva, who expected her to come and clean up Telesheva's home whenever there was a party. Telesheva had a kind of butler and she lived like a great lady—as they lived before the Revolution! Totya Pasha probably exaggerated the faults of Telesheva, for she was like a tigress in defence of Eisenstein, into whom she had once inculcated much of her own quality of simplicity and honesty.

Still the deepest part of Eisenstein was invulnerable. He continued to think his own thoughts and they remained untouched by Telesheva, or the public performance of his 'husband' role. Sergei Mikhailovich continued with his theoretical work and writing and, in collaboration with Alexander Fadeyev, worked on the proposed film of the civil war. The theme was Frunze's drive in 1920 against the White Guards concentrated under Baron Wrangel in the Crimea and it was to be called *Perekop*.

In May 1939, while Eisenstein was at work on this project, the chapter of his creative life which he thought had closed at Yalta with his verbal recreation of *Que Viva Mexico!* was suddenly reopened. Actually, the Mexican film had not been destroyed.

In 1938 I had gone to America and when I arrived in Hollywood in 1939 I learned that the story of the total dismemberment of *Que Viva Mexico!* was not true. The footage remaining after the editing of *Thunder Over Mexico* and the short film *Death Day*, had lain unclassified in a stockshot vault in Hollywood. I also learned that at this time Upton Sinclair was proposing to hand over the whole of the film to Herman J. Kleinhanz for him to cut into a series of travelogues. In order to prevent this, I purchased several thousand feet and took a two-year option on the remainder. I then checked every shot of the footage and, after visiting Mexico, made a complete list of the shots, which I sent to Sergei Mikhailovich through Amkino (Artkino), the Soviet film agency in America. Because there were many retakes of all the material used in *Thunder Over Mexico* and *Death Day*, I knew that Eisenstein could edit *Que Viva Mexico!* substantially as he had outlined it to me at Yalta in 1934.

At first the list of material seemed complete to Eisenstein, and he asked the Soviet film industry if they could make arrangements to purchase the film. Then he looked over the list again. The epilogue—the Day of the Dead—was the one which most concerned him. But under the classification of *Death Day* I had not listed every 'take' individually. He sent a cablegram to Artkino, asking if the Death Day sequence was complete. I assured Artkino that there seemed to be duplicate 'takes' of all the shots. So Sergei Mikhailovich again cabled to Artkino saying that if the whole of *Que Viva Mexico!* could not be purchased, there was one section he wanted very much—Death Day. This he wanted for himself.

Negotiations then slowed down as the threat of war increased during the summer of 1939. At last I sent a letter through Artkino saying that if the Soviet film industry were not going to purchase the material, then I would attempt to edit a film using all sequences of the material. However, the negative would always be at Eisenstein's disposal and I said that I would make an effort to preserve the remaining footage.[1]

[1] After editing the film, *Time in the Sun*, from Eisenstein's *Que Viva Mexico!* material (with Paul Burnford as my assistant), I made an effort to preserve the remaining footage. The Second World War broke out during the early stages of work on *Time in the Sun*. Not having funds of my own with which to pur-

The rediscovery of *Que Viva Mexico!* in 1939 came too late. Sergei Mikhailovich could not escape the realization that he would now have to change his original montage plan since it was based entirely on the aesthetic principles he had repudiated in 1937 following *Bezhin Meadow*. *Que Viva Mexico!* could never become the film he had envisioned during his moments of inspiration in Mexico. Without explanation he dropped the matter.

Yet Eisenstein still loved Mexico with a great passion. What he had experienced there was the deepest emotional and philosophic experience in his life. He had been happier there than at any time.

With the matter of *Que Viva Mexico!* left to other hands, Sergei Mikhailovich changed his immediate creative plans. The civil war film was abandoned. He could not complete *Que Viva Mexico!*, but he could perhaps go forward from its revived image in a new form acceptable to the current style of Soviet films. He flung himself into a project which would take him away from Moscow and into a new and strange world. He began work on a film history of Central Asia from antiquity to the present day called *Ferghana Canal*. The first draft of the script is dated 1–2–3 August 1939. Later in the month he wrote to Jay Leyda:

> Everything is changed—I'm not making *Frunze* [Perekop] (for the moment) instead of that I'm making a big film in Central Asia—starting with Tamerlaine the Great on the background of the architectural marvels of Samarkand, Bokhara etc. And up to today and the building of the enormous Ferghana Canal. It will be the epic of the struggle of humanity against the deserts and sands of Asia. And the struggle for water—highly dramatic and spectacular. Together with Pavlenko (and in no way documentary!). . . .
>
> My correspondence will be transferred to me, so you can write me as always. . . .

And in no way documentary! *Que Viva Mexico!*—'a living history' composed of 'four novels framed by prologue and epilogue, unified in

---

chase the remaining footage, I approached friends of Eisenstein without success. Then I asked the Museum of Modern Art Film Library in New York to purchase the film and keep it for Eisenstein, but they said they were not set up to preserve unedited film. Finally, Upton Sinclair made an arrangement with Bell and Howell, the motion picture equipment company of Chicago, Illinois, to take over the remaining footage (approximately 140,000 feet), and in 1941 and 1942 a series of educational pictures for use in schools were edited under the supervision of William F. Kruse. These pictures, ranging in length from one to two reels, were *Mexico Marches*, *Conquering Cross*, *Idol of Hope*, *Land and Freedom*, *Spaniard and Indian* and *Zapotec Village*. The first five of these films are also sometimes shown together as a feature-length picture under the title *Mexican Symphony*.

conception and spirit, creating its entity'. *Ferghana Canal*, a dramatic film, its prologue, as in *Que Viva Mexico!*, the passing away of a great civilization symbolized by a burial. In Mexico the burial of one man; in Central Asia the burial of thousands. In Mexico the thread of unity —the sarape, the blanket clothing all Indian bodies—in *Ferghana Canal* water, without which man cannot live. Both films unfinished, both commencing with the image of death. In *Que Viva Mexico!* death as a natural phenomenon, mysteriously surrounded by terrifying static images—the gods of death, their dreadful features immobilized in stone. In *Ferghana Canal* death to thousands when their source of water is diverted by the conqueror, Tamerlaine, and, in turn, death to the conquering horde when the water is let loose in flood against them by a group of masons from the stricken city. In each film opening scenes untroubled and suggestive of eternity.

1. (m.s.) The singer Tokhtasin sings, gazing into the desert. . . .
2. (m.s.) . . . singing a song of a flowering land, such as was known in the days of the ancient land of Khoresm. . . .
3. (l.s.) Before Tokhtasin spreads the endless desert. . . .
4. (l.s.) The infinite sands of the desert. . . . Over the words of the song, dissolve to . . .
4A. (c.u.) . . . a spray of a delicately flowering bush . . .
5. (m.s.) . . . surrounded by young trees, clipped and blossoming. . . .
6. (l.s.) And lo! before us a whole shady oasis is disclosed . . .
7. (m.s.) . . . its trees reflected in a broad artificial lake . . .
8. (c.u.) . . . an aqueduct flows into the lake. . . .
15. (l.s.) Water pours from huge reservoirs. It is caught in jars . . .
16. (m.s.) . . . and from these jars it is poured into large vessels. . . .
17. (l.s.) Streams of people pour over the monumental staircase of the ancient city.
18. (m.s.) Suspended in the sky are the pale blue domes of the academy, the mosque, the shrine. . . .

as in far off Yucatan, where the prologue of *Que Viva Mexico!* was set, the Maya observatory, the pyramid temple and the shrine of the warriors shimmered against another tropical sky.

29. (m.s.) Tamerlaine . . .
30. (c.u.) . . . with narrowed eyes. He strokes a sparse beard. Not tall he is slender—almost feeble in appearance. In his simple robe and plain black skull-cap, a common handkerchief for girdle, he seems quite ordinary.
31. (m.s.) Turned towards distant Urganj, like a fearsome wall, stands the army of Tamerlaine.

32. (m.s.) Without looking towards his standing officers—young
and old—Tamerlaine quietly speaks:
'Water is the strength of that city.'
After a moment's silence, he adds:
'Take away the water from Urganj.'
And without pause we hear the cracking of whips in the air. . . .

Thus, Tamerlaine seems to stand like the symbolic priests of *Que
Viva Mexico!*, who cast down the ancient gods and tore apart the
temples at the bidding of the gold-hungry Cortes. From shot No. 33
through to shot No. 118, Sergei Mikhailovich pushed forward to the
dramatic film. It is as if the ravaging of Tamerlaine is 'writing on the
wall' presaging Eisenstein's final film, *Ivan the Terrible*, but without the
subjective undertones which were to be there.

94. (l.s.) The warriors of Tamerlaine burst through the breach in the
city wall, laying waste everything in their path.

95. (m.s.) Hanging across the walls are the defenders, dead of
thirst. . . .

96. (l.s.) Others who have died of thirst are strewn over the flight
of broad stairs. . . .

97. (m.s.) The dried-up lake. At its bottom are more bodies. . . .

100. (m.s.) In the midst of jewelry and precious stones lies a merchant, dead of thirst. . . .

101. (m.s.) In a half-darkened cell of the old academy, an old scholar
has died—resembling a mummy, bent over his withered
parchment.

102. (l.s.) The imprisoned wives of the Emir are dying in their
harem, like quail in festive cages. The rooms have doors of
rare woods and windows of mica.

103. (m.s.) Motionless, they lie naked or dressed in splendid gowns,
upon the rugs and divans of the harem.

104. (m.s.) At the edge of a dried sunken basin, a young wife of the
Emir is dying of thirst. At the bottom of the basin are some
dead fish. Over all these pictures of death expands the music
of roaring and rushing sound. . . .

But with shot No. 119, Sergei Mikhailovich turned back again, to
the past; yet not to *Que Viva Mexico!*, still further back—to the
moment when he had first discovered Leonardo da Vinci's extraordinary writing, *The Deluge*,[1] which was a 'shooting-script' when
there was no more dynamic medium than the fresco. Da Vinci's *Deluge*

---

[1] Quoted in the form of a 'shooting-script' by Eisenstein in *The Film Sense*
(London, Faber and Faber, 1948), pp. 29–32.

and Eisenstein's *Ferghana Canal* are so closely related in approach and use of imagery that when 'intercut' they form a single sequence of dramatic action:

DA VINCI: . . . until the pent-up rivers rise in flood and cover the wide plains and their inhabitants. . . .

EISENSTEIN: 119. (l.s.) Water rushes through the gap, which rapidly widens. The whole canal wall collapses and the river bursts over-overflowing on to the sand.

DA VINCI: . . . And the fields which were covered with water had their waves covered over in great part with tables, bedsteads, boats and various other kinds of rafts . . . upon which were men and women with their children, massed together and uttering various cries and lamentations, dismayed by the fury of the winds which were causing the waters to roll over and over in mighty hurricane, bearing with them the bodies of the drowned. . . .

EISENSTEIN: 121. (l.s.) The wild torrents of water rush towards the army of Tamerlaine, still passing through the gate.

122. (m.s.) The throng of dusty warriors is swept up in the rushing water. . . .

123. (m.s.) The water dashes against the horsemen, rising over them. . . .

DA VINCI: And there was no object that floated on the water but was covered with various different animals. . . .

EISENSTEIN: 130. (l.s.) The water rushes over the desert towards the horizon. People, horses, camels, sheep are swimming and drowning in the flood. . . .

131. (m.s.) The battle elephants circle desperately. Drowning men climb on to them.

132. (l.s.) A tremendous mass of water flows over the desert. Cutting through the noise of the water is a new noise—the howl of the wind . . . of an approaching sand-storm. . . .

133. (l.s.) Howling and whistling the sand-storm attacks the water.

139. (l.s.) The city is buried in sand.

140. (l.s.) The ruined mosque, engulfed by sand. . . .

141. (l.s.) The endless desert. . . .

142. (m.s.) . . . The scattered 'skeletons of people, horses . . .

143. (m.s.) . . . skeletons of camels, half covered with bricks.

144. (m.s.) An overturned chest—scattered gold coins.

145. (c.u.) The gold coins sliding over the sand make an unexpectedly loud sound. . . .[1]

---

[1] S. M. Eisenstein and P. Pavlenko, shooting-script *Ferghana Canal*. Above quotations taken from Jay Leyda's translation, *The Film Sense* (London, Faber and Faber, 1948), pp. 201 *et seq.*

Once before Sergei Mikhailovich had expressed the idea of gold destroying man and nature. It was in *Sutter's Gold*, where:

The sounds of destruction swell to colossal proportions.
Sutter is in an agony of despair.
And the saws continue to whine, and the axes to chop, and the trees to crash and the picks to hammer upon the stones.
The gold-diggers curse in the fever of their hunt.
These things madden Sutter, and he takes refuge in the darkness of the forest. . . .

—the film which had been stopped by the internal politics of Paramount and the external pressure of the Daughters of the American Revolution.

On leaving Hollywood for Mexico, Eisenstein said he had seen man's history telescoped, with decadence and blight writing a last chapter to history. Death and destruction appeared to haunt him, but he could not end the film on this note. Soviet art must be optimistic, so in the scenario the desert came to life once more and in time flourished with the last stage to date—the building of the Ferghana Canal.

Beyond the new turn in his creative work, Sergei Mikhailovich felt compelled to seek escape from the mocking role he had assumed with Elena Telesheva. There was nowhere for him to go except to Pera Attasheva; but she had suffered too much. Though she did not refuse to see the Old Man, she made it clear to him that she would not re-establish the former pattern of their lives.

Yet he persisted. He would come to the Gogolevsky Boulevard in the hope of being able to talk to Pera for a few hours. If Pera was out, he would spend the time with her sister, Zina, who had married and had a small child. As he played with the boy, teaching him to talk and draw, his gruff tone and off-hand manner peeled away and after almost fifteen years, Zina discovered that Eisenstein was a humane man. She came to like him, despite the suffering he had brought to her sister. She felt sorry for him when one day her child was drawing a picture and Eisenstein said to him: 'Mind that you don't become a genius.'

'What's a genius?' asked the boy.

'It is to be someone who is never understood,' Sergei Mikhailovich answered.

Often Telesheva would send Loshka, Eisenstein's chauffeur, to find him and take him to her home so that they could make some public appearance. She acted as if the Old Man were her property. Sometimes he would plead with Zina to say he was not there, for he now loathed the symbolic figure who victimized him, and whom in turn he could only victimize. He expressed his contempt by giving Telesheva no name save that of 'Madame'. She was a 'great lady', the last of 'em. She should send her carriage and a coachman for him, not a car.

In September 1939 Sergei Mikhailovich left Moscow for an exploratory expedition in Central Asia in connection with the making of *Ferghana Canal*. Before leaving, he received information that the film *Time in the Sun*, edited from the footage of *Que Viva Mexico!*, would be previewed early in October at the Academy of Motion Picture Arts and Sciences in Hollywood. The negative would always be held for him and efforts would be made to find a means of preserving the remaining footage. As this news came, Hitler poured his troops into Poland, cutting the world in two. War had come, though the recent German-Soviet Pact was to protect Russia for almost two summers longer.

Suddenly Eisenstein decided to make a gesture of support towards the Academy. He obtained an old 1917 two-dollar bill, put it in an envelope with a sheet of paper bearing his signature and a request for membership in the Academy of Motion Picture Arts and Sciences. He air-mailed the letter to Hollywood, where it arrived on the 8th of September, one week after the outbreak of the Second World War. His act was so unexpected after nine years of total silence that it caused surprise and a search for some explanation.

The expedition to Central Asia produced some footage. But *Ferghana Canal* as an epic film was finally abandoned. It was not a picture particularly suited to the new phase into which the Soviet Union was passing, and all that remained of the great new dream was a short documentary film on the opening of the Ferghana Canal.

Upon his return to Moscow, Eisenstein was confronted with a somewhat ironic set of circumstances. He had ascended to his position of renewed prestige through the success of *Alexander Nevsky*, a film clearly directed against the aggressive intentions of Germany. In connection with the film's release in 1938 he had written an article entitled 'My Subject is Patriotism' in which he attacked Nazism still more violently than in his 'Open Letter to Dr. Goebbels' in 1934.

I do not believe [Eisenstein wrote] that any period in history witnessed such an orgy of violence to all human ideals as has resulted in recent years from the growing insolence of fascist aggression. . . . Nothing could seem more terrible. But every new day brings us news of greater outrages, greater savagery. It is hard to believe your eyes when you read of the unbridled ferocity of the Jewish pogroms in Germany, where before the eyes of the world hundreds and thousands of downtrodden people, shorn of human aid, are being wiped from the face of the earth. . . .
Just as the hounds of fascism are tearing to shreds Czechoslo-

vakian culture . . . so did the Teuton knights of the thirteenth century eradicate everything which each nation or nationality possessed and treasured as its own. . . .[1]

With the signing of the Nazi-Soviet Pact in August 1939, *Alexander Nevsky* became an embarrassing film, even though the Soviet leaders and the Russian people knew that it echoed the truth as to their fate, which the Pact was designed to stave off for a short time. However, *Alexander Nevsky* was withdrawn in the Soviet Union for more than eighteen months.

Eisenstein tried to understand the situation. The Russians had made every effort to form a solid bloc against fascism with the Western powers, who had capitulated to the will of Hitler at Munich. But his ironic turn of mind could only suffer a certain shock when he was asked to play a part in the Soviet-Nazi accord.

Of Russian artists, Sergei Eisenstein was the best-known in Germany. His international reputation had begun in Berlin with the release of *Potemkin*; the Germans had acclaimed him in 1926 and in 1929, when he set forth to discover the world. The Nazi Propaganda Minister, Joseph Goebbels, crowned him in German eyes in 1934 when he had extolled *Potemkin* as the example Hitler's film industry should follow.

So it was proposed to Sergei Mikhailovich that he initiate a suitable Russian-German cultural programme. He was a Soviet citizen first and his feelings as a man, who had received the lash of anti-Semitic epithets in America and would, if in Germany, be branded with the Star of David, or marked with a number in a concentration camp on account of his ancestry, had to be suppressed. On February the 18th, 1940, Eisenstein (which in German means 'iron stone') spoke to the people of Germany over the Comintern Radio Station in Moscow. In his flawless German he said that the Pact of August 1939 formed a solid basis 'for increased cultural co-operation between the two great peoples!'

Eisenstein thus performed his official duties, but at the same time he seized upon the smallest opening to assert his independent views. Just as he had personally challenged Joseph Goebbels in 1934, so in 1940, Sergei Mikhailovich attacked American businessmen for using his name in connection with the re-issue of D. W. Griffith's film *Birth of a Nation*. In a letter to the editors of *International Literature*, Eisenstein said:

> Certain shrewd businessmen, seeking to advertise the film [*Birth of a Nation*], made assertions to the effect that I have praised it and have stated that in its time *Birth of a Nation* greatly influenced my creative work. I emphatically protest against these assertions. True,

[1] S. M. Eisenstein, 'My Subject is Patriotism' (Moscow, *International Literature*, No. 2, 1939).

I've always given Griffith his due as an outstanding master of the bourgeois film. But this can in no way be applied to *Birth of a Nation*. . . .

This film has never been shown here [U.S.S.R.] and I saw it abroad after *Potemkin* appeared and therefore I could in no way have been influenced by *Birth of a Nation*. The disgraceful propaganda of racial hatred toward colored people which permeates this film cannot be redeemed by purely cinematographic effects in this production.[1]

The Comintern broadcast was only the beginning of Eisenstein's association with the German cultural programme, though the further aspect of it had its own intrinsic interest and allowed him to make an excursion into yet another realm of artistic expression—the opera. The management of Moscow's Bolshoi Theatre (the scene of Eisenstein's first triumph, his disgrace in 1935 and the presentation to him of the Order of Lenin) proposed that he direct the production of the Wagnerian opera, *The Valkyrie*. It was not at all a strange digression from Eisenstein's main line of creative work, considering his original experience in the theatre and his development of the pageant-opera form in *Alexander Nevsky*.

The proposal touched Sergei Mikhailovich at several points all at once and each was penetrating. In his early teens he had become absorbed in the saga of the Ring of the Nibelung and had written of it to his mother on a card which was never posted. Since then the saga had assumed further interest: the psychological character of the heroes involved and their relationships to one another, and the saga's portrayal of ancient society in the transitional period between the time when no taboo existed against incest, and the time when the strictest taboo against any such relationship was imposed. There was every reason for Sergei Mikhailovich to desire to direct *The Valkyrie*, for it was a work of art in certain respects expressive of himself, though in an exceedingly disguised and complex form. One fact was obvious: Elena Telesheva, had she been an operatic singer and not an actress, would have been the ideal figure for Fricka, the wife who forces a new morality upon the more ancient amoral Wotan, God of Nature.

Eisenstein, in his own words, approached this adventure 'with indescribable enthusiasm and inspiration'. Apart from the many special interests of *The Valkyrie*, the essentially synthetic character of opera served as a laboratory for experiment where he was able to translate into

[1] S. M. Eisenstein, 'To the Editors of "International Literature"; a communication'. (Moscow, *International Literature*, November–December 1940.) Reprinted in the *Daily Worker* (New York, 14 January 1941).

art-form many of the theoretical ideas developed through his years of research. Beginning at the core, he cast out lines of emotional response to the many problems contained within the whole structure of the opera. The production should in no way be bound to former operatic traditions which accented but two elements, that of music and the singer's quality of voice, leaving all other elements in the work dormant. Since he was free to originate the settings and costumes, no side of the production was beyond his control.

From the beginning he found himself in sympathy with Wagner's musical dramas which gave him the possibility of realizing 'in a new quality' his own constant passion—the 'internal unity of sound and sight'. Whatever he discovered through the production of opera he could later translate into further film development. 'Men, music, light, landscape, colour and motion brought into one integral whole by a single piercing emotion, by a single theme and idea,' was his aim.

He also saw a link between Richard Wagner and himself. Both he and Wagner had been participants in revolutions which had turned them against the bourgeois world whose symbol was gold, the source of evil. Both had subsequently turned to the past in order to enrich their creative work.

Eisenstein recognized that his main problem as a producer of Wagner's opera was his 'direct perception of the music and its answering embodiment on the stage'. In order to 'sense the form in which it should be unfolded on the stage', he immersed himself in the music which called up within him intense visual imagery of an exceedingly dynamic character. As he later wrote, his own feelings were best conveyed in a letter written by Wagner to Franz Liszt: 'Everything in *The Valkyrie* is activity and passion, which, even though it may be chained, is not directed inward; passion that strains outward and breaks out; passion that turns into . . . the saturnalia of elemental passions.'[1]

He found the music for *The Valkyrie* impregnated with the sense of the ancient past of mankind when all men thought and felt in a manner which had survived only among remote tribal people; the spirit as manifested in the Polynesian custom of opening the doors and windows to aid the passage of a new life into the world. To Eisenstein, the gods and men of Wagner's tetralogy appeared to be at the stage where man, 'the author of myths, folk-lore, and epics, pictured nature's participation in his personal life'. Sergei Mikhailovich's concept came from

[1] The excerpts quoted in the analysis of Eisenstein's production of *The Valkyrie* are taken from two articles written by Eisenstein in connection with the production. One, 'Eisenstein Makes his Debut in Opera' (*Moscow News*, 28 November 1940), the other an unpublished article in the possession of Jay Leyda.

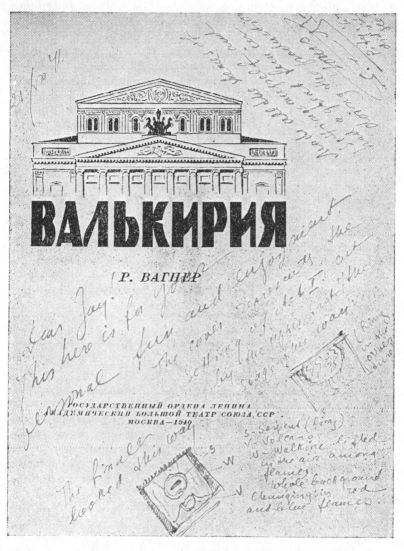

11. First page of 'Valkyrie' brochure with Eisenstein's sketches, and note to Jay Leyda

the years he had spent poring over *The Golden Bough*, and other works on anthropology. At last he had the opportunity to create a work of art expressive of man's early ways of thought.

It seemed to him that previous directors of the opera had regarded the characters merely as voices to sing Wagner's music; but to Eisenstein they were people torn by great passions within a real society. They were his own psychological and social ancestors as well as those of Wagner, who had, in Sergei Mikhailovich's words, felt that folk legends preserve 'the eternal images, born of the wisdom of the people', which enabled 'every generation, every new epoch to understand and appreciate these great images historically'.

Wotan. Costume design by
Peter Williams based on sketches
by Eisenstein

Though Eisenstein's production of *The Valkyrie* was based, as he stated later, more on emotion than reason, he thought that his years of scientific research and his ever-deepening studies of Marxist dialectics anchored his work to reality rather than to unleashed fantasy. As he proceeded, he decided that the heart of *The Valkyrie* was supplied by the story of the relationship between the six characters who represented the clash of three moral and ethical points of view: Wotan, 'the ancient German personification of the forces of nature'; Fricka, his wife, who as a new goddess—that of Marriage—'protects the sanctity of the domestic hearth'; Wotan's daughter, the Valkyrie Brünnhilde, 'the executress of his will'; Siegmund and his twin sister, Sieglinde, representatives of the pre-Fricka morality, where brothers and sisters married each other, and Sieglinde's husband, Hunding, 'the representative of the crudest, atavistic stage of the tribe'. In selecting his singers, Sergei Mikhailovich appears to have chosen tall people. He accentuated their natural height by the style of their costumes and headdresses
[Plate 46]

The two supports for the psychological and sociological drama created through the actions and reactions of the six people was the music on the one hand and the scenic decoration on the other. In order to create unity, every passage of Wagner's music had to be visibly connected with the inner passions of the characters, and the physical motions called up in response. Likewise the settings, expressive of man surrounded by nature, had to respond to the dynamic fluctuations of the characters' passions and the expressiveness of the music. As Sergei Mikhailovich later wrote:

> ... the decoration ... should serve not merely for the ornamentation or artistic arrangement of the stage, not merely as laconic data on the place of the action, but as the support of plastic action, just as that inimitable music which calls the performance as a whole into life serves as the sound support for it ... the decorations would be part of the single dynamic whirlwind that engendered the music to whose lot it fell to congeal fast in the scenic spaces as machines and colours, steps and precipices, surfaces and planes, so as to serve as support for the actions and deeds of the actors.

As part of the scenic design, the *décor* would at certain moments become contiguous to and expressive of the state of consciousness within the characters. This was not new, for Sergei Mikhailovich had planned to have scenery in motion as reflective of the changing state of mind under the influence of intoxication in the last act of the unrealized play, *Moscow the Second*. That was almost six years before. Now in *The Valkyrie* inner emotions, visible action and scenery depicting nature came into a unified relation expressed in dynamic motion in the battle between Hunding and Siegmund, where the lives of the heroes found an echo in the phenomena of nature. As they battled for possession of the woman, sister-mistress to one and wife to the other, two mountains rose up, and having risen within sight of the spectator, oscillated in a rising and falling motion in rhythm with the movements of the men. By such means Sergei Mikhailovich sought to fuse all the elements into one creative scheme of motion. (See p. 404.)

One other element was also introduced: that of original pantomimic choruses, which were to convey 'the feeling that is typical of the period of epics, legends and myths. That is the feeling that man is not yet cognizant of himself as an independent unit set apart from nature as an individual that has already acquired independence within the collective body.' For this reason the pantomimic choruses were brought into a very special and expressive relationship with the characters, revealing the thought processes of primitive man to whom nature appears as another being like himself, a responsive 'being now gracious, now

The battle between Hunding and Siegmund with Hunding's pantomimic chorus.

The two mountains were raising and falling in the rhythm of the battle. Wotan actually stopped the battle by the way shown on picture

austere, at times echoing his own feelings, at others opposing them'. So it came to Sergei Mikhailovich to enfold the characters at certain times within the movement of their own distinctive pantomimic choruses.

Thus Hunding—the representative of [the age] when the tribe is still nothing more than a horde close to the flock, the herd, or the pack—appears surrounded by the myriapodous, shaggy body of his pack, a body which, on falling to the earth, appears to be a hunting pack of a leader, and which, upon rising to its feet, appears to be Hunding's encirclement—kinsfolk, armour-bearers, servants. . . .

14. Hunding   15 Hunding's pantomimic
                            chorus

Costume designs by Peter Williams based on
sketches by Eisenstein

The Hunding chorus projected a most penetrating image of a social period. It served as an objectivization of a stage in the evolution of society and the transposition in art of a transitional stage in man's thinking and social organization. But another chorus had a very different character, one which no one seeing it in stage movement would detect as springing out of the very soul of Sergei Mikhailovich unless they knew of the many strange and painful experiences through which he had passed since he was a little child.

Fricka—who compels her husband, Wotan, to withdraw support from his son, Siegmund, who must do battle with her protégé, Hunding, to retain his sister-mistress, Sieglinde, and thereafter induces Wotan to break his son's sword so that Hunding kills Siegmund and regains possession of the beloved Sieglinde—

comes upon the stage surrounded by a chorus of golden-fleeced half-sheep, half-men—partly like domesticated animals, partly like men who have abjured their own passions and have voluntarily put on the yoke of the tamed instead. Fricka exercises sole sway over them. Fawning servilely, bent to the ground, whipped on by her, they swiftly pull her wraithlike and victorious chariot from the stage.

These were perhaps the only words Sergei Mikhailovich left to record the image born from his own experience as the apparent husband of a woman who, looking the embodiment of the goddess Fricka, sent the chauffeur, Loshka, for him when he was required to go with her as an escort.

The Valkyrie opened at the Bolshoi Theatre on the 21st of November 1940. Working with his emotions rather than reason had liberated Eisenstein from accumulated tension. He was pleased with his production and when a brochure of the opera was published, he sent a copy to Jay Leyda in which he explained his scenic devices and remarked how he 'made all the schemes of settings myself and had a great fun in doing the production. Pity you didn't see it.'

Sergei Mikhailovich may also have better understood his development as a man and an artist as a result of *The Valkyrie*. Certainly time had lessened the bitterness which had made any relationship with Pera impossible. Now they saw each other occasionally but the bond which had once existed between them was never re-established.

Note 1977. Professor H.W. L. Dana told me that he was shocked when, at an evening party at Telesheva's, she and her friends expressed strongly anti-Semitic sentiments in his presence. This was never mentioned by anyone else. For this reason it was omitted from the first edition of this book as a too appalling twist to Eisenstein's life to make public, especially as Pera Attasheva was still alive.

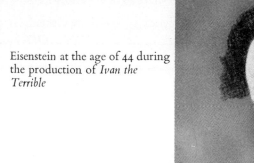

Eisenstein at the age of 44 during the production of *Ivan the Terrible*

Self-portrait drawn at Alma Ata where Eisenstein worked on *Ivan the Terrible*, 1942

From the Prologue of *Ivan the
Terrible*, Part I

'The legs of Ivan hang helplessly from
the throne. They swing about but
cannot reach the floor' (Scenario)

Ivan the Terrible,
Part I, 1941–45

The Prologue: 'An eight-year-old boy, crouching fearfully into a corner.' (Scenario)
(Moved to Part 2)

The Coronation: Ivan (Nikolai Cherkassov) 'stands like one immured as the pronouncement continues: "For Thine is the Kingdom, the Power and the Glory" . . .' (Scenario)

By courtesy of Artkino, New York

'He sees refusal in their eyes. He raises himself on the bed. He is supported by Anastasia . . .' (Scenario)

Ivan the Terrible, Part I, 1941–45

The All-Seeing Eye of God
Anastasia (Ludmilla Tselikovskaya) rejects Kurbsky (Nikolai Nazvanov)

Ivan the Terrible, Part I, 1941–45

Eisenstein's sketch for the shot below

The Coffin of Anastasia

' "I am weary of my crying . . . my throat is dried . . . my eyes fail while I wait for my God . . .' (Scenario)

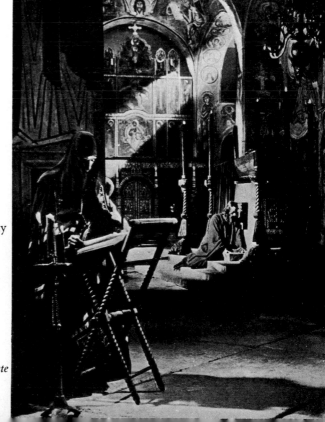

courtesy of the British Film Institute

The people came to Alexander Sloboda to call Ivan back to Moscow. End of Part I

Ivan the Terrible, Part I, 1941–45

Philip the Metropolitan swears before the bodies of his dead brothers: 'To bend the Tsar, humble him . . . crush him with the Church.' (Scenario)

Ivan the Terrible, Part II, 1941–46

The Mystery of the Hebrew Children
'Thrice Ivan bowed his head, Thrice Philip turns away.' (Scenario)

Ivan the Terrible, Part II, 1941–46

'The Tsar and the Priest, above them the Angel—angry—Apocalyptic—its feet trampling the Universe.' (Scenario)

'I ask not as Tsar . . . Leave me not in loneliness. Be with me.' (Scenario)

By courtesy of the British Film Instit

Eisenstein's sketch for the third picture in this sequence

'He [Philip] tore away his mantle uttering coldly . . . "Alone." ' (Scenario)

Ivan the Terrible, Part II, 1941–46

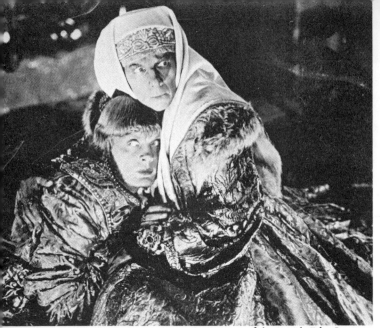

By courtesy of the British Film Institute

Euphrosinia Staritskaya (Seraphina Birman) and Vladimir Andreyevitch (Piotr Kodochnikov)
'Fearful of murder . . . he whispers in terror: "And why are you pushing me to power?"
The powerful old woman embraces her son . . . and sings him a lullaby. A strange,
evil lullaby . . .' (Scenario)

'And from the depths comes slowly towards her . . . Ivan.' (Scenario)

By courtesy of the British Film Institute

By courtesy of the British Film Institute

Ivan the Terrible, Part II, 1941–46

Note the extraordinary resemblance of Eisenstein playing cops and robbers about 1909 with the peaked hoods of the oprichniks. See also pp. 162–63

60

Ivan the Terrible, Part II, 1941–46   The Last Judgement in the Cathedral. See pp. 437–9

From Part III
(un-shot), the end
of the scenario:
'Ivan reaches
the sea of his child-
hood song
     Ocean-sea,
     Azure sea
     Azure sea
     Russian sea'

Two drawings by
Eisenstein

'Roberta sitting on her trunk'
an example of Eisenstein's play
on words drawn while working
on *An American Tragedy*,
Hollywood, 1930

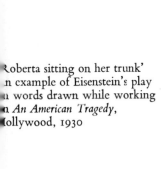

*Eisenstein Collection, Museum
of Modern Art, New York*

'Souvenir d'enfance'
Nostalgia; 1942

By courtesy of Lee Bland

Eisenstein at his 'dacha' outside Moscow, with Lee Bland, July 16, 1946

'The challenging eyes of youth.' Eisenstein as a Spanish conquistador, a portrait by Roberto Montenegro, Mexico, 1931

By courtesy of Artkino, New York

Eisenstein's study in his Potylika flat at the time of his death, February 10, 1948

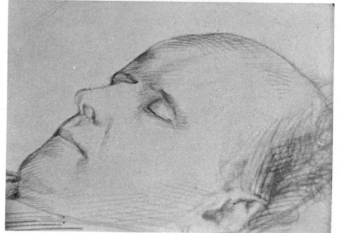

Death mask

Eisenstein lying in state at Dom Kino, Moscow
Standing on the right: Pera Attasheva

The interring of Eisenstein's ashes, Moscow, February 13, 1948
Front row centre: Eduard Tisse and, next to him in a black hat, Pera Attasheva

CHAPTER FIFTEEN

'Ivan the Terrible'

We have no lack of system . . . to parcel out these poor days of ours; wherein it should be our pleasure that they be not squandered or suffered to pass away in vain, and without meed of honour, leaving no record of themselves in the minds of men; to the end that this our poor course may not be sped in vain.

LEONARDO DA VINCI, C.A. 12 v.a.

WHILE Sergei Mikhailovich worked on *The Valkyrie*, war raged to the west. The trend in the Soviet Union towards a revival of national consciousness, reflected in the popularity of *Alexander Nevsky*, continued. Emphasis was laid on historical films which would inculcate a feeling of self-respect and strength in the Russian people. When war came to Russia, the people would require every material and psychological weapon with which to combat the enemy.

But in the years following the Revolution, few, if any, people had been interested in the heroes of Tsarist Russia. Only one figure had retained some features of a hero in Soviet eyes; that was Peter the Great, who attempted to drag the sprawling land of Russia out of the slough of medievalism and barbarity by forcible introduction of Western European ideas, and the building of Petrograd after the defeat of the Swedes. Between 1936 and 1938, Peter appeared as the hero of two films. Another historical figure in whom interest had been revived was Tsar Ivan the Terrible, who had served as the central character in two plays by Alexis Tolstoy.

With these small beginnings the past again became an important factor in the Soviet attitude; this, so far as Eisenstein was concerned, had culminated in his own *Alexander Nevsky*. At the same time, Vsevolod Pudovkin had directed an historical film, *Minin and Pozharsky*, which told of the defeat of the Polish invaders in the seventeenth century.

Historical films were dotted through the Soviet production schedules of 1940 and 1941. In response to this trend, Mosfilm, the Soviet film trust which had produced *Alexander Nevsky*, decided to produce a film on Ivan the Terrible. It was considered an important picture and, because of Eisenstein's success with *Alexander Nevsky*, he was chosen to direct it. The film was placed on Mosfilm's production schedule before the Germans turned eastward to attack the Soviet Union in June of 1941.

In the meantime, following the production of *The Valkyrie* in November 1940, Sergei Mikhailovich had time to concentrate on 'one of the books I'm constantly writing'.

The stack of notes and manuscripts which had been accumulating over the years had grown to huge proportions. It ranged over a vast field and during the years Sergei Mikhailovich had dipped into this reservoir of ideas and observations and distilled a few thousand words for the separate articles which had periodically appeared, first in the Soviet Union and later abroad. In 1939 and 1940 four articles had appeared which he felt were a synthesis of his more important ideas. So he revised and assembled them for a book, which he thought might be called *Film Principles*.

In August 1941, following Hitler's invasion of the Soviet Union, Eisenstein felt the time had come when he could tell Jay Leyda, after a prolonged period of silence, that he was at last approaching the completion of the first of 'the books'. In his cablegram, he suggested that Leyda arrange for publication of the book in America. The cable was followed by a letter:

August 1941

Dear Jay!

First of all my heartiest greetings and the great pleasure that finally our countries are co-operating. And here the preface to the book-let. . . .

Am finishing (at last!) the Greco article. Am making an english version of very large article about Griffith and the history of montage through the arts. Will add to it probably a survey of the idea of the Close-up through art history. These three articles could make another little booklet; first because this one will need illustrations. Secondly because the completion of the articles may take some time and I'd like the first booklet to be published as soon as possible. . . .

The first book was published in America in 1942 under the title *The Film Sense*.[1] A small book, 'booklet' as Sergei Mikhailovich called it, it was the distillation of but a very small part of the great stack of research notes and original ideas contained in his thousands of sheets of manuscript. The 216 pages of print represented years of work.

In his preface, Eisenstein said:

War! . . .

---

[1] S. M. Eisenstein, *The Film Sense* (New York, Harcourt, Brace and Co. 1942, 2nd ed., 1948; London, Faber and Faber, 1943, 2nd ed., 1948).

All that men's souls and the genius of nations have created in these thousands of years is threatened with total annihilation. . . .

That is why, in giving all one's strength to the struggle against mankind's enemy, one must not halt creative work and theoretical analysis. They are factors in that struggle. . . .

For this reason, even though the burden of war is at its heaviest, I have no misgivings in publishing this sequence of essays devoted to one of the most fascinating and typical problems of the film medium.

The perspectives of the possibilities of the film are unlimited.

And I am firmly convinced that we have barely touched these possibilities.

Fully revealed and fully sounded, the definitive rise of an *art of the cinema* and a *cinematographic method* begins with the conclusion of that nightmare through which man now passes. . . .

For that moment we must gather and foster all those accomplishments in cultural fields built through years of creative and physical labor.

Out of that day will come all the forward movements in art, esthetics, and in all spheres of culture. . . .

From one viewpoint this volume is a summation of what has been both practically realized and theoretically clarified in 'montage'— not merely as a stage in the production of a film, but in a broader, esthetic sense.

From another viewpoint this presents a perspective on those possibilities latent in the film medium as yet only slightly explored.

This refers primarily to *audio-visual cinematography*, where a great deal remains to be done.

In the concluding section, containing a concrete example of procedure, I endeavor to demonstrate that the art of the sound-film is as demanding a medium as its kindred arts of music and plastic media, all of which the film is able to fuse in a powerful synthesis.[1]

When published the 'booklet' was divided into four parts:[2] Part I: Word and Image was a corrected version of the article Sergei Mikhailovich had written in 1938; in this section he traced and analysed 'montage' in the literary medium. Part II: Synchronization of the Senses

---

[1] S. M. Eisenstein, *The Film Sense* (New York, Harcourt, Brace and Co., 1942), pp. xi–xv. Eisenstein's Preface was omitted in the second American edition and in the English editions.

[2] The articles contained in *The Film Sense* were: 'Word and Image', originally published as 'Montage in 1938' (*Iskusstvo Kino*, No. 1, 1939); 'Synchronization of the Senses' (*Iskusstvo Kino*, No. 9, 1940); 'Colour and Meaning' (*Iskusstvo Kino*, No. 12, 1940), and 'Form and Content: Practice' (*Iskusstvo Kino*, No. 1, 1941).

was an analysis of audio-visual phenomena in music, poetry and painting. Part III: Colour and Meaning was an argument to prove that the artist's choice of 'correspondences' (not only in colour, but in anything) should be governed by nothing but the needs of the work in hand. Colour here is used more as an example than as a film element. Part IV: Form and Content: Practice again took up the question of audio-visual combinations and led through examples culled from many sources to an examination of what Sergei Mikhailovich had been able to achieve in collaboration with Prokofiev in *Alexander Nevsky*. Though it was to be such a very small book to be grounded on some twenty-five years' patient research, Sergei Mikhailovich knew it reached into the future and could serve cinematography for a very long time. That was his purpose. The quality of thought was the important thing, for now it seemed exceedingly unlikely that he would live long enough to produce the ten great books he had once dreamed about, and spoken of with such passion.

While working on the book Eisenstein received the assignment for the film *Ivan the Terrible*. He began work, and, because of the confidence he had won and the prestige he enjoyed, he worked alone on the scenario, which he knew from the outset would be his most monumental work, and one of the most ambitious films yet conceived in the history of cinematography. Many of the aspects of Ivan's period were familiar to him on account of the research he had done for the film on the history of Moscow, which Shumyatsky had rejected in 1933.

Because of the scope of the projected film, Sergei Mihailovich was granted leave from his duties as a producer and as the artistic head of Mosfilm, a post which he had held since the beginning of 1939. During this period his name appeared as the producer of several films, the most outstanding being *The Artamanov Family* directed by Roshal.

Margaret Bourke-White, who was in Moscow with her husband, Erskine Caldwell, shortly after Hitler attacked the Soviet Union in June 1941, wrote: 'While we were in Moscow we both saw a good deal of Eisenstein, and he was perfectly splendid. He has what is probably the highest film position in the U.S.S.R. because he is consultant for all film organizations. He was very jolly about his efficiency with a fire pump during raids of incendiary bombs. He and Tisse and Alexandrov are busy these days on their propaganda films for the government. Eisenstein was wearing several decorations, chief among them was the Order of Lenin.'[1]

One of the war films on which Eisenstein served as consultant was a newsreel feature-length film made in collaboration with the American war correspondent, Quentin Reynolds. This film, *Moscow Fights Back*

[1] Margaret Bourke-White in a letter to the author, dated December 23, 1951.

(which was also known as *War Against the Nazis* and *The Face of Fascism*), was halted by the evacuation of Reynolds and other correspondents who were sent to the city of Kuibyshev.

When Hitler's army approached Moscow in the autumn of 1941, Mosfilm evacuated its staff to Central Asia and continued film production at Alma Ata. Sergei Mikhailovich and Elena Telesheva travelled on the same train with Grigori Alexandrov, who had become one of the production heads of Mosfilm. [Plate 49]

Since their return from America a deep antagonism had existed between Alexandrov and Eisenstein. Their only contact had at first been in the course of work, and later through Elena Telesheva, who had continued her friendship with Alexandrov and his wife. But Grisha had matured with his independent successes and through the criticism some of his films had encountered. The anger he once felt towards Sergei Mikhailovich had gradually died away, so that in Alma Ata he again felt friendly disposed towards Eisenstein. After Eisenstein's death, Alexandrov told me he realized that he had learned most of what he knew about cinematography from Eisenstein, though for years he had deliberately chosen to develop his own work along quite different lines.

In the strange setting of the Orient, Eisenstein worked to translate his epic scenario into a film which one critic remarked had 'a curious spiritual quality behind the whole composition';[1] while another noted that in contrast to all of Eisenstein's previous films, *Ivan the Terrible* seemed to spring 'against the tensions of near-standstill, [and] it is exciting as if a corpse moved'.[2]

Sergei Mikhailovich had been interested in Ivan Grosny for many years. In his childhood he had read books about him. After the Revolution he had thought of Ivan again. When Joseph Freeman asked him to write a section for *Voices of October* in 1928, Sergei Mikhailovich had analysed Ivan in connection with the current interpretation of history. 'History "in general",' he wrote, 'that is a sweet idealization of bourgeois historians. The "great" and "illustrious" personages of the past ruled the fate of millions according to their limited views. They were "gods" invented out of whole cloth. It is time to reveal the bunk about these paid romantic heroes. The concealed traps of official history must be exposed.'

But ten years later, Eisenstein gave history a different interpretation in *Alexander Nevsky*. Now he had come to Ivan, of whom he had said in 1928 that Ivan 'as a personality in the manner of Edgar Allan Poe will hardly interest the young Soviet worker'; though 'as the creator of the linen trade, the Tsar who enriched and strengthened Russia's eco-

[1] Review of *Ivan the Terrible* (*Observer*, 1 September 1946).
[2] Review of *Ivan the Terrible* (New York, *Time*, 14 Aprtil 1947).

nomic position, he becomes a more interesting figure. The story of Ivan the Terrible should go on to tell how he became absolute monarch, head of a dominant aristocratic class; it should tell of the struggle among the higher classes of society, how they became weakened. On this basis,' he concluded, 'the story would be nearer reality and of more importance than a fantasy about a mephistophelian figure, a Tsar who was a wild beast.'

These were the words of a young man who was very certain what he thought about history. In returning to Ivan, Sergei Mikhailovich, at the age of forty-three, also knew what he thought, but his feelings had undergone a great change as a result of his experiences. Though what he said in 1928 was reflected in his original conception of Ivan, it only served as a base for one of the many levels of thought he was finally to develop in the film.

Nikolai Cherkasov again played the leading role, that of Ivan, and Prokofiev collaborated with Eisenstein on the musical score. He joined Eisenstein in Alma Ata in the summer of 1942. In his biography of Prokofiev, Israel Nestyev says: 'In the international history of the art of the sound film there is no closer creative friendship between director and composer than that between Eisenstein and Prokofiev. . . . Prokofiev was thrilled by Eisenstein's temperament and by his graphic skill in directly or paradoxically formulating his "orders" to the composer: "At this point the music must sound like a mother tearing her own child to pieces", or "Do it so that it sounds like a cork rubbed down a pane of glass". In his turn Eisenstein more than once listened profitably to the keen comments of Prokofiev.

'. . . As in *Alexander Nevsky*, the music was to occupy the role of an active participant in the drama, and was not only to accompany the more important episodes in the film, but also to fill it with a parallel, developing action of emotional sound.'[1]

The Theme of Ivan is introduced at the commencement of the epic with a song symbolic of 'the approaching storm'. The song culminates before any action appears upon the screen with the words:

> Black clouds are surging,
> in crimson blood the dawn is drenched.
> On the bones of enemies
> on the blazing pyres
> Russ united
> gathers strength.[2]

[1] *Sergei Prokofiev, His Musical Life*, by Israel Nestyev (New York, Alfred A. Knopf, 1946), pp. 168–9.

[2] The excerpts quoted in this chapter form Parts I and II of the scenario of *Ivan the Terrible* are from the translation by H. P. J. Marshall published in *Life*

The 'historic envelope' was only the scaffolding of what Eisenstein felt compelled to build from the life of Ivan Vasilievich, Grand Prince of Muscovy, who, like himself, was possessed of 'great natural ability', a man of complex genius. In his historic role, Ivan might be likened to Joseph Stalin, directing the destiny of the Soviet Union in the twentieth century, as Ivan had directed the destiny of Russia in the sixteenth century. But Sergei Mikhailovich was unable to confine himself to the portrayal of history alone.

In the five years Eisenstein worked on *Ivan*, he fought the battles of his own soul in the person of Ivan. As he had been unable to remain objective in his treatment of the father-son conflict in *Bezhin Meadow* because his emotions were too deeply enthralled, so he could not immerse himself in Ivan, a man whose final act in life was to die as a member of the strictest order of hermits—as the monk Jonah—without drawing a subjective parallel between Ivan and himself in a pattern of such complexity that the full meaning of it could never be fully determined by anyone except Sergei Mikhailovich himself. Even the personal parallel, which Grigori Alexandrov later told me he recognized, had more than one level, and the levels interchanged, appearing and disappearing with the fluidity of thought and feeling itself—now commenting objectively upon events of life; now reflecting emotions once experienced; now revealing the deep currents of the unconscious mind; now struggling with life-long problems on both the philosophical and psychological level; now combining, now disguised under the mask of historical, or invented characters, the people who had played a role in Sergei Mikhailovich's own life.[1]

These multiple threads weave in and out, sometimes in a dominant key, sometimes muted, sometimes as an unfinished half-thought, sometimes transformed as in the dream process, often hinting desires unfulfilled, thoughts and speculations never expressed, and every thread strung taut between the inner consciousness of Sergei Mikhailovich and the immutable symbols which stood in his own path determining his fate as a man—the concept of God, which tormented him, and the impeccable enemy who had distorted the whole of his life, the woman filled with hate and the object of his hate—his mother; the small woman transformed into the taller woman who he had led the world to believe was his wife.

and Letters To-day, Part I appearing November–December 1945, and January–April 1946; Part II, May–July 1946. The excerpt quoted from Part III of *Ivan* is from the unpublished translation by Mr. Marshall. The entire scenario was published in book form in the Soviet Union. Another English translation was made by Ivor Montagu.

[1] For confirmation of interpretation see Eisenstein's *Autobiography* (London, Dennis Dobson, 1978).

One thread of the inner pattern—childhood memory—emerged immediately in the Prologue, the first scene of which is 'A Dark Chamber':

> In the darkness a bright spot picks out an eight-year-old boy, crouching fearfully into a corner. Close-up—the frightened face of the boy. Out of the frame—the frenzied cry of a woman. The boy creeps away.
>
> The boy is on the floor. Over him passes the shadow of people with tapers. . . .

People carrying tapers—this was to be one of the symbolic threads of Ivan's life. 'Suddenly a door opens' and the boy's mother appears dying of poison. 'Beware of the Boyars!' The mother is taken away to die. 'It is dark once more' and the mother's death is followed by the murder of her lover by the Boyar Shuisky. 'The boy Ivan trembles alone in the darkness.' Five years pass.

In 'The Reception Hall', the great nobles—the Boyars—and the ambassadors of foreign Powers, who hold the strings of Moscow's destiny, await an audience:

> Above the throne—a fresco; an Angel—angry—apocalyptic—its feet trampling the universe. . . .
>
> From the door through the hall to the grand-princely throne, surrounded by his suite, goes the slim boy Ivan in full Regalia. He is thirteen years old. A thin neck protrudes from a massive gold necklet.
>
> Wide open eyes. Fear in them. He walks timidly. . . .
>
> Ivan hesitatingly approaches the throne. He is guided and sat down. . . .
>
> In fear and confusion Ivan looks at the Boyars prostrate at his feet. At the knee-bent Emissaries.
>
> In deadly fear, but distinctly and clearly, he pronounces at a sign from Shuisky—the triumphant words of the address:
>
> 'We by the Grace of God . . .'
>
> Ivan on the throne. His neck protrudes like a blade of grass from the neck of the heavy gold collar. His young eyes are open wide.
>
> But the surrounding atmosphere begins to act on him. His timidity gradually disappears. The boy sits more firmly on the throne. . . .
>
> In the frightened boy the eaglet awakens. The boy wishes to speak. Shuisky does not let him. Again he speaks for him. . . .
>
> The legs of Ivan hang helplessly from the throne. They swing about but cannot reach the floor . . . [Plate 50]

like the legs of Sergei Mikhailovich when, as the young Tsar of the new art of film, he enthroned himself on the seat of defunct Tsardom in the

Winter Palace in 1927. At the age of twenty-nine his feet had swung like those of the thirteen-year-old Ivan's above the floor. [Plate 50]

And over the Prince of Moscow. The angry Angel of the Apocalypse—threading with firm feet the Universe. . . .

Fade out

The Bedchamber of Ivan

'Sing about the Ocean! The Ocean!' Merrily cries Ivan as he runs around the Bedchamber.

Lifting high his princely robe he hops about on one foot and hurriedly tries to divest himself as he goes.

His old nurse and two maidservants help Ivan to undress.

Ivan is impatient to get out of his gold collar . . .

as the little boy, Sergei Eisenstein, who had been dressed with such elegance in his childhood. He too had listened to the stories of his nurse, as Ivan's 'nurse sings in an old voice':

'Ocean-sea
Azure sea
Azure sea
Russian sea.'

Ivan takes off his princely hat.

'Thou reachest to the very Heavens
Thy waves beat to the highest sun.'

Ivan throws off the heavy, beaten gold collar.

'The Russian rivers run to Thee
On thy shores Cities stand.'

Ivan looks ahead thoughtfully. He ceases to undress. The song has taken him. . . .

The Boyars enter demanding that Ivan make agreements with the Hanseatic League and the Livonians. The old nurse goes on singing the song, which, like the tapers, will become a thread of symbolic sound haunting Ivan throughout his life. And she, as her counterpart in Sergei Mikhailovich's life, was the image of security. When she leaves:

Ivan follows her with appealing eyes.

And Ivan peers from under covered brows at Shuisky

who wishes to pay the Hanseites and Livonians.

Ivan is almost undressed. The maidservants take off the last of his robes. Underneath Ivan has on a simple shirt. He looks almost poor. But in the eyes of the listening Ivan remains something of the look he had on the throne.

Amidst the richly clothed Boyars Ivan looks almost poverty-stricken.

But Ivan's voice rings proudly: 'We are not obliged to pay anyone! . . .'

'The Power of Russia you have squandered,' shouts Ivan, 'that has gone into the Boyars' pockets.'

They roar with laughter. Shuisky with laughter . . . throws his feet on to the bed.

Ivan jumps forward. Breathing heavily with anger he cries: 'Take your feet off the bed! Take them off, I say, take them off my mother's bed. . . .'

'Once I loved my mother very much,' Sergei Eisenstein had said, so much that he had turned to hate himself, imagining that it was he who had driven her away.

Shuisky, rising from the chair like an animal: 'She was a bitch herself! Got involved with that Telepev-Kobel. No one knows who sired you!'

The gigantic figure of Shuisky towers over Ivan. Brandishing over him the heavy iron rod: 'You son of a bitch!'

Ivan covers himself up from the blow with his hands and suddenly, unexpectedly even for himself, shrieks out hysterically: 'Take him away!'

Everyone, including Ivan, is dumbfounded at its unexpectedness. . . .

Though there is no record, this too may have been a part of Sergei Mikhailovich's experience.

Ivan remains alone. He is frightened by his own determination and the unexpectedness of everything that happened. His strength leaves him. Once more he is a weak, helpless boy. He pushes his head into his mother's bed. And sobs as if his head were resting on her breast. His thin shoulders shake.

. . . The door creaks, Ivan shrinks back, frightened to turn round.

. . . The guard guiltily explains: 'We got a bit over-excited . . . and strangled the Boyar.'

Close-up of the face of Ivan. At first at a loss. Then stern and concentrated. The 'princely' look in his eyes and in his glance approval.

'I'll rule myself . . . without the Boyars. . . .'

The guard looks apprehensively at Ivan.

'I'll be a Tsar! . . .' The eyes of Ivan peer into the distance.

[1] This Prologue (which ends with these words) was transferred to Part II to explain Ivan's character. In its final form Part I commenced with Ivan's Coronation.

At seventeen, Ivan is crowned in the Uspensky Cathedral within the Kremlin wall. Here the chief protagonists appear: Ivan's diabolical aunt, Euphrosinia Staritskaya, who forms the fateful hub from which, like spokes, all machinations against Ivan spring, including the poisoning of Anastasia, his wife, the sole person who understands his dreams. These two symbolic women are juxtaposed as the principles of hate and love. Both, though historical, play roles beyond that of history: Euphrosinia by her domination of every faction opposed to Ivan, and Anastasia by appearing as Ivan's only wife, although in fact she had four successors. The other chief protagonists are Andrey Kurbsky and Boyar Kolichev, later Philip, Metropolitan of Moscow, who, commencing as Ivan's closest friends, later conspire against him. They appear only as mute figures standing on either side of Ivan who, in the following scene, enters into his covenant.

> Pimen (Episcope of Novgorod) takes from a gold platter the Tsar's crown—the cap of Monomakh. He gives it to Ivan to kiss. He places it on Ivan's head. He pronounces 'In the Name of the Father, Son and Holy Ghost. . . .'
> Ivan stands up and turns around.
> He is seventeen years old. His eyes shine. Ivan stands like one immured as the pronouncement continues:
> 'For Thine is the Kingdom, the Power and the Glory, in the Name of the Father, Son and Holy Ghost.'
> Ivan looks joyfully at Anastasia. . . .
> The Staritskys gaze gloomily from under their brows. . . .
> Like a young animal, sinuous, well-proportioned, passionate, he glides in the silence up the eight steps to the raised platform in the center of the cathedral.
> He stops in the slanting rays of the sun in the center of the cathedral. Embraced by the vastness. . . . The Tsar is enveloped in a golden halo. [Plate 51]
> All a-quiver. Stronger than the golden chains his moral will-power adorns him. He holds himself back, striving to speak quietly. He holds himself back, striving to speak evenly. But thought surges after thought.
> Words crowd after words . . .

as Sergei Mikhailovich recalled his own voice echoing back over the years, speaking always challenging words in such a quiet tone; as Sergei Mikhailovich had flung his challenge to the whole bourgeois world, so Ivan threw his challenge to the Boyars. As the one, so the other swearing to build a new world.

In directing this sequence, Eisenstein set the character of Ivan as a man possessed by an ecstatic dream. He stands dedicated before God with his dream vaguely comprehended by Anastasia alone. The other characters are stamped, not with the scientific tools of historical perspective, nor the realism of historical materialism, but with the prophetic chisel of mythology. Each is motivated by passions conceived on the scale of Greek tragedy. Every face has the quality of a mask, and no gesture escapes the bonds of symbolic quintessence.

Throughout the succeeding sequences, when the 'line of history' assumes the dominant role, the style of myth never gives way to an interpretation of history in a realistic form, except that the characters Gregory-Malyuta and Basmanov, father and son, emerging as they do from the people, at first appear as men of flesh and blood. But in time even they are absorbed into the mythological pattern. At one point, when the Moscow populace break into the Kremlin in protesting mood they are led by Nikolai, the Great Simpleton, who, foaming at the mouth, cries out that the Tsar is the victim of evil spells. In directing these scenes, Sergei Mikhailovich cast in this role the man who had spread tales about him—Vsevolod Pudovkin. [Plate 36]

The 'line of history' blends with the many personal lines following Ivan's capture (with Kurbsky as his aide) of Kazan, and the rout of the Tartars. It is then that Ivan, ill unto death, seeks to ensure the throne to his son, Dimitri; while Euphrosinia, as spearhead of the Boyar interests, seeks to seduce Kurbsky away from Ivan in support of her son, Vladimir Andreyevich, who all the while sits trying to catch flies.[1] In the bedchamber of Ivan:

. . . extreme unction is being administered.

Pimen takes the New Testament.

Opens its pages, bends it and 'places its pages on the head of the sick one, as if it were the hand of the Saviour himself touching and curing his sickness'.

The face of Ivan is covered with the New Testament.

It is held by seven priests.

Seven candles are burning in their hands.

The pallid lips of Ivan mutter unceasingly from under the New Testament:

'God have mercy on my soul! . . .'

Not mentioned in the scenario is Ivan's fleeting glance, fearful but filled

[1] Eisenstein's portrayal of Prince Vladimir Andreyevich Staritsky as an effeminate, feeble-minded boy completely dominated by his mother, does not appear to coincide with historical fact. It is true that Staritsky played a pusillanimous role in history, but at this period he was very much a man of affairs; he was married and had a daughter who later became the wife of Duke Magnus.

with bravado—like Sergei Mikhailovich's own doubt of the Church.
Ivan becomes aware of the forces waiting for his death; those who will
destroy his son and set on the throne the effeminate Vladimir.

Ivan hardly moving his lips says with great difficulty:
'The end has come, I bid farewell to this world. . . . Swear
allegiance to the legitimate heir . . . Dimitri. . . .'
Ivan grows weaker.
Anastasia cries.
Euphrosinia Staritskaya and Vladimir Andreyevich look at him
challengingly.
Ivan sees refusal in their eyes.
He raises himself on the bed. He is supported by Anastasia.
Ivan pleads: . . .
The Boyars are silent. . . .
Ivan rises from the bed, throws himself on his knees.
On his knees in tears he appeals to the Boyars.
He appeals to each in turn . . .

and all refuse. [Plate 52]
Twice in his life Sergei Mikhailovich had been in the position of
Ivan; but not to defend the right of any child of flesh and blood, only
two of his 'brain children'—when he begged Upton Sinclair to permit
him to complete *Que Viva Mexico!*, and when he waited for the verdict
over *Bezhin Meadow*. On both occasions he had met obdurate rejection. But like Ivan, Sergei Mikhailovich arose through his will-power
and overcame defeat.

Following this scene:
. . . forgetting her timidity, pale Anastasia draws herself up and
turns to the Boyars saying:
'Only in Dimitri his son lies salvation.
'If there be no united power, then be as strong, be as brave, be as
wise as you will—but your rule is doomed to chaos:
'Hating each other you will be but slaves of foreign powers!'
For the great work of her mate she stands like an eagle.
From the door Kurbsky stands adoring Anastasia but hearing not
a word.
Euphrosinia moves forward like an infuriated tigress.
An infuriated tigress bears down on the dove.
A mother—on to a mother rising to defend their young.
'Never shall we Boyars of glorious lineage be under the heel of a
Glinsky!'
The Boyars look on with sympathy:
'Allegiance must be sworn to Vladimir Andreyevich.'

Mother advances on to mother.
Mother retreats from mother.
Mother looks at mother with eyes of hate. . . .
Anastasia covers the cradle of the heir with her body.

Then there follows a sequence not mentioned in the scenario in which
Prince Kurbsky, whose appearance echoes that of Grigori Alexandrov,
calls Anastasia out into a corridor and against the background of a
gigantic icon of God, declares his passion for her. Each shot includes the
all-seeing eye of God. But Anastasia rejects Kurbsky and returns to
Ivan. In the next scene in which Ivan forces himself back to life, Kurbsky
pledges his allegiance to Dimitri. As a reward, Kurbsky is given command of the Russian Army for the campaign to crush Livonia and
reach the sea: [Plate 52]

Ocean-sea
Azure sea
Azure sea
Russian sea.

and Ivan bestows command of his army, which will move against the
Crimean Khan, to Basmanov, a soldier, who warned him of the
Boyars before the walls of Kazan.

Thus, Ivan drives the Boyars back. But Euphrosinia, with the goodwill of the Church in the person of Pimen, the Episcope of Novgorod,
plans to 'take the Tsar firmly in hand'. Pimen instructs: 'Above all we
must take Anastasia away from Ivan. . . .' To which Euphrosinia
replies: 'That I shall take upon myself.' Up to this moment, Euphrosinia
has appeared as chief protagonist of the Boyar class opposed to Ivan's
every political plan; but in the next scenes in which she appears she
passes into a new symbolic relationship to Ivan—the force depriving
him of the wife he loves.

Meanwhile, Ivan's dreams of consolidating Russia are being frus-
trated, and his wrath rises:

'Again the Livonians and the Hanseatic League have detained
English ships!
'My cannon are left without lead, tin, sulphur, and skilled crafts-
men!'

In an adjoining room:

Alongside in her bedchamber Anastasia is ill.
She lies in a burning fever.
Like a black crow Euphrosinia Staritskaya sits over her.
Never taking her eyes off the sick one.
The cries and noise of Ivan's anger reach Anastasia.

Anastasia tries to rise and go to Ivan:
'Let me go to the Tsar. . . . He needs me. I must help him!'
Euphrosinia does not let her go.
Once more she lays her back in the bed.

Ivan is now seen speaking to Osip Nepeya, his Ambassador to the
court of Queen Elizabeth:

'You see, Nepeya, how necessary that military alliance is to me!'
He pushes over to him a luxurious set of chessmen:
'Present this gift to our sweet sister, Elizabeth of England. And
with these chessmen explain to her . . .'
Osip Nepeya places the figures in a silken kerchief . . .
'How her English ships avoiding the Baltic Sea . . . can sail to us
by the White Sea . . . and outwit both Germans and Livonians.
'And remind her that Tsar Ivan of Muscovy is sole merchant here!
'To whom he objects will not enter my State. To whom he loves
he will open the road to the East.'

And when this scene appeared on the screen, a skeletonized globe on the
table, and the head of Ivan, cast a great shadow upon the wall. Some
people saw this sequence as a parallel between the historic aspirations of
Ivan and the contemporary role of Joseph Stalin. Then the Ambassador
departed for England and

Through the windows—rain.
It is cold.
The Tsar shivers.
Wraps himself in his mantle.
Alongside in the bedchamber Euphrosinia Staritskaya still sits like
a black crow over Anastasia.
She watches the Tsar through the door.
Stands back.
Hides in the stairway.
Ivan enters the bedchamber. . . .

He sees Euphrosinia, and makes a most curious gesture to his bitterest
enemy. He lays his arm around her shoulder as if seeking her goodwill
and giving her his own, as if a memory of affection stirred. . . . This
gesture Sergei Mikhailovich did not mention in his scenario; there Ivan
does not notice Euphrosinia's presence. The subsequent action sinks to
deeper levels of unconscious symbolism:

Ivan's head bends over Anastasia.
'Tsar Ivan is troubled?' says the Tsaritsa.
She strokes Ivan's hair.

Through her sickness comforts the Tsar.

Ivan speaks: 'I can trust no one! Kurbsky is far away fighting the Livonians. Fedor Kolichev is still further away—in a monastery. I have only you!'

He bends nearer.

For a moment he wants to forget his troubles.

But they will not let the Tsar forget.

They will not let the Tsar rest.

They run in with messages . . .

which say that Basmanov's campaign against the Crimean Khan has been prevented by the Boyars, who refused to let him defend Riazan.

Anastasia says: '*Be firm!*'

Euphrosinia listens furiously in the darkness to the words of the Tsarina.

She rummages under the black shawl on her breast.

Searching for something . . :

as Malyuta enters to tell Ivan that his army at Nevel has been defeated through the treachery of Kurbsky. Anastasia cries out.

In the corner Euphrosinia stands like a black shadow.

In her hand she holds a cup covered with a handkerchief. . . .

Ivan rushes over to help Anastasia, to give her a drink.

He picks up a cup.

It is empty.

He stumbles, searching for water.

Carefully Euphrosinia hides in the corner and watches.

Anastasia drinks thirstily from the cup.

Her frightened eyes wide open. . . .[1]

Prince Kurbsky has deserted to King Sigismund of Livonia who, in Part II, announces 'a crusade of all Christian states against the Muscovites'. Ivan is once more in the Uspensky Cathedral, where he was crowned and dedicated himself beneath the glowing eyes of Anastasia. Now: 'The coffin with the body of Anastasia.' There are two levels of thought, two levels of emotion—the outward gestures of Ivan and the 'internal monologue', which is supplied by the Psalm of King David intoned by a monk. Interwoven is a third 'line', that of worldly affairs represented by Malyuta, and Basmanov, father and son. The 'lines' weave an extraordinary tapestry of sound and image:

[1] The death of Stalin's wife in the early 1930s called forth speculation that she died of poison.

In the darkness a voice reads a psalm in a whisper.
'Save me, O God . . . for the waters are come in unto my soul.'
The coffin . . . is covered in a black shroud.
The psalm sounds:
'I sink in deep mire, where there is no standing. . . . I come into deep waters . . . where the floods overflow me.'
Ivan stands by the coffin in deep sorrow.
'I am weary of my crying . . . my throat is dried . . . my eyes fail while I wait for my God. . . .'
Whispers the monk behind the lectern.
The words of the psalm merge with the words of Malyuta.
Malyuta is reading a dispatch.
Ivan looks fixedly at one point. [Plate 53]
Hearing neither the prayer nor the dispatch.
And the dispatch is alarming.
'Prince Ivan Mikhailovich Shuisky is hiding on Livonian soil. . . .'
The monk intones:
'They that hate me without cause are more than the hairs of mine head.'
The countenance of the dead Anastasia is calm.
Ivan looks at her with deep longing.
Plunged in sorrow Ivan whispers:
'Am I right to do what I do?
'Am I right?
'May it not be the punishment of God?'
The monk continues:
'I am become a stranger unto my brethren and an alien unto my mother's children.'
Malyuta continues:
'Prince Ivan Ivanovich Turguntai-Pronsky was captured in flight and brought back.'
Ivan rises from the ground and gazes into the dead countenance:
'Am I right in my heavy struggle?' . . .
The dead countenance is silent. . . .

In transferring this sequence on to the screen, Sergei Mikhailovich inserted three shots not mentioned in the scenario. They are a close-up of Euphrosinia standing near the door. A medium shot and a long shot: the long shot revealing the fresco on the wall beside the door. The fresco beside the standing figure of Euphrosinia is that of a man in torment hanging upside down by his heels. Triumphantly Euphrosinia watches as Ivan walks slowly around the coffin, his hand holding the top as he moves. Suddenly:

Tsar Ivan beats his brow on the side of the coffin.

'When I wept and chastened my soul with fasting, that was to my reproach.'

[The] Basmanovs run up to Malyuta.

Whisper in his ear. Malyuta staggers.

'They that sit in the gate speak against me;

'And I was the song of the drunkards.'

Malyuta falls on his knees before Ivan.

He brings news of Kurbsky's treachery. . . .

Ivan raises his head.

A far-away perplexity in his eyes.

Then he apprehends.

And quickly utters:

'Andrei, friend . . . what for?

'What did you lack?

'Or did you aspire to my royal crown?'

'Deliver me out of the mire and let me not sink:

'Let me be delivered from them that hate me and out of the deep waters.'

The monk mutters. . . .

But Malyuta has still worse news for Ivan—that the Boyars are inciting the people against the Tsar. The monk mutters:

'Reproach hath broken my heart, and I am full of heaviness. . .

'And I look for some to take pity, but there was none, and for comforters,

'But I found none.'

And Ivan, turning his head like a wounded beast cries out, as if against his own thoughts: 'You lie!'

Through the whole of the cathedral sounds the affirmation:

'The Tsar of Muscovy is still undefeated!'

Those near ones who have remained run up to Ivan.

But they are few—

Lost in the vast emptiness of the cathedral. . . .

'You are too few!' cries Ivan . . .

and he wishes to call his old friend Kolichev from the Solovetsky monastery, where he made him the Abbot. But Basmanov warns Ivan against the Boyar, urging him instead to surround himself with new people, 'people who have forsworn all ties of family and home to know only the Tsar', and serve his will. And he offers his son, Fedor, as the first member of an 'iron ring'—those who will subsequently become Ivan's Lifeguards—the Oprichniks.

At this moment the character of Ivan begins to harden into 'an iron leader', echoing Joseph Stalin. Quicker almost than thought comes the extraordinary historical resolve to abandon Moscow, to abdicate until 'by the people's summons I shall gain limitless power and re-anointed consummate a great task *mercilessly*'. But, unable to follow this unheard of conception:

Ivan seeks confirmation for his unheard of conception:
But finds it not from his closest friends.
He turns to his true companion and adviser—Anastasia.
But the dead countenance of Anastasia is silent:
The eyelids closed. . . .
But Ivan flies like an arrow to the platform and towers above the coffin.
Looking into the dead features.
The lines of the dead countenance seem to soften.
As if the face of Anastasia shone with approval. . . .
And now no longer with sorrow but determination Ivan gazes on that face. . . .
Music arises:
The theme of Ivan—
'The storm approaches. . . .'
Tsar Ivan straightens up over the coffin.
His eyes burn with new power and determination.
He raises his hand over Anastasia and swears a great oath:
'The voice of the people is the voice of God!
'Into my hand I take the avenging sword of the Lord. . . .'
The theme of Ivan widens in the orchestra. . . .
Ivan kisses Anastasia's brow. . . .

The final sequence of Part I (but not as released) echoes 'in a new quality' the Prologue where, rising from a torturous loneliness and fear, the boy Ivan asserts his will. Alone, prematurely aged and with burning eyes, Ivan weeps in desolation while he waits for the people to come to Alexandrov Sloboda and call him back to Moscow. Ivan's Lifeguards—the Oprichniks—repeat their oath after Basmanov, the Elder, and his son, Fedor:

Like a black shadow towers Ivan. [As Stalin himself towered.]
The oath he hears not.
Lost in thought.
Examining his long fingers.
Only the oath echoes under the arches:

'Before God I swear
a terrible oath:
to execute in Russia the will of the Tsar,
to destroy in Russia savage enemies,
to spill in Russia the blood of the guilty,
to burn out treason with fire,
to cut out treachery with the sword,
sparing neither oneself nor any other—
FOR THE SAKE OF THE MIGHTY RUSSIAN KINGDOM. . . .'

At last the people come with their icons and banners as an endless serpentine crossing the snowy wastes to kneel before the Tsar who, now in truth, will merit the name of Terrible. [Plate 54]

After editing the first part of *Ivan*, Eisenstein removed the Prologue so that the film commences not with Ivan at the age of eight 'crouching fe?.fully into a corner', but with his coronation. It is not clear why Sergei Mikhailovich altered the placing of the Prologue. Perhaps for foreign distribution it was necessary to shorten the film, but this reason would hardly apply in the Soviet Union where audiences were accustomed to long films.

When the first part of *Ivan* was finally released in January of 1945, reactions to the film were strangely mixed. It won the Stalin Prize First Class in the Soviet Union, but it was received abroad with hesitating words. Though it left them confused, many critics felt compelled to praise it; others damned it. What was Eisenstein aiming to achieve? Opera? A patriotic epic? Sergei Mikhailovich's old friend, Maxim Shtraukh, later told me he was entirely baffled. How had Eisenstein come to fashion every character like a marionette? What was the purpose of such stylized movements and formal make-up?

It was all the more confounding since Eisenstein had stamped his mark upon world cinematography by the introduction of realism and the injection of dynamic experiments. Now he had created a film in which every detail was enlarged like the gestures of the Kabuki Theatre. The spectators could only feel themselves as onlookers of intrigue and conflict enacted by men and women of other dimensions than their own who behaved, if it could be imagined, like frescoes come to life.

Every expression, sound and element of *décor* was carefully thought out:

> For days we will struggle with the stubborn cloth [Eisenstein explained] cutting and draping it to capture that rhythm of folds that suddenly struck me when I closed my eyes over that bit of brocade and envisioned a procession of boyars in heavy robes moving slowly to the chambers of the dying Tsar. . . .

Here a viewpoint on that suddenly rising head and ruff is calculated.
Here the characteristic position of fingers and hands in El Greco's
paintings is analysed.[1]

As Ivan moved ever further from the common norm of human
conduct in his endeavour to set Russia upon a new path, so Sergei
Mikhailovich strove in *Ivan* to bring the cinema to a new level of
maturity and grandeur. By employing elements from all the arts and
transfiguring them, he produced a film without parallel; one which
may only come into full perspective when all of its creator's writings
are assembled and published.

Eisenstein's own programme note touched only on the most obvious
facts:

> We have no intention in our film of Ivan the Terrible to white-
> wash him in the people's memory or to make Ivan the Terrible an
> Ivan the Gentle. It is our wish to give Ivan that to which every hero
> of the past is entitled: to show objectively the full scope and range
> of his activities.
>
> For it is only in this way that we can explain all those traits, unex-
> pected, at times harsh, and often terrible, which were indispensable
> in a statesman of an epoch so fraught with passion and blood as was
> the Renaissance of the sixteenth century. . . .
>
> Concealing nothing, smoothing over nothing . . . detracting
> nothing from the formidably impressive romanticism of that splendid
> image of the past, it has been our wish to present it in all its integrity
> to the audience of the whole world.
>
> This image, fearful and entrancing, attractive and terrible, utterly
> *tragic in the inward struggle against the enemies of his country*, will
> become comprehensible to the man of our own day.

It casts no light upon the inner content of Ivan, nor the complex
form in which the slow and inexorable action and atmosphere of hatred
develop. All his real thoughts and feelings Sergei Mikhailovich kept
carefully concealed from friend as well as stranger. [Plate 49]

Telesheva was in Alma Ata with Eisenstein for some months during
the early stages of production. She assisted in directing the acting in
some sequences; even Grigori Alexandrov now and then helped Sergei
Mikhailovich. According to Alexandrov, Eisenstein was singularly
disinterested in his actors: his only concern was the imagery they were
able to create. As he recorded while at work:

> Cherkasov's incomparably lithe and flexible body will practise

[1] *Film Form* by S. M. Eisenstein (New York, Harcourt Brace and Co., 1949
and London, Dennis Dobson, 1950), pp. 262, 263.

long and tiringly to produce the tragic bend of Tsar Ivan's figure so spontaneously fixed on paper [in Eisenstein's own drawings] as camera set-ups. In intent these drawings are no more (but also no less) than those Japanese paper toys that, when cast into warm water, unfold and develop stems, leaves and flowers of fantastic and surprising shape.[1]

Such a method of work took a tremendous toll of the emotions of his actors, particularly those of Nikolai Cherkasov, whose own style of acting was essentially realistic. Cherkasov is said to have been in a state of nervous exhaustion when the second part of *Ivan the Terrible* was completed.[2]

During the time she was in Alma Ata, Elena Telesheva discussed her feelings towards Eisenstein with Grigori Alexandrov. Though they were still living separately, she often said that she loved Sergei Mikhailovich. But when Alexandrov asked Eisenstein about Telesheva, he would not discuss her and turned the conversation aside with the remark 'I am content'. Alexandrov told me after Sergei Mikhailovich's death he was puzzled and never understood the relationship.

After a while Telesheva returned to Moscow, where she rejoined her daughter, who told people that her mother and Eisenstein had parted. Telesheva went on with her life as before; she seemed to enjoy parties and went about gaily with her daughter until, in July of 1943, she contracted typhoid. On the 10th of July she died in Moscow and her death was cabled around the world as international news, because she was believed to be the wife of Sergei Mikhailovich. Pera Attasheva said nothing, although she was still registered at Z.A.G.S. as his wife.

Far off in Alma Ata, Sergei Mikhailovich received the news of Elena Telesheva's death. He was ill, and though he told Grisha he would like to go to Moscow for her funeral, he could not leave. She was buried in Moscow and the strangest, and perhaps the most ironic chapter in Sergei Mikhailovich's life closed. He never mentioned her name again, but went ruthlessly on with the work on his epic film.

In 1942 his book, *The Film Sense*, had been published in America. Now and then he found time to work on articles, some of which were eventually published in his second book. His advice was often sought on films designed to aid the war effort and he appeared in a short film, *To the Jews of the World*.

[1] S. M. Eisenstein, *Film Form* (New York, Harcourt Brace and Co., 1949 and London, Dennis Dobson, 1950), pp. 262, 263.

[2] According to Roger Burford, the British Film Officer in Moscow during the final months of work on *Ivan the Terrible*, Part II. Subsequent to the first publication of this book, in 1952, Cherkasov admitted to an antagonism towards Eisenstein.

For the first time in his life, Eisenstein spoke as a representative of his father's people. In turn, Ilya Ehrenburg and the actor Michoels, of the Moscow Yiddish Theatre, stepped before the camera to appeal to free people in the Allied countries. Eisenstein took his turn before the camera. He appeared nervous and deeply moved. Speaking in English, he said:

> ' As a Russian representative of the Soviet intelligentsia, and work-
> ing, as I do, in a sphere of Russian cinematography and Russian art,
> the very principle of racial hatred is foreign and loathsome to me.
> 'Basing myself on the principles of equal fraternal rights, on spiri-
> tual and material values for each nation, for each people, I regard
> with indignation any phase of national oppression.
> 'But the time for indignation and condemnation has passed.
> 'The time has come to fight.
> 'In the sacred struggle, the Soviet Union is uniting all peoples who,
> with sword in hand, are ready to rise for the right to call themselves
> Czechs, Poles, Dutchmen, Belgians, Russians or Jews, because it is
> not only a matter of saving a Nation that has given Humanity great
> poets, thinkers and artists—because it is not only a matter of saving a
> people numbering many millions of human lives—but because it is a
> matter of the triumph of humanism over brutality, barbarism, in-
> famy, and violence, because it is a matter of a bright future for all
> humanity, irrespective of nationality.'

Then, with the Second World War rising to its crescendo of violence, Sergei Mikhailovich returned to work on *Ivan*.

The scenario of *Ivan the Terrible* had been accepted by Mosfilm in the form of two full-length films. But for some time Eisenstein had been considering dividing the scenario into three films.

He often discussed this change with Alexandrov, who tried to dis-suade him. In Alexandrov's opinion, Part II, as Sergei Mikhailovich now planned it, had an insufficient story and showed little but intrigue, and what Grisha characterized as 'dirty family washing'. Already he thought that Eisenstein was in danger of forgetting history and Ivan the builder of a new, powerful, united Russia and replacing an objective portrayal with a highly subjective excursion into the inner conflicts of Ivan. Some of the characters seemed to have too flimsy a role in history for the part assigned to them by Sergei Mikhailovich. But he would not listen to Alexandrov's warning and persisted in changing the film from two parts to three.[1]

---

[1] Grigori Alexandrov later told me about these conversations with Eisen-stein over the second part of *Ivan*, and his reaction to Part II.—M.S.

Part II of *Ivan*, like the first part, is concerned with Ivan's conflict with the Boyars. Intrigue against him is transmuted into 'a new quality' of complexity and his decisions, put into action by the Life-guards, become ever more merciless, sadistic, as Alexandrov later termed it. Like a serpent the action coils ever tighter. The dialogue is as double as a serpent's tongue as the screws of superhuman torment twist inside Ivan and paralyse his will for a moment, only to drive him forward the next with a murderous thrust towards his goal—the strengthening of Russia—which fills him with a mystical ecstasy.

The Ivan of history was both a man of great ability who brought unity to Russia and one compelled to appalling violence. He was, as his final act in life proclaimed, a man filled with mystic yearnings. In Sergei Mikhailovich's interpretation, Ivan's sense of being ordained by God clashes more and more with the Orthodox Church, which is dedicated to furthering the interests of the Boyars. The whole of Part II reveals the philosophic conflict between the mystic's direct perception of man as God's instrument and the Church's manipulation of ceremonial observance in order to maintain tradition and the power of entrenched interests. Hence the Church, headed in Part I by Pimen and in Part II by Fedor Kolichev, who becomes Philip the Metropolitan, wages an ever more bitter war against Ivan's political schemes. Ivan, in turn, is forced to declare war against the Church as it becomes ever more closely identified with the Boyars, headed by the evil figure of Euphrosinia Staritskaya. Ivan becomes invulnerable, save in his overriding compul-sion towards coming face to face with God—the Tsar of Heaven—in the spirit of an Old Testament prophet. This is the dominant thread intersecting the accumulating intrigue of the Church in Part II entitled The Boyars' Plot. It seems to go hand in hand with Ivan's enormous need to be received with understanding and love and be delivered from his sense of unutterable loneliness.

In the film, as ultimately released, the betrayal of Kurbsky at the Polish court—Livonia—serves as the opening sequence. Livonia is de-picted as culturally aligned to 'the West' and supporting the Boyars' interests. But in the script's opening sequence, Ivan returns to Moscow surrounded by his Lifeguards 'in black cloaks with the Broom and Dog's head Emblem on their saddles', he is overjoyed to meet again his only remaining friend, Fedor Kolichev, who appears as the Abbot.

But Philip is stern.
. . . 'Your undertakings are not from God—but from the Evil One.'
'Silence, Silence, Master!' cries Ivan. . . .
And in the palace the two stand alone . . . one against the other.

The Tsar and the Priest, above them the Angel—angry—Apocalyptic—its feet trampling the Universe.

The Tsar wishes to embrace Philip. But Philip will not permit it.

The Tsar wishes to show affection to Philip. But Philip is stern.

And from the Throne Ivan cries to Philip in anguish: 'Why are you stern with me, Fedor Kolichev? Why cruel? Friend! You should pity me. . . .'

Philip does not look at him. . . .

Ivan sinks back crushed on to the Throne, as once a boy he sat in fear on that very place.

'I had a dearest friend—Anastasia. She left me.

'I had a dear friend. . . .

. . . 'He betrayed me. . . .'

In the finished film, Ivan tells Philip, once his good friend, of his own dedication: 'I will raise new men as God raised Adam from the dust.' Philip fails to sympathize. He understands nothing of Ivan's horror of the Boyars or their betrayal. Ivan tells Philip of his childhood. The Prologue is inserted to explain his experiences in youth. Following this flashback, Ivan assures Philip that he rests on the will of the people. 'I fear not for myself, but for my young cause, just beginning. . . .'

It is not unreasonable to consider that this tortuous scene embodies both Eisenstein's attempts to feel the predicament of Joseph Stalin who had, objectively, caused Eisenstein great suffering according to the dogma of his cause, and Eisenstein's own conflicting suffering in endeavouring to adhere to his own conscience in the cause of his dedication to art.

Ivan confesses, 'I am crushed with the burdens of power.'

. . . Ivan seems about to hide himself with fear in the folds of Philip's mantle. . . .

'I fear not for myself. But for the great work just begun. . . .'

And through the bitter features of the Tsar's yellowing face terror suddenly appears—the terror of a child, an adolescent.

'You do not wish to heed a Priest? Then rule alone. . . .'

And like a bell tolling anathemas: . . . 'reviled, doomed, accursed!'

He [Philip] tore away his mantle.

Uttering coldly: '. . . *alone!*'

He swept towards the door. From the throne Ivan clutches hold of the mantle. . . . The Tsar strides towards him. Trips on the mantle. Falls. Suddenly he finds himself at the feet of Philip. . . . 'I ask you not as Tsar, but as a friend burdened with the heavy load of power. . . . Leave me not in loneliness. Be with me: Help me strengthen the Russian State. . . .'

He [Philip] answers slowly. 'Will you give me the right to intercede before you? To plead for those you have condemned?' . . .

With a heavy heart Ivan gives his agreement to Philip's request.
He submits. . . . Against his will he loses his head and agrees.

. . . He is not pleased with a purchased friendship. Not for such a
friendship is he longing. Not for such a price friendship he seeks. . . .

Philip gives Ivan a confessor, Efstafy, the youngest of the Kolichevs,
who later conspires with Prince Kurbsky. Left alone, Ivan 'stands in
deep thought'. . . . 'Why have you given a priest such power over
you?' demands Malyuta. He offers his services in the swift extermina-
tion of three of Philip's brothers. Once more alone:

Ivan rises slowly from the chair, rises to his full height. Gripping
his head in his hands. Muttering to himself:

'. . . What right have you to judge, Tsar Ivan? And by what right
do you wield the sword of retribution?'
In sorrow, supplication, terror, he stares at the vaults above.
His hands lifted upwards. . . .

Then he rushes to the bedchamber of the long-dead Anastasia.
Malyuta instructs Fedor Basmanov, the first of the Lifeguards, to
watch for Ivan's safety. Following the Tsar into the chamber, Fedor,
who dedicated himself to Ivan beside the coffin of Anastasia, informs
the Tsar that his wife was poisoned—by Euphrosinia—and Ivan had
handed her the cup. Ivan, about to hurl himself to the ground, is caught
be Fedor, who says: 'Be firm!' '*Her very words!*' cries Ivan, recalling
what Anastasia said before she died. 'He catches hold of Fedor and
embraces him.' Together they hurtle down the stairs, along the corridor
to the secret window. In the courtyard below:

. . . In the snow stands Malyuta. . . .
On their knees before him—Boyars. Three of them, all from the
Kolichev family. . . . [Plate 48]
The sabre whistles and the heads fall.
The first Boyar . . . the second. . . . A pause, and then the third—
the youngest. The first two hold themselves up straight with un-
bending necks, and the sword flashes in an arc parallel to the earth.
The third, the youngest, slumps in woe with head bent earthwards,
and the sword flashes vertically downwards.

Going to the courtyard:

The Tsar's eyes do not burn with delight, but sorrow.
The Tsar showers no thanks—but doffs his hat.

And crosses himself with wide gestures, in memory of the fallen. . . .

And suddenly declares: 'Too few!'

With a rush the groundlings [Lifeguards] surge forward, through the storm. . . .

Through the storm the Lifeguards surge with cries and shouts—rough justice to administer. . . .

Boyars are dragged over the ground, with accompanying laughter. . . .

The Church, centred around Philip, and the Boyars around Euphrosinia, swear over the bodies of the dead Kolichevs 'to bend the Tsar, humble him, . . . crush him with the Church'. [Plate 55]

The means chosen by Sergei Mikhailovich is very strange—the enactment in the cathedral of the Biblical miracle of the Hebrew Children and the Fiery Furnace.

The symbolical 'play within a play' is designed to bring Ivan to his knees. A platform, with a furnace, is set on the spot where Ivan was crowned; into it are driven three boys—the Hebrew children—by the 'Chaldeans'. This line of action follows the old miracle play with its mummery. A second line of action is formed by the Boyars and Church representatives who have contrived the performance.

A little lad asks his mother in a ringing voice: 'What is the fiery furnace?'

Alongside stands Euphrosinia Staritskaya. She explains significantly: 'The Chaldean Mystery tells how an Angel of God brought three lads, Shadrach, Meshach, and Abednego—alive and whole—out of the Chaldean fiery furnace. And he who threw them into the fiery furnace was the terrible heathen Tsar. . . .'

Into the Cathedral comes the Tsar.

Philip comes forward to meet the Tsar.

He stops before the furnace.

The three lads sing with their crystal voices.

Passionless, expressionless, without understanding the meaning of the words: a choir of angelic transparency.

And these words fly to meet the Tsar:

> 'Why, then, shameless Chaldeans,
> do you serve the iniquitous Tsar?
> Why then, diabolical Chaldeans,
> do you rejoice
> in a satanic Tsar—
> an outrager, a torturer? . . .'

The Tsar stops, listening to the words in astonishment. . . .

Ivan continues as if he has heard no words. Approaches Philip for the Benediction. Philip turns away. . . .

Thrice Ivan bows his head. Thrice Philip turns away.

And in the dead silence the angelic voices sing:

> 'Now a miracle shalt thou see:
> The Lord of the earth
> Shall be cast down
> By the Lord of the Heavens. . . .'

From the height of the pulpit Philip launches an attack on Ivan.

'Like Nebuchadnezzar, Ivan, you burn your nearest in the fire. But an angel with a sword will come down to them and rescue them from the depths!' In a clear voice a small boy asks if Ivan is the wretched Nebuchadnezzar.

He raises his arm to the dome:

There, hung on a chandelier by a rope, swings a gigantic parchment angel.

The ends of the rope are held by two monks.

'Bow to the Church, Ivan, and submit! Abolish the Lifeguards. Before it is too late!'

Skimming, darting like a swallow through the titanic battle, comes Sergei Mikhailovich's satirical and swift sense of nonsense in preparation for smashing the Church scheme with the unexpected twist. Ivan turns sharply:

'From now on I shall become that which you name me!'

'*Terrible* shall I become!'

Philip is arrested.

In Part I, Euphrosinia, with the Church's blessing, poisons Anastasia. Now she plans the murder of Ivan. Pimen, the Episcope of Novgorod, appoints his own confessor, Peter, to perform the deed and Euphrosinia gives him the knife. Her son, Vladimir Andreyevich,

Fearful of murder, . . . whispers in terror: 'And why are you pushing me to power?'

The powerful old woman embraces her son. Like a child Vladimir clings to his mother. She comforts him. She sings him a lullaby. A strange, evil lullaby. [Plate 58]

Then Ivan invites Vladimir Andreyevich to a banquet where the Lifeguards'

Black jackets dance wildly.

In their midst a girl in a Sarafan.

The girl whirls round like the wind.

The girl's face is covered with a mask.

Alongside the Tsar sits Vladimir Andreyevich.
Ivan pours out wine for him.
Affectionately getting him drunk.
The Lifeguards whirl in a dance.
In their midst—the girl in the Sarafan.
The mask smiles in a dead rapacious smile.
The head suggests the toothed grin of a dog. . . .
Alongside the Tsar's place—Vladimir Andreyevich.
The Tsar affectionately plays with his curls. . . .[1]

The whole sequence in which Vladimir is prepared for death in Ivan's stead has a bizarre atmosphere of make-believe. It extends beyond Ivan's play-acting with Vladimir. Everyone but Ivan, who 'has drunk much, but is absolutely sober', is taken in by their roles in life, while Ivan plays with each like a cat with a mouse.

The Tsar loves Masquerades.
The Tsar loves to dress up others.
They make amusement with mummers, and thus Fedka [who is the 'girl' in the Sarafan] amuses the Tsar.
Fedka hears the Tsar's words [to Vladimir]: 'I am an abandoned orphan with no one to love and pity me. . . .'
Fedka is hurt.

What symbolic thread is this running through the weave of intrigue? Finally Ivan, mimicking Vladimir's drunken words, says:

'Take the crown . . . take the mantle . . . take them. . . .'
The Tsar loves to dress up.
The Tsar loves to dress others.
He orders: 'Bring the Tsarist Regalia!'
Malyuta and Basmanov dress Vladimir in the Tsarist Regalia.
Ivan himself places Vladimir on the throne.
Bends the knee to him.
And this scene appears to be a parody on that in the Prologue, when the youthful Ivan sat on the throne. . . .

Thus, Vladimir is prepared to meet the death his mother has planned for Ivan. The bell for the morning prayer sounds, the banquet ends. Dressed in a bishop's attire beneath a black mantle, Ivan urges Vladimir: 'It is not becoming for a Tsar to retreat. A Tsar must always go forward. . . .' Vladimir passes into the cathedral. And the Lifeguards, in the guise of monks, each with a candle in his hand, chant the oath to

[1] Grigori Alexandrov later told me that when Part II was edited, the dance of the 'girl in a Sarafan' lasted about fifteen minutes.—M.S.

the Tsar: 'I swear before God . . . to serve the Tsar of Russia as a dog,'
as

> The shadow of Peter [the assassin] slips between the columns.
> Vladimir Andreyevich is afraid. The candle in his hand trembles.
> Under the arch of the little door in the darkness stands Peter.
> In his hand a knife glistens. . . .
> Vladimir Andreyevich shuddered and turned aside. And in that
> instant Peter with a swing plunged his knife between his shoulder
> blades.
> Vladimir Andreyevich fell on his face on the stone floor.
> The Lifeguards stand rooted to the spot.
> Through the cathedral runs Euphrosinia triumphantly.
> Comes up to the body. Places her foot upon it.
> Then cries jubilantly: 'People look! It is the end of Ivan.'
> Suddenly she stops. The rows of Lifeguards give way.
> And from the depths comes slowly towards her . . . Ivan.
> [Plate 58]
> Euphrosinia shudders. Looks down. Bends. Turns the body over.
> Recognizes her son. . . .

Dressed in monastic habit, Ivan faces Euphrosinia. Between them is
the body of her effeminate son, whom Eisenstein portrayed with the
characteristics of a homosexual, and an idiot.

> The captured Peter is led to Ivan.
> Around him the other Lifeguards group threateningly.
> But . . . the Tsar is benign. He hugs him by the neck affectionately.
> Saying to Malyuta and Fedor: 'Why are you holding him? He killed
> the clown. Let him go. . . .'
> In astonishment they let him go.
> 'He didn't kill the clown . . . he killed the deadliest enemy of the
> Tsar. . . .'

Of whom was Sergei Mikhailovich thinking when he made Euphrosinia the central protagonist though history gave her no such role? His
mother? In reality he regarded his mother as a class enemy and he felt
that she had injured him over and over again. His early study of Freud
had made so deep an impression upon him because the peculiar insight
he felt in Freud coincided with his own perception of his inner conflicts.

By characterizing Vladimir as a homosexual, Eisenstein involved
Euphrosinia and her son in an entirely psychological interpretation
according to his conception of Freud's teaching. Euphrosinia's interest
in her son becoming Tsar is only a means of gaining power for
herself, and this was the motive Sergei Mikhailovich attributed

to his own mother every time she sought to dominate him. Of what was Sergei Mikhailovich thinking when he has Ivan dress Vladimir in his own robes and, as it were, change places with him so that it is the homosexual who is killed by his mother's plan? Long before, Sergei Mikhailovich had come to the conclusion that homosexuality led to a dead end, to creative death as he had explained to me when he discussed the matter at Yalta. Thus, the symbolism of the mother unwittingly devising her son's death when her aim was Ivan's death is pointed. Sergei Mikhailovich, as he implied to Joseph Freeman in 1928, escaped through sublimation a fate which once could most likely have overcome him. As Grigori Alexandrov later told me, he realized during the production of Ivan that Sergei Mikhailovich had not outgrown the influence of Freud.

In effect Vladimir and Ivan are one; Vladimir being the rejected counterpart of the strong Ivan—'the deadliest enemy of the Tsar'. This duality reflected Sergei Mikhailovich's own duality. He could not tolerate the idea of homosexuality in himself any more than he could tolerate weakness or the 'helpless child' elements in himself. He loved his mother and he hated her for keeping alive the child in him and forcing it to the surface. He had a need to cling to her, but that was the very weakness he felt compelled to reject. It is, of course, Eisenstein himself who symbolically kills the intolerable part of himself in the figure of the clinging, effeminate Vladimir, but in the scenario he transfers the act itself to Euphrosinia, the mother.

In the released picture the action comes to a curiously abrupt end, making the film appear truncated. But in the scenario the action breaks away from the tight knot into which it has been twisted with such horror and violence. The thread of Kurbsky's desertion to the King of Livonia is picked up from Part I. In Part II of the film as released he is shown as the centre of a still wider conspiracy to create uprisings against Ivan in the Russian cities of Pskov and Novgorod. Meanwhile, Peter, the priestly murderer, confesses to Ivan the part played by Pimen, in the conspiracy, and Efstafy, with frightful venom, urges the Tsar to a crusade against Novgorod, where Pimen heads the plot. Swiftly and stealthily Ivan descends upon Pimen. Pimen is arrested. The climax of conspiracy, as well as Ivan's anguish, is reached in a symbolical sequence of the Last Judgement in the cathedral.

> The angry countenance of the Tsar of Heaven
> Sabaoth
> in the fresco of the Last Judgement.
> The Last Judgement is made by the Heavenly Tsar:
> He summons the righteous to him,

he casts sinners into burning Gehenna.
Around the Heavenly Tsar are fiery circles:
The Angelic Hierarchy are depicted.
The winged Lifeguards of the Heavenly Tsar
With fiery swords pointing downwards.
Down to where sinners burn in Eternal Flames
Of Eternal fires.

As in the corresponding sequence in Part I—where Ivan beats his head in torment against the coffin of Anastasia—a monk chants an 'internal monologue' recording the endless names of those whose death Ivan caused, directly or indirectly.

The voice of the monk is heard:
        'Have mercy, O Lord
        'On the Slave of God Vladimir Prince Staritsky;
Out of the darkness emerges the silhouette of the monk:
        'Have mercy, O Lord
        'on Inokina Princess Evdokia,
        'In this world Euphrosinia Staritskaya—
        'drowned in the River Shaxna. . . .'
The monk finishes reading one scroll . . .

In the darkness under the fresco of the Last Judgement, lies pros-
trate Tsar Ivan, inert in a corner where insatiably the Eternal Fire swallows the Sinners.
Prostrate in the dust lies Tsar Ivan.
Over him hovers the Last Judgement. . . .
Over him shines the starry canopy of the Heavenly Court.
At his feet the sinners burn in Eternal Fire.
But more terrible than the Fires of Hell, tortures, burns, gnaws, the tormented spirit of the earthly Tsar of Muscovy.
He holds before him a terrible responsibility.
Sweat pours down his brow, burning tears from his closed eyes.
The Tsar has grown thin and bowed. And seems to have aged a decade. . . .

The monk goes on chanting the names of the dead. And once again Malyuta and Basmanov supply the commentary of fact, remarking to one another:

        'One thousand five hundred and five souls were executed in Novgorod. . . .'
And Ivan's lips mutter as if to justify these terrible deeds:
        'Not in anger, not in malice. Not in fierceness.
        'But for Treason. For betrayal of the whole people's cause. . . .'

He awaits an answer from Sabaoth.

But the walls are silent.

Malyuta informs Basmanov the elder:

'One hundred and seventy monasteries have been pillaged and destroyed. . . .'

And Ivan hastens to explain these bloody deeds:

'Not for myself, not for ambition's sake. But for the Motherland.

'Not out of savagery. But for reasons of state. . . .'

Ivan looks up with entreaty into the eyes of the dark countenance.

But the eyes do not look down:

They look painfully into the distance. . . .

Ivan speaks in anguish: 'You are silent?'

He waits. No answer.

Angrily and threateningly the earthly Tsar challenges the heavenly Tsar: 'You are silent, Tsar of Heaven!' Silence.

And the earthly Tsar hurls the gauntlet at the heavenly Tsar in the shape of his wooden bejewelled staff.

The staff crashes on to the smooth wall, and falls to pieces.

The jewelled stones scatter. Turning to heaven, like Ivan's prayers —in vain. . . . And the earthly Tsar falls, crushed by the mercilessness of the heavenly Tsar.

'So you will not answer the earthly Tsar . . .' mutters Tsar Ivan, banging his fist on the wall in impotence. But stern frescoed Sabaoth stays silent.

And around him the Hierarchy of angels are also silent.

The sinners are silent, writhing in eternal Fire.

On the ground Ivan groans.

His soul is on fire. . . .

Then it is shown that Basmanov, the father, has become corrupt and he is now betraying Ivan by stealing from the Treasury through a serf. But this Ivan does not know as he

Bows to the very earth. Beating his brow on the stones. His eyes become bloodshot. Blood covers his sight. His reason is clouded over. His eyes darken. . . .

His back bent, he sways to and fro.

His hands stretched out—grasping the air—seeking for support.

'Father, Father . . .' his dry lips whisper.

He rises from his knees. . . .

Ivan stumbles through the Cathedral.

'I go to confess,' sounds hoarsely and dully the voice of Ivan.

He goes in the darkness of the Cathedral to the Choir.

Past the impassive Reader.

Past the Golden Gates of the Tsar.
To the little Gate with the Angel.
'Who calls to God?'
Came the clear voice of Efstafy from the Altar.
'The unworthy slave Ivan . . .'
Echoed the Tsar's voice dully from the stone floor.

Alone with Efstafy, Ivan confesses to the killing of Philip the Metropolitan—and the other Kolichevs. Then Efstafy betrays himself as the
last of the Kolichevs. The confession is suddenly turned around with
the confessor confessing to Ivan that he has been Kurbsky's agent and
'all frontier posts have been bribed by the Livonian Ambassador'.

This extraordinary denouement leaves Ivan's inner conflict between himself, as Tsar of Russia, and God, as Tsar of Heaven, un-
resolved. Betrayed by the representatives of the Church, the God-
tormented Ivan is compelled to further actions against them in order
to preserve his State.

The double-edged handling of this conflict within Ivan reveals Eisenstein's own conflicting processes of thought and feeling towards religion
and the Church. In Ivan, Sergei Mikhailovich portrayed his own irresistible pull towards the mysteries of religious experience and his equal
compulsion to destroy the Church. Such a portrayal of Ivan could not
have resulted from thought alone, nor yet emotion. It could only spring
from a sensitive being pulled between the mystic's perception and the
scientist's rationalism, which was the woof and warp of Eisenstein.
[Plate 59]

The little that remained of Part II following the Last Judgement was
a coda drawn from history conveyed through an insinuating sound and
image ballad. A scene in Windsor Castle shows the diplomatic game of
chess played by Ivan the Terrible's emissary, the German Ambassador
and Ginger Bess, the Queen of England. The game, sudden and swift,
is sandwiched between a short sequence in which Kurbsky and Sigismund of Livonia fall into the trap laid for them by Ivan, and the last
scene in which the Lifeguards watch the frontier posts and arrest Ivan's
enemies one by one . . . 'in the darkness move the troops of the Tsar'.

Since Part II of *Ivan the Terrible* was never shown until 1958, it is not
clear whether the closing scenes of Part II of the scenario were included
in the final editing of the film. The scene in Sigismund's Palace between
Kurbsky and Sigismund, King of Livonia, forms the opening sequence
of Part II.

Eisenstein told Richard Lauterbach, who visited Alma Ata with
Eric Johnson in the early autumn of 1944, that he had shot 140,000 feet
of film for Parts I and II of *Ivan*. He showed the two Americans the

sombre, 16th-century sets where authentic icons were blended with papier mâché goblets encrusted with semi-precious stones. Lauterbach says that Eisenstein was concerned with the tremendous task of editing the two films. 'He held his head and gave a bad imitation of Gregory Ratoff imitating a Russian director.'[1]

The scenario for Part III of *Ivan the Terrible*, which was never shot, was originally intended to serve as the end of the second film. It picks up the mood which in Part I characterizes the early scenes of Ivan mastering the inflamed Moscow populace and waging war against the Tartars at Kazan. Military action against Prince Kurbsky and the Livonians and Germans dominate the action. There is a move away from the subjective level. The only intrigue and betrayal that appears is Ivan's detection of the corruption of Basmanov, the Elder, and his execution by his son Fedor. Before executing his father, however, Fedor takes an oath to abandon his loyalty to Ivan and to preserve the Basmanov family interests against those of Ivan's State, but in the end, Fedor pays with his life for his betrayal of Ivan.

Whereas the tempo of the action and conflict of Parts I and II unfold circuitously, the action and rhythm of Part III become martial. Ivan, no longer pondering upon moral questions and freed from 'palace intrigues', has become a man of action:

> On the background of the red glow Tsar Ivan whirls with the cavalry. His hair flying in the wind. Nostrils extended. His eyes burning.
> 'We shall be like our great Ancestor Alexander Nevsky and mercilessly drive the Germans from our land! . . .'
> The Tsar seems to have grown twenty years younger.
> On the background of the red glow Tsar Ivan whirls with the cavalry.

Surrounded by his Lifeguards and the dying Malyuta, Ivan finally approaches the sea of his childhood song: [Plate 60]

> Ocean-sea
> Azure sea
> Azure sea
> Russian sea.

On the horizon lies the Baltic. Malyuta, who has remained loyal to Ivan, dies as they sight the Baltic. Ivan has reached his goal, but he is entirely alone except for Peter, the priest who killed Vladimir Andreyevich, 'the deadliest enemy of the Tsar'.

[1] *These Are the Russians*, by Richard Lauterbach (New York, Harper, 1944–1945), p. 215.

The curious and compelling quality about *Ivan the Terrible*, particularly the scenario of Part II, is that Ivan's character and actions are as open to speculation as those of Hamlet, to whom he was in Part II critically compared. The other most striking feature of the whole treatment is that the spectator, or reader, can see in the action what he himself wishes to read into it. From a political point of view, Eisenstein's *Ivan the Terrible*, Part I, has been interpreted by some people as being a denunciation of dictatorship, while others said 'this vindication of Ivan becomes, by many parallels, a vindication of Stalin and his regime'.[1]

What the scenario as a whole reveals is that Eisenstein had scaled a summit through a lifetime of acute inner experience, made more meaningful by his intensive observation of the world, and the conclusion he reached seemed to be that for the sake of survival men like Ivan were compelled to actions outside the orthodox concepts of 'good' and 'evil'. At last he had fully realized a statement he had made in 1929: 'It is Art's task to make manifest the contradictions of Being.' This he had most surely done, even though the strain of keeping alive 'the first moment of inspiration' year in and year out had taken a mortal toll of his resources.

During the shooting of the second part of Ivan, Sergei Mikhailovich received a terrible blow. According to Grigori Alexandrov, Eduard Tisse, who had worked with Eisenstein for twenty years and had stood by him in all his many troubles, left his unit and joined Alexandrov. Tisse had come to feel that Sergei Mikhailovich's artistic aims and his own had diverged so far that it was impossible for them to work together any longer. On Part I, Tisse had photographed only the exterior scenes.

Now the two people whom Eisenstein had once believed would remain close to him as long as he lived had withdrawn. So he stood alone save for his new cameraman, Andrei Mosvin. Yet he went on.

In the autumn of 1944, Sergei Mikhailovich returned to Moscow, where the film industry had been reorganized. He took up life again in his flat at Potylika and completed the editing of *Ivan the Terrible*, Part I (which, as mentioned before, was released in January 1945). Most of the shooting of Part II had been done in Alma Ata, but the question as to whether or not *Ivan the Terrible* would form two or three films was apparently still undecided. Eisenstein sometimes told people who talked to him about the film that it would be in two parts, at other times he said it would be in three.

Though the war had not ended, the isolation from the outside world which Eisenstein had felt in Alma Ata was now relieved. Renewed

[1] Review of *Ivan the Terrible*, Part I (New York, *Time*, 14 April 1947).

international contact was established in Moscow as a result of the Allied war effort. The Soviet film publishing house, Goskinozdat, prepared a monograph in honour of D. W. Griffith and was planning another on Charlie Chaplin. The article on Griffith, mentioned to Jay Leyda in 1941, had now evolved into a long comparative study of Griffith's films and the novels of Charles Dickens, which Sergei Mikhailovich had re-read with a mature eye and much pleasure. It now became a section of the Griffith monograph. Eisenstein was also working on a section called 'Charlie, the Kid'[1] for the Chaplin book. While he worked to explain his views on Griffith and Chaplin for the Russian people, a select American public had been reading *The Film Sense*. The royalties from this book now enabled Sergei Mikhailovich to buy in America the books he craved. On the 4th of December, 1944, he cabled Jay Leyda a typical book order:

> Buy on honorarium for me books Howard Craft development detective genre Stefan Lorant Lincoln his life in pictures Eisenstein.

Around this time, he also wrote to Roger Burford, the British Film Officer in Moscow:

> DEAR MR. BURFORD,
>   I just got your letter and think it very nice of you to have sent me the copy of my book. Many thanks! I'm crazy about modern english and american plays (and *good* detective stories as well): so if by any chance—besides film stuff—you may happen to dispose of something of this kind—please let me have it to read. (And do not make fun of my bad english!)
>   Always sincerely yours
>   EISENSTEIN.

Eisenstein had met Burford in connection with his work on the three-man Film Committee of V.O.K.S., the Society for Cultural Relations between the U.S.S.R. and Foreign Countries. Together with his fellow members, Pudovkin and Gerasimov, Sergei Mikhailovich served as a liaison between the Soviet film industry and the Film Officers who had been attached to the British and American embassies.

It thus came about that Eisenstein and Pudovkin were thrown into close contact with one another, and foreigners, seeing them together, concluded they were great friends. Perhaps they had reached the conclusion in Alma Ata that their years of antagonism were rather foolish, or that there was no way to escape from one another. Roger Burford, who was introduced to Eisenstein by Pudovkin, was slightly puzzled when Eisenstein insisted he must send him a production photograph

[1] S. M. Eisenstein, 'Charlie, the Kid' (*Sight and Sound*, Vol. XV, Nos. 57, 58, Spring and Summer 1946).

taken during *Ivan the Terrible* in which he was bound in chains to Pudovkin. And Burford could also not understand why Eisenstein sent him only one still of *Ivan*—that of Pudovkin yelling madly as Nikolai, the Great Simpleton. Perhaps Sergei Mikhailovich had heard that Pudovkin had told Burford that he had helped him to write the book *The Film Sense* and this 'still' was his subtle comment. [Pl. 69, p. 418.]

When the first part of *Ivan the Terrible* was released it won much official approval. Finally it was decided that there should be three films on Ivan and, throughout 1945, Sergei Mikhailovich worked to complete the second part. During the first six months he also worked on the 'little booklet' he had mentioned to Leyda in a letter written four years before. On the 20th of June, 1945, Eisenstein sent Leyda a cable (in answer to one Leyda had sent after seeing *Ivan*, Part I):

Many many thanks telegram much love everybody stop am completing new book wire if interested publishing Affections Eisenstein.

Some two months later a great desire arose in Sergei Mikhailovich. He wanted above everything else to see what remained of *Que Viva Mexico!* and, if possible, finally, to edit a film from it. The chain leading from Mexico to Moscow, Moscow to Yalta, Yalta to the rediscovery of *Que Viva Mexico!* flamed in his memory. He had thought that perhaps a print of *Time in the Sun*, the film which I had produced from the material for *Que Viva Mexico!* in 1939, might have been sent to him now the war was ended.

I had not sent a print of *Time in the Sun* because, after the film's completion, it had been impossible to preserve the remaining footage. Without all the material remaining intact, I knew that Eisenstein would suffer if only fragments of his film came into his hands.

But he was unable to forget the Mexican film. Thirteen years had not dimmed his desire to complete the work. Suddenly in September 1945 he decided he must obtain prints of the three films which other hands had edited—*Thunder Over Mexico*, *Death Day* and *Time in the Sun*. The only contact he thought might lead to them was Artkino, the Soviet film agency in America. So he communicated with the New York office and asked them to act on his behalf. On the 27th of September, Mr. Napoli of Artkino sent me a telegram:

Eisenstein much interested securing copy 'Time in the Sun' for own use would be very grateful if you could arrange to make available 16mm or 35mm print stop I will pay all costs stop Am anxious to send copy Eisenstein through Russian friend going Soviet Union next week please wire.

N. Napoli Artkino Pictures
723 Seventh Avenue New York City

Artkino was given a print of *Time in the Sun* and I told Mr. Napoli where he might obtain a print of *Thunder Over Mexico*. The two prints were sent by him to Eisenstein, who waited for them as he worked upon the editing of *Ivan the Terrible*, Part II, during October and November. Soon the work would end and he would be free to rest a while and do other things.

As the work on the second *Ivan* film drew towards completion, Sergei Mikhailovich attended the receptions held in post-war Moscow. He stood about in his impeccable and formal clothes and more often than not spoke only in monosyllables. But however inconspicuous his behaviour, the eyes of strangers were drawn to his hair, which 'spiralled wildly into two horn-like tufts above his bulging forehead', and he appeared 'an amoral gnome, a miniature and intellectual satyr', who was 'a traveller from an unknown land'.

Such was the impression that Eisenstein, at the age of forty-seven, made upon the American dramatic critic Brooks Atkinson and his wife when they met him at a V.O.K.S. reception. Because Atkinson was a link with the theatre and Sergei Mikhailovich had a great hunger to discuss the arts abroad, he suddenly grew friendly. As the year 1945 neared its end, Eisenstein went to dinner several times with the Atkinsons at the Metropole Hotel. They thought it odd that he should always invite them to his flat at Potylika, but then divert the appointment to the hotel. It seemed that the only people who actually visited him at the flat were the few people he had known half his life—Grigori Alexandrov and Maxim Shtraukh. According to Alexandrov, Sergei Mikhailovich met Pera Attasheva occasionally for lunch, but it appears that even she did not go to Eisenstein's flat.

At the Metropole, a place he had once detested, Eisenstein talked volubly to the Atkinsons. He would spin out a web of ideas that sounded as if there were no limits to his many plans. Among his cherished ideas was the creation of a detective magazine. He seemed certain about one thing: *Ivan* would be his last dramatic film. He was avid for news of the American theatre, and it was during a discussion of current American plays that Brooks Atkinson mentioned the play *Harvey*.

Elwood P. Dowd and the six-foot rabbit created out of his unhappy imagination instantly sank into the consciousness of Sergei Mikhailovich. He pleaded with Atkinson to send to America for a script. Each time they met, he asked when the script of *Harvey* would arrive. Atkinson tried to assure him that really *Harvey* was a trifling play. 'You don't understand it!' Eisenstein declared vehemently.

Between discussions of the theatrical form, Eisenstein told the Atkinsons hilariously funny stories of America and Mexico. Apparently nothing serious had ever happened to him in either place. But suddenly his mood would change and he would say that he had never seen one foot of his Mexican film.

Neither *Thunder Over Mexico* nor *Time in the Sun* had been delivered to Eisenstein as the New Year commenced. As the long period of work on *Ivan* drew towards its close, Sergei Mikhailovich wrote to Leyda:

> January 1946
> MY DEAREST JAY!
> Many thanks for your letters. I hope my cable answers reached you. I was (and still am for about 3 weeks) busy like hell: just finishing to shoot and cut the second part of Ivan. This part includes two reels made in color. Color used in quite different a way, than it is usually done—so that it gives a big additional chapter to what is nearly ready in book form. If everything is allright here with the picture I expect to take a vacation and finish the book—3/4 of which are ready for print. Most of the stuff is unpublished (part of it even—unwritten yet!) and is mostly concerned with the development of the principles started by 'Potemkin' during these 20 years in different media (is that the way to say it?)—treatments of sound, music, color. The way of composing ecstatic scenes, etc. 'Ivan' in connection with 'Potemkin'. I will send you a detailed plan as soon as the film goes to the laboratory to be printed. May be it will be allright to include the script of Ivan as well into this book.
> Out of the books you sent me only very few reached me—and according to the list—the less interesting ones! There are lots of things I'd like to write you about—and I'll do it as soon as I get my vacation. Please continue to send books reckoning that still one to six or seven reach me!
> You have a wonderful flair as to what excites me! Take for instance Melville and Steinberg (this book did not reach me!)—so very important for analytical research work. . . .

It is not clear which scenes were in colour because Part II of *Ivan* was not shown. But it may be that one of the two reels in colour, which Eisenstein mentions to Leyda, was the sequence of the masquerade preceding Vladimir's death, and the other, the sequence of the 'Last Judgement'. In such scenes colour could have been used effectively on two levels: first, to heighten the visual effects of costumes, frescoes, etc.; and, secondly, to heighten the emotional content portrayed in the scenes, a subject discussed by Eisenstein in his book *The Film Sense*.[1]

Then came the February day when Sergei Mikhailovich went for the

---

[1] In 1958, when Part II was released, the banquet sequence was in colour but the Last Judgement was not included.

last time to his cutting-room. He took the very last rushes in his hands and completed his montage of Part II of *Ivan the Terrible*. He had ended five years of work, five years of heart searching. Five years of his life had been spent suffering emotions comprehensible only to himself—anguish and ecstasy. He had descended into indescribable hell and ascended to the strange, lone peaks of ecstatic inspiration. He had come face to face with himself and he had also come face to face with the world. He had climbed a mountain and with a part of himself looked down into the valley where the other parts of him wandered, weaving an individual pattern among the men of the world. He had looked into the human heart rather than the heart of history.

For himself, whatever chance he might have had to be a man of the lowlands walking among his fellows as a comrade had died. Too late had come the words of D. Marian: '. . . one must understand simple things. . . .' But he had never been able to follow the advice of his comrades. He left his cutting-room and went to a party given in his honour to celebrate the Stalin Prize First Class won by *Ivan the Terrible*, Part I.

Some months before it had been reported that upon completion of *Ivan the Terrible*, Eisenstein would direct a film in three parts based on the life of Joseph Stalin. The three films would be called *Caucasus*, *Moscow* and *Victory*.[1] In the Soviet Union no greater tribute could have been paid to Eisenstein.

For a short time, Sergei Mikhailovich appeared to be enjoying himself at the party given in his honour. He wore the raffish mask which made him seem like a satyr. He made jokes and danced with pretty women. One, the actress Vera Maretskaya, became his partner for the most macabre dance of his life. As he danced—the guest of honour celebrating his own triumph and the completion of the film which would never be seen—a pain like the grip of a vice closed about his heart. The lights grew brilliant as people and objects in the room began to revolve, spinning in unison with the excruciating pain. Suddenly Sergei Mikhailovich fell to the floor.

He felt very foolish and humiliated lying at the feet of the people who had come to celebrate his triumph. Never before had he been seen helpless in public. A doctor came and told him to remain still. He saw Grigori Alexandrov looking at him. Others stared at him. The sense of humiliation and foolishness grew more intense in his agonized brain. He heard the doctor say they must carry him out. At that his consciousness rebelled. He refused to be carried out of the arena—like a clown.

[1] *To-day's Cinema* (London, 21 August 1945).

'If you move, or if you attempt to walk, you are a dead man,' said the doctor.

But like Ivan, Eisenstein asserted his will. He moved. He stood up. He walked out of the room. Grigori Alexandrov drove him in his car to the clinic of the Kremlin Hospital.

Note 1977. The religious aspects of Eisenstein's film have now been examined in detail by Father Gaston Roberge, S.J., in *Ivan the Terrible, An Analysis,* so far unpublished.

Many people supposed that the second part of *Ivan the Terrible* might be destroyed following the criticism of it (see pp. 457–63) since nothing more was heard of it. This never seemed likely to me. In 1956, two Indian friends of mine, the film director K. A. Abbas and B. Garga, his assistant, went to work at Mosfilm Studio on the Indo-Soviet coproduction, *Padesi.* This was the studio where much of the later work on *Ivan the Terrible* had been done. For five months Abbas and Garga repeatedly requested to see a copy of Eisenstein's *Ivan,* Part II. Repeatedly they were told that there was no copy of the film in Moscow and that it was difficult to bring one to Moscow. But a few days before the end of their work on *Padesi,* a copy of the second part of *Ivan* was discovered in the studio itself and screened for Abbas and Garga.

From Moscow, Abbas and Garga came to London. Garga and I went to see Penelope Houston and it was arranged that Garga write an article for *Sight and Sound* about the rediscovery of *Ivan,* Part II. At the same time I urged Ernest Lindgren to request a copy for the British National Film Archive. Lindgren's letter elicited no response. Then, in 1958, to everyone's astonishment and delight, the Russians announced they would allow the second part of *Ivan* to be world premiered at the Brussels Festival of the Best Films of All Time which was part of the World Fair. *Potemkin* naturally was included in the selection of Best Films. Nikolai Cherkasov came to Brussels for the premiere; so did Nikolai Okhlopkov, the supporting comic hero of *Alexander Nevsky*; and Grigori Kozintsev. The seventh juror was India's Satyajit Ray who, with others, had purchased a copy of *Potemkin* when they founded the Calcutta Film Society in 1948. In a small projection room away from the Festival, we saw the Soviet biographical film of Eisenstein. This reinstated him as a hero of Soviet Cinematography.

Later, in the early 1960s, a collection of Eisenstein's drawings, and sketches mainly for *Nevsky* and *Ivan,* began to be circulated for international exhibition. In 1963, the Victoria and Albert Museum opened its doors to this exhibition which revealed to Londoners the enormous range of Sergei Eisenstein's graphic talent, its pathos and wit.

CHAPTER SIXTEEN

'On Borrowed Time'

Oh thou that sleepest, what is sleep? Sleep is an image of death.
Oh why not let your work be such that after death you become an
image of immortality; as in life you become when sleeping like
unto the hapless dead.

LEONARDO DA VINCI, C.A. 59 r.b.

FOR many days Sergei Mikhailovich hovered between life and
death in a small, bright room overlooking the inner garden of the
Kremlin Hospital. Years of work and strain had culminated in a very
serious heart attack. Only the skill of doctors saved Eisenstein from
immediate death. But no skill could have prolonged his life had he not
wished to live.

He was suffering from a heart condition known as 'infarct', which
develops in the advanced stages of certain types of the incurable and
painful heart disease angina pectoris. Such a condition leads to the
gradual cutting off of the blood supply from the heart and the degene-
ration of the tissue. In the final stages, pain accompanies the slightest
muscular effort and there is difficulty in breathing.

When the doctors told Sergei Mikhailovich that his heart disease was
serious and that he would have to remain in the hospital for some time,
his first decision was that he would continue to work as best he could.
He had his secretary and Loshka, his chauffeur, bring him piles of his
most precious books. He wanted so many that they had to be stacked
on the floor. His second decision was that no one must see how much
he suffered and only very rarely did his resolution break down and fear
come creeping out—the fear of a child to whom something terrible was
going to happen.

For Sergei Mikhailovich, his dependent state was both alluring and
repellent. It was like childhood, only the childhood of a genius who
knew too much. He felt this most keenly when his mother came to see
him once each week. He looked at her and knew that a cycle had completed itself. Once more she had him in her power and now he must
surrender the feelings which had twisted his life since the day she had
rejected him. If he lived it would be with her—as she had plagued him
to do for so many years.

While Sergei Mikhailovich lay utterly still, his mind ravaged by many strange fantasies, criticism of *Ivan the Terrible*, Part II, arose in the Central Committee of the Communist Party. The film was regarded as 'anti-historical' and betrayed an ignorance of historical facts. But on the advice of the doctors attending Eisenstein, the publication of the criticism was held up for several months. Still, many people were aware of the criticism, but Sergei Mikhailovich's friends contrived to protect him from hearing one word about it. Some of them sent him magazines to while away the time and later he was able to arrange for foreign films to be shown to him as he lay in bed. His will to reach out into the world was strong and he exerted great effort to write notes to those who were kind to him. Holding the pencil so that not a single letter betrayed a tremor, he wrote to his acquaintances, among them the Brooks Atkinsons:

> DEAR MRS. ATKINSON
>
> Sorry to say but my heart disease turns out to be pretty serious. I'll have to stay some four–five weeks in bed. (*alone!* you *can* imagine how terrible that is!)
>
> It is terribly nice of you to remember me and send me magazines. I'm quite close to your hotel: in the Kremlin Hospital just opposite the Lenin Library on Komintern Street. . . . I hope in a week or so I might be able to invite you to the lovely room I occupy here.
>
> Sorry that it is not my apartment in the Potilika where we might have much more fun. . . .
>
> Please excuse pencil and handwriting. I am not allowed to sit up even in bed. So many thanks.
>
> SERGEI

He signed this note not with his usual hieroglyphic signature, but as he signed few letters in his life: his name in his ordinary handwriting. This he only did when he was overwhelmed with great trouble, or very strong emotion.

The 'four–five' weeks he thought he would spend in bed was an illusion. Still he did not falter. He read and went on marking his books. He continued to have an insatiable thirst for detective stories and when any new books came to him he was overjoyed. On the 21st of March he cabled to Jay Leyda:

> Just received . . . brilliant selection of books thanks immensely stop am laying sixth week hospital after heart attack the day I made last cut second part Ivan stop looking forward long reconvalescence entirely devoted writing books awaiting cables letters news much love Eisenstein.

A little less than a month later he cabled again saying that he was trying hard to recover and that he was working on his second book. On the 5th of May he sent Leyda another cable full of urgency:

Please send some extraordinarily quick way Laurence Binyon's Spirit of Man in Asian Art and Flight of the Dragon stop in two weeks leaving hospital.

In one of the books, *Idols Behind Altars*, which Sergei Mikhailovich had carried with him in Mexico and back to Moscow, he had marked these lines with three strokes noting his approval: 'The mestizo gesture is the vacilada, a loud laugh, irreverent, sardonic, full of doubt, full of longing, full of despair, in expression a shock, grotesque,' which conceals 'the heroism of thought, the heroism of emotion, and the heroism of expression'.[1] Now more than ever this was a philosophy befitting Eisenstein, for it was the mood in which the Mexicans made laughter on the Day of the Dead.

When anyone went to see him in the hospital he never spoke seriously. He seldom mentioned how he yearned to fulfil just a little more of his great theoretical work, nor did he talk about the people he had known and liked. He was extravagantly gay, although for a long time he was so weak that he could hardly move his once expressive hands. He delighted in telling a fantastic story about being 'a dead man'. He was dead because the doctor had told him that he would be a dead man if he attempted to walk.

'And I did walk. Therefore, I must be dead!' he argued.

When Brooks Atkinson and his wife, Orina, visited him, Sergei Mikhailovich continued to entertain them with stories of the adventures he had had in America and Mexico. He embroidered these tales with bizarre wit.

Eisenstein may have been trying out some of the stories he wanted to include in 'a comic autobiography', an idea which came to him as he lay in the hospital. In a letter to Jay Leyda written shortly after his cable of the 21st of March, he mentioned the 'comic autobiography', which he said he would dictate to a stenographer. However, it is not clear whether any part of the manuscript was ever written.[2] Sergei Mikhailovich did not mention it to Brooks Atkinson or, so far as is known, to anyone other than Leyda, and Jack Chen who saw him in July.

---

[1] In 1934 I copied this sentence from Eisenstein's copy of *Idols Behind Altars*, by Anita Brenner, which he kept in his room at Chysti Prudi 23. It was the phrase which seemed to describe most accurately his attitude when under stress.

[2] Eisenstein did in fact commence his *Autobiography* (London, Dennis Dobson, 1978) in the Kremlin Hospital.

Moscow 17th may
1946
Kremlin
Hospital.

My dear Burford!

Do not consider me as an accomplished swine for my not writing nor thanking for the book.

I have a ..."perfect alibi": having had a very painful heart-attack just a couple of hours after completing the Second part of . Ivan (February) - and am about 3½ months in hospital, suffering of what might sound somewhat strange to the ears of an english talking gentleman - "infarth" (I do not know the exact spelling of this very dangerous kind of plague - may be some

17. Letter from Sergei Eisenstein

other kind of transcription
may free it from those strange
"overtones" the second part of -
"that word has!")

I am always anxious to
hear from you and as soon
as I'll be fairly all right
I'll write you some "bigger
and better" letter!

Much love and best
regards to Ivor, if you should
see him. And make him write
to me. Or is he still in Nüremberg?!

Your

P.S. It's time to have some new stories by yourself
— quit loafing!

to Roger Burford, Moscow 1946.

It seemed that only one thing in his whole life had ever worried him. This he referred to every week when the Atkinsons came to the hospital: he kept saying he had never seen one foot of the Mexican film. But he did not hint that in September 1945 he had asked Artkino in New York to obtain copies of *Thunder Over Mexico, Death Day* and *Time in the Sun*. And he did not know that somewhere in Moscow there were copies of *Thunder Over Mexico* and *Time in the Sun*; but like the criticism of the second part of *Ivan*, they were being kept from him, possibly for the same reason—the condition of his heart.

When the door closed on his mother and his other visitors, the walls of his room fell away and Sergei Mikhailovich passed into a world where he felt in strange symbols the course of his own life. An imprisoned life, because there had been hardly anyone who had dared to cut their way through his defensive armour and come to know him. In a moment of strange fantasy, he wrote to the Atkinsons:

DEAR MRS. BROOKS

I was under such a phantastic spell all this week, getting no news from you. I had the strangest feeling I ever had in my life—that you and Brooks just existed in my imagination and were two-fold, double-sexed (as the ancient Gods have been supposed to be) kind of Harvey miraculously produced by the Moscow soil. I was glad to find out today that I was wrong. Don't you feel sometimes Harvey-ish towards me? If so, you will be disillusioned very soon: tomorrow will be the first part of a great comedy of manners—they'll teach me sitting in a arm chair! In a couple of days we will see act two: my first steps. (I am sorry that the program will not include all the baby performances—for instance that very peculiar devise by which the babies procure natural milk . . . but you can't have everything in this life.) I expect to see both of you, not as shadows of my excited imagination but in true living form.

My love, always expecting news from you,

SERGEI

and he enclosed a drawing of himself and two Harveys. [Reproduced opposite.] Though he had still not read the play, Elwood P. Dowd and his six-foot rabbit haunted his thoughts.

But when he met the Atkinsons again, they came no closer to understanding him than on the first day they met. Towards the end of May he was transferred to the sanatorium outside of Moscow where the leading Bolsheviks were sent when they were ill. It was a beautiful building furnished with modern furniture and decorated in light,

soothing colours with many green plants: a very different setting from
the small, square room at Chysti Prudi 23, where the Old Man had
once been pulled through 'flu by Pera Attasheva. The Atkinsons went
to see Eisenstein at the sanatorium before leaving for America. Though
his contact with them had not become serious, he suddenly decided he
must tell these people what was in his mind. After much laughter and
funny pantomime, he became serious and asked Brooks Atkinson to
take his note-book and he would dictate some ideas, which he still
dreamed to record in a book.

'Aesthetical problems,' he said, 'you understand? Every art has to
have an original method, a specific aesthetic. Cinema is the outlet of all
the arts: the next step after all others. Movies get the dynamic effect in
painting. Movies technically are perfect and finished. Now we must
start creation. Where to look for fundamentals—the constructive
approach?'

He then talked of each art: Sculpture is subject and spirit of construction—the static form of the human body. Painting also static, but it
brings in the rest of the world as background. Literature can enter
inside the human mind—purely mental. Music, unconcrete feeling—
not material, but already dynamic. Theatre, the first synthesis of other
arts and its basic material is human behaviour.

'Every art', continued Sergei Mikhailovich, 'tries to break its limita-

tions and they become unrealistic. The artist has to pay for what he does by destroying his medium. By exaggerating dynamics you break the medium of painting. Sculpture, if it were dynamic, would be crazy. Cinema is the only art where you get outlet for all these arts without losing reality. We must look to process of thought for next step in movies. The laws of cinema must not be copied from the body nor laws of human behaviour. . . .'

The laws of cinematography had now become for Eisenstein 'the inner process of the human mind and human emotion'. In the film medium he had found the expression of man's inner processes.

'Take the "fade-out",' he said, 'and the "flash-back"; they are typical of the processes of the mind. "Focusing" is also a mind process.'

He explained how James Joyce had sought in literature to reproduce the inner life of man, but had broken the medium of literature in the attempt. But the film could translate the inner processes of man in a concrete form.

'The subject', Eisenstein insisted, 'must not be reproduction of man thinking as in *Ulysses*. This is where creation in film begins. It must not be representation. It is wrong to think of cinema as drama.'

He listed the films he had seen in which it appeared to him there were hints of his ideas. They were *How Green is My Valley* and *Lady in the Dark*. Then he declared he would finish the third part of *Ivan the Terrible* and bid farewell for ever to the dramatic film.

'I will build a new language,' he said, 'construct a new way of talking. An idea is more important than a subject. The new spirit of life is one side of the question; new understanding of form the other. Where they cross is where you get outlet for new film.'[1]

Brooks Atkinson had taken down Eisenstein's words and so they said good-bye, as if they would meet again in a little while. Almost his last words to Atkinson were a reminder not to forget to send him a copy of the play *Harvey*. But he never sent it.

'It seems', Atkinson told me later, 'Eisenstein had not seen a foot of his Mexican film in May of 1946. That alone seemed to trouble him.'

Some weeks later, Sergei Mikhailovich was released from the sanatorium. Nothing more could be expected of him as a film director. Now he was free to dedicate the rest of his life to his theoretical work. In June of 1946, he went to the 'little dacha' with its two stories and seven rooms set among tall pine trees. At last the house took on the semblance of the home Sergei Mikhailovich had lost when he was a small boy. For a short time his mother cared for him in this quiet house. To strangers she appeared like a grand dame who was kind and con-

[1] Notes taken by Brooks Atkinson.

siderate towards her son. She took his occasional guests walking in the garden, telling Sergei Mikhailovich he must not tire himself.

But soon Julia Eisenstein died, and with her death another cycle was completed. Whatever Sergei Mikhailovich felt about his mother's death, he kept concealed. His reactions may have been modified by a philosophic acceptance of his own approaching death. The impression he left on the people who saw him after her death, suggests that the image of the clown which the young mind of Sergei Mikhailovich had devised thirty-six years before had died out of his consciousness and was buried with the mother whose actions had, at least in part, called it into being.

Totya Pasha too had departed and no one remained in the dacha, except a new housekeeper, who looked after Sergei Mikhailovich's needs day by day. But he appeared to be at peace and he worked with the same concentrated patience as that truer likeness of himself— Leonardo da Vinci.

When he had strength enough he wrote and when his strength ebbed he sat on the open porch on the second floor which caught the afternoon sun. He seldom dressed, but wore pyjamas and a shirt under them. In the solitude of the country and in this place of his own choice, he was able to lay aside his armour and live in accordance with the deepest levels of his being, for, even though his sole companion was approaching death, he was now free to do exactly what he wished in the house he had built with loving care.

Neither the empty rooms nor his many unrealized dreams could wholly mock him. Despite the cruel frustrations of his life, his un-crushed will made of him at this time that curious thing an optimistic tragedy, an idea once expressed in a play by his friend, Vsevolod Vish-nevsky. Thus, he came ever closer to his innermost self and seemed to consolidate a treasure wrought of his integrity and courage. In a sense, Sergei Mikhailovich had found his own special Holy Grail.

Yet throughout the summer of 1946 impending criticism hung over him. The censure by the Central Committee of the Communist Party had not been made public. However, by now it was quite generally known, but nobody was sure if Eisenstein realized that his final work would not be released to the public. If he knew, he never betrayed it.

Despite the situation, Eisenstein remained in high esteem. It was said that the highest circles of the film industry and the Government at last recognized that no matter how eager Sergei Mikhailovich was to create a film in the general line of Soviet development, once he commenced work he became so deeply immersed in his own complex ideas that he was carried away into regions remote from the public. Hence, it was tacitly understood that for the remainder of his life he should be regarded as a sort of 'elder statesman' and, at the age of forty-eight, left to continue with his theoretical work. If his heart permitted, he should continue to teach.

This possibly explains why Eisenstein, when he was both a very ill man and one whose work was not acceptable for public release, was asked by V.O.K.S. to participate in a recorded interview with Norman Corwin for a broadcast in the United States, though the relations between the Soviet Union and America had already begun to degenerate from war-time allegiance to peace-time hostility.

But when the party arrived at the dacha in mid-afternoon on the 16th of July 1946, Norman Corwin was not with them. He was ill and in his place came his assistant, Lee Bland. After the official interview, in which Sergei Mikhailovich mentioned some of his unpleasant experiences in America, but praised the work of D. W. Griffith, Charlie Chaplin and Walt Disney, the housekeeper brought a light snack and wine for Bland and the two V.O.K.S. representatives who had come with him. Eisenstein drank tea. He asked to be excused from drinking wine on account of his health, which he had earlier said in the interview would keep him 'living six months in pyjamas' and, therefore, 'I use my time, and I have a lot of it now, in working on two of my books'.

It was a pleasant time, easy and friendly, for Sergei Mikhailovich treated his guests with the utmost respect and attention. Bland was charmed by his warmth and cordiality and 'intrigued by his bright, dancing eyes—incongruous for a sick man'. As they talked about art, Lee Bland had the impression that Eisenstein considered *Ivan the Terrible* to be his greatest artistic triumph and that he was eager to return to work. Then he asked Eisenstein if the photographer might take a picture of him in the house, or with the house as a background.

Firmly, but politely, Sergei Mikhailovich refused. It seems 'he had a strong superstition about being photographed in his house, or having his house appear in the background'. Bland asked him why, but Eisenstein appeared quite vague about it. 'He laughed it off, but it was obvious that he meant it.'

The house could not appear in a photograph. Reticence forbade it. The thought of a picture of the dacha being published was something from which he recoiled. For a man to live alone in so large a house was a role in which Eisenstein could not appear. Besides, this was the home he had built when he thought he would not live alone any longer. The least comment about him and his house was what he desired.

Instead, Sergei Mikhailovich suggested that they should take a photograph in the woods near the house. They went out towards a clump of pine trees. Though they did not walk fast there was a certain liveliness about Eisenstein's walk and his fluffy hair shone hazel in the sun. As they walked discussing the picture-taking business, they encountered a horse grazing in the woods. Bland thought it might provide a little local colour and he suggested that they should get the horse into the photograph. But Eisenstein joked about cowboy pictures and said he thought the horse should be omitted, lest he and the equine confuse the viewer! He seemed particularly afraid that the horse might turn around, thus giving his 'Hollywood pals' further ground for comment. So they went on into the woods and shot several pictures. [Plate 62]

Lee Bland then left, thinking that 'Eisenstein was a regular guy', one he would like to see again. 'There was nothing stuffy or upstage about him.' He felt he had been welcome and that Eisenstein had enjoyed their chat. 'He was wonderfully co-operative' and answered every question 'freely and completely'.[1]

Once more Sergei Mikhailovich had become the man whom his friends in Mexico had loved as a dear brother and the Eisenstein of the happy Christmas of 1935 when he had acted as host to Paul Robeson: the Eisenstein who was worthy of the deepest affection and a lasting love.

With Bland gone, he went back to his work on 'the books', and he worked for a few weeks.

On the 4th of September 1946, the resolution of the Central Committee of the Communist Party concerning *Ivan the Terrible*, Part II, was at last made public. In comparison to the attack made by Boris Shumyatsky against *Bezhin Meadow* in 1937, the criticism was mild.

In the resolution, the films *Great Life*, directed by Lukov, *Simple People* directed by Kozintzev and Trauberg, *Admiral Nakhimov*[2] directed by Pudovkin, as well as part two of *Ivan the Terrible*, were censured as 'unsuccessful and erroneous films'. After a severe attack on the film *Great Life*, the resolution said:

What can be the reason for so frequent a production of false and erroneous films? Why have the Soviet producers who in the past created films of high artistic value—as for instance Loukov, Eisenstein, Pudovkin, Kozintzev and Trauberg—been so unsuccessful?

The reason is that many of the leading workers in cinematography, directors, producers, scenario writers, are not sufficiently serious and responsible in their attitude to their work. The chief defect of their

[1] The excerpts quoted are from the transcript of the interview between Eisenstein and Lee Bland, then Director of Special Events, Columbia Broadcasting System, New York, and from letters to the author from Mr. Bland.

[2] *Admiral Nakhimov* was finally released and received the Stalin Prize, First Class, of 100,000 roubles in 1947, after drastic revision.

work is that they do not study the job they undertake. The producer V. Pudovkin, for instance, undertook to produce the film about Nakhimov, but failed to study the details and so distorted historical truth. The result was a film not about Nakhimov but about balls and dances with episodes from Nakhimov's life. . . . The producer S. Eisenstein, in the second series of the film *Ivan the Terrible*, betrayed his ignorance of historical fact by showing the progressive bodyguard of Ivan the Terrible as a degenerate band rather like the Klu Klux Klan, and Ivan the Terrible himself, who was a man of strong will and character, as weak and indecisive, somewhat like Hamlet. . . .

Shortly before the publication of this resolution, an analysis of the censured films had appeared in the magazine *Soviet Art*. Of *Ivan*, Part II, the writer said:

This film never found its way into the cinemas, as it bears all the traces of a superficial interpretation of history, a disdainful attitude to the obligation of art to give an authentic and accurate picture of historical truth. The historical interpretation in this film is false, and the film itself is anti-historical; it fails to give a true image of Ivan Grozny as a progressive statesman, it gives no picture of the people, or of Russia at that period. The whole film is full of court intrigues, and the Oprichniks, who supported Ivan in his struggle against reactionary Boyars, are shown as a band of cut-throats. The film is dedicated not to the efforts of Ivan Grozny to increase the might of Russia, but to the Boyar intrigue and plots going on in Ivan Grozny's court.

In addition it is clear from the very structure of the film that history has been used only as a pretext for formalistic experiments in cinema montage, in the play of contrasts between black and white, etc. The second part of Ivan Grozny provides a very clear illustration of the results to which a lack of responsibility, a disdainful attitude towards the study of essential material, and a careless and arbitrary treatment of historical themes may lead.[1]

In time Eisenstein replied to the resolution concerning his colleagues and himself. Neither before nor after his statement is there any evidence that he suffered a period of 'almost mindless' despair as he did following the banning of *Bezhin Meadow*. The statement appeared in the publication *Culture and Life*:

It is difficult to imagine a sentry who gets so lost in contemplation of the stars that he forgets his post. It is difficult to imagine a tankist

[1] 'Increase the Sense of Responsibility Amongst Cinema Experts' (Moscow, *Soviet Art*, 16 August 1946).

eagerly reading an adventure novel while going into battle. It is difficult to believe there could be a foundry man who, instead of giving
all his attention to the mass of molten metal flowing in prepared
forms, turns aside from his work to contemplate a pattern of his own
phantasy. They would be a bad sentry, a bad tankist and a bad
foundry man. Each would be a bad soldier.

In our Soviet Army and in our Socialist production there are no
bad soldiers.

It is even more difficult to realize that during the stern accounting
caused by demands of our Soviet reality such bad and unworthy
soldiers were discovered in the front lines of literature and art.

Reading again and again the resolution of the party Central Committee about the film *Great Life*, I always linger on the question it put
forth: 'What can be the reason for so frequent a production of false
and erroneous films? Why did such Soviet directors as Comrades
Lukov, Eisenstein, Pudovkin, Kozintzev and Trauberg create failures
while in the past they have created films of high art value?'

I cannot let the question go unanswered. First of all we failed
because at a critical moment in our work we artists forgot for a time
those great ideas our art is summoned to serve. Some of us forgot the
incessant struggle against our Soviet ideals and ideology which goes
on in the whole world. We lost for the time comprehension of the
honourable, militant educational task which lies on our art during the
years of hard work to construct the Communist Society in which all
people are involved.

The Central Committee justly pointed out to us that the Soviet
artist cannot treat his duties in a light-minded and irresponsible way.
Workers of the cinema should study deeply whatever they undertake. Our chief mistake is that we did not fulfil these demands in our
creative work.

Like a bad sentry we gaped at the unessential and secondary things,
forgetting the main things, and so abandoning our post. We forgot
that the main thing in art is its ideological content and historical
truth. Like a bad foundry man, we light-mindedly allow the precious
stream of creation to be poured out over sand and become dispersed
in private unessential side lines. This brought us vices and mistakes in
our creations.

A stern and timely warning of the Central Committee stopped us
Soviet artists from further movement along this dangerous and fatal
way which leads towards empty and non-ideological art for art's
sake and towards creative degradation.

The resolution of the Central Committee reminds us with new
force that Soviet art has been given one of the most honorable places

in the decisive struggle of ideology of our country against the seductive ideology of the bourgeois world. Everything we do must be subordinated to tasks of this struggle.

In the second part of *Ivan the Terrible* we committed a misrepresentation of historical facts which made the film worthless and vicious in an ideological sense.

We know Ivan the Terrible as a man with a strong will and firm character. Does that exclude from the characterization of this Tsar the possibility of the existence of certain doubts? It is difficult to think that a man who did such unheard of and unprecedented things in his time never thought over the choice of means or never had doubts about how to act at one time or another. But could it be that these possible doubts overshadow the historical role of historical Ivan as it was shown in the film? Could it be that the essence of this powerful sixteenth-century figure lies in these doubts and not in his uncompromising fight against them or unending success of his state activity? Is it not so that the center of our attention is and must be *Ivan the builder, Ivan the creator of a new, powerful, united Russian power*, Ivan the inexorable destroyer of everything that resisted *his* progressive undertakings? *The sense of historical truth was betrayed by me* in the second part of *Ivan*. The private, unimportant and non-characteristic shut out the principal. The play of doubts crept out to the front line and the wilful character of the Tsar and his historically progressive role slipped out of the field of attention. The result was that a false and mistaken impression was created about the image of Ivan. The resolution of the Central Committee accusing me of a wrong presentation which disfigures historical truth says that in the film Ivan is presented as 'weak and indecisive, somewhat like Hamlet'. This is solidly grounded and just.

Some historically wrong impressions of the epoch and reign of Ivan the Terrible which were reflected in my film were widely current in pre-Revolutionary literature. This was especially true of the Tsar's bodyguards (oprichniki). Works of classics of Marxism on questions of history have illustrated and made available to us the historically correct and positive evaluation of Ivan's *progressive lifeguards*. In the light of these works it should not have been difficult to overcome the false presentation of the lifeguards in the writing of Traitor, Prince Andrei Kurbsky. It should have been easy to unveil tendentious descriptions of Ivan's activity which were left us by historian spies of the Western Powers, Taube and Kruse or the adventurer Henry Staden. But it was much more difficult to overcome in one's self the remnants of former purely imaginative presentations left over from childhood reading of such books as Alexei Konstantinovich Tolstoy's novel *Prince Serebryani* or the old novel *Kondeyar*. (This Tolstoy, related neither to the playwright Alexei or novelist Leo, died in 1875.)

As a result, in the film the progressive oprichniks were presented as a gang of degenerates something like the Ku Klux Klan. The Central Committee justly condemned this rough misrepresentation of historical fact.

On the basis of the Central Committee's resolution all workers in art should make a most important conclusion as to the necessity of putting an end to all light-minded and irresponsible attitudes towards their work. We must fully subordinate our creations to the interest of education of the Soviet people, especially the youth, and not step aside one jot from this aim.

We must master the Lenin-Stalin method of perception of real life and history to such a full and deep extent as to be able to overcome all remnants or survivals of former notions which although they have been banished from our consciousness a long time, are obstinately and maliciously attempting to infiltrate into our works as soon as our creative vigilance is weakened even for a single moment.

This is a guarantee that our cinematography will be able to eliminate all ideological and artistic failures and mistakes which lie like a heavy load on our art in the first postwar year. This is a guarantee that in the near future our cinematography will again create highly ideological artistic films worthy of the Stalin epoch.

All we workers of art must interpret the hard and just criticism contained in the decision of the Central Committee as an appeal to the widest and most ardent and purposeful activity, an appeal to us masters of art to fulfil our duty before the Soviet people, state and party by creation of highly ideological artistic films.

But Sergei Mikhailovich did not end the matter of *Ivan the Terrible* with this statement. Since 1941, his life had revolved about the Ivan which he had created. Now he felt that he must somehow finish the work he had begun. At last he wrote a letter to Stalin about the second part. In response to this letter, Stalin invited Eisenstein and Nikolai Cherkasov, who played the role of Ivan, to visit him at the Kremlin. Stalin was apparently sympathetic towards Sergei Mikhailovich and his difficulties, and it was arranged that when Eisenstein was well enough he should resume work and complete the third part of the film, incorporating into it certain sequences he had already completed for Part II.[1]

In the meantime, Eisenstein continued to work on the manuscript

[1] The summary of the interview between Stalin and Eisenstein was given to the author by Grigori Alexandrov, who had read the stenographic report of it.

of the second book, which he had mentioned to Jay Leyda in several letters and cables—the 26,000-word study of El Greco and the unpublished material 'mostly concerned with the development of the principles started by *Potemkin* during these twenty years in different media-treatments of sound, music, colour' and 'the way of composing ecstatic scenes, etc. *Ivan* in connection with *Potemkin*'. In a cable to Jay Leyda sent on the 7th of September, he said: 'Shipping you first quarter of my opus very soon.' The months passed, but no manuscripts arrived, not even the manuscript of the 'Comic Autobiography'.

As he worked on the manuscripts for his books, Sergei Mikhailovich turned his attention to a letter he had received from his old friend Leon Moussinac, the French film critic. Moussinac explained how his friend, Armand Panigel, had translated sections of *The Film Sense* and used it in the training of young film workers fighting with the Free French Forces in Egypt during the war. Panigel had become interested in Eisenstein's writing and wanted to know if he would send other manuscripts which could be published in France in addition to *The Film Sense*, which Panigel was translating for the publisher who had purchased the French rights in September 1945.

Sergei Mikhailovich was overjoyed to hear that his book *The Film Sense* had been used for teaching creative methods to young people. He decided to reorganize all of his major published articles and send them to Panigel for publication in France. Gradually he assembled nine hundred pages which included scenarios illustrating the development of his practical work. He corrected each page carefully in his own handwriting and added many special notations in French. The manuscript was divided for publication into four volumes.[1]

[1] In the manuscript S. M. Eisenstein sent to Armand Panigel, he included the following table of contents and his articles were arranged for publication as listed. The prefaces, Items 1 and 2, were ommitted:

Vol. I
   (1) Preface by E. N. Foss.
   (2) Preface by S. M. Eisenstein.
   (3) 'Pride' (*Iskusstvo kino*, Nos. 1 and 2, 1940).
   (4) 'The Cinematographic Principle and the Ideogram', afterword to pamphlet *Yaponskoye Kino* by N. Kaufman (Moscow, 1929).
   (4a) 'The Unexpected' (*Zhizn iskusstva*, 1928).
   (5) 'Through Theatre to Cinema' (*Sovyetskoye kino*, Nos. 11–12, 1934).
   (6) 'Fourth Dimension' (*Kino Gazeta*, 1929).
   (7) 'Sound Manifesto' (*Sovyetskoye ekran*, No. 8, 1929).
   (8) 'New Language', foreword to Russian edition of Guido Seeber's 'Der Trickfilm' (*Technika Kinotrika*, Goskinozdat, 1929).

When his work was finished early in 1947, Sergei Mikhailovich sent the manuscript to Armand Panigel through the Soviet Press Bureau in Paris. He also wrote to Leon Moussinac to thank him for agreeing to supervise the French publication of his work. This was his last letter to the friend he had known for twenty years.

Though Sergei Mikhailovich had now assembled the most important of his published writings, thousands of sheets of manuscript, notes and working sketches remained to be fitted in as part of his great work of synthesis. Thousands of pages reporting his lectures at the Institute of Cinematography still waited to be used in the many books in which he had planned to embody all he knew of the nature of the creative process,

---

(9) 'Film Language (*Sovyetskoye kino*, No. 5, 1934).

(10) 'Detective Work at GIK' (*Proletarskoye kino*, Nos. 17–18, 1932).

Vol. II

(11) 'Film Form: New Problem' (*Za bolshoye kinoiskusstvo*, 1935).

(11a) 'Appendix to the Art' (2 pages) (*Kino Gazeta*, No. 11 3a, 1933).

(12) 'Valkyrie', (*Theatre*, No. 10, 1940)'

(13) 'Montage in 1938' (*Iskusstvo kino*, No. 1, 1939).

(14) 'Synchronization of the Senses' (*Iskusstvo kino*, No. 9, 1940).

(15) 'Colour and Meaning' (*Iskusstvo kino*, No. 12, 1940.

(16) 'Form and Content' (*Iskusstvo kino*, No. 1, 1941).

Vol. III

(17) 'Dickens and Griffith' (*Americkanskaya kinematografiya*: D. W. *Griffit*. Vol. I, *Materialy po istorii mirovogo kinoiskusstva*, 1944).

(18) 'Charlie the Kid', Charles Chaplin book (Goskinozdat, 1945).

(19) 'Fascism Must and Shall be Destroyed' (V.O.K.S., 1941).

(20) 'P-R-K-F-V' (Prokofiev) (V.O.K.S., 1944).

(21) 'On Fascism and the German Cinema' (*Literaturnaysa Gazeta*, 22, III, 1944).

(22) 'Overtake and Surpass' (*Proletarskoye kino*, No. 15, 1932).

(23) 'Programme of Study of the Regisseur' (*Iskusstvo kino*, No. 4, 1936).

Vol. IV

PRACTICE

(24) *Alexander Nevsky* (scenario, 1939).

(25) *Ivan the Terrible* (V.O.K.S. Bulletin, 1945).

(26) *Ivan the Terrible* (scenario, 1944).

(27) *Sutter's Gold* (scenario, 1930).

(27a) Introduction to *Que Viva Mexico!* and the full scenario (1931).

(28) *Ferghana Canal* (scenario, *Iskusstvo kino*, No. 9, 1939).

(29) 'Twenty Years of Soviet Cinema' (Goskinozdat, 1940).

The manuscript sent by Eisenstein to Armand Panigel is still in his possession and he is now working on a plan to publish it along with additional articles.

and of the universe. As he well knew, each of his own works, so few of which had been realized, were as different exercises in his attempt to discover the essence of life itself.

Towards the end of 1946, a bitter-sweet experience suddenly enveloped Eisenstein: the long-withheld prints of *Thunder Over Mexico* and *Time in the Sun* were given to him. The sight of them as they clicked through the projector wounded him to the heart. They were all that was left to him of *Que Viva Mexico!* He must tear them apart and try to build *Que Viva Mexico!* from these fragments. But even this he could not accomplish: he was too weak.

In pain and bitterness he wrote his only words about *Que Viva Mexico!* as an introduction for the Mexican scenario which he sent to Panigel. But even in this sad and bitter document Sergei Mikhailovich could not speak of much that was closest to his thoughts; there were many things he could not bring himself to mention. He dismissed Sinclair and the other people who had helped to bring about the *Que Viva Mexico!* tragedy with these words:

> And in the Dance Macabre which I see, whirling in front of my eyes, are intercut other faces. The faces of those who did not permit the complete realization of my film. Those who do not drop their masks.
>
> I have no need of them.
>
> I know on which side they dance.
>
> And I know what is hidden beneath the cardboard masks which covers their superficial 'radicalism'.[1] (App. Five.)

But even after he had sent this manuscript to Panigel, *Que Viva Mexico!* haunted Eisenstein's thoughts and on the 10th of May 1947 he wrote to the French film critic, Georges Sadoul:

> Très cher Ami!
>
> ... Ma santé est encore assez mauvaise—et c'est la seule chose qui m'empêche actuellement à recommencer mon travail à la dernière partie d'Ivan. Toutes les autres difficultés se sont heureusement dissipées et j'espère a retourner à la manivelle cet été.
>
> Ceci m'empêche de m'occuper à 'Que Viva Mexico!' dont je suis heureux de savoir toutes les copies entre bonnes mains. Je n'ai jamais vu 'Kermesse Funebre'. Et les deux autres [*Thunder Over Mexico* and *Time in the Sun*] il n'y a que ... deux mois (1946! ayant tourné la chose en 1931–1932!) Ce qu'ils en ont fait comme montage est plus que navrant.

[1] S. M. Eisenstein, 'Introduction to *Que Viva Mexico!*' (1947). Original manuscript in the possession of M. Armand Panigel.

Je continue à être professeur à l'Institut du Cinéma. C'est presque la seule chose que j'ai pu faire avec ma méchante santé pendant cet hiver. . . .

Toujours très sincèrement a vous,

EISENSTEIN[1]

In his flat at Potylika, Sergei Mikhailovich had surrounded himself with memories of Mexico. His portrait as a Spanish *conquistador*, painted by Roberto Montenegro, was set into the wall of one of the book-shelves between the volumes. It stared at him with the challenging eyes of his youth. The couch, where he often lay and read, was covered with a Mexican rug and his bed was spread with the sarape he had used at Chysti Prudi. Behind the bed hung a carpet woven with a squat Aztec God of Death. [Plates 62, 63]

The God waited as month in and month out Sergei Mikhailovich kept on writing and reading his books. His craving for books was insatiable. He sent more and more cables to Leyda requesting books. On the 7th of September 1946 he sent two cables:

Steinberg parcel arrived Benesch starts arriving many thanks please send urgently On Borrowed Time script and play stop Guy Named Joe Great Big Doorstep play . . .

and in the second instalment:

Please send Franz Schoenberner Confession of European Intellectual stop Salvador Dali Autobiography stop Anthony How Grow Old Disgracefully. . . .

On Borrowed Time, a strange little play about Death being driven up a

[1] Letter from S. M. Eisenstein to M. Georges Sadoul; translation reads freely as follows:

Very Dear Friend

My health is again rather bad and it is the only thing which actually hinders the resumption of my work on the last part of *Ivan*. All the other difficulties are happily dissipated and I hope to return to the 'crank-handle' this summer.

It hinders me from occupying myself with *Que Viva Mexico!* of which I am happy to know all the copies are in good hands. I have never seen *The Carnival of Death* [*Death Day*] and the two others [*Thunder Over Mexico* and *Time in the Sun*] I saw only two months ago (1946! To have turned [shot] the thing in 1931–32!). What they've done with the montage is more than heart-rending.

I continue to be a professor at the Institute of Cinematography. This was nearly the only thing I could do with my wicked health this winter. . . .

Always very sincerely yours,

EISENSTEIN

tree and kept there for a while in order that an old man could continue
on his self-appointed task. A curious thing to ask for when Sergei
Mikhailovich knew that only medical science was keeping his own
death at bay. And as an echo of humour—'Anthony How to Grow
Old Disgracefully'!

In January 1947, Sergei Mikhailovich felt a little better and in a cable
to Leyda on the 23rd asking for more books, he ended with the word
'recovering'. During the next months he sometimes lectured at the
Institute of Cinematography, and when he was well enough he visited
Grigori Alexandrov at his home.

Late in the evening on the 14th of April, Sergei Mikhailovich was in-
formed that someone in America was trying to reach him by telephone.
The call was from George Kraska who had invited members of the
Press to the Wedgewood Room of the Kenmore Hotel in Boston,
where a loudspeaker was set up so everyone present could hear
Eisenstein. When Eisenstein answered, Kraska told him that *Ivan the
Terrible*, Part I, was opening at Boston's Kenmore Theatre the follow-
ing day.

The Press then questioned him about his historical films and whether
he would visit America again. With his sly, biting humour, Sergei
Mikhailovich countered with the question: 'Would I have to be from
Greece or Turkey if I did?'

Sergei Koussevitsky, the conductor, asked Eisenstein to give his
regards to Prokofiev. His voice was followed by the familiar tone of
H. W. L. Dana, with whom Sergei Mikhailovich had stayed in Boston.
Finally, he heard a voice which he had often wished to hear again. The
thousands of miles suddenly became a reality—an abyss and a bridge
spanning the loneliness of ten years.

Of all the people to whom Eisenstein had confided his ideas, Jay
Leyda, whose shy, slightly double-edged voice he now heard, was the
one who had the most faithfully tried to help him in publishing his
theoretical work. It was to Leyda that he owed the fact that one of his
books—*The Film Sense*—had been published abroad, and now Leyda
had arranged for the publication of another. He was pleased, yet
irritated because Leyda had not told him of his change of address.

As he had done at other difficult moments of his life, he shielded himself behind hopeful and confident words. He said, 'I am taking a rest for
three or four months, then we will go back to work on the second part
of *Ivan*, which we hope to complete by September or October. Some of
it at least will be in the new colour process which we are developing
and about which I am greatly excited.'

The conversation ended. Dana and Leyda were left with the impression of a buoyant Eisenstein who was happy and obviously

recovering. But in reality, Sergei Mikhailovich's heart condition was steadily growing worse.

In the summer, instead of returning to production, he went once more to the dacha, where books were his constant companion. He kept asking Leyda for more and more: Rowley's *Principles of Chinese Painting*, *Painting and Personality*, *Nijinsky* by Magriel, and 'something nicely reproducing old photography daguerrotypes'.

He wanted to complete the manuscript of at least one of the books on which he was working. But the physical strain of writing became increasingly difficult to endure. As the summer of 1947 passed, there came periods when he could scarcely walk and he experienced great shortness of breath. Louis Aragon, the French poet, who went to the dacha to see Sergei Mikhailovich early in September, later said that it had been a most painful visit. He feared that Eisenstein might die at any moment, so great was his difficulty in breathing. Yet at this time, Sergei Mikhailovich determinedly resisted death. He continued to ask for books, and his mind had once more turned to Mexico, to Yucatan where the prologue of *Que Viva Mexico!* was laid. He requested Leyda to send him Morley's *Ancient Maya*.

Mexico! Mexico! He remembered it with such piercing clarity. Mexico had been the turning point in his career. From then on he had been losing his way over and over again. The cards had been stacked heavily against him. He had never explained what happened to him in America. He had wanted to explain, but at the time he had felt himself surrounded by hostility. But now he told his fellow workers some of his experiences.

As the relations between his country and the United States had grown worse, Sergei Mikhailovich had looked across the world from East to West; he realized that the people in America who had persecuted him so long ago and raised a storm against him and called him 'the Red Dog Eisenstein' had now gained greater influence than they had in 1930.

He had found among his papers the twenty-four-page pamphlet written by Major Frank Pease which had helped to drive him from Paramount and put him in gaol in Mexico and, later, turned the American immigration authorities against him. He took this with him to a meeting at Dom Kino and he read excerpts from it to his audience. He told them too that he had encountered difficulties with bureaucratic minds in the Soviet Union—as they all knew—but now he showed them what he had encountered abroad. He let them see both sides and be the judge of him after fifteen years of silence.

Not content with speaking, Eisenstein wrote an article about the American cinema and sent it to the editors of *Culture and Life*. In this he made no mention of his personal experiences; he merely used his critical faculty to reveal the nature of certain recent films: *Going My Way, Anna and the King of Siam* and *Dragonwyck*. These films seemed to him to be the purveyors of spiritual poison. In summing up, he said:

> The ability to take any theme . . . and by means of exaggeration (or some other means) to reduce it—slowly and smoothly to self-destruction and final nothingness—this is probably one of the most cunning characteristics of the American cinema.
>
> Films of this type [those mentioned above] give rise to a cynical inhuman attitude to reality. The men behind Hollywood business-men aim to deprive the average American of all feelings of honour, to make them cynical and egotistical. This is necessary lest he protest against the violation of laws and justice occurring daily, hourly in America. . . . Now all the filthy, dirty, dark elements have come to the surface so that the muddy water obscures the thought of everything fine, pure and progressive.
>
> . . . As regards social problems America belongs not even in the nineteenth century, but rather to the period of the Middle Ages and the crusades, whose bonfires twinkle so familiarly at the bonfires of the lynch courts, fed with high quality petrol.
>
> The skill, inventiveness and technical mastery of the American cinema are used in the service of darkness and oppression funda-mental characteristic features of the cruelty and unjust system of imperialistic society.
>
> American films contribute actively to the consolidation of this society by imposing upon the people.
>
> Thus the most vital of arts—the cinema—is playing the most deadly and destructive role. . . .[1]

Twenty years before, Eisenstein had written a critique for Joseph Freeman and compared the cinema in the Soviet Union and in America. The United States had hardly changed at all; the Soviet Union had grown a great deal and matured. In the process of change, Sergei Mikhailovich had suffered deeply, but he still resolutely believed in the future of the one system and the ultimate death of the other. He had spoken in 1927 of the little fishes composing the collective whale. As part of the collective he had been compelled to renounce many things that he loved—even the second part of *Ivan*—but in the future, far off in the future, there lay a time when there would be greater fulfilment in a socialist society for men like himself. So he concluded:

> When we think of this, it makes us appreciate even more our young healthy growing art. . . .

[1] S. M. Eisenstein, 'Purveyors of Spiritual Poison' (*Sight and Sound*, Autumn, 1947).

As the year of 1947 approached its death, Sergei Mikhailovich continued his research and writing. He was working on the manuscripts of three books: *The Producer's Film Art*, *The Theory of Film Montage* and *The Theory of Colour Films*. He was also preparing analytical studies of Pushkin and Gogol, whose writing he had used as illustration for the general principles of montage in *The Film Sense*.

During the summer he had been corresponding with Jay Leyda about the publication in America of a second book of his collected essays. Leyda had selected and translated a series of articles and, in November 1947, he sent Sergei Mikhailovich a complete outline of the articles to be included in the proposed book. On the 3rd of December Eisenstein replied in a rather strangely worded cable to Leyda:

> Maya Nijinsky Chinese Principles just arrived stop miss you enormously with your energy and cooperation would have completed several books much love many thanks Eisenstein.

Almost ten years before, in February 1937, Sergei Mikhailovich had confessed in his first letter to Leyda that 'strange as it may seem—I'm missing you here!' And in this letter he had spoken about his great dream of synthesis which must be accomplished through many books —'*the* side of my work which is to my opinion the really most important of what I have to do'. Now he admitted that 'with your energy and co-operation would have completed several books'. It was as if he knew that the borrowed time on which he had been living would be short.

When completed, the book, published under the title *Film Form*, traced the development of Eisenstein's work from his early days at the Proletkult Theatre onwards. There was an analysis showing how certain features of Japanese culture contributed to his theories of montage, and the various methods of montage he had devised. As his work proceeded he saw an ever greater connection between montage in the cinema and the genesis of montage in other arts. He selected an analysis of his treatment of Dreiser's *An American Tragedy* to explain how he, as a socially conscious artist, approached his subject in regard to both the content and the form of presentation. Finally, he analysed the films of D. W. Griffith, from which he had once learned, and the montage he found in the novels of Charles Dickens. Included were notes tracing the evolution of ideas during the production of a film—'Notes from a Director's Laboratory'—recorded while he was working on *Ivan the Terrible*.[1]

[1] The articles in *Film Form* are:
'Through Theatre to Cinema' (Moscow, *Sovyetskoye kino*, November–December 1934; in translation, U.S.A., *Theatre Arts Monthly*, September 1936).
'The Unexpected' (Leningrad, *Zhizn iskusstva*, 19 August 1928).

On the 4th of December, Eisenstein cabled approval of the title *Film Form* for his second book, which was published in America in March 1949. On the 15th of December he sent another cable detailing certain changes, and he ordered more books, among them *The Negro in the American Theatre* by Edith Isaacs, the founder of *Theatre Arts Monthly*, who had once long ago in New York given a party for him at which he had remained almost wholly silent because Sara Mildred Strauss had told him the guests would be very formal people.

On borrowed time. Yet there were many things he still wished to do. For months he had been filled with a desire to see once more some of the places he had visited and one he had never seen—Prague. The matter of his going abroad was raised and discussed. As the New Year came, the Government agreed that Eisenstein should go to Prague, Paris and London. He had not really expected this to happen, for he knew that he had been considered as an irresponsible representative of the Soviet Union during his 'Cook's World Tour'. Now at last he was trusted. It signified that for all his failures he was regarded as the 'Soviet

---

'The Cinematographic Principle and the Ideogram', afterword to pamphlet *Yaponskoye kino* by N. Kaufman (Moscow, 1929); in translation as 'The Cinematographic Principle and Japanese Culture' (Paris, *Transition*, June 1930).

'A Dialectic Approach to Film Form': original German manuscript in the Eisenstein Collection, Museum of Modern Art Film Library, New York; first half appeared in translation as 'The Principles of Film Form' (London, *Close-up*, September 1931).

'The Filmic Fourth Dimension' (Moscow, *Kino*, 27 August 1929); in translation as 'The Fourth Dimension in the Kino' (London, *Close-up*, March 1930).

'Methods of Montage', written in London as supplement to preceding essay and in translation as 'The Fourth Dimension in the Kino: II' (London, *Close-up*, April 1930).

'A Course in Treatment' (Moscow, *Proletarskoye kino*, Nos. 17–18, 1932); in translation as 'Cinematography *with* Tears' (London, *Close-up*, March 1933), and 'An American Tragedy' (London, *Close-up*, June 1933).

'Film Language' (Moscow, *Sovyetskoye kino*, May 1934).

'Film Form: New Problems' (Moscow, *Za bolshoye kinoiskusstvo*, 1935); in translation as 'Film Form, 1935—New Problems' (London, *Life and Letters To-day*, September–December 1935).

'The Structure of the Film' (Moscow, *Iskusstvo kino*, June 1939).

'Achievement' (Moscow, *Iskusstvo kino*, January–February 1940); in translation as 'Pride' (Moscow, *International Literature*, April–May 1940).

'Dickens, Griffith, and the Film To-day' (Moscow, *Americkanskaya kinematografiya*): D. W. *Griffit*, Vol. I, *Materialy po istorii mirovogo kinoiskusstva*, 1944).

'Statement' (Leningrad, *Zhizn iskusstva*, 5 August 1928); in translation *Close-up*, London, October 1928.

man' he had aimed to become during the Revolution. But his doctors intervened. They said his heart condition was such that he ought to wait a few months before going abroad. They suggested March as a time when he might be well enough to travel. So, quietly, Eisenstein went on with his research.

But as his fiftieth birthday approached—the 23rd of January 1948— he grew perturbed. Sometimes he paused during his reading or writing and felt that the precarious beating of his heart was going to stop. *It must not stop!* And he fought against the prescience of death. At last he confided to Grisha Alexandrov that he feared the age of fifty. Fifty years . . . What was it about fifty years of life that was so fearful? He could not explain what a strange sensation it was to realize that he, who had once assumed the role of an 'old' man to protect himself from being compared to others, had become in reality a middle-aged man. Yet in the course of life and despite his great 'laboratory of knowledge', Sergei Mikhailovich had never become a wholly adult man.

Writing in 1945 about Charlie Chaplin's art with its 'childish-naïve approach to life clashing with its stern grown-up reprimands', Sergei Mikhailovich mentioned the significance of the nursery rhyme of the 'Ten Little Nigger Boys'. Observing that the fate of the last 'little nigger boy' was to get married, he wrote: 'Marriage is the end of childish infantile existence—the last Negro boy dies and an adult Negro emerges!' He himself had not been able to consummate this symbolic transformation. It appears that only once in his life had he kissed a woman with the passion of a grown man, and that was but moments before he was publicly reprimanded as if he had been playing truant from school and neglecting his 'homework'. In his analysis of Chaplin's art, Sergei Mikhailovich continued:

'Only children are happy, and that not for long', says wise Vasya Zheleznova in Gorky's play of the same name.

And not for long because the stern 'You mustn't' of tutors, and future standards of behaviour, begin to lay their interdiction on the unrestrictedness of children's desires from their very first steps.

He who is unable, in time, to subordinate these bonds and force their limitations to serve himself; he, who having become a man, continues to remain a child—will inevitably be unable to adapt himself to life, will always be placed in a ridiculous situation, will be the cause of laughter, funny.[1]

His forebodings about the 23rd of January 1948 did not come to pass. A party was planned at the flat at Potylika in celebration of the half-

[1] S. M. Eisenstein, 'Charlie, the Kid' (*Sight and Sound*, Vol. XV, Nos. 57 and 58, Spring and Summer, 1946).

century of Eisenstein's life. His birthday came and went. Afterwards he returned to work with the hope that now his life was assured for a time since the fateful day had passed. Once more he looked forward to the future as he worked on a long article on stereoscopic films. Here lay the future of the cinema. Days passed and all the time he kept seeing an ever deeper and wider vista opening up before him. Hopefully he wrote:

> Is not consciousness, in the tireless, post-war struggle, hammering out a more distinct and concrete form of a genuinely democratic international ideal?
> Will all this not call for absolutely new arts, unheard-of forms and dimensions ranging far beyond the scope of the traditional theatre, traditional sculpture and traditional . . . cinema, . . .
> A place must be prepared in consciousness for the arrival of new themes which, multiplied by the possibilities of new techniques, will demand new aesthetics for the expression of these new themes in the marvellous creations of the future.
> To open the way for them is a great and sacred task, and all those who dare to designate themselves as artists are called upon to contribute to its accomplishment.[1]

In the first days of February, Sergei Mikhailovich received Jay Leyda's December letter. It concerned the publication of *Film Form*. At the end of the letter were a few words relating to the past—the first personal words he had received from me in almost eleven years. I had asked Jay Leyda to act as intermediary and transmit a message for me to Sergei Mikhailovich. This was to have been the prelude to telling him what Marcoosha Fischer had said to me in September 1937. But when this letter arrived there was too little time for him to answer Jay and there was no address where he could answer me.

During the second week of February, he was often nervous, but he persisted in working. He was still anxious to find new ways for the development of film through his theoretical writings. He was much alone and, but for his worried references to his heart, he remained silent as to his thoughts. At eight o'clock on the evening of February the 9th, Grigori Alexandrov, who was working at the Potylika Studio, went to see him.

They discussed a book which Alexandrov was writing and it was agreed that Sergei Mikhailovich should write the preface. As Grisha left, Sergei Mikhailovich said he felt rather ill, but not so ill that he could not work. He continued his work when Alexandrov was gone. He worked until midnight, when the telephone rang. He got up to

[1] S. M. Eisenstein, 'Stereoscopic Film' (*Penguin Film Review*, No. 8, London, Penguin Books, 1949).

answer it, leaving on his desk the notes and manuscript for his book *The Theory of Colour Films* on which he was working. It was Alexandrov on the telephone. He wanted to know if Sergei Mikhailovich felt better. Eisenstein answered that he had difficulty in breathing.

He went and lay down on the sofa covered with a Mexican rug. He tried to read and make notes on the use of colour. His writing faltered. The moments ticked away in the silent, empty flat. At twenty minutes past midnight there came a knock on the door. It was Maxim Shtraukh, who had tapped on the wall of Chysti Prudi 23 year in and year out when there was a telephone call for Sergei Mikhailovich. He too was working late at Potylika. [Plate 63]

As Eisenstein got up to open the door, consciousness of colour began to fade, then all consciousness, like a rainbow fading as the sun of great intelligence fell below the horizon. Suddenly Eisenstein's heart broke[1] and he slumped to the floor. . . . Being and non-being. There came the moment when nothing remained of Sergei Mikhailovich Eisenstein but the physical mask he had worn for fifty years—both beautiful and unbeautiful, drawn down to kinship with man's ancestors, yet drawn upwards and stamped with a nobility fitting one of humanity's highest representatives.[2]

When there was no answer, Maxim Shtraukh went away, thinking that Sergei Mikhailovich slept. . . . And he lay on the floor all night in his final sleep which did not erase the pain on his face as sleep had once erased it. He did not look a man set free, rather a dead Prometheus who would never plead for mercy, not even from the Mexican God of the exaggerated features and squat form woven into the carpet under which the next morning he was laid.

Alexandrov found Eisenstein. Now matured, he was capable of understanding and grieving for the man who, as he knew, had once tried to live on the periphery of life through him, because he was handsome and debonair and easily made friends. All envy had passed.

As the body lay in the bed awaiting the final rites, two young artists came and made sketches. They drew the massive skull with the Gothic-like features sharpened so that at last they dominated the once square and heavy outline of the face. While they worked, the funeral of a national hero was prepared. Flowers in profusion were brought into the main hall of Dom Kino—the House of the Cinema Workers—and

[1] In cases of 'infarct', the weakened walls of the heart often actually stretch and the heart bursts, causing death.

[2] The exact time when Eisenstein died is not known, but the position of his body on the floor, and the length of time he had been dead, suggests that he collapsed while trying to reach the door at about the time Shtraukh knocked upon it.

orations were written. Finally, the husk that had been Eisenstein was laid in state beneath a velvet pall embroidered in gold. People filed by the remains of the man whose genius had contributed so much to the transformation of a very elementary form of entertainment into an art worthy to stand beside the older arts.

Thus, this loneliest of men, imprisoned by the magnitude of his dreams, was surrounded in death by crowds of people, most of whom had stood in such awe of him while he lived that they never came to know that he was not an awesome character, but a hypersensitive man who, finding most of humanity of tougher fibre than himself, retreated into his own world of thought and too often closed the door upon the outer world. As he had been deprived of the power to live simply and with affection, so it was his fate to die alone and be greatly honoured. [Plate 63]

People who had injured and deeply wounded the living Eisenstein, because his spirit had appeared incomprehensible to them, now kissed the face without sensation, the hands without motion. Voices to which the corpse was deaf praised Eisenstein. Some were the same voices that when he could hear had criticized him, bewildered him and driven him further into himself. Very few people had been deliberately malicious towards him, for most of them truly could not understand him or his aims since they were so often directed towards a far-off goal and not to objectives close at hand. In truth they valued some of his achievements very highly. Two films, at least, would be reckoned for ever as true Soviet works—*Potemkin* and *Alexander Nevsky*.

Still only a very few people could miss Sergei Mikhailovich for more than a few days or a few months. As a human being he had existed as a friend for too few. His public figure, however much it might be respected, was not one that could easily be liked or loved. He had appeared too formidable.

People passed slowly before his bier. His orations were spoken. And the thoughts of everyone were controlled. Pera Attasheva, who had once loved him with a great passion, stood by his bier quietly. Then suddenly the quietest and most circumspect of his friends broke down. Eduard Tisse wept unashamedly as he kissed farewell to Sergei Mikhailovich with whom he had created so much beauty, truth and power, first with their hand-crank camera and later with the best equipment available. Tisse and Pera, the two people on whom Eisenstein had pinned his faith, had left him; but in death their sorrow was as deep as their love. [Plate 64]

At last, on the 13th of February 1948, the body of Eisenstein was taken to the crematorium and consigned to the flames. It must have taken great heat to reduce his skull to ashes. And the ashes, enclosed in an urn bearing the five-pointed star insignia of the Soviet Union, were carried in a solemn cortège upon the shoulders of Alexandrov and others and buried in the snow-covered ground. Surrounded by other people, Tisse and Pera watched. On Pera's face there was indescribable pain. [Plate 64]

Following the funeral, Pera Attasheva came forward with the certificate from Z.A.G.S. and was recognized as the legal wife of Sergei Eisenstein. His books and papers, and the things that were closest to him, were given into her keeping. All that remained of the Old Man was at last hers.

Pera and Tisse and Grisha had known Sergei Mikhailovich for what he was. And also Maxim Shtraukh, who later said to me: 'He was a great man with a distant vision; but his life was tragic from the days I first knew him. He was seeking to find his way to the home he never knew.'

Yet in his search, Sergei Mikhailovich boldly, gaily extracted the last drop of delight from the living instant. He remained ever hopeful when faced with hopeless odds; he consolidated a resolute faith in the future. Year in and year out while he lived, he said to the coming generations 'Now is the moment of synthesis. . . . Now we stand on the threshold. . . . Now is the beginning. . . .'

Sergei M. Eisenstein—Autobiographical Note

(*International Literature*, No. 4, Moscow, 1933)

THE October Revolution is fifteen years old.

My artistic career dates back twelve years.

Family traditions, upbringing and education intended me for a totally different career.

I was studying engineering. But a subconscious and unformulated inclination to work in the field of art induced me to pick a course within engineering that led, not to mechanical, technical fields but to one closely allied to art—to architecture.

The revolutionary tempest, however, freed me from the inertia of the course marked out, and let me develop inclinations which by themselves did not have the strength to free themselves.

This is the first thing I owe the Revolution.

It took the shattering of the foundations of the country and two years of technical engineering work on the Red fronts in north and west to make the timid student break the chains of the career marked out for him by solicitous parents from early youth, abandon an almost completed education and assured future, and plunge into the unknown future of an artistic career.

From the front I returned not to Petrograd to complete studies begun, but to Moscow to start something entirely new.

And although all about me the thunder of the coming revolutionary art is rolling and scattering I, having broken through to art generally, am totally immersed in art 'in general'.

During my first steps the connection with the Revolution is purely superficial.

However, armed with technical-engineering method, I eagerly delve deeper and deeper into the fundamentals of creative art, instinctively seeking the same sphere of exact knowledge that had succeeded in captivating me during my short experience in engineering.

With the help of Pavlov, Freud, a season with Meyerhold, I get a disordered but hectic hold of some of the mysteries of this new field. Very much reading and first independent steps in decorative and stage work at the Proletcult Theatre mark this single-handed struggle against the windmills of mysticism erected by the solicitous hands of servile sycophants around the approaches to art methods against those who want to penetrate the secrets of art by common sense.

The undertaking proves less quixotical than at first appears. The wings of the windmills break off and one perceives the same dialectics in this mysterious region that are at the basis of all phenomena and all processes.

At this time I had been a materialist for a long time by inner disposition.

And now at this stage I unexpectedly discover the relation between the things I came across in my analytical work and what was going on around me.

My pupils in art, to my great surprise, suddenly point out to me that in the field of art I am following the same method that in the adjoining room is being followed by the instructor in political science and social questions.

This is enough to put on my work table the works of materialist-dialecticians instead of those of aesthetics.

The decisive year 1922—a decade ago.

The essay in personal research in a particular branch of human activity is merged in philosophical research of social phenomena as taught by the founders of Marxism.

But I do not stop there. And the Revolution by means of the works of those geniuses enters my work in a totally different fashion.

My connection with the Revolution becomes a matter of blood and bones and innermost conviction.

In my creative work this is marked by a transition from the rationalistic but almost abstract eccentric *The Sage* (a circus spectacle made over from Ostrovsky's *A Good Deal of Simplicity in Every Wise Man*), through the propagandistic-agitational theatrical poster-play *Hear Moscow* and *Gas Masks*, to the revolutionary screen work *Potemkin*.

The tendency to closer contact with the Revolution calls for ever deeper instilling of the basic principles of militant materialism in art.

The succeeding films, together with the exact requirements carry on the practical experimental work of developing a 'means' for creative film expression, to convey a maximum of positive activization of revolutionary art and arm pedagogically the generation of young Bolsheviks who are to take the place of the cinema masters of the first Five Year Plans of the Revolution.

The centre of gravity of the later work (*Ten Days, Old and New*) lies in the experimental and research fields.

Personal work is intimately bound up with planned scientific and pedagogic practice (the State Institute of Cinematography).

Theoretical works are written on the basic principle of cinema art.

The philosophy of life seems formed. The Revolution accepted. All activity turned completely to its interests.

The question remains, to what extent consciously and with unbending will.

At this stage comes the trip to other countries.

Foreign countries—the ultimate test which one's biography can put to a Soviet citizen grown inseparably with the growth of October. The test of a free choice.

Foreign countries—the ultimate test for the 'masters of culture' to consciously verify 'with whom and against whom'.

Foreign countries—the ultimate test for the creative worker can he create at all outside the Revolution and continue to exist outside it.

Before the gold mountains of Hollywood the test arose and was withstood with no heroic pose of renunciation from earthly charms and goods but a modest organic impossibility of the creative building powers to work under social conditions and in the interests of another class.

And in this impossibility to work creatively beyond the class line of demarcation the full strength and power of the revolutionary pressure came out, the pressure of the proletarian Revolution that sweeps from its path like a storm all that is inimical to it and like even a more powerful storm draws in and holds all those that once chose to go in step with it.

That is how everyone in the galaxy of Soviet workers in art act, and think.

Many of us that came to art by revolution.

All of us that call to revolution by our art.

Note 1977. This 'Autobiographical Note', written in 1933, is not included in Eisenstein's full-scale *Autobiography*, written between 1946 and 1948, and its tenor is very different inasmuch as his first attempt is comparatively concrete, the *Autobiography* a stream of consciousness.

Eisenstein's London Lectures on Film Theory

(Précis notes taken by Basil Wright, November–December 1929)

> *The cinema is not only a new interpretative art form;* it is the only new one mankind has ever known.
>
> ERIC ELLIOT
>
> *Il y a des lois du decoupage qui sont, comme celles de tout composition rhythmique, implacables.* Il s'agit de les decouvrir.
>
> LEON MOUSSINAC
>
> . . . *Rhythmus ist nicht etwas, das hinzugefugt werden konnte, sondern es ist die grundlage der filmpoesie selbst.*
>
> HANS RICHTER

(1) Go the way the material calls you; the scenario changes on location and the location shots change in the montage.

(2) The theatre and the spielfilm [dramatic film] are definitely connected: the spielfilm has several (or unlimited) proscenium openings as a result of camera mobility. In the theatre close-ups can be made, though not exactly in the film sense. (Ex. of Eisenstein's production of the letter scene in *Listen Moscow.*)

(3) Montage can be by:

    (*a*) Motion.

    (*b*) Size.

    (*c*) Light.

    (*d*) The sum of the impression of these elements.

Geometry in Space *and* Time . . . (relativity). . . .

(4) Diagrams.

(5) *Montage of Attraction*

Every film or play produced is structurally an amount of things which attract your attention, the sum of which gives you your effect. A whole programme of different attractions can be made out of the film's subject.

Imitation of

    (*a*) Abstract;

    (*b*) Actors' Motions;

    (*c*) Process which makes the Form,

e.g. cannibals, for primitively if you don't want to die you must prevent your body dying out by eating the stuff *of* which you are made: but in the latest medical theories you have phosphates etc. which are in main things *out of which* the body is made. Here you eat the products which *go to make* the form (of the image of Buddha sucking his foot as opposed to Voronov's gland theories).

Here of ideas of William James. Kuleshov on films makes the mistake of using the cannibalistic method.

Darwin.

Ludwig Klages, *Handshrifft und Charakter*. Good in spite of the errors into which religious beliefs lead him.

Film actor is much to be pitied; his relations with his art are invariably that of *coitus interruptus*.

Kenyon's Proposition. 'Two Opposite Reactions can be provoked by the *same stimulus*.'

These two reactions are the elements of a man's psychological reaction. Either apart cannot be considered psychologically. Importance is when man does both acts at the same moment (even if only mentally). Example of dog to which food is offered together with brandished whip. The dog will wriggle back and forwards. If the stick is removed the dog goes forward; if food removed it goes back. So it is with Hamlet, with his elements for and against activity.

To find psychological expression it is enough to make *one* movement, and at the same time the elements going to make the other reaction. This is mathematically calculable and can be divided into 'Forwards' and 'Backwards'. (Descartes.) You make out of an elusive element TWO elements which are NOT elusive, e.g. representing three-dimensional material on two-dimensional paper. . . .

Duchelle studied movement of every muscle to try and find the secret of the whole human expression. He found himself wrong. ('L'action musculaire *isole* n'est pas dans l'expression humaine.') This isolated action is found only in hysteria etc. Actually it is a conflict in your body exactly the same as above stated. Example of the difference between the mechanical smile of the chorus girl, which is made only with the mouth muscles, and the real spontaneous smile.

So CONDITIONED AND UNCONDITIONED REFLEXES. Conflict occurs because reactions are of different speeds. The same shutting of the eyes can dynamically express two opposite things.

Here of the work of Toulouse-Lautrec and Daumier, especially the portrait of Cissy Loftus by the former, and Oedipus and Sphinx by the latter.

(6) *Montage Analysis*

Montage is (*a*) *Metric*. The building up of a scene in consideration of the absolute length of the celluloid pieces, in a repeated formula (worked as in music 2/4 C, etc. with base constant). This method produces very simple rhythmic effect (cf. the patriotic manifestation in Pudovkin's *End of St. Petersburg*). It works badly if the formula is in too complicated a proportion. Note 'Staircase Shock' in *Potemkin*, however, which is good for spectator.

(*b*) *Rhythmical*. Here the length of the celluloid piece is considered as a multiplication of the stuff in the shot and the length in which the stuff is to be shown. Length is relative here. Three feet of close-up is *quite a different length* to a 3-foot longshot. So considering non-graphically, 3 feet of immobile face in close-up is different from 3 feet of expressive face also in close-up. Also the elements of psychological and dramatic tension come in to modify the length of the pieces. The example of the pillars of Greek temples, which were built on a curve in order to give the impression of level, applies also to montage. Eisenstein nearly always uses pieces which are cut to about the same length, the rhythm being made by *changing the subject of the pieces*. The feeling of *texture* also comes in. The best pieces for montage are those which are *incomplete* or *without balance*. (The succeeding piece makes itself felt both previously and at the actual moment as necessary.) In montage ALWAYS CHOOSE PIECES WHICH DO NOT FIT. If you are showing a movement of the arm and changing from long to close shot, the movement must go back in the close shot and then carry on. Here you are artificially gaining a moment from time. So it is possible to prolong a real movement almost indefinitely. Cf. also in *October*, the door opening three times before Kerenski (corresponding to capital letters in print or special intonation in speech).

(*c*) *Tonic* (Tonal). Elements of movement considered as more delicate of shape. (A diagonal movement across the screen is just as effective when made by picture composition as when it is a genuine motion.) In tonic montage we get what may be called VIBRATION: effects of *light* and *shape* and *form* (cf. fog in *Potemkin*).

If the conflict is tonic *only* you have a 'picture' effect; but this you can combine with another sort of effect, purely dynamic (fog in *Potemkin* again).

(*d*) *Overtonic* (Overtonal). The dominant element in building up montage. This element is invariably *relative*. For it *always* corresponds to a hieroglyph. *The hieroglyph has to be put in combination with other hieroglyphs before a dominating meaning can come through:*

If *a* plus *b* plus *c* equals *a'* plus *b'* plus *c'*
  Then *a* need not equal *a'*
        b „   „   „   *b'*
        c „   „   „   *c'*
So in film if you show successively an:

  Old White Man
  Old White Donkey
  Old White Cat

the meaning is quite indeterminate until you show, say, A White Snowscape, or a title such as '100 years pass'. In the first case you stress the White. In the second you stress the Old.

We have a combining of elements which occurs only when the whole is built (as in music). The 'Dominant' is purely physiological effect. But we can have purely *intellectual* overtones. We can combine association and mental processes. All styles of montage are to be kept on one line, and *considered as a development from ROUGH MOVEMENT UP TO A COMBINATION OF THE MOST DELICATE MOVEMENTS OF THE BRAIN* (*which cannot be called physiological*).

(7) *Reading Material for Training Filmic Feeling*

  (*a*) *Construction*
        du Terrail's *Rocambole*.
        le Blanc's *Arsene Lupin*.

(b) *Psychological details*
   Stefan Zweig's works.
   Zola's works (most important of all).
(c) *Further advanced:*
   James Joyce's *Ulysses* and other works.
   Ben Jonson's *Volpone.*

(8) *Eisenstein's Comments on the Film Society Study Groups*

These groups are the first steps of real practical work undertaken by the Film Society. The *avant-garde* groups have not enough basis to their work, and it is the research into such things which is a very important point. It is necessary to do something for the growing generation of young directors; the amateur groups are also of interest. Criticism as it now is has no connection with practical film knowledge. A course should be arranged for film critics, whose mistaken point of view *causes more harm than directorial ignorance.* These courses are a palliative . . . because in England there are no film schools or colleges. A film study school should be arranged *à la* Moscow.

We have now reached a stage in our Theoretical and Practical work at which we are in a position to work out a Theoretical basis for film.

Only recently have we begun to feel the real type of purely filmic film which is to come. So far films moving in this direction have been purely experimental (intellectual film). But now the historical moment has come at which we are to find *the synthesis of art and science in an entirely new form of picturization.* The new form is not symbolic but vital and picturesque. The method of expression purely dynamic, like music, but not so impressionistic as music. In the new film Sound will play a very big role; but the big new points will *not* come from sound technique. The Sound will enter in as one of the elements of the new montage system. The different elements of art are not opposites; the essential thing is to find out the law belonging to *ALL* forms of impression and expression, and to demonstrate *how* they change their aspects only from one aspect to another. Montage in all its aspects is derived from one and the same principle. . . .

Excerpts from Eisenstein's Lectures at the Institute of Cinematography, Autumn 1934

(Notes taken by the author)

ON MOVEMENT

EACH individual movement has its own logic.

If a doctor operates on a woman at the seventh month, the operation is one of a total vein-like movement.

The simplest of movements is the spring of a tiger which involves but two motives, the animal's psychology and its material weight. Through the evolution of centuries it has become a beautiful movement though mechanical.

When you pass to the human stage, thought enters. Man knows that something will happen, therefore his reaction may contradict his impulse. For example, the mind is behind the biting of the lips. Either the man thinks he has said too much or he is striving to hold something in.

Words and intonations are the highest expression of an expressive movement.

The distribution of movement may result in one word or a whole phrase. Sometimes the movement comes first and then the word, or vice versa, or both may come together. Usually a dull person makes a movement before his words come, while people of temperament speak and gesture together.

The same impulse may be pure instinct or it may turn to the rational.

The play of movement (in a composition) is more important than the perspective.

Do not invent unnecessary things. Your plan of movement must be interesting because of its composition.

Sometimes in the newspapers there are pictures which call forth entirely erroneous ideas. The same thing occurs in the cinema. Hence, we do not only use the movement of the figure, but the figure in relation to the ensemble. The position of the figure is as important as the movement. (Accompanying a diagram of incorrect composition on the blackboard.)

Artistic composition is sometimes harmful where it is not necessary, for example, in a scientific film about horse disease.

Every expressive movement is a conflict between the instinctive reaction and the rationalized reaction.

ON THE USE OF EMOTION IN CREATIVE WORK

You must be infatuated by the ideas and emotions contained within your subject. Without emotion you can create nothing.

Your infatuation is the powder to produce a creative explosion. But an explosion of emotion is not enough. Feelings must be given a definite direction.

Then you must try to find the form which will express the first vivid impressions which moved your whole being. This form must satisfy your consciousness.

My best creative moments were those of improvisation.

Sometimes you remember those things which made an impression many years ago; therefore, you must gather your emotional experiences.

The ordinary man will say 'The sunset is beautiful', but the artist will store the memory away.

I wanted to arouse new and fresh emotions in *The General Line*. That is why I included a whole gamut of emotions. The people who were against the film were those who think rather than feel. Because their emotional and intellectual reactions were not in harmony, the scenes of spring and the pregnant woman evoked emotional protest within them.

You do not require every emotion to be shown in order to move the spectator. You can even remove the man (as the centre of emotion) and replace him, for example, with the Odessa Stairs (as in *Potemkin*) and compare the stairs with Emil Jannings (the actor). You can then take the *principle* of a particular emotion and this principle will serve as the rhythm of the event depicted.

If you go into the street and see a funeral followed by a band, it is the rhythm of the music played by the band which produces an emotional rhythm and this affects you. Likewise, the effect of marching soldiers.

On the stage we do not have the real conditions of emotion, for instance, the feeling of fear for there is no real fire. Therefore, how can we give the real impression of fear on the stage? The technique we employ must be based upon an understanding of real life; that is, an understanding of physical and emotional laws.

Children reflect what they see; that is, they imitate. The impression left by an actor's performance is the result of how he imitates the emotions of life.

IN THE THEATRE

The producer cannot be an actor; the actor cannot be a producer.

The question is whether the actor must feel fear, and if so, where does it come from. If *he really* feels fear why does he not run from the stage? There are two theories, the external and the internal, represented by Vsevolod Meyerhold and Constantine Stanislavsky.

A primitive exposition of Stanislavsky's method is that the actor must feel his role. A primitive understanding of Meyerhold's method is that the actor must have knowledge and develop the technique of expressive movement—the method called Bio-mechanics.

Both the theories of Stanislavsky and Meyerhold pre-date the Revolution and embody the contradictions of their period. These theories reflect the bourgeois origin of Stanislavsky and Meyerhold.

Stanislavsky reflects the attitude of the landowner who is opposed to mechanization. Psychologically, his method reflects the point of view of the introverted individual moving towards mysticism. As a method of commercial relations, Stanislavsky's is the shop where you buy a cabbage for cash.

Meyerhold, on the other hand, reflects the mechanized, urban approach in opposition to Stanislavsky's psychological approach. As a method of trade, Meyerhold sells by cheque his unseen goods.

THE MOSCOW ART THEATRE OF STANISLAVSKY

The details (décor, costuming, make-up, etc.) are connected with the surroundings of the propertied bourgeois. It reflects the thoughts of the merchant with leisure.

In the Art Theatre it is thought unnecessary to consider the body as long as 'the eyes mirror the soul'. Sometimes the productions of the Art Theatre are without a definite form.

The Art Theatre teaches you how to concentrate upon a role through what is called affective remembrance. Instead of concentrating upon the details of only one room, it spreads out over many things. It utilizes the elements of dreaming and fantasy.

The actors think of material which is additional to their role, in order to produce a state of feeling. The additional material they take is that which is emotionally connected with the whole. For example, a character enters a room, takes a glass of water and drinks. In order to characterize that moment, the actor concentrates upon the character in every condition of his life so that he may gather together all the characteristic features of the man. He imagines this person in the street, at the theatre, attending the horse races. Thus, you get the complete person composed of many different images. Involved in this is a kind of hypnosis and it has a certain rhythm, as the rhythm of a drum produces certain states of feeling.

Instead of introducing the most characteristic elements, they introduce all the lines so that a great many elements contribute to the whole. It is a very dangerous theory because it can be developed beyond all limits. Because of the importance of 'dreaming', the Art Theatre developed some pathological elements and it escaped from reality. The Art Theatre may discuss a detail for twenty days.

Still, the system has some good and healthy roots.

THE CONVENTIONAL (STYLIZED) THEATRE OF MEYERHOLD

Though Meyerhold talks of the external basis of his work, internal and external technique is the secret of both his work and that of Stanislavsky.

Both masters lay their stress according to their own philosophy which has come from the social factors of their upbringing.

Of course, there are those people who repeat the theories parrot-like as so many words. These are the one-sided people who kill either theory.

To Meyerhold, the state of feeling has no meaning, but in spite of it he has the emotional basis. Meyerhold stresses automatic imitation and because of this he does not go through each process in the development of the expressive movement.

Meyerhold's actors complain that they are taught to do things which they do not feel. They say they are empty. One of the actors of the Theatre of Revolution said that Meyerhold instructed (when he directed there): 'Say "mother" louder.' In contrast to this the Art Theatre would say 'Say "mother" as if she were a long way off.'

In the conventional theatre you put a gallows on the stage and you have to imagine a forest.

In the Japanese Theatre you have on the one hand a primitive naturalism and on the other constructivism and conventionalism.

The conventional theatre requires from the actors the movement which fills the stage.

In the theatre of convention, the triangle can be the symbol for anything and the result is that a single feature is used to give the impression of the whole.

THE SYNTHETIC THEATRE

We must take what is essential from each school. We should be happy that we come in this synthetic age and that we can create the synthesis.

You must develop in the actor both the elements of Meyerhold and those of Stanislavsky. All actors require to have both techniques. But the schools of each are one-sided and do not consider the elements characteristic of one another.

The school of Meyerhold, with its stress on movement, should call forth a corresponding emotion, that is, movements to create feeling. Sometimes, of course, there are moments when movement must be divorced from psychology and emotion. This is the case with ballet, for the dancer would not be able to stand the double strain.

Now our aim is to create a synthetic school which must embody a natural combination of emotion and movement, the whole being connected with dialectical materialism where two opposites come into synthesis.

'TYPAGE' AND THE COMMEDIA DELL'ARTE

Both the idea of 'typage' and 'montage' were created in the theatre.

Cinema 'typage' and the Theatre of the Commedia dell'Arte are based upon the mask. We replaced eight or ten masks by hundreds of faces. In *Strike*, however, there was expressed the straight transference of the Commedia dell'Arte tradition.

The masks (characters) of the Commedia dell'Arte were conventional and traditional. The Doctor of the Commedia dell'Arte was composed from the 'types' to be found in every university, and the Captain is a figure derived from the history of Italy's struggle for freedom from Spanish domination. The Commedia dell'Arte is an expression of collective work through many years.

'Typage', as we developed it, is neither conventional nor traditional. It is a synthetic method. For example, the Menshevik in *October* has all the biological and emotional characteristics synthesized.

By choosing a human being with the complex physical characteristics of a 'type' we move away from the conventional and approach a realistic tendency which, however, is not naturalistic.

The 'types' in *Potemkin* are not conventional or schematic. They represent the direct connection between the theatre and cinema and between the Theatre of the Mask (Commedia dell'Arte) and 'typage'.

I also used masks in the Proletcult and my own development shows that 'typage' is in the history of the Theatre of the Mask.

The same elements of 'typage' can be found in my scenarios; that is, in the choice of typical events. For example, *October* is a catalogue of events. From the point of view of dramaturgy, the scenario of *Potemkin* has the form of the classical drama in five acts, but it has typical events.

'Typage' is not only the question of characters but the whole development of the action.

The theory of 'typage' is that a good 'type' does not need to act.

In Pudovkin's film *Mother* there were good 'types', but there was a double emphasis because they acted. *Mother* was based on the ideal of Batalov, who was the perfect actor. Since the film was planned upon the basis of theatrical characters there was no need to introduce 'typage'.

All these theories are not the individual creation of myself or Pudovkin or Kuleshov, but the tendency of the time.

Why did 'typage' play such an important part in our early films? The social significance of the idea of 'typage' was the least *organization* of reality, whereas the actor is the greatest expression of organization.

The demolishing of houses in *General Line* was typical for the particular district at that time.

ON JAMES JOYCE

James Joyce took a single figure—Bloom—and put him under a miscroscope during the course of one day. We, however, can put the crowd in the Red Square under the microscope (on a day when there is a demonstration) and you can gain a variety of detail.

This method can be applied if we want to find out everything occurring between midday and one o'clock. The microscopic method is not only a scientific manner of work, but it is the scientific method applied to art.

This is how Joyce works and produces the method of science for art. Joyce takes and exaggerates every feature of his subject to the extent of a whole chapter.

In every normal literary work you have an imitation of sound. But Joyce exaggerates the question of sound. For instance, his editorial office (in *Ulysses*) reads like advertisements in newspapers. And when Bloom thinks of his wife, we have his thoughts without punctuation. Thus, Joyce's book is an organic whole. Like scientists working in other fields, he makes many discoveries in literature.

But critics such as Radek say we don't see people as Joyce sees them and, therefore, we don't want this kind of literature in the Soviet Union, because it has nothing to do with reality. It is wrong to think this, for if you need to understand the nature of microbes you go to the laboratory.

We must study Joyce. For two years there were discussions about translating Joyce for scientific purposes, but this plan was abandoned after the speech made by Radek. Because of this the mass of Russian writers will lose a great deal. I was furious at Radek's speech. When I analysed it, I found it to be a conventional interpretation of Joyce.

Radek complained that Joyce isolated one static character outside its objective context. This can be explained by Joyce's social origin.

He extends the line commenced by Balzac. We require to study his experiments profoundly. I feel that *Work in Progress* is retrogressive; now Joyce can go no further in literature.

ON THE STUDENT TAKING GRAPHIC CLASSES AND THE NATURE OF DÉCOR

If you (students who wish to become film directors) do not attend graphic classes and learn to draw, you will only be able to produce the most primitive drawings of what you require. You must know perspective or you will have to rely upon painters and artists for your designs. Only very few artists understand the medium of film composition.

Many can design a set on paper, but cannot fit it together for practical use. Scenery must be constructed in such a way that the director can take (shoot) it from every angle.

In the theatre the scenery is not so dynamic as in the cinema. I mean by that, that cinema décor can be reassembled and taken at any moment from any angle.

ON REALISM

Historical memoirs impress one beyond their artistic form.

There are tendencies in documentalism and many discussions about films based on facts. One theory is that no art can be compared in beauty with reality.

Andre Malraux has such an idea. When he visited me, he said, 'If I were working here I should be ashamed to write books'. I tried to persuade Malraux that his books are as important documents of the epoch as factories.

Malraux's reaction is typical of the intellectual who comes up against revolutionary reality. Ten years ago we too thought this way, but now it is out of date except among foreign intellectuals. The followers of this line of thought simply took pictures of real life.

Rotating wheels on the screen at first made a great impression. The people using them denied the art of images.

Documentalism appeared just after the destruction of our economy and the adherents liked to show rotating wheels. The wheels were not only a document, but an image of an epoch.

The trouble with the documentalists was that they thought they were only showing facts, but the spectator reacted to the factual images as symbols of the creation of a new economy. The object lost its significance as an image and assumed the power of industrial rhythm.

In *Potemkin* I show the machine as an artistic rhythm not as a document, and in *General Line* I show the machine as tempo.

Now such documental things don't make such an impression on the public because we have the new problem of the socialist man near this machine.

In 1925 it was very important to create collectivity in the cinema. Now it is important to show individuals in the collective.

The tendency in *Potemkin* was correct for its time. It showed the mass; the red and the white. The importance of every picture is that it should solve and reflect the historical problems put forth in its day.

In one book about Flaubert, the author talks about *Salammbo* and how the description of Carthage is a picture of France of Flaubert's time.

When writers give the whole reality and do not organize it, then you in adapting such a book for the cinema must select a form. In *An American Tragedy*, Dreiser included everything. This method is very impressive but it does not equal material which is selected and organized. The writer Mikhail Sholokhov (*And Quiet Flows the Don*) is more significant from the social than the formal point of view.

It is not enough to say that this or that is realistic because for every social system realism is different, with a difference in aesthetics.

In the classic plays of Corneille and Racine action must be within a certain time and there is unity of movement, time and place. They imitated reality in that the movement must take place in certain time for the spectator to see action.

The Romantic Theatre shows thirty years of action moving from place to place with all possible contrasts from poor-house to palace and yet they said they were realists.

The only true realism is the reality of fashion.

Feelings and emotions express the fashion and the psychology of the time.

The Art Theatre has a form of actuality—the windows must have two panes of glass for winter and one for summer. This is the method of 'the fourth wall'.

But all these realisms are limited. Does the synthetic realism come near to our idea of realism? Each class has its own conception, consequently realism and reality on the stage must correspond as near as possible with what is.

The Symbolists think of sensation as reality; this reflects their class, that of nobility.

All the realists are limited.

We demand that Socialist Realism should be as objective as possible, and we inherit all the theories of these realisms. But we must not add eclectically each element together. We don't collect eclectically; we only take the most essential elements.

Now every style had its own feature. From the Art Theatre we take those elements which help us to reflect. From the Symbolists we take sensations. From the Romantic—the elements of emotion and throw away all the unimportant features.

The Naturalists say: what is reality? Canvas and paint. If we take music— the piano and the pressure on the keys. Everything that they call realism is material.

It is interesting for us which theatre stresses the conventional and which the naturalistic, for we are at the commencement of the new Socialist Realism. A man who introduced a naked woman into the cinema was attacked [Alexander Dovzhenko in *Earth*] not only because it was pornographic but because it was outside of the ideology of our society.

Hoffmann divides the world into musicians and non-musicians. The spectator is also divided. On the one side you have actors and on the other the people they work for—and the book-keepers. There are people who react from the point of view of art and people without humour and people with too much.

Everything depends on the social origin of the spectator. For peasants short montage is bad for they have not time to think it over.

Before collectivization the peasants had no idea about machines; now they are used to them.

We have a powerful weapon in emotion. It is more important to react than to be educated.

Realism is a reflection of reality, and in every state of development it is different. The most important demand of realism is that it should be truthful from the dialectical point of view. One must show the typical otherwise the spectator will feel that something is missing.

Our realism, the realism of the future, must embody all the old arts. But the old arts by themselves were not enough. This is not only socialism but it is the complete method of art creation.

In the creative work you do, you must use the entire experience of mankind through the ages. And when you think of something your whole body must take part.

The feeling for art is the whole process by which the result is achieved.

The Films of Eisenstein

(*by* Ivan Anisimov)

(*International Literature*, No. 3, Moscow, 1931)

I

The films of Eisenstein, created during the epoch of the social revolution, attempt to epitomize its content and record its movements. They constitute a form of revolutionary practice in which the genius of the artist works hand in hand with the socialist offensive of the proletariat.

In order to understand and evaluate the art of Eisenstein, we must point out his individual characteristics, and determine his attitude towards the social revolution.

Eisenstein followed a definite path of development. His four films, *Strike*, *Potemkin*, *October* and *The General Line*, represent links in this process. We must seek the driving forces of this development, lay bare the contradictions through which it passed and reveal the relation between the progress of the Revolution and this artist's creative growth.

In outlining the main features of Eisenstein's creativeness, we must first of all point out his tendency to break with the traditions of bourgeois art, and herein lies the revolutionary character of his films, and their close connection with the 'attacking class'.

. . . A striking characteristic of Eisenstein's films is their non-individualistic tendency. This does not mean, however, that he immediately changes his world outlook to that of the proletariat, or that at once having destroyed the fetish of bourgeois individualist art he arrives on the 'virgin shores' of a new proletarian style. No—despite their revolutionary tendency the cinematographic creations of Eisenstein still retain traces of the very bourgeois limitations denounced by him. But although the artist has not as yet fully succeeded in creating an altogether new form, in place of the discarded traditions of individualist art—which as a proletarian artist he should have found—nevertheless his films have for us a very great significance.

In his endeavours to overcome the individualist limitations of bourgeois art, Eisenstein arrives at an original form of social monumental art. Embracing certain great historical processes not as they might have been reflected through individual experiences, but with a wider conception expressed by social movements, Eisenstein strives to show social revolutionary progress in a general, non-individualistic way. . . .

Of primary significance is the fact that he has constantly stressed the importance of the mass rather than that of the individual. In these conceptions expressed in images of the revolutionary epoch, we distinguish not only their positive content but also a characteristic narrowness, a conservatism, despite the fact that these conceptions have arisen during the overcoming of the individual limitations of bourgeois art. Realizing the necessity of the revolutionary negating of bourgeois practice Eisenstein completely denies individualistic principles and thereby transforms himself into a poet of the abstract mass. Indeed one might say that he has moved from one extreme to the other without really finding a true solution of the problem, which he can only learn from the class with whom now lies his destiny. Eisenstein does not think dialectically, and therefore the historic monumentalism of his films often becomes too abstract.

. . . The films of Eisenstein are revolutionary works, but they contain inner contradictions showing the conflict between the old and the new.

The film *Potemkin* is of special significance with regard to the genius of Eisenstein. It is distinguished by its rich content and its completeness.

Here we have a profound interpretation of the Odessa episode of the 1905 Revolution. . . . *Potemkin* presents an extremely interesting solution of the problem of social monumental art, overthrowing individualistic traditions of the past.

The revolutionary rise and fall are portrayed by Eisenstein as profound dramatic actuality, with a vast content. The revolutionary rise, expressed basically as *a drama of the ship and a drama of the steps*, is on the one hand extremely simple and concrete, and on the other receives a monumental interpretation.

The moment of climax (crescendo) and the moment of fall (diminuendo) are the culminations determining the new drama. And by the destruction of the old dramatic construction, based on individual psychological content, new and wider horizons are revealed. . . .

Potemkin has as its subject an episode from history. Understanding of history is determined by the class nature of the artist. One cannot say that an artist of one epoch cannot understand the history of another, but it must not be forgotten that an adequate historical perception is directly related to the class nature of the perceiver. An artist of the revolutionary proletariat, whose world-outlook is dialectical materialism, which consequently conditions his creative power, is of course able to give an adequate historical picture. But the contemporary bourgeois are quite unable to portray their own history in a true light. This class limitation is revealed most clearly in the creative work of a declining class. In all petty-bourgeois interpretations of any historic process we find many limitations. They are retained even where we have to do with those fellow-travellers of the Revolution who have linked their fate with the working class and are re-educating themselves in the common fight. In *Potemkin* we can distinguish traces of such limitations, notwithstanding the fact that this work constitutes an event of first importance in revolutionary art and is connected so closely with the socialist offensive of the proletariat.

In his understanding of the part played by the bourgeois revolution in overthrowing the feudal-landlord regime, Eisenstein is completely logical. His film gives in many ways an adequate reproduction of the historical process. His creation contains some petty-bourgeois features but such a production as *Potemkin* would have been impossible if these petty-bourgeois tendencies had completely dominated the outlook of its author. . . .

Let us examine the opposing contrast of the ship and the steps, and their concrete content. It is not difficult to see that individual distinction could be established only on the steps and not on the battleship. The sailors are presented in a specific aspect—they are envisaged as a scheme of non-psychological phenomena. In essence they are indistinguishable. They are synonyms. We perceive them always in relation to the mechanism and the ship. These external circumstances unite them. This mass is put together mechanically and represents a purely quantitative formation. By this, individualism is cast aside, and Eisenstein, in trying to find his expression, turns to the mass, and overthrows the fetishism of bourgeois individual art. He wants to show the mass in its collective movement. And here appears a very important obstacle. Collectivism includes, of course, individual features. This new art reveals extraordinary possibilities for individual expression, but it proposes in principle a new dialectical approach to the personal. Eisenstein solves the problem by completely doing away with individuality. His mass therefore exists as a scheme which does not find concrete fulfilment. The artist, then, is faced with the necessity of creating some exterior form emphasizing the unity of this broken-up mass. In the film the battleship serves as this central form. The people on the ship are always related to the technical system. The ship is objectively expressed in broad dramatic sequences. Here it is necessary to note not only the traits of technical fetishism but also the fact that the movement of the human masses and the social content of the drama are to a certain extent subordinated to this exterior formation.

If the men on the ship were without individuality, the people on the steps are to be considered in an essentially different way. They are distinguished in their individual peculiarities, they are conceived as part of a psychological drama. Before us are images that are saturated with meaning, nothing superfluous, given in a series of actual incidents. Imagine a long flight of stone steps up a hill, and on them the developing drama: a mother carrying her shot child, or the old wounded grandmother—all these separate expressions of the crushing of the bourgeois-democratic revolution are pieced together in a very complete picture. All of it is the opposite of that on the ship. The drama of the democratic revolution that failed to materialize receives, in the picture of the martyrdom on the steps, a convincing and concrete expression. The steps scene is pathetic. The men on the ship are so related to the people on the steps that they become merely a projection of this drama of suffering. . . . Their external similarity and lack of individuality is in clear opposition to the drama of the individually expressed people shot down on the steps.

Why does the artist thus deny individualism, at the same time revert to it? Eisenstein deprives the sailors on the ship of their individuality because he is unable to give a dialectical exposition of the mass or to understand the unity of the general and the particular. Hence—his schematization and depersonalization. The individualistic portrayal of the people on the steps testifies to Eisenstein's adherence to the principle of individual psychological exposition. The democratic aspect of the 1905 Revolution is particularly accessible to him and receives a deep interpretation. Petty-bourgeois traditions are expressed in the handling of the people on the steps and in the depersonalization and non-psychological treatment of the sailor mass. In these contrasts is revealed the underlying unity of the class content—here is not only a revolutionary affirmation arising during the revolutionary practice of a petty-bourgeois fellow-traveller, but also indications that his class limitations are being overcome, but as yet not fully conquered.

The drama of the battleship has one very characteristic distinction, shown in representing the world opposed to the revolutionary seamen—by means of a physician, a commander and a priest. Here again are images retaining an individualistic colouring. We have the following arrangement: on the one side a drama of the martyred petty-bourgeois radicals given in sequences really understood, and on the other side the Tsarist reaction, expressed very concretely. These circumstances are essential for they show wherein lie the roots of Eisenstein's historical conceptions. The film portrays above all the drama of petty-bourgeois radicalism. . . .

There is true pathos in Eisenstein's portrayal of the 1905 Revolution yet it is not fully conceived as it should have been by a proletarian artist. The events are estranged from the historical development of the proletarian struggle and considered as sufficient in themselves. A characteristic contradiction arises: the event is taken as a monumental historical picture which the artist endeavours to represent as something 'individual-less'—gigantic—and at the very same time the film is given a limited 'esoteric' character. The Odessa episode contains in its treatment traces of esoteric reticence, even renunciation.

It may be affirmed that the style of *Potemkin* represents that stage when the petty-bourgeoisie, collaborating in the Revolution, merge with the proletariat and are beginning to lose their class character. . . .

2

Strike was the forerunner of *Potemkin* and Eisenstein's first film, and in it will be found confirmation of our deductions. The film deals with the class-struggle in an atmosphere of victorious reaction. Factory and proletariat on one hand, and capitalists and Tsarist State on the other. Let us consider these opposing forces, which are the basic factors in the film. First of all we see the capitalist-bourgeoisie represented merely as fiction. They are without content, comprehensible only as a plan of genuine caricatures. The artist's extreme radicalism is thus shown in caricaturing the enemy of the working class. Yet, as a matter of fact, this testifies only to the petty-bourgeois limitations of the picture, to the fact of its being torn away from the revolutionary practice of the working class. Such a falsification of actuality, such an underestimation of the forces of the class enemy, is not at all natural to the proletarian world-outlook.

In *Strike* external aspects of the factory receive full expression. Machines fascinate Eisenstein, they come before everything else. The problem of handling people is dealt with very characteristically—like the sailors in *Potemkin* they are not individualized, but are mechanically united around objects. Therefore the workers are constantly shown in relation to mechanism: men at the anchor, people on the farms, workers on the crane, etc. Things come first of all. Workers and machines are not shown in their productive relationships, but in a scheme of technical fetishism. When it is necessary to represent a meeting,

Eisenstein places his men in most exotic situations, which instead of expressing the social content, appears as a decorative mechanical setting for purely external happenings. . . .

. . . As in *Potemkin* individualism is cast aside and the mass denied its own psychology. For petty-bourgeois thought striving to surmount individualist limitations, this was a peculiar necessity. The struggle with individualism resulted in the elimination of the individual.

Yet there is in *Strike* one aspect of individualism which discloses the inability of the artist to solve dialectically the problem of the general and the particular. Individualization is accomplished by complete isolation from the general. If the mass with Eisenstein is depersonalized then any individual can only be portrayed outside the mass—that is, conceived in the light of petty-bourgeois individualism. As for instance the workers, forced away from the factory during the strike, are considered in terms of: interiors, birds, janitors etc. True unity of general and particular proves impossible for the creator of this film.

He is able to conceive the general, but in no way connected with the particular, or to present the particular in no way connected with the general.

Petty-bourgeois individualism and the depriving of personality: within the confines of these extreme contradictions moves Eisenstein's mentality, still subject to a certain mechanical inertness. He gave in *Strike* the essential characteristics of the proletariat but one must be aware that these have inherent limitations. . . .

The film has for its purpose the portrayal of the proletarian movement. But in many ways it is superficial and far removed from the real content of the events reproduced. The external very often appears as the basic and sole content. Even the spies in *Strike* appear more eccentric than real, thus showing that what is more important to the artist is not the social meaning of the scene but rather its external accidental expression. The lumpen-proletariat participating in the pogrom (one of the culminating scenes in the film) are made into a fetish while taking part in events which should have been natural to them. This rabble is presented as something self-sufficient whose meaning is external to the developing basic movement. The artist accomplishes an original and exotic interlude. The dispersal of the demonstration, by firemen using hosepipes, is also presented as something *outré* and self-sufficient. This episode drags through an appreciable portion of the film, by no means commensurate with the unity of the whole conception.

In *Strike* the artist shows the nature of his connections with the practice of the revolutionary class. It is an attempt to find a new content. An indispensable condition for a real understanding of the revolutionary history of the proletariat is liberation from petty-bourgeois narrowness. In Eisenstein this limitation is still inherent, as is shown in his inability to solve the problem of the general and the particular, not only in the predominance of the external, often misconstrued, characteristics, but also in the technical fetishism of the artist's mentality, in the depersonalization and non-psychological representation of the working class. He approaches reality with very marked mechanistic convictions. Essentially he remains a passive contemplator of reality, always limiting himself to the external: thus Eisenstein's first picture showed that his creative method has a basic bourgeois inclination. . . .

The development of the artist is accomplished through sharpened contradictions. *Strike* and *Potemkin* show that the tasks which the artist set himself, connecting his work with the socialist offensive of the proletariat, are not entirely accomplished. His aspirations go much further than his actual achievements. His class limitations have not yet been overcome. The development of Eisenstein took place under very unfavourable circumstances. His first two films were not subjected to any serious Marxian criticism. He was highly praised and rightly so, but the essential questions concerning the inner contradictions of his creative power were never raised. Eisenstein, like all our cinematography, developed without real criticism. This without doubt hampered and complicated the growth of his creative powers.

3

. . . There is a logical process of development leading from *Potemkin* to *October*. The artist sets himself ever more serious tasks, he aspires to raise his creative power to the level of the high demands imposed upon art by the working class. Here is charted the growth of the revolutionary artist. He does not remain stationary, he develops with the times. One cannot accuse Eisenstein of lagging behind the impetuous tempo of this epoch, he always keeps abreast of it. If his films are examined from the point of view of their general direction, it will be seen that they are in close keeping with the demands of the socialist offensive. . . .

Eisenstein took upon himself an exceptionally difficult problem. *October* is for him a step closer to the world-outlook of the proletariat. This was to be a transition revealing new horizons. Why then is this film, representing such a daring attempt to express the events of October in social monumental art, such a pallid work?

The contradictions inherent in Eisenstein's first films are now repeated even more sharply. His production is still characterized by petty-bourgeois limitations. The measure of his re-education does not satisfy the demands made by the epoch on a revolutionary artist. The very fact of *October's* appearance testifies to the artist's advance, but together with this we may observe the superficial character of his development. Eisenstein is still subject to mechanical thinking, a form of class limitation, and is unable to represent the October events in their real content. It proves to be external and formal. Facts are given but without exposition of their essence. The coldness, stiffness and pomposity of the film prevent the events from appearing in their right relationships and essential content, notwithstanding their documentary reproduction. The film deals with a multitude of external appearances registered with the exactness of a historical document, yet they remain a lifeless mass of phenomena.

We see moving masses, armoured cars tearing along, we see the streets of Petrograd, we see a man photographically resembling Lenin, we witness a multitude of events exactly reproduced, but all of this fails to provide the inner qualities which such a film as *October* should have brought out.

The mass is treated not only in an individual-less aspect, but is often considered allegorically: in other words it is ineffectively emphasized. The artist, powerless to master the movements of the masses—the real heroes of the October epic—finally deprives his picture of concreteness. Depriving reality of its real content he presents merely allegorical schemes. . . .

The external characteristics become of extreme importance—the raising of the drawbridge across the River Neva, the artillery galloping across the court-yard of the Winter Palace—many similar episodes stand out clearly against the dull background of non-individuality. This reveals the nature of his whole conception; incomprehension of the real content of developing events and a purely superficial manner of approaching them.

Objects pour down upon the heads of the spectators in enormous quantities —porcelain, cut-glass, chandeliers, statues, columns, architectural ensemble of the Winter Palace—all these, not conforming to the basic content of the film, are transformed into a real deluge of objects; we might say an 'objective deluge!' The film which was to have been a history of the October Revolution becomes a horde of dead objects covered with the dust of museums. A curious paradox results: the museum objects are individualized and pictured with great exactitude, while the movement of the masses appears drab, deprived of indi-viduality and reduced to mere allegory. This failure to understand essentials leads to a perversion of the content of the film. This deficiency is further brought out in the main contrasts of the film; the Smolny Institute versus the Winter Palace. Externally we have in the Winter Palace the Provisional Governments in Smolny the Revolution. But Eisenstein proves powerless to reveal the content of this antithesis. He makes the contrast absolute. The Winter Palace is con-ceived as a consistent whole, whose elements are architectural, material, external. Here the objective mentality of Eisenstein triumphs, overcoming all obstacles. . . .

Eisenstein in his attempt to portray the October events monumentally is restricted by those identical limitations which characterized *Potemkin*. Externally we have dynamic movement, impetuosity, bustle, abstract dynamics; internally it is static. No attempt is made to present the Revolution as a link in a historic process. Eisenstein limits himself to documental facts, not understanding how to combine them into an integral whole.

Potemkin presents a deeper interpretation of historic reality than was attained in *October*, in spite of traces of petty-bourgeois limitations. If Eisenstein gave us a profound characterization of the bourgeois-democratic revolution, the move-ments of the proletarian revolution proved inaccessible to him. He did not develop quickly enough to interpret the complex problem involved. This circumstance was responsible for the failure of *October* and for its mechanical and external character. The contrast between his external striving and the actual extent of his re-education became clearer. If superficially Eisenstein became more logical and coherent, in the revolutionary sense, by attempting ever more necessary problems, the essence of his first films tenaciously retains traces of class limitations. Their resistance is not yet broken.

4

Eisenstein's latest work, *The General Line*, proved to be such a spineless composition that it became necessary to rename it very unpretentiously *The Old and the New*. It points to an accentuation of the crisis. After *October* the artist should have produced a film solving the contradictions in that unsatisfactory work. This was the only way out. There remained only the alternative of a mere retreat: the artist could have renounced the huge scale of his creations— but it was clear that such a retreat would be for Eisenstein equivalent of creative death.

The General Line in its general tendency is a big step forward. The artist approaches closer to the concrete working of the socialist revolution, aspiring to grasp one of its most important aspects—the reconstruction of the village by socializing the pigmy, individualist farms. Eisenstein addresses himself to the solution of this new problem with great enthusiasm. Yet the result is very poor.

If we examine the images which Eisenstein gives in his new film it will be seen that they are all on an immense, immeasurable scale. Concrete co-relations are violated. Aiming to give prominence to the contemporary village, the artist attains breadth instead of depth, making the images hyperbolic instead of concrete, resulting in purely quantitative presentation. Consideration above all of external appearances is inherent in Eisenstein. In this is shown his incomprehension of the content. But in *The General Line* even the external character of the images are limited by their pure quantitativeness and abstraction. Eisenstein's rich peasant is fabulously rich, extremely tall, monstrously stout. The poor peasantry are similarly expressed in extremes. The pauper's hut reminds one of Dante's Hell. Eisenstein shows swarms of bed-bugs, men at tillage, a hut broken in two. All these pictures are not generalized, they do not become concrete images. They are taken beyond all measure. The cream-separator is conceived as something resembling a turbine of Volkhovstroi (technical fetishism flourishes in full bloom in picturing this modest machine). Addressing himself to cattle-breeding, Eisenstein gives an episode of a 'bull's marriage' which not only takes up a large part of the film but also serves as a most characteristic expression of the boundlessness and excess of his images. All is conceived not in its real contours, but in a scheme of hyperbolization. All becomes abstract, the external torn away from living reality. Immensity serves to express the fact that the artist has not found the essence of phenomena, that he sees them only as accidental, superficial expressions. . . .

. . . Why is this so? Because the artist takes the village outside of its real relations, outside of living connections. He thinks in terms of things. He disintegrates reality into disconnected, unrelated pieces. This makes quite illusory Eisenstein's construction which is proclaimed in principle as arch-realistic. This film, arising from the desire to express a most urgent page of living reality, full of throbbing interest, proves to be a production torn away from reality itself.

The social movements of the contemporary village do not find in this film any deep revelation. So, paradoxical as it may be, the film dealing with the socialist reconstruction of the village is least of all interested in its social content! . . .

The triumph of the external is here just as great as in *October*. Whole portions of this drama represent a mechanical juxtaposition and enumeration of disconnected objects. This explains the peculiar apathy of the film. Dante's Hell of the poor peasantry, and the satiety of the rich peasant, are portrayed by the artist with equal refinement. A lustre and a sparkle cover everything. All becomes peculiarly aesthetic. The poor peasant's hut in the background of the sunset becomes a fact not without a certain elegance. The external approach to the phenomena is expressed by levelling them. Indifference, apathy, a peculiar aesthetic reproduction, all testify that the quality of actuality is inaccessible to the artist. He is in the captivity of poor empty abstractions.

The consequent result of all the creative work of Eisenstein is 'technicism'. The village that is reconstructing itself is perceived under the onslaught of technical progress. The problem of the class struggle is considered secondary and not very essential. The social meaning of the deploying events is alienated. The biggest revolutionary change in the village is perceived as a *technical revolution*. So the tractor is transformed into the cause, the base of social construction, instead of changing class content.

Reducing all events to a purely technical organization is expressed by one of the more substantial images of the film—the agronomist. This person always appears when it is necessary to turn the development into one or another direction. Agronomy is given above all. All the threads of the village's development are in his hands. Here we have a very characteristic perversion of real relations: the technical organizer appears as the essence of the evolving process.

The film is permeated with technical fetishism. If in the previous works of Eisenstein we have seen but traces, in *The General Line* they become quite definite. Their domination hinders the artist from perceiving socialist reconstruction in its essential meaning.

The gigantic social process is represented only in its technical meaning. . . .

. . . The last film of Eisenstein testifies convincingly to his relations with the technical intellectuals.

It reveals the essence of his development, and of those errors in which he still persists. His petty-bourgeois limitation is not overcome during his collaboration with the proletariat but instead passes over into a new quality, becoming a 'technical' limitation. In the initial stages of his development Eisenstein's work is a form of petty-bourgeois practice changing its class nature through participation in the proletarian struggle—but in the actual course of this development it becomes permeated with the ideology of the technical intelligentsia. Such is the concrete character of the history of Eisenstein's genius. Such is his real essence. . . .

. . . It is clear that the revolutionary cinema conceptions of Eisenstein are only external. The artist does not surmount his psychological contradictions by social re-education, by merciless criticism of class conservatism, but attempts to do this through a technical-organizational collaboration with the working class. This keeps him in the captivity of many illusions and hampers him in becoming a dialectical materialist, in becoming one of the greatest artists of our epoch. The crisis of Eisenstein's development has such deep roots that its solution is possible only through a complete revaluaton of values.

As is known Eisenstein made a series of attempts to prove theoretically his views on art. In his remarks, eccentric and fractional in character, there is one very interesting assertion. Theory is always a generalization of practice. However cursorily the formulations are stated, the mechanical quality of Eisenstein's thinking is clearly seen in them. Before us is the philosophy of objective limitation so logically expressed in his films. Of particular interest is the theory of the 'intellectual cinema' which Eisenstein advances as the basis of his method and as a 'perspective' for the development of all revolutionary cinematography. This theory is an expression of organizational-technical fetishism. It is simplicity in the extreme, this theory of new rationalism. It is reduced to fetishizing the primacy of reason as against the psychological 'elementals'. It is well to remember here how Eisenstein, denying bourgeois individualism, attempted to do away with personality. This very same limitation is manifested also in preaching intellectualism. Eisenstein thinks within the limits of mechanical stagnancy, and this brings him to very poor illusions.

For the creative development of Eisenstein, his theoretical reasoning has a negative significance. It not only proves that the artist has moved very little in the direction of re-education but also shows militancy and obstinacy in his defence of these limitations, which serve as a stumbling-block in his revolutionary growth. The theory of the 'intellectual cinema' represents, for him, a peculiar defensive device justifying his limitations. This theory will disappear when he overcomes that inertness in thinking which hinders this great artist from rising to his full height.

What are the perspectives? We have no reason for doubting that Eisenstein can surmount the contradictions of his creative growth and that he will be able to give his work far more completeness and depth than he did in *October* and *The General Line*. If he turns to decisive rearming, overcoming his traits of class limitation, making closer relationships with the 'attacking class', Eisenstein can create real revolutionary cinema productions. But we must on no account minimize the difficulties confronting him. The way out of this crisis is possible only through a stubborn campaign for re-education, through merciless exposure and criticism of his first films. The method of dialectical materialism is a necessary condition for the creative growth of the artist. Only by mastering it, only by conquering the mechanical limitations of his thought, will he produce films worthy of this gigantic epoch. Then will be the authentic achievement of social monumental art.

(Translated by Herbert Marshall)

Eisenstein's Introduction to the Scenario of the Film *Que Viva Mexico!*

(This introduction was especially written for the French publication of Eisenstein's theoretical works and selected scenarios, which is still pending. The unpublished Russian manuscript is in the possession of Armand Panigel whom Eisenstein authorized to edit his works.—M.S.)

WHAT follows is the summary of the first scenario of the film. It was written when our expedition had become familiar with the elements which we envisaged filming.

This first sketch was naturally very superficial; it lacks precision and details as much in the aims as in the tendencies.

Moreover, being destined for the group of which Upton Sinclair was the leader, this summary was intentionally limited to generalizations, because the group which financed the expedition, feared more than anything else any 'radical' content in the film.

On the other hand, the scenario was examined no less carefully by the censors of the Mexican Government.

Any detailed study of social problems (the relationship between the haciendados and the peons, the repression of the rebellious peons) provoked the displeasure of the censors.

To our argument that only a sufficiently precise demonstration of the class struggle on the haciendas could explain and make understandable the revolution against Porfirio Diaz in 1910, we received the reply: 'But the haciendados and the peons are above all Mexicans and it is not at all necessary to stress the antagonism between the different groups of the nation.'

Thus we were left to soften the scenario, and to leave until the time of shooting the vivid delineation of the integral reality to which, at the time, we could only make a passing allusion.

We had to slide over this in the summary while talking about the repressive measures against the peons and the death of Sebastian in the midst of the austere landscape of the plateau where his life of labour had unfolded.

In the shooting, this scene was treated in a complete and detailed manner.

In it is one of the most impressive episodes: the death of the peons beneath the hoofs of horses.[1]

[1] It is well known that the material of *Que Viva Mexico!* was taken away from me by the group who was financing the picture and who refused to ship it to me in Moscow for editing. Later, three films were made from this material, each was fragmentary and independent from the other and badly edited, which deformed the intentions of the original film.

Those who saw the picture well remember this scene, even if the montage leaves much to be desired.

Here briefly are the details:

Sebastian and two of his comrades are buried up to the neck. Then the cavalcade of the haciendado and his guests gallop many times over their heads, trampling them to pieces with the hoofs of their horses.

This scene is not only a document. It is typical of the ferocious repression of the rebellious peons during the epoch of Porfirio Diaz.

For the same reasons, the scenario does not contain the end of the *Fiesta* episode. In this case we feared to wound other sentiments, although the episode was nothing more than the *mise en scène* of a typical 'milagro' (miracle), like those in the popular legends related to this or that saint, or this or that polychrome statue of the Madonna or Christ in all corners of Mexico.

These 'milagros' equal in colour the Miracles of Our Lady (Miracles de Notre Dame), one of the treasures of the French Middle Ages.

The Madonna or Christ in both cases show a very liberal spirit. They are ready to pardon and take under their protection all delinquents, sinners and adulterers as soon as it enters their heads to implore aid and assistance from these superior forces.

All the world knows Maeterlinck's story of *Sister Beatrice*, who was kindly replaced by the Madonna during her peregrinations in the world of sin.

But still more highly coloured are the subjects of other 'miracles' of this odd branch of religious folklore, where the situations recall the serial-novel or detective story.

At every step we find adulterers, swindlers, murderers and deliberate arsonists. We find the Pope making trade out of the Church; a pregnant abbess; an archdeacon the murderer of a bishop, etc., etc.

But all the hardened sinners of both sexes invariably come out of the most difficult situations undamaged thanks to the intervention of 'Redheaded Marion' (Marion la Rousse), the slightly respectable nickname given to the Madonna by the Devils, who are justly vexed at being deprived of their legitimate prey.[1]

Completely in the tone of these 'miracles' is the miracle attributed by legend to the statue of Our Lord of Chalma.

In our novel (*Fiesta*), Señora Calderon, an adulterous wife, is surprised by her husband who finds her in a forest in the arms of her lover.

The woman falls on her knees and addresses her prayer to Our Lord of Chalma.

And the miracle occurs.

The lover is transformed into . . . an altar, on which appears God himself.

The avenging but stunnned husband has nothing to do but kneel down in his turn and pray before the altar.

(See the description of this legend in the very beautiful book by Anita Brenner on Mexico: *Idols Behind Altars*—New York, 1929.)

In using the elements of this legend, we allowed ourselves only one variation:

[1] See *Les Miracles de Nostre Dame par personnages*, edited by Gaston Paris and Ulysee Robert, 1876, 2 vols.

in our text, the lover—a big bronzed boy, not too clever—played by the young picador Baranito (the son of the famous picador Baraño senior), was to be transformed not into an altar, but into one of those old patined crucifixes, which adorn Mexican Baroque in such a decorative manner.

As to the rest, everything was to remain in the absolutely severe line of the canonic design.

In general, this part of the episode was to observe the style of the popular prints of José Guadalupe Posada, the great master-illustrator of Mexican songs on the most diverse subjects: the capture of a famous bandit; the execution of a great rebel general; a drunken citizen murdering his wife; the miracles of one of the local Madonnas! On this plane, José Guadalupe Posada approaches in a remarkable fashion the charming tradition of the French 'images d'Epinal'. It is even possible there is a direct influence, because during the French political adventure of Napoleon III, namely the reign of Maximilian, Mexico was, in all ways, under French influence: from the Presidential park of Chapultepec, which in places is like a copy of the Bois de Boulogne, to the engravings and prints just mentioned in which are mixed the incomparable native folklore of Mexico and unexpected reminiscences of Daumier and even Callot.

But because of all sorts of circumstances, the episode in question was never shot.

If these two episodes were not shown in the scenario because of censorship, two others were not mentioned because, at the moment when the scenario was written, their conception was not yet complete.

Such is the episode of the Civil War—*Soldadera*—in which the direct connection with *Maguey* was masked and in which the traits characterizing it as a movement of rebellion of the agricultural labourers within the frame of the general Mexican revolutionary movement were passed over for the time being in silence.

(As known, the leader of this large stratum of the population and the spokes-man of their ideals was the attractive figure of Emiliano Zapata, whose agrar-ian programme approached in many respects the communist programme.)

However, it is not only in this that the episode is incompletely developed.

The moment at which Pancha passes from her first husband, who has just been killed, to her second husband (the sentinel, according to the scenario), is also incomplete.

Later on, the episode was changed in this sense that, during the funeral of her first husband, Pancha was joined by another man, but this man was not a part of the detachment to which her husband who had been killed belonged, but was of one of the detachments against which the dead man had fought.

Submissive, Pancha follows this man.

This situation had replaced the first version, since it was more typical and at the same time more unexpected.

Let us add that this new version did not seem to us to constitute proof of a lack of political conscience or indifference of the Mexican woman Pancha.

All to the contrary!

Her first husband belonged to the army of Pancho Villa.

Her second—to the detachments of Emiliano Zapata.

There was, in fact, in the intricate imbroglio of the Mexican revolution, a moment at which the partisans of Villa and those of Zapata fought against each other, whereas in principle both were fighting against the reactionary central government of Venustiano Carranza, which, let it be said in passing, had opened the borders of the country to the American interventionist forces, in order to obtain their aid.[1]

This fratricidal and stupid fighting was put to an end when Zapata and Villa allied themselves and, reunited by identical and common aims, defeated the troops of Don Venus and simultaneously made their victorious entrance into the capital of Mexico—Mexico City—from opposite sides.

There is a photograph in which we see the two leaders seated side by side in two golden chairs in the Palacio Naciónal, the government palace, thus symbolizing the unity of Mexico. This was the culminating point in the liberation movement of the Civil War. A very short time after, controversy and disputes arose between the two leaders from which the reactionary forces of the country profited.

In the definitive version of the scenario, Pancha's growth represents Mexico, which, passing from hand to hand, gradually rises to the conception that strength does not reside in dispute, but uniquely in the union of all the people against the forces of reaction.

The triumph, however short, of the united armies of Zapata and Villa and their common entry into Mexico City seemed to represent on the national scale the same motif which unfolded in the destiny of the modest 'daughter of the Revolution' Pancha, who placed humanitarian sentiments and the fraternity of the people above the senseless and sanguinary discord of those whose hatred should have been directed against the forces of reaction and of oppression.

According to tradition of the ancient peoples the widow of one brother should marry the surviving brother. The marriage of the widow of a military leader with his surviving opponent symbolized the end of the war and its replacement by the theme of fraternity and of national union.

However, this episode was not shot either.

Finally, in the scenario there was no mention of the 'gag' climaxing the scene of the Carnival on the Day of the Dead.

Here, the contrast between the prologue and the epilogue symbolizes the general theme and the idea of the film that the biological principle dies and is delivered to death, while the social principle, wider than the limits of animal existence, is immortal and eternal.

If in the prologue we have seen funerals and a desperate submission to the terrible symbol of death, we see, in contrast, in the epilogue this symbol surmounted by the sarcasm of the Carnival of the Day of the Dead.

These sarcastic sentiments towards death are very characteristic and are a particular trait of Mexican *mores*.

The three episodes between the prologue and epilogue represent the three

[1] This did not prevent one of the leaders (Zapata) from being the spokesman of the agricultural labourers and the other (Pancho Villa) from being a 'putschist' general and a typical adventurer.

historical steps of the conception of life from the biological submission to death to the social surpassing of its principle by the immortal power of the collectivity of the people.[1]

The semi-animal, semi-vegetable and biologically unconscious existence is expressed in the episode *Sandunga*. (Historically, it accords to a typically pre-Columbian enviroment, which has been preserved in the tropical provinces up to the present, almost without change.)

It is the theme, brutally introduced into this 'paradise' of colonizing exploitation by the great landlords, which was reinforced with the arrival of the Spaniards. (The almost contemporary epoch of 1910 seems to correspond to the feudalization of Mexico in the time of Hernando Cortes.)

And finally, during the Revolution and the Civil War, the Indian, humiliated and reduced to slavery, makes an attempt to liberate himself from the yoke of the exploiters.

Thus through the episodes of contemporary life one seems to perceive the stages of history.

Above all it is possible in Mexico because there we see existing simultaneously side by side *mores* and ways of living which, socially and culturally, correspond to different stages of human society.

The pre-Columbian stage sleeps lazily in the archaic regions of the tropics.

The immense haciendas of the central plateau show the dark picture of the absence of all rights for the peasant population.

And next to it, in Yucatan, one is amazed to find that the control of the rope industry by the plantation workers is already fully realized, especially if one takes account of the feudal and patriarchal system applied to agricultural labourers in the central states of Mexico. There in Yucatan, the flourishing activity (although deformed by opportunism) still continues as a testimonial of the martyrdom of another brilliant hero of the Revolution, Carillo Puerta.

In the definitive version of the film, the 'apotheosis' of the epilogue was certainly not intended to ring, in this fashion, the triumph of 'progress' and of the 'paradise' of industrialization.

We know very well that as the expansion of the bourgeois countries goes on, the primitive patriarchal forms of exploitation are transformed into more refined and sweated labour forms. Because of this we did not intend to limit the finale of the film to a demonstration of the conquests of the contemporary civilization of Mexico; really considerable conquests, although shown by us otherwise than by concrete factories (which not without irony we have juxtaposed with rugby games). These conquests do not consist only in ranks of generals covered with decorations and parading like 'stars'. They do not consist only in seeing a President with firemen and policemen parading in front of him, at a sports festival, and forming national emblems by their movements on the asphalt.

[1] The episodes *Maguey* and *Fiesta* are closely linked by their colour and their character. In these two episodes, one concerning Sebastian, Maria and the Guest, the other Señor Calderon, Señora Calderon and Baranito, we can see the antithesis of the differing conceptions of the ideal of family and morality according to social classes.

To all this we intended to add a special kind of finale, in the form of a 'Memento', which would have shown that all that glitters is not gold.

And that the life-giving social principle which is self-affirming will still have to struggle for a long time against the forces of darkness, reaction and death, before the realization of the ideal of those who lament beneath the boot of the exploiters.

Flaubert wrote in the *Dictionaire des Citations*: 'D'Alembert is always quoted after Diderot.'

Likewise the word 'Memento' always brings thoughts of the word 'Mori'. Remember that you must die. . . .

To illustrate in our film the problem of such a 'Memento', we chose the symbols which are intimately linked with the idea of 'memento' in general, and more particularly with the image of the most terrifying of these 'mementos', the macabre 'Memento Mori'.

Skulls, cross-bones, skeletons. . . .

So we naturally adopted in the scene the typical and traditional forms for the thought to be transformed into action: the one of the 'Danse Macabre' so popular for centuries in the frescoes in Italian cemeteries and in the prints of Holbein.

And there, in the finale of the film, two motifs were organically interwoven: on the one hand the illustration of thought by the image, on the other, the authentic folklore elements of one of the popular and most characteristic feasts of Mexico.

The Day of the Dead!

I confess completely objectively, and sincerely.

This was it, the Day of the Dead, or more precisely what I knew of it, which in my adult years filled me with passion long before I had the opportunity to visit Mexico. I was like every young boy who dreams of visiting the country of Fenimore Cooper's Red Indians or Marseilles to see the cell, in the Chateau d'If, from which the future Count of Monte-Cristo escaped.

On that day, the 2nd of November, everything takes the form of the symbols of death, the skulls in the foreground.

In the hatters' windows, derbys, top-hats, sombreros and boaters fixed on—skulls, wearing with dignity multicoloured cravats.

The bonbons are in the form of sugar skulls with chocolate coffins bearing the name of the beloved dead.

Puppets on this day are skeletons.

Dolls—skeletons carefully bedizened.

Skulls as tiepins.

Not only the special sheets published on this day, but even the newspapers, are full of epigrams on ministers and other political figures who, always on this day, are supposed to be dead.

These epigrams are written in the form of epitaphs.

And on the caricatures which accompany them, the 'dear departed' are represented as skeletons, with the characteristic attributes of this or that person: a high white collar; a monocle; epaulettes well garnished; moustaches (!), sometimes . . . a nose. And when the personage is particularly dark-complexioned or when he is simply a Negro from the neighbouring island of Cuba, his skeleton is painted black!

The series of political 'calaveras' (as the symbols of death are called in Mexico) by José Guadalupe Posada: Calavera Maderista, Calavera Juertista, Calavera Zapatista, are positively immortal. Some wear moustaches and hats; others have a spider's body; others, finally, are rigged out in top-hats, etc., etc. For the most part they represent in a satiric form the principal figures of the Civil War.

And the masks!

Who on this day does not wear a cardboard mask?

Who does not dance, with his face covered by a mask?

Who does not take part in the joyous banter which unfolds amidst the carousals, the fair stands, the stalls of food and cheap drinks?!!

Who does not whirl around rigged-out in a three-cornered hat of a carnival general; in a broad-rimmed sombrero of a 'dorado' of Villa's army; in a golden cardboard crown or in a plumed helmet of a Spanish conqueror?

And here it is, on the screen, the final joyous farandole. In the dance and medley of masks there naturally appear, dancing also, known figures rigged-out in cardboard masks.

Who?

Here is someone in the clothes of the Haciendado of the *Maguey* episode....

Here is someone wearing the dress of his dead daughter....

Here is someone in the narrow-striped trousers of the Guest....

And here is another one with the mitre of the Bishop, as he appeared in the Spanish *fiesta*.

And here is the black mantilla of Señora Calderon.

Here is a general with a golden three-cornered hat above the same cardboard mask.

And there, in the distance, *horribile dictu*, the Señor President himself, with a broad ribbon across his chest, a star on his side and a very glossy top-hat. And behind him gallops a policeman.

Surrounding them, matadors, picadors, wearing gaudy clothes, workers, and, clad in white, the peons who in the film sang the tragic 'Alabados'.

And above all, good and bad, the humiliated and the oppressors, those who symbolize life and the knights of darkness, all are concealed behind the white cardboard masks of carnival skulls.

And at the most intense moment of the farandole—a pause.

Now comes the moment to drop the masks.

One after the other, the masks of peons, matadors, workers fall.

Their bronzed faces laugh, their teeth glitter, their smiles replace the sneer of the skulls.

Their eyes, black as coal, sparkle joyously.

They roar with laughter—tall, healthy, beautiful, audacious.

But here is the white-gloved hand of a General, stretching towards his mask.

The elegant mittens of the daughter of the Haciendado stretch towards hers.

Likewise the Bishop and the President.

Following them, all those who, in our film, represented the figures of shadow.

Señora Calderon hurries to follow their example.

Their masks are swiftly removed.

But they are not only cardboard carnival masks.

It is something more powerful!

Other masks are removed.

Under the masks of Señora Calderon, of the President, of the General, of the Policeman, of the Bishop and the Haciendado appear not faces of the living, but . . . real skulls.

Not carnivalesque, not cardboard.

Real not clowns.

Real, skulls.

They are no longer clownish 'Calaveras'.

But death and putrefaction.

Cadavers.

The cadavers of a socially dead class.

The skull, a new symbol.

Not only of the dead.

But the dead who bind the living. (*Mais du mort qui saisit le vif.*)

The skull, a terrible symbol. Memento of the power of the dead over the living.

The skull, memento of terror for those who oppose life. It reminds them that quickening life will sweep them away without leaving any trace!

But what is sparkling amidst these terrible symbols of a moribund class which seeks, before its death, to strangle the life-giving and the ascending?

Another cardboard face.

What is hiding behind it?

The mask falls.

And on all the width of the screen, pushing away the shadows and nightmares of reaction and death, appears the laugh of a little brown child.

Would it be the child of Pancha?

Will it be the one who will see the real liberation of Mexico?

It is on this last 'Memento', the most important for the great Mexico of the future, that the film was supposed to end.

Thus was to be constructed the finale.

Instead of this, by the will of those who had invested money in the film, 'The Day of the Dead' became a film of two hours,[1] separate, independent, and, moreover, documentary.

And in the *Danse Macabre* which I see, in my mind, whirling in front of my eyes, are intercut other faces. The faces of those who did not permit the complete realization of my film. Those do not drop their mask.

[1] The short film *The Day of the Dead* (*Death Day*), edited from Eisenstein's *Day of the Dead* footage by Sol Lesser's concern, is two reels (2,000 feet). Eisenstein, who never saw this version called *Death Day*, apparently had been misinformed about its length.—M.S.

I have no need of them.
I know on which side they dance.
And I know what is hidden under the cardboard mask which covers their superficial 'radicalism'.

Moscow, 1947.

Correspondence between the Author and Upton Sinclair

March 20, 1950

Mr. Upton Sinclair
Monrovia, California.

Dear Mr. Sinclair:

I am taking the liberty of writing to you because I have just written a biography of Eisenstein which will be published in England this fall.

Naturally I cover the matter of *Que Viva Mexico!* The account is given as objectively as possible, the facts having been gained from all available sources here and in Mexico and in Europe. I think all aspects are covered and only a few matters remain speculative. . . .

You told people during the difficulties over the film [*Que Viva Mexico!*] that you had received a cablegram from Stalin declaring that Eisenstein was considered a deserter and that you had also received letters and cablegrams from Soviet officials in Moscow to that effect, but at that time you did not wish to make these matters public. This led to debate and recriminations.

Now that Eisenstein is dead, the only consideration is historical fact. Would you, therefore, be kind enough to loan me photostatic copies of these, or any other documents to include in my biography?. . .

Sincerely yours,
Marie Seton.

Monrovia, California,
March 26, 1950

Dear Miss Seton

I'd send you the cablegram if I could. All that mass of material was put into boxes and stored in one of three warehouses on this place—I'd guess there must be 500 carton boxes full of papers from 4½ years of my life—ever since the Helicon Hall fire. I've no idea which box, and it would take weeks to find the stuff. All I can give you is this letter, which you may print, giving my word that there was a long cablegram from Stalin, telling me that the Soviet people considered Stalin [*sic*] a renegade and had no more use for him.

At this time he had been trying to get a director job in half a dozen different countries.

Sincerely
Upton Sinclair

PS.

About six months at a guess, after Thunder appeared, I wrote a letter to the New Republic in which I gave the main facts, and I suggest you publish that. I send you American Outpost, which has a lot about it.

U.S.

March 31, 1950

Mr. Upton Sinclair,
Monrovia, California.

Dear Mr. Sinclair,

Many of the documents I am using, including telegrams, etc., which you sent to Eisenstein have been in my possession since 1933 and 1934, although at Eisenstein's request I never used them at that time or made reference to them.

Two press reports which I am using . . . plus a letter of Eisenstein . . . show that he was in Mexico with the permission of Moscow which was given prior to August 1931 and that the permission was extended to January 1932. Only Stalin's cable to you can support your word that Eisenstein was regarded as a renegade.

Perhaps now that I have explained . . . you will feel that it is worth while unearthing the Stalin cablegram. If you will do this, I will be most grateful, and also for any other documents which you would care to give me in support of your various statements.

One more question: did you ever have any correspondence with Boris Shumyatsky at this time or later in connection with the film? If so, could you possibly lay your hands upon it?

April 1, 1950

P.S. Since receiving 'American Outpost', for which I thank you, I have re-read with great care the statements, letters and telegrams in my possession which you wrote in connection with the film . . . The material shows so great a change of sentiment on your part between October 1931 and August 1933 that I feel that I must ask you to help me. Will you be so kind as to give me answers to some personal questions in order to aid me to understand the record?

1. What did you think and feel about Eisenstein when you first knew him and entered into this project?

2. What specific acts of Eisenstein led you to distrust him?

3. Did you halt work on the film solely because there were no funds available as you suggest in your account in 'American Outpost' and elsewhere? If so, this appears to contradict a report on the film dated November 2, 1931, in which you state: 'The total estimated cost of the picture is $90,000 and of this $10,000 has still to be raised.'

4. Can you possibly tell me what Mr. Kimbrough reported to you concerning Eisenstein's conduct in Mexico?

5. Why did you tell Eisenstein in two telegrams that the film would be sent to him to Moscow to edit when such arrangement had apparently not been *definitely* made with the Soviet authorities? Was this, as you stated later, because you wanted to help the Soviet authorities get Eisenstein back to Russia? Or was this, as you also stated, because the Soviet authorities were not interested in Eisenstein or getting the film to Moscow for him to edit?

6. I appreciate the position of the investors and your financial difficulties, but was the whole core of the trouble financial?

7. Can you tell me why a print of the film was not sent to Eisenstein

after the release of *Thunder* in 1933? You stated in a cable at that time: 'Print will be made available after Thunder release as promptly as distribution agreement makes possible.' The record shows many negotiations were entered into after this for the disposal of the film, but no attempt to send it to Eisenstein. Can you explain this contradiction?

Thanking you again for your co-operation.

Marie Seton.

Monrovia, California.
April 5, 1950.

Dear Miss Seton,

I have yours of Mar. 31 and am taking time off from the book I am writing to answer your questions. You must excuse my typing. Also my slip of the pen in writing Stalin when I meant Eisenstein. I think also I have to change the word renegade to deserter; this comes to my mind as I think it over. All this was nearly twenty years ago, and it was the most painful experience of my life, and thinking about it is like raking in a garbage heap.

Of course I do not know what permission the Russians gave to E. I only know what several of their officials told us, that he had been ordered back and had not obeyed. We knew that he had been trying to get a film job in half a dozen different countries. I recall especially Japan and Spain. I do not recall the name Shumyatsky, but there was a string of agents and officials, at least eight or ten, all trying to get the film away from us.

When E. first came to Hywd. I paid him a call. He was polite but showed no special interest in me and did not ask to see me again. When he lost his job he sent some one to me, and then came himself. He was good company and I liked him. He signed a contract to make a picture for $25,000 and we raised that. What first led us to distrust him was that when the money was spent he wrote us that we'd have to send more or we'd have no picture. He kept that up, over and over, and we realized that he was simply staying in Mex. at our expense in order to avoid having to go back to Russia. All his associates were Trotskyites, and all homos. No doubt you know that, and I'll be interested to see if it's in your book. Men of that sort stick together, and we were besieged by them for several years.

Question 3. I made a joke of our troubles in Amer. Outpost. I didn't want to attack E. personally. I never did, except so far as was necessary to answer the falsehoods he supplied to his journalist friends. We stopped the work because first my wife and then I had come to realize that E. was a man without faith or honor, or regard for any person but himself. Also because we had no more money and couldn't raise it. I had to earn the money to cut the film and I had no advance knowledge that I'd be able to earn it.

4. Yes, by God, I can! K. was a young Southerner with very old fashioned ideals of honor. He was told that E. was a great artist, and expected to honor and help him. I doubt if he had ever heard of such a thing as a homo and he was bewildered to find himself in such company. He discovered that E. wanted money, money, money, and never had the slightest idea of keeping any promise he made. When K. obeying my orders, tried to limit the money and the subjects

shot, there were furious rows, and the upshot was that K. disarmed a Mexican who tried to kill him, and took from the man E's. gun which E. had given the man for the purpose. I'll get you an affidavit from K. about his observations of E.—PROVIDED that you'll agree to publish it in the book. It will include the fact that E. spent a lot of his time and our film in shooting pictures of animals copulating and of human beings in degrading positions, and he used his leisure in making elaborate drawings of pornography. K. had the job of getting E's. trunks out of Mex. to be shipped to Germany as per E's. request. The customs people opened the trunks and inspected the contents and said it was the vilest stuff they had ever seen—and they see a lot. K. persuaded them to let us have a few samples—for our own protection against the flood of lies these degenerates were pouring out against us. You have asked for it, so I give you one example, a parody of Christian paintings showing Jesus and the two thieves hanging on crosses; the penis of Jesus is elongated into a hose, and one of the thieves has the end in his mouth. This is Art—an elaborate drawing in colored crayons, in E's. unmistakable style—and some of them signed.

6 and 7. Some Russ. officials said they wanted E. and some not; one or two said he might be shot. The head of their film industry [Boris Shumyatsky-M.S.] came from Moscow, a highly educated man, and sat in our Pasedena home and heard the story of how he had treated us, and at the end he smiled and remarked: 'Well, he outsmarted you, that's all.' And we had thought we were dealing with idealists and comrades!

After we had got the film back from Mex. we made a precise deal with Amkino in N.Y. The stuff was to be sealed and shipped to them and they were not to open it but ship it direct to Moscow where E. was to cut it and the government would then ship the negative back to us. Two or three weeks later we learned from friends that E. was still in N.Y. and running the film for all his friends. We had our lawyer in N.Y., B. M. L. Ernst, recover the film and ship it back to us, and of course that was the end of both E. and Russ. for us. We never had any idea of shipping him a print or anything else after that. We'd as soon have shipped it to the devil. Any negotiations after that were for the purpose of trying to get back some of the money our friends had put in at our urging. The total cost was about $90,000 and the receipts about $30,000. My wife and I lost about everything we had, and that was all right, it had happened to us before and has happened since, for causes. What hurt was being 'outsmarted'. That caused my wife to predict the deal between Stalin and Hitler, several years before it was made.

Upton Sinclair

In my answer to this letter, I pointed out to Mr. Sinclair that I could not include Hunter Kimbrough's affidavit without also including the affidavits of other people concerning Mr. Kimbrough's conduct in Mexico. Moreover, it would be unjust to include Mr. Kimbrough's affidavit, made today, since Eisenstein was dead and could not answer it. However, I said: 'I still extend to you the invitation to send me letters, cables or anything you wish written at the time of the events in question and I will publish them no matter how damaging to Eisenstein. . . .' But Upton Sinclair did not reply.—M.S.

The Stalin Cable and the Sinclair Denouement

On October 26, 1931, Upton Sinclair wrote a letter to Joseph Stalin telling him of his financing of the Mexican film. He said that this had brought him into touch with a young Russian technician, Fred Danashevsky, whose father in Moscow had been convicted of sabotage. Sinclair had been responsible for the father's employment in the Soviet Union.

On November 21, Stalin cabled the following reply:

WESTERN UNION

Received at   1931 NOV 21 AM 11 35

SA155 VIA RCA=CD MOSCOU 118 21 2030

UNITED STATES OF AMERIKA UPTON SINCLAIR STATION A=
PASADENA (CALIF)=

LETTER RECEIVED STOP BODY OF SURVEILLANCE ACCUSES DANASHEVSKY
OF SABOTAGE STOP MATERIALS WE HAVE IT SEEMS TO ME DONT SPEAK
IN FAVOUR OF DANASHEWSKY STOP IF YOU INSIST I CAN SOLICITE
BEFORE THE HIGHPOWERED BODY FOR THE AMNESTY STOP EISENSTEIN
LOOSE HIS COMRADES CONFIDENCE IN SOVIET UNION STOP HE IS
THOUGHT TO BE DESERTER WHO BROKE OFF WITH HIS OWN COUNTRY
STOP AM AFRAID THE PEOPLE HERE WOULD HAVE NO INTEREST IN
HIM SOON STOP AM VERY SORRY BUT ALL ASSERT IT IS THE FACT
STOP WISH YOU TO BE WELL AND TO FULFILL YOUR PLAN OF COMING
TO SEE US STOP MY REGARDS STOP 2783 21/11 31=
         STALIN.

Sinclair wrote a long letter to Stalin on November 22, 1931, arguing that Eisenstein was not disloyal to the Soviet Union. At this time no disagreement had arisen between Sinclair and Eisenstein.

The two Sinclair letters with a photostat of Stalin's cable were published in the Summer 1965 issue of *Sight and Sound* by Ronald Gottesman who, with Professor Harry Geduld, has edited the Sinclair-Eisenstein correspondence into a book published in 1970 by Indiana University Press under the title *Sergei Eisenstein and Upton Sinclair The Making and Unmaking of Que Viva Mexico!* The originals were left by Sinclair, with other papers, to the Library of Indiana University where they form the Upton Sinclair Archive.

In 1952, an early review by Dwight Macdonald of the first American edition of this Eisenstein biography evoked protest from Upton Sinclair in a letter to the *New York Times*, although he admitted he had not read the book. His letter provoked me to send him a copy. My thought was that he had probably never really known the facts of what took place in Mexico, nor the effects on and for Eisenstein of his actions. I did not expect an acknowledgement for the book. I had judged Upton Sinclair too stiff necked to be able to admit he might have been in the wrong in his treatment of Eisenstein. Yet, all the same, I hoped that, however much he might detest the book and me, this biography might induce him to feel less harshly towards the memory of Eisenstein.

After some considerable time there came a sign of life and seeming mellowing from Upton Sinclair: he handed over all that remained of *Que Viva Mexico!* to the Museum of Modern Art Film Library. This gesture opened the way for the devoted Jay Leyda to receive a grant through Lincoln Kirstein to assemble a selection of the remaining rushes for the study of Eisenstein's unedited material. More recently, the residue of the Mexican material has been acquired by Moscow.

Finally, early in 1969, Upton Sinclair died. In the long obituary in the London *Times*, no mention was made of the Mexican tragedy which left such deep scars upon Sinclair and Eisenstein who, because of the structure of their inner natures, should have had the insight never to have become entangled with one another. Their attitudes to life and their respective personalities were inimical.

Index